Mass
Media
Bibliography

Mass
Media
Bibliography

An Annotated Guide to Books
and Journals for Research
and Reference

Eleanor Blum
and
Frances Goins Wilhoit

UNIVERSITY OF ILLINOIS PRESS
Urbana and Chicago

Library of Congress Cataloging-in-Publication Data

Blum, Eleanor.
  Mass media bibliography : an annotated guide to books
and journals for research and reference / Eleanor Blum and
Frances Goins Wilhoit—3rd ed.
    p.   cm.
  Rev. ed. of: Basic books in the mass media.
  2nd ed. 1980.
  ISBN 0-252-01706-4 (alk. paper)
  1. Mass media—Bibliography. I. Wilhoit, Frances Goins.
II. Blum Eleanor. Basic books in the mass media. III. Title.
Z5630.B55 1990
[P90]
016.30223—dc20   89-39705
                                                      CIP

Contents

Preface

This successor to the 1972 and 1980 editions of *Basic Books in the Mass Media* has been updated to 1987, and extensively revised and expanded. The new title removes the word "basic", which the constantly increasing number of publications about the numerous and varied aspects of mass communications makes too constricting. Reflecting this growth, the present bibliography contains 1,947 entries as against 1,179 in the 1980 edition and 665 in 1972. The majority of new titles were published between 1980 and 1987, the cutoff date. A number of titles from the earlier editions have been deleted, and of those retained some of the annotations have been rewritten to take into account new editions or to combine with later works by the author. With the wisdom of hindsight we have also included certain titles previously omitted which have not dated or now possess historical significance or are classics in their fields. Although only books published before 1987 are annotated, the existence of 1987 and 1988 editions are noted in the annotations where appropriate.

This bibliography, like its predecessors, has three primary purposes: to serve as a reference tool; to suggest materials for research or reading; and to act as a checking or buying list. A secondary purpose is to provide a work which will allow the user, through the use of the subject index and judicious browsing, to piece together an informal history of the literature of mass communications in the English speaking areas of the world and the authors and scholars who have shaped its direction.

All titles give information about some aspect or aspects of mass communications—theory, structure, economics, function, research, content, effects. Many are reference works. Only a few discuss technique or methodology—content analysis, being the exception. Most contain footnotes and bibliographies. When they do, this is noted. All entries have one common factor: they treat the subject in broad general terms. For example, we have included books about news agencies, but not about a specific agency; histories of the newspaper, but not of individual newspapers. For this reason there are no biographies, either personal or institutional, and no books presenting a narrow aspect of a subject unless it serves to reflect a broader view. Also, the entire contents must concern communications; those having only partial treatment are excluded.

Selecting headings under which to group the entries presented problems because of media overlap. For instance, news, at one time synonymous with newspapers and certain periodicals, now includes broadcasting to an equal extent. Likewise, film and television often intersect. Therefore we have classified titles by form rather than function. The first section is general, dealing with titles about two or more media. The other sections treat broadcast media (radio and television together); print media (newspapers, book publishing, and periodicals); film; and advertising and public relations, which cut across all media. It is worth noting the growth of the broadcasting and film sections in this edition, reflecting the increasing importance of and interest in these areas. Following the monographs are four sections organized by type of publication: bibliographies, yearbooks, journals, and indexes. Each entry has an annotation discussing its contents and relevance to the field.

A partial list of subjects covered includes popular culture; children; women; politics and government; ethics; history; developing countries; public broadcasting; blacks, American Indians, Hispanics, and other minorities; violence, crime, war, and terrorism; religion; training and education for a career. A detailed topical and geographical subject index provides a key to the contents of all titles. There is also an author index and a title index.

Certain subjects are not included in this bibliography—among them, censorship, law, copyright, printing, the post office, instructional broadcasting, and telephone and telegraph, although some of these are discussed in connection with broader subjects, such as printing with history; telephone and telegraph with telecommunications; law with regulation. Others like propaganda and public opinion, though important, have not been treated in depth.

In any work of this kind some titles could have been included which were not, and conversely, some could have been omitted. Selection inevitably becomes somewhat eclectic and arbitrary, reflecting the compilers' knowledge and inclinations. Our criteria for inclusion varied. Sometimes, although not always, a criterion was that elusive attribute, quality. The determination of quality, however, is selective as well as elusive, and some books which we felt lack it to a greater or lesser degree have their place because little else exists on the subject or because they cover aspects not covered elsewhere. Also, to limit a bibliography to works of undisputed merit (and opinions differ as to what constitutes merit) would narrow its scope and usefulness. Even hackneyed anthologies may contain some essays of value, and mediocre surveys may give factual material not easily found elsewhere.

A number of the books included here are out of print—a fact no longer so important because of the prevalence of paperback and hardcover reprints and the possibility of borrowing through interlibrary loan.

Because prices vary with edition or availability on the secondhand market, we have not attempted to include them, nor the various editions of a title. Nor have we given publishers' addresses, most of which can be easily obtained through such sources as *Literary Market Place* and the *American Book Trade Directory*, or their foreign equivalents, or by contacting the reference department of a library.

In conclusion we would like to thank Professor George Gerbner of the Annenberg School of Communications, University of Pennsylvania, for his suggestion years ago that a bibliography on the mass media was needed, and Professor Theodore Peterson of the University of Illinois, who—again years ago—convinced the University of Illinois Press that it should be published. During the years of preparing this book, we received extensive support and assistance from our respective institutions, the University of Illinois and Indiana University. We would like to acknowledge the contributions of Nena Thomas of the University of Illinois Communication Library for her very valuable and willing help in verifying and locating materials. Thanks also go to Carla Heath, Angharad Valdivia, Ronald Bettig, Susan Wroblewski and Michael Rogalla, graduate students at Illinois, who assisted ably and beyond the call of duty. Their help was made available through grants from the Graduate College, the Institute of Communications Research, and the Graduate College of Library and Information Science at the University of Illinois. We are grateful for grant support from the Indiana University Office of Research and Graduate Development and from the Indiana University Libraries Faculty Research Support. The Indiana University School of Journalism and the Indiana University Libraries have contributed staff and computer support. We would like to thank Dawn Hornbeck, Journalism Library Coordinator, and the student staff for creating and maintaining records, securing materials, and proofreading. Among those students are several who along with Ms. Hornbeck performed major tasks; they are Cynthia Erb, Patty Werner, and Lorré Levy. We are also indebted to two persons at the School of Journalism, Don Baker, Coordinator of Technical Services, for programming, and Cathi Norton, Editorial Assistant, for editing and typing.

General Communications

This chapter contains books relating to two or more media.

1

Abel, Elie, ed. **What's News: The Media in American Society**. San Francisco, CA: Institute for Contemporary Studies, 1981. 296p.

Abel and his contributors address issues important to the present and future of the media, among them the role of the marketplace and the heavy dependence on advertising revenues; obligations toward the community; effects of chain ownership; decline of the family owned newspaper; social changes new communications technology may bring about; and monopoly aspects of publishing and broadcasting. The contributors are Ithiel de Sola Pool, Theodore Peterson, Edward Jay Epstein, William Porter, Benno Schmidt, James Rosse, William Henry III, Robert Bartley, John Hulteng, George Comstock and Abel. Although some of the articles are dated, especially those dealing with technology and regulation, most of the comments and predictions are still pertinent. Notes and index.

2

Abuse of Women in the Media. Penang, Maylasia: Consumers' Association of Penang, 1982. 85p.

This booklet contends that the lifestyle of women in the Third World, including Malaysia, has been influenced by the Western media which represent "the interests and values of an alien and dominant culture" and project a Western brand of consumption which is discriminatory, oppressive and male-oriented. Chapters discuss the use of women in advertising, pornography, sex tourism (a form of prostitution with Westerners), women's magazines, novels, television and film, and newspapers. References, the great majority of which are from Western sources.

3

Adams, Valerie. **The Media and the Falklands Campaign**. London: Macmillan, 1986. 224p.

Using the Falkland campaign as an example and applying her examination to potential future campaign coverage on a larger scale, Adams explores the issues raised in wartime between the media, the government and the public. She examines the conflict from two perspectives: sources of military information, and the ability of the interested and intelligent layman to grasp its specialized and often technical presentation. Although she does not come up with answers, her analysis indicates the scope of the problem. Appendixes give a list of sources; a list of main commentators on military aspects of the Falkland campaign; and a chronology. Bibliography and index.

4, 5

Agee, Warren K., Phillip H. Ault, and Edwin Emery. **Introduction to Mass Communications.** 8th ed. New York: Harper & Row, 1985. 599p.

Agee, Warren K., Phillip H. Ault, and Edwin Emery, comp. **Maincurrents in Mass Communications**. New York: Harper & Row, 1986. 457p.

Introduction to Mass Communications is the silver anniversary edition of this undergraduate text. The authors say that in this as in previous editions the purpose is "to give readers a full description of the mass communications, to introduce them to all the areas of professional work in journalism and mass communications and to demonstrate the importance of the communicator in modern society." The latest edition has an added chapter, "The Communications Explosion," synthesizing the many ways in which the computer and satellite are revolutionizing the transmission of information and entertainment. Also new is a 200-item glossary, "The Language of Mass Communications." There is a bibliography and an index.

Maincurrents in Mass Communications, the revised edition of **Perspectives on Mass Communications** (1982), contains more than 70 short essays, interviews, surveys, commentaries, speeches and descriptions designed to show how electronic technology and the evolving audience desires are reshaping the traditional forms of the mass media, and how new methods of delivering information and entertainment emerge. The focus is contemporary—what the media do, the criticisms they receive, the people who operate them and their methods, and the ways in which the media influence the lives of individuals. Taken as a whole, it gives the beginner a brief and provocative glimpse into the way the various media interrelate financially, technically and ethically with each other and with various business and social institutions. Index.

6

Ainslie, Rosalynde. **The Press in Africa: Communications Past and Present**. New York: Walker, 1967. 264p.

Despite its publication date, this book is considered among the best general description of mass communications in Africa, providing historical background for the study of international news flow. See also Mytton's **Mass Communication in Africa** (No. 312).

7

Alisky, Marvin. **Latin American Media: Guidance and Censorship**. Ames: Iowa State University Press, 1981. 265p.

Alisky discusses the press systems of the various Latin American countries in terms of governmental restrictions, dividing them into three groups according to extent: "Nations with Media Guidance"—Mexico, Peru and Brazil; "Nations with Media Freedom"—Venezuela and Columbia; and "Nations with Censorship"—Cuba, Argentina, Uruguay, Chile, and the Central American states. Extensive chapter notes constitute a bibliography. Index.

8, 9

Altheide, David L. **Media Power**. Beverly Hills, CA: Sage, 1985. 287p.

Altheide, David L., and Robert P. Snow. **Media Logic**. Beverly Hills, CA: Sage, 1979. 255p.

Media Power "deals with a very simple paradox that cuts through complexities of the modern world," says Altheide. "In other times, people would communicate in order to do something; today, we must first do something before we communicate. The role of the mass media in establishing, polishing, and shaping basic communication formats is what I wish to examine. Along the way, I offer a theoretical perspective for beginning a coherent analysis of social time and space." In exploring how the mass media provide formats for perception, expectation and action, he emphasizes TV and analyzes examples, among them the crisis of the American hostages in Iran. Chapter notes, references and index.

In an earlier book, **Media Logic**, co-authored with Robert Snow, media logic is defined as a process through which media present and transmit information in specific formats with their own institutional strategies that have become part of the total media culture. The authors examine the influence of this logic on entertainment, news, politics, religion, and sports, making reference to pertinent literature throughout. Bibliography and index.

10

Altschull, J. Herbert. **Agents of Power: The Role of the News Media in Human Affairs**. New York: Longman, 1984. 355p.

A philosophical and historical analysis of the folklore of the power of the press. A major conclusion is that the press does not exercise the tremendous independent power usually assigned to the mass media, especially television. Rather the media are influenced by their respective governments and the politicians and statesmen who run them. Altschull identifies three types of world press systems—market, Marxist, and advancing. In his opinion, none of the premises of the three systems reflect the reality of the influence, the effect or the power of the press.

11

Anani, Elma Lititia, Alkaly Miriama Keits, and Awatef Abdel Rahman. **Women and the Mass Media in Africa: Case Studies from Sierra Leone, the Niger and Egypt**. Addis Ababa, Ethiopia: United Nations, Economic Commission for Africa, 1981. 38p.

Three studies, each backgrounding the press as a whole, its image of women, and their professional status in the mass media.

12

Arterton, F. Christopher. **Media Politics: The News Strategies of Presidential Campaigns**. Lexington, MA: D.C. Heath, 1984. 220p.

"What are the influences of news reporting on the conduct of election returns?" and, "What are the consequences of this influence?" These two questions are the focal points for Arterton's study of the role of journalism in contemporary politics which centers around presidential campaigns. Principal data comes from over 100 interviews with presidential campaigners in 1976 and 1980. Chapter notes cite both oral and print sources. Indexed.

13

Asian Mass Communication Institutions: Directory. Singapore: Asian Mass Communication Research and Information Centre, 1986. Looseleaf.

Identifies many of the Asian institutions engaged in teaching, training, and research, with details such as address, telephone number, date founded, objectives, activities, names of staff, type of research, publications, research reports, and facilities. Ninety institutions have been included from Bangladesh, Hong Kong, India, Indonesia, Japan, Korea, Lebanon, Malaysia, Pakistan, Philippines, Singapore, Sri Lanka, and Thailand. The first directory of Asian institutions was published in 1973.

14

Aspen Handbook on the Media: A Selective Guide to Research, Organizations and Publications in Communications. New York: Praeger and the Aspen Institute, biennial. (1973–1977.)

This valuable reference book, which unfortunately

concluded with the 1977–1979 edition, brings together extensive factual material about the media not available in any other single source, such as lists of research programs in communications and organizations supporting programs; communications organizations with communications broadly defined to include advertising and public relations, broadcasting, educational/instructional media, film and photography, journalism and other print media, and new technologies; actions groups; government policymaking bodies in the U.S. and Canada; law courses; special libraries and other resources; a selection of films; and a selected bibliography. All entries are annotated and give appropriate information to enable the user to get in touch with a given source or order specific materials. The 1977–79 edition is edited by William L. Rivers, Wallace Thompson, and Michael J. Nyhan. Index. Although no new editions have appeared, much of the material still holds good, and it gains historical value. For a companion volume see **The Mass Media: Aspen Institute Guide to Communication Industry Trends** (No. 416).

15

Atwan, Robert, Barry Orton, and William Vesterman. **American Mass Media: Industries and Issues**. 3d ed. New York: Random House, 1986. 470p.

Intended to serve either as the basic text for introductory-level college courses in mass communications or as a reader to supplement standard texts, this collection of articles concerns the industries that design and sustain the major channels of mass communication and the significant social, political and cultural issues that shape, and are in turn shaped by, these industries. Articles are divided by media into five sections: (1) "The Environment of Media Industries," including audiences, advertising and government regulation; (2) "The Print Media," including books, newspapers and magazines; (3) "The Sound Media," including radio and recordings; (4) "The Visual Media," including film and television; and (5) "Personal Media," including VCRs, self-publishing, telephones, computers, and satellite television. Articles range from classic to contemporary; authors, drawn from the social sciences and the arts include Leo Bogart, Daniel Boorstin, Ithiel de Sola Pool, Carol Caldwell, Ben Bagdikian, John Dessauer, Michael Schudson, Nora Ephron, Benjamin Compaine, Larry King, David Mamet, Michael J. Robinson, John Wicklein, and Av Weston. Suggestions for further readings and index.

16

Atwood, Rita, and Emile G. McAnany, eds. **Communication and Latin American Society: Trends in Critical Research**. Madison: University of Wisconsin Press, 1986. 220p.

A collection intended to give American communication scholars a better idea of Latin American communication research. In four parts: "An Introduction to Latin American Critical Communication Research," "Critical Theory, Transnational Communication and Culture," "The Effects of Transnationals on Culture," and "Alternatives for Latin American Cultures." Chapter notes and index.

17

Atwood, L. Erwin, Stuart J. Bullion, and Sharon M. Murphy, eds. **International Perspectives on News**. Carbondale: Southern Illinois University Press, 1982. 203p.

A symposium in which participants and individual speakers addressed ideological and empirical approaches to national development, international perceptions, global news flow, and education from a mass communication perspective. Presentations reflected a wide range of sometimes conflicting views on the issues. Speakers, representing a number of countries, included Joseph Ashcroft, Jeremy Tunstall, Kaarle Nordenstreng, Sylvanus Edwelie, Hanno Hardt, Reda M. Khalifa, Jasper Hsu, Chin-Chuan Lee, Georgina R. Encanto, and the editors. References, author index, and subject index.

18

Audley, Paul. **Canada's Cultural Industries: Broadcasting, Publishing, Records and Film**. Ottawa: Canadian Institute for Economic Policy, 1983. 386p.

An economic study, giving an overview of all sectors of Canada's "cultural industries." Separate sections on daily newspaper, periodical, and book publishing, the recording industry, radio, theatrical film, and television analyze the state of each industry, its market and distribution, its economic impact, its content, its current public policy, its policy issues and proposals, and other pertinent factors. A concluding section draws the information together. Audley, a consultant and policy analyst in broadcasting and publishing, emphasizes throughout problems of specifically Canadian content and control. Contains notes for each chapter, but no bibliography per se and no index.

19

Bachman, John W. **Media: Wasteland or Wonderland: Opportunities and Dangers for Christians in the Electronic Age**. Minneapolis, MN: Augsburg, 1984. 175p.

This book has three aims: to help Christians understand the culture in which they live, work, and consume the products of the media; to sort out the uses—both good and bad—to which the media have been put; and, as Martin Marty aptly says in his Introduction, to "Provide a kind of 'do it yourself' kit so that Christians can interpret and intervene in a world that so often seems beyond the range of understanding, beyond a zone in which they can have effect." Contains a bibliography and a list of helpful organizations.

20, 21, 22

Bagdikian, Ben H. **The Media Monopoly**. Boston: Beacon Press, 1983. 282p.

Bagdikian, Ben H. **The Information Machines: Their Impact on Men and the Media**. Harper & Row, 1970. 359p.

Bagdikian, Ben H. **The Effete Conspiracy and Other Crimes by the Press**. New York: Harper & Row, 1972. 159p.

Bagdikian, a Pulitzer Prize winner, whom Ralph Nadar has called the "conscience of American journalism" and the American Society of School Administrators has called "journalism's most perceptive critic," has written three appraisals of the press. Two of them, **The Media Monopoly** and **The Information Machine**, are documented studies; the third, **The Effete Conspiracy and Other Crimes by the Press** is a collection of perceptive essays from the 1960s and very early 1970s, most of which appeared in the **Columbia Journalism Review** and several in **Harper's** and the **Atlantic Monthly**. Taken together, the three works offer a provocative assessment of the America press—its economic control, its technology, and its social aspects.

In the most recent of the three, **The Media Monopoly**, he contends that 50 media corporations control what the U.S. audience sees, hears and reads. He lists corporations involved in the various media, their holdings, and their complex interconnections that go beyond individual media into a subtle cooperation among giant industries which influences the quality of information and entertainment available to the public through newspapers, magazines and broadcasting. While data of this sort constantly change, the implications, specific and fully substantiated, do not. Chapter notes and index. An extensively revised edition was published in 1987.

The Information Machine, sponsored by the Rand Corporation, considers "the most likely technologies that will change the way in which the next generation receives its news." In the ensuing years some of its predictions have come true, some have not. But the importance of the study lies not so much in its forecasts as in its analysis of the nature of news in America and of its audience, and the ways in which methods of delivery can affect both. Reference and index.

The essays in **The Effete Conspiracy and Other Crimes of the Press** are useful for three purposes: historical insights into issues affecting journalism of the 1960s and early '70s; analyses of the forces causing them; and fine examples of journalistic reporting. Index.

23

Bailey, Charles W. **Conflict of Interest: A Matter of Journalistic Ethics. A Report to the National News Council**. Minneapolis: Minnesota Journalism Center, University of Minnesota, 1984. 55p.

A study focusing on "outside activities of journalists, on the conflicts of interests these outside activities set up, and of the effects of those conflicts both on the performance of and the public perception of the news media."

24

Bakr, Yahya Abu, et al. **Development of Communication in the Arab States: Needs and Priorities**. Paris: UNESCO, 1985. 60p. (Reports and Papers on Mass Communication No. 95)

Taking a broad view, this report focuses on the need for communication planning and for recognition by Arab countries that communication must be placed in the larger context of comprehensive development planning. Several sections also consider the importance of developing capacity for production of communication materials, along with an analysis of what is actually being produced. The facilities discussed are broadcasting, print media, news agencies, telecommunication network and technology. The imbalance in the flow of information is dealt with throughout. Appendixes tell the status of district and local media, telecommunications linkages, Intelsat ground stations, and centers for information and communication research in the various Arab states.

25

Ball-Rokeach, Sandra J., and Muriel G. Cantor, eds. **Media, Audience, and Social Structure**. Beverly Hills, CA: Sage, 1986. 400p.

A sociological interpretation of the mass media consisting of several kinds of essays: "one set to illustrate the complex relationships that can exist among political, cultural, and economic contexts in which content is produced and distributed; another examining the role of audiences as part of the larger media system; and still another that examines not only how people depend upon and use the media to obtain information and entertainment, but also how audiences are both affected by and find meaning in media content"—Introduction. Media include television, radio, film, the live theater, and print media, especially newspapers and magazines, which the authors examine in light of the social system which produces them. All in all, the articles illustrate the expansion of the field of mass communication in interdisciplinary and subject terms. Each chapter has prolific references, and there is an author and a subject index.

26

Barber, James David. **The Pulse of Politics: Electing Presidents in the Media Age**. New York: Norton, 1980. 342p.

The book traces the critical role of journalists "as the major advancers and retarders of Presidential ambitions . . ." The author says, "Smart candidates recognize that power and hurry to adapt their strategies to it. They learn to **use** journalism, as journalism uses them. They and the journalists grapple in a reciprocal relationship of mutual exploitation, a political symbiosis." President by president, from Theodore Roosevelt in 1900 through Richard Nixon in 1968, Barber shows the connection between 20th century political elections and their connection with journalism. Bibliography and index.

27

Barton, Frank. **The Press of Africa: Persecution and Perseverance**. New York: Africana Publishing Co., 1979. 304p.

"As political freedom came to the Continent, so did press freedom disappear," is Barton's opening sentence. Although his attitude is definitely colonial, this statement is not as prejudiced as it first appears, for he attempts to put it in a historical perspective by making the case that this trend in Africa has happened in many non-African countries which today claim some sort of press freedom. Against this background he surveys in breadth rather than depth first the white colonial press and then the emergent black press in French-speaking Africa, East and Central Africa, Portuguese Africa, "the White South," Swaziland, and "unconquered Africa"— Liberia and Ethiopia. He omits Arab Africa because he feels the cultural differences to be too great. Bibliography and index.

28

Beasley, Maurine, and Sheila Silver. **Women in Media: A Documentary Source Book**. Washington, DC: Women's Institute for Freedom of the Press, 1977. 198p.

The authors, out of their experience in teaching a "Women and Mass Communications" course, have assembled the kinds of documents they feel best tell the historical development of women's role in communications in the United States from colonial times forward. Bibliographical footnotes.

29

Becker, Jörg, ed. **Information Technology and a New International Order**. Lund, Sweden: Student litteratur AB; Bromley, Kent, England: Chartwell-Bratt Ltd., 1984. 141p.

Papers from an international conference held by the Protestant Academy of Arnoldshain (Schmitten, FRG), the Protestant Association for Media Communication (Frankfurt, FRG) and the World Association for Christian Communication (London), with the common theme that all people are entitled to equal rights of access to information technology.

Articles discuss concentration of the media in both state and private hands, with its inevitable result on public opinion as it becomes more and more powerful; the danger that the increasing internationalization of media may prevent democratic control; and a final article, "Advertising and the Creation of Global Markets," contending that the new information technologies are creating an infrastructure that is making the 20th century "information age" a "commercial age" at a global level. References.

30

Becker, Jörg, Göran Hedebro, and Leena Paldén, eds. **Communication and Domination: Essays to Honor Herbert I. Schiller**. Norwood, NJ: Ablex, 1986. 278p.

Scholars from various countries of the socialist and capitalist—the developing and developed—world, and representing many of the disparate areas that make up the interdisciplinary field of communication, have contributed articles centering around Schiller's dominant theme—the use and misuse of power. In six parts: "The Formative Functions of Information Technology," "Information, International Relations, and Warfare," "Modes of Cultural Domination and Resistance," "The New Information Order: Struggles and Reconsiderations," "Reconstructing Information Patterns and Practices," and "Meeting the Future: Research and Action." Among the 27 contributors are Cees Hamelink, Tapio Varis, Dallas Smythe, Vincent Mosco, Stuart Ewen, Enrique González Manet, Yassen Zassoursky, William Melody, Kaarle Nordenstreng, Breda Pavlić, George Gerbner and James Halloran. Countries represented by the contributors are Germany, Sweden, Finland, Denmark, India, the United States, the U.S.S.R., Cuba, England, Holland, Canada, Ireland, Australia, Peru, Sri Lanka and Kenya. About half the articles contain "Notes" or "References." An author and a subject index.

31

Beharrell, Peter, and Greg Philo, eds. **Trade Unions and the Media**. London: Macmillan, 1977. 150p.

"This collection of essays is about the mass communications system of our society. It deals with the ownership and control of the mass media and the kind of messages that it broadcasts and prints. The common interest of the contributors here is in how the organization of the media, and what it produces, reflects the power of dominant interests in society at large."—Introduction. The essays make this point through analyses of various aspects of the relationship of British labor unions and the media. Contributors come from universities, labor organizations, and journalism. An appendix gives the National Union of Journalists' Code of Conduct. Bibliography.

32

Bennett, Susan, et al. **Media Studies in Education**. Paris: UNESCO, 1977. 92p. (Report and Papers on Mass Communication No. 80)

Covers aspects of media education in the secondary schools in certain European countries where it is emphasized: France, Italy, Federal Republic of Germany, The Netherlands, the United Kingdom, Denmark, Finland, Sweden, the U.S.S.R. (cinema only), and the U.S.A. In all countries except the U.S. film is stressed to the exclusion of other media. A final section is on organizations. Bibliography. (A new edition was published in 1988.)

33

Bennett, W. Lance. **News: The Politics of Illusion**. New York: Longman, 1983. 161p.

Although intended for a college textbook this readable, well-written book is also well-suited for laymen curious about how news is created, interpreted and packaged by the media. Bennett discusses in detail the structural conditions in the political system that determine news, calling it a "battle for information" among interest groups, government and the public, with the public increasingly losing ground for reasons he expands upon. Emphasis is political rather than cultural. Each chapter is copiously footnoted. Index.

34

Berelson, Bernard. **Content Analysis in Communication Research**. New York: Free Press, 1952. 220p.

The first book on content analysis, the then-new quantitative research technique frequently applied to mass media content. Berelson, on the faculty of the University of Chicago at the time of the book's publication, develops its history, methodology and application. See also, Pool, Ithiel de Sola, ed. **Trends in Content Analysis**, (No. 339).

35

Berger, Arthur Asa. **Media Analysis Techniques**. Beverly Hills, CA: Sage, 1982. 159p.

Media Analysis Techniques is a college-level text designed to acquaint students with explanations of four basic perspectives for interpreting various popular media and other texts—among them literature, advertisements, and political propaganda. The first part, "Techniques of Interpretation," explains the Marxist, psychoanalytical, semiological and sociological viewpoints as applied to critical analysis; the second, "Applications," applies them to specific case studies—an analysis of **Murder on the Orient Express**, fashion advertising, all news radio, and football, showing how varying techniques can result in quite different analyses of the same material. Annotated bibliographies follow each chapter.

36

Berger, Arthur Asa. **Television as an Instrument of Terror: Essays on Media, Popular Culture and Everyday Life**. New Brunswick, NJ: Transaction, 1980. 214p.

Readers of **Television as an Instrument of Terror** should not be misled by the word "terror" in the title. These are light-hearted essays which sometimes seem like, and are often intended to be, take-offs on more

serious articles about popular culture subjects and the study of popular culture itself.

37

Berger, Arthur Asa. **Signs in Contemporary Culture: An Introduction to Semiotics**. New York: Longman, 1984. 196p.

The theory of semiotics—the art of signs—is becoming more and more widely used in the study of the mass media, popular culture, the arts, and culture in general. Here Bergner has written "a personal (perhaps even idiosyncratic) explanation" for the general reader or beginning student. Each chapter is divided into two sections—the first dealing with a theoretical topic or topics, and the second applying a concept from it to some aspect of the media. Arcane terminology is kept to a minimum and, when used, carefully explained. Although simplified, it is not written down, and is quite interesting. There are references, a bibliography, a dictionary of concepts, and an index.

38

Bhasin, Kamla, and Bina Agerwal, eds. **Women and Media: Analysis, Alternatives and Action**. New Delhi, Kali for Women in collaboration with Isis International and the Pacific and Asian Women's Forum, 1984. 132p.

Articles, drawn mainly from the Asian and Pacific region, grouped in two parts: "Analysis," reflecting the portrayal of women through myth and the arts in the past and the mass media in the present; and "Action/Alternatives," focusing on attempts made by various women's groups both to protest against existing negative portrayals and to create alternatives. In conclusion is an annotated list, "Resources and Networks," and a bibliography.

39

Blumler, Jay G., and Elihu Katz, eds. **The Uses of Mass Communications: Current Perspectives on Gratifications Research**. Beverly Hills, CA: Sage, 1974. 318p.

The Uses of Mass Communications is a reader in which the authors treat the subject from a variety of viewpoints to show that there is room in the research for a number of approaches, including psychology, sociology, anthropology, ethnography, and philosophy. There are also a few cogent critiques of the uses and gratification position. Each of the 15 articles contain bibliographical references.

40

Bonney, Bill, and Helen Wilson. **Australia's Commercial Media**. Melbourne: Macmillan, 1983. 331p.

An in-depth study intended primarily as a college text in which the authors integrate factual, analytic and theoretical material. Their way of accomplishing this derives largely from recent British work on media and culture, especially at Birmingham's Center for Contemporary Cultural Studies and Leicester's Mass Communication Research Program, and they have attempted, "more deliberately than most work in media studies, to give equal weight to the analysis of media texts and the study of their general economic, political, technological and ideological determinants." The first chapter, "Studying the Media," explains their approach, and is valuable in itself. This is followed by chapters on the media and world capitalism in relation to Australia; ownership, control and regulation of the Australian media; technology and economy in the press; several chapters on advertising as a crucial factor in media economics; women's magazines and their packaging; and the marketing of news.

41

Boorstin, Daniel J. **The Image: A Guide to Pseudo-Events in America**. New York: Atheneum, 1961. 315p.

Published originally as **The Image, or What Happened to the American Dream**, Boorstin's insightful analysis of news and public relations and the thin line between has become a classic. He contends, with numerous examples, that the creation of news by publicists—the pseudo event as he terms it—has become as much a part of journalism as the coverage of the spontaneous events, and can turn into a self-fulfilling prophesy. In a section that follows the text, "Suggestions for Further Reading (and Writing)," he claims three purposes: to give further information about and insight into the topics; to acknowledge the books, articles, and other materials he has used; and to point out some unexplored territories. Index.

42

Boyd-Barrett, Oliver. **The International News Agencies**. Beverly Hills, CA: Sage, 1980. 284p.

A systematic inquiry into world news agencies, with a focus on the relationship between those of the developed and developing world. Boyd-Barrett examines the four major Western-based news agencies in particular—Reuters, the Associated Press, United Press International and Havas Agence France Press—in their dual role as both national and world news agencies, discussing their history, ownership, control, revenues, resources and range of services. The book shows that while the news agencies' role in the Third World is an important issue, it must also be seen in relation to their viability in their own developed world and points out the various pitfalls involved in the delivery of international news. All in all, this is one of the best possible sources for a critical examination of news agencies and their service role and for an explanation of the production of news, itself a fragile commodity.

43, 44

Braestrup, Peter. **Big Story: How the American Press and Television Reported and Interpreted the Crisis of Tet 1968 in Vietnam and Washington**. abr. ed. New Haven, CT: Yale University Press, 1983. 613p.

Braestrup, Peter. **Battle Lines: Report of the Twentieth Century Fund Task Force on the Military and the Media**. New York: Priority Press, 1985. 178p.

Braestrup is one of the most precise American reporters on military coverage by the media. **Big Story** is his detailed and in-depth assessment of the U.S. press in Vietnam during the period when he was Saigon Bureau chief for the **Washington Post**. The two-volume edition contains 700 pages of documentation, including transcripts of news conferences, briefings, key TV programs, and special studies, among which is an analysis of published news photographs and a detailed chapter by Burns W. Roper on public opinion polls before, during and after Tet. It is illustrated with 110 photos of newsmen and others involved in the Tet action. The abridged edition, which is itself more than 600 pages, contains 60 pages of notes but no photographs.

Battle Lines, his report of the Task Force's findings about media coverage during the U.S. attack on Grenada, raises the issues of media access to U.S. forces in combat, which "provoked fresh arguments over relations between the military and the media, with their sometimes conflicting goals of defending the nation and informing the citizenry," and other crucial issues as well. A background paper provides an overview of U.S. military-media relations in overseas battle zones from World War II to Grenada, followed by a chapter on "Press Freedom: Rhetorical and Constitutional Issues," and "Two Cultures," exemplified by the world of the soldier and the world of the journalist. An appendix gives the recommendations in the report, which was issued by the Joint Chiefs of Staff Media-Military Relations Panel, known as the Sidle Panel. Chapter footnotes.

45

Brantlinger, Patrick. **Bread & Circuses: Theories of Mass Culture as Social Decay**. Ithaca, NY: Cornell University Press, 1983. 307p.

"My chief purpose has been to provide a critique of the methodology of negative classicism as it has developed over the last two centuries in relation to 'mass culture': the mass media, journalism, mass education, the cultural effects of the processes of democratization and industrialization," says Brantlinger in his Introduction. He has focused chronologically on major patterns and major cultural theorists from their Greek and Roman origins to Harold Innis, Marshall McLuhan and the Frankfurt Institute. In conclusion he points out that today television is seen as one of the causes in the alleged decline and fall of contemporary culture—a view which he feels obscures the potential of the new communications technology. Notes and index.

46

Briggs, Asa. **Mass Entertainment: The Origins of a Modern Industry**. Adelaide, Australia: The Griffin Press, 1960. 30p. (John Fisher Lecture in Commerce, University of Adelaide)

This brief pamphlet gives a deeper insight into popular culture than many much longer works. Briggs approaches the development of mass entertainment from an economic and technological viewpoint, analyzing underlying conditions that make it an industry, and specifically tracing its growth in the nineteenth and twentieth centuries, with emphasis on film and broadcasting in the latter.

47

Brogan, Patrick. **Spiked: The Short Life and Death of the National News Council**. New York: Priority Press, 1985. 129p.

A brief history of the National News Council, 1979–1984—why it was attempted and why it failed—commissioned by the Twentieth Century Fund and written by an editorial writer on the New York **Daily News**. An appendix gives an account of the British Press Council whose success influenced the founders of its American counterpart. Other appendixes include the Task Force's recommendations; a cast of characters; a memorandum from A.O. Salzberger; contributors; publications (**In the Public Interest I**, 1973–75; **In the Public Interest II**, 1975–78; **In the Public Interest III**, 1979–83, Nos. 206, 207, 208); and revenues and expenses for 1975–78.

48

Brookeman, Christopher. **American Culture and Society Since the 1930s**. New York: Schocken, 1984. 241p.

Brookman's analysis centers around various interpretations of mass society and mass culture in the U.S. over the past 50 years, as exemplified by the theories and criticisms that emerged from certain individuals and schools representing academics, writers, film makers, journalists—among them being Daniel Bell, Southern Agrarianism, Dwight Macdonald, Marshall McLuhan, Herbert Marcuse, Tom Wolfe, the Frankfurt School (Paul Lazarsfeld, Leo Lowenthal, Max Horkheimer, Theodore Adorno), David Riesman, Norman Mailer, the auteur theory, and Susan Sontag.

49

Brown, Allan. **Commercial Media in Australia: Economics, Ownership, Technology, and Regulation**. St. Lucia, Queensland, Australia: University of Queensland Press, 1986. 240p.

Following an examination of the mainstream literature on the economics of newspaper publishing and commercial broadcasting, Brown, a professor of economics at the University of Queensland, analyzes their structure, ownership, technology and economic performance, and investigates and evaluates government policy on control and regulation. The discussion of policy takes into account the need for diversity. Whenever possible he has avoided jargon. Appendixes give figures on the four major newspaper groups. Notes, bibliography and index.

50

Brucker, Herbert. **Communication Is Power: Unchanging Values in a Changing Journalism**. New York: Oxford, 1973. 385p.

Brucker's commentaries, representing half a century of experience, in which he expounds his theories about the role of journalism in society: that its primary function is to disseminate and interpret news to the layman, "whether through print, electronics, or other means; and that it serves best if it also makes the governors—economic and moral governors as well as political governors—aware of what the governed think and feel." Using these standards, he accesses journalism's successes and failures, and the broad underlying factors that contribute. Specific aspects as shown by some of the chapter headings are "Newspapers Shouldn't Play God," "What Is News?" "Reporting Crime," "A Conscience for the Press," "Mass Man and Mass Media," "The Prophet Motive," "Should an Editor Edit?" "Who Should Own Newspapers?" Notes and index.

51

Bruun, Lars, ed. **Professional Codes of Journalism**. Prague: International Organization of Journalists, 1979. 127p.

This is not a compilation of codes of ethics, but rather a compilation about them, with chapters by journalists and journalist/educators from Eastern and Western Europe and Latin America. Chapters include: "The History of Written Codes of Ethics—A Chronology of Events" and "Contemporary Codes—A Review," both by Lara Bruun (Finland); "Media Councils in the Western Hemisphere" by J. Clement Jones (England); "Journalists' Responsibility for the Destiny of Peace" by Spartak Beglov (U.S.S.R.); "Toward an International Code of Ethics" by Cees Hamelink (Holland); "Journalistic Ethics in Latin America" by Hernan Uribe (Chile); and "The International Ethics of Journalists" by Jean-Maurice Hermann (France). Appendixes contain a number of relevant documents from various nations and the UN. There are no indexes or references.

52

Bryant, Jennings, and Dolf Zillmann, eds. **Perspectives on Media Effects**. Hillsdale, NJ: Erlbaum, 1986. 358p.

Although a preponderance of empirical research on media effects has appeared in scholarly journals very little of it has consisted of single volumes, say the authors, who tell us that this one is the first to appear since the classic **The Process and Effects of Mass Communication**, edited by Wilbur Schramm and published in 1954 (with a revised edition co-edited with Donald Roberts in 1971, No. 389). But whereas Schramm emphasized general aspects of political communication, persuasion, and advertising effects in the print media and reflected the "state of the art" of empirical research several decades ago, many of these articles center around television in its various aspects—among them, aggression, addiction, effect on children, educational impact, personality of viewer, presentation of minorities, psychological theories, and advantageous use. Other more general articles concern entertainment, news, gratification theory, election projections, and the parameters for information society research. Each contains extensive references which review the literature. There is an index to the authors whose work is mentioned and a subject index.

53

Budd, Richard W., Robert K. Thorp, and Lewis Donohew. **Content Analysis of Communications**. New York: Macmillan Company, 1967. 147p.

One of the earlier texts on the application of content analysis to forms of human communication, full of examples from research about the media. A lengthy, annotated bibliography, divided by books and articles, provides a history of the development of the technique.

54

Bures, Oldrich, ed. **The Children and the Mass Media**. Prague: International Organization of Journalists, 1980. 128p.

Essays by authors from Communist countries which consist largely of the writers' opinions, with occasional references to studies but with no documentation. There is, however, a "A Selective Analytical Bibliography" which abstracts 49 books and articles on the subject. All of the essays are heavily value-laden.

55

Burgess, Jacquelin, and John R. Gold, eds. **Geography, the Media and Popular Culture**. London: Croom Helm, 1985. 273p.

Essays which are interesting not only for their content but because they suggest ways in which geographers specializing in the study of people have used the media as a focus to explore a wide variety of popular culture forms. Theoretical and methodological orientations differ widely, but all the essays concern themselves with material and symbolic expressions of the 'everyday' lives of 'ordinary' people and the places in which they live. One, for example, analyzes the impact of changing technology on the gathering, processing and dissemination of "non-local news" during the 19th and early 20th centuries in the **Cincinnati-Enquirer**, using theoretical formulations of Harold Innis; another essay, straddling physical and human geography, studies disaster fiction and films to discover its appeal to producers and audience; another explores the urban visions of films

produced during the inter-war periods. The 10 essays all have in common an exploration of the media one way or another for geographic purposes. The editors have written an excellent introductory essay on various approaches both American and British frequently used in communication studies. Bibliography and index.

56

Burnet, Mary. **The Mass Media in a Violent World**. Paris: UNESCO, 1974. 44p. (Reports and Papers on Mass Communication No. 63)

This, one of the earliest studies on the subject, is a report of a symposium conducted by 23 specialists in various disciplines of the social sciences who represent 18 countries. Emphasis is worldwide as members attempt to answer three questions: (1) What is meant by violence? (2) What is commonly assumed and what is actually known about the relation between violence in the mass media and violence in real life? (3) How can the media carry out their traditional mission of informing, educating, and entertaining in such a way that their influence will tend to reduce rather than increase violence? The developing countries come in for special attention. Discussion centers around structure and theory rather than empirical studies.

57

Butler, Matilda, and William Paisley. **Women and the Mass Media: Sourcebook for Research and Action**. New York: Human Sciences Press, 1980. 432p.

Intended to serve as a framework for study groups interested in various aspects of the treatment of women in and by the media. In a series of chapters the authors summarize various pertinent materials, with notes leading back to the source for each, on such subjects as sexism in language, in image and in media content, institutional sexism in the media, sexism and media audiences, the history of the struggle for women's rights, and a discussion about research. In conclusion are suggestions for types of action which can be pursued. An appendix gives additional resources for research and action. There is an extensive bibliography, and separate name and subject indexes.

58

Carpenter, Edmund, and Marshall McLuhan, eds., **Explorations in Communication: An Anthology**. Boston: Beacon, 1960. 210p.

Before Marshall McLuhan became well known, he and Carpenter were using a journal, **Explorations**, published at the University of Toronto between 1953 and 1959, as a sounding board for new and different approaches to communication. (Issues are now rare items.) All the essays in this anthology appeared in **Explorations**. They probed the grammars of such languages as print, the newspaper format, and television, arguing that revolutions in the packaging and distribution of ideas and feelings modified not only human relations but also sensibilities. They further argued that we are largely ignorant of literacy's role in shaping Western man, and equally unaware of the role of electronic media in shaping modern values. These ideas are current today, but were for the most part pioneered by the contributors who included, in addition to Carpenter and McLuhan, David Reisman, Robert Graves, S. Gideon, Stanley Edgar Hyman, and Gilbert Seldes, among others.

59

Cater, Douglass. **The Fourth Branch of Government**. New York: Houghton Mifflin, 1959. 194p.

Cater was one of the early writers to realize the importance of the reporter's role in government, as exemplified by the Washington journalist. As a Washington reporter himself who was working at the time for **The Reporter**, an analytical fortnightly, he observed and participated, so that his book is written from first-hand knowledge. His analysis is a thought-provoking contribution to the literature, which includes Leo C. Rosten's **The Washington Correspondents** (Harcourt, Brace, 1937, probably the first book on the subject, No. 952) and, more recently, the works of William L. Rivers and Stephen Hess's **The Washington Reporters** (No. 184) in the **Newswork** series. Footnotes.

60

Cawelti, John G. **The Six-Gun Mystique**. Bowling Green, OH: Bowling Green University Popular Press, 1971. 138p.

Cawelti has used the Western genre as an example to show the basic principles of interpretation and explanation relevant to popular formula narrative and drama, discussing how a number of factors have interacted in the complex process of its evolution. This methodology, he believes, can be used to explicate other formula genre. In making the case he discusses various methodologies—their strengths and weaknesses. He concludes with a bibliographic essay featuring books and film, illustrating "the nineteenth century shaping and twentieth century practice of a certain kind of fiction which might loosely be described as stories and novels of the romantic or legendary West, a type of fiction that has centered around the sort of literary and cultural formula defined in the preceding essay." There is no index.

61

Chaffee, Steven H., ed. **Political Communication: Issues and Strategies for Research**. Beverly Hills, CA: Sage, 1975. 319p. (Sage Annual Reviews of Communication Research, v. 4.)

Articles by social scientists brought together in an attempt "to assume, in some degree or another, that the study of political communication needs to be approached from fresh intellectual perspectives, and with new tools." Their goal, they say, "is not the achievement of

positive certitude about human behavior; it is the more pragmatic aim of developing vigorous and challenging fields of inquiry" by devising new kinds of questions about communication and politics, and sharpening methodological procedures. Contributors are Lee Becker, Maxwell McCombs and Jack McLeod; Karen Siune and Gerald Kline; Garrett O'Keefe; Jay Blumler and Michael Gurevitch; Sidney Kraus, Dennis Davis, Gladys and Kurt Lang; William Rivers, Susan Miller and Oscar Gandy; John D. Stevens; Donald Gillmor and Everette Dennis; and the editor.

62

Chafee, Zechariah, Jr. **Government and Mass Communications**. Chicago: University of Chicago Press, 1947. 2 vols.

An in-depth review of governmental restrictions which affect freedom of the press. These are companion volumes to Hocking (No. 192) in which he discusses the foundations of press freedom and law, and both are part of the larger Commission on Freedom of the Press study (No. 81). Both volumes are indexed.

63

Chafets, Ze'ev. **A Double Vision: How the Press Distorts America's View of the Middle East**. New York: Morrow, 1985. 349p.

As yet, no impartial scholar (if one is to be found) has made an assessment of press coverage of the Israeli-Arab wars. Lacking that, present assessments of press coverage are likely to bring with it the author's point of view, governed by his nationality. This book is no exception; its author, director of Israel's Government Press Office, cautions the reader that as an Israeli veteran of the Middle East press wars he is sometimes critical of his country's policies but generally sympathetic to its point of view. With this disclaimer, he describes and explains through various stories, the subtleties of press coverage in the Middle East with its problems for the Western reporter such as censorship, ignorance of Middle Eastern languages, history and culture, physical danger, instructions from the home front, and other difficulties that can stand between journalism and reality. He also includes a discussion of the Iran-Iraq war. This is an excellent book from the standpoint of foreign news coverage in particular and even reporting in general. Notes and index.

64

Chambers, Iain. **Popular Culture: The Metropolitan Experience**. London: Methuen, 1986. 244p.

In this college text Chambers defines popular culture broadly as a whole way of life based on everyday happenings and objects rather than as literature and the arts. In the greater part of the book he suggests through picture and text the vast and complicated array of sights, sounds, tastes, choices, sentiments and politics which have formed British culture over the past 30 years, and in a final chapter summarizes the theoretical underpinnings—linguistic, semantic, semiotic, Marxian, and structuralist—by which the culture can be analyzed. He has succeeded admirably in making a complex subject understandable. "References," "Further Materials" and an index.

65

Chibnall, Steve. **Law-and-Order News: An Analysis of Crime Reporting in the British Press**. London: Tavistock, 1977. 288p.

"Newspapers and television do not merely monitor the events of the real world; they construct representations and accounts of reality which are shaped by the constraints imposed upon them: constraints emanating from the conventions, ideologies, and organization of journalism and news bureaucracies," says Chibnall, who uses crime reporting to prove his point. The aim of his study is to examine the values, ideologies, and interests that go into the construction of crime news by using two main areas of inquiry: the ownership and control of newspaper businesses, and the world of the professional communicator. In making his points he surveys the literature; traces the development of crime reporting as a field of journalism; analyzes law-and-order news during 1965–1975; discusses the symbiotic relationship between crime reporters and police sources and examines specifically the goals and techniques of news management by the police in Britain and the army in Ulster; and finally, explores the wider implications of the study. A chronology of law-and-order events helps the reader to place the happenings mentioned in a context. Notes, bibliography and index.

66

Chimutengwende, Chenhamo C. **South Africa: The Press and the Politics of Liberation**. London: Carleton House, 1978. 197p.

An analysis of the mass media in South Africa as instruments of oppression or liberation and their role in effecting change or perpetuating the status quo. Chimutengwende examines the operation of the press within the South African socio-economic and legislative system and in relation to the blacks' struggle for liberation, ending with conclusions as to role of the press in affecting change or maintaining the status quo. For the latter he has drawn heavily on communication theory. This is a measured and well-reasoned study that challenges some Western concepts of freedom of the press. Emphasis is on print media. Bibliography.

67, 68

Christian Communication Directory. Africa. Franz-Josef Eilers, et al., eds. Paderborn, Munchen, Vienna, Zurich: Ferdinand Schoningh in connection with the Catholic Media Council, Lutheran World Federation, and World Association for Christian Communications, 1980. 544p.

Christian Communication Directory. Asia. Franz-Josef Eilers, et al., eds. Paderborn, Munchen, Vienna, Zurich: Ferdinand Schoningh in connection with the Catholic Media Council, Lutheran World Federation, and World Association for Christian Communications, 1982. 1,036p.

These two volumes represent a systematic effort to collect all relevant information on Christian media institutions for the whole of Africa and Asia except the Near East, with emphasis on institutions related to the three organizations compiling the data. Classification in both volumes is in nine categories: Church Communication Centres, News and Information Services, Publishing Houses, Printing Presses, Periodicals, Radio/TV Stations, Radio/TV Production Studios, AV/Film Centres, Research and Training Institutions—all listed by country with an index of names. Information for each country varies according to the degree of organization within it. The three institutions responsible for the directories plan eventually to include Latin America and perhaps other regions.

69

Christian, Harry, ed. **The Sociology of Journalism and the Press**. Keele, England: University of Keele, 1980. 395p. (**Sociological Review Monograph** 29)

Christian remarks in his Introduction on the shift in perspective in the study of mass communication in the past decade as it has moved away from attempts to develop a specialized theory which treated it as a field analytically distinct from the rest of society toward a more integrated view of the media as social institutions forming interdependent parts of the wider society and therefore requiring to be incorporated into general sociological and political theories. "The questions raised have become broader in scope and less amenable to positivistic and quantitative methods, so that instead historical, interpretive or dialectical approaches have found greater favor," he continues. This shift in perspective was exemplified in 1977 by **Mass Communication and Society**, edited by James Curran, Michael Gurevitch and Janet Woollacott (No. 91) and **Culture, Society and the Media** by Michael Gurevitch, et al. (1982) (No.163).

70

Christians, Clifford G., and Catherine L. Covert. **Teaching Ethics in Journalism Education**. Hastings-on-Hudson, NY: Institute of Society, Ethics and Life Science, 1980. 71p.

Moral considerations have been incorporated into journalism courses from the time they first became a formal study in the early decades of the century. In their examination of the subject Covert and Christians consider the development historically of news reporting and of journalism education in reference to matters of ethics and discuss the state of the art in media ethics instruction, along with substantive issues in ethics courses and instructional objectives. Chapter notes and bibliography.

71

Christians, Clifford G., Kim B. Rotzoll, and Mark Fackler. **Media Ethics: Cases and Moral Reasoning**. New York: Longman, 1983. 331p.

A textbook involving case studies and their analyses. Under the headings of news, advertising and entertainment the authors discuss, in prose that could serve as a model for textbook writing, such pressing issues as truth telling, reporters and sources, violence, invasion of privacy, censorship, financial improprieties, what kinds of advertising to accept and how to write the ads, triviality and escapism, what to do about offensive material, and other problems involving ethics. Case studies illustrate each issue. The "Recommended Reading" includes a listing of codes and guidelines issued by the various media organizations, with addresses. (A second edition was issued in 1987.)

72

Chu, Godwin C., ed. **Popular Media in China: Shaping New Cultural Patterns**. Honolulu: Published for the East-West Center by the University of Hawaii Press, 1978. 263p.

Eight articles which focus on the structure and content of China's "popular media," adapting old traditional forms of art and entertainment to create a new culture and transform basic patterns of thought and behavior. The studies deal with folk songs, opera, comic books, short stories and wall newspapers, showing how they are used and what values and ideas they attempt to convey. For a descriptive analysis of the mass media, see John Howkin's **Mass Communication in China** (No. 198).

73

Clarke, Peter, and Susan H. Evans. **Covering Campaigns: Journalism in Congressional Elections**. Stanford, CA: Stanford University Press, 1983. 151p.

A nation-wide survey of political journalism which, the authors say, "represents an important shift in a long-standing media-and-politics research tradition. Instead of media-reliance patterns among voters, we look at work patterns among a national sample of media professionals. Instead of presidential elections, our eye focuses on congressional contests." Research is limited to print which for congressional elections they say is the main source of coverage. There is a list of references, an index, and appendixes showing the questionnaire given to reporters and the newspapers surveyed.

74

Clutterbuck, Richard. **The Media and Political Violence**. 2d ed. London: Macmillan, 1983. 191p.

Clutterbuck, a former general turned academic, believes that media coverage of riots, violent picketing and terrorism in the British press has played into the hands of the instigators. In this somewhat controversial book he examines the evidence. A substantial part of the examination consists of case studies. In a final chapter, "The Media in a Reasonable Society," he suggests governmental regulations which journalists feel would be inhibiting. Chapter notes and references, a bibliography and an index.

75

Cockerell, Michael, Peter Hennessy, and David Walker. **Sources Close to the Prime Minister: Inside the Hidden World of the News Manipulators**. London: Macmillan, 1984. 255p.

"This book is about news management: about the suppression and dissemination of official information, and about the political manipulation of what journalists report," say the authors in this examination of the British press which they feel has institutionalized a penchant for secrecy. Although they take a long hard look at the Thatcher government in particular, they also attribute it to the political collaboration between journalists and politicians in former governments. The book ends with calls for reform. Much of the material is based on interviews, some of which were with "moles" in Whitehall and among the Westminster Lobby correspondents— "Those unknown warriors in the cause of openness." Index.

76

Cohen, Bernard C. **The Press and Foreign Policy**. Princeton, NJ: Princeton University Press, 1963. 288p.

A quarter of a century has not diminished the timeliness of Cohen's penetrating analysis of the place of the press in American foreign policy-making as it revolves around the competing demands of diplomacy and democracy on the organization and conduct of foreign affairs reporting. One by one he takes up the alternative viewpoints embedded into the structure of the American political system, as for instance the claims of diplomacy which often involve secrecy versus the claims of journalists which traditionally involve the peoples' right to know—a conflict which can affect the quality both of policy-making and of news. He also discusses the effects of the journalistic policy of gearing foreign affairs reporting to a general audience rather than to the relatively small policy and opinion elites, and of the organizational pattern by which news is collected and distributed. Neither these or the other issues which Cohen discusses have dated, nor have his comments and suggestions. Notes and index. For another excellent older book treating the same problem from a different angle, see Theodore Kruglak's **The Foreign Correspondents: A Study of the Men and Women Reporting for the American Information Media in Western Europe**, 1955 (See No. 238).

77

Cohen, Phil, and Carl Gardner, eds. **It Ain't Half Racist, Mum**. London: Comedia in conjunction with Campaign Against Racism in the Media, 1982. 119p. (Comedia series, No. 10)

Short, specific, down-to-earth articles cover various aspects of racism as practiced by the British media, grouped under three headings, "Media Racism in Action," "The Colonial View," and "Campaigning in the Media." Appendixes give codes and guidelines formulated by the National Union of Journalists and other concerned organizations, and a list of such organizations with addresses.

78

Cohen, Stanley, and Jock Young, eds. **The Manufacture of News: Social Problems, Deviance and the Mass Media**. Rev. ed. Beverly Hills, CA: Sage, 1981. 506p.

Thirty articles, each of which is designed to show the mass media's conceptions of deviance and social problems and the implicit view of society behind these conceptions. The editors have organized the articles around two very different theories—or models: the mass manipulative model in which the public is seen as being manipulated by powerful groups, and the commercial or market model which argues that diversity of media and consequently of information opts against manipulation. Articles illustrate how these models work in three areas of social problem imagery: selection, presentation and effects. A number of the articles are case studies. This revised edition has been considerably changed from the earlier (1973) one. Chapter headings.

79

Cohen, Yoel. **Media Diplomacy: The Foreign Office in the Mass Communication Age**. London: Frank Cass, 1986. 197p.

A study based on 250 interviews in Britain and abroad with government ministers, parliamentarians, civil servants, editors, journalists, and interest group leaders which examines the ways events in recent British diplomatic history have been presented to the media and covered by press and television. Cohen has pinpointed the areas where the media impinge on the foreign policy process either in terms on public opinion, new information to policy makers, or use by officials as channels of information to other governments and to the public at home and abroad. One of the features is a detailed account of "the British government's nervous news management of the Falklands War." Notes, bibliography and index.

80

Collins, Richard, et al., eds. **Media, Culture and Society: A Critical Reader**. Beverly Hills, CA: Sage, 1986. 346p.

Articles from the journal **Media, Culture and Society** published between its foundation in 1979 through 1985, and "grouped to illustrate the major intellectual themes and concerns that distinguish the approach of **Media, Culture and Society** to the analysis of the mass media from other approaches—for example, the classical tradition of empirical 'effects' studies, with which many, especially non-British readers, may be more familiar." Part One, "Approaches to Cultural Theory," analyzes the mass media in a very broad cultural and social context. Part Two, "Intellectuals and Cultural Production," examines the composition and social role of a specific social group—the intellectuals or cultural producers—in its relationship to cultural consumers and to other centers of social power. Part Three, "British Broadcasting and the Public Sphere," gives concrete examples of general theoretical positions within a national and historical context. An introduction explains in some detail the genesis and development of the critical tradition and helps to place the collection of articles in their specific historical and socio-cultural context. Editors, in addition to Collins, include James Curran, Nicholas Garnham, Patty Scannell, Philip Schlesinger and Colin Sparks. Additional articles are by Stuart Hall, John Corner, Michele Mattelart, Philip Elliott, Raymond Williams (with Garnham), Pierre Bourdieu, David Cardiff, and David Cheney. Notes and bibliographies for each article.

81

Commission on Freedom of the Press. **Reports**. 6 vols. Chicago: University of Chicago Press, 1946–47.

The following studies resulted from an inquiry financed by Time, Inc., and Encyclopedia Britannica, Inc., with funds disbursed through the University of Chicago. The aim of the Commission, composed mostly of some of the leading university educators of the day and chaired by Robert M. Hutchins, chancellor of the University of Chicago, was to investigate the flow of public information through the press as comprised of radio, newspapers, motion pictures, magazines, and books. Equal emphasis was placed on the flow of ideas. Recommendations, although not drastic enough for some, went further than freedom of the press, and urged owners and managers to be aware of their responsibility to American culture and the American people—in short, they formulated the social responsibility theory. Even though this has generally not worked out in practice, the studies listed below go deeply into history, structure, problems, and principles of individual media and press freedom and provide a landmark. They are:

A Free and Responsible Press: A General Report on Mass Communication: Newspapers, Radio, Motion Pictures, Magazines and Books (No. 130)].

Peoples Speaking to Peoples: A Report on International Mass Communication. By Llewellyn White and Robert D. Leigh (No. 452).

American Radio: A Report on the Broadcasting Industry in the United States. By Llewellyn White (No. 836).

Freedom of the Press: A Framework of Principle. By William Ernest Hocking (No. 192).

Government and Mass Communications. By Zechariah Chafee, Jr. (No. 62).

Freedom of the Movies: A Report on Self Regulation. By Ruth A. Inglis (No. 1298).

In 1950 Frank Hughes issued a sharp—often shrill—rebuttal of the Commission's Report: **Prejudice and the Press: A Restatement of the Principle of Freedom of the Press with Specific Reference to the Hutchins-Luce Commission** (Devin-Adair. 642p.)

82

Communication Policies . . . . Paris: UNESCO, 1974–.

A series of studies whose aim is an analysis of communication policies in various countries as they exist at public, institutional, and professional levels, with information presented in a way that enables comparison. Countries covered thus far are the following:

Furhoff, Lars, Lennart Jonsson, and Lennart Nilsson. **Communication Policies in Sweden: A Study Carried out by the Swedish Journalism School**. 1974. 76p.

Mahle, Walter A., and Rolf Richter. **Communication Policies in the Federal Republic of Germany: A Study Carried out by the Arbeitsgemeinschaft fur Kommunikationforschung**. 1974. 86p.

Szecsko, Tamás, and Gabor Fodor. **Communication Policies in Hungary**. 1974. 58p.

Stapleton, John. **Communication Policies in Ireland: A Study Carried out by the Institute of Public Administration, An Foras Riarachain**. 1974. 73p.

Camargo, Nelly de, and Virgilio B. Noya Pinto. **Communication Policies in Brazil**. 1975. 80p.

Leković, Zdravko, and Mihailo Bjelica. **Communication Policies in Yugoslavia: A Study Carried out by the Yugoslav Institute of Journalism**. Rev. ed. 1976. 66p.

Desai, M.V. **Communication Policies in India**. 1977. 88p.

De Silva, M.A., and Reggie Siriwardene. **Communication Policies in Sri Lanka: A Study Carried out by a Committee Appointed by the Ministry of Education**. 1977. 59p.

Fonseca, Jaime M. **Communication Policies in Costa Rica**. 1977. 89p.

Kato, Hidetoshi. **Communication Policies in Japan**. 1978. 57p.

Ortega, Carlos, and Carlos Romero. **Communication Policies in Peru**. 1977. 68p.

Alajmo, Alberto Carrizosa. **Communication Policies in Columbia**. 1977. 50p.

Las Politicas de Comunicación en Venezuela. 1977. 109 p. (Not published in English)

Pae-Ho, Hahn. **Communication Policies in the Republic of Korea**. 1978. 50p.

Mwaura, Peter. **Communication Policies in Kenya**. 1980. 94p.

Ugboajah, Frank Okwu. **Communication Policies in Nigeria**. 1980. 67p.

Bokonga, Ekanga Botombele. **Communication Policies in Zaire**. 1980. 59p.

83, 84

Compaine, Benjamin M., et al. **Who Owns the Media? Concentration of Ownership in the Media Communications Industry**. 2d ed. White Plains, NY: Knowledge Industries, 1982. 529p.

Compaine, Benjamin M., ed. **Understanding New Media: Trends and Issues in Electronic Distribution and Information**. Cambridge, MA: Ballinger, 1984. 378p.

The primary objective of **Who Owns the Media?** is "to bring together as much relevant data as feasible on the nature and degree of competition and ownership in the mass media business . . . in order to provide an empirical context for the continuing debate on the structure of the traditional media segments," says Compaine. Other objectives are to specifically identify the owners of media and to explore the extent of concentration today compared to previous periods. Medium by medium the authors examine the information industry. Compaine writes about newspapers and magazines; Christopher Sterling, television and radio broadcasting and cable and pay TV; Thomas Guback, theatrical film; and J. Kendrick Noble, books. In a final chapter, "How Few Is Too Few?" Compaine discusses implications. Text is accompanied by many tables; chapters have "Notes," and there is a lengthy bibliography of books and articles. Index.

Understanding New Media takes a hard look at the social and technological forces shaping the information industries, broadly defined—their extent; trends and forces in distribution; strategic implications; and possible future developments. Among issues discussed are the extent of the information business as a whole; its shifting boundaries; present and future effects of new technologies on broadcasting and newspapers; regulation; and computer literacy. Each is treated within the framework of oral and print literacy. This is an excellent sourcebook for interested laymen, for workers within some part of the industry who would like to see it as a whole, and for beginning students. The authors of the various articles have managed to keep their writing clear and simple, although the issues are neither. Chapter notes; appendixes; brief bibliography; index.

85

Comstock, George, ed. **Public Communication and Behavior**. v.1. Orlando, FL: Academic Press, 1986. 319p.

First of a series designed to cover portions of research and theory development from within a wide range of disciplines and fields—advertising, child development, education, journalism, political science, sociology, and social psychology which Comstock considers basic to all the topics. Emphasis is and will continue to be on "theory—guided by empirical fact." Contents of volume one include "An Evaluation of the Models Used to Evaluate Television Series" by Thomas D. Cook and Thomas Curtin; "A Synthesis of 1034 Effects of Television on Social Behavior" by Susan Hearold; "More Than Meets the Eye: TV News, Priming, and Public Evaluations of the President" by Shanto Iyengar and Donald Kinder; "The Myth of Massive Media Impact: Savagings and Salvagings" by William J. McGuire; and "The Found Experiment: A New Technique for Assessing the Impact of Mass Media Violence on Real-World Aggressive Behavior" by David P. Phillips. References for each article. Index.

86

Connor, Walter D., and Zvi Y. Gitelman, with Adaline Huszezo and Robert Blumstock. **Public Opinion in European Socialist Systems**. New York: Praeger, 1977. 196p.

Concentrates on the U.S.S.R., Poland, Czechoslovakia, and Hungary, describing the emergence of opinion polls, the ups and downs and the reasons behind them, and the ways in which they are conducted. Although data obtained from the polls occupies a large space, primary emphasis is on a social analysis of the process and its effects, with the regimes of the four countries examined both as subject acting to maintain itself and as object being evaluated by the public. Contains chapter notes and an index.

87

Connors, Tracy Daniel. **Longman Dictionary of Mass Media and Communication**. New York: Longman, 1982. 255p.

On the theory that technical jargon or slang for the same terms can have different meanings in various communication specialties, Connors has amassed this dictionary to help communicators communicate with each other by bringing together in one alphabet the terms most often used and indicating specific area or areas of communication in which the meaning belongs. Subjects covered are advertising; television and radio broadcasting; computerized information management; data processing; film; graphic arts; magazine, newsletter and newspaper journalism; marketing; photojournalism and photography; printing; public relations and communication; publishing; theater.

88

Covert, Catherine L., and John D. Stevens, eds. **Mass Media Between the Wars: Perceptions of Cultural Tension, 1918–1941**. Syracuse, NY: Syracuse University Press, 1984. 252p.

A collection of 12 essays about the cultural dimensions of the new mass media forms between the two world wars. Although not limited to this theme the essays discuss and illustrate the interaction of the mass media public with the new technology of the era—slick photography magazines, radio, the newsreel, tabloids,

and the growth of the wire services. The authors are a blend of historians of the mass media from programs in mass communication and historians from American history programs. As Covert says in her introduction, the vitality of the book "comes in juxtaposing the views of the academic historians, on the one hand, with those of historians in communication schools, on the other." The book ends with an unusually comprehensive bibliographic essay by Jennifer Tebbe of the Massachusetts College of Pharmacy, Boston.

89

Crawford, Nelson Antrim. **The Ethics of Journalism**. New York: Knopf, c1924, 1969. 264p.

This is among the earliest—probably *the* earliest—effort to discuss standards of the press—their formation, development, and acceptance. Crawford's description of his aim in the Preface is still timely: "The function of the volume is not to lay down a series of rules for the guidance of the young journalist, but rather to aid him in the formulating for himself an ethical philosophy of his profession that will be realistic, discerning, intellectually honest, and applicable to the press as social institution." Among the areas he discusses are journalism as a profession, indictments of the press, objectivity, and setting standards. An appendix consists of codes of ethics and rules adopted by organizations of journalists and by newspapers. Bibliography and index.

90

Crouse, Timothy. **The Boys on the Bus**. New York: Random House, 1972. 383p.

A descriptive book about the national political press corp as it worked to cover the presidential primaries, the political party conventions, and the presidential campaigns of Richard Nixon and George McGovern. Crouse describes in lively detail the way the political journalists work together on the campaign trail (on the bus), sketches the working lives of the acknowledged leaders among the journalists, and probes critical issues about the relationships these journalists have with politicians and staff members. The events center around the 1972 presidential campaign, but the value of the book goes beyond its story of one campaign to become a discussion of issues of political reporting.

91

Curran, James, Michael Gurevitch, and Janet Woollacott, eds. **Mass Communication and Society**. London: Edward Arnold in association with The Open University Press, 1977. 479p.

"The central concern of this Reader is with whole societies, their class structure and forms of class dominance and an exploration of the role of the media as ideological and signifying agencies within that whole. The concept of ideology is therefore of central concern," say the editors in their anthology. This is a very different approach from the empirical Lasswellian research formula: "Who says what in which channel to whom with what effect?" Divided into three sections: Section I presents the relationships between the media and society from different ideological perspectives; Section II focuses on the organizational structure of the media; Section III reflects a variety of approaches to "ideology" and the communication of "culture." Most of the articles were especially commissioned. Each is followed by extensive references. Among the authors are Graham Murdock and Peter Golding. Denis McQuail, Oliver Boyd-Barrett, Philip Elliott, Anthony Smith, Michael Tracey, James Carey, Jay Blumler, Stuart Hall, and the editors.

92

Curran, James, and Jean Seaton. **Power Without Responsibility: The Press and Broadcasting in Britain**. 2d ed. London: Methuen, 1985. 396p.

An examination of British broadcasting within the context of British journalism, and its relation to its role in politics, which is also an examination of the British press as a whole. The authors contend throughout that the relationship between the media and society varies with the climate of the times and the changing technologies, and that commonly held theories about them need reassessment. They trace historically the forces that lead to the present structure and to popularly held conceptions, ending their analysis with proposals for specific reforms. Overall, their conclusions are pessimistic. A 31-page bibliography broken down by subject; chapter notes; and an index.

93

Curran, James, et al., eds. **Bending Reality: The State of the Media**. London: Pluto Press in association with the Campaign for Press and Broadcasting Freedom, 1986. 242p.

"This book has been organized into three sections. The first examines the ways in which the media represent—and misrepresent—what is happening in the world. The second debates what concrete steps should be taken to rectify these distortions, and the third considers alternative approaches to campaigning for reform."—Introduction. A common theme in the first section, "Whose Reality," is that the media regularly portray negatively and sometimes pejoratively minority groups, including among others gays, blacks, Irish nationalists, and women; the second, "The Politics of the Media," considers approaches and proposals to improve conditions; and the third, "Campaigning for Media Freedom," reviews some of the issues involved in organizing and mobilizing public pressure for media reform. Unlike many books on the media which are written wholly by academics, here articles by academics are interspersed equally with those by practitioners and those whose only role is consumer. Although viewpoint is British, it nonetheless relates to countries throughout the western world.

94

Curtis, Liz. **Ireland: The Propaganda War; The British Media and the 'Battle for Hearts and Minds'**. London: Pluto Press, 1984. 336p.

A detailed examination of the British media coverage of Ireland from 1971 to 1984. Curtis indicts the government, supporting the indictment with detailed and extensive research. An appendix lists and describes 48 television programs from 1958 through 1983 which were banned, censored or delayed by the British. Extensive chapter notes and index.

95

Cutten, Theodore E. G. **A History of the Press in South Africa**. Capetown: National Union of South African Students, 1935. 160p.

A chronological account of the development of the press in South Africa in which the author emphasizes its struggle for freedom from the government, particularly in the Transvaal Republic where he was a journalist. There is also a good deal of other rare or useful description—i.e., "The Bantu Press," "Press and the Police," "Press and the Pulpit." Footnotes but no bibliography.

96

Czitrom, Daniel J. **Media and the American Mind: From Morse to McLuhan**. Chapel Hill: University of North Carolina Press, 1982. 254p.

A lively intellectual history of modern communication in America. Czitrom is concerned to know: "How have the attempts of Americans to comprehend the impact of modern communication evolved since the mid-nineteenth century? How have these efforts fit into the larger realm of American social thought? What has been the relationship between these ideas and changing communications technologies and institutions? What role did early popular responses play in the development of new media forms?"

His inquiry is divided into two parts: "Contemporary Reactions to the New Media" in which he traces the development of the telegraph, American motion pictures, and radio; and "Theorists of Modern Communication," in which he discusses the social thought of Charles Horton Cooley, John Dewey and Robert Park; the development of communication research as behavioral science between 1930 and 1960; and the ideas of Harold Innis and Marshall McLuhan.

This is not a book to approach merely for facts, although they are abundant, but rather to gain historical perspective on the development of the media within the broad context of American culture. Apart from its other virtues, it makes fascinating reading.

97

Da Costa, Alcino Louis, et al. **News Values and Principles of Cross-Cultural Education**.

Paris: UNESCO, 1980. 51p. (Reports and Papers on Mass Communication No. 85)

In four parts: "New Criteria for the Selection of News in African Countries" by da Costa; "Toward an Intro-Cultural News Exchange in the Arab States" by Yehia Aboubakr; "Asian News Values: A Barrier or a Bridge" by Pran Chopra; and "Concept of News in Latin America: Dominant Values and Perspectives of Change" by Fernando Reyes Matta. The major conclusion is that information flows are far more strongly influenced by historical and cultural links, including those remaining from colonial times, than by ideological affinities and geographical proximity. It includes an excellent discussion of the international press agencies. Bibliographical notes.

98

Davis, Dennis K., and Stanley J. Baran. **Mass Communication in Everyday Life: A Perspective on Theory and Effects**. Belmont, CA: Wadsworth, 1981. 217p.

"Why does so much existing social science research appear of so little practical use to intelligent, interested students in mass communication? Why are most research findings so fragmentary and contradictory? Is a broad, unified, coherent approach to understanding mass communication possible?" ask the authors, whose aim is to create a synthesis of what they consider the best work that has been done in the field. Although they emphasize the humanistic approach, drawing on scholarly methods and concepts more common to the humanities than the social sciences, they also cite and rely upon empirical findings and theories to guide their own theory building. Each of the nine chapters has notes and a bibliography; in addition there is a useful "Reference Guide to Mass Communication Theories" both critical and empirical.

99

Davis, Howard, and Paul Walton, eds. **Language, Image, Media**. London: Blackwell, 1983. 317p.

The editors have assembled articles from areas of communication—the nature of advertising, the construction of fact by radio and television, reading photographs—which seek to answer a methodological question: "how can one move from what C. Wright Mills called the 'grand social problems' to small-scale empirical questions without losing sight of the propositions and assumptions which inform the larger problems?" As a whole the collection illustrates some of the results of crossing disciplines as it examines the relationship between signs and symbols, the visual and verbal, the senders and receivers in a variety of areas. No attempt has been made to provide a general theory, but rather to concentrate on communications and cultural questions involved in analyzing contemporary cultural practices, whether small-scale or large-scale. Chapter notes, references and index.

100

Davison, W. Phillips, James Boylan, and Frederick T. C. Yu. **Mass Media: Systems & Effects**. 2d ed. New York: Holt, Rinehart & Winston, 1982. 264p.

Part One of this undergraduate text deals with media systems: how they developed in the U.S., how they function in other countries, and how news content in the U.S. is shaped. Part Two concerns communication effects: what messages are generally available, how we select from them, and what can happen as a result. An epilogue gives practical information about the effect of the media upon our daily lives and the citizen's role in influencing policy. In conclusion, we get a glimpse of the future and the changes new communication technologies will bring about. Each chapter ends with suggestions for further reading. There is a lengthy list of references and an index.

101

Deakin, James. **Straight Stuff: The Reporters, the White House and the Truth**. New York: Morrow, 1984. 378p.

James Deakin began his political reporting career covering President David Eisenhower. This book gives the details of his experience reporting the presidency as a member of the Washington press corps for the **St. Louis Post-Dispatch**. Unlike Crouse's book, **Boys on the Bus** (No. 90), a detailed story of the reporters working the campaign trail following presidential candidates, this book analyses the communication skills of the presidents and their respective press secretaries. Index included.

102

DeFleur, Melvin L., and Everette E. Dennis. **Understanding Mass Communication**. Boston: Houghton Mifflin, 1981. 516p.

Beginning text which first examines the nature of communication as a whole, then introduces the student to the various media and assesses their influence on individuals, society, and culture. Finally, it discusses three major practical activities of mass communication—news, advertising, and public relations—along with possible careers. Glossary, chapter notes and references, and index. (A revised edition was published in 1987.)

103

DeFleur, Melvin L., and Sandra Ball-Rokeach. **Theories of Mass Communication**. 4th ed. New York: Longman, 1982. 263p.

"From the first through the fourth editions, **Theories of Mass Communication** has, in the clearest terms articulated a world view of mass communication study while creatively integrating the fragmented work of many scholars into a cohesive and understandable pattern," says Everette Dennis in the Foreword. The authors have focused on three areas: the impact of a society on its mass media; the process of mass communication in relation to direct interpersonal communication; and the effect of human exposure to mass communication. Because they feel that the third area has received more scholarly attention than the first two they have paid special attention to discussions of ways in which social and cultural conditions in the United States have had a role in shaping its media, and have attempted to draw together what is known about the nature of the communicative act. However, they have not neglected the third area; effect studies are discussed at some length. In the final chapter they come up with a communication theory of their own. This new edition has been extensively revised to take account of the growth of the field since the first edition in 1975. (The fifth edition was published in 1989.)

104

Del Mundo, Clodualdo, Jr. **Philippine Mass Media: A Book of Readings**. Manila: Communication Foundation for Asia, 1986. 286p.

An introduction to the Philippine media, with emphasis on its popular culture aspects—film, radio and television in particular. The various readings present an overview of development; discusses practical economic aspects; makes critical analyses from sociological, political, economic and aesthetic viewpoints; and assesses the various possible roles of the media in a developing country like the Philippines. There are notes and an index. The editor is Chairman of Communication Arts at De La Salle University and a documentary film maker.

105

Dennis, Everette E., and John C. Merrill. **Basic Issues in Mass Communication**. New York: Macmillan, 1984. 201p.

Is the American press free? Should the media and government be adversaries? Has the public a right to know? Is journalistic objectivity possible? Is the U.S. guilty of communications imperialism? Is journalism a profession? These are six issues out of the 13 which Dennis and Merrill argue pro and con, each explaining the issue and assembling evidence from separate viewpoints. Designed for college and university undergraduates or beginning graduate students, it would also be valuable to laymen wanting to learn more about contemporary journalism. A bibliography follows each issue. Index.

106

Dennis, Everette E., and William L. Rivers. **Other Voices: The New Journalism in America**. San Francisco: Canfield Press, 1974. 218p.

Comprehensively surveys trends away from traditional journalism as it has existed for most of this century, and describes new and alternate forms, as well as the revival of an old form. Covers muckraking, journalistic nonfiction, advocacy journalism, the counterculture, alternative broadcasting, and precision journalism. There is also a chapter on journalism reviews. The authors have compiled an extensive annotated bibliography of articles and books. Indexed.

107

Denton, Robert E., Jr., and Gary C. Woodward. **Political Communication in America**. New York: Praeger, 1985. 364p.

Using an approach that is both descriptive and empirical, and drawing on such first hand sources as private memoranda, memoirs, speeches, and journalistic accounts, the authors take a broad look at the use and role of communication and mass communications in the political process. The book is divided into three parts: "The Variables of Political Communication," "The Presidency, the Congress, and the Mass Media," and an "Epilogue," discussing "Politics, Communication, and Public Trust." Chapter notes and index.

108

Directory of Communication Research Centers in U.S. Universities 1983–1984. Comp. by Barry S. Sapolsky, assisted by Deborah Wool. Tallahassee: Communication Research Center, College of Communication, Florida State University, 1985. 48p.

A profile of 40 Communication Research Centers responding to a national mail survey in which centers were queried as to: location, phone number, director, years in operation, governance structure, staffing, facilities, funding (1983), publications, special activities, research organizations, methodologies, issues, directions, short/long-term goals.

109

Dizard, Wilson P. **The Coming Information Age: An Overview of Technology, Economics, and Politics**. New York: Longman, 1982. 213p.

In this study of the new technologies of communication as they relate to the U.S. (and therefore affect the rest of the world), Dizard contends that America's ability to solve the political and social problems of the information age has not kept pace with its technological development. In stating his case he explains in non-technical language the technologies of computers, semiconductors, satellites and guide lights, and describes the historical, economic and political issues involved in the communications revolution, from the invention of the telegraph to the immediate present. One of the chapters, "Exporting the Information Society," deals with the relationship between the U.S. and developing nations. His final chapter is a plea for American reassessment of our present resources and policies. Chapter notes, bibliography and index. (A second edition was published in 1985 and a third in 1989.)

110

Dorfman, Ariel, and Armand Mattelart. **How to Read Donald Duck: Imperialist Ideology in the Disney Comic**. Tr. and Introduction by David Kunzle. New York: International General, 1975. 112p.

The authors analyze Disney's comic "to reveal the scowl of capitalist ideology behind the laughing mask, the iron fist beneath the Mouse's glove." This has become a classic in Third World countries, especially in Latin America, where it is regarded as a touchstone for the interpretation of American media. The authors have included a lengthy bibliography of additional Marxist studies on the two principal themes they treat in **Donald Duck**—cultural imperialism and the comic book.

111

Douglas, Sara U. **Labor's New Voice: Unions and the Mass Media**. Norwood, NJ: Ablex, 1986. 310p.

An examination and appraisal of the relationship between organized labor and the mass media in the United States, and in a larger context, a look at the extent to which not-for-profit associations of all types in America are affected by their relationship with mass media. The approach is from four perspectives: a broad description of the environment in which labor operates in terms of its public relations; a specific example as illustrated by an in-depth case study of the Amalgamated Clothing and Textile Workers Union's campaign against the J.P. Stevens Corporation; a further analysis of the case study within a framework that conceptualizes the relationship between labor and media in general in a labor-management conflict situation; and finally, a consideration of certain aspects of the structure of the media systems in the U.S. in terms of their accessibility and responsiveness to organized labor. Chapter notes; extensive bibliography including books, documents, periodicals, pamphlets, reports, speeches, unpublished materials and personal sources; and index.

112

Duke, Judith S. **Religious Publishing and Communications**. White Plains, NY: Knowledge Industry Publications, 1981. 272p.

An analysis of the religious communications industry circa 1980—the demographic, economic and social trends affecting it and the economics of the industry itself. It then narrows to analyses of trends within various markets—Jewish books, Bibles, general religious books, book clubs, records, magazines, and broadcasting which is the largest sector. Although the author bolsters facts with statistics where possible, she found that some areas lack statistical information, and in others there is conflicting data. Even so, she has put together a substantial picture of the industry. At the end are sections giving "Profiles of Organizations in Religious Communications" and a brief bibliography. Indexed.

Dusiska, Emil. **Historical Development of Media Systems II: German Democratic Republic** (See No. 213.)

113

Dye, Thomas R., and Harmon Zeigler. **American Politics in the Media Age**. 2d ed. Monterey, CA: Brooks/Cole, 1986. 396p.

The authors describe their book as "a basic introduction to American government with a special focus on the political role of the mass media." It tells how the elements of American political system—beliefs and ideologies, constitutional arrangements, federalism, interest groups, parties and elections, Congress, the Presidency, the bureaucracy, the courts, civil liberties and civil rights—are symbolized and communicated to mass audiences and how these audiences respond to the symbols. Two short bibliographies follow each chapter—one with "Notes," the other with "Close-Up and Depth Analyses." Name and subject indexes.

114

Edgar, Patricia, and Sued A. Rahim, eds. **Communication Policy in Developed Countries**. London: Kegan Paul in association with East-West Center, Honolulu, 1983. 297p.

Studies of the communication systems of seven developed countries: the United States, by Anne Branscomb; the United Kingdom, by Anthony Smith; Canada, by Jean McNulty and Gail M. Martin; Sweden, by Goran Hedebro; the Federal Republic of Germany, by Ed Wittich; Australia, by Geoff Evans; and New Zealand, by Donald Stewart and Logan Moss. "Each chapter combines a description of present-day policies with critical discussion of those policies and methods of policy formation. Each chapter reflects the background of the author(s) and thus approaches taken differ. The variety of approaches illustrated the scope for policy analysis from different perspectives. The seven chapter overviews, while they reveal different trends within industrial countries, demonstrate how unique communication systems have emerged as a result of cultural differences."—Introduction. Of the seven, only Sweden has a specific policy; the rest have acted pragmatically.

115

Elliott, Deni, ed. **Responsible Journalism**. Beverly Hills, CA: Sage, 1986. 187p.

Essays by professors in journalism and related fields, which set forth their views, sometimes from competing perspectives, about the source of journalistic responsibilities, how these responsibilities fit in with legal and press theories, and how they work in specific contexts. Authors are Louis W. Hodge, John Merrill, Ralph Barney, Theodore Glasser, Everette Dennis, Clifford Christians,

Martin Linsky, Howard Ziff, and the editor. References follow each article and in conclusion is a "Selected Bibliography." Index.

116

Ellul, Jacques. **Propaganda: The Formation of Men's Attitudes**. Tr. from the French by Konrad Kellen and Jean Lerner. New York: Knopf, 1971. 320p.

"The principal difference between his [Ellul's] thought edifice and most other literature is that Ellul regards propaganda as a sociological phenomenon rather than as something **made** by certain people for certain purposes"—Introduction. In this classic analysis Ellul deals with its characteristics, conditions for existence, necessity for being, and psychological and socio-political effects. Throughout he dissects classic misconceptions. Two appendixes: one discussing the effectiveness of prop aganda; the other, Mao Tse-tung's propaganda. Bibliography and index.

117

Emery, Edwin, and Michael Emery. **The Press and America: An Interpretive History of the Mass Media**. 5th ed. Englewood Cliffs, NJ: Prentice-Hall, 1984. 774p.

"With words and pictures the book surveys the landmark events in communications history, probing significant issues, personalities, and media organizations, all the while tracing how major events in American history were covered by reporters, editors, and broadcasters and how other writers, advertisers, and advocates influenced American life," so the co-authors describe their tried-and-true text which has been going strong since its first edition in 1954. The American press is placed within the context of trends and their coverage, showing how one has influenced the other. In this fifth edition the first half, from European beginnings to the present century, has been expanded, and the second half has been rewritten and reorganized. "Press" is interpreted broadly to cover new and less new technologies, including film. In addition to other virtues this encyclopedic text is a valuable reference tool. Each chapter has notes and extensive annotated bibliographies of both books and articles. Author-subject index. (The sixth edition, with Michael Emery as first author, was published in 1988.)

118

Epstein, Laurily Keir, ed. **Women and the News**. New York: Hastings House, 1978. 144p.

An examination of various aspects of the status of women vis à vis the news in terms of three concepts in news media research: agenda setting, access to the media, and definitions of the news.

119

Ernst, Morris L. **The First Freedom**. New York: Macmillan, 1946. 316p.

One of the earliest examinations of monopoly in the communications industry, which was then chiefly press, radio, and motion pictures. Updated by Bryce W. Rucker in 1968 at Ernst's request, **The First Freedom** (Southern Illinois University Press). The new edition concentrates on newspapers and broadcasting monopoly.

120

Ettema, James S., and D. Charles Whitney, eds. **Individuals in Mass Media Organizations: Creativity and Constraint**. Beverly Hills, CA: Sage, 1982. 259p. (Sage Annual Reviews of Communication Research, v. 10.)

Articles which explore the theory that those who create the form, content and meaning of the media in terms both of information and entertainment work, for better or worse, within the constraints of organizational structure. Among those who bring various points of view to bear are John Ryan and Richard Peterson; William Powell; Anne Peters and Muriel Cantor; Horace Newcomb and Robert Alley; Joseph Turow; Robert Pekurny; Lee Becker; John Robinson, Haluk Sahin and Dennis Davis; Michael Gurevitch and Jay Blumler; Peter Clarke and Susan Davis; Mark Fishman; and the editors.

121

European Aid to Third World Media: A Survey of Assistance by the Commission of the European Community and Its Member States to the Media in Developing Countries. Prepared by John Roper and Cornelia Goeyvaerts. Manchester, England: University of Manchester, European Institute for the Media, 1986. 100p. (Media Monograph No. 4)

A report prepared by the European Institute for the Media to assess the scale and quality of the aid given by the various organizations in its member states to Third World countries. The ten EIM members involved reported on capital sent to developing countries and training programs available. Member states included Belgium, Denmark, Federal Republic of Germany, France, Greece, Ireland, Italy, Luxembourg, the Netherlands, and the United Kingdom. Tables chart sources of organizational assistance rendered continent by continent. Courses offered to trainees are also listed.

122

Eysenck, H.J., and D.K.B. Nias. **Sex, Violence and the Media**. London: Maurice Temple Smith, 1978. 306p.

The authors, both connected with the Institute of Psychiatry at the University of London, have painstakingly analyzed a wealth of literature—roughly 250 articles—on the effects of media portrayal of violence and overt sex on the individual, and have described in readable terms the results of individual studies and of the studies as a whole. One of the most interesting features is the discussions of methodology of this sort where it is difficult to control variables. The list of articles, reports, books, etc. that they examined, along with some that they examined but did not analyze, form a valuable bibliography. Author-subject index.

123

Facts about the IOJ. Prague: International Organization of Journalists, 1973. 95p.

Gives the purpose and activities of the International Organization of Journalists, including its centers of professional education, publicity, statutes, executive committees, and the composition of its membership.

124

Farrell, Brian, ed. **Communications and Community in Ireland**. Dublin: Mercier, 1984. 133p.

The Thomas David Lectures dealing with the role of communication in the evolution of the modern community in Ireland. Taken as a whole, they present an eclectic collection, with five articles on mass media history, both print and broadcast; one on censorship; one on the political role of the media in contemporary Ireland; one on the media and Irish culture; a general article on new technological developments, applicable anywhere; and a final one on the topic of the series, discussing problems and prospects. Chapter notes.

125

Fischer, Heinz-Dietrich, and Stefan Reinhard Melnik, eds. **Entertainment: A Cross-Cultural Examination**. New York: Hastings House, 1979. 330p.

Entertainment, an ambiguous, many-faceted term, has many forms and uses, differing with cultures and individuals. In this wide-ranging reader the editors deal with its importance as supplied by the media. The scope is international, with contributors from a number of countries, and the emphasis is on theory and research. Various forms are discussed—newsreading, advertising, popular literature, television, the record and tape industry, story telling and traditional folk forms, often in relation to theory and in the context of a specific country. Intended for the college or university audiences and for people involved in the production of entertainment, or the general reader interested in the subject. Notes at the end of each article; a bibliography; and an index.

126

Fishburn, Katherine. **Women in Popular Culture: A Reference Guide**. Westport, CT: Greenwood, 1982. 267p.

In this comprehensive and useful work on women in America as portrayed in the media and in popular culture generally, Fishburn covers the subject historically from Colonial times to the present, showing their treatment in literature, in magazine fiction and nonfiction, in film, television, advertising, fashion, sports and comics. She begins with a general discussion as background and ends with theories about women in relation to popular culture. Each of the seven chapters contain notes, and appendixes list pertinent periodicals, with a further list of issues and special sections of periodicals. A full bibliography includes other bibliographies, biographies, and information guides; and there is a list of important research centers and institutions. Index.

127

Fisher, Glen. **American Communication in a Global Society**. Norwood, NJ: Ablex, 1979. 165p.

Fisher, who has been involved in a number of American governmental communication agencies in connection with Third World countries, including the International Communication Agency, the U.S.I.A., and as a Foreign Service Officer, has drawn upon both his professional experience and the academic disciplines of sociology, anthropology, and social psychology to seek a rationale which would enable him "to produce the kind of 'think piece' analysis that would sharpen the focus on trends and new factors which might affect the logic of a wide range of programs directed toward mutual understanding objectives." He does not pretend to have the answers, only the questions. Footnotes, bibliography and index. (A revised edition was issued in 1987.)

Fishman, Joshua A. **Language Resources in the United States. Vol. I. Guide to Non-English-Language Print Media**. (See No. 1048.)

Fishman, Joshua A. **Language Resources in the United States. Vol. II. Guide to Non-English-Language Broadcasting**. (See No. 605.)

128

Fishman, Mark. **Manufacturing the News**. Austin: University of Texas Press, 1980. 180p.

Concerned with the process by which "a very special and important reality is socially constructed: the public reality of mass media news," Fishman observed the journalistic process as a novice reporter and as a researcher to learn more about the social facts reporters produce every day and the methods they use to do so. His study is organized in four stages: the methods by which newsworkers detect occurrences; their interpretation of them as meaningful events; how they investigate them as facts; and how they assemble them into stories. Notes, references and index.

129

Fiske, John. **Introduction to Communication Studies**. London: Methuen, 1982. 174p.

Fiske's ability to make complicated ideas clear and understandable without oversimplifying them makes this short text an outstanding introduction to the study of communication. He explains the two schools of thought involving process and semiotics and follows with discussions of theories, models, meaning and signs, codes, signification, semiotic and empirical methods, and ideology and meanings. An excellent source to equip the beginner with the necessary background to examine thoughtfully the products of the various media for latent meanings. Bibliography and index.

Francis-Williams, Edward Francis William, Baron. See Williams, Francis (Nos. 457, 458, 459, 460).

130

A Free and Responsible Press: A General Report on Mass Communication: Newspapers, Radio, Motion Pictures, Magazines, and Books. Chicago: University of Chicago Press, 1947. 138p.

A summary and critique of the findings of the six-volume report of the Commission of Freedom of the Press (No. 81), with "press" interpreted broadly. It emphasizes the responsibilities of owners and managers to use their media for the common good—the "social responsibility" theory.

131

Friedman, Sharon M., Sharon Dunwoody, and Carol L. Rogers, eds. **Scientists and Journalists: Reporting Science as News**. New York: Free Press, 1986. 333p.

This is by no means a simple "how to" book. Its aim is to describe the complex connections between scientists and journalists today to a wide readership that includes scientists, journalists and students which will give the scientists a better grasp of journalism, and journalists a better grasp of science, and the layman a better grasp of both. In four parts, with contributors from journalism and science it includes: "Understanding the Actors," "Analyzing the Interactions," "Critiquing the State of the Art," and "Talking to the Public: Scientists in the Media." Appendixes include "The Scientist's Responsibility for Public Information: A Guide to Effective Communication"; "Nuclear Waste: A Problem That Won't Go Away"; "Mrs. Kelly's Monster" (a Pulitzer Prize-winning article exemplifying science writing, with notes for the novice); "Examples from 'Science Notebook'"; a bibliography, "Research on Mass Media Science Communication"; and "Science in the Mass Media: A Selected Guide" to documentaries, series and other sources of reporting. All in all, this is a most informative addition to an area where too few books exist.

132

French, Blaire Atherton. **The Presidential Press Conference: Its History and Role in the American Political System**. Lanham, MD: University Press of America, 1982. 47p.

An analysis of the factors that have formed the presidential press conference as we know it today. Notes and bibliography.

133

Fry, Don, ed. **Believing the News**. St. Petersburg, FL: Poynter Institute for Media Studies, 1985. 301p.

The report of a group of prominent print and TV journalists and executives who gathered at the Poynter Institute in 1985 to discuss the credibility of newspaper and television news with specific emphasis on "public distrust of all branches of the media; the perception that journalists are arrogant and biased; the inevitable conflict between inquiring reporters and evasive government officials; the manipulation of the press by unnamed sources and special interest groups; the difficulties of maintaining traditional news values in a media world increasingly influenced by elements of entertainment." The first section is a well-edited transcript of the three-day meeting; the second part consists of appended essays. In conclusion is a brief chapter, "Some Approaches to Heightened Credibility" and a "Bibliography of Sources of Media Credibility."

134

Gallagher, Margaret. **Unequal Opportunities: The Case of Women and the Media**. Paris: UNESCO, 1981. 221p.

Gallagher has brought together research results culled from hundreds of worldwide reports (many of them in mimeographed forms), articles, fugitive materials, and a lesser number of books (which are much scarcer), to address certain basic questions about the relationship between women and the media. The questions: What are the issues? What do we know already? What has been done so far? What remains to be done? She has then related her findings to the needs and possibilities of action. One of the most valuable features of the book is the bibliography of her materials. Appendixes list international feminist publications; directories and guidebooks; seminar proceedings and reports; groups and organizations; formats for media analysis; and the list of references previously mentioned.

The Gallup Poll. (See No. 1753.)

135

Gandy, Oscar H., Jr. **Beyond Agenda Setting: Information Subsidies and Public Policy**. Norwood, NJ: Ablex, 1982. 243p.

Gandy is concerned with the way media content, or

information, is selected. Who sets the agenda? What is its relation to the distribution of power and values in society? As he focuses on the processes of selection he looks for organizational inequities whereby various groups and interests gain control of the flow of information through subsidies in pursuit of their goals. The introduction is a discussion of agenda setting as traditionally explored by students of mass communication. In the chapters which follow he develops a perspective on the role of subsidized information in the policy process in general and explores the use of information subsidies in specific policy areas such as health, education, science and technology, and national economic planning. The final chapter identifies some theoretical issues and suggests some potential approaches to structured research into the role of information subsidies in the public-policy process. Chapter notes, bibliography and index.

136

Ganley, Oswald H., and Gladys D. Ganley. **To Inform or to Control? The New Communications Networks**. New York: McGraw-Hill, 1982. 250p.

"What we are witnessing on every hand today is the beginning of the collapse of the economies based on traditional industries, *traditionally managed*, and the rise of economies based on or assisted by new communications and information resources," say the Ganleys in their Preface, backing up the assumption with facts and figures to show the worldwide ferment as familiar boundaries of industry, natural resources, recreation, arms control and communications enlarge to become more and more global. The important role, both positively and negatively, that new communications and information developments play in the changing area of international economics is described. A case history of the relationships between Canada and the United States is used as a specific example. Notes, bibliography, a list of acronyms and an index.

137

Gans, Herbert J. **Deciding What's News: A Study of CBS Evening News, NBC Nightly News, Newsweek and Time**. New York: Pantheon, 1979. 393p.

Result of a ten-year study in which Gans sat in on the day-to-day life of the studios and the newsrooms, witnessing the decision-making process. He examines the values of the journalists and the values in the news itself, and finds definite "enduring values" built into it which support a certain social order. While it is non-ideological and impartial, it actually defends implicitly a conservative, although reformist, vision of America. Notes, bibliography, and index.

138

Gans, Herbert J. **Popular Culture and High Culture: An Analysis and Evaluation of Taste**. New York: Basic Books, 1974. 179p.

Gans, advocate of cultural pluralism and devil's advocate to those who maintain that popular culture threatens the existence of high culture, here states his case. Within a sociological framework he defends popular culture against some of its attackers, arguing for cultural democracy and against the idea that only the cultural expert knows what is good for people and for society. Finally, he makes policy proposals for more cultural pluralism. Footnotes and index.

139

Gao, Guo-Gan, ed. **China Press and Publishing Directory, 1985**. Beijing and London: Modern Press and Longman, 1985. 360p.

"... this directory is the first of its kind ever published in China, the only reference tool so far available in this respect," says Wang Yi, Advisor to the Bureau of Publishing Administration, Ministry of Culture. It contains 2,353 entries of publishers, booksellers, newspapers and periodicals throughout the country, with information collected through questionnaires to the end of 1983, and a few from early 1984. Information for each entry includes name in both Chinese and English, address, telephone, date founded, subject/s (where pertinent) or whatever brief background information is useful. Listing of publishers and booksellers is by province; of newspapers and periodicals, by subject. Each of the two main categories has its separate index.

140

Garbo, Gunnar. **A World of Difference: The International Distribution of Information: The Media and Developing Countries**. Tr. by Gail Adams Kvam. Paris: UNESCO, 1985. 114p. (Communication and Society 15)

This study is especially interesting because Garbo, a Norwegian, writes not only from his own association with the United Nations, UNESCO and the International Programme for the Development of Communication, but also from a broad knowledge of flow-of-information literature. The story of his involvement in the futile efforts to remedy the uneven distribution of communication technology, news, and entertainment through international organization is, to a large extent, the history of the opposing viewpoints between the have's and have-not's. In the telling he reviews the research on content and possible effects, especially in regard to American television programs popular in developing countries. This is one of the best sources to gain a long-term perspective on media development in the Third World.

141

Gardner, Carl, ed. **Media, Politics and Culture: A Socialist View**. London: Macmillan, 1979. 197p.

A collection of essays from a series of open public forums in London on the mass media delivered by members of the National Union of Journalists and Equity in the International Marxist Group. According to the editor, it "represents probably the first 'overview' of the various strategies being offered by the socialist and feminist movements, for a genuine opposition to and eventual transformation of the mass media." Essays deal with the role and growth of the media, television, pop music, film, newspapers, sexism, racism and certain more general topics. All represent various aspects of socialism, which can and do differ greatly. Although some of the contributors are or at one time have been academics, "most are either political activists in and around the media and/or media practitioners of various sorts, with a commitment to socialism." The lead article is by an academic, Raymond Williams. Gardner is a journalist and political activist. Chapter notes and references, bibliography and index.

142

Gerald, J. Edward. **The Social Responsibility of the Press**. Minneapolis: University of Minnesota Press, 1963. 214p.

"This book intends to describe the market and its journalistic products, to observe their influence on other social institutions important to self-government, and to seek out ways in which the media may contribute more to the development of our civilization." Since the times in which Gerald stated these aims in the early 1960s the press has changed vastly, so that his descriptions and observations have taken on historical value which enables us to measure the present against the past.

143

Gerbner, George, and Marsha Siefert, eds. **World Communications: A Handbook**. New York: Longman, 1984. 527p.

Brings together 54 articles on research and policy on communications in the "three worlds" by scholars and policy makers from the U.S., Western Europe, the socialist countries including the U.S.S.R. and Eastern Europe, and the developing world, including Africa, Asia, and Latin America—25 countries all told. The editors' goal was "not to orchestrate the voices but to select papers that are well-argued and representative of the diversity of opinion on various issues." Thus there are case studies as well as policy statements and critiques. In five parts: "Global Perspectives on Information," "Transnational Communications: The Flow of News and Images," "Telecommunications," "Mass Communications: Development within National Contexts," and "Intergovernmental Systems." Appendixes include a bibliography, international and intergovernmental events and documents on the subject, acronyms and other terms used, and global satellite systems. Chapter references and notes.

144

Ghareeb, Edmund, ed. **Split Vision: Arab Portrayal in the American Media**. Washington: Institute of Middle Eastern and African Affairs, 1977. 171p.

Eleven taped interviews with American journalists as to their views on bias in coverage of the Middle East, all of whom, by accident or selection, find bias toward Israel. In conclusion there are chapters on "Zionist bias on American Editorial Pages," "A Survey of Political Cartoons Dealing with the Middle East," and "The Image of the Arab on American Television." The editor is press adviser for the United Arab Emirates Embassy and correspondent for **Il-Ittihad** newspaper in Abu Dhabi.

145

Gibbons, Arnold. **Information, Ideology and Communication: The New Nations' Perspectives on an Intellectual Revolution**. Lanham, MD: University Press of America, 1985. 219p.

In calm and reasoned prose that digs beneath the surface, Gibbons explores the relationship between the rich and poor countries—the have's and have not's—which has resulted from an enormous gap in information technology. His aim is to create a better understanding between the old order and the new on a domestic and international level and in terms of economics and ideology. Throughout the discussions he describes the various conferences on the subject, as well as the development of UNESCO's interest. Each chapter lists sources. One of the appendixes gives the text of "The Declaration of Fundamental Principles Concerning the Contribution of the Mass Media to Strengthening Peace and International Understanding, the Promotion of Human Rights and to Countering Racialism, Apartheid and the Incitement of War," adopted in 1978 by the UNESCO General Conference.

146

Ginsberg, Benjamin. **The Captive Public: How Mass Opinion Promotes State Power**. New York: Basic Books, 1986. 272p.

A provocative analysis of the power of public opinion in modern government. Ginsberg's thesis: that to an important extent the contemporary western state is ruled by opinion and that ultimately the state ruled by opinion is not necessarily different from the state that rules opinion. Chapter notes and index.

147

Gitlin, Todd. **The Whole World Is Watching: Mass Media in the Making and Unmaking of the New Left**. Berkeley: University of California Press, 1980. 327p.

In this analysis of the complex relationship between the mass media and the New Left, Gitlin shows not only the way the media affected that particular movement and vice versa but also gives a sharp understanding of the interaction between mass media and social movements in general and of the construction of news. Selected bibliography.

148

Golding, Peter. **The Mass Media**. London: Longman, 1974. 134p.

Golding, a sociologist at the Leicester University Center for Mass Communication Research, analyzes evidence produced by the social sciences about the mass communication process in contemporary Britain and its development and structure, the media's relationship to one another and to other agencies of society, and wider sociological implications of organizational and technological changes taking place within them. Contains a bibliography and an index.

149

Goldstein, Jeffrey H., ed. **Reporting Science: The Case of Aggression**. Hillsdale, NJ: Lawrence Erlbaum, 1986. 121p.

Described by its editor as "a nonscientific book about science," and specifically about research on various forms of aggression and violence, **Reporting Science** presents problems of communication and understanding between scientists and journalists and a discussion of their respective roles, their conflicts of interest, and the ambiguities of their relationship. Chapters include: "Social Science, Journalism, and Public Policy," "The Social Responsibility of the Scientist," "How to Publicize Science: A Case Study," "How Not to Publicize Research: the UCLA Violence Study," "Determinants of Science Reporting in Europe," "Science Journalism in Asia," "When Science Writers Cover the Social Science," "What Is 'The Media' and Why Is It Saying Those Terrible Things About Aggression Research?," "Prospects for Science Journalism," and an appendix, "A Guide to Effective Communication with the Media," prepared cooperatively by scientists and science writers to aid in understanding the writer's problems, which differ with the various media. Name and subject indexes.

150

Goldstein, Tom. **The News at Any Cost: How Journalists Compromise Their Ethics to Shape the News**. New York: Simon and Schuster, 1985. 301p.

Goldstein, a former reporter and now a journalism teacher, dissects the press to show practices—often dubious—used in collecting news, and gives examples of how the press frequently gets the news wrong yet is reluctant to issue corrections. Although critical of much of the press he praises certain journalists who are honest and careful, and he suggests ways to minimize mistakes. His evidence is based on a comprehensive survey, internal media documents, and many interviews. Copious chapter notes and a detailed index.

151

Goodell, Rae. **The Visible Scientists**. Boston: Little Brown, 1977. 242p.

This is an interesting and unusual book about science and the media which grew out of a dissertation. The author contends that the image of the scientist has changed over the past decades from recluse to public personality. Exploring "the rapidly changing visibility system," she sets out to answer the following questions: "What kinds of scientists now reach public attention? What role do the media play in singling them out? What forces within science bring them to visibility? What do their more traditionally minded colleagues think of them? Do their scientific careers suffer? What influence do visible scientists in turn have on the media? Do they deliberately cultivate publicity? How serious are the many criticisms leveled against them?" Her answers give an insight into the subtle and not-so-subtle part modern media play in creating the public image of science.

152

Goodfield, June. **Reflections on Science and The Media**. Washington: American Association for the Advancement of Science, 1981. 113p.

A critical essay about "the mutual and often uneasy relationship between two distinguished professions," says Goodfield, who uses four case studies to show how scientists and journalists have worked together and with what results. These are preceded by a discussion of the built-in constraints on the media, both print and broadcast, and on the scientist as they cooperate to report to the public. The cases, beautifully recorded, read like a cross between science fiction and detective stories. Notes and references.

153

Goodwin, Eugene. **Groping for Ethics in Journalism**. Ames: Iowa State University Press, 1983. 335p.

Goodwin's aim: ". . . to assess the current status of ethics and present it in a way that might help journalists think through their ethical problems." His methodology: examining pertinent literature and interviewing about 150 print and broadcast journalists, including executives, along with a few media watchers, whose opinions he felt would be significant. Focus is on newspaper, wire service and television journalism. He has not pretended to place journalistic ethics in an underlying ethical philosophy, but has given us an eminently practical survey full of interesting case studies and examples. Chapter notes, a bibliographic essay, and an index.

154, 155, 156

Graber, Doris A. **Mass Media and American Politics**. 2d ed. Washington: Congressional Quarterly Press, 1984. 385p.

Graber, Doris A., ed. **Media Power in Politics**. Washington: Congressional Quarterly Press, 1984. 348p.

Graber, Doris A. **Processing the News: How**

People Tame the Information Tide. New York: Longman, 1984. 241p.

Graber is concerned throughout these three books with the symbiotic relationship between politics and the media. **Mass Media and American Politics** examines the ways in which electronic and print media shape Americans' political beliefs and social values. Among issues discussed are government control; ownership, regulation and guidance of media, newsmaking and reporting; press freedom and the law; impact on individual attitudes and behavior; election in the television age; the struggle for control of news waged by the White House, Congress and the courts; the media as policymakers; crisis and foreign affairs coverage; and trends in policy. Notes and readings at the end of each chapter, and name/subject index. (A third edition was published in 1988.)

Media Power in Politics is an interdisciplinary reader intended as a text for courses on mass media and politics, public opinion, political communication, and mass media and society. Representing the work of 62 authors, it is divided into six sections, prefaced by an introduction: "Mass Media Effects: From the Past to the Future," "Shaping the Political Agenda," "Influencing Election Outcomes," "Affecting Political Actors and the Balance of Power," "Guiding Public Policies," and "Controlling Media Effects." Essays are cut, but Graber says that they follow the originals in all essential matters. The general idea is to give students as sweeping a view as possible on the subject and to acquaint them with samples of the work of scholars in the field. Chapter notes.

In **Processing the News** she uses empirical methodology to deal with the ways people select and process information from the vast flow the media flood them with to form opinions about current political issues. Taking her data from a sample of 200 registered voters from Evanston, Illinois, she investigates information-processing patterns, allowing for the social and cultural contexts of the various respondents. Chapter notes, bibliography and index.

157

Greenberg, Bradley S., Michael Burgoon, Judee K. Burgoon, and Felipe Korzenny. **Mexican Americans & the Mass Media**. Norwood, NJ: Ablex, 1983. 290p.

An empirical study, funded by the Gannett newspaper chain and carried out by communication research at Michigan State University. The result is an analysis of how Hispanic Americans and their Anglo counterparts use and evaluate the media and how the media in turn treat members of each group. The first section consists of two chapters that summarize existing research literature on Mexican Americans' mass communication and interpersonal communication practices and evaluations. Other chapters explain methodology, summarize results, and give conclusions, recommendations, and implications. Extensive bibliography and author-subject index.

158

Grewe-Partsch, Marianne, and Gertrude J. Robinson, eds. **Women, Communication, and Careers**. Munich, Germany: Saur, 1980. 138p.

A systematic interdisciplinary exploration of the interconnections between women, communication, and careers consisting of nine articles by authors from social psychology, mass communications, management, and law, who probe the role of sex in media programming, career patterns and strategy, and in everyday communication strategies. Each article lists references.

159

Grossman, Michael Baruch, and Martha Joynt Kumar. **Portraying the President: The White House and the News Media**. Baltimore: Johns Hopkins University Press, 1981. 358p.

An analysis of the organizations of the White House information offices and the news media covering the White House, and of the relationships between the public officials and the reporters, which points out that there is more cooperation than conflict between them. The description of the two organizations is given in detailed entries, almost in a handbook format. Also included are detailed analyses of the role and importance of specific members of the White House press corps. Analyses and information are carefully presented in a historical context. The book offers both theoretical conclusions about the relationship between the U.S. President and the press along with specific information about the organization and personalities on both sides. According to the authors, the only other book to date (1981) adequately covering the subject is Elmer Cornwell's **Presidential Leadership of Public Opinion**. (Bloomington: Indiana University Press, 1965. 370p.)

160

Guback, Thomas, and Tapio Varis. **Transnational Communication and Cultural Industries**. Paris: UNESCO, 1982. 55p. (Reports and Papers on Mass Communication No. 92)

An examination of the transnational production and distribution of information and flow of mass media material, with special attention to the role by corporations. Emphasis is on film and television, and to a lesser degree on the print media. There are also case studies of Argentina and Thailand. Bibliography.

161

Guiley, Rosemary. **Career Opportunities for Writers**. New York: Facts on File, 1985. 246p.

Intended to help both aspiring writers seeking entry-level jobs as well as experienced writers interested in a career change, this gives detailed descriptions of 91 job possibilities in eight fields of the major media—media and information services, including newspaper and news services, videotex services, magazines, television and radio; book publishing; arts and entertainment; business communications and public relations; advertising and marketing; federal government and politics; scholastic, academic and non-profit institutions; and freelance, specialized, and writing-related fields. Each job description follows a basic format, with duties, salaries, prerequisites, opportunities for employment and advancement, opportunities for women and minorities, and organizations to join. Appendixes list some of the educational institutions offering pertinent degrees; professional, industry, and trade associations and unions; major trade periodicals; and a bibliography. Index.

162

Gumpert, Gary, and Robert Cathcart, eds. **Inter/Media: Interpersonal Communication in a Media World**. 3d ed. New York: Oxford, 1986. 666p.

A popular text which focuses on the symbiotic relationship between the media and the individual in modern society, and, on another level, between mass communications and speech communication. The 40 essays, 19 of which were written especially for this volume, illustrate the editors' belief that the traditional division of communication study into interpersonal, group and public, and mass communication is inadequate to deal with the pervasiveness of the media and the complexities of the process. The essays, which cover a variety of media and disciplines, are grouped under four headings: "The Interpersonal and Media Connection," "Media, Intimacy, and Interpersonal Networks," "Mediated Reality," and "Media Values." The contributors are a mix of academics, professional writers, and an occasional practitioner. Among them are Elihu Katz and Tamar Liebes, Gerald R. Millen, Edmund Carpenter, Gaye Tuchman, Michael Novak, Seri Thomas, Ellen Wartella, Sherry Turkle, Anthony Smith, Lee Thayer, Elizabeth S. White, S. J. Ball-Rokeach and Melvin DeFleur, Michael Arlen, Susan Sontag, Karl Erik Rosengren and Sven Windahl, and the two editors. Walter Ong has written a postscript.

A group of essays by Gunmpert, **Talking Tombstones and Other Tales of the Media Age**, was published in 1987.

163

Gurevitch, Michael, Tony Bennett, James Curran, and Janet Woollacott, eds. **Culture, Society and the Media**. London: Methuen, 1982. 317p.

An in-depth examination of the various theories about the role and processes of mass communication in society by the writers of England's Open University course on the subject. They do not opt for any single theory; rather, they analyze various alternative and sometimes competing ones, focusing in particular on the division and opposition between the liberal-pluralist and Marxist views of the media. Central to the discussions is the question of power. How should it be defined? How and by whom

is it wielded? Have previous approaches to the question proved adequate? In three parts: "Class, Ideology and the Media," "Media Organizations," and "The Power of the Media." Contributors are James Curran, Michael Gurevitch, Janet Woollacott, Tony Bennett, Stuart Hall, Graham Murdock, Margaret Gallagher, J.O. Boyd-Barrett, Jay Blumler and Tony Bennett. Chapter references and index.

164

Hachten, William A. **Muffled Drums: The News Media in Africa**. Ames: Iowa State University Press, 1971. 314p.

Examination of the news media—newspapers, radio, television, magazines—in contemporary Africa, focusing on them as institutions, and describing their establishment, their effectiveness, and their relations with the government. Emphasis is on news and public information rather than cultural and educational roles.

Hachten has also compiled **Mass Communication in Africa: An Annotated Bibliography** (University of Wisconsin, Center for International Communication Studies, 1971, 121p.), which is a comprehensive guide to his source material.

165

Hachten, William A., and C. Anthony Giffard. **The Press and Apartheid: Repression and Propaganda in South Africa**. Madison: University of Wisconsin Press, 1984. 336p.

"This is a study both of measures taken by the South African government to control its mass media and of the efforts of its journalists and others to express their views and resist those restraints,"—Introduction. The authors examine the conflict between government and press in a social, economic, and political context derived from forces rooted deeply in history, showing the depth of hostility and describing in detail the various organizations used by government to influence opinion and to censor. One chapter is devoted to "The Afrikaans Press, Freedom within Commitment." The two authors draw upon different backgrounds—Hachten, a specialist on mass communications in Africa and Giffard, a South African journalist now at the University of Washington. Contains notes, a brief glossary of unfamiliar South African terms, and a bibliography of books and articles. Indexed.

166

Hachten, William A., with the collaboration of Harva Hachten. **The World News Prism: Changing Media, Clashing Ideologies**. Ames: Iowa State University Press, 1981. 133p.

"This book describes and analyzes the dramatically altered role of today's transnational news media in the technetronic age," says Hatchen, who probes how the current clashes and disputes over international communication between the West, the Socialist nations, and the Third World affect transnational journalism and mass communication. Chapters include "Communication for an Interdependent World," "International News System," "Communication Satellites and New Technology," "Internationalizing the World's News Media," "Clashing Ideologies: Five Concepts of the Press," "Western Perspective on World News," "Third World Views of News Flow," and "Moving Together or Further Apart?" Bibliography and Index. (A new edition was published in 1987.)

167

Hall, Stuart, ed. **Culture, Media, Language: Working Papers in Cultural Studies, 1972–79**. London: Hutchinson in association with the Centre for Contemporary Cultural Studies, University of Birmingham, 1980. 311p.

The work being done at the University of Birmingham's Centre for Contemporary Cultural Studies is pivotal to an understanding of important dimensions to communication theory. This volume is a selection of articles drawn from the first nine issues of the Centre's journal, **Working Papers in Cultural Studies**, from its list of **Stencilled Papers**, and from some more recent work. It is divided into four main sections—ethnographic work, the media, language, and English studies—which, as is pointed out in the Preface, do not "accurately reflect the *present spread* of the Centre's work." Nor does it offer "a consistent theoretical position . . . nor even a unified set of findings." But while not definitive, it reveals "the necessarily open, provisional nature of work in a novel and emergent area" and underscores "the diversity of approaches, the sense of developing from position to position, which has characterized our approach throughout." Interesting not only because of the individual studies included, but also because it shows—even though partially—the Centre's scope and its methodology which might be considered unorthodox by certain American standards. Bibliography.

168

Hall, Stuart, et al. **Policing the Crisis: Mugging, the State, and Law and Order**. New York: Holmes and Meier, 1978. 425p.

This is not primarily a book about muggings, nor is it primarily about the media. Rather, using one particular instance of a mugging in Birmingham, England, it analyzes various social conditions in some way responsible for the climate that produces crime, including the press, to which the authors devote three chapters: "The Social Production of News," "Balancing Accounts: Cashing in on Handsworth" (a discussion of press treatment of the mugging), and "Orchestrating Public Opinion." Contains "Notes and References."

169

Hall, Stuart, and Paddy Whannel. **The Popular Arts**. Chicago: Hutchinson Educational, 1964. 480p.

This book is intended to educate younger readers, or for that matter any interested layman, about today's mass culture, and even though it was written some years ago it is so firmly grounded in verities that it has not dated. Part I defines the media's relation to society, minority art, folk art, and popular art and relates popular art to mass culture. Part II suggests topics for study—"Violence on the Stage," "Falling in Love," "Fantasy and Romance," "Popular Forms and Popular Artists," among others. Part III discusses social themes—the institutions, the critics and defenders of mass society, society and the hero, and the world of pop, and so on. Some of these topics are suggested as teaching projects. Appendixes contain bibliographies of books and journals, records, films and television materials, and organizations. Indexed.

170

Hallin, David C. **The "Uncensored War": The Media and Vietnam**. New York: Oxford, 1986. 285p.

Conventional wisdom has it that the media opposed the Vietnam war—"the living room war"—and that their coverage played a part in America's defeat. In a detailed examination of what Americans read and watched over a 12-year period Hallin investigates this charge, studying accounts in the **New York Times** from 1961 to 1965, watching hundreds of television reports from 1963–73, and conducting interviews. The result is a scrupulous analysis that not only probes the role of the media in Vietnam but also the larger role of the relation of the media to government in contemporary American politics. Chapter notes, an appendix dealing with methodology, an extensive bibliography, and an index.

171

Halmos, Paul, ed. **The Sociology of Mass-Media Communicators**. Keele, Staffordshire, England: University of Keele, 1969. 248p. (**The Sociological Review**: Monograph No. 13)

Emphasis here is divided between the theoretical and the practical. Some of the essays broadly examine the factors which underlie a number of aspects of the communications system as it functions today; others concentrate upon television. All articles probe beneath the surface. There are footnotes at the end of each article but no bibliography.

172, 173, 174, 175, 176

Hamelink, Cees J. **The Corporate Village: The Role of Transnational Corporations in International Communication**. Rome: IDOC International, 1977. 233p.

Hamelink, Cees J. **Finance and Information: a Study of Converging Interests**. Norwood, NJ: Ablex, 1983. 170p.

Hamelink, Cees J. **Cultural Autonomy in Global Communications: Planning National In-**

formation Policy. New York: Longman, 1983. 143p.

Hamelink, Cees J. **Transnational Data Flows in the Information Age**. Lund, Sweden: Studentlitteratur AB; Bromley, Kent, England: Chartwell-Bratt Ltd., 1984. 115p.

Hamelink, Cees, J., ed. **Communication in the Eighties: A Reader on the "MacBride Report"**. Rome: IDOC International, 1980. 62p.

Cees Hamelink, a prolific analyst of international communication with emphasis on developing nations, makes a case that capitalism as practiced by developed nations thwarts effective communication in the Third World. The first four titles analyze the way this comes about; the fifth is a critical examination of the MacBride report.

Hamelink's thesis in **The Corporate Village**, international communication, far from turning the world into McLuhan's "global village," has instead created a one-way flow of culture, a communication imperialism of political-economic structures dominated by capitalistic nations. Documenting corporate interests and concentration of the transnationals as they affect the Third World, he shows the cultural dependency this has caused. He concludes with a discussion of the signs of cultural resistance and an exploration of countervailing power of national governments, the UN, labor unions, churches, universities/research institutes, and action groups. Parts of the book consist of excerpts from other works by various authors, including among others, Armand Mattelart, Herbert Schiller, Oliver Boyd-Barrett, Thomas H. Guback, and Tapio Varis. Contains tables, chapter notes, a bibliography and an index of corporations.

Hamelink followed **The Corporate Village** with a further exploration of the role of transnational corporations in international communication in **Finance and Information, a Study of Converging Interests**. In this he concentrates on an analysis of the relationship of contemporary information systems to the financial center and to the worldwide process of transnationalization.

In **Cultural Autonomy in Global Communications** Hamelink feels that cultural diversity, so necessary for development in the Third World, is being increasingly threatened by large-scale export of the cultural system of advanced industrial states and must be countered by new models of development, especially in the area of information. Here he makes a proposal for planning national information policies in a way that protects and stimulates the cultural autonomy of Third World countries—a proposal, so he says, which will undoubtedly be interpreted in some quarters as controversial. References, bibliography and index.

Because data is the raw-stuff of information, and information is of primary importance in national development, the free flow of data becomes increasingly necessary for social development. In **Transnational Data Flows in the Information Age** Hamelink looks closely at its worldwide distribution and finds, not surprisingly, that data, along with the accompanying social benefits resulting from technological information "normally do not befall the poor majority of the Third World." He enumerates the situation in detail, discussing the information age, telematics, transnational corporations and transnational data flows, the impact and disparities in the telematics, data regulation, and consideration of policy. Although emphasis is on the Third World, the background is of necessity general, including Western Europe and the U.S. Chapter notes, bibliography and index.

In **Communication in the Eighties**, Hamelink offers critical reflections intended to contribute to an understanding of important points that the MacBride Report (No. 210) "rightfully stressed or unfortunately omitted." Contributors include Alfred Opubor, Kaarle Nordenstreng, Tamàs Szecskö, Rafael Roncagliolo, Oswalda Capriles, Nabil H. Dajani, Eapen K. Eapen, Jörg Becker, Herbert Schiller, Charles Foubert, and Hamelink.

177

Handbook of International News Agencies Around the World. Prague, Czechoslovakia: International Organization of Journalists, 1986. 167p.

Lists approximately 80 news agencies by continent and country. Data, which is supplied by the agency, vary according to pertinence, including some or all of the following: address; telephone, cable, telex; branches in country of origin; branches abroad; staff; number of transmission hours; extent of daily service; way of transmission; special services; number of foreign agencies received and number of recipients; central editorial office; character of agency.

178

Hannah, Gayle Durham. **Soviet Information Networks**. Washington: Georgetown University, Center for Strategic and International Studies, 1977. 80p.

A close examination of the sources through which the Soviets control information. Hannah discusses such aspects as public opinion; the extent and confines of the various media and sources of information, broadly interpreted to include such diverse ones as writers and the postal and telephone services; the spreading of the Communist philosophy through agitation and propaganda; private and foreign communication networks; censorship; changes since Stalin; and the possible future path. Although Hannah cites many facts and figures, she gives no notes or bibliography, and there is no index.

179

Harasymiw, Bohdan, ed. **Education and the Mass Media in the Soviet Union and Eastern Europe**. New York: Praeger, 1976. 130p.

Studies selected from among those presented at the First International Slavic Conference held in Banff, Canada, in 1974 which are concerned with public policy in Communist countries as it involves education in relation to the mass media (particularly the news agencies) and public opinion (especially in the Soviet Union).

180

Hardt, Hanno. **Social Theories of the Press: Early German & American Perspectives**. Beverly Hills, CA: Sage, 1979. 239p.

For years Germany and the United States approached theory and research in journalism from different directions, with the German tradition older and grounded in philosophy and the newer American tradition, operating in the narrower context of psychology and the small group. In his philosophical inquiry, Hardt traces the migration of ideas from Germany to America and, more recently, from America to Germany, detailing their modification and adoption by both countries. Bibliography and index.

181

Hartley, John. **Understanding News**. London: Methuen, 1982. 203p.

Intended to provide undergraduates with "some of the discursive concepts and strategies for approaching news texts" through semiotics. This is also excellent for anyone who wants to become more knowledgeable on the subject without (or before) going into depth with original sources. In the next-to-last chapter Hartley gives an annotated list of books for further reading and study, and in conclusion, a bibliography. Index.

182

Hartmann, Paul, and Charles Husband. **Racism and the Mass Media: A Study of the Role of the Mass Media in the Formation of White Beliefs and Attitudes in Britain.** Totowa, NJ: Rowman & Littlefield, 1974. 279p.

An examination of the beliefs and attitudes toward race held by sections of the white British population, as well as of the treatment of race and color issues by the mass media. The authors start from the value position that racial discrimination is a social evil and briefly discuss the history of colored immigration to Britain, British images of the black man, and prejudice in general. Later chapters report the findings from the surveys on attitudes and the content analysis of the media. Appendixes detail the methodology. Chapter notes and index. For a complementary, more intensive study of the coverage of race in the British press between 1963–1970, see **Race as News** (Paris: UNESCO, 1974. 173p.) by Hartmann, Husband, and Jean Clark. For a shorter study emphasizing the local evening paper and local radio see Barry Troyna's **Public Awareness and the Media** (No. 430).

183

Hepple, Alex. **Press Under Apartheid**. London: Information Department, International

Defense and Aid Fund, Information Department, 1974. 67p.

An analysis of freedom of the press in South Africa, including the long war against the free press, the laws that restrain and control it, relations with the police, press ownership, and the role of the press in an apartheid society. Appendixes give circulation figures and group ownership.

Another, and much older, book on the South African book is Cutten's **A History of the Press in South Africa** (No. 95) in which the author emphasizes its struggle for freedom from the government, particularly in the Transvaal Republic where he was a journalist. There are also other rare descriptions such as "The Bantu Press," "Press and the Police," "Press and the Pulpit." It carries footnotes.

184, 185, 186

Hess, Stephen. **The Washington Reporters**. Washington: Brookings Institution. 1981. 174p. (Newswork: 1)

Hess, Stephen. **The Government/Press Connection**. Washington: Brookings Institution. 1984. 160p. (Newswork: 2)

Hess, Stephen. **The Ultimate Insiders. U.S. Senators in the National Media**. Washington: Brookings Institution, 1986. 151p. (Newswork: 3)

Companion volumes in a four-part series (the fourth is in preparation) examining how the press fits into the public life of the capital. In the first volume Hess surveys over half of the 1,250 Washington-based journalists as to their backgrounds, their work habits, their freedom to choose their own stories, and the means they use to get information. In the second volume he investigates the jobs of public information officers at five executive agencies—the Food and Drug Administration, the Pentagon, the Department of Transportation, the State Department, and the White House—to consider their efficiency, their relations with reporters, and their influence on the news that got reported. In the third volume, he focuses on high-prestige news outlets—a handful of newspapers and newspaper groups, wire services, news magazines, and television and radio networks, which make some senators more newsworthy than others, looking at coverage in terms of personality and position as well as—on the other side of the coin—possible bias within the media. All volumes contain statistics, and all are indexed. The fourth volume will deal with the Senate and local news media.

Several earlier analyses of the Washington media which are still pertinent are Leo Rosten's **The Washington Correspondent**, 1937 (No. 952) and Douglass Cater's **The Fourth Branch of Government**, 1959 (No. 59) and the works of William L. Rivers, **The Opinionmakers** (No. 356), **Adversaries: Politics and the Press** (No. 357), and **The Other Government** (No. 358).

187

Hetherington, Alastair. **News, Newspapers and Television**. London: Macmillan, 1985. 329p.

"It's like riding a bicycle: if you stop to think about it you'll fall off," said the deputy editor, BBC television news, when interviewed about the news process by Hetherington, who, as a former journalist, agrees. "The pace of journalism leaves little time for introspective contemplation," Hetherington continues. "Nevertheless, for many years I had felt that it would be useful to try to persuade journalists to explain how they reached their decisions—especially on what was or was not news, and on how it should be handled." With the cooperation of decision-makers at BBC and ITV news staffs and those of several national dailies he has analyzed how such judgments are made. He has also included a case study of newspaper and television news in the 1984–85 coal dispute, and a chapter on coverage of war and terrorism. Appendixes briefly outline ownership, work stoppages, outstanding personalities and staffing of the newspapers studied. Glossary, notes and references, bibliography and index.

188, 189

Hiebert, Ray Eldon, Donald F. Ungurait, and Thomas W. Bohn. **Mass Media IV: An Introduction to Modern Communication**. New York: Longman, 1985. 684p.

Hiebert, Ray Eldon, and Carol Reuss, eds. **Impact of Mass Media: Current Issues**. New York: Longman, 1985. 515p.

Mass Media IV is the fourth edition of a text first published in 1974, whose aim is to assist students to become critical consumers of mass media by giving them a basic understanding of the theories, elements, functions and effects of mass communication, along with discussions of the various media in chronological order from books through sound recording. Contains a useful list of research materials, a bibliography and a subject index. Among the research materials listed are general reference, mass communication organizations, and a selected bibliography of periodicals by media. (The fifth edition was published in 1988.)

Though not intended as a companion volume, **Impact of Mass Media** might well supplement the introductory text, **Mass Media IV**. It deals with some of the controversial issues on which, for better or worse, mass media coverage appears to have impact, and examines the coverage and probable influence from different perspectives, with some authors defending, some criticizing, and some taking a balanced approach. Among the 16 issues discussed are mass media and ethics, religion, access and pressure groups, crime and violence, sex and sensationalism, politics, government management of the media, media management of government, business and media, war and media, media and culture, and media and minorities, women, and religion. All articles have been published previously; some have lists for further reading. (The second edition was issued in 1988.)

190

Hindley, M. Patricia, Gail M. Martin, and Jean McNulty. **The Tangled Web: Basic Issues in Canadian Communications**. Vancouver, B.C.: Douglas, 1977. 183p.

Much of the writing about Canadian communications concerns the effect on the system, both cultural and economic, of the U.S.—"the giant to the South." This book, however, has a different approach. Its thesis is that "the instabilities and uncertainties which currently afflict this country because it has still not decided whether it is a true confederation or an old-style nation-state, also beset the country's communications system." From this vantage point it explores, in the following order, publishing, films, broadcasting, cable, telephone, data transmission and satellites. The authors are core members of the Telecommunications Research Group in the Department of Communications Studies at Simon Fraser University. "Chapter Notes" and "Recommended Reading."

191

Hinds, Harold E., Jr., and Charles M. Tatum, eds. **Handbook of Latin American Popular Culture**. Westport, CT: Greenwood, 1985. 259p.

Contributors discuss popular religion, popular music, comics, television, sports, photo-novels, film, festivals and carnivals, cartoons and newspapers. Most of the approaches are critical-methodological within the various disciplines of the writers, including literature, cultural anthropology, sociology, philosophy, music, mass communications and history. Two approaches in particular emerge—the cultural imperialist and the semiological—based mostly on the works of Umberto Eco. There are chapter notes and an index.

192

Hocking, William Ernest. **Freedom of the Press: A Framework of Principle**. Chicago: University of Chicago Press, 1947. 239p.

Seeking principles on which the Commission on Freedom of the Press (No. 81) might base its work Hocking examines the foundation of freedom of the press in philosophy and law. Index. This is a companion volume to Chafee's **Government and Mass Communication** (No. 62) in which he reviews governmental restrictions.

193

Hoggart, Richard. **The Uses of Literacy: Aspects of Working-Class Life with Special Reference to Publications and Entertainment**. New York: Oxford University Press, c1957, 1970. 319p.

In the earlier (1957) publication, this socio-literary

study was subtitled **Changing Patterns in English Mass Culture**. It concerns changes in working-class culture during the last 30 or 40 years preceding the 1960s, telling in particular how these changes were being encouraged by mass publications. Emphasis is on periodicals and popular music, although the author believes he would have obtained similar results if film and commercial broadcasting had been used. Contains "Notes and References," "A Select Bibliography," and an index.

194

Hohenberg, John. **The Pulitzer Prizes: A History of the Awards in Books, Drama, Music and Journalism, Based on the Private Files over Six Decades**. New York: Columbia University Press, 1974. 434p.

This is an analysis as well as a history, describing mistakes along with achievements. Appendixes give members of the Advisory Board, awards by category, and a summary of the dates prizes were withheld and in which categories. Notes and comments, bibliography, and detailed index.

195

Hollander, Gayle Durham. **Soviet Political Indoctrination: Developments in Mass Media and Propaganda Since Stalin**. New York: Praeger, 1972. 244p.

Against the background of the Soviet political system the author analyzes the structure, content, and audience of book publishing, newspapers and magazines, broadcasting, film, and agitation and propaganda. Notes follow each chapter, and there are maps, tables, notes on Soviet sources, and an extensive bibliography.

Honey, Maureen. **Creating Rosie the Riveter**. (See No. 1051.)

196

Hooper, Alan. **The Military and the Media**. Aldershot, Hants, England: Gower, 1982. 247p.

Hooper, an officer in the British Royal Marines, bases his study largely on first-hand research consisting of personal observation of the news process in the press, radio and television, interviews with various personalities in the military and the media, and visits to a number of military establishments to see what they teach about the media. From this he has culled case studies of the news process as practiced in print and broadcast news; a review of the current depth of knowledge which journalists and military personnel possesses of the other; an analysis of the portrayal of the military on television; and a study of the reporting of conflict which includes an examination of some examples from the Vietnam war, Northern Ireland and the Falkland crisis. Footnotes, an extensive bibliography and an index.

197

Hopkins, Mark W. **Mass Media in the Soviet Union**. New York: Pegasus, 1970. 384p.

As the **Milwaukee Journal**'s Soviet affairs specialist since 1964, the author has spent much time in Russia and has attended Leningrad University. He possesses insights into what are in his opinion the good and bad elements of the Soviet system, which he frequently compares with the good and bad elements of our own. Focus is on the newspaper press. Contains detailed footnotes and an excellent bibliography as well as maps, lists, tables, and an index.

Horowitz, Irving Louis. **Communicating Ideas**. (See No. 1065.)

198

Howkins, John. **Mass Communication in China**. New York: Longman, 1982. 160p.

An inside look at the media since the fall of Mao Tse Tung, based largely on first-hand evidence the author collected on the spot. After an analysis of the role of communications in today's China, Howkins deals with the various media—broadcasting, film, publishing, telecommunications ("From Beacon Fires to Satellites"), and advertising—a new development. Appendix A is "A Chronology—1900–1980's"; other appendixes include "A Note on the Language," "Population," and "Names and Addresses of Selected Media Organizations." Contains a bibliography and an index. See also Godwin C. Chu's **Popular Media in China: Shaping New Cultural Patterns**, (No. 72).

199

Hudec, Vladimír. **Education and Training of Journalists at Higher Educational Establishments in the Czechoslovak Socialist Republic**. Prague: Charles University, 1984. 31p.

Hudec traces the development of journalism education and its present state in Czechoslovakia, emphasizing the curriculum and discussing the background of its faculty and the cooperation of journalists and journalistic institutions within the community of Communist-oriented countries.

200

Hudson, Michael C., and Ronald G. Wolfe, eds. **The American Media and the Arabs**. Washington: Center for Contemporary Arab Studies, Georgetown University, 1980. 103p.

Articles derived from a symposium at Georgetown University, organized around four main themes: popular perception of Islam and the Arabs; Arab stereotyping in television entertaining; practices and constraints in American journalism; and American journalists in the Arab world. In a concluding article Hudson summarizes the papers, analyzing trends which seem to dominate media treatment of Arabs and cautiously suggesting two modest steps which would lead to improvement.

Hughes, Frank L. **Prejudice and the Press: A Restatement of the Principle of Freedom of the Press with Specific Reference to the Hutchins-Luce Commission**. (See No. 81.)

201

Hulteng, John L. **The Messenger's Motives: Ethical Problems of the News Media**. 2d ed. Englewood Cliffs, NJ: Prentice-Hall, 1985. 239p.

Through use of pertinent problems that have arisen, Hulteng examines ethical issues confronting journalists on a number of fronts—among them, matters of taste, use of photographs, abuse of trust, protection of source, influence of advertisers. His central purpose is to make practitioners, students, and the general public more knowledgeable about the nature of such problems and thus better equipped to find solutions. Notes and an annotated bibliography. Index.

202

Inkeles, Alex. **Public Opinion in Soviet Russia: A Study in Mass Persuasion**. 2d ed. Cambridge, MA: Harvard University Press, 1958. 393p.

Although three decades old, this analysis of the structure, function, and contents of the Soviet press, broadcasting, and film still provides useful background. Contains bibliographic notes, a bibliography, and an index. The fact that there have been more recent studies—Hopkins's **Mass Media in the Soviet Union** (No. 197) and Markham's **Voices of the Red Giants** (No. 266)—in no way invalidates its usefulness. Contains bibliographic notes, a bibliography, and an index.

203, 204, 205

Innis, Harold A. **Empire and Communication**. Rev. ed. by Mary Q. Innis. Toronto: University of Toronto Press, 1972. 184p.

Innis, Harold A. **The Bias of Communication**. Toronto: University of Toronto Press, 1951. 226p.

Innis, Harold A. **Changing Concepts of Time**. Toronto: University of Toronto Press, 1952. 142p.

One of Marshall McLuhan's outstanding contributions has been to bring into prominence the works of the late Canadian economist, Harold Innis, whose early insights into the importance of media to economics and culture have become increasingly pertinent. His thesis is that the communications systems of empires have influenced their rise and fall. In **Empire and Communication** he discusses the possibility, with emphasis on economics, that communication may occupy a crucial position in the organization and administration of government and in turn of empires and of Western civilization. **The Bias of Communication** is a collection of papers supporting this theory in more detail. **Changing Concepts of Time** attempts to show that the communication system of a given culture can affect the way in which its people regard space-time concepts.

206, 207, 208

In the Public Interest: A Report by the National News Council, 1973–1975. New York: National News Council, 1975. 163p.

In the Public Interest—II: A Report by the National News Council, 1975–1978. New York: National News Council, 1979. 437p.

In the Public Interest—III: A Report by the National News Council, 1979–1983. New York: National News Council, 1984. 610p.

These three volumes are a record of the decade of the Council's existence. The majority of each volume is given over to an analysis of complaints handled, with (in volumes I and II) shorter discussions on the defense of press freedom. Volume I tells how the Council came into existence; in volume III, Richard Salant, president, gives his personal view of the Council's past and possible future role. Volume III contains an Index of Complaints 1973–1983.

209

International Commission for the Study of Communication Problems. **Documents for the Study of Communication Problems**. 90 parts (approx.) Paris: UNESCO, 1979.

Series of pamphlets of varying lengths from eight to 50 pages, resulting from a mandate by the Commission to make a critical analysis on a global level of the state of communication in the world today. Among topics treated are: summary of statistics and recent research; various aspects of news agencies, with analysis of 19 specific ones; dissemination of information in a pluralistic world; treatment of information and imbalances among nations; planning; strengthening the Third World press; technology; communication in traditional societies as illustrated by some of the African and Asian nations and the Arab states. Emphasis is on the needs of the developing nations. Pamphlet No. 7 is a bibliography.

210

International Commission for the Study of Communication Problems. **Many Voices, One World: Communication and Society Today and Tomorrow**. Paris: UNESCO, 1980. 312p. (The MacBride Report)

A UNESCO report headed by Sean MacBride of Ireland in which representatives from Canada, Chile, Columbia, Egypt, France, India, Indonesia, Japan, the Netherlands,

Nigeria, Tunisia, the U.S., the U.S.S.R., Yugoslavia and Zaire were mandated "to study the totality of Communication problems in modern society" in order to formulate "a more just and more efficient world information and communication order," keeping in mind particularly the differences among nations in culture and resources. The result of this hard, if not impossible, charge to reconcile divergent viewpoints represents a compromise which can wholly please none of the three worlds, but it does offer a wide-ranging investigation with varying viewpoints. Appendixes include a list of international organizations active in communications, and there are, in addition, a list of about 100 available background papers. Index.

For a discussion of the report giving some of its strengths and weaknesses see **Communication in the Eighties: A Reader on the "MacBride Report"**, edited by Cees J. Hamelink (No. 176). A 244-page paperback abridgement, **Many Voices, One World**, was published in 1984 by UNESCO.

211

Isaacs, Norman E. **Untended Gates: The Mismanaged Press**. New York: Columbia University Press, 1986. 258p.

A critique of contemporary journalism in which Isaacs, a well-known editor and educator, examines the shortcomings of the press in ethical terms, using actual cases involving top and lesser journalists to illustrate how and why the press falls short of its responsibilities. His provocative analysis is directed not only to professional journalists, educators and students, but also to the non-involved layman. Among the case studies: the Janet Cooke Pulitzer Prize hoax at the **Washington Post**, the Sharon and Westmoreland libel trials, the insider-trading episode at the **Wall Street Journal**, and the criticism about television's role in the Arab terrorist seizure of the TWA plane and the holding of hostages in Beirut. Chapter notes and index.

212, 213

Ito, Shinichi, et al. **Historical Development of Media Systems I: Japan**. Paris: UNESCO, 1979. 69p. (Communication and Society 1)

Dusiska, Emil. **Historical Development of Media Systems II: German Democratic Republic**. Paris: UNESCO, 1979. 35p. (Communication and Society 2)

Studies of the mass communication systems in two countries which offer an interesting contrast in content and presentation. The Japanese study provides an insight into indigenous media forms and the introduction of modern media which are then followed through World War II and the Occupation up to the present. The German study concentrates to a large extent on the ideological and political bases of the mass media as they developed after World War II. Both are summaries of larger studies.

214

Jacobs, Norman, ed. **Culture for the Millions? Mass Media in Modern Society**. Princeton, NJ: Van Nostrand, 1961. 200p.

One of the earliest works on the subject which asks whether pure culture can survive the mass media and mass society. This question is considered by a notable list of contributors whose comments do not date: Paul Lazarsfeld, Edward Shils, Leo Lowenthal, Hannah Arendt, Ernest van den Haag, Oscar Handlin, Leo Rosten, Randall Jarrell, James Baldwin, Stanley Edgar Hyman, Arthur Schlesinger, among others.

215

Janowitz, Morris. **The Community Press in an Urban Setting: The Social Elements of Urbanism**. 2d ed. Chicago: University of Chicago Press, 1967. 275p.

First published in 1952, this sociological study places the community press within the larger process of communication and a system of values. Janowitz finds it to have a double aspect as both a reflection of underlying social organization and at the same time an active ingredient in social change. His examination includes its growth and organization; its image of the community; its readers and their selection of information from the local newspapers; the social role of the community publisher; and the dynamics of the local community. An appendix includes the methodology of the content analysis used; the readership survey; and basic data on three sample communities. In an article, "Post script: Communication and Community," Scott Greer comments on the findings and the methodology. Index.

216

Janowitz, Morris, and Paul Hirsch, eds. **Reader in Public Opinion and Mass Communication**. 3d ed. New York: Free Press, 1981. 440p.

The first edition of this anthology, co-edited by Bernard Berelson and Janowitz, was one of the earliest to link public opinion with mass communication. In this present edition some of the articles from the first (1953) edition have been retained—classics like Walter Lippmann's "Stereotypes," James Bryce's "Nature of Public Opinion," and Harold Lasswell's "Nations and Classes: The Symbols of Identification," for instance. In both the second (1966) edition and this one, new authors reflect the contemporary scene—among them Jay Blumler, Michael Robinson, Ben Bagdikian, Gaye Tuchman, Jeremy Tunstall, George Gerbner and Larry Gross, Horace Newcomb, Denis McQuail, and Kurt and Gladys Lang. Articles in the 1981 edition are grouped under "Theories of Public Opinion," "Formation of Public Opinion," "Public Opinion and the Political Process," "Mass Media: Organization, Structure and Control," "Communication Content," "Theories of Mass Media Impact," "Mass Media Effects," and "Advertising and

Opinion Change Over Time." The topic of advertising is new. Like the two previous editions, this is a standard. Together the three provide insight into a quarter of a century of trends in mass communication research. References follow each article. Index.

217

Jensen, Klaus Bruhn. **Making Sense of the News**. Aarhus, Denmark: Aarhus University Press, 1986. 392p.

Jensen, a faculty member at the University of Copenhagen, explores the theoretical bases from which to study the audience of the mass media. In the preface, he writes, "The present work proposes a comprehensive model of reception and places it in the broader framework of a theory of communication." The concept of "meaning" is attended from the viewpoints of the audience as producers of meaning as well as the mass media institutions as producers of meaning. The process of meaning is traced empirically in a study of American television news viewers, hence the book's title. The data of the research of American television news viewers are meticulously presented. Also included in the book is an essay on audience rights with relation to mass media news content, "The ABC of Communication Rights." A final chapter discusses political and educational implications of the mass media audience research. Extensive bibliography. No index, however, the list of contents is exceedingly detailed.

218

Joan, Polly, and Andrea Chesman. **Guide to Women's Publishing**. Paradise, CA: Dustbooks, 1978. 296p.

Comprehensive coverage of feminist journals; women's newspapers; feminist "small press" publishing, including all-women print shops and women printers; the non-sexist children's press (which concerns itself with sons as well as daughters); and distribution outlets for feminist writing, with a listing of women involved in distribution. Ends with a section on additional resources of directories, review publications, libraries and archives, organizations, bookstores, and mail order. Index.

Journalism Career and Scholarship Guide (See No. 1764).

219

Johnstone, John W. C., Edward J. Slawski, and William W. Bowman. **The News People: A Sociological Portrait of American Journalists and Their Work**. Urbana: University of Illinois Press, 1976. 257p.

In this, the first systematic treatment of newsmen at large, based on extensive interviews with more than 1,300 practicing journalists, the authors say that their main concern is "to present a representative overview of the nature of newsmen and newswork in contemporary America." "News people" is interpreted broadly to include those who work in radio and TV, wire services and syndicates, news magazines, daily and weekly newspapers, as well as some of the journalists in the alternative media. Data is analyzed to show social characteristics, education and training, career patterns, political affiliations, division of labor, the ways in which news men and women perceive their journalistic responsibility, and the rewards and satisfactions they find in their work. Finally, the authors draw their conclusions as to *who* and *where* the news-gatherers are and how this affects the quantity and quality of their work. Extensive appendixes give charts and tables of data. Bibliography and person-subject index. Winner of the National Association of Public Broadcasters' Award in 1977.

This has been updated by **The American Journalist: A Portrait of U.S. News People and Their Work** by David H. Weaver and G. Cleveland Wilhoit (No. 445).

220

Jones, Greta, Ian Connell, and Jack Meadows. **The Presentation of Science by the Media**. Leicester, England: University of Leicester, Primary Communications Research Centre, 1978. 76p.

A study whose aim is to show how interpretations of science in the media are constructed. The authors have concentrated on an examination of the activities of those people involved in the presentation of science to the public by means of newspapers, radio, or broadcasting. Contains a bibliography.

221

Jones, J. Clement. **Mass Media Codes of Ethics and Councils: A Comparative International Study of Professional Standards**. Paris: UNESCO, 1980. 80p. (Reports and Papers on Mass Communication No. 86)

With information from governments, media councils, journalists and broadcasts, Jones has compiled a succinct study of codes generally and of a few specifically. His aim is "to bring together some of the background information and to advance some of the arguments needed to help media people and others concerned to make up their own minds in accordance with their own needs and circumstances." In a "World Survey" he has chosen 49 countries for an analysis of their codes and the conditions underlying them, and in an appendix has given the codes for Australia, Canada, Egypt, India, Japan, Sweden, Great Britain, and the U.S.A., along with organizational codes for the International Federation of Journalists, the European Community, the International Organization of Journalists, and the UN and UNESCO. There is also a section on "Mass Media Councils in Third World Countries." This is excellent source material for any individuals or countries interested either in devising or revising journalistic codes of ethics.

222

Jones, Nicholas. **Strikes and the Media: Communication and Conflict**. Oxford, England: Blackwell, 1986. 224p.

Jones, radio correspondent for BBC News who has covered all major industrial disputes in England for the last six years, uses the 1984–85 miners' strike to show how the battles between industry and labor have moved away from the negotiating table to the propaganda war in newspaper columns and TV news programs. The news media, he contends, sometimes find that in addition to reporting the news, they help to create it. This is a thoughtful analysis based on practical observation and personal experience. Index.

223

Joslyn, Richard. **Mass Media and Elections**. Reading, MA: Addison-Wesley, 1984. 313p.

Although intended as a text, this detailed account of the media's role in contemporary elections serves as an excellent general source book. Joslyn deals with one segment of the increasingly important and complicated relationship between the media and politics—the role of the media in contemporary elections, with emphasis on their interaction with the candidates, the public, and the electoral process itself. His account is detailed and well documented, and although it is intended as an undergraduate text it also serves as an excellent source book, with chapter notes and a bibliography to take an inquiring reader further. Indexed.

224

Jowett, Garth S., and Victoria O'Donnell. **Propaganda and Persuasion**. Newbury Park, CA: Sage, 1986. 234p.

Intended as a guide to further reading on specific issues, this succinct text gives an overview of the history of propaganda as well as a review of the social scientific research on its effects. In the authors' words: "We chose to present in this book both a digest of important and classic ideas on the subject and our original ideas." Chapter headings reflect its scope: "What Is Propaganda and How Does It Differ From Persuasion?," "Propaganda Through the Ages," "Propaganda Institutionalized," "Propaganda and Persuasion Examined," "Propaganda and Psychological Warfare," "How to Analyze Propaganda," "Propaganda in Action: Five Case Studies," and "How Propaganda Works in Modern Society." References comprise a substantial bibliography. Index.

225

Kato, Hidetoshi. **Japanese Research on Mass Communication: Selected Abstracts**. Honolulu: University of Hawaii Press, 1974. 128p.

Contains 98 abstracts of statistical studies giving data on a variety of subjects, among which are audience, children's media, "the politically concerned public," the use of radio by the blind, and changes in media taste throughout the years of television's growth. Contains a list of Japanese periodicals on mass communication and a subject index.

226

Katz, Elihu, and Paul F. Lazarsfeld. **Personal Influence: The Part Played by People in the Flow of Communications**. New York: Free Press, 1955. 400p.

One of the classics in the literature of mass communication, this theoretical analysis, backed by empirical data, studies the effect of face-to-face personal communication as distinguished from the effects of mass communication, and shows their important interrelationships. Contains bibliographic notes, a bibliography, and an index.

227

Katz, Elihu, and Tamás Szecskö, eds. **Mass Media and Social Change**. Beverly Hills, CA: Sage, 1981. 271p.

A compilation of the papers of Symposium VII of the 9th World Congress of Sociology whose central theme asks whether the mass media should be agents of change or agents of the status quo. Central to the articles are discussions from varying viewpoints as to the nature of news and the factors that shape it. Among the contributors are Peter Golding, Gaye Tuchman, Paul Hirsch, Elihu Katz, Tamás Szecskö and Elisabeth Noelle-Neumann. A list of reference follows each article.

228

Kent, Ruth K. **The Language of Journalism: A Glossary of Print-Communications Terms**. Ohio: Kent State University Press, 1971. 186p.

A dictionary of journalistic and many printing terms, preceded by a discussion of the meaning and origins of such associated words as *muckraker*, *tabloid*, and *yellow journalism*, and followed by a list of abbreviations, a list of proofreaders' marks, footnotes, sources consulted, and a bibliography. Although the author says that she does not attempt to present a complete journalism glossary, her scope is extensive. Emphasis is mainly on editorial journalism, with a scattering of entries having to do with paper, book production, the electronic media, statistical research, law of the press, and photography.

229

Kessler, Lauren. **The Dissident Press: Alternative Journalism in American History**. Beverly Hills, CA: Sage, 1984. 159p.

"This book investigates a handful of the many fringe groups—political, social, and cultural—who, denied access to the mainstream media marketplace, started marketplaces of their own," says the author, who explores various groups: Black Americans, utopians and communitarians; feminists; the ethnic groups; radical groups—populists, anarchists, socialists, communists, and pacifists. The approach is historical.

230

Kesterton, W. H. **A History of Journalism in Canada**. Toronto: McClelland and Stewart, 1967. 304p.

One of the first studies of the press in Canada. Fact-filled, descriptive and chronological, it is especially valuable for its meticulous detail. Beginning with the earliest newspapers in 1752, Kesterton chronicles press development and, in the early decades of the 19th century, the development also of radio and television. Chapter notes, and a lengthy name/subject index to lead back to precise information.

231

King, Josephine, and Mary Stott, eds. **Is This Your Life? Images of Women in the Media**. London: Virago, in association with Quartet Books, 1977. 199p.

A group of women writers investigate the attitudes and images various media (radio, advertising, newspapers, comics, bestselling fiction, films, television, pop music, and erotic and women's magazines) offer readers, viewers, and listeners. Comparing the version of women's roles they found with the realities of changing times, the editors attempt to identify stereotypes and to search for ways in which attitudes are conditioned and perhaps manipulated. Illustrated by cartoons. Index.

232

Klapp, Orrin E. **Overload and Boredom: Essays on the Quality of Life in the Information Society**. Westport, CT: Greenwood, 1986. 174p.

Insightful essays in which the author, a sociologist, uses information from such diverse areas as psychology, communication studies, information science, economics, and literature to theorize about how a society could become boring in spite, or rather because, of huge loads of information which can lead to a combination of noise and banality. His ultimate focus is not on boredom per se, which he considers merely a symptom, but on degradation of information due to overload. This is one of the few books devoted entirely to this important subject. Bibliography and index.

233

Klapper, Joseph T. **The Effects of Mass Communication**. New York: Free Press, 1960. 302p.

Klapper's book now seems simplistic in light of the new techniques developed since it was published, but it remains important as the initial effort to synthesize existing empirical knowledge gleaned from effect studies. The first part is a report of the way the mass media change or reinforce opinions and the differences among the various media in bringing this about; the second deals with probable effects of specific types of material—for example, crime and violence and escapist categories, and adult TV fare when viewed by children. Contains a bibliography and an index.

234

Kline, F. Gerald, and Phillip J. Tichenor, eds. **Current Perspectives in Mass Communication Research**. Beverly Hills, CA: Sage, 1972. 320p. (Sage Annual Reviews of Communication Research, Vol. I)

Articles in this anthology are selected to illustrate research perspectives in major departments and schools of journalism dealing with mass communication—the subjects they are treating and the methodologies they are using. Among the subjects are gatekeeping, information diffusion, socialization, political campaigns, the urban poor, sex, and violence. There are also chapters on the interpersonal context of mass communication and on communication theory. Bibliographies at the end of each chapter, a general bibliography, and a subject index. Further volumes of the series deal with other aspects of communication research, both interpersonal and intrapersonal. (See No. 1786.)

235

Knightley, Phillip. **The First Casualty: From the Crimea to Vietnam: The War Correspondent as Hero, Propagandist, and Myth Maker**. New York: Harcourt Brace Jovanovich, 1975. 465p.

The title indicates the scope of this excellent history of the war correspondent, including photographers, as Knightley traces him (and a few hers) from the beginning of this type of journalism in the Crimea in the 1850s to the war in Vietnam over a century later. In between he covers various wars, little and big, in various parts of the world. He describes not only the correspondents but also the political and ideological climate that produced and set the course of the particular war, and analyzes the media coverage. This is useful not only for research and reference, but also as history. In addition it makes fascinating reading, although some parts are true horror stories which can be hard to take. There are 12 pages giving numerous sources, a bibliography and an index. (The 1982 edition omits two chapters in the 1975 edition on the Boer War and on Algeria.)

236

Kraus, Sidney, and Dennis Davis. **The Effects of Mass Communication on Political Behavior**. University Park: Pennsylvania State University Press, 1976. 308p.

"Our purpose is to provide students, scholars and even politicians who study political communication with a review and commentary on what is known about the field, what is not yet known, what ought to be known, and how we assess and evaluate the effects of mass communication on political behavior." Chapters relate mass communication to socialization, the electoral process, political information, the political process, and the construction of political reality in society. There is also an examination of methods of political communication research. The authors conclude with a discussion of the current state of knowledge. Each chapter contains abstracts and a bibliography. Author index and subject index.

237

Krippendorf, Klaus. **Content Analysis: An Introduction to Its Methodology**. Beverly Hills, CA: Sage, 1980. 191p.

In this sophisticated text Krippendorf introduces the reader to ways of analyzing data as symbolic communications. Its content can be grouped into three main concerns—the theoretical, the methodological, and the critical. The theoretical part gives a brief history of content analysis, develops a definition distinguishing it from other methods, and illustrates its practical application. The methodological begins with the logic of content analysis designs and continues with procedures involved—unitizing, sampling, recording, construction of data languages, analytical constructs, computational techniques, and use of computers. The critical concerns the two principal quality criteria—reliability and validity. In conclusion, a practical guide summarizes the special perspective of this method. References.

238

Kruglak, Theodore Edward. **The Foreign Correspondents: A Study of the Men and Women Reporting for the American Information Media in Western Europe**. Geneva, Switzerland: E. Droz, 1955. 163p.

Kruglak, in his introduction to this work now over three decades old, but still timely, points out the difficulty American correspondents had in covering foreign news, particularly in understanding and backgrounding problems. In his words: "What do we know about the correspondents who write for our newspapers, news agencies and magazines, or broadcast over our radio stations? Do they have the necessary training, background and experience for the vital task of interpreting Europe to Americans?" Looking for answers he compiled a basic list of accredited correspondents in 18 countries of Western Europe to whom he sent a questionnaire, and he conducted interviews with a selective number of bureau chiefs and correspondents. Using these as data he analyzes the media represented and the social, professional and political composition of the correspondents, along with their views on specific international political and economic problems; and finally the problems of news gathering in Western Europe and the performance of the correspondents corps stationed there. Appendixes give the questionnaire and the raw data obtained from it. There is a glossary of journalistic terms, footnotes and a bibliography but no index. For another book written a

decade later which treats the quality of foreign news produced by American correspondents at home, see Bernard Cohen's **The Press and Foreign Policy** (No. 76).

239

Kurian, George Thomas, ed. **World Press Encyclopedia**. 2v. New York: Facts on File, 1982.

This is a definitive survey of the state of the press in 180 countries which brings together in easily consultable form available information and statistics on the history of the world's press as well as the political and economic climate in which it functions. In both scope and size it is probably the most comprehensive survey on the subject. The survey is in four sections: Section I, "The International Press"; Section II, "The World's Developed Press Systems"; Section III, "Smaller and Developing Press Systems," and Section IV, "Minimal and Underdeveloped Press Systems." Coverage is alphabetical by country within the sections, and each article is by one or more specialists who in some cases are nationals. Discussions and data for the various countries in the first three sections are under the following headings: "Basic Data: Background and General Characteristics"; "Economic Framework"; "Press Law"; "Censorship"; "State Press Relations"; "Attitude Toward Foreign Media"; "News Agencies"; "Electronic News Media"; "Education and Training"; and in conclusion "Summary," with a discussion of trends and prospects; followed by "Chronology." Preceding each country is a table of basic data, and following it a bibliography. Section IV, "Minimal and Underdeveloped Press Systems," treats each country briefly in tabular form. Appendixes list 50 of the best known daily newspapers, the news agencies of the world, selected periodicals dealing with the press, media multinational, press-related associations, unions and organizations, advertising expenditures, radio transmitters and receivers, and television transmitters and sets. There is also a one-page discussion of media multinationals, with two outstanding examples. The 31-page author-subject index by Marjorie B. Bank and James Johnson should be especially helpful.

240

Lambeth, Edmund B. **Committed Journalism: An Ethic for the Profession**. Bloomington: Indiana University Press, 1986. 208p.

Through an examination of past and present philosophies, case studies, events, and judgments—all of which relate to the news media—Lambeth suggests relevant guides (as distinct from guidelines) for the modern journalist in search of a framework. Chapter notes, a bibliography, and name and subject indexes.

241

Läpple-Wagenhals, Doris. **A New Development Model—A New Communication Policy? On Communications in Nicaragua Before and After July 19, 1979**. Frankfort am Main, West Germany: Peter Lang, 1984. 165p.

How have the overthrow of the Somoza regime in 1979 and a new and very different political approach to government affected Nicaragua's communication system? To discover the effects the author has studied not only the structure and development of the communication system—print, broadcasting and film—but also the history and political, socio-economic, cultural and educational system behind it. This is all brought together in a final "Interconnections between Communication and other Subsystems of Nicaragua." Most of the research was done in the country itself through numerous interviews with a wide variety of Nicaraguans. In conclusion is a bibliography which includes books and papers, decrees, and newspapers, newsletters and magazines. This is a very thorough study.

242

Lasswell, Harold D., Daniel Lerner, and Hans Speier, eds. **Propaganda and Communication in World History**. 3 vols. Honolulu: University of Hawaii Press, 1979–80. v.1 **The Symbolic Instrument in Early Times**; v.2 **Emergence of Public Opinion in the West**; v.3 **A Pluralizing World in Formation**.

Scholars from many disciplines examine the impact of communication on history from its beginnings in primitive and tribal communities to modern times and the contemporary world situation, reconstructing the ways in which social communication was practiced, codified, and transmitted. Each volume contains chapter notes and an index.

Lasswell, Harold., et al. **Propaganda and Promotional Activities**. (See No. 1664.)

243

Lawler, Philip R. **The Alternative Influence: The Impact of Investigative Reporting on America's Media**. Washington, DC: The Media Institute, 1984. 92p.

"The Purpose of this book," says the author, "is . . . to appraise the life of the American mass media from one very specialized angle"—that of investigative reporting. Because investigative reporting can be arduous, controversial, expensive and sometimes difficult to place, a number of individuals and supporting institutions have banded together in consortia to assist. Lawler describes nine such organizations and reflects on the genre and its influence on American journalism. Chapter notes.

244

Lee, Jung Bock. **The Political Character of the Japanese Press**. Seoul, Korea: Seoul National University Press, 1985. 198p.

"With a view to examining two major conceptions of the political orientation of the Japanese press, either as an oppositional leftist or as an apologist for the conserva-

tive establishment, Professor Lee has analyzed the origins, the structure, and the attitudinal inclinations of the Japanese Press." (Foreword) In doing so, he has employed the historical approach, institutional analysis, empirical survey, case study, and content analysis. Footnotes, bibliography and index.

245

Lee, Philip, ed. **Communication for All: New World Information and Communication Order**. Maryknoll, NY: Orbis, 1985. 158p.

An anthology sponsored by the World Association for Christian Communication, whose articles examine the MacBride Report and expound the philosophy that communication is a basic human right to be shared by the developing and developed countries alike. There is a 24-page bibliography of books, pamphlets, documents, periodicals and articles on the NWICO by Colleen Roach.

246

Lendvai, Paul. **The Bureaucracy of Truth: How Communist Governments Manage the News**. London: Burnett, 1981. 285p.

"A dispassionate analysis of Soviet-type Communist communication policies reveals a yawning gap between rhetoric and realities, claims and facts," says Lendvai whose intention "is to avoid sweeping generalizations and to provide a truthful and dispassionate account, even of policies which I deplore." Part I deals with Communist mass media, their structure, function and control, and combines common features and variations in each country; Part II, with the problems connected with international broadcasting to Eastern Europe, including a description of major broadcasters, audience impact and counter moves by the Soviet bloc, among them jamming; and Part III, with the significance and consequences of the Helsinki accords and the Eastern method of implementation in 1975–80, which he describes and analyzes. Much of the material is based on primary sources such as Soviet and Eastern European publications, information collected during visits to the area, and interviews with Western and Communist newsmen. Books used are cited in a section, "Bibliographical Notes." Index.

247

Lent, John A. **The New World and International Information Order**. Singapore: Asian Mass Communication Research and Information Centre, 1982. 103p.

Lent states as his purpose to "1) concisely background the issues and form of the debate in its evolution during the past decade and a half; 2) briefly critique the literature of the controversy; 3) provide a comprehensive bibliography of books, monographs, documents and periodicals that deal with the issue; and 4) list the major conferences, symposia and meetings on any aspect of the debate up to 1980."

248, 249

Lent, John A. **Philippine Mass Communications Before 1811, After 1966**. Manila: Philippine Press Institute, 1972(?) 179p.

Lent, John A. **Third World Mass Media and Their Search for Modernity: The Case of Commonwealth Caribbean, 1717–1976**. Lewisburg, PA: Bucknell University Press, 1977. 405p.

Philippine Mass Communications . . . is a historical survey touching on the newspaper press, the provincial press, press freedom, magazines, radio, television, film, book publishing, advertising and journalism education.
Third World Mass Media attempts "to examine historical, cultural, economic, and political aspects of all Commonwealth Caribbean mass media, from the time of the first newspaper in 1717 until 1976." Both this and **Philippine Mass Communications** have comprehensive bibliographies.

250

Lewels, Francisco J., Jr. **The Uses of the Media by the Chicano Movement: A Study in Minority Access**. New York: Praeger, 1974. 185p.

Chicanos feel that they and other minority groups are denied access to the media because they lack funds and for other reasons. This book documents the steps they have taken and are taking to gain access, especially (although not exclusively) to broadcasting. Contains detailed footnotes and a bibliography.

251

Lewis, Peter M., ed. **Media for People in Cities: A Study of Community Media in an Urban Context**. Paris: UNESCO, 1984? 239p.

Although rural development, especially in the Third World, is a major concern of UNESCO, emphasis here is upon those uses of media which support community initiatives in urban settings or were introduced to help resolve tensions and problems. Media are not limited to newspapers and broadcasting; they also include such other forms as wall posters, mimeographed newsletters, audio cassettes and portable video equipment. Emphasis, however, is not upon the medium or its mode of delivery, but rather upon its function within a community program to focus upon the urban problem. Scope is international and arrangement is by country: Africa, the Arab world, Australia, the Caribbean (a case study), Europe, India, Japan, Latin America, North America and the Philippines. An appendix includes extracts from the Final Report of the Urban Community Media Consultation, UNESCO: "Proposals for related activities," and "Proposals for future activities and research programmes."
A 1977 study edited by Frances J. Berrigan, **Access: Some Western Modern Models of Community Media**

(UNESCO), is a discussion accompanied by case studies of different ways in which communities in the U.S., Canada and some European countries have provided access for audience participation in broadcasting programming for both television and radio.

252

Lewis, Roger. **Outlaws of America: The Underground Press and Its Context: Notes on a Cultural Revolution**. Harmondsworth, England: Penguin, 1972. 204p.

The author, an Englishman who attended an American university, traveled across the U.S. gathering his material. He has identified the main groups and tied in their publications with various of the counter-culture movements of the 1960s. One chapter discusses the underground press in England. There is a listing, "Underground Press Syndicate—Members and Friends, June, 1971," and a name and subject index.

253

Lichter, S. Robert, Stanley Rothman, and Linda S. Lichter. **The Media Elite**. Bethesda, MD: Adler & Adler, 1986. 342p.

On the contention that today as never before the major media stand at the center of the struggle for social influence, the authors have conducted an empirical study which systematically examines the life situations of newspeople and the nature of their product to determine whether the two are linked, and if so, in what ways. Media whose personnel were examined through a random sample and include the **New York Times**, **Washington Post**, **Wall Street Journal**, **Time**, **Newsweek**, **U.S. News and World Report**, ABC, NBC, CBS and public television, with the questionnaire centering on social background, political opinions, motivations, and orientations toward the news. The book also presents the results of an in-depth content analysis of three major public issues covered by the national media during the 1970s and early 1980s: bussing to achieve integration, the safety of nuclear power, and the oil industry's role in the energy crisis. An appendix survey research procedures. Notes and index.

254

Linsky, Martin. **Impact: How the Press Affects Federal Policymaking**. New York: Norton, 1986. 260p.

This is a study of aspects of government in relation to the press, and not a study of the press per se, with government defined as the national U.S. government, and press defined as editors and reporters who cover Washington for general circulation print media and for network TV. Methodology included a broad mail survey of senior policy makers for the last 20 years; lengthy interviews with 20 policymakers and 16 journalists nominated by their peers as having been particularly competent in making policy and covering the federal government; and six case studies providing detailed examination of different press roles and impacts in significant federal policy decisions over the past two decades. (The six case studies are contained in a separate book by Linsky and others, **How the Press Affects Federal Policy Making: Six Case Studies**, Norton, 1986. 373p.) The adversary role of the press toward government is downplayed, and its responsibility and accountability emphasized. Likewise, Linsky attempts to help public officials understand the constructive role the press can play in developing more sound policies. Appendixes give the methodology. Notes and index.

255

Lippmann, Walter. **Public Opinion**. New York: Macmillan, 1922. 272p.

Years have not dated nor dimmed Lippmann's basic concepts. His discussions of stereotypes, of the role of newspapers, and of various other aspects remain classic and have shaped much of today's thinking about the role of the media in society. Indexed.

256

Lipstadt, Deborah E. **Beyond Belief: The American Press and the Coming of the Holocaust, 1933–45**. New York: Free Press, 1986. 370p.

History has brought to light that America could have saved thousands or even hundreds of thousands of Jews during the 1930s and 1940s but did not do so. On the assumption that press coverage of Nazi anti-semitism—the space allocated, the location of the news in the paper, and the editorial opinions—shaped American reaction, Lipstadt analyzes its role as a conduit of information and finds its coverage lacking in ways and for reasons she details. Her conclusions are based on an examination of the daily **Press Information Bulletin** which digested reports and opinions from 500 of the largest American newspapers; news and opinions in a number of major daily newspapers and journals of the period; files from government and private agencies; and interviews with reporters who covered the story in Europe. Her study reaches deeply into the behavior of the press, the reaction of the American people to it, and the interrelationship of the one to the other. Notes cover 79 pages. Index.

257

Literary Taste, Culture and Mass Communication. Ed. by Peter Davison, Rolf Meyersohn, and Edward Shils. 14 vols. Teaneck, NJ: Somerset House, 1978.

In this imaginative and wide-ranging collection of over 200 articles, books, lectures, and reviews reprinted in 14 volumes, the editors had several purposes in mind. They wanted to highlight the different approaches taken by American, British, and to some extent Continental scholars to the study of the mass media and popular culture, and to do so in such a way that readers of this generation would better understand the development of what they were studying and what it has meant to those writing in earlier decades. They also wanted to present material from a number of viewpoints. In the words of the editors: "In selecting what should be reprinted it was thought there would be considerable advantage if work from many different standpoints could be juxtaposed: literary, sociological, cultural, and political; American, British, and Continental; initial groupings and final analysis; scholarly studies, journalistic articles, and the comments of creative writers," and "that the very juxtaposition of materials might provide new insights." Because their approach is historical (although not chronological), the materials begin as far back as the 1920s and carry through the 1960s, but seldom into the 1970s, mainly because recent works tend to be readily available and also because in some cases there were copyright difficulties. Vol. XIV contains a bibliography and an index, and each volume has a "Further Reading" section, as well as individual bibliographies accompanying some of the articles.

A partial list of authors gives an idea of the quality of the series: Theodor Adorno, Dwight Macdonald, Susan Sontag, F. W. Bateson, Robert Escarpit, Richard Hoggart, F. R. Leavis, E. M. Forster, Stuart Hall, Leslie Fiedler, Max Horkheimer, Maurice Janowitz, Bernard Berelson, Richard D. Altick, Raymond Williams, H. G. Wells, Marshall McLuhan, George Orwell, Andre Malraux, Stephen Spender, George Steiner.

Volumes include: v.1 **Culture and Mass Culture**, v.2 **Mass Media and Mass Communication**, v.3 **Art and Social Life**, v.4 **Art and Changing Civilization**, v.5 **Literature and Society**, v.6 **The Sociology of Literature**, v.7 **Content and Taste: Religion and Myth**, v. 8 **Theater and Song**, v.9 **Uses of Literacy: Media**, v. 10 **Authorship**, v. 11 **The Writer and Politics**, v.12 **Bookselling, Reviewing and Reading**, v. 13 **The Cultural Debate Part I**, v.14 **The Cultural Debate Part II and Indexes**.

258

Liu, Alan P. L. **Communications and National Integration in Communist China**. Berkeley: University of California Press, 1971. 225p.

Although the primary purpose of this study is to define the roles that the mass media play in achieving integration in China, it also serves as an excellent survey of radio, the press, book publishing, and film. In addition it details propaganda methods. Appendixes give statistics. Contains notes, a bibliography, and an index.

259

Lowenthal, Leo. **Literature and Mass Culture**. New Brunswick, NJ: Transaction Books, 1984. 301p. (Communication in Society, Vol. 1)

A collection of Lowenthal's essays on communication in society, written at various times ranging from the 1930s to the 1960s. He has centered upon literature from a broad sociological viewpoint, drawing from history and philosophy rather than experimental methodology ("approaching sociological research from a humanistic angle while retaining a sociological view of the humanities," as he puts it). "Literature," he says, "is a particularly suitable bearer of the fundamental symbols and values which give cohesion to social groups and its members. . . . Perceived in this way, literature embraces two powerful cultural complexes: art on the one hand, and a market-oriented commodity on the other." This present volume deals primarily although not exclusively with literature as a commodity. Part I, "Historical and Empirical Studies," contains "Historical Perspectives of Popular Culture," "The Debate over Art and Popular Culture: A Synopsis," "Notes on the Theater and the Sermon," "Eighteenth Century England: A Case Study," "The Debate on Cultural Standards in Nineteenth Century England," "The Reception of Dostoevsky in Pre-World War I Germany," "The Biographical Fashion," "The Triumph of Mass Idols," and "Some Thoughts on the 1937 Edition of **International Who's Who**." Part II, "Contributions to the Philosophy of Communication," contains "On Sociology of Literature (1932)," "On Sociology of Literature (1948)," "Humanistic Perspectives of David Riesman's **The Lonely Crowd**," "Popular Culture: A Humanistic and Sociological Concept." Chapter notes.

260

Lowery, Shearon, and Melvin L. DeFleur. **Milestones in Mass Communication Research: Media Effects**. New York: Longman, 1983. 398p.

A backward glance at 11 large-scale research projects from the 1920s to the present which the authors consider integral to the mainstream of communications effects research. Studies chosen for analysis are the Payne Fund series; "The Effects of Movies on Children"; Hadley Cantril's **Invasion from Mars**; **The People's Choice** by Paul Lazarsfeld, Bernard Berelson and Hazel Gaudet; "The American Soldier" by Carl Hovland, Arthur Lumsdaine and Fred Sheffield; **Communication and Persuasion** by Hovland, Irving Janis and Harold Kelley; **Personal Influence** by Elihu Katz and Paul Lazarsfeld; **Project Revere**, a group of studies carried out under the leadership of Stuart C. Dodd; Frederick Werthem's **Seduction of the Innocent**; **Television in the Lives of Our Children** by Wilbur Schramm, Jack Lyle and Edwin Parker; **Violence in the Media**, edited by Robert K. Baker and Sandra J. Ball; and "The Surgeon General's Report on Television and Social Violence." Each study is summarized and analyzed as to conception, purpose, techniques, findings, and theoretical contribution. An introductory chapter discusses major social trends of the decades covered, the development of research technology, and emerging theories of media effects. "Notes and References" follow each chapter. Indexed. (A second edition was published in 1988.)

MacBride Report (See No. 210).

261

Machlup, Fritz. **The Production and Distribution of Knowledge in the United States**. Princeton, NJ: Princeton University Press, 1962. 416p.

Machlup, an economist, approaches knowledge in its many varieties as an industry and analyzes it from this viewpoint. In the 1962 book he defines the types of knowledge, knowledge production, the knowledge-producing industries, and the occupations involved, breaking the industries down into education, research and development, the mass media, information machines (of which the "electronic computer" is a subdivision), and information services, with a final summary on the total production of knowledge as related to the national product and occupational structure. Although statistics, most of which were for 1958, as well as some of the facts, are out of date, the definitions and theoretical analyses still hold.

262

MacKenzie, John M. **Propaganda and Empire: The Manipulation of British Public Opinion 1880–1960**. Manchester, England: Manchester University Press, 1984. 277p.

An analysis of the cultural and institutional expressions of propaganda used to "sell" and perpetuate the concept of imperialism to the British people. In exploring this theme MacKenzie examines the theater, cinema, school textbooks, juvenile literature, imperial exhibitions, youth movements and radio to show how they were manipulated. Chapter notes, bibliography and index.

263

Malik, Madhu. **Traditional Forms of Communication and the Mass Media in India**. Paris: UNESCO, 1983(?) 101p. (Communication and Society 13)

"The purpose of the present study is to focus precisely on the relationship between folk and mass media, on actual experiments that have been conducted in India to receive an integration of the two, on problems that were encountered in the process of integration." The author lists documentary films produced by the Films Division of India viewed in connection with the study.

264

Mankekar, D.R. **One-Way Free Flow: Neo-Colonialism Via News Media**. Dehli, India: Clarion, 1978. 171p.

Mankekar is concerned with the charges made against the Western media by the Third World and, likewise, the reaction of Western *journalists to their concept of a new information order for developing countries. Combing data and evidence from diverse sources he has analyzed the anatomy and function of international news media to test the validity of the Third World's accusations and has traced the Third World's struggle in the United Nations, UNESCO and their own councils to rid themselves of what they consider the hold of world news monopoly by the four international news agencies. The potentialities of modern electronic media in bringing this about are also examined, and there is a chapter on the Third World news pool. Appendixes include a discussion of "News Agencies in the World" and a short bibliography.

265

Marbut, F. B. **News from the Capital: The Story of Washington Reporting**. Carbondale: Southern Illinois University, 1971. 304p.

A history of governmental reporting in the U.S. from the early 1800s to the mid-1960s. Contains bibliographical notes and an index.

266

Markham, James W. **Voices of the Red Giants: Communications in Russia and China**. Ames: Iowa State University Press, 1967. 513p.

Investigation of Communist mass communication systems as exemplified by the Russian Soviet and Communist Chinese models. The author covers magazines, newspapers, radio and television, the news agencies, and advertising. A drawback is the use of secondary rather than primary sources. Contains bibliographic notes and an index.

267

Martin, L. John, and Anju Grover Chaudhary, eds. **Comparative Mass Media Systems**. New York: Longman, 1983. 356p.

Analyzes media systems from the viewpoints of the West, the Communist countries, and those developing countries lumped together as the Third World. Six key concepts or functions of the media are treated: the concept of news; the concept of the role of the mass media; the educational, persuasive and opinion-making function; the entertainment function; press freedom; media economics. Notes and references at the end of each chapter. Indexed.

268

Marx, Karl, and Frederick Engels. **Marx & Engels on the Means of Communication**. Ed. by Yves de la Haye. New York: International General, 1979. 173p.

A collection of basic texts concerning the movement of commodities, people, information and capital, showing how Marx and Engels used the analytical method of historical materialism to understand the complex relations between the media and society during the 19th century. De la Haye has written a 46-page introduction:

"Contribution to a Materialist Analysis of the Media." He has also included a "Selected Bibliography."

Marxism and the Mass Media: Toward a Basic Bibliography. (See No. 1671.)

Marzolf, Marion. **Up from the Footnote: A History of Women Journalists**. (See No. 933.)

269

Mass Media in C.M.E.A. Countries. Budapest: Nemzetkozi Ujsagiro Szervezet (International Organization of Journalists), 1976. 255p.

Facts and figures about press, radio, and television in Council of Mutual Economic Assistance (C.M.E.A.) countries—Bulgaria, Cuba, Czechoslovakia, East Germany, Hungary, Mongolia, Poland, Romania, and the U.S.S.R. Data include concentrated information about central and regional papers, weeklies and magazines (title, publisher, circulation, thumbnail profile), press agencies, and radio and television, with a brief description of programming. Material on each country differs somewhat.

270

Mass Media and Violence: A Report to the National Commission on the Causes and Prevention of Violence. Comp. by David L. Lange, Robert K. Baker, and Sandra J. Ball. Washington: Superintendent of Documents, U.S. Government Printing Office, 1969. 613p. (Staff Report 9 to the National Commission on the Causes and Prevention of Violence.)

Vol. IX in a series dealing with the various aspects of the problem of violence in American society. This one is concerned with the media. First it approaches the problem from a historical perspective. Then it analyzes factually and often critically certain accepted values and practices such as function and credibility, intergroup communication, the marketplace myth (access to the mass media), coverage of civil disorders, journalism education. And finally it deals with television entertainment vis-à-vis violence, with emphasis on our limited knowledge of effects. Programming is analyzed and contrasted with the reality of violence in daily life.

Each section has discussions, conclusions, and recommendations, as well as factual appendixes. Among these are: codes, guidelines and policies for news coverage; a review of recent literature on psychological effects of media portrayals of violence; the content and context of violence in the mass media, with opposing views as to possible effects; content analysis procedures and results; the views, standards, and practices of the television industry. Includes bibliographical references.

271, 272, 273

Mattelart, Armand, ed. **Communicating in Popular Nicaragua**. New York: International General, 1986. 140p.

Mattelart, Armand. **Transnationals & the Third World: The Struggle for Culture**. South Hadley, MA: Bergin & Garvey, 1983. 184p.

Mattelart, Armand, and Seth Siegelaud, eds. **Communication and Class Struggle**. New York: International General, 1979, 1983. 2 vols. v.1 **Capitalism, Imperialism**; v.2 **Liberation, Socialism**.

Mattelart is one of the best exponents of the Marxist viewpoint in relation to developing nations.

Communicating in Popular Nicaragua is a critical anthology of 12 articles by authors from Nicaragua and the United States who give a Marxian analysis of numerous aspects of communication, broadly defined to include mural expression and literary and social movements as well as the more traditional journalism, the press, radio, film and video. A number of the articles are published here for the first time. In conclusion is a bibliography of "Left" studies on the media and culture in Nicaragua and Latin America in general.

The United Nations, through the Center on Transnational Corporations, commissioned two separate reports on the sociocultural impact of transnational firms on developing countries. One was to analyze the positive impact; the other, the negative. Both reports were "to allow foundations for policies within the framework of self-reliance." In **Transnationals & the Third World** Mattelart has focused on the negative aspects, examining the structure and process of transnationals as they penetrate the Third World with entertainment, information and advertising. Notes and index. The positive report has not, at this writing, been published independently.

Communication and Class Struggle is an anthology containing more than 120 articles originating in over 50 countries since the mid-nineteenth century which were selected by the editors to explain three interrelated questions about the mass communication process from the Marxist viewpoint: 1) how communication is conditioned by basic economic, social, ideological and cultural factors; 2) how capitalistic production affects communication practice and theory in bourgeois society; and 3) how the underprivileged and the working classes have reacted in certain countries by developing their own communication theory and practice. Selected bibliography.

274

Mattelart, Michele. **Women, Media and Crisis: Femininity and Disorder**. London: Comedia, 1986. 123p.

"This is my first approach to the theme of 'women and the media,' an attempt to elucidate or analyze continuities and ruptures in the way in which the symbolic order processes the relationship between femininity and modernity in normal times, and in times of crisis," Mattelart explains in her Foreword. "Part One: Everyday Life" discusses the role of the media in shaping women's reality, including their habits as consumers; "Part Two:

Modernity" deals with the feminine ideal and the myth of modernity; and "Part Three: Crisis," with an analysis of the decisive ideological role of women in the Chilean coup d'etat of 1973. "Notes and References."

275

McAnany, Emile G., ed. **Communications in the Rural Third World: The Role of Information in Development**. New York: Praeger, 1980. 222p.

Several decades ago communication research about the Third World centered largely around the diffusion-of-innovation theory which measured elements of social structure but drew no policy implications from its findings. This anthology brings together research with a new perspective involving the rural poor, and reexamining communication's role in terms of equity (who benefits from information) and productivity (what impact information has on agriculture productivity, health, and income, as well as knowledge, attitudes, and behavior of rural people). Studies are grouped in three parts: "Information in Rural Development: General Social Issues," with articles by McAnany and Larry Shore; "Information within Structural Constraints: Three Case Studies" which includes the Ivory Coast by Frans Lenglet, Guatemala by Jeremiah O'Sullivan, and Brazil and Guatemala by Eduardo Contreras; and "Information and Education in Rural Development: Economic Analysis" by Jacqueline Ashby, Steven Klees, Douglas Pachico and Stuart Wells. Bibliography and index.

276

McAnany, Emil G., Jorge Schnitman, and Noreene Janus, eds. **Communication and Social Structure: Critical Studies in Mass Media Research**. New York: Praeger, 1981. 341p.

"What this volume illustrates is that communication technology and institutions are disseminated and take root in an increasing variety of social and cultural settings," says McAnany. "Once in place," he continues, "the technology and institutions are difficult to change," and mass communication scholars should aim toward a critical research agenda which will broaden the research perspective to meet the challenge. His introduction gives an overview of the articles that follow, which illustrate U.S. mass communication research in an international context, the role of social change and social structure, themes for an agenda in critical communication, and future directions for studies in change. An important aim of the anthology is to suggest perspectives that expand the typical research agenda of U.S. mass communication studies to include critical studies of how the communication system works as a whole rather than to concentrate, as much American research does, on how it functions in terms of individual effects. Authors include the editors Schnitman and Janus, James Halloran, Vincent Mosco and Andrew Herman, Josiane Jouët, Timothy Haight and Laurie Weinstein, Armando Valdez, Félix Gutiérrez and Jorge Reina Schement, Oscar H. Gandy, Jr., June Fisher, and Ingrid Sarti. Studies contain notes and references. Index.

277

McDonald, Robert. **Pillar and Tinderbox: The Greek Press and the Dictatorship**. New York: Marion Boyers, 1983. 231p.

A study of the press under a dictatorship (1967–1974) which backgrounds prior conditions—press law, newspaper economics, trade unions—and relates the aftermath. Although emphasis is on newspapers it contains a chapter on broadcasting. Each chapter is footnoted; appendixes give censorship regulations; and there is a bibliography and an index.

278

McGaffin, William, and Erwin Knoll. **Anything But the Truth: The Credibility Gap—How the News Is Managed in Washington**. New York: Putnam's Sons, 1968. 250p.

A digest of examples of lies issued from the federal government to the press woven together by the thread of an idea about the effect of a credibility gap in a democratic society. The detailed examples focus on the Vietnam War, but the book is not limited to that era.

McLuhan, Marshall, ed. **Explorations in Communication**. (See No. 58.)

279, 280

McLuhan, Marshall. **The Gutenberg Galaxy: The Making of Typographic Man**. Toronto: University of Toronto Press, 1962. 293p.

McLuhan, Marshall. **Understanding Media: The Extensions of Man**. New York: McGraw-Hill, 1964. 365p.

These are McLuhan's two best-known books. **The Gutenberg Galaxy** is a lively and unconventionally organized history of print, beginning with Gutenberg's press and skipping about eclectically through time and literature. For example, here are a few headings for brief chapters: "King Lear Is a Working Model of the Process of Denudation by Which Men Translated Themselves from a World of Roles to a World of Jobs," "Schizophrenia May Be a Necessary Consequence of Literacy," "The Greek Point of View in Both Art and Chronology Has Little in Common with Ours but Was Much Like That of the Middle Ages."

Understanding Media is the best single source of McLuhan's unconventional taxonomy of media as "hot" (print) and "cool" (television) and his controversial theory. "The medium is the message," he argues. "The formative power in the media are the media themselves." Global in its purview, the book spans everything from comics to military weaponry, and it is deep in literary and historical metaphor. This book, more than any other, rediscovered media for a generation of students who had been schooled on the minimal effects model. It made

McLuhan famous among the general public and established his reputation as a savant of media, particularly television.

281, 282, 283, 284

McQuail, Denis. **Communication**. 2d ed. New York: Longman, 1984. 266p.

McQuail, Denis. **Mass Communication Theory: An Introduction**. Beverly Hills, CA: Sage, 1983. 245p.

McQuail, Denis, and Sven Windhal. **Communication Models for the Study of Mass Communications**. London: Longman, 1981. 110p.

McQuail, Denis, ed. **Sociology of Mass Communication**. Harmondsworth, Middlesex, England: Penguin, 1972. 477p.

In all of his writings McQuail approaches the study of communications, both with and without the "mass," from a humanistic-sociological viewpoint. In his own words in the Foreword to the second edition of **Communication**: "At a time when much attention is directed to the immense technical power and capacity of new means of communication it is worth affirming that the consequences for relationships of social power deserve more attention."

Communication, a part of the Aspect of Modern Sociology series, deals with communication as a social process—its relation to society, the various theories about it, its operation, structure, and influence. A final chapter summarizes theory and research. There is a bibliography, "References and Further Reading," and an index.

Mass Communication Theory: An Introduction, was first conceived as a successor to **Toward a Sociology of Mass Communications** (Collier Macmillan 1969) in which McQuail viewed the subject sociologically on the grounds that mass media study was a field of research to which many disciplines contributed but which was not itself a discipline and consequently had no theory of its own. But in the intervening years he found that the study of the media had developed a body of theory which made it more than a collection of research problems, and in response he organized a framework which summarized work "according to its theoretical yield rather than its empirical substance." After an overview and a discussion of alternative approaches to mass communication theory, he examines its research and the theory underlying its various aspects in terms of function and purpose, institution and organization, content, audience, effects, and finally, themes of media theory and issues of media policy. References, and name and subject indexes.

Communication Models for the Study of Mass Communications, an anthology, has a dual purpose: it assembles many of the various communication models, past and present, designed to explain the communication, and particularly the mass communication, process; and it presents the main lines of thought about the latter over the past 30 years of research, thereby making it a form of historical review. The authors also draw their own models "which reflect important conceptual developments or relatively new fields of enquiry." References follow each chapter and there is an index.

Separately, each in its own way, and certainly together, these three books are an invaluable guide to a burgeoning field.

285

McQueen, Humphrey. **Australia's Media Monopolies**. Melbourne, Australia: Visa, 1981. 218p.

Aiming at the layman reader, McQueen examines the Australian media in the context of Marxist theory applied to monopoly capitalism. Bibliography and index.

286

Meadow, Robert G. **Politics as Communication**. Norwood, NJ: Ablex, 1980. 269p.

Meadow feels that while much has been done in a narrow sense on the effects of mass communication on political behavior, particularly at election time, conceptual and theoretical questions have been neglected. His aim in this book is to move away from election-based research toward a broader view. In his words: "I propose communication research be viewed two ways: first as the role that *communication* plays in political institutions and processes, and second as the role politics plays in shaping communication processes. The former issue has been well considered; the latter less so. One of my aspirations for this volume is that it may help put the two in better balance." He discusses communication in relation to political concepts and institutions; and communication as a political issue in relation to language, popular culture, the media, and the role of government. Throughout, he demonstrates that there can be no politics independent of communication processes. Bibliography and author and subject indexes.

287

Media Studies in Education. Paris: UNESCO, 1977. 92p. (Reports and Papers on Mass Communication No. 80)

Report on the teaching of the mass media in the secondary schools in France, Italy, the Federal Republic of Germany, the Netherlands, the United Kingdom, Denmark, Finland, Sweden, the U.S.S.R. and the U.S. Contains a list of international organizations and a bibliography.

288

Melody, William H., Liona Salter, and Paul Heyer, eds. **Culture, Communication and Dependency: The Tradition of H.A. Innis**. Norwood, NJ: Ablex, 1981. 264p.

A compilation of 18 articles, some of which are derived from a symposium held at Simon Fraser University in 1978 entitled "Harold Adams Innis: Legacy, Context, Direction," designed to put his scholarship in broad perspective. In three parts, "Assessing the Contribution," "Institutions and Development, A Focus on Political Economy," and "Communication, Culture and the Interdisciplinary Perspective," the book considers the body of Innis' work, relating him both to communications and to Canadian economics. Those concerned primarily with communications are "Culture, Geography and Communications: The Work of Harold Innis in an American Context" by James W. Carey; "Communications: Blindspot of Economics" by Dallas W. Smythe; "Innis, Marx, and the Economics of Communication: A Theoretical Aspect of Canadian Political Economy" by Ian Parker; "'Public' and Mass Media in Canada: Dialectics in Innis' Communication Analysis" by Liora Salter; "The Other Side of Empire: Contact and Communication in Southern Baffin Island" by Gail Guthrie Valaskakis; "Exploration in Communications Since Innis" by Donald F. Theall: "Harold Innis and the Modern Perspective of Communications" by David Crowley; and "Innis and the History Communication: Antecedents, Parallels, and Unsuspected Biases" by Paul Heyer. Bibliographic notes and indexes.

289, 290, 291, 292

Merrill, John C., and Ralph D. Barney, eds. **Ethics and the Press: Readings in Mass Media Morality**. New York: Hastings House, 1975. 338p.

Merrill, John C. **The Imperative of Freedom: A Philosophy of Journalistic Autonomy**. New York: Hastings House, 1974. 228p.

Merrill, John C. **Existential Journalism**. New York: Hastings House, 1977. 158p.

Merrill, John C., and S. Jack Odell. **Philosophy and Journalism**. New York: Longman, 1983. 190p.

In these four books spanning almost a decade Merrill has concerned himself with underlying philosophical concepts which apply to the practice of journalism. In Part I of **Ethics and the Press** contributors consider problems of quality, objectivity and truth, among other abstracts; in Part II they deal with specifics. There is a lengthy bibliography. **The Imperative of Freedom** develops Merrill's own philosophy of journalism, treating it by means of concepts such as libertarianism, individualism, rationalism, self-interest, self-control, pluralism, competition, duty, sensitivity and existentialism—some of which are contradictory and must be connected meaningfully. The book contains a bibliography and an index.

Existential Journalism is a follow-up of **The Imperative of Freedom**, with its scope limited somewhat and concentrated on the relevance of the philosophy of existentialism to the profession. It is, he feels, "a frame of mind—an attitude—which is thrust by individual journalists into their journalism, imbuing it with a vitality, a depth, a commitment, a character of flux, a creativity and originality which is almost universally lacking in modern 'corporate' journalism." Unlike Merrill's other works, and in keeping with his theme in this one as illustrated by the quotation, it is an "angry" book. He has included a bibliography and an index.

Philosophy and Journalism was co-authored with S. Jack Odell, a philosophy professor. In the first part, "Foundations," Odell covers some fundamentals of philosophy—deductive and inductive reasoning, conceptual analysis, ethics, and the theory of knowledge, illustrating these principles in a journalistic context. In the second part, "Implications," Merrill uses philosophical themes to discuss the nature and state of the art of journalism. The book is intended for journalism students interested in philosophy or philosophy students interested in journalism. A list of suggested readings follows each chapter. Indexed.

293

Merrill, John C., ed. **Global Journalism: A Survey of the World's Mass Media**. New York: Longman, 1983. 374p.

Merrill and contributors take a sweeping look at global journalism and mass communications by regions of the world. In Part 1, "The Global Perspective," Merrill himself does an overall survey of problems, news flow, philosophies, relations with government for both print media and telecommunications, and ends with his analysis of the demand by developing nations for a new information order. In Part 2, "The World's Regions and Journalism" Paul S. Underwood treats Europe and the Middle East; John Luter and Jim Richstad, Asia and the Pacific; L. John Martin, Africa; Marvin Alisky, Latin America, and Ralph D. Barney and Deanna Nelson, the U.S. and Canada. All regions receive the same broad treatment as the general section, with no emphasis on particular newspapers, magazines or broadcast agencies, but rather on philosophy and structure. Education and training for journalism in each area is discussed. Although there is a great deal of pertinent data about journalism throughout the world, the book is geared to "the neophyte, the inquisitive beginner" rather than the specialist. It is also intended as a text. For those desiring more extensive information about the various countries, see Kurian (No. 239). Or for what has now become historical information, see an earlier book Merrill co-authored with Carter R. Bryan and Marvin Alisky, **The Foreign Press: A Survey of the World's Journalism** (2d rev. ed. Louisiana State University Press, 1970) in which the authors treat the press country by country. **Global Journalism** contains an excellent bibliography.

294

Merrill, John C., and Ralph L. Lowenstein. **Media, Messages, and Men: New Perspectives in Communication**. 2d ed. New York: Longman, 1979. 264p.

Rather than provide a broad substantive overview, the authors have selected issues and problems of modern journalism and communication intended to stimulate the novice to think, argue and read further. Contents are grouped under three headings: "Media: A New Look at Changing Roles," "The Communicator and His Audience," and "Media Concepts and Ethics." Within this context they discuss various facets in short provocative takes which will serve the purpose, they hope, of arousing the reader's curiosity to pursue the subject. For those who do, there is an excellent annotated bibliography. This is one of the best surveys in the field; the first edition won the Society of Professional Journalists/Sigma Delta Chi national award in 1972. Chapter notes and index.

295

Metha, D.S. **Mass Communication and Journalism in India**. Bombay: Allied Publishers, 1979. 313p.

A manual intended for the Indian journalist or layman needing quick information on a variety of aspects, but also useful to non-Indians as a guide to the state of the art in India. Along with information about techniques which are similar everywhere Metha also covers those specific to India for mass communication, print media, broadcasting, audio-visual media, news agencies, advertising, newspaper organization, press and public relations, professional organizations, press council, freedom and law of the press, research, and education. There is also a chronology of development of mass communication in India. Appendixes include a bibliography, the commercial broadcasting code, excerpts from Code of Ethics for Advertising, rules for accreditation of news media representatives, procedure for starting newspapers and periodicals, universities/colleges and institutions conducting courses in journalism, and a selected list of Indian periodicals on mass communication. Bibliography and a list of selected foreign publications on journalism. Index.

296

Meyer, Philip. **Precision Journalism: A Reporter's Introduction to Social Science Methods**. 2d ed. Bloomington: Indiana University Press, 1979. 430p.

Meyer pioneered when in 1973 he wrote the first edition of this book on the uses of social science methodology in journalism reporting. Updated to 1979 to include later changes, both editions introduce the student to the subject, dealing with new concepts like hypothesis testing, statistics, computers, surveys, field experiments, public records and other basic tools of the social science trade. In no sense, however, is it "how to." The author's description is "half handbook, half mild-mannered polemic," written to "get the show off the road." Appendixes include "Suggestions for Further Reading," "A Guided Tour of the Data Trip," and "Three Case Studies: An Analysis of Data from Public Records, An Election-Day Survey, and a Telephone Survey." Notes and index.

297

Mickiewicz, Ellen Propper. **Media and the Russian Public**. New York: Praeger, 1981. 156p.

An examination of the mass media available in Soviet Russia and of attitudes toward the various ones. Although the author was somewhat hampered because partisan and political subjects were not considered appropriate for opinion surveys, she was nevertheless able to learn not only about media exposure and use by the general public but also within different groups—for example, migrants and super-activists. Chapter notes and index.

298

Miller, Abraham H., ed. **Terrorism: The Media and the Law**. Dobbs Ferry, NY: Transnational Publishers, 1982. 221p.

Acts of terrorism bring up complex issues for the media, confronting them with extremely difficult ethical, moral and legal choices involving press freedom. Here, journalists, lawyers, political scientists, psychologists and law enforcement officers discuss the issues, concluding with recommendations for covering terrorism. Appendixes give existing media guideline documents and describe the project on media coverage of terrorism which summarizes national surveys and other investigations. In conclusion is a 24-page bibliography of books and periodicals. Index.

An interesting pamphlet—shorter and less structured—is **Terrorism and the Media in the 1980's** (1984, 67p.), the proceedings of a conference in 1983, co-sponsored by the Transnational Communications Center, The Media Institute, Washington, DC (the publishers) and the Institute for Studies in International Terrorism, State University of New York. Participants representing a number of nationalities and interests discuss media representation in the U.S. and abroad. An appendix gives statistics on acts of terrorism.

299

Miller, Roger LeRoy, and Arline Alchian Hoel. **Media Economics Sourcebook**. St. Paul, MN: West, 1982. 169p.

". . . directed specifically at journalists and their need for some basic tools with which to pursue major economic and business stories," this is an attempt to acquaint the uninitiated with first facts about inflation, profits, interest rates, unemployment, the value of the dollar in international trade, and the scope and influences of government. There is also a chapter on the accuracy

of economic statistics and tips on compiling an inexpensive financial or economics resource library. The co-authors are economics professors at the University of Miami.

300

Modleski, Tania, ed. **Studies in Entertainment: Critical Approaches to Mass Culture**. Bloomington: Indiana University Press, 1986. 210p.

In recent years the study of mass culture has become increasingly popular, with a number of diverse and interesting theories emerging. Here Modleski has brought together some of them which, taken as a whole, reflect "a critical view of mass cultural production and mass cultural artifacts and concentrates on texts without disregarding contexts." Contents include "Traditions of Mass Culture," "Studies in Television," "Feminist Studies in Entertainment," and "Redrawing the Boundaries between Art and Entertainment," under which the authors discuss, among other subjects, rock 'n' roll, situation comedy, television news personality and credibility, advertisements, popular novels for women, fashion, and contemporary horror films. Notes follow each article.

301

Morgan, David. **The Flacks of Washington: Government Information and the Public Agenda**. Westport, CT: Greenwood, 1986. 165p.

Using data gathered from extensive questionnaires followed by interviews and buttressed by literature on the subject, Morgan has examined the federal government as a source of information below the White House level over the decade 1974–1984 in terms of the daily relationship between the government agency and the departmental officials who cover the news. Part I looks at the micro-relationships between reporters and press information officers; Part II looks to micro-political relationships among the White House, the media, and the public. The concluding chapter reviews both parts of the study and addresses itself to questions raised by it. Data from the questionnaire are given, and chapter notes indicate the wealth of literature consulted. There is also a comprehensive bibliography. Index.

302, 303, 304

Mosco, Vincent, and Janet Wasko, eds. **Labor, the Working Class and the Media**. Norwood, NJ: Ablex, 1983. 312p. (Critical Communications Review, Volume I)

Mosco, Vincent, and Janet Wasco, eds. **Changing Patterns of Communications Control**. Norwood, NJ: Ablex, 1984. 299p. (Critical Communications Review, Volume II)

Mosco, Vincent, and Janet Wasco, eds. **Popular Culture and Media Events**. Norwood, NJ: Ablex, 1985. 323 p. (Critical Communications Review, Volume III)

The first three volumes of a series whose aim is a critical examination of certain specific aspects of mass communication in terms of its underlying power structure. Subjects the editors have chosen to explore are labor, the information industry, and popular culture.

Volume II examines labor in terms of "History," "Media Unions," "Media Content and Working People," and "New Communications Technologies for the New Workplace." Contributors include Stuart and Elizabeth Ewen, Hans Fredrich Folton, Brian Winston, Michael Goldhaber, Mike Nielsen, Kevin Robins and Frank Webster, Dennis Chamot and Kevin Murphy, Jennifer Daryl Slack and the editors. Volume II deals with control under "Global Considerations," "Canada, U.S. and Labor America," and "Europe," with articles by Herbert Schiller, Dallas Smythe, Noreene Janus, Giovani Cesareo, Robert Jacobson, Timothy Haight, Howard Frederick, Manjunath Pendakur, Emile McAnany, Armand Mattelart and Jean-Marie Piemme, Patrice Flichy, Morten Giersing, Graham Murdock and the editors; Volume III discusses "History: Popular Culture, Commodity Culture," "Media Events: Stars and Star Wars," and "The Public Sphere and Social Struggle." Among contributors are Susan Davis, Paul Swan, Kenneth Fones-Wolf, Richard Butsch, Jeanne Allen, Levon Chorbajian, Michael Real, James Buston, Terri Toles, Anders Hansen and Graham Murdock, T.B. Young and Rosalind Bresnahan. In each volume references follow the articles and there is a name and subject index.

305

Moses, Sir Charles, and Crispin Maslog. **Mass Communication in Asia: A Brief History**. Singapore: Asian Mass Communication Research and Information Centre, 1978. 85p.

This does as much as can be expected—perhaps more—from an 85-page history of mass communication in Asia. Divided into three sections, it consists of very short chronological accounts of print media in 16 countries, broadcast media in 25, and film in six. This is particularly useful because the facts, although scant, go back to beginnings, and because leading newspapers in their respective countries are identified by name. As might be expected, the section on print media is by far the longest, with 50 pages, even though it deals with fewer countries; broadcast media takes up 24 pages; and film only nine. Footnotes.

306

Mousa, Issam Suleiman. **The Arab Image in the US Press**. New York: Peter Lang, 1984. 187p.

Current research on the Arab image in U.S. media tends to be strictly contemporary, linked to Israel and the Middle East conflict. This research, however, begins in 1917 with the downfall of Ottoman control and ends in 1948 with the creation of Israel. By means of a content analysis of the **New York Times** it shows how the image changed from a romantic one, fostered by the **Arabian Nights** and reinforced by the early movie industry, to the present more realistic portrayal. Contains a review of the research literature, chapter notes, and a bibliography.

307, 308, 309

Mowlana, Hamid. **International Flow of Information: A Global Report and Analysis**. Paris: UNESCO, 1985. 74p. (Reports and Papers on Mass Communication No. 99)

Mowlana, Hamid. **Global Information and World Communication: New Frontiers in International Relations**. New York: Longman, 1986. 248p.

Mowlana, Hamid, ed. **International Flow of News: An Annotated Bibliography**. Paris: UNESCO, 1985. 272p.

Three works by a specialist in international communication. **International Flow of Information** synthesizes relevant research by different individuals, institutions and organizations, with special emphasis on the areas of mass media, transborder data flow, and satellites and planetary resources. Mowlana also identifies and evaluates critically major approaches, theories, concepts and propositions in an effort to point out problems of analytical integration within the field and problems of interdisciplinary contribution and coherence. Finally, he proposes a framework of analysis to serve as a possible guideline for a methodology to be used in future evaluations. The hundreds of studies he has examined are listed in his chapter notes. These, along with a long "Selected Bibliography," constitute a valuable reference resource.

Global Information and World Communication emphasizes culture and communication as fundamental to the process of creating understanding among peoples. In addition to reviewing works by communication researchers, he draws on studies conducted in allied areas— among them economics, political science, sociology, cultural anthropology, and international relations. Material is based on research and lecture tours in Europe, Asia, Africa, Latin America and the Middle East. Notes, bibliography and index.

Finally, **International Flow of News** provides a selected, annotated, divided bibliography on the subject. The first part includes studies international in scope, or deal with general theoretical, methodological and policy issues. The second part contains studies treating the regional or national flow of news by country for Africa, the Arab States, Asia, Eastern Europe, Western Europe, North America, and South and Central America. While studies on news flow in Latin America and Asia are numerous, there are fewer for Africa and the Socialist countries, which makes their inclusion especially valuable. Certain of the works are supported with systematic data, while others are historical and analytical. Entries, which are extensively annotated, cover monographs, periodical articles, and theses, and are by contributors from around the globe.

Hamid Mowlana compiled an earlier bibliography, **International Communication: A Selected Bibliography** (Dubuque, IA: Kendall/Hunt, 1971), well-organized but not annotated.

310

Murphy, Sharon. **Other Voices: Black, Chicano, and American Indian Press**. Dayton, Ohio: Pflaum/Standard, 1974. 132p.

Surveys these three minority presses, with brief histories and extensive use of quotes from personnel and prominent personalities within the minorities. Lists newspapers and other existing media, briefly analyzes treatment of minorities in some of the standard histories of journalism, and suggests further readings.

Sharon Murphy, with James E. Murphy and Neva S. Lehde-White, has also compiled the **Directory of American Indian Print and Broadcast Media** (University of Wisconsin-Milwaukee, 1978[?]), which lists by states the names, addresses, and frequency of Indian newspapers and magazines currently publishing, as well as the call letters and addresses of radio stations which broadcast Indian programs.

311

Murray, George. **The Press and the Public: The Story of the British Press Council**. Carbondale: Southern Illinois University Press, 1972. 243p.

Murray, a well-known British journalist who was prominent in the activities of the Press Council, has written the history of its development from 1953 until 1970. Three appendixes list founder members and constitution, 1953; original members of the 1964 Press Council and its constitution; and names and descriptions of the organizations forming the Press Council. There is a bibliography and an index.

312

Mytton, Graham. **Mass Communication in Africa**. London: Edward Arnold, 1983. 159p.

The first half places African mass communications in a broad social context, touching on their history, technology, politics, etc.; the second half consists of three case studies: Zambia, Tanzania and Nigeria. A final chapter discusses roles and controls. The North African countries are not included. Contains extensive chapter notes, a bibliography and an index.

Nafziger, Ralph O., comp. **International News and the Press . . . An Annotated Bibliography**. (See No. 1678.)

313

Nair, Basskaran. **Mass Media and the Transnational Corporation: A Study of Media-Corporate Relationship and Its Consequences for the Third World**. Singapore: Singapore University Press, 1980. 172p.

Do negative news reports on Third World countries have an adverse effect on the business climate, diverting transnational corporation investment away from those countries? In an exploratory study Nair has investigated the question, using data collected through library research and interviews with 30 media and corporate executives in the U.S. Appendixes list some of the data. Bibliography and index.

314

The News Agency in the System of Mass Media. Prague: International Organization of Journalists, 1980. 64p.

An analysis of news agencies as part of the information system, by journalists from the Eastern Bloc countries.

315

Ng'wanakilala, Nkwabi. **Mass Communication and Development of Socialism in Tanzania**. Dar es Salaam: Tanzania Publishing House, 1981. 149p.

Mass media in Tanzania are scarce and, as the title implies, their main role is informational and instructional, designed to clarify and develop national direction and consciousness rather than to be a source of entertainment. To this end the author surveys the main communication channels—what they are, their availability, what they carry, and perhaps most important, how well they fulfill their function to promote the country's ideology and development policies. There are two bibliographies—"Publications on Socialism and Self-Reliance and the Implied Role of Communication," and "On Communication Theory and Practice."

316

Niamsuren, D., and D. Urzhinbadam. **Mongolia and Its Mass Media**. Prague: International Organization of Journalists, 1980. 48p.

"The aim of this booklet is not only to inform; we tried in the first place to give a journalistic view of a country, that only some decades ago was a backward feudal country and by now is able to regard with satisfaction the remarkable results of its socialist construction," explains the editor. Twenty seven of its 44 pages are devoted to this transformation of Mongolia, followed by brief summaries of the role of the various media. Useful in spite of the scarcity of information because so little exists on mass communications in Mongolia.

317

Niazi, Zamir. **Press in Chains**. Karachi, Pakistan: Karachi Press Club, 1986. 252p.

"The central theme of this book [about suppressive journalism practices in Pakistan] is the persecution of newspapers and punitive actions taken against dissenting journalists. The first chapter deals with the one and three-quarters of a century of the ruthless repression and suppression under foreign domination. The rest deal with the four distinct phases of our checkered history and offers an objective account of the captivity of the Press, and roles of various regimes and agencies, including proprietors of newspapers, editors, working journalists, their associations and unions"—Preface. In concentrating on the issue of freedom, this also shows much of the structure of Pakistan's contemporary press. Index.

318

Nimmo, Dan D., and Keith R. Sanders, eds. **Handbook of Political Communication**. Beverly Hills, CA: Sage, 1981. 732p.

"We believe that the essays in this volume capture what we now accept as the state of the art in political communications studies—rapid development and pluralistic emergence. They are not intended as articles to provide a definitive statement of where the field is or where it is going. But they do represent a cross-section of the key theoretical approaches, areas of inquiry, and methods of study in this burgeoning field. They combine to form a summary statement on which to build." (Preface) In the Introduction Nimmo and Sanders discuss the emergence of political communication as a field; in the remainder of the book various contributors deal with some contemporary theoretical approaches; modes and means of persuasive communication in politics; political communication settings; and methods of study. Among the 30 or so contributors are James Combs, Jack McLeod and Lee Becker, Maxwell McCombs, Doris Graber, Lynda Lee Kaid, Sidney Kraus and Dennis David, L. John Martin, Jay Blumler and Michael Gurevitch, and Richard Hofstetter. In an appendix, Richard Fitchen comments on European literature, and Kaid gives a guide to print and non-print sources. Chapter notes and index.

319

Nimmo, Dan D., and James E. Combs. **Mediated Political Realities**. New York: Longman, 1983. 240p.

This is a study about the ways in which we structure our world, and especially our political world, by means of mediated reality as presented by the mass media through news and entertainment. The authors identify specific types of programming which they believe help in the creation of political "fantasyland," and specific groups which make use of the media for this purpose. Among the types of programming: TV news; election campaign coverage; melodrama through the re-presentation of history; popular magazines through their presentation of political celebrities. Among the groups: those engaged in decision-making, group-thinking, gatekeeping, pack journalism; religious movements; radical ideologies. References, author index, subject index.

320

Nimmo, Dan D. **Newsgathering in Washington: A Study in Political Communication**. New York: Atherton, 1964. 282p.

Nimmo focuses on the interaction between news channels and news sources in Washington where he believes that they interact to form a set of complicated relationships crucial in the linkage of citizen and official in a democracy. His evidence is in the form of personal interviews with Washington correspondents and the official news sources—the public information officers of executive agencies and Washington reporters. Although primarily a report of what he calls his "exploratory" research, he has drawn significant conclusions explaining the officer-reporter relationship, and has assessed the consequences of that relationship for the opinion-making processes of American democracy. Although decades have passed since Nimmo made this survey and additional political opinion-making techniques have been developed, this remains a benchmark study. Appendixes give the nature and method of his analysis, including research literature, and his interview questions to public information officers and to newsmen. Bibliography and index.

321

Noelle-Neumann, Elisabeth. **The Spiral of Silence: Public Opinion—Our Social Skin**. Chicago: University of Chicago Press, 1984. 200p.

A probe of public opinion as it relates to the social nature of human beings. The author approaches from two vantage points: the historical and philosophical, going back as far as Plato, and the much newer approach through statistical methodology. Contains a nine-page bibliography and an index.

322

Nordenstreng, Kaarle, with Lauri Hannikainen. **The Mass Media Declaration of UNESCO**. Norwood, NJ: Ablex, 1984. 475p.

In 1978 UNESCO drew up the **Declaration on Fundamental Principles Concerning the Contribution of the Mass Media to Strengthening Peace and International Understanding, to the Promotion of Human Rights and to Countering Racialism, Apartheid and Incitement to War**. Here Nordenstreng analyzes the **Declaration**. His analysis is divided into three parts. The first focuses on the diplomatic process of formulation in the context of a "new international information order." The second reviews the international law applicable to the field of journalism and mass communication. The third covers the social ethics and philosophical foundation of mass communication. There are 27 appendixes. The first gives the text of the **Declaration**; Appendix 2 through 27 give the text of previous statements, reports, draft declarations, letters, etc. that led up to it. Name index and subject index.

323

Nordenstreng, Kaarle, and Herbert I. Schiller, eds. **National Sovereignty and International**

Communication. Norwood, NJ: Ablex, 1979. 286p.

Sixteen experts representing Latin America, the third world, Europe, Israel, Canada, and the U.S. examine from their various viewpoints the new problems that have arisen in international communications. Their articles challenge conventional thinking on concepts such as free flow of information, cultural integrity, the role of communications in national development, the right of nations to control their own cultural/communication space, and the current makeup of the international system of information transfer.

324

Nye, Russel. **The Unembarrassed Muse: The Popular Arts in America**. New York: Dial, 1970. 497p.

The author terms this "a historical study of certain American popular arts, the arts of commercial entertainment." It relates many aspects of mass culture today and yesterday: popular fiction (the Tarzan series and Zane Grey, among other novels), the pulps, radio and television, comic books and comic strips, the Wild West show, vaudeville, film, musical comedy, poetry, even the "dream palace" architecture of movie theaters in the 1930s. He explores some of the myths about our culture not widely discussed elsewhere. In addition to its reference value, the book makes interesting reading. Contains a "Bibliography and Sources" and an index.

325

O'Brien, Rita Cruise, ed. **Information, Economics, and Power: The North-South Dimension**. London: Hodder and Stoughton, 1983. 156p.

Essays on the political economy of information which show how the management of complex new technological sources dramatically alter the nature of international business, adding a new dimension to trade and posing increased difficulties to developing countries. Authors analyzing the problem and suggesting possible remedies are from South America, Europe and the U.S.A. Chapter notes and index.

326

Ochola, Francis W. **Aspects of Mass Communication and Journalism Research on Africa**. Nairobi, Kenya: South African Book Services (EA), 1983. 103p.

An examination of the numerous major socioeconomic, cultural and methodological problems that exist in the area of mass communication and journalism research, and selected priority research areas on African media problems. There is also a brief discussion of African versus overseas training in journalism. Chapter references, a bibliography and an index.

327

Ochs, Martin. **The African Press**. Cairo, Egypt: American University Press in Cairo, 1986. 138p.

Although a number of books have been written on African journalism, this, according to Ochs, a professor of mass communication at the American University in Cairo, is the first to take an overall look at the continent as a whole, notwithstanding the lack of data and frequent change of ownership which made his task difficult. The first 50 pages survey the continent, following which are case studies of seven countries offering representative yet contrasting languages and press situations: Tanzania and Nigeria (English-speaking), the Ivory Coast and Senegal (French-speaking), Morocco and Algeria (Arabic and French-speaking), and Egypt (Arabic-speaking). Throughout he has attempted to show the effect on the press of the extreme diversity of peoples, countries, cultures and politics. The term "press" includes broadcast as well as print media, but in the case of the former the "almost monolithic government control makes research here less productive." Tables, bibliography and index.

328

O'Sullivan, Tim, John Hartley, Danny Saunders, and John Fiske. **Key Concepts in Communication**. London, Methuen, 1983. 270p. (Studies in Communication)

To beginners in the study of communication bewildered by some of the terminology of the discipline, the authors have assembled "a fieldguide . . . designed to put together in an accessible form some of the most important concepts that you will encounter in communication studies, and to show some of the ways in which these concepts have been (or might be) used." They have explained as simply as possible the origin and range of the terms, many of which are interdisciplinary and international and others from ordinary language used in unaccustomed ways, and have managed to do so understandably but without over-simplifying.

Definitions can be lengthy to include the different meanings of the terms in their various context, ranging from the familiar and widely used ("gatekeeper," "feedback," "propaganda") to the more theoretical ("semiotics/semiology", "symbolic interactionism," "metonymy") and such often deceptively simple terms as "popular culture" and "literacy" which lend themselves to various interpretations.

This is an invaluable aid to the novice in the field of communication, although its usefulness is by no means limited to beginners. Contains a 13-page list of references and an index.

329

O'Sullivan-Ryan, Jeremiah, and Mario Kaplum. **Communication Methods to Grassroots Participation: A Summary of Research**

Findings from Latin America, and an Annotated Bibliography. Paris: UNESCO, 1980(?) 155p. (Communication and Society No. 6)

A survey of the various communication strategies through which the Latin American people as a whole can participate in national development and which gives the Latin American perspective toward the problem. It tells the role of international aid agencies, lists and discusses participatory projects country by country, and in conclusion assembles a 65-page annotated bibliography of literature on the subject.

330

Paletz, David L., and Robert M. Entman. **Media, Power, Politics**. New York: Free Press, 1981. 308p.

The main issue of this book is to understand the role of the media in power politics. Although not described in these terms by the co-authors who are political scientists from Duke University, the central question concerns the agenda-setting role of the media in Washington politics. The book is stimulating and generates general hypotheses about the role of the press in political power. Content analysis is the methodology, but the data are available only from the authors and are not presented in the book. The political press studied include the prestige press (**New York Times, Washington Post**, NBC, ABC, CBS, **Time**, and **Newsweek**), but some examples of media are less well known. For example there is a case of race riot reporting in North Carolina.

331

Parenti, Michael. **Inventing Reality: The Politics of the Mass Media**. New York: St. Martin's, 1986. 258p.

"In the pages ahead we will explore the way the press distorts and suppresses the news about major domestic and foreign events and policies, the hidden and not so hidden ideological values, the mechanisms of information control, the role of newspeople, publishers, advertisers, and government, the way patterns of ownership influence information output, and the instances of dissent and deviancy in the major media," says Parenti in this mass media critique which grants no middle ground. He concentrates on national and international politico-economic class issues rather than racist and sexist biases in media content or on the entertainment media which, he says, await another volume. Confirmed advocates of the status quo won't like this book; confirmed critics will find it useful, especially its numerous examples, many of which are from the media themselves and others from more scholarly sources in chapter notes.

332

Pavlić, Breda, and Cees J. Hamelink. **The New International Economic Order: Links between Economics and Communications**. Paris: UNESCO, 1985. 65p. (Reports and Papers on Mass Communication No. 98)

In tracing and analyzing the relationship between economics and communication with reference to the Third World, the authors define the obstacles caused by inequalities and imbalances standing in the way of a new economic order and describe various perspectives on the problems, along with suggestions of practical implementation for policy and action. They also consider the consequences for information and communication if such an order is established.

333

Peck, Abe. **Uncovering the Sixties: The Life & Times of the Underground Press**. New York: Pantheon, 1985. 364p.

Peck, who was part of the underground press movement in the days of the hippie, writes from both experience and research about the times and its coverage by radical participants, showing how "new journalists responded to the causes, adventures, challenges and repressions surrounding life in the underground press." A final chapter, "After the Revolution: Who Are They Now," is an interesting follow-up of the present status of about 100 writers, editors and activists who were part of the movement. Chapter notes, bibliography and index.

334

Pelfrey, Robert, with Mary Hall-Pelfrey. **Art and Mass Media**. New York: Harper & Row, 1985. 380p.

An art appreciation book for students which emphasizes the mass media as the provider of the forms most familiar to them. Tracing both Western fine art and popular art as they stem from a common artistic tradition, it shows how they draw upon other times and other cultures. Format is chronological under the headings of "Perspective Age," "Photographic Age," "Film Age," and "Television Age." The latter chapters show how the interaction between the mass media and contemporary art creates problems as well as opportunities. A final chapter treats the problem of image-versus-reality which Pelfrey believes extends far beyond the field of art. There are many illustrations, chapter notes, a bibliography, and an author-subject index.

335

Penney, Edmund. **A Dictionary of Media Terms**. New York: Putnam, 1984. 160p.

". . . about that new lingo that grew up with film hardware, hard and soft, and sprouted into and through the at first unwanted child Video," says Ray Bradbury in his introduction to this dictionary intended to update the workaday vocabulary of the professionals who work in film, tape, radio or the new media. Definitions are brief, and include slang. However, the title is misleading, for the print media are not included.

336, 337

Phelan, John M. **Disenchantment: Meaning and Morality in the Media**. New York: Hastings House, 1980. 191p.

Phelan, John M. **Mediaworld**. New York: Seabury, 1977. 169p.

"Instead of rehearsing the familiar litany of controversial issues that pass for moral awareness in media studies or of targeting one or more trade association codes, it seems more useful to examine three major contexts wherein communications can be related to the perennial humanistic concerns of history, philosophy, and literature," says Phelan in the preface to **Disenchantment**.... His first context concerns methodology, in which he suggests a humanistic analysis as a means to study the media rather than a methodology tied to functionalism and figures. The second concern he describes as "the contemporary collusion between Censorship and Consumerism," i.e., media monitoring to serve advertising or political interests. His third concern, labeled "Cassettes and Consumerism," focuses on the communications version of technological determinism. Only by taking a hard look at methodology and social values, he feels, can we get to the heart of meaning and morality in the media. Each of the three parts has a selective bibliography, and there is, in addition, a "Bibliographic Commentary on Method." Index.

Mediaworld gives Phelan's insights into the influence of the media upon today's culture, popular and otherwise, as it creates what he contends is a superficial life style and climate of opinion, or, in his words, "a cultural and cognitive counter-ecology that increasingly permeates our mental and moral environment."

338

Picard, Robert G. **The Press and the Decline of Democracy: The Democratic Socialist Response in Public Policy**. Westport, CT: Greenwood, 1985. 173p.

In this exploration of the democratic socialist theory of the press ("the fifth theory"), Picard contends that democracy has declined in the Western democratic world in recent decades because public participation in originating policy proposals and deciding public policy has been eroded. Reasons for this erosion are the growth of bureaucracy and technology in decision-making apparatuses and increasing elite control and manipulation of the vehicles of public opinion and political expression. He reviews the ways that economic intervention by the state has worked in various Western democratic nations to the advantage of press freedom, and suggests principles to guide press policy away from such threats as private concentration of media ownership which can restrict the marketplace of ideas. Notes, a long bibliography and an index.

Pollard, James. **The Presidents and the Press**. (See No. 424.)

339

Pool, Ithiel de Sola, ed. **Trends in Content Analysis**. Urbana: University of Illinois Press, 1959. 244p. (Papers of the Work Conference on Content Analysis of the Committee on Linguistics and Psychology, Social Science Research Council)

This book follows Berelson's **Content Analysis** (1952) which established the standard codification of the research method and presents interdisciplinary approaches that were new in the mid-1950's. The central issue of the book is the problem of inference. Pool summarizes the contributed chapters in a final chapter on trends in content analysis.

340

Pool, Ithiel de Sola, Wilbur Schramm, and others, eds. **Handbook of Communication**. Chicago: Rand McNally, 1973. 1,011p.

Each of the 31 chapters of this 1,000-page handbook is a review of the studies and findings in a different area of communication research. Part I describes the basic process; the concept of a system; verbal, nonverbal, and interpersonal communication; the mass media and their audience; the impact of communication on children, and on persuasion and propaganda. Part II examines the operation of the process in various settings: the mass media; small groups; bureaucracies; advertising; political parties; scientific institutions. It also compares communication in Western democracies, Communist countries, the developing world. Part III reviews current methods of communication research, particularly aggregate data analysis and experimental studies of communication effects. Contains a name and a subject index.

341

Pool, Ithiel de Sola. **Technologies of Freedom**. Cambridge, MA: Belknap, 1983. 299p.

"The causal relationships between technology and culture are a matter that social scientists have long debated," says Pool in his opening chapter. As technological changes bring about social changes, as communication other than face-to-face conversation become increasingly electronic, what regulation is necessary for the common good and how shall such regulation be effected? Pool addresses himself to these issues. Chapter notes and index.

342, 343

Postman, Neil. **Amusing Ourselves to Death: Public Discourse in the Age of Show Business**. New York: Viking, 1985. 184p.

Postman, Neil. **The Disappearance of Childhood**. New York: Delacorte, 1982. 177p.

Among media analysts Postman is a pessimist. He describes **Amusing Ourselves to Death** as "... an inquiry into and a lamentation about the most significant

American cultural fact of the second half of the twentieth century: the decline of the Age of Typography and the ascendancy of the Age of Television." He believes that the change-over has dramatically and irreversibly shifted the content and meaning of public discourse, "since two media so vastly different cannot accommodate the same ideas," and all public business must be recast in terms suitable for television. Drawing widely from history, literature and philosophy he makes a case that we will become a trivialized culture, amusing ourselves to death. Notes, bibliography and index.

In **The Disappearance of Childhood** he says "The observation that the dividing line between childhood and adulthood is rapidly disappearing is common enough among those who are paying attention, and is even suspected by those who are not. What isn't so well understood is where childhood comes from in the first place and, still less, why it should be disappearing." He proceeds with a series of conjectures as to how media of communication affect the socialization process and in particular, how the printing press created childhood and how the electronic media are "disappearing" it. He gives no solution because, he says, he knows none. Notes, bibliography and index.

344

Press Councils and Press Codes. 4th ed. Zurich: International Press Institute, 1966. 134p.

Summary prepared by the IPI Research Service on the basis of texts published in **IPI Report** and other documents. Part I gives 88 pages of background information on press codes and councils in Austria, Belgium, Canada, Denmark, Germany, India, Israel, Italy, the Netherlands, Norway, Pakistan, the Philippines, South Africa, South Korea, Sweden, Switzerland, Turkey, the United Kingdom, and the U.S. Part II gives texts of international codes for the United Nations and the Inter-American Press Association, and texts of national codes for Australia, Belgium, Canada, Chile, Denmark, France, Germany, India, Israel, Italy, Nigeria, Norway, Pakistan, South Africa, South Korea, Sweden, Turkey, the United Kingdom, and the U.S.

345

Press, Film, Radio. 5 vols. and supps. 1–2. Paris: UNESCO, 1947–51. (Reports on the Facilities of Mass Communications)

A UNESCO survey originally designed to determine the extent of damage suffered by the equipment of news agencies, newspaper printing works, broadcasting stations, and cinemas during World War II in the war-devastated countries, as well as the nature and extent of those countries' technical needs in these fields of communication. This original purpose was later broadened to include all countries and territories, and information was extended to cover existing technical resources of mass communication. At the completion of the study 157 countries and territories had been surveyed. A few could not be surveyed—Albania, Bulgaria, Byelo-Russian SSR, U.S.S.R., and Yemen. In addition, certain British and Portuguese colonies failed to respond in time for inclusion of their data.

Information, especially for the larger countries, is detailed and thorough, with historical background, tables, figures, and maps.

Subsequent publications have supplemented the data. **World Communication** in its several editions was an authoritative reference book and a textbook in journalism schools. **World Communications: A 200-Country Survey of Press, Radio, Television, and Film** was last issued in a fifth edition by UNESCO in 1975 (533p.). The first (1950) and second editions (1951) were published by the Division of Free Flow of Information of UNESCO, and the third edition (1956) was published by the Department of Mass Communications of UNESCO. The fourth edition of **World Communications: Press, Radio, Television, Film** was published in 1964 (New York: UNESCO. 380p.).

Television: A World Survey (Paris: UNESCO, 1953. 51p.) and a **Supplement** (Paris: UNESCO, 1955) were also published in the series "Reports on the Facilities of Mass Communication."

For a follow-up concerned with newspapers only, see **The Daily Press: A Survey of the World Situation in 1952** (No. 883).

346

Press Laws and Systems in ASEAN States. Ed. by Abdul Razak. Jakarta, Indonesia: The Confederation of Asean [sic] Journalists, Gedung Dewan Pers, 1985. 458p.

A survey of press laws in Indonesia, Malaysia, the Philippines, Singapore, and Thailand, this handbook presents the information in two parts: (1) a descriptive survey of the press system for each country, and (2) transcripts of the national laws. A final chapter compares the five national systems. The first chapter is a philosophical discussion of press systems. ASEAN is the acronym for the Association of Southeast Asian Nations, founded in 1967.

347

Raboy, Marc. **Movements and Messages: Media and Radical Politics in Quebec**. Tr. by David Homel. Toronto: Between the Lines, 1983. 165p.

This study of the struggle by Quebec's French majority against its domination by the English-speaking minority during the 1960s and 1970s deals with one particular aspect: the relationship of different types of communications media to the social and political movements of the period in general and the impact of alternative communication in particular. Raboy reviews the social history of the period chronologically, isolating and evaluating the major attempts to use communications for radical social change, both within and without the mainstream media. Although theoretically influenced by the Marxist analysis of the role of mass media in capitalist society, he has broadened his bias to look for a communication strategy that is anti-authoritarian as well as socialistic. In an appendix he states his omissions: regional Quebec in favor of metropolitan Montreal; the counter-culture; the women's movement; and the English-speaking minority. Another appendix gives a chronology of events. Contains chapter notes and a bibliography.

348

Radical Science Collective, eds. **Making Waves: The Politics of Communications**. London: Free Association Books, 1985. 176p. (Radical Science No. 16)

"We may well ask: Will 'communications' mean prosthetic substitutes for real human contact? Will making waves mean more commoditisation and policing of daily life? Or might oppositional designs and uses be possible? Toward answering these questions, the essays here explore both the oppressive and liberatory possibilities of communication technologies." They include "Terminal Isolation" by Ursula Huws; "High Tech Alternativism: The Case of the Community Memory Project" by Tom Athanasiou; "Community Radio in Britain" by Richard Barbrook; "Public Access Television: Alternative Views" by Douglas Kellner; "Nicaraguan Video: 'Live from the Revolution'" by DeeDee Halleck; "The Reuters Factor" by Michael Chanan; "'E.T.': Technology and Masculinity" by David Albury; "International Meeting of Radical Science Periodicals" by Les Levidow. This is the communications issue Number 16 of a British series, **Radical Science**.

349

Rafferty, Keen. **That's What They Said about the Press**. New York: Vantage, 1975. 137p.

For whatsoever reason are you in need of a quotation about the press? If so, here is a handy collection of more than 500 made by "the famous, the infamous and the nondescript," a wide range which includes such strange bedfellows as Lord Acton, Cicero, Jane Austin, Turner Catledge, Erasmus, Shana Alexander, Stalin, Shakespeare, Oscar Wilde, and so on ad infinitum (well, not quite). Apart from the fact that it is fun, it provides a reference tool when occasions call for such quotes. Arrangement is topical, with an author index.

350

Read, William H. **America's Mass Media Merchants**. Baltimore: Johns Hopkins University Press, 1976. 209p.

The author, an experienced journalist and former regional director for the Voice of America, examines implications as the mass media penetrate the globe, bringing American values into ethnic cultures. He begins with an overview of our transnational mass media and follows with more detailed exploration of the "visual media merchants" and the "print media merchants." Next he discusses the various influences of the media and the ill will they often generated. He concludes with a critique. A well-documented scholarly work with many footnotes. Indexed.

351

Real, Michael. **Mass-Mediated Culture**. Englewood Cliffs, NJ: Prentice-Hall, 1977. 289p.

What cultural images in the form of symbols, rhythms, beliefs and practices do the media—television, radio, records, films, books and periodicals, among other forms—transmit in a mass manner from a single source to many anonymous receivers? asks Real. And how nutritious is it for the mind, the imagination, the feelings and the social systems? He explores these questions in a comparative framework, including the U.S., Canada, Western Europe, Japan, and many Third World countries. His approach is cross-cultural; his conclusions pessimistic. "Mass mediated culture," he says, "primarily serves the interests of a relatively small political-economic power elite that sits on the top of the social pyramid." And for this reason he does not find it improves the quality of life.

352

Resource Book for International Communications. Washington, DC: The Media Institute, Transnational Communications Center, 1983. 62p.

Provides a broad overview of the international communications field by furnishing names and descriptions of relevant public and private sector people, organizations, and programs based in Washington, as well as libraries, periodicals and other directories. Includes specifically Congress, Federal Departments and agencies, the media; selected associations, firms, foundations and institutes; special government boards and commissions; universities; book and document collections; periodicals; selected directories and source documents; and foreign embassies. There is an index to individuals.

353

Richstad, Jim, and Michael H. Anderson, eds. **Crisis in International News: Policies and Prospects**. New York: Columbia University Press, 1981. 473p.

Authors from the three worlds offer a wide range of perspectives as they examine ways in which the New International Information Order concepts are—for better or worse, according to viewpoints—interacting with international news processes and structures. Appendixes give texts of important documents that have emerged from conferences. Bibliography and index.

354

Righter, Rosemary. **Whose News? Politics, the Press and the Third World.** New York: Times Books, 1978. 272p.

An analysis of the struggle between the Western concept of the press as a means through which the public is freely informed about those in authority so that it can form judgments and act accordingly, and the Third World concept that the press should be a national voice functioning to make a better life for the people in terms of such things as nutrition and literacy. Bibliographical notes and index.

355

Rivers, William L., Wilbur Schramm, and Clifford G. Christians. **Responsibility in Mass Communication.** 3d ed. New York: Harper and Row, 1980. 378p.

Although several books on the ethics—and in a broader sense, the responsibility—of journalism appeared in the 1920s, the Rivers/Schramm study in 1957 was the first to deal with the subject in the era of mass communication. Since then a second edition appeared in 1969 and now a third, with Christians, a specialist in the field of ethics, joining Rivers and Schramm. It discusses the role of the press in society, broadly speaking and including the popular arts, in terms of ethical issues both direct and indirect. Appendixes give texts of the codes of the American Society of Newspaper Editors, Sigma Delta Chi, the **Chicago Sun Times** and the **Washington Post**; the annual 1979 Movie Rating System as defined by the Motion Picture Association of America; the Radio Code, the Television Code; the Declaration of Principles of the Public Relations Society of America; and the Standards of Practice of the American Association of Advertising Agencies. "Suggested Readings" for each chapter and an index.

356, 357, 358

Rivers, William L. **The Opinionmakers.** Westport, CT: Greenwood, 1965. 207p.

Rivers, William L. **Adversaries: Politics and the Press.** Boston: Beacon, 1970. 273p.

Rivers, William L. **The Other Government: Power & the Washington Media.** New York: Universe, 1982. 240p.

Rivers, a Washington reporter before he became a journalism and communications professor, has a long-standing interest in modern political journalism as practiced by the Washington media, which is reflected in this trilogy spanning almost two decades. The first, **The Opinionmakers**, sketched the relationship between government officials and journalists in Washington. **The Adversaries**, five years later, theorizes that there is an ideal relationship, not limited to Washington, between government and journalism, and that it is adversarial. The most recent, **The Other Government**, deals with the growing power of the Washington press as news makes its complex way through government and media organizations. Throughout he draws upon specific events as examples on which to make his point. All three books are indexed, but there is no bibliographic documentation.

359

Robertson, Geoffrey. **People Against the Press: An Enquiry into the Press Council.** London: Quartet, 1983. 182p.

The Press Council was set up in Britain to prove to the public that it is better to rely upon a system of voluntary self-regulation than on a set of statutory principles, powers and penalties which can be applied to the press. But in recent years there have been complaints that the Council is not effective in improving the quality of press performance. This study evaluates its achievements against its constitutional objectives and comes up with recommendations which might reconcile the right to freedom of expression with the right of persons who are somehow misrepresented by the press. An appendix lists other organizations which have an interest in self-regulation. There are references and an index.

360, 361

Robinson, Gertrude Joch. **News Agencies and World News in Canada, the United States and Yugoslavia: Methods and Data.** Fribourg, Switzerland: University of Fribourg, Institute for Journalism and Mass Communication Research, 1981. 225p.

Robinson, Gertrude Joch. **Tito's Maverick Media: The Politics of Mass Communication in Yugoslavia.** Urbana: University of Illinois Press, 1977. 263p.

The five essays about world news production contained in **News Agencies** are presented in three parts: I. "The Yugoslav Tanjug Agency and World News"; II. "News Flow: Theory and Methods"; and III. "The Canadian Press Agency and World News." Taken together, they are interesting both as information and as methodology. As information, the essays show an interwoven system of news agencies on three geographic and functional levels: world global agencies, as illustrated by the United States; world regional agencies as illustrated by Canada; and national agencies as illustrated by Yugoslavia. As a study of methodology, each illustrates the use of communications techniques when applied to research of news agencies. In an epilogue Robinson discusses the essays as a whole, calling them "working papers" rather than systematic coverage. The epilogue also contains a penetrating analysis of the "New Information Order Debate." Tables and chapter notes.

In **Tito's Maverick Media** Robinson discusses the development and operation of the press and broadcasting, against the background of the sociopolitical factors that have shaped this multinational, multilingual Communist state. She details the history of communications from 1945 to 1975; analyzes the national news agency, Tanjug; examines the way in which characteristic news values have evolved; and describes the role of the media in nation-building in a country with widely diverse ethnic groups. In conclusion she explores the composition of readers, listeners, and viewers. Appendixes give the journalism code, the content of three geographical foreign policy registers (1964), and a comparison of overlapping subject matter in Tanjug and the Associated Press. There are footnotes and a bibliography.

362, 363, 364

Rogers, Everett M. **Diffusion of Innovations**. New York: Free Press, 1962. 367p.

Rogers, Everett M., and F. Floyd Shoemaker. **Communication of Innovations: A Cross-Cultural Approach**. 2d ed. New York: Free Press, 1971. 475p.

Rogers, Everett M. **Diffusion of Innovations**. 3d ed. New York: Free Press, 1983. 453p.

In 1963 when Rogers published the first edition of **Diffusion of Innovations**, summarizing and evaluating research results on the spread of ideas, his literature search revealed about 500 studies ranging from "new drugs among physicians to hand tools among primitive tribes to hybrid corn among farmers." These he described and synthesized, along with unpublished research and personal discussions with American and European researchers in the area. Many of the studies involved cultures other than Western, and many were done by scholars in anthropology, sociology and related disciplines. Rogers concluded his survey with this statement: "This book is the first of two volumes. The second volume, co-authored with Shoemaker, can perhaps be written in ten or fifteen years after the leads for research suggested here have been followed and expanded upon.

In the 1971 edition of **Communication of Innovations: A Cross-Cultural Approach**, research had almost quadrupled, and its nature had become more varied and more involved with developing countries, necessitating a change in generalization about the theory. Twelve years later, in 1983, with the total number of diffusion publications grown to almost 4,000, Rogers published the third edition which further revised the theoretical framework and introduced new concepts and theoretical viewpoints. All three editions have extensive bibliographies of works cited and are indexed.

365

Rogers, Everett M., ed. **Communication and Development: Critical Perspectives**. Beverly Hills, CA: Sage, 1976. 148p.

In the 1960s communication scholars believed that the spread of communication and its new technologies into developing countries would insure further development. This has not proved the case. This anthology considers various alternative conceptions. References accompany each article.

366

Rogers, Everett M. **Communication Technology: The New Media in Society**. New York: Free Press, 1986. 273p. (Communication Technology and Society, no. 1)

The first of a series of texts, **Communication Technology and Society**, this book has as its purpose "to define the scholarly field of communication technology for readers who want a non-technical introduction." Against a background of the history of communication science Rogers discusses the nature and adoption of the new technologies, their implications and social impact, and the new theories and research methods they have spawned, along with their practical applications. Emphasis is on the empirical. There is a long list of references and a name and subject index.

367, 368

Rosenberg, Bernard, and David Manning White, eds. **Mass Culture: The Popular Arts in America**. New York: Free Press, 1957. 561p.

Rosenberg, Bernard, and David Manning White, eds. **Mass Culture Revisited**. New York: Van Nostrand-Reinhold, 1971. 473p.

Mass Culture: the Popular Arts in America, a collection of 51 essays designed to show the interplay between the mass media and society, was the first anthology to deal with popular culture, and remains, in spite of its age, one of the best. Contributors include literary critics, social scientists, journalists, and art critics whose work in this area has been scattered in relatively inaccessible scholarly journals and "little magazines." Not all are contemporary; for example, there are essays by de Tocqueville and Walt Whitman. Among more contemporary authors are Ortega y Gasset, Dwight Macdonald, Edmund Wilson, David Reisman, George Orwell. Among topics are books, magazines, detective fiction, comics, radio and television, motion pictures, and advertising. Contains a list of further readings at the end of each section and bibliographic notes following most of the articles.

Mass Culture Revisited updates its predecessor, with 27 articles, some appearing for the first time. It takes into account the many changes between 1957 and 1970, including the increased impetus of television, comic strips in the underground press, and new trends in established media like films, magazines, and newspapers. One section, "The Overview," is general. Among the contributors are Hannah Arendt, Nicholas Johnson, Mordecai Richler, Nathan Blumberg, Diana Trilling, and Fred Friendly.

369

Rosenblum, Mort. **Coups and Earthquakes: Reporting the World for America**. New York: Harper, 1979. 230p.

Rosenblum, who reported abroad for the Associated Press from 1967 to 1979, has drawn upon his experience and knowledge to write "an insider's look at foreign reporting, . . . a consumer's guide to foreign news" in which he shows the pitfalls and pratfalls of presenting an accurate picture of the news, and describes a number of them in interesting detail, along with other cases where the stories were covered well, although sometimes with difficulty. Not all the obstacles are made by humans. Some are technological, some have natural causes. In conclusion he presents a case for a better system of international reporting. Index.

370

Rosengren, Karl Erik, ed. **Advances in Content Analysis**. Beverly Hills, CA: Sage, 1981. 283p. (Sage Annual Reviews of Communication Research, v. 9)

This selection of 13 papers from the first Scandinavian Conference on Content Analysis is international in its interest, drawing from both the quantitative and qualitative traditions. Some of the articles are general, dealing largely with methodology; others relate to specifically Scandinavian issues. The introductory article by the editor, "Advances in Scandinavian Content Analysis," gives a brief history of opposing trends in both content analysis and the social sciences in general in Europe and North America, and tells how each has influenced the other. Chapter references.

371

Rosengren, Karl Erik, Lawrence A. Wenner, and Philip Palmgreen, eds. **Media Gratification Research Current Perspectives**. Beverly Hills, CA: Sage, 1985. 311p.

Essays grouped around a wide range of theoretical and methodological issues, new research paradigms, and key research areas which use media gratification theory to examine the present state of development of empirical research and point out future possibilities. In four parts: "Looking Back"; "Perspective on Theoretical Issues"; "Perspectives on Key Research Areas"; and "Looking Ahead." Contributors include the editors, Jay Blumler, Maxwell McCombs, David Weaver, Lennert Weibull, Denis McQuail, Alan Rubin, James Lull, Frederick Williams, Amy Friedman Phillips, Patricia Lum, Michael Gurevitch and Elihu Katz. References.

372

Roshco, Bernard. **Newsmaking**. Chicago: University of Chicago Press, 1975. 160p.

A sociological analysis of the newsmaking process in which the author seeks answers to two basic questions:

How do the relationships the press maintains with other institutions determine what it defines as news, where it seeks news, and how it presents news? And, how is the news content of the American press shaped by the dominant values in American society? Roshco, a former Washington newsman, is both well-qualified and an excellent writer. Chapter notes, bibliography and index.

373

Rubin, David M., and Ann Marie Cunningham. **War, Peace & the News Media**. New York: New York University, Department of Journalism and Mass Communications, 1983. 285p.

Verbatim proceedings of a discussion about press coverage of the superpower rivalry and threat of nuclear war, sponsored at New York University by the Gannett Foundation, with participants from the U.S., Canada and Mexico, among them journalists, government officials, academicians, clergymen, citizen-activists and students. Among news organizations represented were the **New York Times**, **Washington Post**, **Newsweek**, **Time**, AP, UPI, NBC, ABC, CBS, PBS, NPR, **Washington Monthly**, **Commentary**, **Bulletin of the Atomic Scientists**, **Mother Jones**, and the **Nation**.

Rubin, Rebecca B., Alan M. Rubin, and Linda J. Piele. **Communication Research: Strategies and Sources**. (See No. 1691.)

374

Rugh, William A. **The Arab Press: News Media and Political Process in the Arab World**. Syracuse, NY: Syracuse University Press, 1979. 205p.

Unlike more recent books dealing with the press in the Middle East which focus upon the treatment of the Arab Israeli conflict, this one analyzes the news media as institutions, "to see what forms they have taken in the independent Arab states, how the self-governing Arab societies have chosen to control them, and how they relate to the political processes in the Arab world." The author, counselor for public affairs at the U.S. Embassy, Cairo and an expert on the region, looks in particular at the relationship between the mass media and the government with an eye to the extent of freedom that exists. Countries dealt with are the 18 nation states where Arabic is the official language of the people and the media. Much of the material is based on interviews and Arabic-languages sources. Notes and index.

375

Rutherford, Paul. **The Making of the Canadian Media**. Toronto: McGraw-Hill Ryerson, 1978. 141p.

"My book," says Rutherford, "is intended to fill a gap in our understanding of the Canadian experience: to trace the evolution of the media and the impact of communications." He makes two qualifications: his study does not apply any theory or model, although it has been conditioned by the findings of communications theorists, notably Innis and McLuhan and in particular their emphasis upon the cultural importance of communications systems; and his arguments rest upon secondary material—"the enormous wealth of reminiscences, accounts, criticisms, reports, and monographs pertinent to the development of the media" rather than on primary research except to fill in gaps. His "story" as he calls it is organized into three essays. "The Rise of the Newspaper" tracing the press from Conquest to Confederation when the press had matured; "The Golden Age of the Press" covering the next 60 years and looking at the supremacy of the big city daily and the impact of mass communications upon Canada; and "Triumph of the Multimedia" which ends with the present. In a brief "Conclusion" he tells why he disagrees with McLuhan and Innis. Chapter notes and an extensive bibliography. Index.

376

Said, Edward W. **Covering Islam: How the Media and the Experts Determine How We See the Rest of the World**. New York: Pantheon, 1981. 186p.

This is far more than an analysis of the way the U.S. covers the Islamic world. A penetrating study by a scholar and a humanist it goes much deeper than an examination of what he considers a biased treatment of Islamic news by the American press. Using illustrations from the media, he makes the point that we do not—perhaps are not properly trying to—understand "the new horizons being opened up everywhere in the nonwhite, non-European world" which have roots in history and involve deep cultural differences. The first third of the book deals with "Islam as News," the middle section with "The Iran Story," and the final section with "Knowledge and Power." He contends, "Knowledge and coverage of the Islamic world are defined in the United States by geopolitics and economic interests on—for the individual—an impossibly massive scale, aided and abetted by a structure of knowledge production that is almost as vast and unmanageable." But until we somehow overcome these difficulties and acquire a knowledge in depth the American press cannot cover Islam properly.

377

Salinas, Raquel. **Communication Policies: The Case of Latin America**. Stockholm: Institute of Latin American Studies, 1978. 39p. (Paper No. 9)

The author's aim is to relate Latin America to a search for a new information order in the context of both the developed and underdeveloped countries. She discusses the nature of the forces opposing change and how they are also manifest in industrialized countries. There is a bibliography of references.

378

Sandford, John. **The Mass Media of the German-Speaking Countries**. London: Oswald Wolff, 1976. 235p.

An introduction to the mass media of West and East Germany, Austria, and Switzerland which discusses for each country the historical background and the present structure of the press and broadcasting systems. Comparisons are drawn between the media systems within the four countries dealt with and between their systems and those of the English-speaking world. An appendix briefly describes 11 of the major magazines and newspapers. There is also a glossary of German words and abbreviations used in the text, a bibliography, and an index.

379

Schiller, Dan. **Objectivity and the News: The Public and the Rise of Commercial Journalism**. Philadelphia: University of Pennsylvania Press, 1981. 222p.

How did the concept of objectivity in news reporting, which arose in the 19th century and is with us today, become a standard in America? Schiller reviews critically various theories and their proponents, and carefully sets the groundwork for a theory of his own through an examination of the news in the **National Police Gazette 1845–1850** in relation to the social milieu of its readers. Chapter references, bibliography and index. (See also, Schudson, No. 392.)

380

Schiller, Herbert I. **Information and the Crisis Economy**. Norwood, NJ: Ablex, 1984. 133p.

A challenging book in which Schiller contends that information—"the nucleus of culture in a highly industrialized society"—is becoming an item of commerce, up for sale. The information technologies with their extensive capabilities are being manipulated to benefit large private corporations in a push toward a corporate-controlled information society; for the common good human values and social criteria must be introduced. He analyzes and documents the evidence to prove his thesis. Chapter notes and author-subject index.

381, 382, 383

Schiller, Herbert I. **Mass Communications and the American Empire**. New York: Augustus M. Kelley, 1969. 170p.

Schiller, Herbert I. **The Mind Managers**. Boston: Beacon Press, 1973. 214p.

Schiller, Herbert I. **Communication and Cultural Domination**. White Plains, NY: International Arts and Sciences Press, 1976. 127p.

All of Schiller's writings are Marxist-oriented, well-documented, and skeptical of the status quo of the communications industries. In **Mass Communications and the American Empire** he critically examines the economic and political structure of the broadcasting industry in the U.S., from the period of radio to the period of the satellite, and finds it organized primarily to serve the military-industrial complex.

In **The Mind Managers** he makes a case that America's media managers "deliberately produce messages that do not correspond to the realities of social existence." In **Communication and Cultural Domination** he is concerned with the "sources, character, and contents of the communication stream that passes between nations and on the flow that is generated inside national states." Here again he feels the "haves" tend to influence and sometimes dominate the "have nots." All three volumes are copiously footnoted and are indexed.

384

Schiller, Herbert I. **Who Knows: Information in the Age of The Fortune 500**. Norwood, NJ: Ablex, 1981. 187p.

Schiller offers his evidence that although the information technology in the U.S. changes vastly in a post-industrial society, the infrastructure remains the same or is even strengthened, while at the same time it spreads over the developing and under-developed world. He has used the expression "The Fortune 500" as a generic term for the largest corporations in the country, as he examines not only the manufacturing firms they represent but banks, insurance companies, utilities, etc. as well. Chapter notes and author and subject indexes.

385

Schilpp, Madelon Golden, and Sharon M. Murphy. **Great Women of the Press**. Carbondale: Southern Illinois University Press, 1983. 248p.

Biographies of 18 women journalists spanning the 18th, 19th, and 20th centuries, presented within the framework of family background and the socio-economic environment of their times. Granted the paucity of women journalists in the two earlier centuries, it is nevertheless hard to make a selection, and much harder in the present one when they are no longer a rarity and much more material exists. Consequently the book seems especially valuable for the earlier period—not only for the facts about the women but also for the light it throws on the role of women in the history of journalism. Notes, bibliography and index.

386

Schmid, Alex P., and Janny de Graaf. **Violence as Communication: Insurgent Terrorism and the Western News Media**. Beverly Hills, CA: Sage, 1982. 283p.

The authors' thesis: that terrorism is in itself a means of communication, a means of insuring public attention and even of channeling particular messages to chosen targets. To this end they explore the ways the media are used both by the terrorists and the authorities. Along the way they examine established structures and practices of news journalism under conditions of high competition for audiences, with emphasis on the news value placed upon violence. In conclusion they make detailed recommendations and judgments and offer a global perspective on the problem. Notes and a selected bibliography.

387

Schmuhl, Robert, ed. **The Responsibilities of Journalism**. Notre Dame, IN: University of Notre Dame Press, 1984. 138p.

Report of a conference to explore the moral dimensions of contemporary journalism. Contributors include print and broadcast journalists, theologians, academicians, and one executive—Elie Abel, Lisa Sowle Cahill, John G. Craig, Jr., Georgie Anne Geyer, Jeff Greenfield, Max Lerner, Robert J. McCloskey, Rev. Edward A. Malloy, Edwin Newman, Robert Schuhl, Leonard Silk, Rev. Oliver F. Williams, and John E. Swearington (the executive). The article by Elie Abel deals with the Hutchins Commission (No. 81)—"Hutchins Revisited: Thirty-five Years of Social Responsibility Theory." The excellent "Selected Bibliography" will be of especial value to those interested in media ethics.

388

Schramm, Wilbur, ed. **Mass Communications: A Book of Readings**. 2d ed. Urbana: University of Illinois Press, 1960. 695p.

Communications students of the 1950s and 1960s grew up on the articles in this anthology (the first edition came out in 1949). For this if nothing else it is important. But there are other reasons. The articles, which are as a whole well-chosen, represent the thinking of some of the scholars who were then shaping the study of mass communication, and much of what they said holds today in spite of the fact of new technology, theory, and research. Among topics dealt with are development, structure, function, control and support, process, content, audience, effects, and responsibility of newspapers, broadcasting, magazines, and film. A number of articles in the 1949 edition are not duplicated in this one. Appendixes in the first edition give statistical data, outdated but historically useful, a brief analysis of mass communication in other countries, accompanied by figures; and an excellent bibliography. Both are indexed.

389

Schramm, Wilbur, and Donald F. Roberts, eds. **The Process and Effects of Mass Communication**. Urbana: University of Illinois Press, 1971. 586p.

First published in 1954, this revised edition contains only four articles from the original volume. It represents the examples of communication research and theory produced during the preceding 15 years, as well as work done earlier in this century by prominent social scientists. Subjects discussed include media, messages and audiences of mass communication; the effects of communication on attitudes, politics, public opinion, and social change; and the technological future of mass communication. Contains a bibliography of 100 titles for further reading and an index.

390

Schramm, Wilbur, and Erwin Atwood. **Circulation of News in the Third World: A Study of Asia**. Hong Kong: The Chinese University Press, 1981. 352p.

A quantitative content analysis in which Schramm and Atwood focus on the flow of news into and out of the Third World, with emphasis on the four Western news agencies—Reuter, the Associated Press, United Press International, and Agence France Presse. Part of the project measures quantity of news, part quality. Appendixes give basic data. In conclusion is a list of references used.

391

Schramm, Wilbur, and William E. Porter. **Men, Women, Messages, and Media: Understanding Human Communication**. 2d ed. New York: Harper & Row, 1982. 278p.

This undergraduate text, useful to layman as well as student, emphasizes a holistic approach which provides "an introduction to mass communication as a part of human life and society, reflecting modern knowledge of the field but still readable without advanced knowledge of social science or research methods." The first third deals with communication in the abstract—how it developed, what it does, how it works (process), signs and codes, and pathways (who talks to whom). The remainder concerns communication, both via media and person to person—its dimensions, its audience, its social control and its effects. A final chapter is on "The Information Revolution." Schramm and Porter synthesize theory and research throughout. There are chapter references, a name index, and a subject index. Indicative of the nine years that have lapsed between the first edition and this second one: the title of the first, **Men, Messages, and Media: A Look at Human Communication** (1973) has been changed to **Men, Women, Messages, and Media, Understanding Human Communication**.

392

Schudson, Michael. **Discovering the News**. New York: Basic Books, 1978. 228p.

An outstanding analytical history of American journalism which deals with it in terms of the concept of objectivity—its origin and development. To come up with a theory, Schudson has examined the relationship between the institutionalization of modern journalism and the general currents in economic, political, social, and culture life in America from Colonial times to the present. This is distinguished for its style and readability,

and although probably not intended for a history-of-journalism text it is widely used for one. Contains extensive notes and an index. (See also, Schiller, No. 379.)

393, 394

Seldes, Gilbert. **The Seven Lively Arts**. New York: Harper, 1924. 306p.

Seldes, Gilbert. **The Great Audience**. New York: Viking, 1951. 299p.

Gilbert Seldes was one of the first people in the twentieth century to take modern mass culture seriously. In a period when film had just come into its own, it held great promise to him as an innovative art form. He was also excited about the quality of entertainment in general—the comic strip, popular music, the Broadway comedians. Among the "lively arts" he even includes Picasso.

In the years that followed he lost much of his optimism. But **The Seven Lively Arts** stands as one of the best descriptions of popular mass culture during and preceding the 1920s.

When, a quarter of a century later, he reexamined the state of mass entertainment in **The Great Audience** its character and the character of the special type of audience it had created—he found it wanting. Much emphasis is on radio and on television, which was just appearing. Both books are perceptive studies which have held up over the years.

395

Severin, Werner J., and James W. Tankard, Jr. **Communication Theories: Origins—Methods—Uses**. New York: Hastings House, 1979. 286p.

Addressed specifically to undergraduate students, this text has as its aim to put into perspective the pragmatic uses of communication theory research and the methods by which such research can be practiced. First the authors discuss scientific method and also models, analyzing some of the best known. Then in the bulk of the book they describe types of research and some representative studies—among them, general semantics, measurement of readability and of connotative meaning (the semantic differential), propaganda, group behavior, attitude change, interpersonal communication and the media, the role of the mass media in modern society, newspaper chains and media conglomerates, and effects. Chapter notes and index. A second edition was published by Longman in 1988. See also Alexis S. Tan, **Mass Communication Theories and Research**. 2d ed. (New York: Wiley, 1985. 400p.)

396

Seymour-Ure, Colin. **The Political Impact of Mass Media**. London: Constable; Beverly Hills, CA: Sage, 1974. 296p.

The author believes that **effects** has commonly been defined too narrowly. Using a broader framework he has examined and illustrated varieties of political effects caused by the mass media. Illustrations are drawn mainly from Britain and the U.S. Part I is an analysis of what media effects comprise, the different ways they are produced, and the kinds of political relationship that may result. Part II explores in some depth specific examples. These complement Part I, but can be read on their own. They include a study of the relationship between press systems and party systems; a survey of the impact of the media on British elections and electioneering since 1945; studies of the mass media vis-à-vis Enoch Powell; the political role of **Private Eye**; the role of the London **Times** in the appeasement of Hitler; and the mutual influence of broadcasting and Parliament. Contains a list of references, a bibliography, and an index.

397

Shannon, Claude E., and Warren Weaver. **The Mathematical Theory of Communication**. Urbana: University of Illinois Press, 1949. 117p.

When communications emerged in the late 1940s from the hard sciences into the social sciences and humanities, this was one of the first theories. Using a mathematical model devised by Shannon in an article in the **Bell Telephone System Technical Journal**, Weaver applies it in a broad way to include all the procedures by which one mind may affect another, including not only written and oral speech, but also the arts and human behavior in general.

398

Shanor, Donald R. **Behind the Lines: The Private War on Censorship**. New York: St. Martin's Press, 1985. 179p.

An examination of the unofficial news networks used by Soviet citizens to penetrate official control of information, along with an investigation of the officially controlled media to show the reasons for their weaknesses, both organizational and technological.

399

Shanor, Donald, and Donald H. Johnston, eds. **Third World News in American Media: Experience and Prospects**. New York: Columbia University, Center for Advanced Study of Communication and Public Affairs, Graduate School of Journalism, 1983. 63p. (Journalism Monograph No. 4)

Report of a conference sponsored by the Ford Foundation. Nineteen short essays by academics and journalists, all of whom have interest and/or experience in news coverage about the Third World, discuss what America is doing in reporting it and how, perhaps, it can be done better. Topics are discussed under the following headings: "The Information Gap Controversy," "Will Americans Accept More Third World Information?," "Current Patterns of Third World Coverage," "Education

and Training of Journalists," and "New Approaches to Presenting Third World News."

400

Sharp, Nancy W., et al. **Faculty Women in Journalism and Mass Communications: Problems and Progress**. Columbia, SC: Association for Education in Journalism and Mass Communications, College of Journalism, University of South Carolina, 1985. 66p.

A publication honoring the late Cathy Covert of the Newhouse School of Public Communications at Syracuse University analyzes the progress of women in communications education and problems still remaining. A quantitative study, it is based on a survey of current women faculty, doctoral students or doctoral graduates in journalism and mass communications education; a content analysis of leading communications journals to document the extent of women as authors of research articles; and interviews with leaders in communication education, equally divided between men and women. The five women authors were her colleagues at Newhouse.

401

Siebert, Fredrick Seaton. **Freedom of the Press in England 1476–1776: The Rise and Decline of Government Controls**. Urbana: University of Illinois Press, 1952. 411p.

"Since most of our constitutional and political concepts of the late eighteenth century were inherited directly from English forbears, it seems reasonable to begin with a study of the English origins and backgrounds of our American Press," says Siebert in his Introduction to this detailed history of the first 300 years of press control in England under the Tudors, the early and later Stuarts (interrupted by the Puritan Revolution) and the first three quarters of the 18th century. He describes the number and variety of controls operated by the central government, the efforts made to enforce regulation both with and without success, and the degree of public compliance, either voluntary or enforced by policy. This will interest readers not only for the light it sheds on policy involving freedom of the press in the U.S., but also as a social history of the first three centuries of the printing press in England. Footnotes and author/title/subject index.

402

Siebert, Fredrick Seaton, Theodore Peterson, and Wilbur Schramm. **Four Theories of the Press: The Authoritarian, Libertarian, Social Responsibility, and Soviet Communist Concepts of What the Press Should Be and Do**. Urbana: University of Illinois Press, 1956. 153p.

One of the most quoted books in the literature of press freedom, this defines it in terms of four types, with historical background and broad implications of each.

Siebert is the author of the chapters on the authoritarian and libertarian theories; Peterson, the social responsibility theory (advocated by the Hutchins Commission, No. 81), and Schramm, the Marxist theory. The basic thesis is that the social and political structures of a society shape and control its press.

403

Siegel, Arthur. **Politics and the Media in Canada**. Toronto: McGraw-Hill Ryerson, 1983. 258p.

Newspapers, radio and television industries in Canada are studied in relation to the political, social and economic environment in which they operate, with particular attention to their role in Canadian nation-building. Provides a documented overview of the present and a review of past history. Footnotes and index.

404

Sigal, Leon V. **Reporters and Officials: The Organization and Politics of Newsmaking**. Lexington, MA: Heath, 1973. 221p.

A descriptive study of the press journalists' role in reporting national political affairs. The information is gleaned from an extensive reading of the memoirs and essays of journalists and from interviews with editors, columnists, and elite reporters at the **New York Times** and the **Washington Post**. The central question is the collaborative relationship between the politicians and government policy employees, particularly the State Department professionals, and the elite members of the Washington press corps.

Unlike **Boys on the Bus** (No. 90), which is an engaging narrative, exceptionally written, **Reporters and Officials** is a more scholarly analysis, and the author takes care to consider the formal dimensions of professional journalists' work. For example, he gives the professional codes, the organization and routines at the **NY Times'** Washington Bureau office. Sigal does occasionally describe power struggles among the journalists, i.e., Turner Catledge's attempt to oust Tom Wicker as head of the **Times** Washington Bureau in 1966.

405

Singer, Benjamin D., ed. **Communications in Canadian Society**. 2d ed. Reading, MA: Addison-Wesley, 1983. 342p.

As in his 1983 edition, Singer's anthology concentrates on the impact of communication on Canada. Essays are grouped under five headings: "Social Forces and Communications Media," "Control of Communications Media," "Identity, Unity and Mass Communication," "Social Problems and Communication," and "Participation and the Communications Media." The majority of the papers are original; many are new to this edition, or substantially revised. Overall, they provide a variety of perspectives on the past, present, and future of Canadian communications. Among the 25 authors are

Garth Jowett, Wilfred Kesterton, Thelma McCormack, Thomas McPhail, Alvin Toffler, Frank Peers and Maxwell Cohen. About two-thirds of the articles have notes. Index.

406

Sinha, Arbind K. **Mass Media and Rural Development: Study of Village Communication in Bihar**. New Delhi: Concept, 1985. 134p.

"India has to reach to the level, where it can provide food, clothing, and shelter to each individual, within the shortest possible time. Thus, it has become necessary to gear up the developmental process in India, where almost 80 percent of the population lives in rural areas isolated from the urban centres and have low rates of literacy," says Sinha in his Introduction. Using the village of Bihar as a case study, he explores the role and relevance of the mass media, especially television, and face-to-face communication. His introduction contains a very brief history of television. "Bibliographical References" and index.

407

Smith, Anthony. **The Politics of Information: Problems of Policy in the Modern Media**. London: Macmillan, 1978. 252p.

In this group of perceptive essays about various aspects of broadcasting and the print press, Smith's theme is that the media could serve the public better than they are doing. He proceeds to tell why he feels this to be the case. Orientation is British and continental, but comments are applicable to Western countries in general. Indexed, with notes and references.

Smith, Bruce Lannes, et al. **Propaganda, Communication, and Public Opinion**. (See No. 1665.)

Smith, Bruce Lannes, and Chita M. Smith, comps. **International Communications and Political Opinion**. (See No. 1666.)

408

Smith, Stephen A. **Myth, Media, and the Southern Mind**. Fayetteville: University of Arkansas Press, 1985. 207p.

The North American South has always been and still is a breeding ground for various cultural myths which have influenced history. In this study Smith says that he has tried "to demonstrate the rhetorical nature of public myths, to show that the South has developed a new mythology to define and explain contemporary reality, and to lay bare the relationship between myth and media." To analyze the role of the media he has used a socio-cultural model of mass media persuasion posited by Melvin DeFleur and Sandra Ball-Rokeach, along with George Gerbner's Communication, theory. This is an interesting treatment of an interesting subject. Chapter notes, bibliography, and index.

409

Smythe, Dallas W. **Dependency Road: Communications, Capitalism, Consciousness, and Canada**. Norwood, NJ: Ablex, 1981. 347p.

"This is a study of the process by which people organized in the capitalist system produced a country called Canada as a dependency of the United States, the center of the core of the capitalist system," says Smythe in his Introduction. Focus is on the role of communications institutions—press, magazines, books, films, radio and television broadcasting, telecommunications, the arts, sciences, and engineering—in legitimatizing Canada's dependency by producing the necessary consciousness and ideology. Contains an appendix: "The Electronic Information Tiger, or the Political Economy of the Radio Spectrum and the Third World Interest." Footnotes, extensive bibliography, and name/subject index.

410

Snow, Robert P. **Creating Media Culture**. Beverly Hills, CA: Sage Publications, 1983. 263p.

Using as a model theoretical principles of symbolic interaction—i.e., an analysis of the language of the mass media as an important part of the ways in which people symbolically construct the meanings of their lives—Snow, after a discussion of media strategy in general, takes up the individual mass media: newspapers, "the daily institution"; novels and magazines, "dreams and subcultures"; radio, "the companion medium"; television, "the cultural medium"; and film, "the emotion medium." In a concluding chapter, "The Power Source," he speculates upon some possible effects the media have on the public. There are two appendixes: "Social Psychological Dimensions of Communication" and "Advertising." References are listed, and Snow gives a short list of recommended readings. Index.

411

Soderlund, Walter C., et al. **Media & Elections in Canada**. Toronto: Holt, Rinehart & Winston, 1984. 163p.

A study, part empirical, part overview, of the relationship between Canadian politics and the media. After a sketch of the development of the media in Canada comes a content analysis of the gatekeeping process and news agenda in the 1979 and 1980 campaigns. This is followed by a review, "The Other Side of the Coin: Government Regulation of the Media," and a concluding chapter of the major issues relating to media and politics. All in all, this provides the uninitiated with an overview of the subject, with references to pertinent literature for those who might want to follow up with the sources. Chapter notes, bibliography and index.

412

Soderlund, Walter C., and Stuart H. Surlin, eds. **Media in Latin America and the Caribbean: Domestic and International Perspectives**. Windsor, Ontario, Canada: University of Windsor, 1985. 272p.

Report of 14 papers presented at the proceedings of the Ontario Cooperative Program in Latin American and Caribbean Studies, organized under four thematic sections: the New World Information Order and the MacBride Report; media performance in Latin America and the Caribbean; media coverage of Latin America and the Caribbean in the American press; and a special section focusing on various aspects of the American military invasion of Grenada. Ideological points of view vary throughout the papers. References follow each.

413

Sreberny-Mohammadi, Annabelle, et al. **Foreign News in the Media: International Reporting in 29 Countries**. Paris: UNESCO, 1985. 96p. (Reports and Papers on Mass Communication No. 93)

A comparative study on how the media present other countries, peoples and issues to readers, listeners and viewers. Using quantitative content analysis, teams followed the news in selected countries representing various communication systems in North America, Africa, the Middle East, Asia, Eastern and Western Europe and Latin America during one week in 1979. Two methods were employed: one measured the amount of foreign news while the second balanced measurement with a qualitative analysis of the material, fleshing out the content, drawing attention to omissions, and showing the flavor of the kinds of news coverage available within each media system. Appendixes give the participating teams; the coding of the study; a section on "Other Research and the World of News" by Robert L. Stevenson which not only lists the research from other studies but breaks the material down into tables and draws overall conclusions; and a final appendix: "The News of the World in Four Major Wire Services: A Study of Selected Services of the Associated Press, United Press International, Reuters, and Agence France-Press" by David Weaver, Cleveland Wilhoit, Robert Stevenson, Donald Lewis Shaw, and Richard Cole.

414

Stempel, Guido H.,III, and Bruce H. Westley, eds. **Research Methods in Mass Communication**. Englewood Cliffs, NJ: Prentice-Hall, 1981. 405p.

Articles defining the scope of study and research in mass communication in the 1980s. Whereas in the not too distant past concentration would have been on the quantitative, articles here reflect the growing trend toward the qualitative as well. The first three are general and explanatory; the remaining 17 discuss the application of the various types of present-day research, both empirical and nonempirical, and represent related disciplines often involved, such as ethics, law and history.

An older book with a similar aim which makes interesting comparison is **An Introduction to Journalism Research** edited by Ralph Nafziger and Marcus Wilkerson (Baton Rouge: Louisiana State University Press, 1949) and a 1958 update, **Introduction to Mass Communication Research** (also published by Louisiana State University Press).

415

Stephenson, William. **The Play Theory of Mass Communication**. Chicago: University of Chicago Press, 1967. 225p.

Stephenson's theory has been called "a brilliant explication of the play-pleasure aspects of communication." Applying his notions of work and play to media content and using data gathered by Q-sort methodology from individuals and groups, he theorizes that mass communication, for the first time in history, can be used to manipulate the individual through entertainment, which he equates with play—i.e., such media fare as fiction, stories, comics, radio music, television drama, art museums, stage and film plays, ballet, rock concerts, etc. Bibliography and index to names and subjects.

416

Sterling, Christopher H., and Timothy R. Haight. **The Mass Media: Aspen Institute Guide to Communication Industry Trends**. New York: Praeger, 1978. 457p.

Brings together in a single reference source the most significant statistics describing communication industry trends in the U.S. from the 1930s well into the 1970s, with more than 300 tables of data supplemented by a brief interpretive text, an analysis of source reliability and validity, and a listing of sources of further information in each subject area. Figures were gathered from government, business and trade, academic, and private correspondence. Media covered include books (publishing, bookstores, book clubs, and libraries); newspapers; magazines; motion pictures; radio and television. Those government publications most frequently used for communication statistics are discussed in a special section, and there is an extensive bibliography. Organizations which are a fruitful source of statistics are also given. Contains a subject index. Sterling's later book, **Electronic Media** (No. 798) expands and updates the information for the electronic media.

417

Stevens, John D., and Hazel Dicken-Garcia. **Communication History**. Beverly Hills, CA: Sage, 1980. 157p.

The title is somewhat misleading. This text is not a history of communication (a monumental task!) but an analysis of its methodologies. In the first section, by Dicken-Garcia, "Toward a Redefinition of the Discipline," she critiques histories of American journalism and finds the approaches used in most of them too limited, in ways in which she elaborates. Although certainly not intended as such, her text provides an interesting bibliographical essay on the history of American journalism histories.

The second section differs. In "Media Effects from an Historical Perspective" Stevens gives two examples of unconventional approaches to research on aspects of the mass media. Taking public opinion as a subject he reverses the usual approach and considers how public opinion influences the media rather than how the media influences public opinion. Taking distribution systems as another example, he demonstrates how the history of print media and film can be researched from that angle rather than the more frequently used angle of production systems.

While both Dicken-Garcia and Stevens have offered provocative discussions, the two parts somehow don't seem to fit together. Chapter references and index.

418

Stevenson, Robert L., and Donald Lewis Shaw, eds. **Foreign News and the New World Information Order**. Ames: Iowa State University Press, 1984. 243p.

In the debate between the developing and developed world over the function and structure of the mass media, this collection consolidates and interprets primary findings of an international study funded by the U.S.I.A. that analyzes content and dissemination of foreign news by the mass media of 17 Third World countries and the four major Western news agencies. Among contributors are the editors, Richard Cole, Kirsten Thompson, Gary Gaddy, J. Walker Smith, Anne Cooper, Emmanuel Paraschos, David Weaver, Cleve Wilhoit, Jere Link, Robert Haynes, Jr. and Thomas Ahern, Jr. Bibliographies at the end of chapters. Index.

419

Stokke, Olav, ed. **Reporting Africa**. Uppsala: Scandinavian Institute of African Studies. New York: Africana Publishing Corp., 1971. 223p.

Report of a seminar which explored the manner in which African news is presented by the European press. In two parts: "The Mass Media in Africa" and "Reporting Africa by the International Mass Media." In the first part, emphasis is on the English-speaking African nations— Ghana, Kenya, and Nigeria—although there are chapters on the African mass media as institutions of African political systems, and on the freedoms and functions of mass communications in Africa. The second part deals with the way selected European nations present African news, with a chapter each on the British, French, and North American mass media, a single chapter on the Soviet and Czechoslovak presses, and four chapters on Scandinavian broadcasting systems, including Finnish.

Part II also contains sections on the problem of cultural translation in the reporting of African social realities, and other problems confronting correspondents specializing in Africa.

420

Stoler, Peter. **The War Against the Press: Politics, Pressure and Intimidation in the Eighties**. New York: Dodd Mead, 1986. 226p.

Stoler, a senior correspondent for **Time**, believes that a dangerous attitude about the press and its credibility is occurring in America both by the government and the people which threatens its freedom. How much of the criticism is justified, he asks, and how much is based on misunderstanding? In his search for answers he examines contemporary issues and attitudes toward the press and its coverage in terms of recent events—among them, Vietnam, Watergate, the Iranian hostage situation, Grenada, the Sharon and Westmoreland libel suits, the growing hostility between the press and the Reagan administration. He also goes into the weakening of the Freedom of Information Act, the crackdown on leakers, and such less tangible attitudes as the growing public belief that the press is elitist. The final chapters suggest how the media can regain public confidence, support itself against its attackers, and assure its survival. A thoughtful analysis based on the author's personal knowledge and careful research, which is both informative and interesting. Source notes, bibliography index.

421

Surrette, Ray. **Justice and the Media: Issues and Research**. Springfield, IL: Charles C. Thomas, 1984. 337p.

As the media have become more sophisticated and differentiated they have also become more intrusive and important in many areas of society, among them crime and criminal justice. In this collection of essays, contributors survey the state of knowledge pertaining to the media in relation to crime and criminal justice in order to relate it to some of the new issues that have arisen, to review existing research, and to point to directions for future research. In the first section contributors discuss the issues; in the second they discuss research under two headings: media research on public attitudes, and media research on crime and violence. References accompany each article. Subject index.

422

Sussman, Leonard R. **Glossary for International Communications**. Washington, DC: The Media Institute, 1983. Unpaged. (Communications in a Changing World, v. 3)

In this politically oriented glossary, common key words and terms frequently used on an international level are each defined under four headings: The First World, the Second World (Marxist), the Third World, and UNESCO. Forty-eight terms are included, beginning with "Access" and ending with "War of Liberation." The comparative usage of the same word is revealing.

423

Switzer, Les. **Media and Dependency in South Africa: A Case Study of the Press and the Ciskei "Homeland"**. Columbus: Monographs in International Studies, Ohio State University, 1985. 72 p. (African Series No. 47)

The Ciskei "Homeland" has long been a center of African nationalism and of conflict between whites and blacks. Switzer's examination of the press in this area also shows on a larger national scale, how the South African privately owned commercial press promotes dependency of blacks upon whites by perpetuating the values of the white governing class. The introduction briefly surveys South Africa's communications industry. Bibliography.

Tan, Alexis S. **Mass Communication Theories and Research**. (See No. 395.)

424

Tebbel, John, and Sarah Miles Watts. **The Press and the Presidency from George Washington to Ronald Reagan**. New York: Oxford, 1985. 583p.

A historical study of the presidency, including the personalities of the presidents, and of the changing character of the press. The thesis is that the presidency has evolved into an imperialistic institution now capable of manipulating and controlling the media, and through them the public, in ways the Founding Fathers never intended. Though intended for a general audience, the authors have appended a list of their primary and secondary sources. Index.

A pioneer study which explores the subject in less depth is James Pollard's **The Presidents and the Press** (New York: Macmillan, 1947. 566p.) which carried the story through Franklin Roosevelt, with a paperback supplement updating it to Truman.

425

Tehranian, Majid. **Socio-Economic and Communication Indicators in Development Planning: A Case Study of Iran**. Paris: UNESCO, 1980(?). 126p. (Communication and Society No. 5)

This case study of Iran focuses on those indicators crucial to an understanding of an evolving communication system. These include environmental factors such as population, geography, history, and legal and social systems; data on national development objectives, resources and technologies; communication structures—the press, broadcasting, printing and publishing, film, advertising, telecommunications, theater, tapes and records, libraries and documentation centers, data publication, and storage and retrieval systems; and communication policies for gathering, processing and distributing information. Organized at a time of revolutionary change in Iran, it focuses primarily on the pre-revolutionary period and includes only brief references to the major post-revolution developments. There are numerous statistics and a bibliography.

426

Thomas, Sari, ed. **Studies in Mass Communication & Technology**. Norwood, NJ: Ablex, 1984. 278p. (International Conference on Culture and Communication, v.1)

An anthology which explores both structural (institutional and artifactual) and systemic (behavioral) functions of mass communication and related technological issues. In five parts: Part I "International Communication," Part 2 "Institutions," Part 3 "Mass Media Content," Part 4 "Behavior and Acculturation," Part 5 "Technology." References follow each article. Author and subject indexes.

427

Thomson, James C., Jr. **Journalistic Ethics: Some Probings by a Media Keeper**. Bloomington, IN: The Poynter Center, Indiana University, 1978. 15p.

Report of a brief but penetrating talk in which the author, who calls himself "a Curator or Keeper of journalists" at Harvard's Nieman Center, points out the power journalism has attained today as a profession and some of the self-doubts on the part of journalists which have resulted as journalists have assumed the responsibilities involved. Appendixes give the "Code of Ethics or Canons of Journalism" (1923), the American Society of Newspaper Editors' "A Statement of Principles" (1975); and Sigma Delta Chi's "Code of Ethics" (1973).

428

Training for Mass Communication. Paris: UNESCO, 1975. 44p. (Reports and Papers on Mass Communication No. 73)

A highly practical report, intended for developing countries, which surveys in general terms the status of communication training, pinpointing deficiencies and identifying potentially influential trends. Discusses the nature of training, the institutions, the operational problems, and course planning and curriculum. Appendixes include "A Program for Action"; "Module Specification Sheet"; and "ETV Training Modules."

429

The Training of Journalists: A World-wide Survey on the Training of Personnel for the Mass Media. New York: UNESCO Publications Center, 1958. 222p. (Press, Film, and Radio in the World Today)

Gives training programs for journalists in 21 countries and contains discussions of UNESCO's role in jour-

nalism education and a series of eight articles by authorities on various aspects of journalism training, including a comparative analysis of curricula trends. Useful both historically and for comparison with present day trends.

430

Troyna, Barry. **Public Awareness and the Media: A Study of Reporting on Race**. London: Commission for Racial Equality, 1981. 95p.

An analysis of the presentation of race-related material in local British media, particularly radio and the evening paper—its amount, prominence and content. The research also involves a survey of the nature and sources of racial beliefs, and the political sympathies of a sample of the white adult population. An earlier and longer study is **Racism and the Mass Media** by Paul Hartmann and Charles Husband (No. 182).

431

Tuchman, Gaye, Arlene Kaplan Daniels, and James Benet. **Hearth and Home: Images of Women in the Mass Media**. New York: Oxford University Press, 1978. 333p.

"Many question of just how the media do construct their messages and why they do it that way (e.g., what is really newsworthy?) are not yet answered," say the editors in their *Preface*. This collection examines treatment of women on television, in women's magazines, on women's pages of newspapers, and television's effect on sex-typing in children and youths. The studies and essays not only are informative but also provide models for further work. Includes an annotated bibliography by Helen Franzwa, "The Image of Women in Television." Indexed.

432

Tuchman, Gaye. **Making News: A Study in the Construction of Reality**. New York: Free Press, 1978. 244p.

Tuchman argues that news media set the context in which citizens discuss public issues; that news has an even greater impact upon policy makers and politicians than upon ordinary readers; and that it is created by interchange among politicians and policy makers, newsworkers, and their organizational superiors. Through her own observations and through the research of other social scientists she presents concrete descriptions, examples, and analyses of newswork. Notes and index.

433

Tunstall, Jeremy. **Journalists at Work**. London: Constable, 1971. 304p.

Tunstall's concern is with the journalist who specializes in a subject field. For his research he has collected data from the approximately 200 full-time specialists employed by the 23 general news organizations at the national level in Britain in the fields of politics (lobbying), aviation, education, labor, crime, football, fashion and motoring. Also included are foreign correspondents working for London news organizations and stationed in Bonn, Rome, New York and Washington. Using this data Tunstall systematically investigates specialist newsgatherers at work and compares specialists from different fields of news, examining their roles as employee, as newsgatherer, and as competitor/colleague. His book is aimed first at sociologists, secondly at journalists themselves and other communicators, and thirdly at a wider audience, especially those people from other areas of work who in some fashion have a connection with journalism. Chapter references, bibliography, an appendix on methods, and an index.

434

Tunstall, Jeremy, ed. **Media Sociology**. Urbana: University of Illinois Press, 1970. 574p.

Anthology of 25 essays intended for students taking introductory courses dealing with the media, which in this anthology include newspapers, magazines, radio, records, television, and books. Although intended primarily for British students, articles by and about the American media are included. Contains a section citing "Notes and Sources" on which the articles are based, a bibliography, and name and subject indexes.

435, 436

Tunstall, Jeremy. **The Media Are American: Anglo-American Media in the World**. New York: Columbia University Press, 1977. 352p.

Tunstall, Jeremy. **The Media in Britain**. New York: Columbia University Press, 1983. 304p.

As its title indicates, Tunstall's theme in **The Media Are American** is cultural imperialism. To quote him: "This book covers a lot of media, a big time span and most of the world's larger countries. . . . The main thesis is mainly at the beginning and the end, while particular countries come in the middle." Among countries he discusses are the British Commonwealth and ex-Commonwealth, which includes India and portions of Africa; Italy; Germany; France; Japan; the Communist countries; the Arab countries; the Middle East; Latin America; and of course the U.S. The big question he poses: Can countries, especially developing ones, find other forms and content for their media more suited to their culture than the form and content of ours? He also goes into detail about the structure of the present system from the standpoint of economics and distribution. There are a number of tables, an extensive bibliography, and an index.

The Media in Britain is a survey of the main books, official reports, and unpublished surveys and research studies concerning British film, television, radio, newspapers and magazines which gives facts but goes beyond them into a critical examination of policy—past, present and possible future. The period covered is primarily between 1945 and 1953, with occasional backward glances

at the 1930s or even earlier, along with some forward glances. Tunstall is not afraid to be critical. "The book is also deliberately opinionated," he says as he explores myths and exposes errors with common sense and high style.

There are numerous charts and tables throughout, and much economic information. The evaluative bibliography, too, merits special consideration. There are also chapter notes and references and a detailed index.

437

Turow, Joseph. **Media Industries: The Production of News and Entertainment**. New York: Longman, 1984. 213p.

How is the content of the mass media decided and produced? Who wields the power and control, and why? Turow analyzes these questions by examining the industrial and organizational processes through which power and control are exercised on a range of mass media industries including newspapers, books, television, movies, records, video cassettes and even billboards. The conclusions involve such facets as finance and support, distribution and exhibition, government regulation, public advocacy groups, personnel policies, and day-to-day nitty gritty—to name some of the complex factors involved. Chapter notes, bibliography of books and articles, and index.

438

Ughoajah, Frank Okwu, ed. **Mass Communication, Culture and Society in West Africa**. New York: Hans Zell, 1985. 329p.

A collection of 26 papers, about two-thirds of which are by West Africans, designed to put the development of mass communication into a cultural and historical overview of the development of the region, which includes Nigeria, Liberia, Ghana, the Ivory Coast and Senegal. Among the subjects are ownership and control, the New World Information and Communication Order, cultural programs and language use in the media, professionalism, information diffusion, media use, and the trend of mass communication research. Among the essays is an extensive bibliographic essay containing several hundred items. Each article contains references.

439

Ullmann, John, and Steve Honeyman, eds. **The Reporter's Handbook: An Investigator's Guide to Documents and Techniques**. New York: St. Martin's Press for Investigative Reporters & Editors, Inc. (IRE), 1983. 504p.

A unique handbook for reporters, this maps out "paper trails" to follow when a reporter is researching an investigative project. The 16 chapters cover the most common areas of paperwork pursued by investigative reporters. Although information centers on documents and other paper sources, such reporting techniques as interviews and legwork are included in each chapter. A few details from the first chapter illustrate the unusual approach of this handbook: "How to Organize the Paper," "What to Do After the Tip," "Using Telephone Records," "Keeping Tabs On an Elected Official." Included in the details of the chapter are explanations about using bank credit card payments, campaign contribution reports, planning and zoning records, business licenses and applications, and audit reports, local and federal.

440

Variety: Major U.S. Showbusiness Awards. Ed. by Mike Kaplan. New York: Garland, 1982. 571p.

Covers the five major show business awards—Oscars, Emmys, Tonys, Grammys, and Pulitzer Prize Plays—and every individual category within these awards in chronological order from inception through December 1981. A separate section is devoted to each award. A master index lists all winners and nominees.

441

Viet, Jean. **Thesaurus: Mass Communication**. Paris: UNESCO, 1975. 2 parts. 158p, 58p.

This multilingual thesaurus in English, French, and Spanish provides a "documentation language" developed at the request of the Division of Communication Research and Planning of UNESCO. Precise terms designed to be used in post-storage retrieval of computerized documents are consistent with international documentation systems in related fields. The first part is a subject arrangement; the second part, an alphabetical listing.

442

Wade, Graham. **Film, Video and Television: Market Forces, Fragmentation and Technological Advance**. London: Comedia, 1985. 77p. (Comedia's Media and Communications Industry Profile)

A look at the operating dynamics of the film, video and television industries in Britain by a freelance journalist specializing in the mass media, who examines their histories in order to explore the present and predict the future of public service broadcasting, the new surge of film production, the rise of independent facilities and production companies, and the phenomenal spread of the domestic video recorder. He has also made case of studies of some of the UK's prominent companies. A final section, "Forward View: The Privatization of Entertainment and Information," deals with things to come. Two appendixes: lists of "Useful Organizations" and "Useful Publications."

443

Wasserman, Steven R., ed. **The Lively Arts Information Directory: A Guide to the Fields of Music, Dance, Theatre, Film, Radio and Television, for the United States and Canada, Covering National, International, State and** **Regional Organizations, Government Grant Sources, Foundations, Consultant Special Libraries, Research and Information Centers, Education Programs, Journals and Periodical Festivals and Awards**. Detroit, MI: Gale, 1982. 846p.

A comprehensive guide to the lively arts which "provides factual information on more than 6,700 organizations, agencies, associations, programs, publications, institutions, government activities, and other services and facilities." Divided into sections, with each varied in format and arrangement to suit the subject and separately indexed.

444

Watson, James, and Anne Hill. **A Dictionary of Communication and Media Studies**. London: Edward Arnold, 1984. 183p.

Although the authors have designed this dictionary primarily for British students in media studies, their criteria is so broad and wide-ranging that it should have much wider use. Some examples from architecture, psychology, language, theater and sociology are included. Many of the definitions are quite lengthy; all are clear and to the point.

445

Weaver, David H., and G. Cleveland Wilhoit. **The American Journalist: A Portrait of U.S. News People and Their Work**. Bloomington: Indiana University Press, 1986. 216p.

Today a wealth of literature exists on news—its infrastructure, its effects, its role in American society. But very little exists on journalists and journalism as a profession. Until now the only research was done in the early 1970s—**The News People: A Sociological Portrait of American Journalists and Their Work** (1976) by Johnstone, Slawski, and Bowman (No. 219), which provided baseline information on their demography, education, job situation, and professional attitudes. Weaver and Wilhoit have updated Johnstone, et al., gathering new data for comparison of backgrounds, work situations, and professional attitudes with those in the earlier study, and in addition covering some new territory, such as technology, values and ethics. Information was compiled from a survey research involving over 1,000 journalists; appendixes give a detailed account of the methodology and the questionnaire. Contains notes, a bibliography and an index. Winner of the Sigma Delta Chi Award for Research in 1986.

446

Webster, Frank, and Kevin Robins. **Information Technology: A Luddite Analysis**. Norwood, NJ: Ablex, 1986. 387p.

Luddism, say the authors, has been much abused both as a movement and as a pejorative term. Defining it as a well-organized, well-disciplined attempt of working people to exert some control over changes that were felt to be fundamentally against their interests, they analyze the present-day "microelectronics revolution" in this light as part of a social process which should not be opposed per se, but rather should be examined in terms of values and choices. In three parts: "Conceptualizations of Information Technology," "The Social Contexts of Information Technology," and "The 'Information Revolution': From Taylorism to Neo-Fordism." A special feature is the array of apt quotes from various sources which introduce each chapter and are too good not to be mentioned. Chapter notes, an impressive bibliography, and author and subject indexes.

447

Weibel, Kathryn. **Mirror, Mirror: Images of Women Reflected in Popular Culture**. New York: Anchor (Doubleday), 1977. 256p.

From a historical perspective Weibel examines the portrayal of women over time in fiction, television, movies, women's magazines and magazine advertising, and in fashions, dealing with their images within the context of their creators and in the broader cultural context of the times. In an interesting Epilogue she concludes that when men control the media they create women as passive, whereas when women are in control, they create them in more active and forceful roles. Notes and index.

448

Welch, David, ed. **Nazi Propaganda: The Power and the Limitations**. London: Croom Helm, 1983. 228p.

"Propaganda, propaganda, propaganda. All that matters is propaganda," Hitler is quoted as saying. Here authorities make a detailed examination of Nazi manipulation of the media in terms of theory, practice and effectiveness, giving examples of specific programs not only in Germany but also in the occupied countries. Even Hitler's use of architecture is discussed. Footnotes, glossary and bibliography.

449

Whale, John. **Journalism and Government: A British View**. Columbia: University of South Carolina Press, 1972. 113p.

"Journalists," says Whale, "are stewards of the word" even though they find it is difficult to live up to the stewardship. Here Whale gives reasons, as well as the importance of journalists to society as interpreters of events and their shortcomings and those of society. Although his remarks are aimed specifically at Britain they are universally applicable.

450

Whale, John. **The Politics of the Media**. Manchester, England: Manchester University Press, 1977. 176p.

This is a thoughtful examination of the delicate balance maintained by the state, the proprietors, the unions, the advertisers and the law as each in its way influences journalism in Britain. Whale's writing in this and in his other works is notable for its clarity of style and elegant turn of phrase as well as for its incisive content.

451

Whetmore, Edward Jay. **Mediamerica: Form, Content, and Consequence of Mass Communication**. 3d ed. Belmont, CA: Wadsworth, 1985. 374p.

An undergraduate text in three parts: "Print: The Gutenberg Galaxy," "Electronic Media: Edison Came to Stay," and "Beyond the Media: The Phenomena of Mass Communication." Whetmore touches—of necessity lightly—on books, newspapers, magazines, radio, recordings, television, film, advertising and public relations, popular culture, international mass communications, and mass communication research, and the new technologies which include satellites, computers, and home video. He backgrounds the history and current status of each medium, along with well-known examples of their products, from the traditional **New York Times** to the sensational **National Enquirer**. Throughout there is emphasis on today's popular culture and its good and less good offshoots. Chapter headings are catchy and euphonious—"Magazines: A Mass Menagerie" and "Sunset and Scenarios: Film as Popular Art." Whetmore writes simply (sometimes too simply) and covers a large territory. His text should give beginners food for thought, pleasantly presented. Index. (Revised editions issued in 1987 and 1989.)

452

White, Llewellyn, and Robert D. Leigh. **Peoples Speaking to Peoples: A Report on International Mass Communication from the Commission on Freedom of the Press**. Chicago: University of Chicago Press, 1946. 122p.

A detailed analysis of the means by which information, especially news, is gathered, controlled, and distributed internationally. Source notes.

453, 454, 455

Williams, Francis. **Dangerous Estate: The Anatomy of Newspapers**. London: Longmans, 1957. 304p.

Williams, Francis. **The Right to Know: The Rise of the World Press**. London: Longmans, 1969. 336p.

Williams, Francis. **Transmitting World News: A Study of Telecommunications and the Press**. New York: Arno, c1953, 1972. 95p.

In these studies of various aspects of the press, Williams always places it in a broad context. **Dangerous**

Estate shows the social role of newspapers, past and present, with press history woven around the issues of society as they affect and are affected by the papers of the time and by the men responsible for them. **The Right to Know** treats the media as barometers of time and geography, assuming various shapes in various countries. Here Williams shows the switch from political control to business orientation in certain parts of the world; the growth of radio; the place of TV; the press in the new nations; and public interest and commercial ownership. **Transmitting World News** investigates the system of rates and priorities as well as other technical factors affecting the dispatch of press messages. Although Williams discusses the physical means of news transmission, he goes beyond this to show the human elements: the competence, integrity, and judgment of those who collect and distribute news, and the readiness of governments and peoples to allow or forbid objective reporting. He also takes cost factors and availability of newsprint into account.

456

Williams, Frederick. **The Communications Revolution**. Beverly Hills, CA: Sage, 1982. 291p.

Among the many forces in the contemporary world that are changing our total environment are the communications technologies which, although not a sole cause, are catalysts or intensifiers. Here Williams explores the impact and its consequences. In the first section, "The Communications Explosion," he points out the frightening rate of acceleration as the explosion creates a living and working environment that is artifactual and electronic. In the second section, "The Electronic Environment," he dissects its components, and in the third, "Living in the Communications Future," he explores the impact of the new technologies in such traditional areas of our lives as leisure, transportation, health, politics, work, and education. Throughout, he points out the differences between "muddled" change and "managed" change, and opts for the latter. References and index.

457

Williams, Raymond. **Communications**. Rev. ed. London: Chatto & Windus, 1966. 196p.

This book first appeared in 1962 as a part of Penguin's Britain in the Sixties series. Its contents, however, have a much broader application than a given country or decade, and summarize much of Williams's philosophy of communication, which he defines in broad terms of social and cultural policy. His approach is basically Marxist, although in no party sense. From this vantage point he examines the history and content of the various media, and differing ideas about mass and class culture. He concludes with a chapter on proposals which relates more directly to England than the rest of the book. There is a

bibliography, "Further Reading," and two appendixes: "Methods in TV Education" and "A Policy for the Arts."

458

Williams, Raymond, ed. **Contact: Human Communication and Its History**. New York: Thames and Hudson, 1981. 272p.

In his organization for this intellectual coffee-table style book which serves as a fascinating introduction to communication, Williams takes a long view beginning with language and ending with "The Electronic Cornucopia." In between are sections on non-verbal communication; signs and symbols; alphabets, writing and printing; sounds and images; and communications technologies and social institutions. Authors of the articles are Ferruccio Rossi-Landi and Massimo Pesaresi, Robyn Penman, Donis A. Dondis, Jack Goody, Henri-Jean Martin, Ithiel de Sola Pool, Garth Jowett, Ederyn Williams and Raymond Williams. Illustrations are numerous, beautiful, and colorful. Each article has its own bibliography. Index.

459, 460

Williams, Raymond. **Culture and Society, 1780–1950**. New York: Columbia University Press, 1958. 363p.

Williams, Raymond. **The Long Revolution**. Westport, CT: Greenwood, c1961, 1975. 396p.

"The organizing principle of this book is the discovery that the idea of culture, and the word itself in its general modern uses, came into English thinking in the period which we commonly describe as that of the Industrial Revolution. The book is an attempt to show how and why this happened, and to follow the idea through to our own day. It thus becomes an account and an interpretation of our responses in thought and feeling to the changes in English society since the late eighteenth century. Only in such a context can our use of the word **culture**, and the issues to which the word refers, be adequately understood," explains Williams of **Culture and Society**, in which he pursues this thesis in terms of the novelists, the economic and political philosophers, and the critics of the nineteenth and twentieth centuries.

He follows this with **The Long Revolution**, in which he further examines factors which have shaped culture, with particular emphasis on the Industrial Revolution in relation to print media. The first part of the book deals with the nature of the creative mind, and with culture and society in general. The second part is concerned with education, the reading public, the popular press, the novel, and writers. The third part surveys the 1960s.

Although Williams's orientation is British throughout both books, his analyses are universal. A Penguin edition of **The Long Revolution** appeared in 1965 with a few revisions and amendments, and added notes. Both books have reading lists and indexes.

461

Wilson, Clint C., II, and Félix Gutiérrez. **Minorities and Media: Diversity and the End of Mass Communication**. Beverly Hills, CA: Sage, 1985. 247p.

When the co-authors, a black and a Latino, went looking for work in the news media in the 1960s they found jobs virtually closed to non-whites. This book which examines the relationships between mass communications media and the four largest racial minority groups—native Americans, blacks, Latinos and Asians—was inspired by experience. The major portion is concerned with portrayal and activism—portrayal, past and present, by the press and in movies, television, and advertising; and activism of several sorts used as a means to gain access. The conclusion suggests a media mosaic more diverse than in the past. Each of the five chapters contain notes and a list of suggested readings.

462

Wimmer, Roger D., and Joseph R. Dominick. **Mass Media Research: An Introduction**. Belmont, CA: Wadsworth, 1983. 397p.

Designed for beginning mass media research courses, this text concentrates entirely on statistical methodology. In five parts: "The Research Process," "Research Approaches," "Basic Statistics," "Research Applications," and "Analyzing and Reporting Data." Each chapter concludes with problems and questions for further consideration. An appendix of tables and a glossary appear at the end of the book. A revision will appear in 1987. Name index and subject index.

463

Windschuttle, Keith. **The Media: A New Analysis of the Press, Television, Radio and Advertising in Australia**. Ringwood, Victoria, Australia: Penguin, 1985. 436p.

In his discussion of Australian media, which is also pertinent to the media in other countries and other cultures, Windschuttle rejects arguments that the media are dominated by market forces, designed to "give the people what they want," or contrarily that they are primarily instruments of domination rather than communication. Nor does he believe that the traditional literary concepts of "high culture" are appropriate for the study and criticism of the popular culture of the media. His own argument is that they should be seen as an arena of conflict between social classes, and that economics establish a framework within which relatively independent cultural factors are played out. In three sections: "Political Economy," "Culture," and "Hegemony." In the third section he supports his class-based conflict theory as opposed to American structural functionalism of the 1950s and 1960s, and French structural Marxism

of the 1970s. Whenever possible he has used concrete evidence and examples to make his point and has avoided jargon and arcane terminology. Chapter notes and index.

464

Winston, Brian. **Misunderstanding Media**. London: Routledge and Kegan Paul, 1986. 419p.

"The information revolution is an illusion, a rhetorical gambit, an expression of profound ignorance, a movement dedicated to purveying misunderstanding and disseminating disinformation," says Winston in this stimulating and provocative thesis in which he uses television, telephones, the computer and satellites to make a case that the more things change the more they stay the same; despite our so-called information revolution the major institutions which underpin technology remain unchanged. His orientation is historical; to make his point, he draws heavily on the history of technology placed within the context of social history. This is most interesting reading, not only because of Winston's challenge to prevailing wisdom but also because of the scope of his knowledge and the sparkle of his style. Chapter notes and index.

465

Wolfe, Tom, and E. W. Johnson, eds. **The New Journalism, with an Anthology**. New York: Harper & Row, 1973. 394p.

Although, as Wolfe says in his article, he was not the founder of the "new journalism"—that daring and unconventional type of feature reporting which broke with time-honored journalistic conventions in the 1960s—his name has become synonymous with it. In the first 53 pages of this anthology he describes what exactly it is and how it came to be. The rest of the anthology is devoted to examples by some of its outstanding practitioners.

466

Wolfson, Lewis W. **The Untapped Power of the Press: Explaining Government to the People**. New York: Praeger, 1985. 202p.

Wolfson pulls no punches in this analytical examination of government coverage and press-official relations. Component by component he discusses the Presidency, Congress, the Judiciary, the Federal regulatory agencies, the agencies which control access to information, state and local agencies, and press coverage of political events and elections. The press, he feels, should do a better job of covering government and likewise government should do a better job in dealing with the press. In conclusion he makes recommendations for both. Bibliography of sources and index.

Wolseley, Roland E., and Isabel Wolseley. **The Journalist's Bookshelf**. (See No. 1708)

467

World Communication Facts: A Handbook Prepared for the International Conference on World Communications: Decisions For The 80's. Comp. by Richard Jay Solomon. Philadelphia: Annenberg School of Communications, University of Pennsylvania, 1980. 33p.

A fund of information about mass communications, in which facts and figures tersely are presented by means of graphs and charts and selected data about the world's human resources; the uses and users of the media; the information business, including its impingement upon other businesses; material resources and their limitations; person to person communications as represented by transportation, migration and tourism; and barriers and opportunities in communications technology. Sources for data are always included, and there is a brief but excellent bibliography and an index.

468

World Directory of Mass Communication Researchers. Comp. by Walery Pisarek, et al. Cracow, Poland: International Association for Mass Communication Research, Bibliographic Section, 1984. 300p.

The objective of this directory, conceived at a meeting of the Bibliographic Section of the International Association for Mass Communication Research, is "to facilitate and increase interpersonal contacts between individual researchers interested in the same problems in various countries of the world," with data based on replies to questionnaires sent to members of the IAMCR, to individual members of other international and national organizations involved in mass communication research, and to university mass communication programs and institutes.

The project was ambitious, and results were disappointing. Many researchers did not reply; some who did wrote illegibly; and translation from a dozen languages into English proved difficult. For these reasons the compilers consider this a draft version rather than a first edition. Information requested includes name, address, telephone number, biographical data, research interests, memberships, and chief publications. Not all this information was always provided, and in some cases where it was the editors were forced to cut. As they themselves acknowledge, the results leave a lot to be desired. Nevertheless it is an ambitious beginning and the only one of its kind.

469

Wright, Charles R. **Mass Communication: A Sociological Perspective**. 3d ed. New York: Random House, 1986. 223p.

This time-honored text, first published in 1959, is one of the best in the field. It gathers together a number of recent and "classic" sociological studies of mass communication that deal with important research problems and groups them under ten headings: "Nature and Function of Mass Communication," "Mass Communications as Social Institutions," "Sociology of the Mass Communicator," "Sociology of the Audience: Interpersonal Communication and the Mass Audience," "Sociology of the Audience: Selected Characteristics of Audience and Communication Behavior," "Cultural Content of American Mass Communication," "Social Consequences of Mass Communication: Studies of News and Mass Persuasion," "Social Consequences of Mass Communication: Public Concern Over Mass Entertainment," "Social Consequences of Mass Communication: Mass Communication and Socialization," and "The Social Impact of the Communication Technology." Footnotes, "Additional Selected Readings," name index and subject index.

Broadcasting Media

Abundo, Romeo B. **Print and Broadcast Media in the South Pacific**. (See No. 849.)

470

Adams, William C. **Television Coverage of the Middle East**. Norwood, NJ: Ablex, 1981. 167p.

Eight previously unpublished studies which examine patterns of coverage and summarize attitudinal findings. The first chapter is a summary of content findings in later chapters, with more detailed discussion of coverage of Afghanistan and Iran; the next five chapters center upon Israel and Arab nations; the two final chapters deal with the coverage of the Soviet occupation of Afghanistan and the big news story of 1980—the seizure of American hostages by Iran. References follow each chapter. Short subject index and a name index.

471

Adams, William C., ed. **Television Coverage of International Affairs**. Norwood, NJ: Ablex, 1982. 253p.

How adequately and fairly does U.S. television treat foreign news? This issue is addressed in 13 content analyses grouped in five parts: "Global Coverage," "Third World," "The West and Presidential Diplomacy," "Southeast Asia," and "Audience." The contributors also survey pertinent literature. Bibliographic information is repeated with complete entries following each chapter. Index.

472

Adams, William, and Fay Schreibman, eds. **Television Network News**. Washington: George Washington University, School of Public and International Affairs, 1978. 231p.

Brings together from a variety of disciplines discussions of some of the more important issues in the study of network news content. The three areas emphasized are the status of existing research, methodological issues, and future directions of research.

473

Adler, Richard and Walker S. Baer, eds. **The Electronic Box Office: Humanities and Arts on the Cable**, New York: Praeger and Aspen In-

stitute, 1974. 139p. (Sponsored by the Aspen Program in Communication and Society.)

A retrospective look at what was considered in the early seventies to be cable's potential for increasing the diversity and quality of television programming available to the public. Adler, Baer and Douglass Cater and other authorities give pros and cons such as the financial boost cable could lend the performing arts as opposed to the opposition it would probably meet from commercial broadcasters and theater owners, and specific FCC rules designed to keep off pay cable programs that might threaten them. Also discussed are unions, the economics of pay TV, experimental video groups and the danger that no "bold vision of what can be accomplished" will present itself or be accepted if it does. Economics are emphasized throughout. Indexed.

474

Aitken, Hugh G. J. **Origin and Spark—the Origins of Radio**. New York: Wiley, 1976. 347p.

An important technological/economic history of radio in which Aitken shows how the complex and particularly autonomous systems of science, technology and economics have interacted with one another and with various other elements in society to create it. Three of the six chapters deal with the work of Hertz, Lodge, and Marconi specifically. Though limiting himself to radio Aitken sheds light on creativity in general. In chapter notes he gives references to his many sources. Index.

475

Alexeyeva, Ludmilla. **U.S. Broadcasting to the Soviet Union**. New York and Washington, D.C.: U.S. Helsinki Watch Committee, 1986. 136p.

A commissioned report on the work of the Russian-language broadcasting services of Radio Liberty and the Voice of America by a former Soviet historian who was one of the founders of the Moscow Helsinki Watch Committee, emigrated to the U.S. and is now a consultant to the U.S. Helsinki Watch Committee. Contains an overview, a general background, a section of each of the services, general conclusions and two appendixes: "Russia Yesterday, Today and Tomorrow" and a discussion of "Religious Programs." The author's conclusions are highly critical of the organization and content of the programs. Footnotes.

476

Alfred I. Dupont-Columbia University Survey of Broadcast Journalism. Marvin Barrett, ed. 8 v. New York: Grosset & Dunlap, Vols. 1–2; Crowell, Vols. 4–6; Lippincott & Crowell, Vol. 7; Everest House, Vol. 8. (1969–1982.)

The aim of this series is to consider and critique broadcast news of the preceding twelve months—how TV and radio report the news; how they serve the public; and how they live with politicians, advertisers, and the FCC. Appraisals of the coverage of years that saw assassinations, student unrest, Vietnam, Watergate, Three Mile Island and similar events are a running commentary on the strengths and weaknesses of American journalism. Individual volumes in chronological order include:

Survey of Broadcast Journalism , 1968–1969. 132p.
Survey of Broadcast Journalism, 1969–1970: Year of Challenge, Year of Crisis. 159p.
Survey of Broadcast Journalism, 1970–1971. A State of Seige. 183p.
Survey of Broadcast Journalism, 1971–1972. The Politics of Broadcasting. 247p.
Survey of Broadcast Journalism: Moments of Truth. 1975. 274p.
Survey of Broadcast Journalism: Rich News, Poor News. 1978. 244p.
Survey of Broadcast Journalism: The Eye of the Storm. 1980. 240p.
Survey of Broadcast Journalism: Broadcast Journalism 1979–1981. 1982. 256p.

The first five volumes are edited by Barrett; the sixth and seventh are written by him—the seventh coauthored with Zachary Sklar; the eighth is written by Barrett. No more volumes are planned, but educational materials may be issued in the future in the form of video cassettes.

477

Allard, T.J. **The C.A.B. Story 1926–1976: Private Broadcasting in Canada**. Ottawa: Canadian Association of Broadcasters, 1976. 68p.

A commemorative booklet, published by the Canadian Association of Broadcasters on its 50th anniversary telling the history of the organization of stations existing outside of the framework of nationalization. Appendixes give officers and officials of the C.A.B. for the years covered, and a summary of structural changes in the Board of Directors. There is also brief biographical material on C.A.B. presidents and chairmen.

478

Allen, Robert C. **Speaking of Soap Operas**. Chapel Hill: University of North Carolina Press, 1985. 245p.

Allen has two goals: the first, to examine American

soap opera as a narrative form, cultural product, advertising vehicle, and source of aesthetic pleasure to an enormous audience; the second, to demonstrate how soap operas and their audiences have been and might be studied, and by extension, how other types of broadcast programming might be examined. In pursuing the first aim he discusses, among other aspects, the origins of soaps, their fictive world, their method of production, their tremendous popularity, and their enormous and diverse audience. In pursuing the second aim he says, "my goal is polemical. I join those who argue for a thorough reassessment of the manner in which traditional mass communications research in the United States has attempted to 'explain' the complex relationship between viewers and fictional programming and for a reconsideration of the consequences of forty years of domination by a single research paradigm upon the current state of 'knowledge' about television and radio programming and viewing." He himself has used critical methods drawn from the study of literature and film, and he explains in detail why he does not hold with exclusively quantitative analysis. As a whole this book is important not only for its findings about soap opera but also for the questions it raises about mass communication methodology in the United States. Bibliography and index.

479

Altheide, David L. **Creating Reality: How TV News Distorts Events**. Beverly Hills, CA: Sage, 1976. 220p.

In the belief that the nightly newscasts are distorting what they claim to represent, the author has as his aim "to clarify how the news process works in order to improve certain inadequacies." Many of his points, he feels, can also be applied to print journalism. He looks particularly at the organization of news which carries a built-in bias that simplifies events. This he traces through its roots in commercialism, scheduling, technology, and competition, offering partial solutions and suggesting ways for the viewer to interpret what he sees on the screen.

The American Film Institute Guide to College Courses in Film and Television. (See No. 1133.)

480

Anderson, Kent. **Television Fraud: The History and Implications of the Quiz Show Scandals**. Westport, CT: Greenwood, 1978. 228p.

The $64,000 Question, television's first big-money quiz show back in the 1950's, is forgotten today by older generations and unknown to younger ones. But in its days its popularity was immense, and the revelation of the fraud behind it rocked the public. Anderson tells the story and places it in the context of commercial television and of popular culture in America—the use of leisure, the manipulation of technology, the philosophies of Protestant (or capitalist) work ethic, upward mobility, and self-help. Chapter notes, appendixes giving some of the documents, a bibliography, and an index.

481

Ang, Ien. **Watching Dallas: Soap Opera and the Melodramatic Imagination**. Tr. from the Dutch by Dalla Couling. London: Methuen, 1985. 148p.

What gives **Dallas** its worldwide popularity? In a study that is both lively and scholarly, Ang takes as a starting point for her investigation letters to her from viewers telling why they liked or disliked the program. Drawing on methods from psychology and semiotics, she analyzes both their reactions and the serial itself in terms of the melodramatic imagination, the ideology of mass culture, and the place of women in contemporary society. Notes and index.

482

Anwar, Muhammad, and Anthony Shag. **Television in a Multi-racial Society: A Research Report**. London: Commission for Racial Equality, 1982. 84p.

An analysis of the number and type of ethnic minority appearances in sample television output and of the opportunities for employment of ethnic minorities, along with attitudes and practices of producers and others in control of programming. Contains numerous statistical tables and "Notes and References."

483, 484, 485, 486

Arlen, Michael J. **The Camera Age: Essays on Television**. New York: Farrar, Straus & Giroux, 1981. 337p.

Arlen, Michael J. **Living-Room War**. New York: Viking, 1969. 242p.

Arlen, Michael J. **Thirty Seconds**. New York: Farrar, Straus & Giroux, 1980. 211p.

Arlen, Michael J. **The View from Highway 1**. New York: Farrar, Straus & Giroux, 1976. 293p.

Michael Arlen, who regularly contributes about television to the **New Yorker**, has the ability to put his critiques into a larger and penetrating context. **The Camera Age, Living-Room War**, and **The View from Highway 1** are compilations of essays first published there. In a wry, readable, half-humorous way that sometimes employs short story techniques, he discusses specific programs and genres, or sometimes more general aspects of American television, which he feels as a whole to be rather sorry. Whatever his approach, he leaves the reader with a broader understanding of TV and its role in American society.

Thirty Seconds, which also appeared in the **New Yorker**, is different. It is a case history of the making of one of the Bell Telephone commercials which has as a theme, "Reach Out and Touch Someone." Narrating the process chronologically and without personal comments, he follows from casting to conclusion, providing a penetrating insight into the sort of thinking—and money—behind the creation of commercials.

487

Armstrong, Ben. **The Electronic Church**. Nashville, TN: Thomas Nelson, 1979. 192p.

Armstrong, executive director of National Religious Broadcasters which establishes standards for religious stations and program producers and represents three-fourths of U.S. religious broadcasting, highlights ministries representative of specific trends and discusses pros and cons of broadcast religion, with his evaluations heavily weighted toward the pros, as might be expected. His book provides a broad general description of the audience type and the reasons for its appeal, as well as his theory of why liberal churches which use traditional methods to spread their message have their doubts and fears of the evangelical broadcasters. He also goes into fund raising. Appendixes give "The NRB Code of Ethics," "Principles and Guidelines for Fund-Raising, Accounting, and Financial Reporting by Christian Organizations," and a list of "Awards and Honors." Chapter notes.

Aterton, F. Christopher. **Media Politics: The News Strategies of Presidential Campaigns**. (See No. 12.)

BBC Annual Report and Handbook. (See No. 1720.)

488

Baggaley, Jon, and Steve Duck. **Dynamics of Television**. Farnborough, Hants, England; Lexington, MA: Saxon House, 1976. 180p.

Believing that our concern with research centered upon "mass" communication with emphasis upon content is the wrong approach, the authors advocate an "analysis of the effects upon the individual that stem from the conventions and forms of a medium as opposed to its declared content—forces which affect the individual's processes of cognition and social judgment." From this perspective they analyze television as a medium—its imagery, its persuasiveness, its power to teach, its control. Since their analyses are based on a number of studies, the book is an excellent source of review for the empirical literature in the field. There are long lists of references at the end of every chapter. Indexed.

489

Baldwin, Thomas E., and D. Stevens McVoy. **Cable Communication**. Englewood Cliffs, NJ: Prentice-Hall, 1983. 416p.

"This book is written for all those who have a need or a desire to learn about the cable communications industry," say the authors, who enumerate possible users from college students to professionals seeking a single source of information about all aspects of cable, to citizens and government officials who have become involved, to program producers, to the general public. It is encyclopedic in its scope, including technology, services, public policy, organization and operations, and a glimpse into cable's future. Appendixes give specific examples of franchise proposals, public access and community channel rules, and instructions about procedure for assessment of communication needs. The National League of Cities Code of Good Cable Television Franchising Conduct are also included. Indexed. A new edition was published in 1988.

490

Ball-Rokeach, Sandra, Milton Rokeach, and Joel W. Grube. **The Great American Values Test: Influencing Behavior and Belief Through Television**. New York: Free Press, 1984. 190p.

A study which brings together mass media and social psychology researchers to address two main theoretical issues—who uses the mass media, why, and with what effects and under what conditions will people's important beliefs and behaviors undergo change, especially relatively enduring change? The authors set up an elaborate experiment in the form of a 30-minute television program revolving around the issues of racism, sexism and environmental pollution which a random sample of adults watched in the privacy of their homes, with effects checked by the researchers. Evidence of previous studies is reviewed, and results and methodology of this study are described at length, along with their methodological and ethical implications. References and index.

491, 492

Barcus, F. Earle, with Rachel Wolkin. **Children's Television: An Analysis of Programming and Advertising**. New York: Praeger, 1977. 218p.

Barcus, F. Earle. **Images of Life on Children's Television: Sex Roles, Minorities, and Families**. New York: Praeger, 1983. 217p.

Two content analyses. The first, **Children's Television: An Analysis of Programming and Advertising** made for Action for Children's Television, which includes descriptions of racial, cultural, and sexual representations; a measure of the incidence of aggressive behavior; and a breakdown of advertising themes and formats. Data is accompanied by an introduction and references to other studies, and interpretation of findings. An initial chapter explains methodology.

Basing **Images of Life on Children's Television** on the rationale that children learn from their environment and that today television is an important part of that environment, Barcus has conducted studies in which he analyzed a sample of nearly 50 hours of network and independent station programs for the child audience during a week in January 1981. The studies are in four parts: investigation of the programs as a whole and studies of sex-role behaviors of the characters, minority-character portrayals, and family and kinship relations. A major question is the extent to which television is reflecting traditional and changing patterns of family life. Each part concludes with a summary of pertinent research literature, and a substantial bibliography of further sources.

493

Barlow, Geoffrey, and Alison Hill, eds. **Video Violence and Children**. London: Hodder and Stoughton, 1985. 182p.

In 1983 an informal British Group of Parliamentarians and Churchmen promoted an academic research project to find out what videos children were seeing throughout the country. The result is a body of research on contents and effects which examines violence as a sociopsychological phenomenon and discusses television violence; findings from a National Viewers' Survey and a survey made by the National Society for the Prevention of Cruelty to Children; case studies by a group of psychiatrists; a pediatrician's survey; a report by educators; and in conclusion a pessimistic summary. Appendixes include the definition of a term used in England—'video nasty'—those videos on the list of the Director of Public Prosecutions, and several synopses of examples. Articles have references where pertinent. Index.

494, 495, 496

Barnouw, Erik. **A History of Broadcasting in the United States**. Vol. I. **To 1933: A Tower in Babel**. New York: Oxford University Press, 1966. 344p.

Barnouw, Erik. **A History of Broadcasting in the United States**. Vol. II. **1933–53: The Golden Web**. New York: Oxford University Press, 1968. 391p.

Barnouw, Erik. **A History of Broadcasting in the United States**. Vol. III. **From 1953: The Image Empire**. New York: Oxford University Press, 1970. 396p.

A chronological overview of American broadcasting which touches upon practically every major event, trend, and personality in its history. The author's style makes for good reading. Appendixes in each volume include a chronology in outline form, text of the major laws relating to broadcasting, an extensive bibliography, and an index by performer, program, and topic.

In 1978 Barnouw condensed the three volumes into one, which he updated, **The Tube of Plenty** (Oxford, 518p.). Like its predecessor, it "stresses the emergence of television as a dominant factor in American life and a component of American influence in many nations." Here, too, a chronology, bibliographical notes, and an index follow the text.

Barnouw, Erik. **The Sponsor: Notes on a Modern Potentate**. (See No. 1538.)

497

Baron, Mike. **Independent Radio: The Story of Commercial Radio in the United Kingdom.** Lavenham, Suffolk, England: Terence Dalton, 1975. 192p. (Sound Radio Series.)

A strictly factual history of Britain's independent radio from the early days of "wireless broadcasting" to the mid-seventies, with much attention to broadcasting politics. Also contains a map, history, and description of the 18 or so local stations. Appendixes list addresses, telephone numbers, and top personnel of the stations; addresses of associations; technical information about the various stations; and a discussion of the job market with emphasis on disc jockeys. Indexed.

498

Barr, Trevor. **The Electronic Estate: New Communications Media and Australia.** Ringwood, Victoria, Australia: Penguin, 1985. 271p.

Barr shows how the new technologies—the domestic satellite, videotex, cable television, electronic funds transfer, and microcomputers—are changing Australia's traditional publishing, broadcasting and communications industries. He points out their international connections which have political implications at home and abroad. "Endnotes," "A Select Bibliography," "Major Official Reports," and "Index."

499

Baruah, U.L. **This Is All India Radio: A Handbook of Radio Broadcasting in India.** New Delhi: Minister of Information and Broadcasting, Publications Division, 1983. 367p.

The author, a former Director-General of All India Radio, has provided an in-depth study of its history and development, an analysis of the organizational structure covering administration, engineering and personnel, and a detailed account of the program services including home, commercial and overseas broadcasts and developments in progress. Tables provide specific data on its various aspects. Index. (See also, Luthra, No. 697.)

500

Beck, Kirsten. **Cultivating the Wasteland: Can Cable Put the Vision Back in TV?** New York: American Council for the Arts, 1983. 249p.

Will cable save the arts? Beck found, not unexpectedly, that it wouldn't, but she also found that local cable companies held promise by putting television within the reach of regional arts through local origination channels and their policy of access. So this book, which was originally intended to explore national cultural cable services is instead about community prospects for cable and the arts. In it she discusses cable's basic technology (how signals get from here to there); the business side of a complicated industry and major considerations of people doing business with it; issues involved in programming, and in particular, the job of putting the arts on cable. A final chapter, "A Guide to Understanding Television Deals," is written by several lawyers who instruct those organizations creating or anticipating cable deals as to how they should proceed. Contains a list of cable trade and service organizations and a bibliography of books and periodicals.

501

Bell, Philip, Kathe Boehringer, and Stephen Crofts. **Programmed Politics: A Study of Australian Television.** Sydney: Sable Publishing, 1982. 164p.

A study on the representation of politics on Australian news and current affairs programs which concentrates particularly on the period prior to the 1980 Federal Election and analyzes certain well-known programs in the light of critical social theory. Contains "References" and index.

502

Belson, William A. **Television Violence and the Adolescent Boy.** Westmead, Farnborough, Hampshire, England: Saxon House, Teakfield, 1978. 529p.

Description and results of a study sponsored by Columbia Broadcasting System and carried out in England, in which Belson measured the effects on adolescent boys of exposure to TV violence. Findings lend support to the case for making major changes. Belson's methodology is interesting; he uses a naturalistic, or real-life, approach instead of a laboratory one. This is fully described.

503

Bennett, Tony, et al., eds. **Popular Television and Film.** London: BFI [British Film Institute]. Published in association with The Open University Press, 1981. 353p.

Readings, designed initially for use by Open University students for a popular culture course. Rather than emphasizing the structure of the broadcasting and film industry the editors have chosen to emphasize the structures of the texts which broadcasting institutions and the film industry circulate. The authors have applied the techniques of structuralist and semiological criticism, along with psychoanalysis, across a wide range of television programming and a smaller range of films. All share a common concern with the ideological and political significance of the areas of television programming and film practice with which they deal. Part I treats the various genres of television fiction; Part II, with types of television nonfiction; Part III, with entertainment as exemplified in popular film; and Part IV, with the treatment of history on television. Some of the articles contain chapter references. Index of names and titles.

504

Bergreen, Laurence. **Look Now, Pay Later.** New York: Doubleday, 1980. 300p.

A history of American broadcasting networks in the pre-cable period, which argues that the networks occupy a kind of Jekyl-Hyde universe that has "fed off programming, technology, local stations, and even government regulation," with the entrepreneur as king. Bergreen concludes that the networks represent both public trust and a private enterprise which has played a significant part in 20th-century social history. Much of his data comes from interviews with personalities who have helped shape the networks. A final chapter, "From Broadcasting to Narrowcasting," examines the future. Source notes, bibliography and index.

505

Berry, Gordon L., and Claudia Mitchell-Kernan, eds. **Television and the Socialization of the Minority Child.** New York: Academic Press, 1982. 289p.

These articles are intended to bridge the gap between the prolific general literature on television and social behavior and the increased examination social scientists are giving to special issues of minority-group socialization in a television-oriented society, with particular attention to Afro-Americans, American Indians, Asian Americans, and Hispanics. Part 1 provides a basic framework by focusing on concepts and theories about television and the socialization process; Part 2, on minority children and personal identity problems such as mental health, identity formation, and self-concept development; Part 3, on special socialization concerns for each ethnic group; Part 4, on questions related to the minority child, television, and selected research issues; and Part 5, on specific findings of available material for future study. Contributors from such fields as communication, education, linguistics, history, psychiatry, sociology, and the television industry bring a multidisciplinary approach. Notes and references following each essay, and there is a name and a subject index.

506

Beville, Hugh Malcolm, Jr. **Audience Ratings: Radio, Television, Cable.** Hillsdale, NJ: Erlbaum, 1985. 380p.

"I have been intimately involved in rating throughout a professional lifetime of over 50 years," says Beville, who joined NBC as a statistician in March 1930, the month when the first rating survey was conducted, and has continued to work on ratings systems in various capacities ever since. From this vantage point he documents the growth and research behind today's audience measurement infrastructure, with personal highlights of the early years and early pioneers. He traces the history of ratings through radio to television today, including cable; examines methodologies comparatively; discusses quantitative vs. qualitative ratings; tells how the data is used; explores the concept of ratings as both servant and master; and examines government intervention. In conclusion he sums up what has been learned in almost 55 years and looks at the future. Appendixes include "Ratings Basics: Terms, Calculations, and Relationships," "Offices and Services of Principal Syndicated Ratings Companies Operating on a National Basis," "Audience Measurement Highlights," "Significant Methodological Studies and Assessments." There is an extensive bibliography of books, articles, periodicals and reports, and an index.

507

Biryukov, N. S. **Television in the West and Its Doctrines.** Moscow: Progress Publishers, 1981. 207p.

"What is television like in the advanced capitalist countries today, what do its programmes show the audience? What stages did it go through in its evolution? How does it interact with other mass media and what is its organizational structure? And the main question: How does it serve the ideological interests of the ruling class, the big bourgeoisie, and what are its doctrines and methods?" Drawing mainly upon the works of Walter Emery, Timothy Green, James Halloran, Marshall McLuhan, Jean Cazneuve, Erique Mellon-Martinez, and Takeo Furu, along with specialized factbooks and periodicals, Biryukov discusses from the Communist viewpoint various aspects of television in the Western world, touching sometimes on other media. Chapters include: "A Short History of Television in Capitalist Countries," "Television and Other News Media," "The Structure of Television in Capitalist Countries," "Television and Monopoly Capitalism"; "Television and Ideology," "Television as the Object of Research," "The Impartiality Doctrine in Bourgeois Television," "The Doctrine of 'Mass Culture' and Television," and "'Free Flow of Information' and Television's International Relations."

508

Bittner, John R. **Broadcasting and Telecommunication: An Introduction.** 2d ed. Englewood Cliffs, NJ: Prentice-Hall, 1984. 526p.

An introductory text, encyclopedic in scope, which, in the author's words, "Incorporates a total approach to the study of electronic communication, examining everything from the history of the telegraph to the future of personal computers." He has the knack of loading a great deal of information into a small space in simple—sometimes almost too simple—language. At the end of each of the 23 chapters is a bibliography, "Opportunities for Further Learning." Also contains a glossary, a list of journals and trade publications, and extensive notes. Author and subject indexes.

509

Black, Peter. **The Mirror in the Corner: People's Television**. London: Hutchinson, 1972. 232p.

An insightful account of the BBC's losing struggle against ITV to maintain its television monopoly which tells why the monopoly was created and why it went; the rise of ITV; its effect on BBC; and finally, the effect on television of having two competing services. Black, a television columnist who has a way with words, is concerned with quality in television, and poses some interesting questions about it against the background of the system's change from monopoly to competition. Chapter notes, bibliography.

An earlier book covering in detail and from a Left viewpoint one aspect of ITV history—the intraparty conflict over the introduction and passage of the legislation founding it—is H. H. Wilson's **Pressure Group: The Campaign for Commercial Television** (London: Secker & Warburg, 1961. 232p.).

510

Black, Peter. **The Biggest Aspidistra in the World: A Personal Celebration of Fifty Years of the BBC**. London: British Broadcasting Corp., 1972. 243p.

An informal history written around accounts of programs and people associated with the BBC rather than around its policies. It is especially useful for the insight into BBC radio and television content. Contains a bibliography and an index.

511

Blakely, Robert J. **To Serve the Public Interest: Educational Broadcasting in the United States**. Syracuse, NY: Syracuse University Press, 1979. 274p.

In case the term "educational broadcasting" misleads, it should be explained that Blakely is referring to noncommercial broadcasting, both "educational" as in earlier days and "public" after the Public Broadcasting Act of 1967. His purpose is to detail its history which is "necessarily a kind of history of broadcasting in the United States" as well, though in this case with emphasis on noncommercial broadcasting. Having been connected with educational broadcasting since 1922 he writes out of first-hand experience along with the necessary secondary sources. At present this is the only full-length history of the rise of public broadcasting and its predecessors, which alone increases its importance, but even if others existed or will exist in the future this would remain especially valuable because of Blakely's years of experience which constitute a primary source. Chapter notes and index.

512

Blanchard, Simon, and David Morley, eds. **What's This Channel Four? An Alternative Report**. London: Comedia, 1982. 186p.

A 33-page historical background by Blanchard deals with the emergence of the two Fourth Channel organizations—Welsh and British—and is followed by articles by a number of contributors which as a whole offer suggestions for a critique of quality to be used as an alternative to the critique required by the Independent Broadcasting Authority and the Welsh Fourth Channel Authority. Appendixes give brief biographies of officials in charge, to be read in conjunction with organizational charts in Blanchard's background article, "Channel Four Television Company Limited Terms of Reference," and a list of useful addresses and publications. Chapter notes.

513

Bluem, A. William. **Documentary in American Television: Form. Function. Method**. New York: Hastings House, 1965. 311p.

Treating the subject historically, Bluem has emphasized the role of informal drama and dramaturgical structure in relation to the documentary (an aspect he feels has been neglected), along with special conditions of documentary production and distribution introduced by broadcast communication. In five parts: "The Documentary Heritage," "Television News Documentary," "Television Theme Documentary," "Documentary Departures" and "Television and the Documentary Quest." Appendixes include "Documentarists on Documentary," "Memorandum from a Television News Man" (a lengthy memorandum by Rueven Frank, then the executive producer), and "TV Documentaries for Review and Analysis" which includes 100 important documentaries produced in America and abroad from the early 1950s until the time the book was written in the early to mid-sixties. Although decades have passed, Bluem's analysis remains pertinent. Selected bibliography and index.

514, 515, 516, 517

Blumler, Jay G., ed., and Anthony D. Fox, asst. ed. **Communicating to Voters: Television in the First European Parliamentary Elections**. Beverly Hills, CA: Sage, 1983. 387p.

Blumler, Jay G., and Anthony D. Fox. **The European Voter: Popular Responses to the First Community Election**. London: Policy Studies Institute, 1982. 183p. (Study in European Politics 6.)

Blumler, Jay G., Michael Gurevitch, and Julian Ives. **The Challenge of Election Broadcasting**.

Leeds, England: Leeds University Press, 1978. 91p. (Report of an Enquiry by the Centre for Television Research, University of Leeds.)

Blumler, Jay G., and Denis McQuail. **Television in Politics: Its Uses and Influence**. Chicago: University of Chicago Press, 1969. 379p. (U.S. edition.)

Blumler's works divide themselves into two areas: mass communications in relation to politics and mass communication in relation to the satisfactions the mass media provide their audiences. In the bulk of his work he is particularly concerned with voting behavior and the use and influence of television in elections. Two of the books are European-based; two, British. **Communicating to Voters** is a series of articles concerning the 1979 Direct Election to the European Parliament. The first of its kind, it analyzes the way in which television networks operated and the rule they placed in the campaign. **The European Voter** is a survey of voter attitudes and behavior in the same election, broken down by the various countries and by each major group of the national electorates, with discussion of the activities of the news media.

Television in Politics studies the role of television in the 1964 British election, based on interview data and shaped by two central questions: How do voters wish to use political programs when following a campaign? and How does televised propaganda influence their political outlook? It is the second major research project on the subject done in 1961 by the Television Research Unit at the University of Leeds, the first having appeared in **Television and the Political Image** by Joseph Trenaman and Denis McQuail (London: Metheun, 1961. 287p.). Although both studies are now years old they are still pertinent.

The Challenge of Election Broadcasting, drawing extensively on interviews held with many news and current affairs broadcasters and with leading politicians, examines the main strengths and unsolved problems of the British system of election broadcasting as it functioned in 1974 and suggests certain lines for future improvement. All have bibliographies, and all except **The Challenge of Election Broadcasting** are indexed.

518

Bogart, Leo. **The Age of Television: A Study of Viewing Habits and the Impact of Television on American Life**. 3d ed. New York: Ungar, 1972. 515p.

This book, first issued in 1956, discusses the development of television as a cultural factor in American life and details patterns of viewing habits; programming; interrelation with radio listening, reading, movies, spectator sports, and advertising; political effects; and the juvenile audience. The author has updated it with a new introduction, a set of notes to be read with the text, the latest statistics, and a new supplemental bibliography. Indexed by name and subject.

519

Boretsky, R. A., and A. Yurovsky. **Television Journalism**. Prague: International Organization of Journalists, General Secretariat, 1970. 204p.

The authors, both members of the Department of Journalism at Moscow University, seek to explain TV reporting as a system of mass information; to specify its place in society (in this case, in a Communist society); and to discuss its particular idiom as a genre, or rather, as a compound of genres, because the authors feel that journalism is closely akin to literature. There are also some pointers on news gathering and production. All in all, we get the Communist viewpoint in countries with a different ideology.

520, 521

Bower, Robert T. **Television and the Public**. New York: Holt, Rinehart and Winston. 1973. 205p.

Bower, Robert T. **The Changing Television Audience in America**. New York: Columbia University Press, 1985. 172p.

Both of these are continuations of the systematic study of popular attitudes toward the mass media that began with Paul Lazarsfeld's **Radio and the Printed Page** (1940), followed by his **The People Look at Radio** (1946), **Radio Listening in America** and **The People Look at Radio—Again** (1948) with Patricia Kendall, and Gary Steiner's 1963 **The People Look at Television: A Study of Audience Attitudes** (No. 797). Bower's two surveys in 1970 and 1980 are follow-ups of Steiner's, with necessary modifications to take care of changes in the structure and technology of television. Results of both reflect changes in public attitudes over ten-year periods—changes in the composition of audiences and changes in their reactions to programming. Other sections cover television news and television in the family. Appendixes give details about sampling procedures and other methodological information, along with statistical notes, references, and indexes.

522

Boyd, Douglas A. **Broadcasting in the Arab World: A Survey of Radio and Television in the Middle East**. Philadelphia: Temple University Press, 1982. 306p.

Against a background of the historical, religious, geographical, climatic, political, economic and linguistic factors that make radio and television unique as they affect its development, Boyd discusses broadcasting in the Arab League countries—Egypt, the Sudan, Lebanon, Syria, Jordon, North Yemen, South Yemen, Iraq, Kuwait, Saudi Arabia, Bahrain, Qatar, the United Arab Emirates, Oman, Algeria, Libya, Morocco, and Tunisia (omitting Somalia and Mauritania). Egypt and Saudi Arabia are covered in more detail than the other countries. The bulk of the book is taken up with these individual descriptions; an introduction discusses Arab broadcasting in general—its developments, trends and constraints—and concluding sections are concerned with international radio broadcasting in Arabic and with problems within Arab broadcasting. There is a bibliography of printed sources of various kinds and a listing of the author's personal communications. Index.

523

Brack, Hans. **The Evolution of the EBU Through Its Statutes from 1950 to 1976**. Geneva, Switzerland: European Broadcasting Union, 1976. 179p. (EBU Monograph 11, Legal and Administrative Series.)

An analysis of the European Broadcasting Union—its founding, its structure, its financing, its achievements—traced through its statutes. Appendixes give the statutes, 1950 version (Torquay) and 1976 version (Helsinki), and a table of the organizations that have held seats on the Administrative Council between 1950 and 1976, together with the names of the administrators and their alternates. Subject and name index.

524, 525, 526, 527, 528

Briggs, Asa. **History of Broadcasting in the United Kingdom**. Vol. I. **The Birth of Broadcasting**. New York: Oxford University Press, 1961. 525p.

Briggs, Asa. **History of Broadcasting in the United Kingdom**. Vol. II. **The Golden Age of Broadcasting**. New York: Oxford University Press, 1965. 663p.

Briggs, Asa. **History of Broadcasting in the United Kingdom**. Vol. III. **The War of Words**. New York: Oxford University Press, 1970. 766p.

Briggs, Asa. **History of Broadcasting in the United Kingdom**. Vol. IV. **Sound and Vision**. New York: Oxford University Press, 1979. 1,096p.

Briggs, Asa. **The BBC: The First Fifty Years**. New York: Oxford University Press, 1986. 439p.

In his detailed four-volume official history of British broadcasting up to the 1950s, Briggs, one of England's foremost historians, has recorded the facts as they occurred, based on archival records and concluding with the end of the BBC monopoly and the emergence of television as a major force. **The BBC: The First Fifty Years**, written 16 years after the completion of the four-volume history and concluding in 1972 with the BBC's fiftieth birthday, is much more than abridgement and extension. In his words: "In my four volumes I wanted to explain how the activities of broadcasting were organized and judged in their own generation. . . . In this single volume, by contrast, I am concerned with the longer-term view." In short, **The First Fifty Years** is an interpretative history which "seeks to explain not only the rise and influence of broadcasting, a universal activity, on Britain, but why

Britain chose to organize it through a particular national institution, the BBC." An appendix lists "BBC Milestones: The First Fifty Years." This is followed by 14 pages of detailed bibliographical notes of evaluative references. Index.

529

Briggs, Asa, and Joanna Spicer. **The Franchise Affair: Creating Fortunes and Failures in Independent Television**. London: Century Hutchinson, 1986. 226p.

"Our book takes the form of a narrative, but it tells several stories, not one," say the authors of this critique of the establishment and operation of Britain's Independent Television Authority. Against a background of the allocation of franchises by the Independent Broadcasting Authority in 1981 behind closed doors and by criteria not made public, they discuss the past, present and possible future of independent television in the UK, and challenge the position of an IBA which does not have to explain its decisions to the public. Briggs, a social and cultural historian, was a director of Southern Television from 1968 to 1984; Spicer worked for the BBC for 20 years and is now a consultant in the field of international communications. Because of their reputations their sharply critical analysis of the motives and procedures of the IBA cannot be taken lightly. Presumably they write from wide personal knowledge rather than documentation. Index.

Broadcasting Bibliography: A Guide to the Literature of Radio and Television. (See No. 1640.)

530

Brooks, Tim, and Earl Marsh. **The Complete Directory to Prime Time Network TV Shows 1946-Present**. New York: Ballantine, 1985. 1,123p.

"We have set out to give you the most complete and accurate history of night-time television series ever assembled," say the authors of this popular and comprehensive encyclopedia of programs aired on ABC, CBS, NBC and from the early days on Dumont. Although the title says "prime time" (the authors say they are stuck with it) they complain that it is not sufficiently inclusive; in later editions they have added all network series that aired after six p.m. as well as the top syndicated programs that ran predominately in the early evening and late night. The major portion of the directory is an alphabetical-by-title listing of each series, with generic series such as news entered under News, sports events entered under the specific name of the sport, and feature film series under Movies. Only network shows are included. Information for each entry contains type (musical variety, documentary, etc.); inclusive dates; schedule on air; cast or performers; and a discussion of each series. This is followed by a year-by-year chart scheduling prime-time programs; a chronological list of Emmy Award winners;

top-rated programs by seasons, with network and ratings; a list of longest running series; series airing in prime time on more than one network; song hits from television; and hit theme songs from series. Finally, there is an extensive index to personalities and performers. In their introduction the authors give a succinct history of network television. This reference work is a winner of two national awards, one of them the prestigious American Book Award.

531, 532, 533, 534

Brown, Les. **Television: The Business Behind the Box**. New York: Harcourt Brace Jovanovich, 1971. 374p.

Brown, Les. **Keeping Your Eye on Television**. New York: Pilgrim Press, 1979. 84p.

Brown, Les, and Savannah Waring Walker, eds. **Fast Forward: The New Television and American Society; Essays from Channels of Communication**. Kansas City, KS: Andrews and McMeel, 1983. 213p.

Brown, Les. **Les Brown's Encyclopedia of Television**. New York: New York Zoetrope, 1982. 496p.

Les Brown, who has covered television for both **Variety** and the **New York Times**, is one of its most perceptive and provocative critics who, in addition to scrutinizing its inner workings with a caustic eye, has also written a valuable reference book.

"I set out in January 1970 to write on how the American television system works, and about the men who work in it, using as a framework the events that would take place in that calendar year. My expectation was that, whatever occurred, it would be in most respects a typical year," he says of **Television: The Business Behind the Box**. Although the events are long past, Brown's description of them remains a timeless picture of the structure of the industry and the mentality of American broadcasting. It is also great reading. Index.

Keeping Your Eye on Television is a slim volume questioning the status quo of broadcasting which, in Brown's opinion, serves as a "money machine" rather than a forum for debating controversial public issues and a medium for cultural enrichment." Packed with provocative facts, it is an excellent source for individuals and groups to learn more about the social issues that lie behind the control of broadcasting, whether by government or industry.

In **Fast Forward** Brown and his co-author, Walker, have assembled perceptive articles on television as business, information, and entertainment in the 1980s, as seen by experts from industry and academe. Typical among the 25 essays: "Are the Networks Dinosaurs?" and "Living in a Nielsen Republic" by Brown; "Stanley Hubbard and His Magnificent New Video Flying Machine" by Julie Talen; "Television's Way with Words" by Edwin Newman, "What Harm to the Children?" by Robert Coles; "Living with a Satellite Dish" by Steven Levy; "Escape

Realism" by Brian Winston; "The New Enemies of Journalism" by Charles Kuralt, "Birth of a Wired Nation" by David Burnham; and "America's Global Information Empire" by Herbert Schiller. They and the rest of the contributors perceive clearly and write lightly.

Les Brown's Encyclopedia of Television updates his **Brown's New York Times Encyclopedia of Television**. It contains thousands of items, 400 of them new, which bring together in well-written thumbnail sketches the various facets of television: its history, technology, programs, stars, creative talents, executives, special language, FCC regulation, landmark legal cases, government decisions, network and station groups, industry organizations, unions, citizen's groups, syndications, cable TV, pay TV, video public television, ratings, and the structure and content of foreign broadcasting systems. All this information is arranged in neat chronological form and tightly packed prose, with illustrations here and there. There is a brief bibliography of important books, magazines and yearbooks. Appendixes give the "Highest Rated Programs of All Times," and in tabular form, the number of TV stations on the air, 1946–81, as well as numerous other pertinent pieces of information.

535

Brown, Ray, ed. **Children and Television**. Beverly Hills, CA: Sage, 1976. 368p.

Articles are grouped in three parts: Part One: "Children as Audience," is an assessment of the extent children watch television and why; Part Two, "Individual and Social Factors Which Shape the Viewing Experience," concentrates on two influences—the family, and the child's own expectations as to what he hopes to get from watching; and Part Three, "Effects," upon which much more research has been done than on the other two areas. Authors are British, American and Scandinavian. Notes, author index and subject index.

536

Browne, Donald R. **International Radio Broadcasting: The Limits of the Limitless Medium**. New York: Praeger, 1982. 369p.

Browne calls this book a selective history of international radio broadcasting designed to help the reader "understand better the reasons for the birth and growth of international stations in particular and international radio in general, the sorts of internal and external pressures that bear upon stations, the sorts of messages they broadcast, and the types of listeners they reach." Documentation varies because it is sometimes unavailable, but it is richest for the Western stations, including Communist ones, and thinnest for the Third World stations. Contents include a general discussion of structure and growth; stations in specific countries or parts of the world; religious stations; audience research; and conclusions, speculations and suggestions. Appendixes give: International Broadcasting Program Categories; Language Services Added (and dropped) by Six Major International Broadcasters—1960–1980; Estimated Weekly

Broadcast Hours for Some Leading International Radio Stations; and Six Major Broadcasters and Their Services in Some of the World's Major Languages. There is also a bibliographical essay and an index.

537

Bryant, Jennings, and Daniel R. Anderson, eds. **Children's Understanding of Television: Research on Attention and Comprehension**. New York: Academic Press, 1983. 370p.

The book brings together research on the fundamental nature of children's television viewing, including such aspects as attention, comprehension of content and format, and application of these findings to produce effective television programs or to mediate potentially harmful effects of viewing television. Each chapter presents the assumptions, methodologies, theories, and major findings of a particular research program or tradition. The first four deal with attention; chapters five through nine are oriented toward comprehension; and chapters 10 through 14 with research application or intervention. In the final chapters the editors draw on all the chapters to provide a "state-of-the-art" report, with suggestions as to areas where clarification, integration, and/or future research is needed. Notes follow each article. Index.

538

Buckman, Peter. **All for Love: A Study in Soap Opera**. London: Secker & Warburg, 1984. 226p.

A high-brow exploration of a low-brow cultural form which investigates "What working in such a high-pressure business does to all those involved: the writers, actors, directors, technicians, producers, reviewers and critics, and—last but not least—the public. . . . Who runs the industry, what kind of people work in it, how do they operate? Is it, like the old Hollywood, a sweat-shop cranking out fantasies. . . .? Or is it a form of neo-realism, reflecting some of our longings and most of our frustrations? . . . What I am offering will be selective, partisan, and personal: an exploration of how we see and hear ourselves." Buckman confines himself to the soaps in England and the U.S. although as these sell worldwide, he feels that he is dealing with attitudes that transcend these two cultures. Buckman is an elegant writer; his stylish prose contrasts with the corniness of the plots and people he succinctly describes. In addition to its other values, this makes fascinating reading.

539

Bumpus, Bernard, and Barbara Skelt. **Seventy Years of International Broadcasting**. Paris: UNESCO, 1985. 117p. (Communication and Society, 14.)

Traces the history of international broadcasting—broadcasting outside national frontiers—from the early days of radio to the present, with a look at the impact of these broadcasts and how they can be measured. The authors also examine some of the problems inherent in the practice, including jamming, and they consider the future of the medium. They explain that they have made the study as comprehensive as possible, but because of the wide range of the subject, the number of stations involved, and the difficulty in getting facts, there are inevitable omissions. There is a bibliography and an appendix, "Estimated Total Programme Hours Per Week of Some External Broadcasters."

540

Bunce, Richard. **Television in the Corporate Interest**. New York: Praeger, 1976. 150p.

The author, a research sociologist, questions the structure of commercial television in relation to the public interest. Does it properly represent the diverse and often antagonistic segments of our society? How responsible are business corporations to these diverse segments? Is regulation by government the answer? These issues are examined and evidence presented, much of it economic. Part I, "The Logic of FCC Policy," discusses business pluralism and cross-ownership; Part II, "The Logic of Corporate Practice," discusses the meaning of business control, multinational empire building, conglomerates, and television in the public interest. There are tables, footnotes, and a bibliography.

Bunzlová, Alice, and Leopole Slovák. **Socio-Economic Aspects of National Communication Systems. II. Radio Broadcasting in Czechoslovakia**. (See No. 786.)

541

Buxton, Frank, and Bill Owen. **The Big Broadcast, 1920–1950**. New York: Viking, 1972. 301p.

A new, revised, and expanded edition of **Radio's Golden Age** (1966) which lists alphabetically network radio programs of the period. Information about each necessarily varies, being very scanty for some, but always including the type of program and, in almost every case, the date the program began and the leading characters. In some cases there are complete casts, director, writer, network, a synopsis of the plot, and considerable other information. Now and then the history of the program is included, as, for instance, "Grand Ole Opry." All entries are series. In spite of its unavoidable unevenness, it is useful because so little information of this sort exists for radio. There are also pictures of some of the performers, a bibliography, and a name index.

542

Cable and Satellite Television: Risk, Reward and Reality. London: Spencer House, 1984. 76p.

Proceedings of the Economist Intelligence Unit (EIU) conference at Birmingham (England), Sept. 12–14, 1983, in association with the CAST 83 cable and satellite television exhibition which gives a clear and concise discussion of the state of cable and satellite television in Britain, the U.S.A and western Europe—its present uses and future potentials, its economics, regulation, and programming. Participants are mainly British, with Brenda Maddox, Home Affairs editor of **The Economist**, chairman.

Cable and Station Coverage Atlas. (See No. 1733.)

543

Cable Capsules. 7th ed. New York: J. Walter Thompson, USA. 1986. 74p.

Designed for the use of the advertising staff of the J. Walter Thompson agency, this is one of the finest all-round sources of information of cable audiences available. Contents include: Cable Universe; Cable Profile and Penetration; Cable, Pay and VCR Penetration in NSI Markets; Viewing in Cable Homes; Viewing by Daypart: TV Viewing by Daypart and Source (annual); Share of Audience Trends by Source; Network TV Audience Comparison, by Cable Status, by Quarter; Service Universe Estimate Comparison, including Basic Cable Services, Pay TV & STV; Guide to Satellites; % Household Rating Comparison by System; Household Rating Trends—NTI (for all channels); Nielsen and Estimated Viewers Per Viewing Household by Network; Commercial Cable Vehicles—Summary; Regional Sports Services; Cable Network Terminations; Religious and Text Services; Pay Cable Networks. Copies are available by making a $25 donation by check made out to The Help to Retarded Children to the Media Department, J. Walter Thompson, 466 Lexington Ave., New York, NY 10017.

544

Cable Communications and the States: A Sourcebook for Legislative Decision-Makers. Albany: New York State Senate, 1975. 487p.

A compendium of information about cable television in the 50 states in the mid-'70s. Included are the following: background; intergovernmental relations; state involvement in regulation; legislation; pros and cons; guiding development (a broader view); and a bibliography.

545

A Cable Primer. Washington: National Cable Television Association, 1984. 43p.

Divided into six sections, each intended to serve as a basic guide to a specific facet of the cable industry. "The Origins of Cable" outlines the past, present and future growth; "Cable Technology" explains basic mechanics of the cable system and covers the new technological services and advances in the industry; "Cable Economics" presents the basic criteria for a cable system, including capital costs, operating revenues and expenses, and system profitability; "The Franchising Process" gives an overview of what happens when a community decides it wants cable service; "Cable Programming" focuses on

presentations; and "Cable Regulation" provides an overview of the regulatory history of the industry. Five appendixes: "Satellite-Delivered Cable Programming" listing channels; "Government and Foundation Sources," "State Regulatory Bodies," "Cable Bibliography," and "Cable Television Glossary of Terms."

546

Cable Television: Franchise Provisions for Schools. Washington: National Education Association, 1973. 33p.

In addition to recommended franchise provisions, this book gives ownership options, a glossary, and appendixes, "Rules and Regulations," and "Franchise Provisions at Variance with FCC Cable Television Rules."

547

Cable Television in the Cities: Community Control, Public Access, and Minority Ownership. Ed. by Charles Tate. Washington: Urban Institute, 1972. 184p.

Information concerning the technology, franchising, local program origination, strategies for community control, community ownership arrangements, business development procedures and prospects, and other pertinent data. A final section is an 80-page Reference and Resource Guide which gives a glossary of terms; facts and figures on the CATV industry; CATV regulation and policy development; special ordinance/franchise provisions; FCC regulations and New York access rules; important federal agencies; organizations and associations; research and demonstration projects; information and technical assistance; trade journals and industry publications; and a bibliography of selected articles and books.

548

Canadian Radio-Television Commission. **Directory: Multi-lingual Broadcasting in Canada**. Ottawa: Information Canada, 1974. 117p.

A listing of Canadian stations which broadcast in languages other than English. Includes cable TV, off-air TV, AM radio and FM radio.

549

Canadian Radio-Television Commission. Research Branch. **Symposium on Television Violence: Colloque sur la Violence à la Télévision**. Ottawa: Printing and Publishing Supply Services, 1976. 252p.

Report of a forum hosted by the Canadian Radio-Television and Telecommunications Commission, in which representatives of the television industry, writers, social science scholars, and legal and lay experts voice diverse opinions, areas of agreement, and analyses of problems and possible solutions. Contents include "The

Public Issue," "The Social Effects of Television Violence," "The Industry Perspective," and "Control and Improvement." Contains four bibliographies and footnotes, and the Canadian Code of Broadcast News Ethics of the Radio Television News Directors Association of Canada.

550

Canadian-U.S. Conference on Communications Policy. **Cultures in Collision: The Interaction of Canadian and U.S. Television Broadcast Policies**. New York: Praeger, 1984. 207p.

Report of a conference sponsored by Syracuse University, the University of Toronto, and the Americas Society, these papers present a comparative study highlighting differences and similarities in Canadian and U.S. broadcasting policies and the factors which have contributed to them. Chapter notes and bibliography.

551

Cantor, Muriel G. **Prime-Time Television: Content and Control**. Beverly Hills, CA: Sage, 1980. 141p. (Sage COMMText Series.)

A detailed analysis of the ways in which legal, political, organizational and occupational factors in production determine the final drama we see on the television screen. Drama is defined to include situation comedies and action, adventure and family series. Chapter notes, bibliography and index.

Cantor is also the author of **The Hollywood TV Producer: His Work and His Audience** (New York: Basic Books, 1971. 256p.), which focuses on the work of the people creating prime-time series and how they are constrained by the organizational milieu and their work relationships.

552

Cantor, Muriel G., and Suzanne Pingree. **The Soap Opera**. Beverly Hills, CA: Sage, 1985. 166p.

Cantor and Pingree give this tried-and-true genre serious treatment. Their aim is to integrate it into the field of communications, examining its distinct aspects in terms of format, content and audience; roots in fiction and radio; possible effects; and built-in production restraints. A valuable feature is the bibliography bringing together much of the scholarly research on the subject. An earlier book, also serious, is Madeleine Edmondson's and David Rounds' **From Mary Noble to Mary Hartman: The Complete Soap Opera Book** (New York: Harmony, 1978) which discusses appeals, writers and players, economics and regulations.

553

Cardwell, Jerry D. **Mass Media Christianity: Televangelism and the Great Commission**.
Lanham, MD: University Press of America, 1984. 213p.

Watching the electronic preachers perform on television, interviewing and observing them and their workers at their headquarters, comparing preaching styles, backgrounds and emphases, Cardwell, a sociologist, makes a dispassionate analysis of the power, influence, and potential for social change embodied in mass media Christianity. Chapter notes and index.

554

Case Studies on Broadcasting Systems. London: Routledge and Kegan Paul in association with the International Institution of Communications, irregular. (1977–.)

A series of monographs, sponsored by the International Institute of Communications, which points out the main features of the communications patterns of a number of different countries. Emphasis is on the various structures and how they came into existence, landmarks in their histories, and alternative possibilities envisioned for the future. Studies thus far include:

Broadcasting in Sweden by Edward W. Ploman. 1977. 90p.

Broadcasting in Canada by E. S. Hallman and H. Hindley. 1977. 90p.

Broadcasting in Peninsular Malaysia by Ronny Adhikarya with Woon Ai Leng, Wong Hock Seng, and Khor Yoke Lim. 1977. 102p.

Broadcasting in the Netherlands by Kees van der Haak with Joanna Spicer. 1977. 93p.

Broadcasting in Ireland by Desmond Fisher. 1978. 120p.

Broadcasting in Guyana by Ron Sanders. 1978. 76p.

Broadcasting in Japan by Masami Ito. 1978. 125p.

Broadcasting in India by P. C. Chatterji (projected for 1987, to be published by Sage Publications).

555

Cassata, Mary, and Thomas Skill. **Life on Daytime Television: Tuning-In American Serial Drama**. Norwood, NJ: Ablex, 1983. 214p.

Using broad surveys and case studies of several soap operas, Cassata and Skill, with co-authors for some of the chapters, explore various facets, including the life-style and demography of the characters; their problem-solving strategies; the image of old age; presentations of life, death and sex; plots and characterizations; the environment (music, sets, fashions); and concerns and relationships of the characters. Vintage radio as well as television soaps are discussed. The authors think the audience survey data have as much to say about the character of the persons doing the viewing as about the characters themselves. In the Introduction George Comstock presents "A Social Scientist's View of Daytime Serial Drama" and Horace Newcomb counterbalances with "A Humanist's View of Daytime Serial Drama." One of the most valuable features are two excellent bibliographies,

"The Daytime Serial: A Bibliography of Scholarly Writings, 1943–1981" by Patricia Tegler and one by the authors, "The Soap Opera: A Bibliography of Popular Writings, 1960-March 1982." An author and a subject index.

Cassata, Mary, and Thomas Skill. **Television: A Guide to the Literature.** (See No. 1643.)

556

Castleman, Harry, and Walter J. Podrazik. **Watching TV: Four Decades of American Television.** New York: McGraw-Hill, 1982. 314p.

Useful for reference or nostalgia trips, this factual and chronological blow-by-blow account of television's development with emphasis on its programming takes it season by season from 1944–45 through 1980–81, describing and charting each season, with a backdrop of events both within the industry and the nation. Index.

557, 558

Cater, Douglass, ed.; Richard Adler, Project ed. **Television as a Social Force: New Approaches to TV Criticism.** New York: Praeger, 1975. 171p. (Published with the Aspen Institute on Communications.)

Cater, Douglass, ed.; Richard Adler, Project ed. **Television as a Cultural Force.** New York: Praeger, 1976. 191p. (Published with the Aspen Institute.)

The first of these titles contains essays which analyze from varying viewpoints TV's impact and its potential for influencing our concept of reality. Among the subjects considered are TV vis à vis "thinking people"; TV and public health; TV as a medium for communicating ideas; newspaper news and TV news; electronic journalism and politics; and the electronic community—a new environment.

In the second title, eight participants from the Aspen program's Workshop on Television examine the significance of its first 25 years in America, with special reference to American culture. Some of the areas discussed are TV as dream, as cultural document, as melodrama, as moral force, as news. There is a bibliography and a name and program index.

559

Cater, Douglass, ed.; Michael J. Nyhan, Project ed. **The Future of Public Broadcasting.** New York: Praeger, 1976. 372p. (Published with the Aspen Institute Program on Communications and Society.)

Experts examine the many serious policy questions facing public broadcasting into the 1980s, identifying problems, exploring possible solutions, and proposing

future directions. Topics include the difficult business of building public broadcasting into an institution, the stations, public radio, instructional television, audience involvement, financing, audience and programming research, programming, program funding, the new technology. Christopher Sterling has compiled "A Selective Guide to Sources on Public Broadcasting." Glossary and index.

560

Cavalli-Sforza, Francesco, Agnes Donati, and Hew Evans. **Independent Television Networks in Italy at the Turning Point from Cable to Broadcasting.** Strasbourg: Committee for Out-of-School Education and Cultural Development, Council for Cultural Cooperation, Council of Europe/Conseil de l'Europe, 1977. 36p.

Describes the emergence of local television, with six case studies and some evaluation of the development and the momentum at the time of writing. A map shows the distribution of independent TV networks as of October 1976, with brief information about each.

Chaikin, Judy, and Lucinda Travis, comps. **Film/Television: Grants, Scholarships, Special Programs.** (See No. 1196.)

561

Charren, Peggy, and Martin W. Sandler. **Changing Channels: Living (Sensibly) with Television.** Reading, MA: Addison-Wesley, 1983. 272p.

Simple without being simplistic, this is the perfect book for the uninitiated who, as individuals or groups, need a broad overview as to what television is all about. Charren and Sandler discuss its aspects accurately, objectively and as a bonus, entertainingly with many illustrations in the form of graphics and text. Even though Charren is best known as founder of the highly critical Action for Children's Television, here she and her co-author take pains to show what is right along with what is wrong. Their aim is to help the viewer watch it creatively as well as critically, sorting out the good and the bad, and learning how to make complaints felt. "Resources," following each chapter list pertinent sources for further information. Bibliography and an index.

562

Cheney, Glenn Alan. **Television in American Society.** New York: Franklin Watts, 1983. 88p.

An excellent elementary introduction to the structure of television which poses questions that will give laymen something to think about. Brief bibliography and index.

Chin, Felix. **Cable Television: A Comprehensive Bibliography.** (See No. 1645.)

563

Chronology of Telecommunications and Cable Television Regulation in the United States. Cambridge, MA: Program on Information Resources Policy, Center for Information Policy Research, 1984. 57p.

Consists of tables, with each page divided into two parts: by subject across the page according to Industry Developments; State Regulation; State Judicial; Federal Legislation; Federal Administrative; Federal Judicial, and chronologically in columns down the sides, beginning with 1835 when Morse invented the magnetic telegraph and ending with 1983. Thus the user can see precisely what was happening when.

564

Codding, George Arthur, Jr. **Broadcasting without Barriers**. New York: UNESCO Publications Center, 1959. 167p.

A study to determine the extent to which radio broadcasting is available throughout the world as a means of communicating information and to examine ways of overcoming political, economic, and technological obstacles that impede its availability. It describes broadcasting systems in the various countries, broadcasting between countries, use of the radio spectrum, the sharing of frequencies, the quest for better techniques, and the impact of television on radio broadcasting. Contains a bibliography and an index.

565, 566

Codding, George Arthur, Jr. **The International Telecommunication Union: An Experiment in International Cooperation**. Leiden, Netherlands: E. J. Brill, 1952. 505p.

Codding, George Arthur, Jr. and Anthony M. Rutkowski. **The International Telecommunication Union in a Changing World**. Denham, MA: Artech House, 1982. 414p.

"The aim of this work," says Codding of **The International Telecommunication Union: An Experiment in International Cooperation**, "is to give a comprehensive and up-to-date picture of the evolutional, structural and functional control of communications," with telecommunications defined as telegraph, telephone and radio. Beginning in 1865 with the founding of the Telegraph Union, he details the development of international cooperation over years which spanned the development of telephone and radio, the subsequent restructuring of the organization into the International Communication Union in 1932, the post-World Ward II reorganization in 1947, and the important developments from 1947 to 1951. Because technical aspects are equally involved with political, economic, and social interests, Codding includes explanations of technical terms for those with minimum knowledge; for those with no previous knowledge he warns that they will do well to acquire

minimum knowledge before reading. Four appendixes include, "Definitions," "Agreement Between the United Nations and the International Communication Union," "Position of Countries in Relation to the acts of the Union," and "International Telecommunication Union Organization." Bibliography and index.

Intended as a "current, comprehensive and readable treatise on the ITU and what it does," **The International Telecommunication Union in a Changing World** examines the organization from the point of view of its ability to adapt to changing technologies, the changing needs of member states, and the changing international political environment in which it operates. The first section is historical, the second deals with its decision-making apparatus, the third presents a critical analysis of activities, and the final section evaluates performance, with future directions of communication technology explored in relation to possible future functions. The authors also offer suggestions for structural change and methods of operations. Appendixes contain charts and lists, with a great deal of detailed information, including organizational structure and members with dates of admission. Bibliography; Abbreviations and Acronyms; and Index.

567

Cole, Barry, and Mal Oettinger. **Reluctant Regulators: The FCC and the Broadcast Audience**. Reading, MA: Addison-Wesley Publishing Co., 1978. 303p.

An in-depth study of the FCC showing conflicts and compromises that influence it and various forces that operate behind these conflicts and compromises—the lobbyists, the Washington law firms handling FCC cases, the trade press, the concerned citizens' groups. In dealing with these latter, the authors pay particular attention to the efforts to improve children's television. They thoroughly examine the inner workings of the FCC and measure what it is supposed to do against the ways it actually operates. Appendixes give an organizational chart, forms relating to license renewal, and the FCC Children's Policy Statement. There is no bibliography, probably because most of the material comes from close firsthand observation. This is one of the best possible sources for an overall picture of the agency.

568

Cole, Barry, ed. **Television Today: A Close-Up View. Readings from TV GUIDE**. New York: Oxford, 1981. 480p.

Sixty-four articles which, taken together and with Cole's introduction, provide an overview of popular television in the 1970s: its content; how it is determined; the audience and its importance as evidenced by ratings; its role and significance in our society; the regulation and control of programming; and speculations on its future. Among contributors are Isaac Asimov, Daniel Boorstin, David Brinkley, David Chagall, Edith Efron, Louis

Kronenberger, Robert MacNeil, Martin Mayer, Arthur Schlesinger, Alvin Toffler. Most of the readings appeared in 1970, with a few from the 1960s. Index. For readings from the 1950s and 1960s Cole edited an earlier anthology, **Television: A Selection of Readings from TV Guide Magazine** (Free Press, 1970).

569

Colino, Richard R. **The INTELSAT Definitive Arrangements: Ushering in a New Era in Satellite Telecommunications**. Geneva, Switzerland: European Broadcasting Union, 1973. 196p. (Legal and Administrative Series. Monograph No. 9.)

The assistant vice-president in charge of international affairs and later director general for Communications Satellite Corporation discusses in detail the arrangements, giving the background, the process of negotiation, an analysis of key features, and a commentary on the controversy between INTELSAT and other satellite systems. Elaborate footnotes and supplementary materials accompany the text of the agreement.

570

Collins, Richard. **Television News**. London: British Film Institute, Educational Advisory Service, 1976. 56p. (BFI Television Monograph 5.)

Investigates some dominant assumptions and practices which govern the production of news on British TV. Among topics discussed are formation, function, and financing; news values, principles and practices; gatekeepers; analysis of style and structure; and audience. Appendix 1 is a one-page rundown on the Eurovision News Exchange; Appendix 2, a geographic chart. Bibliography.

Commercial Radio in Africa. (See No. 1551.)

Commonwealth Broadcasting Association Handbook. (See No. 1738.)

571

Comstock, George. **Television in America**. Beverly Hills, CA: Sage, 1980. 154p.

In this short but broadly based undergraduate text Comstock skillfully uses empirical evidence, theory, and speculation in the areas of psychology, political behavior, broadcasting, sociology and communication to show how television as an institution influences our lives. Contains references.

572

Comstock, George, Steven Chaffee, Natan Katzman, Maxwell McCombs, and Donald Roberts. **Television and Human Behavior**. New York: Columbia University Press, 1978. 581p.

The co-authors have attempted "out of vanity and with a touch of arrogance" to cover the entire relevant scientific literature on television in English, examining more than 2,500 books, articles, reports, and documents, including some that fall beyond the usual boundaries of science, and recording their conclusions (some of which are tentative) and their speculations. They have grouped their material under the following headings: "Overview," "What's On," "The Audience," "Living with Television," "One Highly Attracted Public" (children), "Four Highly Attracted Publics" (women, blacks, the poor, and the elderly), "Politics and Purchases," "The Psychology of Behavioral Effects," and "The Future." There are 47 pages of references, a name index, and a subject index. This vast and important book is part of a body of national studies of empirical evidence about television and behavior, including the Surgeon General's Report in 1972 (No. 808), a follow-up report in 1980 (No. 809) and a 10-year update in 1982 (No. 810).

Contemporary Theatre, Film & Television: A Continuation of *Who's Who in the Theatre*. (See No. 1204.)

573

Contreras, Eduardo, et al. **Cross-Cultural Broadcasting**. Paris: UNESCO, 1976. 49p. (Reports and Papers on Mass Communications No. 77.)

A discussion of transnational broadcasting which explores conditions, possibilities, and problems. Among them: regional communications systems and cooperation in program production; use of satellite broadcasting to achieve a wide diffusion of television programming to multi-cultural audiences; and international program sales which insure that programs are suitable for the cultures which they reach. Political, cultural, linguistic and psychological implications and possible effects are taken into consideration. Footnotes and bibliography.

574

Crane, Rhonda J. **The Politics of International Standards: France and the Color TV War**. Norwood, NJ: Ablex, 1979. 165p.

Focusing on the adoption of color TV standards in France, the author examines the politics, technology, international trade relations and bargaining involved in standard-setting, showing the degree to which technical standards are the result of political and economic factors. Some of the evidence is drawn from never-before-released declassified documents. Appendixes, a bibliography, and an author and a subject index.

575

Crisell, Andrew. **Understanding Radio**. London: Methuen, 1986. 236p.

Criswell's first purpose is to determine the distinctive characteristics of radio as a medium by locating it among other modes of communication, individual and collective, literary and visual; by examining its historical development in Britain; and by exploring the way it conveys or mediates messages of any kind. His other purpose is to investigate its characteristics in terms of such users as the journalist, the teacher, the dramatist, and the listener who seek its potentialities as a medium of information, culture and entertainment for both broadcasters and audience. Although Crisell writes in terms of British institutions his study of the way radio mediates its messages is universally pertinent. Bibliography and index.

Critchley, R.A. **Television and Media Effect**. (See No. 1553.)

576

Cullingford, Cedric. **Children and Television**. Aldershot, Hampshire, England: Gower, 1984. 239p.

A survey of children's response to television, based on more than 5,000 children, in which the author investigates the nature of their reactions—their attitudes as they watch, their ability to distinguish the true from the false; in short, he seeks to gain insight about their inner world as they respond to television. Cullingford does not critique individual programs. In his words, "The Programmes are ephemeral; children's learning is not." Throughout, he compares and correlates his findings with those of other pertinent social science studies. A 39-page bibliography of books and articles. Index.

577

D'Agostino, Peter, ed. **Transmission**. New York: Tanam, 1985. 326p.

Provocative essays encompassing television aesthetics, social commentary and application of new technologies which as a whole are intended as "one more step to redefine the map of television/video studies" by dealing with form and content within the context of new television/video practice, and with quality rather than commercialism as a criterion. Programs discussed are those which do not usually appear on commercial prime-time TV but which, the editor and authors feel, give a better idea of the medium's possibilities than the conventional sit-com, soaps, and sports genres. Among the 22 essayists are John Fiske and John Hartley (co-authoring), Hal Himmelstein, Todd Gitlin, Sol Worth, Vincent Mosci, Erik Barnouw and Bill Moyers. The final essay, by Barbara London, is a brief history and selected chronology of video. Contains a videography, a bibliography, and a selected index.

578, 579

Davis, Richard H. **Television and the Aging Audience**. Los Angeles: Ethel Percy Andrus Gerontology, University of Southern California Press, 1980. 107p.

Davis, Richard H., and James A. Davis. **TV's Image of the Elderly: A Practical Guide for Change**. Lexington, MA: Lexington, 1985. 264p.

In **Television and the Aging Audience**, Davis, a gerontologist, uses facts, figures and research concepts to describe in simple language evidence from studies on both TV and geriatrics in order to disabuse some popular misconceptions about aging, and to explain to the novice something about the world television creates both in general and with reference to the old, including the role advertising plays. He also gives concrete ways TV can be used to advantage by both workers and interest groups. Chapter references.

TV's Image of the Elderly has as its purpose to improve the television portrayal of the elderly. The first section, "Television and the Aging Audience," describes the present situation. It discusses the aging society, broadcasting as a medium, the composition of an aging audience, and the way the elderly are presented on programs. The second part, "Helping Shape Television Coverage," tells what the elderly can do, with explanations and instructions to enable them actively to influence television by developing and producing their own creative senior-oriented programs. The co-author is also a gerontologist.

580

DeGooyer, Janice, and Farfalla Borah. **What's Wrong with This Picture? A Look at Working Women on Television**. Washington, DC: National Commission on Working Women, 1982. 22, 4p.

The first segment of this study looks at 10 years of prime time programming to discover how television has portrayed women who work outside the home during 1972–1981; the second and shorter segment examines current programming on cable and satellite.

581

The Development of Wireless to 1920. Ed. by George Shiers. New York: Arno Press, 1977. Variously paged. (Historical Studies in Telecommunication.)

An anthology containing 20 articles published between 1890 and 1967 on the "pre-history" of radio, showing the experimental and technological work.

582

De Vera, Jose Maria. **Educational Television in Japan**. Tokyo: Sophia University; Rutland, VT: Tuttle, 1967. 140p.

De Vera's aim is to provide both information and interpretation, with the term *educational* covering both instructional TV to schools and more general instructional TV to a wider audience. He first discusses the concept and philosophy of educational broadcasting in Japan, including its history, then he proceeds to its content and audience, and its effects and effectiveness in the learning process. Finally he gives an overall appraisal. Notes and bibliography.

583

Diamant, Lincoln, ed. **The Broadcast Communications Dictionary**. 2d ed. New York: Hastings House, 1978. 201p.

"This handy quick reference book is designed for everyday assistance," says the author over-modestly about his comprehensive dictionary of more than 4,000 terms intended to assist both beginner and professional. Included are technical, common, and slang words and acronyms in current use in radio and TV programming and production; network and station operations; broadcast equipment and engineering; audio and video tape recording; performing talent; advertising procedures; media usage; research; and government and allied groups. There are cross references to British terminology.

Directors Guild of America. **Directory of Members**. (See No. 1743.)

584

Donnelly, William J. **Confetti Generation: How the New Communications Technology Is Fragmenting America**. New York: Holt, 1986. 239p.

What will the new electronic media—satellites; broadcast, cable, and pay television, videocassettes, video games, video discs, computers, etc.—do to our culture and to us personally? Donnelly asks. Drawing on McLuhan, Daniel Bell, David Riesman and other media commentators and soothsayers, he analyzes the effect of television on past generations and predicts the future with the new media. His message: control their effects on our culture or be controlled (a not-too-happy fate). Donnelly resigned as a senior vice-president of Young and Rubicam to write this book.

585

Dorr, Aimée. **Television and Children: A Special Medium for a Special Audience**. Beverly Hills, CA: Sage, 1986. 160p.

This text provides students and laymen as well with a survey of pertinent research on the ways children receive television and can be affected by it. Chapters include: "A Special Medium for a Special Audience," "Making Sense of Television," "Influences on Understanding," "Effects of Television Content," "Refining the View of Television Content Effects," "The Medium as the Message," and "Influencing Television's Role in Children's Lives," which gives practical advice. References and index.

586

Drummond, Phillip, and Richard Paterson, eds. **Television in Transition: Papers from the First International Television Studies Conference**. London: BFI Publishing, 1986. 280p.

A report sponsored by the British Film Institute and the University of London Institute of Education, which attempts "to bring together as many different examples of TV research from as many different countries as could be accommodated," (Anthony Smith in his Foreword). Representing not only a range of countries but also of disciplines, methodologies and levels, the essays span the fields of sociology, politics, economics, literary criticism, and semiotics. Content emphasizes three broad areas: political economy and cultural imperialism; the development of American television; and the relationship of television to the viewer. In the Preface the editors succinctly point out other areas in need of exploration. Articles are footnoted and there is a name/subject index.

587

Dunkley, Christopher. **Television Today and Tomorrow: Wall-to-Wall "Dallas"?** London: Penguin, 1985. 160p.

Bit by bit new technologies are bringing changes to the British television system in terms of quality. Will it be for better or for worse? "Greater choice, more specialization, an increasing shift of power from the broadcaster to the audience, greater convenience in timing and format . . ." or wall-to-wall **Dallas**? This is the question Dunkley poses as he assesses the possible impact of the increasing deregulation against a background of past and present policy and programming in Britain, with comparisons with U.S. Programming in the U.S., incidentally, does not come off too badly. Dunkley is a television critic and "occasional television presenter" and writer. Much of what he says is provocative and challenging, and apparently comes from his own wide knowledge and experience. No notes; no index.

588

Dunn, Gwen. **The Box in the Corner: Television and the Under-Fives**. London: Macmillan, 1977. 160p.

A British study in which the author observed children in their own homes to determine their reactions to television. Quoting extensively from their comments and reactions, she focuses on the intentional and unintentional effects of television on the mental and physical development of pre-school children and how it can best be used to the child's advantage. Bibliography.

589

Dunning, John. **Tune in Yesterday: The Ultimate Encyclopedia of Old-Time Radio, 1925–1976**. Englewood Cliffs, NJ: Prentice-Hall, 1976. 703p.

Intended as historical reference, a nostalgia reader, and an entertainment review, this book covers drama, comedy, and variety shows, listing them alphabetically, discussing each, and often going into considerable detail for well-known series. (**One Man's Family** runs to nine pages, complete with family tree.) Dunning explores interrelationships of characters and includes full biographical data on many of the stars. Among other items of information are dates, networks, sponsors, time changes, and personnel. Newscasters are covered only when they were billed regularly as semi-entertainment (for example, Walter Winchell and Hedda Hopper), and band leaders only when they had a regularly sustained variety show. Although the author says that a number of shows are discussed here for the first time, not all series from radio history are included. There is a name-show index.

590, 591

Durham, F. Gayle. **Radio and Television in the Soviet Union**. Cambridge, MA: Massachusetts Institute of Technology, Center for International Studies, Research Program on Problems of Communication and International Security, 1965. 122p. (Distributed by Clearinghouse for Federal Scientific and Technical Information, U.S. Dept. of Commerce.)

Durham, F. Gayle. **Amateur Radio Operation in the Soviet Union**. Cambridge, MA: Massachusetts Institute of Technology, Center for International Studies, Research Program on Problems of Communication and International Security, 1956. 71p.

Radio and Television in the Soviet Union gives information on many aspects of Soviet broadcasting: structure, equipment, production and repair, subscription fees, programs and hours, educational television, relations with Intervision, and audience. Detailed notes refer to the original sources; and numerous charts, graphs, and tables illustrate the text.
Amateur Radio Operation in the Soviet Union is a companion piece which discusses the importance, structure, and extent of amateur radio and contains bibliographic footnotes.

592

Durkin, Kevin. **Television, Sex Roles and Children: A Developmental Social Psychological Account**. Philadelphia: Milton Keynes for Open University Press, 1985. 148p.

Durkin's aim is to assemble and evaluate the main findings of recent work on television and sex role acquisition, pointing to gaps and limitations in the research, and suggesting a framework for future study. He has targeted his work toward students in the social sciences and mass communications, and as the subtitle indicates, his viewpoint is that of a social psychologist. References and an author and a subject index.

593

Dyer, Richard. **Light Entertainment**. London: British Film Institute, 1973. 43p. (BFI Television Monograph No. 2.)

Relates the practice of TV light entertainment to the ideals of abundance, energy, and community, and poses the question of how far it is able to live up to these ideals. Starting from an examination of the notion of light television, Dyer considers the nature of the television entertainment situation, the kind of aesthetics needed for its analysis, and the ways in which we may attempt to understand its place in contemporary society.

Edmondson, Madeline, and David Rounds. **From Mary Noble to Mary Hartman**. (See No. 552.)

594

Efron, Edith. **The News Twisters**. Los Angeles: Nash, 1971. 355p.

In the belief that the three networks have a liberal bias in their political coverage Efron devised "a simple analytical method for ascertaining the presence or absence of such bias, to apply this method to the network product, and to arrive at a documented answer." Her study, which she replicates in appendixes, proves her assumption to her satisfaction. Within the context of the times—1969 when Vice President Spiro Agnew delivered his famous speech charging the networks with a bias toward liberalism her name and her book became synonymous with the far-right accusation against television news.

595

Eisner, Joel, and David Krinsky. **Television Comedy Series: An Episode Guide to 153 TV Comedies in Syndication**. Jefferson City, NC: McFarland, 1984. 866p.

The authors have included "every prime time situation comedy series, live or animated, broadcast from 1949 to 1980 and still available for syndication"—some 150 series and over 11,000 total episodes. Excluded are live shows, shows not in syndication, banned shows, and recent shows which had not produced enough episodes to include at the time material was gathered. Entries are alphabetical by title, with a general description including dates, cast, writers and theme, followed by a listing of episodes with a four or five line description. An index contains the names of players and others concerned with the production.

Ellis, John. **Visible Fictions: Cinema, Television, Video**. (See No. 1234.)

596

Ellmore, R. Terry. **The Illustrated Dictionary of Broadcast-CATV-Telecommunications**. Blue Ridge Summit, PA: G/L TAB Books, 1977. 396p.

This is much more than a dictionary of terminology; it contains identifying descriptions of law cases, commissions, associations—to name a few of the areas. It even defines *catharsis* as the term is used in relation to broadcasting, and there are countless acronyms. A few hundred engineering terms are included, but it is not intended to be primarily technical. It interprets telecommunications broadly, even dealing with advertising, sales, scenery, research, history, and other wide-ranging aspects. Contains some illustrations.

597

Elving, Bruce F., comp. **FM Atlas and Station Directory: A Handy Reference to the FM Stations of the United States, Canada and Mexico**. 9th ed. Adolph, MN: FM Atlas Publishing Co., 1984. 144p.

In three parts: 1) a directory of state maps indicating location of FM stations in the U.S. in geographical order east to west; a two-part map of Canada, east and west; and single maps of Mexico, Puerto Rico and the Virgin Islands; 2) a state by state geographical directory, city by city within the U.S. also including Puerto Rico and the Virgin Islands; province by province for Canada; and with Mexico treated as a whole; and 3) a directory of all stations by frequency. Symbols indicate coverage, type of station, network, language, and programming.

598

Emery, Walter B. **National and International Systems of Broadcasting: Their History, Operation and Control**. East Lansing: Michigan State University Press, 1969. 752p.

Country-by-country examination of the broadcasting systems of 29 countries and one continent, giving origin, development, regulation, programming patterns, quantitative dimensions. While some of the material has dated, much still holds. Countries include the U.S., Mexico, Canada, the United Kingdom, Ireland, Belgium, the Netherlands, Luxembourg, Denmark, Iceland, Norway, Sweden, Finland, France, Italy, Greece, Germany, Austria, Switzerland, Spain, the U.S.S.R., Hungary, Yugoslavia, Turkey, India, China, Japan, Australia, and the continent of Africa (an overview).

An appendix gives various broadcasting laws and acts, codes for several nations, membership of the European Broadcasting Union, and information on satellite communications. Detailed bibliography and subject index.

599

Ensign, Lynne Naylor, and Robyn Eileen Knapton. **The Complete Dictionary of Television and Film**. New York: Stein and Day, 1985. 253p.

"Covering everything from words such as 'apple box,' coined in the early days of silent film, to television jargon of the '70s and '80s such as 'backdoor pilot,' we present a volume that attempts to compile, define, and standardize the language of television and film. It is the first book in English to do so," say the authors. They present the working language of a fluid industry in simple to-the-

point terms intended to interpret it to film and television professionals, lay people, and students. The most common definition, subordinate meanings, and slang are included.

600

Epstein, Edward Jay. **News from Nowhere: Television and the News**. New York: Random House, 1973. 321p.

In this work which has become classic, Epstein studies the effect of the processes of a news organization on the news product, using the three major networks, with emphasis on NBC. Among topics he examines: the relation of the news to reality; the structure imposed on network news by government regulations, affiliates, parent networks and economic realities; the effect of internal procedures and structure; and finally, a composite picture of American society as depicted on network news over a three-month period. Source notes, bibliography, and index.

Gans, Herbert J. **Deciding What's News**. (See No. 137.)

601

Faenza, Roberto. **The Radio Phenomenon in Italy**. Strasbourg: Committee for Out-of-School Education and Cultural Development, Council for Cultural Cooperation, Council of Europe/Conseil de l'Europe, 1977. 29p. (CCC/DC (76) 93-E)

A brief survey of the present state of broadcasting in Italy, with an analysis of the use of radio as a social force, its power, and its consequences in the Italian context.

602

Fifty Years of Japanese Broadcasting. Tokyo: Japan Broadcasting Corp. (Nippon Hoso Kyokai) Radio & TV Culture Research Institute, with cooperation of the Mainichi Newspapers, 1977. 429p.

Although compiled and edited by Japan's public broadcasting organization, NHK, this relates the history and development of commercial broadcasting as well. The editors say that an additional aim is to bring into relief the relationship between broadcasting and Japanese society. Appendixes include the provisions of the broadcast law, standards of NHK's domestic and overseas broadcast programs, and 32 pages giving the annals of Japanese broadcasting, 1885–1975. A map shows the NHK GTV network.

603

The First 50 Years of Broadcasting: The Running Story of the Fifth Estate. New York: Broadcasting Publications, 1982. 297p.

The editors of **Broadcasting Magazine**, which has served the broadcasting industry since 1931, have compiled a year-by-year factual account of the growth of the industry for 50 years, as culled from their magazine. Emphasizing events, not statistics, the story unfolds chronologically and neatly, with many illustrations. There is an excellent name/subject index.

604

Fischer, Stuart. **Kids' TV: The First 25 Years**. New York: Facts on File, 1983. 289p.

"This book—with entries on every children's show to air on network television during the medium's first 25 years—traces the history of children's programming and, I hope, brings to life some of the great old shows and characters so many of us grew up watching." In this introductory statement Fischer sets the scope and tone of his chronological descriptions of the Saturday morning "children's hours" on commercial television from 1946 through 1973. Each entry, alphabetical by title for the year covered, gives networks, scheduled time, dates from debut to cancellation, producers, hosts, casts and whatever other facts are pertinent. This is followed by an uncritical and often lengthy description of plot, characters and cast and many, many illustrations. Useful to pinpoint shows and characters, or on a more serious level, as a starting place for further research, giving names and dates. Index.

Fisher, Kim N. **On the Screen: A Film, Television and Video Research Guide**. (See No. 1649.)

605

Fishman, Joshua A. **Language Resources in the United States. Vol. II. Guide to Non-English-Language Broadcasting**. Rosalyn, VA: Inter-America Research Associates, Inc., National Clearinghouse for Bilingual Education, 1982. 112p.

A profile that includes call letters, address, language, and any of the following information available: transmitting wattage (day or night), program length (by language), commercial or noncommercial status, and contact person. This is preceded by an alphabetical listing, and followed by indexes to geographical locations and languages served.

606

Fiske, John, and John Hartley. **Reading Television**. London: Methuen, 1978. 223p.

The authors contend that we cannot properly analyze the content of television in depth because we have never established proper criteria. Through the use of semiotics, which they skillfully explain for the benefit of laymen, they demonstrate how this can be done so that we can better understand the role television plays in our culture as it both creates and reflects reality. Contains a bibliography, an annotated list of further readings, and an index.

607

Fletcher, James E., ed. **Handbook of Radio and TV Broadcasting: Research Procedures in Audience, Program and Revenues**. New York: Van Nostrand Reinhold, 1981. 336p.

"This book has been prepared not as a manual for the researcher but as a manual for the non-researcher who must understand what a researcher is talking or writing about, and as a manual for the occasional researcher who, because of financial constraints, wishes to undertake a research study without the services of a commercial research," says Fletcher. Articles by authorities, including a number by Fletcher himself, contain the various aspects of broadcast measurement research in simplified language, with many charts and graphs to illustrate. As examples, appendixes contain extracts of an Arbitron radio and a television report, "Basic Statistical Routines: A Self-Study Course" by Fletcher, and "Mathematical and Statistical Tables." Index.

608

Fowles, Jib. **Television Viewers vs. Media Snobs: What Television Does for People**. New York: Stein and Day, 1982. 253p.

In this ardent defense of television Fowles knows no middle ground. He amasses the research evidence con and pro, diminishing the con and proclaiming the pro. What television does for people is all to the good; snobs have given it a bad name. Selected chapter headings indicate his affinity: "Television Is Good for Your Nerves," "Television Is Good for Your Spleen," "Television Is Good for Your Heart," "Television Is Good for Your Brain," "Television Is Good for Your Children," and finally, "Television Heals." Books dispassionately examining the research on television effects are always needed, but this is not it. Rather, it suggests a tie-up with the industry as Fowles notes in his bibliographical section, "Much of the research for this book was done at the library of the Television Information Office in New York City." Index.

609, 610

Frank, Ronald E., and Marshall G. Greenberg. **The Public's Use of Television: Who Watches What and Why**. Beverly Hills, CA: Sage, 1980. 368p.

Frank, Ronald E., and Marshall G. Greenberg. **Audiences for Public Television**. Beverly Hills, CA: Sage, 1980. 230p.

Initially Frank and Greenberg set out to analyze audience patterns for public television, but soon realized that a specialized TV audience could be better understood in relation to TV audience characteristics and behavior in general. This resulted in two volumes—one researching patterns for commercial television as a whole with public television a segment, and the other devoted wholly to the public television audience. Thus the first book deals with audience interest segmentation for all television, including public, and for magazines, books, movies, newspapers as well, though not so intensively. The second elaborates, discussing specific audience interest segmentation, viewing behavior, media usage among above- and below-average audience segments, program preferences, funding, and minority audiences. Each contains a number of tables and gives their research designs. **Audiences for Public Television** concludes with a list of references which seems to hold for both.

611

Frederick, Howard H. **Cuban-American Radio Wars: Ideology in International Telecommunications**. Norwood, NJ: Ablex, 1986. 200p.

Through content analysis Frederick examines the ideological confrontation between the United States and Cuba as seen in their respective international radio newscasts on Voice of America and Radio Havana Cuba, accompanied by detailed explanations of his methodology. Chapter notes, a 16-page bibliography and an index.

Gable, Jo. **The Tupenny Punch and Judy Shows**. (See No. 1568.)

612

Garay, Ronald. **Congressional Television: A Legislative History**. Westport, CT: Greenwood, 1984. 195p.

"This book is devoted to one particular aspect of political broadcasting, that of televising the proceedings of the U.S. Senate and the U.S. House of Representatives. Using a format that closely resembles a legislative history, it traces some sixty years of efforts by individual legislators to implement first radio and then television coverage of congressional hearings, meetings and chamber deliberations." Preface. Chapter 1 tells how and why television is so important to House and Senate members; chapters two through six give a legislative history of television; chapter seven examines its impact upon members' conduct, legislative procedures, and the congressional television audience. Chapter notes, a bibliographical essay, and an index.

613

Garnham, Nicholas. **Structures of Television**. Rev. ed. London: British Film Institute, 1980. 54p. (BFI Television Monograph No. 1.)

An analysis of the organizational structures of British television which examines it in terms of its own specifically determined political, social and ideological problems and in relation to wide issues of social, and especially economic, policy. The revised edition contains a new section on the implications for broadcasting structures of the Annan Committee's Report. Bibliography.

Geis, Michael L. **The Language of Television Advertising**. (See No. 1569.)

614

Gelfman, Judith S. **Women in Television News**. New York: Columbia University Press, 1976. 186p.

The author has based her findings on interviews and on-the-job observation of 30 women who have succeeded in television news. Among topics discussed are: breaking ground, background for a career, dimensions and expectations of a career, being a women in television news, double tokenism, career versus home life, career guidance and advice. Bibliography and index.

615

Gerani, Gary, and Paul H. Schulman. **Fantastic Television: A Pictorial History of Sci-Fi, the Unusual and the Fantastic from Captain Video to the Star Trek Phenomenon and Beyond**. New York: Harmony Books, 1977. 192p.

In two parts. The first, "Fine Tuning," focuses on 13 shows which the authors feel to be the "very best" in the science fiction/fantasy genre, and follows them from birth and development to eventual demise. The second, "The Full Picture," is a brief treatment of other representatives of the genre including children's fantasy programming, giving in five or six lines primary credits and a "nutshell" synopsis. Profuse illustrations and index.

616, 617, 618, 619

Gianakos, Larry James. **Television Drama Series Programming: A Comprehensive Chronicle, 1947–1959**. Metuchen, NJ: Scarecrow, 1980. 565p.

Gianakos, Larry James. **Television Drama Series Programming: A Comprehensive Chronicle, 1959–1975**. Metuchen, NJ: Scarecrow, 1978. 794p.

Gianakos, Larry James. **Television Drama Series Programming: A Comprehensive Chronicle, 1975–1980**. Metuchen, NJ: Scarecrow, 1981. 457p.

Gianakos, Larry James. **Television Drama Series Programming: A Comprehensive Chronicle, 1980–82**. Metuchen, NJ: Scarecrow, 1983. 678p.

The object of this series is to follow television drama as it has progressed since its beginnings in the late 1940s. Its chronology needs explanation. Gianakos compiled the 1959–1975 volume first, then backtracked to cover 1947 to 1975—therefore the discrepancy in publication dates. The first (1957–75) volume is in two sections: "Days and Times for Network Prime Time Programming, fall, 1959—spring, 1975," which lists programs and their episodes by seasons and networks, giving day of week, time, name and date year by year. The second section, "Television Drama Series Programming: A Comprehensive Chronicle, 1959–1975" which constitutes the bulk of the book, again lists shows alphabetically by season with different information, beginning with descriptions of the show, followed by the cast of regulars, and a list of episodes. In conclusion is a list of programs appearing irregularly. Subsequent volumes contain new features. **. . . 1957–1959**, in which he backtracked, has a section, "The Overview," which discusses programming trends seasonally and significant specials; and the "Days and Times" section includes non-network programming, drama and otherwise. **. . . 1980–82** has an appendix giving teleplays adapted from Pulitzer Prize fiction and plays; by Nobel literature laureates; and taken from classical Greek drama, Shakespeare, and selected 19th and 20th century writers. Each volume picks up titles previously omitted and each has a cumulative index of series titles. (Volumes published in 1987 and 1988 update the series.)

620

Gibson, George H. **Public Broadcasting: The Role of the Federal Government, 1912–76**. New York: Praeger, 1977. 263p.

Tells of the expansion of the role of the federal government in noncommercial educational broadcasting since about 1912 and describes in detail the work that presidents, congressmen, the FCC, commissioners of education, the Department of Health, Education and Welfare, foundations, and educational broadcasters have done at the federal level with regard to public broadcasting. Footnotes at the end of each chapter and an index.

621

Gitlin, Todd. **Inside Prime Time**. New York: Pantheon, 1983. 369p.

Gitlin takes as his themes "power, politics, and the nature of the decision-making process governing prime-time network television. . . . How much does a show's commercial success depend upon its 'fit' with social trends abroad in the land?" he asks in this enlightening and readable study. Gitlin's data comes largely from interviews with 200 industry people from various levels, and he recounts a number of their stories at length, often in the words of the people telling them. The final product is a study of the social and political pressures that govern production and content of television serials. Ratings, too, come in for discussion. Chapter notes and index, but no bibliography as such, since much of the data is first-hand.

622, 623, 624, 625

Glasgow University Media Group. **Bad News**. Vol. 1. London: Routledge & Kegan Paul, 1976. 310p.

Glasgow University Media Group. **More Bad News**. Vol. 2. Routledge & Kegan Paul, 1980. 483p.

Glasgow University Media Group. **Really Bad News**. London: Writers and Readers Cooperative Society, Ltd., 1982. 170p.

Glasgow University Media Group. **War and Peace News**. London: Open University Press; Philadelphia: Milton Keynes, 1985. 335p.

In this series, a research team, initially based at Glasgow University and composed largely of sociologists, use "critical" insights, textual analysis, semiology and sociolinguistics to analyze television news for bias. The first two studies focus on coverage of labor, industry and the economy for a six-month period in 1975, with particular emphasis on trade unions. The third deals with the representation of politics in the news and concludes with comments on historical and social factors which shape television's view of the world. A fourth analyzes coverage of war and peace, concentrating on the Falkland conflict, defense and disarmament. The series as a whole—and particularly the first two volumes—criticize TV coverage as biased against trade unionism and the working class. Among the researchers contributing to the four volumes are Peter Beharrel, Lucinda Broadbent, Howard Davis, John Eldridge, John Hewitt, Gordon Kimmett, Jean Oddie, Greg Philo, Malcolm Spavin and Brian Winston. Each volume contains notes and an index. Richard Hoggart introduces the first volume.

For a critical view of the Group's conclusions, especially of the first two volumes, see Martin Harrison's **TV News: Whose Bias? A Casebook Analysis of Strikes, Television and Media Studies** (No. 647).

626

Glut, Donald F., and Jim Harmon. **The Great Television Heroes**. New York: Doubleday, 1975. 245p.

"We do not claim to have written a history of the medium, but rather a nostalgic look back upon the greatest and most exciting years of television—its infancy," the authors tell us in the Foreword. Even though strictly a nostalgia trip, the book nonetheless contains some useful information about the early heroes—and heroines and character actors and actresses and programs as well.

627

Godfrey, Donald G., comp. **A Directory of Broadcast Archives**. Washington: Broadcast Education Association, 1983. 90p.

A listing of radio-television program archives for the U.S. and Canada, giving for each collection the institution with address, phone number and curator; a content description including type of recordings, program types, and subject; the accessibility of the collection in terms of indexes, catalogs and regulations; and any further comments the respondent made. All known institutional, private and commercial sources were surveyed, but some responded less fully than others and some did not respond, making the compilation necessarily incomplete. Even so it is a valuable contribution.

628

Golding, Peter, and Philip Elliot. **Making the News**. London: Longman, 1979. 241p.

An investigation of the production and content of broadcast news in Nigeria, Sweden and Ireland to shed light on two questions: What picture of the world is provided by broadcast news, and how is this picture related to the routine demands of news production in broadcasting organizations? Answers, which involve discussions about the social role of journalism, the ideological nature of news, and the possibility of change, indicate that news is shaped by a variety of organizational, cultural, economic and normative restraints. The authors find that news is more nearly a reflection of the forces that produce it than of the events and processes in social reality. Charts, notes, bibliography, and index.

629

Goodhardt, G.J., A.S.C. Ehrenberg, and M.A. Collins. **The Television Audience: Patterns of Viewing**. Lexington, MA: Lexington Books, 1975. 157p.

This consists of data from a continuing program of British audience research undertaken by the three authors for the Independent Broadcasting Authority, with the intent to get beyond the specific information supplied by audience studies to a more general description about viewer behavior. They examine loyalty to particular programs or types of programs and to particular channels, the nature of switching from channel to channel, the intensity of viewing, and repeat viewing and other factors which have little to do with measurement of audience size. An appendix describes their methodology. References, further readings, and index.

Gormley, William T., Jr. **The Effects of Newspaper-Television Cross Ownership on News Homogeneity**. (See No. 900.)

630

Gordon, George N. **Educational Television**. New York: Center for Applied Research in Education, 1965. 113p.

History and appraisal which takes into account growth, financial structure, public service function, open- and closed-circuit television, television in schools, and effect studies. Contains a brief bibliography and an index.

631

Gould, Peter, Jeffrey Johnson, and Graham Chapman. **The Structure of Television**. London: Pion, 1984. 177p., 135p.

This two-part work could more accurately be titled **The Structure of Television Programming**, for the authors deal exclusively with this aspect. The first half, entitled "Television: The World of Structure," discusses the problems of classification of programs on a worldwide basis. The authors point out the difficulty in finding the right descriptors, especially when values are involved; and they emphasize the need for monitoring. This is explained in straightforward, nontechnical language with numerous examples of specific programs and different systems within certain countries. Part 2, "Structure: The World of Television," is a complete switch. Highly technical, it is aimed to provide social scientists, particularly those in communication research, with an introduction to an algebraic and topological 'language of structure' that focuses the methodological core of the research on international television programming. Neither part is dependent on the other. Both sections are indexed.

632

Green, Timothy. **The Universal Eye: The World of Television**. New York: Stein and Day, 1972. 276p.

A comprehensive work which surveys in detail the state of TV in every nation that has TV available to any extent. Covering Europe, Asia, Africa, North and South America, and Australia, it examines programming, financing, the availability of talent, the role of government, and the possible future course of TV. Written by the former head of **Time**'s London Bureau, it is also extremely readable. Contains a bibliography and an index.

633

Greenberg, Bradley S. **Life on Television: Content Analysis of U.S. TV Drama**. Norwood, NJ: Ablex, 1980. 204p.

The primary purpose of this statistical content analysis of TV fiction by Greenberg and 13 collaborators is to identify, document and trace some major dimensions which might have potential significant social implications. Areas where treatment was examined include people (Hispanic-Americans, blacks, the elderly, and the demography of fictional characters); sex portrayals; social behavior (anti- and pro-social, sexual intimacy, use of alcohol and drugs); and family structures and interactions. Although Greenberg makes no attempt to research possible effects of content, he sees conflict in the fact that what the industry, with its dual goal of entertainment and profit, sees as obvious make-believe may be seen by some viewers as guidance and values, and may lay the groundwork for further examination. References and author and subject indexes.

634

Greenfield, Jeff. **Television: The First Fifty Years**. New York: Abrams, 1977. 275p.

An outsized, coffee-table-type book of 500 pictures accompanied by text which, in spite of its appearance, is a serious and critical analysis of television. It examines news, sports, commercials, soap operas, situation comedies, and practically all kinds of programming in terms of what the medium may be doing to us, for better or worse. The pictures are chosen to illustrate points in the text rather than vice versa. Greenfield laments his inability to document as fully as he would have liked the earliest programs and commercials because broadcasts were live at that time with no kinescopic recording or else the recordings have been lost. Bibliography and index.

635

Greenfield, Patricia Marks. **Mind and Media: The Effects of Television, Video Games, and Computers**. Cambridge, MA: Harvard University Press, 1984. 210p.

On the assumption that the damaging effects the electronic media can have on children are not intrinsic to the media but grow out of the ways they are used, Greenfield explores the relationship between the media of communication and the development of thought. Theoretically, she discusses film and television literacy and its relationship to learning and to social responsibility; practically, she focuses on the constructive use of media at home and at school. The last chapter deals with multimedia education. References, suggested readings, and index.

636

Grundfest, Joseph A. **Citizen Participation in Broadcast Licensing before the FCC**. Santa Monica, CA: RAND, 1976. 195p.

"Describes some of the avenues open to citizens seeking to influence FCC policies; describes the history of citizen participation, through partition and settlement, in broadcast licensing; traces the evolution of an FCC policy statement regarding citizen agreements and analyzes it, especially in the light of four recent cases before the FCC; makes recommendations for future commission policy which suggest that considerable leeway remains for commission approval of citizen settlements, without infringing on the rights and obligations of broadcasters." Preface. Footnotes.

637

Guimaryst, Donald L. **Citizens' Groups and Broadcasting**. New York: Praeger, 1975. 170p.

Surveys citizen involvement in commercial broadcasting from the standpoint of the citizens, industry leaders and the FCC, and assesses the meaning and possible implications of such groups. Contains a bibliography and an index.

638

Gunter, Barrie. **Dimensions of Television Violence**. London: Gower, 1985. 282p.

An experimental study made at the request of Britain's Independent Broadcasting Authority in which Gunter has investigated the ways ordinary viewers perceptually differentiate and evaluate television violence shown them from current British and American crime-detective series, westerns, science fiction programs and cartoon shows. The viewers' reactions were examined in a variety of ways, linking various aspects of the production to the personality of the viewer. Bibliography and index.

639

Gunter, Barrie. **Television and Sex Role Stereotyping**. London: John Libbey, 1986. 80p.

Gunter, Research Officer for the Independent Broadcasting Authority, critiques research in the area under four headings: "Portrayal of the Sexes on Television," "Perceptions of the Sexes," "Social Effects of Television and Sex Stereotyping," and "Counter-Stereotyping through Television." His concentration, however, is more on methodology than results; he feels that the study of television's influence needs to be put into a broader social and psychological context than has characterized most research so far, and should be considered alongside and in relation to other factors concerning individuals examined and the social environment in which they operate. References.

640

Hadden, Jeffrey K., and Charles E. Swann. **Prime Time Preachers: The Rising Power of Televangelism**. Reading, MA: Addison-Wesley, 1981. 217p.

The co-authors—Swann, an ordained Presbyterian minister who is currently managing WRFK-FM for the Virginia Theological Seminary, and Hadden, a professor of religious sociology at the University of Virginia—have made an intensive and critical study of religious broadcasting—examining its roots, its vast organization, its programming and messages, its electronic underpinnings, its audiences, and, most significantly, its broader implications for society. Contains bibliography and index.

641

Hale, Julian. **Radio Power: Propaganda and International Broadcasting**. Philadelphia: Temple University Press, 1975. 196p.

An introduction to the practice of overseas broadcasting as propaganda and the various ideological philosophies back of it, in terms both of sender and receiver. Analysis centers around Nazi Germany, the Communist countries, the U.S.'s Voice of America, Britain's BBC, and the undeveloped parts of the world. A large section is devoted to factors affecting success or failure. Appendixes give a table of radio sets and ownership around the world in 1973; external broadcasting statistics in 1950, 1960, 1970, and 1973; extracts from Internal Policy Guidelines of Radio Free Europe and

Radio Liberty; and extracts from a BBC unpublished monitoring report. Contains chapter notes, a bibliography, and an index.

Hall, Jim. **Mighty Minutes: An Illustrated History of Television's Best Commercials**. (See No. 1572.)

642

Halliwell, Leslie, with Philip Purser. **Halliwell's Television Companion**. 2d ed. London: Granada, 1982. 713p.

"Television is a vast and frightening wasteland in which treasures are occasionally to be found by the keen explorer. This book is an alphabetical catalogue, wherein some of these treasures are to be found," says Halliwell in this compilation of 10,000 items in which he aims "to include all English-speaking TV movies, bland as most of them are," as well as series, individual plays, documentaries, people who have made significant contributions, companies and networks, technical and trade terms, a few general subjects, and books on television. For each movie is given ratings by asterisks, country and year of origin, running time, color or black and white, principal cast, synopsis, appraisal (frequently caustic), and additional and critical notes, if any. (For some items much of this information was unavailable.) Not included are lesser-known foreign-speaking programs, news and magazine items, sports coverage, music and art critiques, and a few other minor categories. Halliwell has included an introductory essay, "What's the Matter with Television," and a postscript, "What's Right with It." The first (1979) edition was called **Halliwell's Teleguide**.

Hanhardt, John G., ed. **Video Culture**. (See No. 1279.)

643

Harmon, Jim. **The Great Radio Heroes**. New York: Doubleday, 1967. 263p.

A lighthearted book which gives an excellent though informal account of the popular radio serials of yesteryear. The title, incidentally, is sexist; heroines are included as well.

644, 645

Harmonay, Maureen, ed. **Promise and Performance: Children with Special Needs. ACT's Guide to TV Programming for Children**. Vol. 1. Cambridge, MA: Ballinger, 1977. 255p.

Harmonay, Maureen, ed. **Promise and Performance: The Arts. ACT's Guide to TV Programming for Children**. Vol. 2. Cambridge, MA: Ballinger, 1979. 216p.

The purpose of Action for Children's Television in these two volumes is to heighten awareness on the part of broadcasting professionals about the uses of television programming both for children who have disabilities and as a means for promoting the arts. The first volume, after an introduction on attitudes and images, deals with specific handicaps: mental retardation, sight and hearing impairment, mental health, and—more generally—preparing the child for the hospital, tools of the trade, programming prospects, and parent education. The second volume concerns ways to bring the performing arts, the visual arts, music, and the literary arts to children. A final section in volume 2, "Audience Building and Diversity," discusses ratings versus creativity, and funding. There are five or six articles in each section—all by experts. In both volumes print and organizational resources are listed.

646

Harris, Paul. **Broadcasting from the High Seas: The History of Offshore Radio in Europe, 1958–1976**. Edinburgh: Paul Harris Publishing, 1977. 361p.

The mid-twentieth century has witnessed a new type of piracy—unlicensed shipboard radio broadcasting. The author (and publisher) of this history describes minutely the growth and development of these stations—their squabbles with each other and with the authorities, the legislation against them, the pros and cons of their existence in social terms. Much of Harris's material is based on an earlier work, **When Pirates Ruled the Waves**. (London: Impulse Publications, 1970. 216p.)

647

Harrison, Martin. **TV News: Whose Bias? A Casebook Analysis of Strikes, Television and Media Studies**. Hermitage, Berkshire, England: Policy Journals, 1985. 408p.

Harrison writes in refutation to the Glasgow University Media Group's critiques of British TV coverage of labor news and the working class generally (**Bad News, More Bad News** and **Really Bad News**, Nos. 622, 623, 624), which he feels constitute a representation of ideology rather than an accurate reflection of facts. To make his point he has sampled the evidence, "just as the original volumes did, concentrating on coverage of industrial disputes by Independent Television News between January and April 1975"—amounting to some 1,700 pages of running orders, scripts and transcripts from ITN's microfilm record." The pertinent items from these pages are reproduced as evidence (in fine print). Index.

648

Havick, John J. **Communications Policy and the Political Process**. Westport, CT: Greenwood Press, 1983. 223p.

Nine articles are presented to discuss issues concerned with American politics, a subject broadly defined and not to be limited to political parties or campaigns.

Many of the papers focus on the political arena of the FCC and the rewriting of the Federal Communications Act of 1934. Some of the papers are historical analyses, but others look forward to describe the role of government in the changing technology of communication. The editor's introduction provides a summary of technical and policy changes in telecommunications or broadcast policy. For example, the change in the corporate holdings of AT&T are reviewed. In his preface, the editor observed the dearth of material available on the study of politics involved in policy decisions about communications. The bibliography created for the book as a whole appears to be complete.

649

Hawes, William. **American Television Drama: The Experimental Years**. Tuscaloosa: University of Alabama Press, 1986. 272p.

From a historical perspective this traces in detail the roots of television drama during its first two decades from its beginning in 1928 through 1947, the year of the first dramatic anthology series, showing the trends in American culture that led to a drama for the mass public, as well as the effect on it of the new technologies and changing entertainment industries. Appendixes include "Production Personnel at Commercial Television Companies in 1946," "BBC Television Dramas Relevant to American Television, 1936–1946," "CBS Television Dramas, 1931–1946," and "Firsts in Television Drama, 1925–1947." Chapter notes, selected bibliography, and index.

650, 651, 652

Head, Sydney W., ed. **Broadcasting in Africa: A Continental Survey of Radio and Television**. Philadelphia: Temple University Press, 1974. 453p.

Head, Sydney W., and Christopher H. Sterling. **Broadcasting in America: A Survey of Television, Radio, and New Technologies**. 4th ed. Boston: Houghton Mifflin, 1982. 642p.

Head, Sydney W. **World Broadcasting Systems: A Comparative Analysis**. Belmont, CA: Wadsworth, 1985. 457p.

Head's knowledge of the structure of television worldwide is monumental, as is his ability to organize it into books. In **Broadcasting in Africa** 35 authors, including Head himself, have contributed essays which give a comprehensive picture of African broadcasting country by country, and the role which non-Africans play in shaping it. Information given for each African nation includes population, receivers per thousand, radio transmitter sites, area per site. Otherwise information varies a bit, with longer discussions for larger countries. The authors discuss the system against the background of such factors as geography, politics, and language, and include broadcasting history and, when available,

audience data. The second half of the book is concerned with the ways in which other nations are influencing African broadcasting. Here are discussions of international broadcasting agencies and programs, religious broadcasting, foreign aid, training, research, educational uses to which broadcasting is put, and the commerce of broadcasting. Head concludes with an agenda for further study. Appendixes give technical problems of spectrum utilization, the uses of broadcasting in African political crises, historical and demographic data, a summary of system facilities, and languages used in broadcasting. There is a lengthy bibliography and a comprehensive index. In 1974 Head, with Lois Beck, also published **The Bibliography of African Broadcasting: An Annotated Guide**. (See No. 1653.)

Broadcasting in America is a frequently revised landmark which first appeared in 1956; since then it has gone through four editions and acquired Sterling as a co-author. Descriptive and analytical, each volume is increasingly comprehensive, matching the growth of the field. In the fourth edition the authors set the stage with a chapter on "National Contrasts" which gives a concise world view, and continue with a technological explanation of radio and television broadcasting, its development in the U.S. in terms of commercial, noncommercial and cable; economics and advertising; audience measurement; social control; law; freedom, fairness, the FCC, and non-regulatory influences; and effects and effects research. Sterling has provided a lengthy bibliographical section, "Further Reading," in which he cites background reading for each chapter, with valuable comments, and an alphabetical bibliography including both the titles in "Further Reading" and the textual citations. There is an index of names and subjects. (The fifth edition was published in 1987.)

"Instead of describing typical systems in their entirety . . . ," says Head in his Foreword to **World Broadcasting Systems**, "I decided to organize the text on the basis of the common problems faced by *all* systems" to show the basic, universal demands and dilemmas they all must face as each interacts with its particular national setting. His purpose is to enable students, after allowances for limitations imposed by national settings, to appraise the system critically by comparing reality with the ideal possibilities. Thus, he discusses, in terms of the various systems, their origins, their politics of both ownership and access, their laws, regulation, economics, facilities, programming and programs, audience research, transborder broadcasting, and broadcasting and freedom. Although intended as a text, this has much wider uses. There are chapter notes, a "Glossary of Acronyms and Special Usages," an extensive bibliography of citations from books and periodicals, and an index.

653

Heller, Melvin S., and Samuel Polsky. **Studies in Violence and Television**. New York: American Broadcasting Co., 1976. 503p.

A 500-page volume which gives the results of five

years of empirical testing by the American Broadcasting Company to try to determine the effect of television violence upon the normal child and the emotionally disturbed child.

Higgins, Gavin, ed. **British Broadcasting 1922–1982: A Selected and Annotated Bibliography**. (See No. 1654.)

Hill, George H. **Black Media in America: A Resource Guide**. (See No. 1655.)

Hill, George H., and Silvia Saverson Hill. **Blacks on Television: A Selectively Annotated Bibliography**. (See No. 1656.)

Hill, George H., and Lenwood Davis, comps. **Religious Broadcasting 1920–1983: A Selectively Annotated Bibliography**. (See No. 1657.)

654

Himmelstein, Hal. **On the Small Screen: New Approaches in Television and Video Criticism**. New York: Praeger, 1981. 206p.

"Are there no clearly defined critical approaches to television? Are television critics clearly lacking when compared with literary, visual arts, and contemporary film critics? Is video criticism parochial, dogmatic, and confused? These are a few of the questions this volume will address.... Above all else, the volume highlights the work of a variety of television and video critics who are, in their individual ways, facing up to the task of decoding television—the most ephemeral and perhaps our most socially powerful contemporary art form." The five critics chosen are John J. O'Connor of the **New York Times**, Bernie Harrison of the **Washington Star**, Horace Newcomb of the University of Texas—all of whom represent television; and David Ross, a museum video curator, and Douglas Davis, an artist working video and a video critic. Chapter notes, bibliography and index.

655

Himmelstein, Hal. **Television Myth and the American Mind**. New York: Praeger, 1984. 336p.

In this lively book, originally developed for a basic television criticism university course, Himmelstein uses myth analysis to examine his thesis that television in its various forms—the commercial, the situation comedy, the melodrama, news, the documentary, sports, religious programming, the talk show—is manipulated to construct the dominant ideology of our society. Or, in other words, to persuade the viewer that "the way things are now is the way they should remain." In the last chapter, "Toward an Oppositional Television: Strategies for Change," he suggests remedies which may be found in new technologies like Low-Power Television Stations (LPTV) which allow more available channels for opposi-

tional groups who have been denied means of public access. But first, he says, we must cultivate "the true critical viewer who welcomes oppositional work," which he concedes is no easy task. Chapter notes and author-title-subject index.

656

Himmelweit, Hilde T., A. N. Oppenheim, and Pamela Vince. **Television and the Child: An Empirical Study of the Effect of Television on the Young**. London: Oxford, 1958. 522p.

A very early study based on a large sample of children in five British cities who were questioned about their attitudes, interests and behavior and reexamined a year later to test changes that might have occurred. The authors looked for reactions to conflict, crime, and violence, and for effects on values, outlook, knowledge, school performance, leisure, interests, and so on. Appendixes describe methods, and there is a bibliography, glossary, and index. For another of the earlier studies see **Television in the Lives of Our Children** by Schramm, Lyle, and Parker (No. 771).

657

Hodge, Robert, and David Tripp. **Children and Television: A Semiotic Approach**. Cambridge, England: Polity Press, 1986. 233p.

The authors argue that television viewing is not necessarily a passive mindless activity for children, but is an important aspect of their cognitive and social development. Calling for further recognition of the positive role it could play in their lives, they draw upon recent work in linguistics and semiotics and the findings from an informal study they conducted over three years with 600 children to show that children are sophisticated viewers, bringing a shrewd sense of fact and fantasy as they actively interpret plot. References and index.

658

Hoggart, Richard. **On Culture and Communication**. New York: Oxford University Press, 1972. 111p.

". . . a broadcaster is in all his decisions involved with the moral life of his society, with its pattern of values, with the stresses and changes these patterns of values are undergoing at any particular time. This kind of engagement has to be recognized if broadcasters are to do justice to their own cultures and to the capacities of the individuals who make up their audiences." These are challenging requirements which Hoggart puts forth in six gracefully written BBC Reith lectures for 1971 concerned with our understanding of other individuals, other cultures and of ourselves as basic to building a good broadcasting program.

659

Hoggart, Richard, and Janet Morgan, eds. **The Future of Broadcasting: Essays on Authority,**

Style and Choice. London: Macmillan, 1982. 166p.

Essays derived from papers at a symposium on The Foundations of Broadcasting Policy in which Britain's broadcasting systems are discussed in terms of authority, style and choice. Contributors include Richard Hoggart and Janet Morgan who introduce the essays, Shirley Williams, Asa Briggs, Jeremy Isaacs, a separate essay by Janet Morgan, Dennis Lawrence, Randolph Quirk, Karl Deutsch, and a collaborative essay by Mary Douglas and Karen Wollaeger. Janet Morgan summarizes the discussions, and Richard Hoggart gives closing observations. Taken as a whole, the essays provide an excellent overall picture of British broadcasting. Index.

660

Hollins, Timothy. **Beyond Broadcasting: Into the Cable Age**. London: Published for the Broadcasting Research Unit by BFI Pub., 1984. 385p.

A debate is going on today about possible effects of cable on the structure of broadcasting which sheds more heat than light. In an effort toward greater understanding Hollins has described the issues and placed them in a context of actual experience and developments. Part One examines the wider telecommunications background and cable's place within it in terms of technological, social and commercial pressures and political motivations. Part Two deals with the history of cable broadcasting in Britain from the late 19th century to 1982, with emphasis on experiments in cable programming and recent debates. Part Three moves to North America and the differences in control and regulation. Part Four analyzes the situation in the United States. Part Five examines future prospects in England. Indexed.

661

Homberg, Erentraud, ed. **Pre-School Children and Television: Two Studies Carried Out in Three Countries**. New York: K. G. Saur; Munich: Verlag Dokumentation Saur, 1978. 78p.

Presents summaries of two major studies: "Pre-School Children and Television," carried out by the Centre for Mass Communication at the University of Leicester under James D. Halloran, and "The Role of Television and Other Media in the Lives of Pre-School Children," carried out by Sveriges Radio, Weiden, and directed by Leni Filipson from its Audience and Research Department. Each study presents the following information: significance, influence, position relative to other media, response to contents, and popularity of particular programs.

662

Horsfield, Peter G. **Religious Television: The American Experience**. New York: Longman, 1984. 197p.

What has been the influence of television on religion, and vice versa? Horsfield studies the institutional structure of television with this question in mind. Part I provides a historical overview of the development of religious television and an analysis of its structure; Part II is a survey of relevant empirical research; Part III is a projection of the future as indicated by current trends, and a suggested strategy for a realistic use of television by the church. His conclusion is that religious broadcasting has been overly influenced by television's institutional structure. Chapter notes, bibliography and index.

663

Hosley, David H. **As Good As Any: Foreign Correspondence on American Radio, 1930–1940**. Westport, CT: Greenwood, 1984. 165p.

A history of foreign correspondence as it developed in the first dozen years of network radio in America when many of the present standards were established by the men and women who worked for the networks in the 1930s. Hosley identifies the pioneers and describes their techniques and values. Material comes from interviews, oral histories and broadcast recordings as well as the usual print sources. Bibliography and index.

664

Howe, Michael J. A. **Television and Children**. Camden, CT: Linnett Books, 1977. 157p.

A study by a British psychologist in which he deals with what we know about television's various influences on children: their viewing habits; the kind of world they view; the informal learning that occurs; the effects of television violence; specific children's programs, including those like **Sesame Street** which are intended to help them learn; and finally, suggestions for dealing with problems the survey has brought to light. A bibliography follows each chapter.

665

Howell, W. J., Jr. **World Broadcasting in the Age of the Satellite**. Norwood, NJ: Ablex, 1986. 329p.

A comprehensive and succinct description of the many aspects of world broadcasting which is both descriptive and analytical. Howell puts together concepts, trends, and facts and figures in interesting new patterns. His classification of world broadcasting systems is an example; instead of the classic four theories—authoritarian, libertarian, Soviet Communist, and social responsibility—he suggests authoritarian, western, communist, revolutionary and developmental. The book is in three large sections: "Frames of Reference in World Broadcasting," in which he discusses a rationale, a framework, a methodology, and governmental and non-governmental organizations; "The Four Worlds of National Broadcasting"—the English-speaking West, the Soviet Union and Communist Bloc countries, developing countries, and pluralistic societies; and "Previewing and

Reviewing World Broadcasting"—international broadcasting via short wave and satellite, and global trends in broadcasting, cable, and VCR within a national framework. Chapter notes are extensive, and there is an author and a subject index.

666

Howkins, John. **New Technologies, New Policies?** London, BFI Institute, 1982. 74p.

"Reading as a layman, I found the report most helpful—dispassionate, level-headed, well-informed and very shrewd, a most compact and clear guide to the new technological jungle," says Richard Hoggart in the Introduction to this first report of Britain's Broadcasting Research Unit (set up by the BBC, the Markle Foundation, and the British Film Institute). Descriptive rather than prescriptive, it is an accurate and comprehensive survey of developments in cable, video, and satellite technology which keeps in mind their implications for policies on information and communication that will satisfy social needs.

667

Huesmann, L. Rowell, and Leonard D. Eron, eds. **Television and the Aggressive Child: A Cross-National Comparison**. Hillsdale, NJ: Erlbaum, 1986. 314p.

The editors' aims in this study are three-fold: to devise a psychological process model to explain how television violence affects aggression; to integrate media violence research with other aggression research; and to study cultural norms and programming differences which might interact with age and gender of children to produce different effects in different countries. The results are two general studies by the editors: "The Development of Aggression on Children of Different Cultures: Psychological Processes and Exposure to Violence," and "The Cross-National Approach to Research on Aggression: Measures and Procedures"; followed by cross-cultural studies on five countries: the U.S., (the editors), Finland (Kirsti Lagerspetz and Vappu Viemerö), Poland (Adam Fraczek), Australia (Peter Sheehan), and Israel (Riva Bachrach). Huesmann draws some commonalities, and Jo Groebel finishes with "International Research on Television Violence: Synopsis and Critique." Chapter reference, and author and subject indexes.

668

Hutchinson, Robert. **Cable, DBS and the Arts**. London: Policy Studies Institute, 1984. 104p.

In three parts, cable and DBS (direct broadcasting), cable and the arts in North America, and cable and the arts in England. The first summarizes the debate surrounding cable and DBS developments in the U.K.; the second describes the aims, fates and fortunes of arts channels available on cable in North America, and the programming and other plans for such channels in the U.K.; and the third considers the proposed developments in the structure, financing and programming of British

TV in relation to film policy and other aspects of arts policy. There are numerous references and four appendixes: "Cable Systems in the UK"; "Home Video"; "Major UK Performing Arts Companies: Their Work on Television and Video"; and "Copyright Reform—A Levy on Blank Tapes."

INICO (Institute of Communication Research, Central University of Caracas). **Socio-Economic Aspects of National Communication Systems: III, Radio Broadcasting in Venezuela.** (See No. 787.)

Johnstone, John W. C., Edward J. Slawski, and William W. Bowman. **The News People**. (See No. 219.)

669

Kaatz, Ronald B. **Cable Advertiser's Handbook**. 2d ed. Lincolnwood, IL: Crain, 1985. 262p.

A "how to" guide which gives the ABC's of cable advertising and as background the ABC's of cable itself. Good for the totally uninitiated. The author is Senior Vice President-Director of Media Concepts, J. Walter Thompson. Contains a list of standard organizations and trade papers concerning themselves with cable; a glossary of advertising terms; and an index.

670

Kahn, Frank J., ed. **Documents of American Broadcasting**. 4th ed. Englewood Cliffs, NJ: Prentice Hall, 1984. 501p.

A collection of primary source materials in the field of public policy formulation in broadcasting and related media. Includes laws, commission materials, court decisions, and other documents that range chronologically from the pre-history of electronic media development to the 1980s. However, Kahn has made an exception of governing statutes in his arrangement, placing them last. Each document is put in perspective by an introductory headnote, and a "Related Reading" section suggests further sources. Documents are minimally edited and reproduced in their entirety. A feature new to this edition is a glossary of legal terms. There is a dual table of contents—one arranged by page order and the other based on thematic patterns—and two indexes—one a guide to cited cases and the other a general index. A thorough revision, with much new material and a rearrangement of some of the old.

671

Kaminsky, Stuart M., with Jeffrey H. Mahan. **American Television Genres**. Chicago: Nelson-Hall, 1985. 220p.

An exploration of possible ways to study various television genres. First comes a discussion of definitions and the nature of the problem, followed by an examination of historical, structural, psychological, sociological and anthropological approaches. Specific shows are used at random to illustrate various types of methodology. Bibliography and author-title index.

672

Katz, Elihu, and George Wedell. **Broadcasting in the Third World: Promise and Performance**. Cambridge, MA: Harvard University Press, 1977. 305p.

"The emphasis of our study is on *process*, on the dynamics of accommodating the phenomenon of broadcasting and its institutional forms to the surroundings of a developing country for which it was not in the first instance designed," say the authors. They are also interested in side effects, some of which were not anticipated. Basing their work on an extensive review of statistical and documentary data concerning broadcasting in 91 developing countries and on case studies of 11 of these, they assess the status quo in terms of structure, control, and social and cultural patterns. The 11 countries include Algeria, Brazil, Cyprus, Indonesia, Iran, Nigeria, Peru, Senegal, Singapore, Tanzania, and Thailand. Contains a number of tables of data throughout and an appendix of supplementary tables. Two other appendixes give methodology and levels of development of the 91 selected countries. There are numerous footnotes and an index. Winner of the 1977 National Association of Education Broadcasters Award.

673

Kaye, Evelyn, with the cooperation of the American Academy of Pediatrics. **The ACT Guide to Children's Television or . . . How to Treat TV with T.L.C.** Rev. ed. Boston: Beacon Press, 1979. 226p.

Evelyn Kaye, the AAP, and the ACT (Action for Children's Television) have designed this guide for concerned parents. Accepting the view that the affinity between children and television is a fact of life, they provide information and tips—to watch or not to watch; professional opinions; advertising; violence; TV and the classroom; children's programming; and other such valuable items. The index contains still more: "A Short Course in Broadcasting," "Violence in Children's Television Programs," a valuable "Resource Directory," and an equally valuable bibliography. Although published some years ago, this has lost none of its usefulness.

Kittross, John M., comp. **A Bibliography of Theses and Dissertations in Broadcasting, 1920–1973.** (See No. 1661.)

674

Koenig, Allen E., ed. **Broadcasting and Bargaining: Labor Relations in Radio and Television.** Madison: University of Wisconsin Press, 1970. 344p.

A study on broadcasting unions covering four major areas: a historical overview, legal decisions rendered by the National Labor Relations Board and the courts, specific problem areas confronting the industry and unions, and a look at the future. Contains appendixes: "Report and Order of the FCC on Nondiscrimination in Broadcast Employment Practices," and "Further Notice of Proposed Rulemaking on Nondiscrimination in Broadcast Employment Practices." Indexed and with footnotes at the ends of sections.

675

Krasnow, Erwin G., Lawrence D. Longley, and Herbert A. Terry. **The Politics of Broadcast Regulation**. 3rd ed. New York: St. Martin's Press, 1982. 304p.

The central point made by this book is that the regulation of the broadcast industry is a complicated political process which serves as the "basic framework for analyzing broadcast regulation. . . ." Six factors involved in broadcast regulatory policy are identified and analyzed: FCC, Congress, the courts, the President, industry representatives, and citizen groups. The latter is a newcomer among the active forces in this political environment. Five case studies and an excellent bibliographic essay are included.

676

Kuhn, Raymond, ed. **Broadcasting and Politics in Western Europe**. London: Frank Cass, 1985. 174p.

Individual studies of eight countries and one cross-national comparative article provide a survey of present trends and potential developments, both political and technological, in Western European broadcasting. Articles include: "Politics, Parties and Media in Britain" by Jean Seaton; "Proclaiming the Republic: Broadcasting Policy and the Corporate State in Ireland" by Desmond Bell, "France and the 'New Media'" by Raymond Kuhn; "Political and Market Forces in Italian Broadcasting" by Donald Sassoon; "Pluralism in the West German Media: The Press, Broadcasting and Cable" by Arthur Williams; "Broadcasting and Politics in the Netherlands: From Pillar to Post" by Kees Brants; "Broadcasting in Spain: A Study of Heavy-Handed State Control" by Estaban López-Escobar and Angel Faus-Belau; and "Greece: A Politically Controlled State Monopoly Broadcasting System" by Dimitrios Katsoudas. The cross-national study, "The Politics of Cable and Satellite Broadcasting: Some West European Comparisons," is by Kenneth Dyson. Each article contains chapter notes and an abstract. For a more general survey, see **New Media Politics: Comparative Perspectives in Western Europe**, by Denis McQuail (No. 717).

677

Kuhn, Raymond, ed. **The Politics of Broadcasting**. London: Croom Helm, 1985. 305p.

Describes and analyzes the problems faced by politicians and broadcasters in eight democracies as they respond to radical new developments in telecommunications and information technology, coupled with governmental changes, which together effect the nature and quality of national broadcasting systems. Countries are Great Britain, France, West Germany, Italy, the U.S., Canada, Australia and Japan. Intended for laymen. References at the end of each article. Index.

678

Kuo, Eddie C. Y., and Peter S. J. Chen. **Communication Policy and Planning in Singapore**. London: Kegan Paul in association with East-West Communication Institute, 1983. 111p.

After providing an overview of the Singapore society and its communication system as background, the co-authors examine the main aspects of communication policy in Singapore, and conclude with a case study of communication planning at the Radio and Television Singapore and the Singapore Family Planning and Population Board. Appendixes include "The Communication Network in Singapore," "Breakdown of Television Singapore Programs, by Language, Type of Program, and Location of Production," and RTS's [Radio Television Singapore] Requirements for Advertising Material." Contains references.

Kurtz, Bruce. **Sports: The Popular Art of American Television Commercials**. (See No. 1583.)

Labeau, Dennis. **Theatre, Film and Television Biographies**. (See No. 1328.)

679

Lackmann, Ron. **Remember Radio**. New York: Norton, 1970. 128p.

Intended to provide entertainment and provoke nostalgia through photographs, scripts, and radio listings of programs in pre-television days, this covers a range of popular programs. Among other things, it contains about 300 pictures of character known by voice rather than by face.

680

Lambert, Stephen. **Channel Four: Television with a Difference?** London: British Film Institute, 1982. 178p.

Lambert tells the story of the British Channel Four—its philosophy, the struggle to get it started; the aims and objectives; the organization and financing; and the ways in which it differs from the other channels. Appendixes give terms of reference and program policy statement for Channel Four, a chart of the executive structure, and a list showing personnel and organizational structure. Chapter notes and index.

681

Lang, Gladys Engel, and Kurt Lang. **Politics and Television Re-VIEWED**. Beverly Hills, CA: Sage, 1984. 221p.

"In this book we examine some ways in which television, through its live coverage of major political events, has shaped public images of politics and political personalities, and in so doing, has influenced the nature and course of political life."—Preface. A 1968 book, **Politics and Television** (Quadrangle, 315p.) took readers through election night 1964; the present volume continues through Watergate and the Carter-Ford debates, with implications of these events for 1984 and beyond. Chapter notes.

682

Larson, James F. **Television's Window on the World: International Affairs Coverage on the U.S. Networks**. Norwood, NJ: Ablex, 1984. 195p.

An examination of television network news which focuses on three broad areas. The first and principal focus is on the content of international affairs coverage provided by ABC, CBS and NBC on week-night news broadcasts from 1972 through 1981; the second is on influences which affected the presentation of reality—among them, satellites, improved equipment and patterns of deployment of news personnel; and the third is on the consequences of television's coverage of international news, particularly in relation to foreign policy process. To gather his information Larson used as his primary method quantitative content analysis based on data gathered from Vanderbilt University's Television News Archives. All in all, he analyzed over 7,000 international news items contained in more than 1,000 early evening network broadcasts. Six appendixes show the breakdown of his data. Bibliography and an author and a subject index.

683

Lazarsfeld, Paul F. **Radio and the Printed Page**. New York: Duell, Sloan & Pearce, 1940. 354p.

Lazarsfeld pioneered in examining the role and effect of broadcasting, at that time limited to radio. In this, the first of half a dozen or more studies, he discusses its interplay with reading.

684, 685

Lazarsfeld, Paul F. and Harry Field. **The People Look at Radio**. Chapel Hill: University of North Carolina Press, 1946. 158p.

Lazarsfeld, Paul F., and Patricia Kendall. **Radio Listening in America: The People Look at**

Radio—Again. New York: Prentice-Hall, 1948. 178p.

Two studies conducted by the National Opinion Research Center in cooperation with the Bureau of Social Research are analyzed and interpreted by Paul Lazarsfeld (and Patricia Kendall in the latter). Both concern radio content and the communication behavior of the American people, with discussion on the role of criticism. Appendixes give statistics. Indexed. Updated to 1963 by Steiner's **The People Look at Television**. (No. 797.)

686, 687, 688

Lazarsfeld, Paul F., and Frank N. Stanton, eds. **Radio Research, 1941**. New York: Duell, Sloan & Pearce, 1941. 328p.

Lazarsfeld, Paul F. **Radio Research, 1942–43**. New York: Duell, Sloan & Pearce, 1944. 599p.

Lazarsfeld, Paul F. **Communications Research, 1948–1949**. New York: Harper, 1949. 332p.

These are among the earliest anthologies (especially the first two volumes) in the new subject field of mass communications. The 1942–43 volume contains such classics as the articles on soap operas by Herta Herzog and by Rudolf Arnheim and Leo Lowenthal's "Biographies in Popular Magazines." It also has a section about radio in World War II.

The 1948–49 volume as well has some classic studies, among them "The Children Talk about Comics" by Katherine M. Wolf and Marjorie Fiske and "What Missing the Newspaper Means" by Bernard Berelson. Alex Inkeles has analyzed domestic broadcasting in the U.S.S.R. and Robert Merton and Lazarsfeld discuss research methodology. Both volumes are indexed.

689

Lee, Chin-Chuan. **Media Imperialism Reconsidered: The Homogenizing of Television Culture**. Beverly Hills, CA: Sage, 1971. 276p.

An analysis of media imperialism with a middle-range focus. Capitalist exploitation, Lee contends, is not limited to the Third World but extends to advanced capitalist countries as well. The real questions should resolve around "(1) the extent to which Marxist-Leninist theory of 'media imperialism' withstands vigorous historical tests and empirical verification; (2) the extent to which liberal rhetoric of 'free flow' refutes its formidable critics; and (3) the extent to which socialist centralized control, as some Marxian adherents claim, constitutes a viable alternative to the media imperialism of advanced capitalism." He centers upon three countries—Canada, Taiwan and China—for his inquiry. Although the analysis is of television specifically, it examines divergent theoretical and ideological structures common to other media as well. Notes, an extensive bibliography and a subject and an author index.

690

Lent, John A., ed. **Broadcasting in Asia and the Pacific: A Continental Survey of Radio and Television**. Philadelphia: Temple University Press, 1978. 429p.

Asian and Pacific national broadcasting personnel and international communication scholars, trainers, and practitioners contributed to this anthology, which covers the instructional and functional foundations of broadcasting in 44 countries, territories, and dependencies, ranging from Afghanistan on the periphery of West Asia to the South Pacific islands. All chapters are original except the introductory one, which is reprinted from the 1974 **Asian Press and Media Directory**, and many are by nationals from the countries described. For the most part topics covered are oriented to historical development, control, ownership and pressures, programming and performance, facilities, financing and advertising, external services, audiences, training, and research. There is a long section on cross-system functions which includes specialized program services and international, regional, and national assistance and cooperation. The bibliography lists primarily sources cited in the text; for further references Lent refers us to his **Asian Mass Communications: A Comprehensive Bibliography** (No. 1667). Indexed.

Lentz, Harris M., III. **Science Fiction, Horror & Fantasy Film Television and Credits**. (See No. 1337.)

691, 692

Levin, Harvey J. **Broadcast Regulation and Joint Ownership of Media**. New York: New York University Press, 1960. 219p.

Levin, Harvey J. **The Invisible Resource: Use and Regulation of the Radio Spectrum**. Baltimore: Johns Hopkins Press, 1971. 432p.

Broadcast Regulation and Joint Ownership of Media discusses the character of intermedia competition, the pattern and trend of joint media ownership, the case for separate ownership, economics of joint ownership, impact of old media on new, competition in price and quality, broadcast regulatory policy. Although some of this material has dated and the statistics have become historical, its verities hold. An appendix giving sources of statistical data forms a bibliography, and there are indexes to cases cited and to subjects.

The Invisible Resource is a detailed account with emphasis on technical and economic aspects. In four parts: 1) the spectrum system, which discusses the technical basis of the problem, the major users of spectrum, and potential goals of spectrum management; 2) the alternatives in spectrum allocation and management, which examines a free-market rather than a regulated approach; 3) the level of spectrum development; and 4) allocations-regulation-prices-service, which examines the potential of competition as a means of preserving resources.

Lewels, Francisco J., Jr. **The Uses of the Media by the Chicano Movement**. (See No. 250.)

Lichty, Lawrence W., comp. **World and International Broadcasting: A Bibliography**. (See No. 1668.)

693

Lichty, Lawrence W., and Malachi C. Topping, comps. **American Broadcasting: A Source Book on the History of Radio and Television**. New York: Hastings House, 1975. 723p.

An anthology of 93 selections (one third of which were never before published), chosen to give "as complete and accurate" a picture as possible of American broadcasting from its pre-history to 1975. Divided into eight parts: technical, stations, networks, economics, employment, programming, audiences, and regulation, each preceded by the compilers' commentaries. There is a second table of contents which is chronological, and more than 50 original tables.

694

Liebert, Robert M., Joyce N. Sprafkin, and Emily S. Davidson. **The Early Window: Effects of Television on Children and Youth**. 2d ed. New York: Pergamon Press, 1982. 251p.

The authors' purpose: "to provide an account of the theory and research which now bears on television and children's attitudes, development, and behavior, and to explore the social, political, and economic factors that surround these issues." Discussions include television as business; violence; the Surgeon General Report and its aftermath; TV advertising and children; race and sex on TV; and TV's potential benefits. The bibliography is unusually detailed, and an appendix lists obtainable government documents on the subject. Index.

695

Lisann, Maury. **Broadcasting to the Soviet Union: International Politics and Radio**. New York: Praeger, 1975. 199p.

Deals chronologically with Soviet radio as it is influenced by governmental policies, and in a final chapter probes opinion and trends. Each chapter is footnoted and there is a lengthy bibliography and an index.

696

Lodziak, Conrad. **The Power of Television: A Critical Appraisal**. New York: St. Martin's Press, 1986. 217p.

Although prevailing wisdom has it that television has considerable power to affect society for better or worse, research has not established this with any degree of certainty, says Lodziak, who believes that its power has been overemphasized and misplaced, so that it has come to prescribe research practices and theoretical reasoning. The problem can be understood only by considering the full impact of non-media forces in determining the range of actions available to individuals. In a final chapter he gives a number of implications of his arguments for television research within critical social theory. Chapter references and index.

697

Luthra, H. R. **Indian Broadcasting**. New Delhi: Minister of Information and Broadcasting, Publications Division, 1986. 531p.

Luthra brings to his history of broadcasting in India more than 50 years of personal involvement, along with documents from the National Archives and correspondence and notes in files at the Directorate General of All India Radio. Emphasis is on the early years because, he says, "very little is now remembered of that period," and it is important that those who lived through it recapture it for history. This is a straight chronological account of events and the people who took part in them, with no effort to place the growth of Indian broadcasting in a social or cultural context, but which nevertheless serves as a useful starting place for research. An earlier book along the same lines is by **Broadcasting in India** (Bombay: Allied Publishers, 1965. 268p.) by G. C. Awasthy, a former AIR employee.

Lyle, Jack. **The People Look at Public Television, 1974**. (See No. 774.)

698

Lyman, Peter. **Canada's Video Revolution: Pay-TV, Home Video and Beyond**. Toronto: James Lorimer in association with the Canadian Institute for Economic Policy, 1983. 173p.

In language which the interested layman can understand, Lyman describes the impact of the new communications technologies on the evolution of Canada's cultural industries.

699

MacCabe, Colin, and Olivia Stewart. **The BBC and Public Service Broadcasting**. Manchester, England: Manchester University Press, 1986. 116p.

On the assumption that the kind of public service broadcasting Britain offers is central to the national culture, this volume brings together the varying perspectives of academics, researchers and practitioners from major networks to discuss present and future possibilities resulting from technological developments and a changed political climate likely to affect funding and quality. Contributors include Anthony Smith, Janet Morgan, William Maley, Krishan Kumar, Charles Jonscher, Brenda Mattox, David Elstein, Margaret Matheson, Jeremy Isaacs, John Caughie, and MacCabe.

700

MacCabe, Colin, ed. **High Theory/Low Culture: Analyzing Popular Television and Film.** Manchester, England: Manchester University Press, 1986. 171p.

This collection of essays grew out of a dissatisfaction with widely used definitions of popular culture and forms of analysis employed to interpret it. Focusing on film and television, they offer new approaches in terms of both content and methodology with emphasis on popular culture and politics, popular culture and genre, and popular elite culture. Authors, from both Britain and America, include Laura Kipnis, Tania Modleski, Simon Frith, Douglas Gomery, Laura Mulvey, Jane Feuer, Gillian Skirrow, Andrew Tolson, John Caughie, and the editor. Chapter notes.

701

MacDonald, J. Fred. **Don't Touch That Dial! Radio Programming in American Life, 1920–1960.** Chicago: Nelson-Hall, 1979. 412p.

Through an examination of the content of radio programming from 1920 to 1960 in relation to developments in national life during that period MacDonald offers a perspective which sees culture—and especially the commercialized mass culture of the United States in the present century—as "a reflector and creator of popular values, attitudes, fantasies and realities." The book is divided into two complementary sections. The first traces the history of radio and its programs, seeking to understand the ways in which broadcasting arose and collapsed during those 40 years; the second looks more closely at distinct types of programs or social themes within radio during the time span. In addition to scholar sources, fan magazines, newspapers and **Variety**, the author has drawn upon his private collection of more than 8,000 hours of tape-recorded vintage shows. Chapter notes, bibliography, an index to radio programs, and a general index.

702

MacDonald, J. Fred. **Television and the Red Menace: The Video Road to Vietnam.** New York: Praeger, 1985. 277p.

Far from regarding television as a primary force responsible for the American public's ultimate distaste for our participation in the Vietnamese war, MacDonald contends that years of misrepresentation on television prepared the U.S. to participate. Analyzing news and information and entertainment programming, he builds a case, beginning with the emergence of television during the Cold War era and its subsequent politization which sold a view of the world and America's role in it.

703

Maclauren, W. Rupert, with R. Joyce Harman. **Invention and Innovation in the Radio Industry.** New York: Arno Press, c1940, 1971. 304p.

A history of radio and early TV, first published by Macmillan, from the time of the scientific pioneers of radio to 1940, with emphasis on the technology involved. Appendixes include "The Elements of Modern Radio Communication" and "Radio Patent Litigation." Bibliography and index.

704

MacNeil, Robert. **The People Machine: The Influence of Television on American Politics.** New York: Harper & Row, 1968. 362p.

MacNeil grasps eternal verities out of the grab bag of political events of the mid- to early 1960s. Over a passage of time his analysis of the role of television in image creation, political campaigning and government in general does not date. Apart from the value of his incisive insights, his book makes interesting reading for scholar or layman. Notes and index.

705

Macy, John W., Jr. **To Irrigate a Wasteland: The Struggle to Shape a Public Television System in the United States.** Berkeley: University of California, 1974. 186p.

A capsule history of public broadcasting in America, with an inside account of recent developments and consideration as to how it may be financed without commercials or partisan control. Appendixes give, among other things, a glossary of organizational terms, public TV licenses, call numbers, locations; text of Public Law 90–129, Public Broadcasting Act of 1967; growth pattern—1969–72; characteristics of PTV station types, 1971; U.S. noncommercial compared with U.S. commercial TV stations; source of funds by PTV station type, 1966–71; TV service cost by country; public TV programming sources, 1971. Indexed.

706

Maddison, John. **Radio and Television in Literacy: A Survey of the Use of the Broadcasting Media in Combating Illiteracy among Adults.** Paris: UNESCO, 1971. 82p. (Reports and Papers on Mass Communication No. 62.)

Gives information on the uses of radio and TV in connection with literacy work in 40 countries in various parts of the world.

707

Mander, Jerry. **Four Arguments for the Elimination of Television.** New York: Morrow, 1978. 371p.

From a great deal of soul searching, much of it based on his own experience as an advertising executive, Mander opts for the elimination of television because it distorts reality and makes for automatic control by those already in power who will use it to maintain the status quo. In short, the medium has no democratic potential; the ideology comes with the technology. He writes entertainingly and with challenge, and although his arguments are for the most part simplistic, they possess kernels of truth.

708

Mankiewicz, Frank, and Joel Swerdlow. **Remote Control: Television and the Manipulation of American Life**. New York: Times Books, 1977. 308p.

A damning array of facts compiled and conclusions drawn from a wide variety of sources, including thousands of studies and a number of intensive interviews with men and women in the profession. The authors examine TV in the light of violence, family-hour programming, news, sex roles, reading, learning and behavior in children, consumerism, and our political and quasi-political institutions. Their conclusions about the part TV plays in our lives are not reassuring. There is a sizable bibliography and an index.

709

Mansell, Gerard. **Let Truth Be Told: 50 Years of External Broadcasting**. London: Weidenfeld and Nicolson, 1982. 300p.

A tightly written history of BBC's external broadcasting system written from primary sources supplemented by extensive conversations with many retired BBC officials, among them some of the earliest members of the first foreign language services and many who worked in the European and Overseas Services in wartime. Prolific notes, bibliography and index.

Marill, Alvin H. **Movies Made for Television**. (See No. 1369.)

Marzolf, Marion. **Up from the Footnote: A History of Women Journalists**. (See No. 933.)

710

Masterman, Len, ed. **Television Mythologies: Stars, Shows and Signs**. London: Comedia, 1984. 143p.

Short critical essays focusing primarily on light entertainment, comedy and game shows, music and sports programming, the two authors have leaned upon Roland Barthes's method of analysis which asserts that popular culture must be assessed within a broad social framework rather than a narrow one based on popular mythologies. The programs analyzed are English, but the critiques are universally applicable.

711

Mattelart, Armand, Xavier Delcourt, and Michele Mattelart. **International Image Markets: In Search of an Alternative Perspective**. Tr. by David Buxton. London: Comedia, 1984. 122p.

This is the final report of the research commission "toward a Latin Audiovisual Space." The term "Audiovisual Space" marks the emergence of a new diplomatic vocabulary to indicate the rapid new developments of communication and information systems, particularly television, which demand new strategies, policies and both national and international projects. "Space" indicates geographic boundaries which in this case includes countries speaking French and Spanish or some variation thereof. The report is in four parts: 1) an analysis of the imbalance of the international flows of culture, information, and communications; 2) a linkage between culture and industry to show the main tendencies in the restructuring of the international economy which condition to a large extent the search for audiovisual space; 3) an evaluation of efforts already undertaken to find potential partners and forms of cooperation not only between countries of the North and South, but also South and South; 4) a discussion of the contradictions of reconciling the conquest of foreign markets with the value of domestic expression of national individuality. In the introduction Nicholas Garnham points out this book's relevance to Anglo Saxon readers. He says, "It deals cogently with two of the central contemporary cultural debates, the future of European audiovisual culture and the New World Information." The authors reject the simplistic view that sees the "South as Good and the North as Bad." The individual histories of each country are considered on the recognition that cultural, like economic imperialism, works through the specificities of the local power structure. Chapter notes.

McArthur, Colin, ed. **Scotch Reels: Scotland in Cinema and Television**. (See No. 1376.)

712

McCavitt, William E. **Broadcasting Around the World**. Summit, PA: TAB, 1981. 336p.

Description of broadcasting systems in 18 countries: South Africa, Poland, Russia, Japan, South Korea, Israel, Canada, the United States, Brazil, Guyana, India, Federal Republic of Germany, Britain, Ireland, Italy, the Netherlands, Sweden and Australia. Each chapter has been written by an individual involved in broadcasting in that particular country or has been contributed by the official broadcast system of the country. Information varies for each, but concise and fairly extensive. An appendix suggests additional reading. Index.

713

McLoone, Martin, and John MacMahon, eds. **Television and Irish Society: 21 Years of Irish**

Television. Dublin: Radio Telefis Eireann, 1984. 151p.

A group of essays of RTI television programming which grew out of Ireland's new media studies program and are intended both to offer systematic analyses of television's various forms and to open up fresh ideas on its potential. Each essay is footnoted. There are two appendixes, one containing "DeValera's Address on the Opening of Telefis Eireann—31 December 1961," and another giving scant statistics on television programs and audiences.

714

McMahon, Morgan E., comp. **Vintage Radio: Harold Greenwood's Historical Album Expanded with More Old Ads, Illustrations, and Many Photos of Wireless and Radio Equipment**. 2d ed. Palos Verdes Peninsula, CA: Vintage Radio, 1973. 263p.

In the early days of wireless and radio, a man named Harold Greenwood put together a collection of pictures from many sources illustrating the state-of-the-art apparatus used for broadcasting and receiving, with textual explanations when necessary. This book is now out of print. Morgan McMahon has compiled a similar one, described in the sub-title, with illustrations and materials of all sorts, drawn mainly from old ads and catalogs, which should prove useful to those interested in equipment used between the late nineteenth century and the first two decades of this one. In addition to the main text, which shows the many types of receivers and transmitters, there is a survey at the beginning and a guide to collecting. Indexed. A second book, **A Flick of the Switch, 1930–1950**, also published by Vintage Radio (1975), takes up where the earlier book leaves off, covering early television as well as radio.

715

McNeil, Bill, and Morris Wolfe. **The Birth of Radio in Canada: Signing On**. Garden City, NY and Toronto: Doubleday, 1982. 303p.

Signing On, a celebration of half a century of Canadian public broadcasting, contains 125 interviews with broadcasters, producers, technicians, entrepreneurs and ordinary listeners from both the private and public sector in all ten provinces. Material is divided into seven parts—the first three geographical ("The Maritimes," "Quebec-Ontario," and "The West"), followed by "The C.N.R. [Canadian Radio Broadcasting Commission]," "The CBC [Canadian Broadcasting Corporation]," and a brief "The Coming of Television." There are many illustrations, including photographs, ads, cartoons and newspaper clippings. Useful for reference and entertainment. Chronology and index.

716

McPhail, Thomas L. **Electronic Colonialism: The Future of International Broadcasting and Communication**. Beverly Hills, CA: Sage, 1981. 259p.

Much of the writings about the New World Information Order (NWIO) is heated, with rhetoric by the Western industrialized nations and the Third World countries governed by their differing viewpoints in the context of their disparate pasts and conflicting philosophies. McPhail approaches the debate with delicate balance, discussing the objectives of the NWIO, freedom of the press, media and development research traditions (which he calls "a misguided start"), the role of UNESCO, International Telecommunications Union and the World Administration Radio Conference, wire service, DBS and related international issues, and the MacBride Report. An appendix charts the ideological alignments of developing countries in terms of "radical," "conservative" or "independent" political orientations. A second appendix contains the text of the "Draft Declaration on Fundamental Principles Concerning the Contribution of the Mass Media in Strengthening Peace and International Understanding, the Promotion of Human Rights, and to Countering Racialism, Apartheid and Incitement to War." Chapter notes, references, and author index. (A revised edition was published in 1987.)

717

McQuail, Denis, and Karen Siune, eds. **New Media Politics: Comparative Perspectives in Western Europe**. Beverly Hills, CA: Sage, 1986. 216p.

This book is the first to come from a project which originated as a Workgroup of the European Consortium for Political Research, consisting of a group of European social scientists and professionals in the field of mass media. They came together, they say, "to uncover underlying dynamics of policymaking and disclose long term patterns, rather than provide an up-to-date report on matters of ever-changing detail. Unlike most other work in this area, we have sought to develop a comparative framework and to provide an integrated, rather than country-by-country, assessment of what is happening in Europe in the mid-1980s." Within the framework of the European continent they discuss policy-making, the transnational context of the media, broadcasting, cable, satellites, video, mass telematics, monopoly, and the issues of culture and commercialization. A final chapter raises the question: "A New Media Order?" Chapter notes and name-subject index. See also **Broadcasting and Politics in Western Europe**, edited by Raymond Kuhn, for a discussion of specifics in eight countries (No. 676).

718

Meetings of Experts on the Development of News Agencies in Africa, Tunis, 1963. Paris: UNESCO, 1963. 225p.

An examination of measures to promote the development of existing news agencies, the establishment of agencies in areas not yet possessing them, and the flow of news within the region, as well as in other regions of the world.

Mehr, Linda Harris. **Motion Pictures, Television and Radio: A Union Catalog of Manuscripts and Special Collections in the Western United States**. (See No. 1381.)

719

Melody, William H. **Children's Television: The Economics of Exploitation**. New Haven: Yale University Press, 1973. 164p.

Should children's television be declared an area that requires the establishment of special protections for children and positive responsibilities toward them? This early study, commissioned by Action for Children's Television, examines the economic aspects of commercial children's television and the relation to the FCC public-policy options. Melody analyzes the economic characteristics of advertising practices and the ways in which they affect programming, traces the history of children's programming from TV's early years to the present, and suggests alternative modes of financing it. Contains notes; an extensive bibliography of articles, documents, and other materials; an appendix: "FCC News Release Announcing Its Notice of Inquiry and Proposed Rule-making into Commercial Children's Television."

Merrill, John C., ed. **Global Journalism**. (See No. 935.)

720

Meyer, Manfred, ed. **Children and the Formal Features of Television: Approaches and Findings of Experimental and Formative Research**. Munich, Germany: K. G. Saur, 1983. 333p. (Communication Research & Broadcasting, No. 6.)

Articles which present research into the ways children perceive and understand the formal features and visual codes of television such as zooms, camera movements, cuts, montage techniques, ellipses and programming pacing, music, special sound effects, peculiar voices, etc., in order to determine the extent they arouse and sustain attention, support comprehension, or encourage intended learning processes. Contributors are interdisciplinary from the U.S., Europe and Israel. Each article has a bibliography.

721

Meyrowitz, Joshua. **No Sense of Place: The Impact of Electronic Media on Social Behavior**. New York: Oxford University Press, 1985. 416p.

An analysis of the ways electronic media affect social behavior in which the author contends that their main impact is not through their messages but rather through a reorganization of the social settings in which people interact and a weakening of the relationship between physical place and social "place." A larger purpose, he says, is to offer a new approach to the study of both media effects and social change, and he gives credit to Marshall McLuhan whose theories stimulated his own theorizing. Notes, 15-page bibliography, and index.

Miller, Randall, M., ed. **Ethnic Images in American Film and Television**. (See No. 1387.)

722

Moody, Kate. **Growing Up On Television: The TV Effect**. New York: Times Books, 1980. 242p.

"My purpose," Moody says, "is to promote thinking about what it means to grow up on television." To stimulate awareness, she examines effect studies on various aspects: physical well being, learning and perception, aggressive behavior, health and life style, social relationships, and action at home, at school, and in public in the hope the findings may serve as guidelines to adults on children's TV-watching. Appendixes recommend aids to help compete with TV in capturing the child's interest—"Read Aloud Books" and "Suggested Equipment and Materials"; a brief chronological history of Action for Children's Television; and a list of local children's television committees and of national research and reform groups. Notes, recommended booklist, and index.

723

Mosco, Vincent. **Broadcasting in the United States: Innovative Challenge and Organizational Control**. Norwood, NJ: Ablex, 1979. 168p.

Mosco makes a case that established interests—primarily the owners of radio and TV stations—have induced the FCC to respond conservatively to FM radio, UHF TV, cable TV, and subscription TV. He contends that this has resulted in the concentration of political and economic power in the hands of the broadcasting industry and has restricted the audiences' choice of programs. He then reviews proposals that have been made to change the regulatory structure, and suggests new alternatives. Contains appendixes, a bibliography, and an author and subject index.

724

Mosco, Vincent. **Pushbutton Fantasies: Critical Perspectives on Videotext and Information Technology**. Norwood, NJ: Ablex, 1982. 195p.

Using critical theory, Mosco applies "new ways of seeing," as he terms it, to the development of information technology and, more specifically, to videotext which he feels is the key to a powerful new communication system combining television, computers, and in some of its applications, telephone or coaxial cables. From this perspective he analyzes its future within a critique of post-industrialism in the workplace, mass society in the home, pluralism in government, and developmentalism in international relations. Contains figures and tables, footnotes, a chapter by chapter bibliography and an index.

Müller, Werner, and Manfred Meyer, comps. **Children and Families Watching Television: A Bibliography on Viewing Processes**. (See No. 1675.)

725

Murphy, Brian. **The World Wired Up: Unscrambling the New Communication Puzzle**. London: Comedia, 1983. 155p.

Murphy writes about the "tools of a new era" in terms of products and markets—the products being the tools of the information revolution, the markets being the global environment in which they operate. Most materials currently available, he says, talk about the tools alone, which is a balance he has set out to redress. After an "Introduction: Marketing the Electronic Future," he breaks down his examination worldwide: "The United States: Global Communications Inc."; "Canada: The Most Wired Nation on Earth"; "Europe: Swimming Against the U.S. Tidal Wave?"; "Japan: A Yen for the Micro Market"; "The Third World: Spectators at the Feast"; and "The UK: Cabling Up for the Depression." His assessment points toward a world—Northern as well as Southern hemispheres—in which "information technology, which holds so much potential for assisting the development of equality, has already started to increase the efficiency and intensity of repression," an argument he buttresses with extensive background information preceding each chapter. His facts are carefully footnoted, and there is a glossary of technical terms and a brief bibliography.

Murray, John P. **Television & Youth: 25 Years of Research & Controversy**. (See No. 1676.)

726

Murray, John P., and Gavriel Salomon, eds. **Future of Children's Television**. Boys Town, NB: The Boys Town Center, Communications and Public Service Division, 1984. 174p.

Discussions and papers resulting from a conference on children's television held at Boys Town which "summarizes much of what is known, raises questions that need to be answered, and examines the evolving future of television." The papers detail the considerable knowledge available about effective educational and social uses of television, but point out that for various reasons this knowledge has not been put to sufficient use.

727

Musolf, Lloyd D., ed. **Communications Satellites in Political Orbit**. San Francisco: Chandler, 1968. 189p.

Beginning with the organization of the Communica-tion Satellite Corporation in 1962 and progressing through the next half-decade, the editor has traced its history through the use of official documents—testimony of interested parties, both public and private, before Congressional committees; reports made by these committees; interchanges between protagonists on the floor of the House or Senate; presidential messages and statements; and policy pronouncements by administrative agencies. Through use of these excerpts, he has been successful in revealing some of the decision-making processes that structured an important technological innovation. A valuable sourcebook.

728

Negrine, Ralph, ed. **Cable Television and the Future of Broadcasting**. London: Croom Helm, 1985. 211p.

Surveys cable television in nine modern industrialized countries—the U.S., Canada, Belgium, Holland, Great Britain, France, Western Germany, Australia, and Japan. The editor's objective is to provide a general survey of developments in specific countries, and to give the reader the opportunity to assess the promise of cable television, gage its rate of development, and measure its likely impact on existing broadcasting services. Contributors are Vernone Sparkes, Andre H. Caron and James R. Taylor, Kees Brants and Nick Jankowski, Claude-Jean Bertrand, Michael Schact and Rolf Fudiger Hoffman, Geoffrey Caldwell, and Michael Tracey, all of whom are nationals or living in the country each writes about. Notes and references, glossary, and index.

729, 730

Newcomb, Horace, ed. **Television: The Critical View**. 3d ed. New York: Oxford University Press, 1982. 549p.

Newcomb, Horace. **TV: The Most Popular Art**. New York: Anchor, 1974. 272p.

In both of these books Newcomb approaches TV from a humanistic and aesthetic vantage point, and seeks to establish and define its role in American culture. **Television: The Critical View** consists of 30 essays by practitioners and scholars who examine specific genre through specific programs, assessing their values, perceptions, characterizations, and artistic techniques. The book's ultimate aim is to teach viewers how to watch their television fare with a more observant and discerning eye. In addition to the editor, writers are Robert S. Alley, David Antin, Michael Arlen, Karin Blair, Muriel Cantor, Richard Corliss, Robert Craft, Martin Esslin, John Fiske, Todd Gitlin, John Hartley, Paul Hirsch, Robert Hofeldt, Douglas Kellner, Michael Kerbel, Jerzy Kosinski, Daniel Menaker, Michael Novak, Dennis Porter, Michael Real, Roger Rosenblatt, Anne Roiphe, Michael Schudson, Robert Sklar, David Sohn, David Thorburn, Bernard Timberg and Peter Wood. Some of the articles have bibliographies. (A fourth edition was published in 1987.)

In **TV: The Most Popular Art**, his earlier book, Newcomb himself applies humanistic analysis to TV as popular culture, examining soap opera, Westerns, mystery and detective, sports, news and various other genres in TV programming in search of aesthetic dimensions which will help to establish some of its social and cultural functions. He believes that the aesthetic and social-scientific viewpoints are not necessarily at odds, but might supplement one another in an attempt to fully comprehend the medium. Bibliography.

731

News Agencies Pool of Non-aligned Countries: A Perspective. New Delhi: Indian Institute for Mass Communication, 1983. 303p.

In the mid-1970s News Agencies of Non-Aligned Countries joined in a cooperative system which they called the Pool for the purpose of strengthening mutual relations by an information exchange system and by other actions which would increase the quality and quantity of information through technological means, training of personnel, reduction of tariffs, and other appropriate measures. Here the Committee has brought together documents, declarations and decisions which concern context and style of Pool news, the progress of the Pool over the years, and its plans for future development, including its role within a New International Information Order. Bibliography and list of documents.

732

Nimmo, Dan D., and James E. Combs. **Nightly Horrors: Crisis Coverage by Television Network News**. Knoxville: University of Tennessee Press, 1985. 216p.

On the theory that what people define as real can be real in its consequences, and that television supplies many definitions of reality for many people, Nimmo and Combs have searched for key patterns in the way the three major television networks in the U.S. covered six major crises in their nightly news reports: the mass murders and suicides by members of The People's Temple in Guyana in 1978; the "accident" at the Three Mile Island nuclear plant in 1979; the disastrous American Airlines crash at O'Hare Field in Chicago in 1979; the death of three persons from taking the pain reliever, Extra Strength Tylenol, into which poison had been introduced through tampering with the package; the taking of American hostages by Iran in 1979; and the eruption of Mount St. Helens volcano in 1980. Findings are based on observation and content analysis of the coverage. Although crisis news is emphasized, the study gives insight into factors involved in general television coverage. References and index.

733

Noble, Grant. **Children in Front of the Small Screen**. Beverly Hills, CA: Sage, 1975. 256p.

A synthesis of literature by a social psychologist on the subject of children and television. Noble has some interesting theories, influenced by his experiences as a Westerner contrasted with time he spent in India observing peoples whose lives were complete without mass media and even without literacy. This is a very interesting book. Bibliography and index.

734

Nordenstreng, Kaarle, and Tapio Varis. **Television Traffic—A One-Way Street? A Survey and Analysis of International Flow of Television Programme Material**. Paris: UNESCO, 1974. 63p. (Reports and Papers on Mass Communication No. 70.)

The first part of this study made at the University of Tampere is a 62-page international inventory of the composition of TV programs, particularly from the point of view of material imported to a country from outside, and a survey of the international networks for sale and exchange of program material for TV. Included are numerous tables, charts, and graphs. The second part is the essence of a symposium held at the University of Tampere which comments upon the hard facts contained in the study.

735

O'Conner, John E., ed. **American History/American Television: Interpreting the Video Past**. New York: Ungar, 1983. 420p.

Essays by a group of cultural historians, each of whom probes the long-range historical meaning of our television fare through examination of a specific genre or series of phenomenon. As a whole, the essays add up to an assessment of the many-faceted medium and the relevance of coupling it with a long-established discipline to gain a broader understanding of American culture. Contains notes; a selective chronology of television's history; a guide to archival and manuscript sources for the study of television; a bibliographic essay; and an index.

736

O'Neill, Michael J. **Terrorist Spectaculars: Should TV Coverage Be Curbed?** New York: Priority Press, 1986. 109p.

An analysis commissioned by the Twentieth Century Fund to examine some of the dilemmas posed by television coverage as it balances a free press and the public's right to know against the terrorist's desire for publicity. The author, a veteran print journalist who is a former editor of the **New York Daily News** and a former president of the American Society of Newspaper Editors, concludes that "what is needed more than new rules for covering terrorism . . . is a new journalism," which seeks in its reporting to prevent disasters, not merely to report them. Chapter notes form a bibliography.

737

Owen, Bruce M., Jack H. Beebe, and Willard G. Manning, Jr. **Television Economics**. Lexington, MA: Lexington, 1974. 218p.

"Glamour and social influence notwithstanding, television is a business," say the authors of this book intended to make the intricacies of TV economics understandable to the general reader. It is in two parts, the first emphasizing theory and analysis, the second emphasizing policy. Among topics included are programming supply, theories of program choice, behavior of networks, improving TV performance with both limited and unlimited channels, public TV, and related policy issues. There are many tables, a bibliography, and an index.

Paletz, David L., et al. **Politics in Public Service Advertising on Television**. (See No. 1603.)

738

Palmer, Edward L. and Aimee Dorr, eds. **Children and the Faces of Television: Teaching, Violence, Selling**. New York: Academic Press, 1980. 360p.

Teachers, researchers, production managers, consumer group lobbyists and advertising agency executives join forces to discuss uses and abuses of television in relation to children. Each of the three sections, "The Teaching Face of Television," "The Violent Face of Television," and "The Selling Face of Television," discuss history, current emphasis, content and production, effects, individual differences in effects, and politics of change, ending with a look toward the future. Chapters are based on research and its implications, and contain references to the sources cited.

739

Palmer, Patricia. **The Lively Audience: A Study of Children Around the TV Set**. Sydney, Australia: Allen & Unwin, 1986. 166p.

What do children make of the TV they watch? This is the question Palmer asks, contending that children have by and large been treated as passive receivers whose minds are controlled by the medium. Using the theoretical framework of symbolic interaction and letting the child be its own interpreter, she probes the ways in which children define and discuss television content; what they do when they watch; and the part it plays in relationships with friends and family, and in games and other activities. Appendixes reproduce the catchy cartoons used as questionnaires and gives criteria for children's programs. Bibliography and index.

Parish, James R. **Actors' Television Credits**. (See No. 1418.)

740

Parker, Everett C., David Barry, and Dallas Smythe. **The Television-Radio Audience and Religion**. New York: Harper, 1955. 464p.

This marks the first serious attempt to understand the effects of religious programs broadcast over radio and television. Using New Haven, Connecticut, as a laboratory, the authors assess its cultural, social and religious environment as a background for broadcasting, as well as the potential audience and the availability of programs and their selection. Design for the research is empirical, including methods that range over various social sciences and include "some that may as yet only dubiously be designated as scientific and precise," in order to classify listener characteristics and factors and to probe patterns of personality that indicate susceptibility to certain broadcasts and with what effects.

741

Patterns of Discrimination against Women in the Film and Television Industries: Special Report by the Association of Cinematograph and Television Technicians. London: The Association, 1975. 62p.

A thorough investigation of all aspects of the problem. The first part deals with such generalities as attitudes, educational and social training and facilities, job structure and security, right to work and rights of work, representation in the ACTT, and economic and legal position. The second part deals more specifically with types of position—laboratory, TV (ITV and BBC), film production. Appendixes include "Women in the BBC," "Educational Television," "Women in the French Film Industry," "The Working Women's Charter," "Maternity Leave Schedules," "Sources of Information" (few of them books), "Glossary," "Recommendations," and tables on which much of the data is based.

742

Patton, Phil. **Razzle Dazzle**. New York: Dial, 1984. 230p.

Patton follows the history of televised football to prove his contention that TV has turned the game into theater—"razzle dazzle." Carefully researched and popularly written.

743

Paulu, Burton. **Television and Radio in the United Kingdom**. Minneapolis: University of Minnesota Press, 1981. 476p.

In 1956 and 1961 respectively Paulu published **British Broadcasting: Radio and Television in the United Kingdom** (Minneapolis: University of Minnesota Press, 1956. 457p.) and its sequel, **British Broadcasting in Transition** (Minneapolis: University of Minnesota Press, 1961. 250p.). Although following in the same format, this

1981 volume is more than a rewriting and updating, being new in most respects and taking into account world changes and changes in Britain. In general it surveys and appraises the salient features of British broadcasting, describing the system and judging its performance. Specifically it deals with the constitutions of the BBC and IBA; their economic bases; physical plants and electronic facilities; personnel; radio and television programs; audience reaction; and the external broadcasting done by BBC for reception abroad. Written by an American, this is nonetheless one of the best of the histories of British Broadcasting. Chapter notes, bibliography and index.

744

Paulu, Burton. **Radio and Television Broadcasting in Eastern Europe**. Minneapolis: University of Minnesota Press, 1974. 592p.

Describes and appraises the theory and practice of radio and TV broadcasting in the Soviet Union, East Germany, Poland, Czechoslovakia, Hungary, Romania, Yugoslavia, and Albania. Covers the following: basic information theory, legal structure, finance, technical facilities, stations and networks, program objectives, principal program areas, audience research, and broadcasting for listeners. Among program types discussed are news, current affairs, drama, music, documentaries, educational and entertainment film, and sports. There are comprehensive footnotes; a bibliography; and an index of persons, places, and subjects.

745, 746

Peers, Frank W. **The Politics of Canadian Broadcasting, 1920–1951**. Toronto: University of Toronto Press, 1969. 446p.

Peers, Frank W. **The Public Eye: Television and the Politics of Canadian Broadcasting, 1952–1968**. Toronto: University of Toronto Press, 1979. 459p.

The Politics of Canadian Broadcasting traces the beginnings and development of Canada's mixed system of private and public ownership of broadcasting, which was then almost exclusively radio. Peers gives particular attention to the reasons that Canadian radio diverged from the primarily commercial U.S. model and shows how and why it reflects values different from those prevailing in the British or U.S. system. Index.

A sequel dealing with TV only, Peers' **The Public Eye** outlines the growth of TV from 1952 to the passing of the Broadcast Act in 1968, focusing on decisions made by governments on broadcasting activities and the circumstances under which they were made. Indexes.

747

Piepe, Anthony, Miles Emerson, and Judy Lannon. **Television and the Working Class**. Lexington, MA: Saxon House/Lexington, 1975. 170p.

An attempt to measure the social consequences of TV in the flow and distribution of values in society—specifically, British society—as it relates to class and stratification. Findings are based on the results of two surveys. Of special interest is a lengthy review of the literature, much of which deals with TV effects.

748

Pitts, Michael R. **Radio Soundtracks: A Reference Guide**. 2d ed. Metuchen, NJ: Scarecrow, 1986. 337p.

Pitts' goal is to provide information on radio programs from its "golden age"—from the late 1920s to the early 1960s. The first and largest section lists available programs on tape recordings; the second itemizes radio specials on tape; the third lists the programs on long playing records; the fourth gives performers' radio appearances on discs; and the last lists compilation albums made up of radio material. Each entry gives sources where the program may be obtained. An appendix contains these sources with their addresses. Name/title index. This should be very useful to radio buffs or anyone who for whatsoever reason wants to obtain early programs.

Pitts, Michael R. **Western Movies: A TV and Video Guide to 4200 Genere Films**. (See No. 1433.)

Poteet, G. Howard. **Published Radio, Television, and Film Scripts: A Bibliography**. (See No. 1686.)

749

Powers, Ron. **The Newscasters**. New York: St. Martin's, 1977. 243p.

As Ron Powers watched television news in the 1970s he became increasingly concerned by its drift into entertainment—"toward the end of determining what gratifies, as opposed to what is useful or necessary." Here he documents the who's, why's and how's, naming names and pulling no punches. Although his illustrations are dated his insights are not. A Pulitzer-prize-winning journalist and television critic, he writes from first-hand experience and knowledge. Index.

750

Powers, Ron. **Supertube: The Rise of Television Sports**. New York: Coward-McCann, 1984. 288p.

"The memories, the personal records and the informed analysis of nearly 100 sources, both active in and retired from network television, advertising, public relations and financial research, form the journalistic spine of this book" says Powers of his informal history of TV's coverage of sports. With a discerning eye and well-turned phrases he hits the high spots, beginning briefly with the late 1930s (radio) and ending with America's 1984 Olympics ("America on the eve of the 1984 Olympics is a nation seemingly stupefied on sports."). Bibliography and index.

751

Pragnell, Anthony. **Television in Europe: Quality and Values in a Time of Change**. Manchester, England: University of Manchester; European Institute for the Media, 1985. 125p. (Monograph No. 5.)

A report which discusses the strategies which should be adopted to stimulate domestic production of programming in Europe. Pragnell suggests that broadcasters, governments and European institutions take stock of what Europe can and should do to preserve its culture and values in television, pointing out that new kinds of broadcasting services are emerging which will put existing standards under pressure. He stresses that it is essential to seek alternatives rather than relying upon increased use of ready-made material, much of which would come from the United States. Parts of the findings and recommendations come from a questionnaire sent to all European-based members of the European Broadcasting Union, asking for information about the use of and attitude toward television material from the U.S.A. and other sources, European and non-European. Glossary of terms.

752, 753

Public Television: A Program for Action. New York: Harper & Row, 1967. 254p.

A Public Trust: The Report of the Carnegie Commission on the Future of Public Broadcasting. New York: Bantam, 1979. 401p.

Two reports made 12 years apart, both of which examine public TV in its various aspects. The earlier one concerns prospects for a broader base. It defines the term, summarizes the report, and discusses the opportunity, the present system, the Commission's proposal, and the specific type of programming that could emerge. There is a list of various stations operating as of the end of 1966, and supplementary papers by various experts concerning technology, costs, legal aspects, relations of stations with FCC, financial and operating reports for the previous year, and estimates of audiences for 1965 and 1966.

The later report designs a new structure for public television around four areas: programming, public participation, financing, and technology dissemination. This is preceded by a summary of findings and recommendations.

754

A Qualitative Study: The Effect of Television on People's Lives. Washington: Corporation for Public Broadcasting, Communications Research, 1978. 91p.

A four-city (Philadelphia, Minneapolis, Denver, Houston) study, conducted by means of discussion groups, to discover how representative television viewers "interacted with their television sets, what their viewing habits were, how they planned for their viewing time, which members of the family had a strong say-so in program selection, what type and what specific programs were liked and disliked and what programs or televised events had made a strong impact on them." Also, how they felt about the time spent watching, and their attitudes toward public television.

755

Quicke, Andrew. **Tomorrow's Television: An Examination of British Broadcasting, Past, Present and Future**. Berkhamsted, Herts., England: Lion, 1976. 240p.

"... intended to give the general reader an insight into the complexities and the politics of the television world, and to explain some of the problems affecting the future of television in Britain that will have to be solved by the Committee looking into the future of television under the chairmanship of Lord Annan," says the author. Among aspects he treats are "The Populists Versus the Elitists," "The New Priesthood," "Television and Politics," "Television and Belief," "Sociology and the Mass Media," "Cassettes, Cable and Satellites," "Control and Censorship." Quicke is a television producer. Indexed.

Quinn, James. **The Film and Television as an Aspect of European Culture**. (See No. 1442.)

Rachty, Gehan, and Khalil Sabat. **Importation of Films for Cinema and Television in Egypt**. (See No. 1443.)

756

Rader, Benjamin G. **In Its Own Image: How Television Has Transformed Sports**. New York: Free Press, 1984. 228p.

Combining sports history, media research and cultural analysis, Rader, a professor of history at the University of Nebraska, describes the radical transformation television, with its hype, high financial involvement, and sophisticated packaging, has brought to sports over the last 40 years.

Radio Financial Report. (See No. 1782.)

757

Ranney, Austin. **Channels of Power: The Impact of Television on American Politics**. New York: Basic Books, 1983. 207p.

Television has had a profound influence upon American politics in terms of the public, the politicians, and the system, argues Ranny, a distinguished political scientist, as he outlines changes it has brought about. Television alone is not responsible, but the medium *does* influence the message and on a deeper level alters American politics. Notes and an index.

758

Reed, Maxine K., and Robert M. Reed. **Career Opportunities in Television, Cable, and Video**. 2d ed. New York: Facts on File, 1986. 266p.

Intended as an introductory guide for high school and college students to some of the most common occupations in the field, this describes 100 jobs based on data gathered from printed job descriptions, employment documents, research studies, salary surveys, and tables of organization from more than 100 sources in the communications field, along with discussions with the authors' professional colleagues. In two parts: "Television, Broadcasting," and "Cable, Video, and Media," it gives a career profile and career ladder for each job, followed by position description, salaries, employment prospects, advancement prospects, education, experience/skills, minority/women opportunities, and unions/associations. Types of jobs listed run the gamut from the technical to managerial to the creative. The Introduction contains relevant statistical information about the growth patterns of the industry, its employment opportunities, and its trends for the 80s. No radio positions are listed, and jobs in public relations, film, journalism and theater are included only as they relate to television broadcasting and video. Appendixes include "Degree and Non-Degree Programs," "Unions and Associations," and "Bibliography" of books and periodicals. Index.

759

Report of the Task Force on Women in Public Broadcasting. Comp. by Caroline Isber and Muriel Cantor. Washington: Corporation for Public Broadcasting, 1975. 141p.

A report, authorized by the CPB board of directors, in which a task force monitored programs, collected and analyzed data, interviewed, discussed, and recommended. Appendixes describe methodologies and instruments, and present program content analysis tables, employment tables, and other related tables. Somewhat out of date but still useful.

Researcher's Guide to British Film and Television Collections, Ed. by Elizabeth Oliver. (See No. 1446.)

760

Rice, Jean, ed. **Cable TV Renewals & Refranchising**. Washington, DC: Communications Press, 1983. 212p.

A practical discussion of the issues involved in contracts between cable companies and municipalities. Among the topics are negotiating procedures, programming, legal issues for refranchising, community access channels and protecting consumer privacy.

761

Roberts, Stevens, ed. **International Directory of Telecommunications: Market Trends, Com-** panies, Statistics, Products, and Personnel. London: Longman, 1984. 282p.

Intended primarily as a buying guide to telecommunications products and services, this directory also is useful for its background information on worldwide developments in telecommunications technology, application, penetration, regulation and competition. Divided geographically into Africa, Asia and Oceania, Australia and New Zealand, Canada, Eastern Europe, Western Europe (EEC countries), Western Europe (non-EEC countries), Japan, Latin America and the Caribbean, Middle East, United Kingdom, and U.S.A., it first gives statistics for the entire area in terms of population, size, number of telephones, radios and television sets, and similar data, followed by a survey and listing of telecommunications facilities in each country which includes detailed information on pertinent organizations and on companies manufacturing and/or distributing equipment. There are four indexes: Companies and Organizations Index; Product Area Index; Registered Trade Name Index; and Personal Name Index.

762

Robinson, John P., and Mark R. Levy. **The Main Source: Learning from Television News**. Beverly Hills, CA: Sage, 1986. 272p.

What is the basis for the popular belief—the "myth," as the authors call it—that the public gets most of its news from television? They contend that this assumption is shallow, and does not allow for the complex ways the mass media as a whole diffuse public awareness and understanding of news events. Fortifying their hypothesis, they evaluate some new and old research into how, what, and where the public learns about the news. Their study, they say, "is not intended to denigrate television's potential as a news medium, but to question the mythology surrounding its influence on the audience," and they offer "an evolving state-of-the-art assessment of what we know, and do not know, about public learning from the news media." Assisting Robinson and Levy are Dennis K. Davis, W. Gill Woodall, and Michael Gurevitch. Methodology is described in three appendixes. Chapter notes, references and index.

Roper, Burns W. **Public Attitudes Toward Television and Other Media in a Time of Change**. (See No. 1785.)

763

Rose, Brian G. **Television and the Performing Arts: A Handbook and Reference Guide to American Cultural Programming**. Westport, CT: Greenwood, 1986. 270p.

"My goal has been to offer, for both scholars and students of broadcasting, a comprehensive guide to the development, innovations, trials, and achievements of American television and the performing arts, from the 1930s through the close of the 1984–85 TV season," says

Rose of this decade-by-decade chronicle of the evolution and treatment of cultural programming and how the arts have been transformed by television. An introductory chapter discusses the fate of the arts as a group on CBS, NBC, ABC and PBS, and four other chapters deal with dance, classical music, opera and theater individually. Supplementing this discussion, each chapter includes a survey of reference material, a bibliography, and a videography which lists the production credits of the dozen or so shows cited for their significance and merit. In conclusion is a name index.

764

Rose, Brian G., ed. **TV Genres: A Handbook and Reference Guide**. Westport, CT: Greenwood, 1985. 453p.

A systematic examination of the central elements of 19 television genres, showing how they have reshaped previously existing formulas to the specific demands of the medium's relatively small screen, lack of visual clarity, time restrictions, influence of sponsors and standards presumed to be held by the public. Nineteen formats are included, with each article containing an overview, historical development, themes and issues, and a final section with notes, a bibliographical survey, lists of books and articles, and a videography. There is also a final name and subject index.

Rose, Ernest, D. **World Film and Television Resources: A Reference Guide to Major Training Centers and Archives**. (See No. 1450.)

765

Rothafel, Samuel L., and Raymond Francis Yates. **Broadcasting: Its New Day**. New York: Arno Press, c1925, 1971. 316p.

In this book, written when radio was almost brand new, the authors have tried to present "the bigger and more vital issues on broadcasting and commercial radio." They discuss directions it is taking, some of which are "Radio and National Sport," "The New Force in Politics," "What Radio Can Do for Education," "The Broadcast Drama, A New Art," "Can We Talk to Mars?," "Radio and the Future of America's Commerce," "Radio: The Invisible Crusader" (its use in religious broadcasting). They also go into technological problems, such as interference, and technological possibilities, such as communication with Mars and the wire telephone.

766

Rowland, Willard D., Jr., and Bruce Watkins, eds. **Interpreting Television: Current Research Perspectives**. Beverly Hills, CA: Sage, 1984. 293p. (Sage Annual Review of Communication Research, Vol. 12.)

A collection of articles which, according to the editors, "represent a solid sample of new directions for

research on television and attempts to understand its cultural meanings and resonances." Its aim is to illustrate by example how current changes in communication research are helping to redefine the issue of television as a cultural institution. Approaches focus primarily on television as a creator and conveyor of meaning, by means of which the culture and societies in which it exists can be interpreted. Much of the research stems from debates between traditional mainstream positivistic research and the conflicting trends in cultural and critical studies. A list of references follow each article.

767

Rowland, Willard D., Jr. **The Politics of TV Violence: Policy Uses of Communication Research**. Beverly Hills, CA: Sage, 1983. 319p.

An investigation into the interaction of public concern about violence on television with the research about its effect and the use of this research in the policymaking process for broadcasting. Rowland probes deep into the problem, treating the concerns with violence and television as "essentially symbolic issues, as problems bespeaking the uncertainties of the modern era." He focuses on the role of legislators, commissions and bureaucracies; on spokespersons for researchers; on reformers; and on the management and research figures in the broadcasting industry. An important contribution is his account of the early history of mass communication research against a background of the growth of American social science, and his history of violence effects research. This in-depth study provides an excellent source to anyone investigating the problem of television violence and the factual and symbolic efforts of society to stem it. Chapter notes and references.

768

Schemering, Christopher. **The Soap Opera Encyclopedia**. New York: Ballantine, 1985. 358p.

"This book tells the story of the television soap opera—a history of the phenomenon for the student, a reference guide for the librarian, a fact-filled binge for the fan," is how Schemering describes his successful account of the soap opera world in all its unreality. The A to Z program entries give background information on all the daytime and prime-time TV soap operas broadcast on CBS, NBC and ABC, as well as a selection of syndicated, cable, and foreign efforts. Appendixes include "The Emmies," "The Neilsen Ratings," "Famous Graduates of Daytime Drama," "Famous Guest Stars in Daytime Drama," "Longest-Running Performers in TV Soap Opera," "Black in Daytime Drama," "Chronology of Television Serial Drama," "Longest-Running Daytime Dramas," and "Current and Long-Running Serials: Broadcast History, Production Credits, Addresses." There is also a bibliography and an index of personalities. Schemering is a stylish writer and gets in some subtle and not-so-subtle cracks in his accounts of convoluted plots and characters that inhabit the genres. His book reads as though he enjoyed writing it; the reader coming to it for trivial or not so trivial pursuits will likewise enjoy using it.

769

Scheuer, Steven H., and the staff of **TV Key. Who's Who in Television and Cable**. New York: Facts on File, 1983. 579p.

Concise biographical data on more than 2,000 individuals in the TV, video and cable industry. Scheuer says that a majority of the entries include leading executives of CBS, NBC, ABC, public television, and the major national cable services such as Home Box Office and Cable News Network, as well as "hundreds of on-air television journalists, actors and actresses and dozens of important executives employed by local TV stations in New York, Washington and Los Angeles." Information, in abbreviated form and based on questionnaires, includes position, address, birth date, education, career highlights, achievements and awards, and "Personal," which may be interpreted any way the respondent wishes. Indexes by corporation with which the respondent is connected, and by job title or position.

Schiller, Herbert I. **Mass Communications and the American Empire**. (See No. 381.)

770

Schlesinger, Philip, Graham Murdock, and Philip Elliott. **Television 'Terrorism': Political Violence in Popular Culture**. London: Comedia, 1983. 181p.

An examination of the coverage of television political violence in Britain, written to shed light on the question: should it be censored? The authors think not, and give reasons for their opinion in this lucid analysis which is, however, not a tract but rather an attempt to provide material for intelligent debate. Notes and references.

771

Schramm, Wilbur, Jack Lyle, and Edwin S. Parker. **Television in the Lives of Our Children**. Stanford, CA: Stanford University Press, 1961. 324p.

Although many new books on the subject with much new data have appeared since 1961, this is historically important as the first in the United States. In the 1980 edition of **Basic Books in the Mass Media** we said of it: "This standard work analyzes the effects of television, based on a study of over 6,000 children and on information obtained from some 2,300 parents, teachers, and school officials. An appendix gives statistics and tabulations and data on related topics (including children's use of other mass media). There is an annotated bibliography, an index of names, and a general index. For its British counterpart see Himmelweit's **Television and the Child: An Empirical Study of the Effect of Television on the Young**." (No. 656.)

772

Schramm, Wilbur L., and Lyle Nelson. **The Financing of Public Television**. Palo Alto, CA: Aspen Program on Communications and Society, 1972. 59p.

Gives concise facts and figures on the economic status and structure of public TV—its program services and coverage from its beginnings to the early 1970s, its cost estimates, and its funding.

773, 774

Schramm, Wilbur, Jack Lyle, and Ithiel de Sola Pool. **The People Look at Educational Television: A Report on Nine Representative ETV Stations**. Stanford, CA: Stanford University Press, 1963. 209p.

Lyle, Jack. **The People Look at Public Television, 1974**. Washington: Corporation for Public Broadcasting, Office of Communication Research, 1975. 66p.

Schramm, Lyle, and Pool conducted more than 30,000 interviews measuring audience composition and size, programs viewed and why, and how audiences felt about ETV. They also discussed potential audience. Bibliography and index. Twelve years later in a study for the Corporation for Public Broadcasting, Lyle handles the same subject, presenting an overview based on a number of studies, some of which were part of an ongoing series sponsored by CPB. It contains charts about audience preferences and composition, and a listing of public television stations.

775

Schreibman, Fay C., and Peter J. Bukalski. **Broadcast Television: A Research Guide**. Los Angeles, CA: American Film Institute, Educational Services, 1983. 62p. (Factfile 15.)

Identifies print and institutional sources of information on domestic broadcast television: archives, special libraries and other institutions containing television materials and/or provide informational services about television; and reference works or books and periodicals. Selection of print materials was made on the basis of the quality of the work and the inclusion of substantial bibliographies. General mass communications and media theory books are not identified but are referred to in many of the bibliographies. Memoirs and biographies of television personalities are also excluded. Entries are annotated. There is an author and a title index, but no subject index because this is intended to identify sources rather than specific topics.

776

Schwartz, Meg, ed. **TV & Teens: Experts Look at the Issues**. Reading, MA: Addison-Wesley, 1982. 222p.

"To explore television's potential to help young

viewers and to foster more and better programming for the ten-to fifteen-year-old adolescent, Action for Children's Television (ACT) went to educators, developmental psychologists, medical and health practitioners, researchers, and producers of teen-age programming for answers to key questions such as: What are the facts about adolescence in our society? How can television help young adolescents in their search for identity? What are some things to remember when producing for young teens?" Introduction. The essays, well-written and interesting, deal with eight aspects: "The Young Adolescent," "TV as Entertainment and Information," "Role Models," "The World of Work," "Sex and Sexuality," "Youth in Crisis," "Radio," and "Advertising and the Teen Market." As a whole they provide an unbiased picture of television programming, American adolescents, and for better or worse, the culture that is producing them both. Those essays based on research give their references; some of the others suggest further reading. There is an index.

777, 778

Sendall, Bernard. **Independent Television in Britain: Origins and Foundations 1946–62**. Vol. 1. London: Macmillan, 1982. 418p.

Sendall, Bernard. **Independent Television in Britain: Expansion and Change, 1958–68**. Vol. 2. London: Macmillan, 1983. 429p.

The first two volumes of a projected 3-volume series designed to trace the story of Independent Television from its origins through the new Broadcasting Act and the franchise decisions of 1980. The first volume deals extensively with political issues and problems of structure, finance and organization, and program developments. It also describes the establishment and growth of the regional companies, or contractors, which comprised the independent system, some of which did not survive. Volume 2 continues the account of the founding and sometimes the failure of other regional contractors. Sendall also assesses the Report of the Committee on Broadcasting 1960 (the Pilkington Report) which was critical of the ITA. Both volumes are highly detailed, Volume 1 contains two appendixes: "The Nature of the System: Extract from the ITA Annual Report, 1961/2"; and "Some Contemporary Publications." Each has chapter notes and are indexed. Volume 3 was expected to be published under the title **Recognition and Responsibility, 1968–80**.

779

Settle, Irving. **A Pictorial History of Television**. 2d ed. New York: Ungar, 1983. 290p.

Pictures and text cover the history of television in breadth rather than depth. Indexed.

780

Shaheen, Jack G. **The TV Arab**. Bowling Green, OH: Bowling Green State University Popular Press, 1984. 146p.

Beginning with the 1975–76 television season and continuing for eight years, Shaheen, an American of Arabic descent, documented over 100 different popular entertainment programs, cartoons and major documentaries telecast on network, independent and public channels, totaling nearly 200 episodes, that related to Arabs. He concludes that TV in its various genre perpetrates four basic myths: they are all fabulously rich; they are barbaric and uncultured; they are sex maniacs with a penchant for white slavery; and they revel in acts of terrorism. Chapter notes and index.

Short, K. R. M., ed. **Film, Radio Propaganda in World War II**. (See No. 1470.)

781

Short, K. R. M., ed. **Western Broadcasting over the Iron Curtain**. London: Croom Helm, 1986. 274p.

Articles by authorities on broadcasting systems to Iron curtain countries from Canada, the U.S., Britain and West Germany in particular. Notes, a bibliography and an index.

782, 783

Shulman, Milton. **The Least Worst Television in the World**. London: Barrie and Jenkins, 1973. 180p.

Shulman, Milton. **The Ravenous Eye**. London: Coronet, 1975. 349p.

Shulman, a caustic and perceptive critic of TV, describes his 1973 book as "... a personal survey of how television in Britain has developed and, in my opinion, has deteriorated. In such a tale of rise and decline, the compromises, the shortcomings, the scandals of the medium tend to overshadow the achievements and successes. If they do, my book may act as some counterweight to the load of complacency and self-congratulation that is pumped out by the press officers of the BBC and the commercial companies."

In the latter volume he has not changed his mind. "Six years of working in television and eight years of writing about it have convinced me that in its present primitive phase in countries like Britain and America it does, on balance, more harm than good." He proceeds to document his views with surveys, studies, and statistics. Notes and index.

784

Siepmann, Charles A. **Radio, Television and Society**. New York: Oxford University Press, 1950. 410p.

Siepmann, one of the first to realize the broad-ranging implications of broadcasting, best tells in his own words the scope of his analytical study, calling it an attempt "to describe the facts about radio and television and to combine these facts with a consideration of the social and psychological effects of broadcasting." His first purpose is "to bring to the general reader the history of a cultural revolution and to show what has been discovered by research concerning the effects of radio and television upon our tastes, opinions and values." His second is "to deal with broadcasting as a reflection of our time and to throw light upon the problems of free speech, propaganda, public education, our relations with the rest of the world, and with democracy itself." He has succeeded well; over the decades his book remains an excellent examination of the role of broadcasting—radio in particular—in society. Bibliographies for each chapter and an index.

785, 786, 787

Signitzer, Benno, and Kurt Luger. **Socio-Economic Aspects of Communication Systems. I. Radio Broadcasting in Austria**. Paris: UNESCO, 1983? 57 p. (Communication and Society 10.)

Bunzlová, Alice and Leopole Slovák. **Socio-Economic Aspects of National Communication Systems. II. Radio Broadcasting in Czechoslovakia**. Paris: UNESCO, 1982? 73p. (Communication and Society 11.)

INICO (Institute of Communication Research, Central University of Caracas). **Socio-Economic Aspects of National Communication Systems. III. Radio Broadcasting in Venezuela**. Caracas, INICO, 1983? 104p. (Communication and Society 12.)

This series examines the role of radio broadcasting in the process of socio-economic and cultural change in three countries with different types of broadcasting organization: Czechoslovakia—public; Venezuela—private: Austria—public ownership and management, but with a Board of Trustees as highest decision-maker and organ of program control. It takes up cultural implications of these broadcasting structures, their ownership and financing, and pays special attention to advertising, both commercial and noncommercial. Each study has a short description of the historic and legal development of its system.

788

Silverstone, Roger. **The Message of Television: Myth and Narrative in Contemporary Culture**. London: Heinemann, 1981. 248p.

Silverstone describes this study as "... an oblique, but hopefully illuminating approach to the study of television." Drawing on theories and evidence in various disciplines and modes of thought—linguistics, mythology, theories of narration, and sociology—he suggests ways to analyze television programming which will "break through the crust of familiarity which makes television so inescapably invisible despite its constant presence" and show how it "translates history, political and social change, into manageable terms." Emphasis is on narrative. Chapter notes, bibliography and index.

789

Singleton, Loy A. **Telecommunications in the Information Age: A Nontechnical Primer on the New Technologies**. 2d ed. Cambridge, MA: Ballinger, 1986. 256p.

Describes in plain language for the layman: cable television (system features and operation; programming; two-way services); low power and subscription television; multi-point distribution service; communication satellites; direct broadcast satellites; satellite master antenna television; high-definition; television; videotext; teletext; video cassette recorders; videodisc; personal computers; new business communication networks; teleconferencing; telecommuting; and portable telecommunications; cellular mobile and radio paging. For each of these it gives background (how it was developed and when); how it works (a non-technical description in everyday language); applications (real-life examples); and forecast (upcoming developments, including legal and social issues). A glossary defines frequently used acronyms, abbreviations and terminology, and a topical bibliography lists books and other readings that expands the condensed treatment in the text. Index.

790

Skornia, Harry J. **Television and Society: An Inquest and Agenda for Improvement**. New York: McGraw-Hill, 1965. 268p.

Skornia contends that a TV system controlled wholly by business cannot be expected to put public interest before profit. Bolstering his thesis with documents, he discusses the structure of commercial TV—its leadership, its hidden economics, its rating system, its possible effects, including those on international relations. The picture he presents has changed surprisingly little over the decades. Chapter notes and index.

Slide, Anthony, ed. **International Film, Radio, and Television Journals**. (See No. 1480.)

791

Smith, Anthony, comp. **British Broadcasting**. London: Newton Abbot; Devon: David & Charles, 1974. 271p.

"The purpose of this book is to show, through documents from official and other sources, how the institutions of broadcasting in Britain were created and developed in a context of public discussion," says the author. He has selected nearly 100 key documents, concentrating on certain areas often inaccessible to the ordinary reader or student, including Parliamentary Papers, Acts, memoirs, and commission reports. The introduction and commentary are useful for those who need a historical explanation of today's issues. Arrangement is chronological, beginning with the 1863 Electric Telegraphy Act and ending with documents and BBC statements of principles in the 1960s. There is an essay bibliography, "Suggestions for Further Reading," and an index.

792

Smith, Anthony. **The Shadow in the Cave: The Broadcaster, the Audience and the State**. Rev. and enl. ed. London: Quartet, 1976. 335p.

In this carefully documented analysis of the role of broadcasting in society, the author's aim is to show the ways in which it does not fulfill its potential to serve the people. Using as examples the systems in Britain, the U.S., France, Japan, Holland, and, more briefly, several other countries, he makes a case that the arguments besetting it—bias, taste and lack of it, trivialization, balance and fairness, control of access—are part of a larger problem threatening democratic freedom. There are copious notes, a long and detailed bibliography, and an index.

793

Smith, Anthony, ed. **Television and Political Life: Studies in Six European Countries**. New York: St. Martin's Press, 1979. 288p.

In this anthology, political journalists and media experts use six examples to examine ways in which television has affected national society and political culture. They show how this is brought about formally by means of the structure and execution of the programming and, more informally, by the interaction between political leaders and television journalists and by the influence on public opinion exerted by "styles" of politicians and broadcasters. Countries assessed are Britain, France, Germany, Italy, Holland, and Sweden. Indexed.

794

Smith, Delbert D. **Communication via Satellite: A Vision in Retrospect**. Leyden and Boston: Sijthoff, 1976. 335p.

The author's intent is to trace the strategy of communication satellite development from its origins in the 1800s, when its possibilities were undefined, to its present advanced state. Studying satellite progress in an institutional, legal, and social context, he interprets it in the light of governmental concern about its role in technological society, or "technology integration" as he terms it, referring to a complex economic, legal, and social process he claims is unique in the context of government-industry relationships. There is a list of acronyms and abbreviations, 41 pages of footnotes, a twelve-page bibliography, and an index.

This is a companion work to the author's earlier **International Telecommunication Control: International Law and the Ordering of Satellite and Other Forms of International Broadcasting** (Sijthoff, 1969. 231p.), which investigates legal controls and provides a framework for alternative concepts through "an examination of the

relevant general principles of international law, the activities of the International Telecommunication Union and other organizations, unauthorized international telecommunication and the applicable control theories and legislation, regional broadcasting groupings and national policy alternatives, and the problems created by satellite telecommunication."

Smith, Myron J., Jr., comp. **U.S. Television Network News: A Guide to Sources in English**. (See No. 1697.)

A Sourcebook on Radio's Role in Development. (See No. 1699.)

795

Stedman, Raymond William. **The Serial: Suspense and Drama by Installment**. 2d ed. Norman: University of Oklahoma Press, 1977. 574p.

This is a good reference source to pinpoint popular serials over a period of years. From **What Happened to Mary** in 1912 through **The Adams Chronicles** in 1976, Stedman describes the births, deaths and intervening developments of an infinite variety of movie, radio, and TV serials covering a number of genres. Appendix A lists daytime network serials on radio, with sponsor, writer, cast, dates, and sometimes musical theme; Appendix B lists by date of origin daytime network serials on TV. A bibliography contains books, pamphlets, magazine and newspaper articles, and unpublished sources on the subject. There is a general and a title index.

796

Stein, Aletha Huston, and Lynette Kohn Freidrich. **Impact of Television on Children and Youth**. Chicago: University of Chicago Press, 1975. 72p.

Review of a large body of literature on observational learning and TV which is not limited to the study of violence, but discusses pro-social TV, cognitive function, and social knowledge and stereotypes as well. Contains an extensive bibliography of articles, books, theses and dissertations, documents, and other types of material.

797

Steiner, Gary A. **The People Look at Television: A Study of Audience Attitudes**. New York: Knopf, 1963. 422p.

Report of a study at Columbia University's Bureau of Applied Social Research in which the author conducted personal interviews with a sample of about 2,500 adults to determine each respondent's attitude toward programs and commercials as well as toward himself as a viewer. This is intended as an update of Paul Lazarsfeld's **The People Look at Radio** (1946) and with Patricia Kendall, his **Radio Listening in America—The People Look at Radio Again** (1948). (See Nos. 684 and 685.)

798

Sterling, Christopher H. **Electronic Media: A Guide to Trends in Broadcasting and Newer Technologies 1920–1983**. New York: Praeger, 1984. 335p.

". . . intended as a handy single reference source providing the most significant and/or interesting quantitative trend data on electronic media over the longest possible time periods. Its purpose is to create and refine something of a census, or benchmark, of currently available data, allowing researchers of all kinds reader access to what we now know—and suggesting areas where further data generation is still needed." In eight sections—growth of electronic media; ownership; economics; employment and training; content trends; audience; international aspects; regulation. Tabular information provides data for as many years as possible—sometimes going back to the 1920s—and is accompanied by an analytical and critical text that assesses the source (much of it comes from government), tells how the data was gathered, and what its value is. Concludes with "Sources" and "References," which discusses pertinent government statistical publications providing economic data, and lists pertinent books, periodicals and newspapers. (A new edition is to be published in 1989.)

Sterling, Christopher H. **Foreign and International Communications Systems: A Survey Bibliography**. (See No. 1702.)

Sterling, Christopher H. **Mass Communication and Electronic Media: A Survey Bibliography**. (See No. 1701.)

Sterling, Christopher H. **Telecommunications Policy: A Survey Bibliography**. (See No. 1700.)

799

Sterling, Christopher H., and John M. Kittross. **Stay Tuned: A Concise History of American Broadcasting**. Belmont, CA: Wadsworth, 1978. 562p.

"Our goal is to tell how American broadcasting got where it is today, and, by analyzing principles, events, and trends, suggest what directions it may take in the future," say the authors of this comprehensive one-volume history which emphasizes broad trends, important individuals, and basic principles rather than isolated facts. Events are interrelated with developments in technology, organization and structure of the industry, economics, programming, audience research, public policy, and regulation. Arrangement is topical within a chronological context. There are two tables of contents, one chronological and one topical. Appendixes give a short chronology of American broadcasting, a glossary, historical statistics, and a selected bibliography. Indexed.

800

Stewart, Donald E. **The Television Family: A Content Analysis of the Portrayal of Family Life in Prime Time Television**. Melbourne, Australia: Institute of Family Studies, 1983. 65p.

Part of an international project on **Television and the Family** involving Australia, Hungary, Denmark and the United Kingdom. An analysis of television shows featuring family life in which 551 (human) major speaking characters in 191 programs were studied. Conclusions suggest distortion and unreality on most levels.

801

Stone, David M. **Nixon and the Politics of Public Television**. New York: Garland, 1985. 370p.

A detailed examination of public television's struggle during its controversial first years of existence in the early 1970s to maintain its independence from the federal government, with emphasis on its stormy relations with President Nixon and the effect of the struggle on both the institution and the president. Sources include White House documents dealing with public television as well as personal interviews and documents from the Public Broadcasting Service and the Corporation for Public Broadcasting.

802

Summers, Harrison B. **A Thirty-Year History of Programs Carried on National Radio Networks in the United States, 1926–1956**. Columbus: Ohio State University, Department of Speech, 1958. 228p. (Reprinted by Arno Press, 1971.)

Programs are listed by year and, within this framework, broken down by type—comedy, variety, general variety, hillbilly, minstrel, concert music, musical variety, drama, thrills, news, commentary, public affairs talks, religious, talk programs of various sorts. Information about each includes as much of the following data as available: sponsorship, number of seasons on the air, network, program length, day, hour, and ratings.

803

Swerdlow, Joel L. **Beyond Debate: A Paper on Televised Presidential Debates**. New York: Twentieth Century Fund, 1984. 89p.

Television debates between presidential candidates are becoming an important part of the election process, but thus far they have been organized on an ad hoc, unpredictable basis that must be renegotiated every four years. Believing that these debates are in the public interest and should occur regularly, the 1979 Twentieth Century Fund Task Force on Televised Presidential Debates asked Swerdlow, a Washington journalist, to examine them and make suggestions for ground rules.

After a hard look at the 1960–1980 experience with emphasis on the Carter/Reagan/Anderson triangle he offers suggestions on a regular format, on the participation, of candidates in their own interests, on the question of non-major-party candidates, and on sponsorship. Twenty-six pages of notes indicate the extent of his research. Although the Reagan/Mondale debate in 1984 and the continuing series of 1988 debates are not included, Swerdlow's work presents valuable background.

Taplin, Walter, **The Origin of Television Advertising in the United Kingdom**. (See No. 1624.)

804

Taylor, Laurie, and Bob Mullan. **Uninvited Guests: The Intimate Secrets of Television and Radio**. London: Chatto & Windus, 1986. 218p.

Don't be put off by "intimate secrets" in the title. This is no titillating exposé, but a serious audience research study by two British sociologists, designed to show how confirmed viewers of popular TV regard what they are viewing. Data is provided by groups of eight or nine confirmed watchers, recruited on the basis of age, sex and social class, who discuss their reactions to various kinds of programs, including sitcoms and soap operas, and the characters who inhabit them. Comments—many of them are quoted verbatim—are interpreted in connection with statistics from IBA and BBC. Non-Britishers who use this book will find some of the British programs unfamiliar; however, a number of U.S. programs popular in Britain are included. Bibliography and index.

805

Technical Development of Television. Ed. by George Shiers. New York: Arno, 1977. 500p. (Historical Studies in Telecommunications.)

A collection of 30 items which, taken as a whole, surveys technical progress from the early proposals of the late 1870s to the inception of modern color TV. Materials include original papers by pioneers, contemporary articles, reports on individual and corporate activities, accounts by historians, and national committee records. The selections constitute a record of developments in Britain, Germany, Russia, and the U.S. Material is divided into four sections: General History, Mechanical Systems, Electronic Television, Color Television. The introduction includes a comprehensive list of references to contemporary materials and a chronological list of 91 books published from 1925 to 1975.

806, 807, 808

Television and Social Behavior: A Technical Report to the Surgeon-General's Scientific Advisory Committee on Television and Social Behavior. Ed. by John P. Murray, Eli A. Rubenstein, and George A. Comstock. 5 v. Washington: Superintendent of Documents, U.S. Government Printing Office, 1972.

Television and Social Behavior: An Annotated Bibliography of Research Focusing on Television's Impact on Children. Ed. by Charles K. Atkin, John P. Murray, and Oguz B. Nayman. Rockville, MD: National Institute of Mental Health, 1971. 150p.

Television and Growing Up: The Impact of Televised Violence. Washington: Superintendent of Documents, U.S. Government Printing Office, 1972. 279p.

The editors of this series, **Television and Social Behavior: A Technical Report . . .**, popularly known as the Surgeon General's Report on Violence, call these five landmark volumes "a broad scientific inquiry about television and its impact upon the viewer." To this end more than 50 scientists participated in research which produced over 40 scientific reports, with major emphasis on the relationship between televised violence and the attitudes and behavior of children. Vol. I, **Media Content and Control**; Vol. II, **Television and Social Learning**; Vol. III, **Television and Adolescent Aggressiveness**; Vol. IV, **Television in Day-to-Day Life: Patterns of Use**; Vol. V, **Television's Effects: Further Explorations**. Each volume contains an overview paper which summarizes and relates the papers in that volume. There are references at the end of most chapters.

A part of the series, although not included as a volume, is **Television and Social Behavior: An Annotated Bibliography of Research Focusing on Television's Impact on Children**, edited by Charles K. Atkin, John P. Murray, and Oguz B. Nayman and containing approximately 300 annotated and 250 unannotated citations.

Television and Growing Up: The Impact of Television Violence is a summary of the five volumes of the report, with a lengthy bibliography of books and articles upon which the authors of the articles drew.

809

Television and Social Behavior: Beyond Violence and Children: A Report of the Committee on Television and Social Behavior, Social Science Research Council. Ed. by Stephen B. Withey and Ronald P. Abeles. Hillsdale, NJ: Lawrence Erlbaum, 1980. 356p.

A follow-up of the Report of the Surgeon General's Scientific Advisory Committee on Television and Social Behavior (No. 808), in which a Social Science Research Council committee considers the advantages and disadvantages of various measurements of television violence in general as well as for children, and, going beyond the issue of violence, assesses the current state of research into television and social behavior. Among the 13 articles presented are: "Beyond Violence and Children" by Ronald Abeles, "On the Nature of Media Effects" by Jack McLeod and Byron Reeves, "The Audience for Television—and in Television Research" by Herbert Gans, "Social Influence and Television" by Hilde Himmelweit, "Television and Afro-Americans: Past Legacy and Present Portrayals" by Gordon L. Berry, and "Social Trace Contaminants: Subtle Indicators of Racism in TV" by Chester Pierce. Appendixes include "A Profile of Televised Violence," and reports on the entertainment function of television and on television and ethnicity. Each article contains references. Author index and subject index.

810

Television and Behavior: Ten Years of Scientific Progress and Implications for the Eighties. Vol. 1: Summary Report; Vol. 2: Technical Reviews. Rockville, MD: U.S. Department of Health and Human Services, National Institute of Public Health, 1982. 94, 362p.

These two volumes update and elaborate upon information in the 1972 Report of the Surgeon General's Advisory Committee on Television and Social Behavior (No. 806). In the intervening ten years more than 2,500 titles have appeared researching the subject—some dealing with aggression but more dealing with television viewing and its influences on other aspects of development and behavior. Focusing on this broader spectrum rather than violence alone, as in the earlier edition, this new report addresses such issues as cognitive and emotional aspects of television viewing; television as it relates to socialization and viewers' conceptions of social reality; television's influences on physical and mental health; and television as an American institution. Orientation is toward research and public health issues as reflected in entertainment television rather than in television news and news reporting, political programs, public affairs broadcasting, or television advertising. Volume I contains comprehensive, critical, and integrative scientific literature reviews on specific topics which will be of interest to the researcher and scholar; Volume II is largely an assessment and integration of these reviews, written in nontechnical language for the general reader. Consultants for the two new volumes come from communications, psychiatry, education, and psychology, and include Steven H. Chaffee, George Gerbner, Beatrix A. Hamburg, Chester Pierce, Eli A. Rubinstein, Alberta E. Siegel, and Jerome L. Singer. Reviews in the second volume are by these and other well-known researchers—among them Aletha Huston, John C. Wright, Dolf Zillmann, Aimée Dorr, Larry Gross, George Comstock, and Muriel Cantor. Both volumes contain prolific notes and references.

Television Financial Reports. (See No. 1783.)

811

Television Yearbook of the Republic of China, 1961–1975. English ed. Taipei, Taiwan: Television Academy of Arts and Sciences of the Department of China, 1976. 253p.

This reference book (the use of the word **yearbook** is a misnomer) is the first publication of its kind in Taiwan and has as its aim to provide "a systematic presentation of all the pertinent data about the development and growth of the television enterprise in the country." Contents include a brief history; a 140-page analysis of programming broken down by categories such as news, dramas, etc.; engineering and industry; training of personnel; administration and pertinent regulations; international cooperation activities; advertising; a chronology of events; and appendixes containing (1) Broadcasting and Television Law of the Republic of China; (2) Moral Code for the Television Enterprise in the Republic of China; (3) List of Television Organizations and Advertising Agencies in the Republic of China; (4) TV Books and Publications in the Republic of China (in the Chinese language). The book contains numerous illustrations and a great deal of data in the form of tables, graphs, and maps.

812, 813, 814

Terrace, Vincent. **Encyclopedia of Television: Series, Pilots and Specials, 1937–1973**. Vol. I. New York: Zoetrope, 1986. 480p.

Terrace, Vincent. **Encyclopedia of Television: Series, Pilots and Specials, 1974–1984**. Vol. II. New York: Zoetrope, 1985. 458p.

Terrace, Vincent. **Encyclopedia of Television: Series, Pilots and Specials: Index**. Vol. III. New York: Zoetrope, 1986. 662p.

Together the first two volumes contain a total of 7,460 items spanning 50 years and representing experimental programs as well as the series, pilot films and special broadcasts indicated in the title. Inclusion is limited to original entertainment programming; feature films are excluded because they do not fall under the "original" category, and news and sports are excluded because in a strict sense they are not "entertainment." Each entry includes cast information and a detailed story line; credits for writers, producers and directors; number of episodes for each completed series; running time and network, and syndication and/or cable information. Terrace says that "You will also find such trivia as titles of theme songs, vocalists, musicians, and art directors and photographer." This is a useful reference tool which also has its appeal to nostalgia and Trivial Pursuit buffs. Volumes I and II are arranged alphabetically and can be approached by name or subject through the Index, Volume III.

815

Terrace, Vincent. **Television 1970–1980**. San Diego, CA: Barnes, 1981. 322p.

A smaller version of the author's **Encyclopedia of Television Series, Pilots and Specials, 1937–1984** (Nos. 812, 813, 814), this covers the same ground for the decade of the 1970's, with almost 2,000 entries.

816

Terrace, Vincent. **Radio's Golden Years: The Encyclopedia of Radio Programs 1930–1960**. San Diego, CA: Barnes, 1981. 308p.

An alphabetical listing of 1,500 nationally broadcast network and syndicated entertainment programs, including adventure, anthology, children's, comedy, crime (police, detective), drama, game (quiz, audience participation), gossip, human interest, interview, musical variety, mystery, science-fiction, serial, talk-interview, variety, westerns, and women's programs. Entries, in outline form, provide story line information, cast lists, announcer and music credits, sponsors, program openings, network and/or syndication information, and length and date of broadcast. Arrangement is alphabetical by title. Name index.

817

Thomas, Ruth. **Broadcasting and Democracy in France**. Philadelphia, PA: Temple University Press, 1976. 211p.

Explores the history, structure, and economics of French broadcasting from 1945 onward; examines relations between broadcasting and government on the one hand and between broadcasting as a state monopoly and various commercial interests on the other; and analyzes the two central features of a democratic broadcasting system: information and citizen participation. Contains footnotes and a bibliography.

818

Thompson, Kenneth W., ed. **The Media**. Lanham, MD: University Press of America, 1985. 241p. (The Credibility of Institutions, Policies and Leadership, Vol. 5.)

Professionals in one sector or another of news interpreting and reporting comment on good and bad aspects of political news reporting. Discussions include "The Media: Power and Responsibility" by Kenneth W. Thompson; "The Media and Politics," Sander Vanocur; "The Media and the Presidency," Paul Duke, Ray Scherer and Jody Powell; and "Presidents I Have Known," with Thomas Reston and Richard Stout speaking generally; George Juergens on Wilson and the press; Chalmers Roberts on Franklin Roosevelt; Charles Roberts on John Kennedy; and Helen Thomas on Reagan. In spite of the broad title, emphasis is on television. This is not a researched or documented work, but rather a series of discussions by qualified professional, transcribed from tapes.

Trenaman, Joseph, and Denis McQuail. **Television and the Political Image**. (See No. 517.)

819

Tuchman, Gaye, ed. **The TV Establishment: Programming for Power and Profit**. New York: Prentice Hall (Spectrum book), 1974. 186p.

An anthology in which the articles, taken as a whole, explore the ways in which American commercial television legitimizes the status quo and limits the range

of ideas admissible to the legendary free marketplace of ideas. Contributors in addition to Tuchman are Edward Jay Epstein, Harvey Molotch, Marilyn Lester, Mindy Nix, Philip Elliott, Les Brown, Muriel Cantor, David Sallach and Herbert Schiller. Notes.

820

Turow, Joseph. **Entertainment, Education, and the Hard Sell: Three Decades of Network Children's Television**. New York: Praeger, 1981. 153p.

In this study of series programming for children that appeared on the ABC, CBS and NBC television networks from commercial television's earliest days in 1948 through 1978, Turow has "poured over bi-yearly series for changes and continuities, tracked diversity and the shape of programming, placed them alongside developments in the television industry, and confronted the meaning of it all." Throughout he keeps in mind the struggle that the groups outside the industry who monitor quality have with network programmers and advertisers. Appendixes detail procedures and list network series for children during the period covered. Chapter notes and index.

Twomey, John E. **Canadian Broadcasting History Resources in English**. (See No. 1705.)

821

Tydeman, John, and Ellen Jakes Kelm. **New Media in Europe: Satellites, Cable, VCRs and Videotex**. New York: McGraw-Hill, 1986. 260p.

This is intended for anyone in Europe or elsewhere who is interested in or involved with the new European market and particularly with consumer electronic media. It describes the state of the art by late 1985, assesses its present developments qualitatively and quantitatively, and offers a basis for evaluating opportunities. The authors define the many facets of Europe as a market; discuss the importance of television broadcasting, especially in relation to advertising and its growth through cable, satellite and video cassette recorders; examine the likely market potential of direct broadcast (DSB) in relation to entertainment and information content; and finally, identify possible political, ethical and regulatory uncertainties. Chapter references and index.

822

Tyson, James L. **U.S. International Broadcasting and National Security**. New York: Ramapo Press, 1983. 153p.

Tyson examines one of America's least publicized international relations strategies—Voice of America and Radio Free Europe/Radio Liberty—explaining the history, components, and relationship to the broader issues of international security. Finally, he draws conclusions about the place of official radio in a democratic society, and offers recommendations for upping quality and cost effectiveness. Notes and appendixes giving some financial and employment statistics.

823

U.S. Foreign Broadcast Information Service. **Broadcasting Stations around the World**. Pts. I-IV. 26th ed. Washington: Superintendent of Documents, U.S. Government Printing Office, 1974.

Lists all reported radio broadcasting and TV frequency assignments with the exception of those in the U.S. which broadcast on domestic channels. Part I, "Amplitude Modulation Broadcasting Stations According to Country and City"; Part II, "Amplitude Modulation Broadcasting Stations According to Frequency"; Part III, "Frequency Modulation Broadcasting Stations," in two sections—one alphabetical by country and city and the other by frequency; Part IV, "Television Stations," also in two sections and with the same information as in the preceding parts plus additional data to distinguish audio, video, polarization, and other technical factors that apply. Appendixes in Parts I and II give call-sign allocations and world time chart; an appendix in Part IV gives characteristics of VHF and UHF TV systems. This document has not been updated.

824

Vedin, Bengt-Arne. **Media Japan**. Stockholm, Sweden: Nord Video, 1977. 119p.

A report on the development of the Japanese information society which encompasses TV, video, telefacsimile, and major experiments such as the Tama New Town "cable community" and the Higashi-Ikoma optical fiber venture.

825

Victorian Ministry for the Arts. **Tomorrow's TV: Cable Television and the Arts**. Melbourne, Australia: Cable Press, 1983. 114p.

Report of a conference which addresses various options offered by cable to the Australians, with pros and cons. Of equal concern: will the ability to watch art programs over cable—a sedentary pursuit—hurt the performing arts? Contains a glossary of cable terminology.

Wade, Graham. **Film, Video and Television: Market Forces, Fragmentation and Technological Advance**. (See No. 442.)

Wasserman, Steven R., ed. **The Lively Arts Information Directory**. (See No. 443.)

Ward, Scott, et al. **How Children Learn to Buy**. (See No. 1628.)

826

Ward, Scott, Tom Robertson, and Ray Brown. **Commercial Television and European**

Children: An International Research Digest. London: Gower, 1986. 243p.

Report of a conference whose object was "to provide leading academics in Europe with an opportunity to exchange knowledge about advertising and children and identify appropriate avenues for future research." Twenty participants from eight European countries and two speakers from the U.S., representing a variety of disciplines from economics to psychology, child psychiatry and media education, discussed 1) age-related differences in children's reaction to television advertising; 2) micro-processes of children's response to advertising; 3) parent-child relations relating to TV advertising; and 4) consumer-socialization and TV advertising. Emphasis is on empirical research with theoretical models. References.

827

Wartella, Ellen, ed. **Children Communicating: Media and Development of Thought, Speech, Understanding**. Beverly Hills, CA: Sage, 1979. 286p. (Sage Annual Reviews of Communication Research, Vol. 7.)

Research containing investigations of the growth of children's communicative behavior and ability both in terms of their interaction with media and their communication with others around them. All of the studies have a common interest in associating qualitative change with age, while recognizing the involvement of cognition. Among the articles: "Children's Comprehension of Television Content" by W. Andrew Collins; "Shape, Not Only Content: How Media Symbols Partake in the Development of Abilities" by Gavriel Salomon; "Children's Attention: The Case of TV Viewing" by Robert Krull and William Husson; "Children's Understanding of Television People" by Byron Reeves; "Coming of Age in the Global Village: Television and Adolescence" by Ronald J. Farber, Jane Brown and Jack McCleod, and "The Young Child as Consumer" by Wartella, Daniel Sackman, Scott Ward, Jacob Shamir and Alison Alexander. Chapter References.

Weaver, David H., and G. Cleveland Wilhoit. **The American Journalist: A Portrait of U.S. News People and Their Work**. (See No. 445.)

828

Wedell, George, ed. **Making Broadcasting Useful: The African Experience**. Manchester, England: Manchester University Press, 1986. 306p.

In two parts. The first deals with practical issues in African broadcasting, such as "Program Building on Limited Budgets," "Broadcasting and Multilingualism," "The Organization and Managing of a Broadcasting Service," "Radio as a Tool for Development," and similar topics of concern, with broadcasters in Zambia, Kenya, Tanzania, Zimbabwe, Ghana, the Sudan, Lesotho,

Swaziland, the Seychelles and Ethiopia discussing the problems facing them as new nations. The second part grew out of the Symposium of Broadcasting Organization and Management held in 1984 at the request of UNESCO, The U.K. Overseas Development Administration, and the British Council, in which a group of directors of broadcasting organizations and permanent secretaries of ministries of information dealt with such matters of policy as shifting cultural boundaries, economic constraints, and technological change. Countries are limited to anglophone Africa; Wedell says that financial constraints prevented a bilingual meeting with colleagues in francophone Africa. Notes, maps and index.

829

Wedlake, G.E.C. **SOS: The Story of Radio Communication**. New York: Crane, Russak, 1973. 240p.

Beginning with Michael Faraday's discoveries in the field of electrical science, this simply written account for laymen traces developments in radio communication, with attention to technical as well as social developments. It is illustrated by both figures and photographs throughout. Appendixes give particulars of early instruments and a chronological table. There is a brief selected bibliography of books and an index.

830

Weir, Earnest Austin. **The Struggle for National Broadcasting in Canada**. Toronto: McClelland & Stewart, 1965. 477p.

Lengthy history of Canadian broadcasting from 1919 to 1965. The author, who was with the Canadian Broadcasting Corporation from its beginnings to his retirement, has used all available materials (he laments that many sources have not been preserved) and has interviewed a number of people who played prominent parts in the development of Canadian broadcasting.

831

Wells, Alan. **Picture-Tube Imperialism? The Impact of U.S. Television on Latin America**. Maryknoll, NY: Orbis, 1972. 197p.

A sociologist examines the cultural penetration of Latin America by U.S. telecorporations, TV programs, and foreign branches of Madison Avenue ad agencies. The first half of the book deals with various aspects of communication, with emphasis on consumerism; the second half with conscious and unconscious manipulative uses by various agencies and the media themselves. There is a 12-page bibliography and tables and diagrams.

832

Wenham, Brian, ed. **The Third Age of Broadcasting**. London: Faber & Faber, 1982. 139p.

With Britain expanding television distribution to permit new channels and with the explosion of program-ming this expansion would involve, nine Englishmen and one American concerned in various ways with television programs put together their thoughts in essays "offered, not as definitive statements but as an initial probe into tomorrow's broadcasting interior . . . designed to mark out new paths for further examination and inquiry so that—at the end of the day—the better to choose." The single American is Robert MacNeil, the commentator who worked for years with BBC. The essays deal with such topics as the place of the arts, televised films, video education, portrayal of prejudice in programs, and the risk of news overkill on the new channels. MacNeil takes a hard look at cable television programming in the U.S.

833

Wertheim, Arthur Frank. **Radio Comedy**. New York: Oxford University Press, 1979. 439p.

Discussion, accompanied by excerpts and photographs, of many of the comedies of the 1930s and 1940s. Wertheim explores the relationship between social history and radio comedy, believing that it was popular not because it was escapist fare but because much of it dealt with social issues.

834

Whale, John. **The Half-Shut Eye: Television and Politics in Britain and America**. Westport, CT: Greenwood, 1969. 219p.

Whale's intriguing title comes from Pope's **The Rape of the Lock**, in which Pope pretended that the politician had the ability to "see through all things with his half-shut eyes." Translated into television times, Whale believes that it is a condition of democracy that the governed constantly watch their governors, and television has become the main tool of surveillance. "Yet," he contends, "the round, unwinking gaze of the television camera is not as all-vigilant as it may seem. Natural and artificial causes conspire to ensure that its eye too, like the politician's in Pope, is no more than half open." Elaborating on this theme, he points out television's limitations—some imposed, some inherent—as a primary source of political information. Although his examples are from the 1960's his logic remains pertinent. Notes and index.

Whatmore, Geoffrey. **The Modern News Library.** (See No. 976.)

835

Whetmore, Edward Jay. **The Magic Medium: An Introduction to Radio in America**. Belmont, CA: Wadsworth, 1981. 246p.

Although a great deal has been written about radio, most of it concerns technology, policy or economics and is often part of a larger work, and is not intended as a text. Consequently this introductory text, concerned solely with radio as a whole, fills an empty spot. Three chapters tell of its history from technical beginnings through the

"Golden Age" of the 1920s to the mid-1950s. Other chapters examine news, sports and music (the latter heavily emphasized); the place of commercials in radio's economics; production; programming; audience research; and aesthetics. Whitmore writes well, which adds to the interest of the subject matter, as does the format with interesting illustrations and special pages featuring thumbnail sketches of some of radio's prominent characters, past and present. Most of the chapters end with a brief annotated list of readings. Index.

836

White, Llewllyn. **The American Radio: A Report on the Broadcasting Industry in the United States from the Commission on Freedom of the Press**. Chicago: University of Chicago, 1947. 260p.

A study of radio from its inception until the late 1940s made by the Commission to determine the possible need for regulation and control. White discusses history and structure, the attempts to establish educational broadcasting, academic and industrial research, and the efforts toward regulation both by government and by the industry itself. Appendixes give regional networks and excerpts from the codes of 1929 and 1939. There are notes on sources.

837

Who's Who in Broadcasting. 2d ed. London: Carrick, 1985. 210p.

This paperback crowds a lot of bare-bone facts about British media personnel into a small amount of space. **Who's Who in Broadcasting** lists position, date of birth, address, education, experience, and sometimes recreational pursuits for about 1,000 broadcasters throughout the British Isles. In selecting individuals, the editors "limited the number of on-air faces in favour of a greater proportion of production staff."

838

Who's Who on Television. Compiled and produced by ITV Books. London: Independent Television Books in association with Michael Joseph, 1982. 272p.

Contains background and credits and photographs for approximately 1,000 actors and actresses on television and in film. Editors apologize for the omission of many who either did not want to be included or could not be reached. All are British except for a few Americans—among them the full cast of **Dallas**.

839

Wicklein, John. **Electronic Nightmare: The New Communications and Freedom**. New York: Viking, 1981. 282p.

"In writing this book, I tried to find and describe specific examples of the major [new] developments in communication, to illustrate the point that the blessings and threats are already upon us," says Wicklein, adding that he has concentrated on concepts and techniques rather than the specific pieces of hardware that made them possible. Aware that the new technologies have their blessings, he is equally aware that they pose dangers, especially to individual liberty and privacy. To make his points he takes examples—two-way cable, video text, the electronic newspaper, satellites—from around the world; and he discusses privacy in terms of Sweden and government control in terms of Brazil. Although he suggests some possible answers to his concerns, his main aim is to raise thought-provoking questions. Chapter notes and index.

840

Williams, Arthur. **Broadcasting and Democracy in West Germany**. Philadelphia, PA: Temple University Press, 1976. 198p.

Traces the development of the German broadcasting system from 1945 onward, as its democratic foundations evolved. Material is presented in the context of West German society. Contains notes, a bibliography, and an index.

841

Williams, Raymond. **Television: Technology and Cultural Form**. New York: Schocken, 1974. 160p.

An exploration and a description of some of the relationships between TV as a technology and TV as a cultural form, in which Williams uses the medium as an outstanding example to comment not only upon it but also upon the interaction it brings about between technology, social institutions, and culture in general. He also discusses alternative technology and alternative uses of the medium. Throughout he brings a depth few writers on the subject can match. Bibliography and index.

Wilson, H.H. **Pressure Group: The Campaign for Commercial Television**. (See No. 509.)

842

Williams, Tannis MacBeth, ed. **The Impact of Television: A Natural Experiment in Three Communities**. New York: Academic Press, 1986. 446p.

Does television affect its child and adult viewers, and if so, how? To attempt an answer the authors studied several thousand people in each of three Canadian communities on two occasions, just before one of the towns obtained television for the first time and again two years later. The results are larger than a description of who was studied, and when, how, and what was found; they also examined the processes involved in television's influence and the complexities of relationships between TV and human behavior. Although results will be of most interest to researchers, teachers and students in communication studies, psychology, education and sociology, it is intended equally for parents, educators, policy makers, advertisers and workers in the television industry. To this end the authors have avoided jargon when possible and presented results straightforwardly in text, tables and figures, with more involved statistical details in the appendixes and chapter notes. The final chapter, "Summary, Conclusions, and Implications," provides a quick overview. Each chapter has references as well as notes, and there is an author and a subject index.

843

Window Dressing on the Set: Women and Minorities in Television; A Report of the United States Commission on Civil Rights. Washington: U.S. Commission on Civil Rights, 1977. 181p.

Findings and recommendations derived from two content analyses which show the portrayal of women in dramatic programs and news, along with facts and figures concerning employment. Appendixes give methodology used in collecting data on network entertainment programming; non-white characters identified by program, race, ethnicity, sex, and occupation, 1973 and 1974; network entertainment program sample, 1973 and 1974; sources of labor force and population data; and comments by the FCC on the report. This has been followed by **Window Dressing on the Set: An Update** (1979, 96p.), which deals with the late 1970s.

844

Winn, Marie. **The Plug-in Drug: Television, Children and the Family**. 2d ed. New York: Viking, 1985. 288p.

A well-documented study in which the author contends that the act of watching TV can be bad, regardless of the nature of the content. Interviewing families, teachers, and child specialists and examining scientific studies, she addresses herself to such questions as the effect of television on children's use of free time and on family relationships, the role of TV as surrogate parents, the possible mental and physical dangers of passivity, and some of the ways schools deal with television. She also suggests possible solutions which parents and schools might consider. Contains footnotes and an index.

845

Women in the Media. Paris: UNESCO, 1980. 119p.

During International Women's Year in 1975 one of the problems studied was the role of women vis-à-vis the media. This slim book approaches the problem eclectically: Part I. "Inquiry on Participation of Women in Radio, Television and Film in Four Countries (Australia, Canada, United Kingdom and United States)" by Jerzy Toeplitz, Director of the Australian Film and Television School, and Part II. "Women in Cinema," the account of a symposium in which women film workers from many different countries exchanged views on practical and theoretical considerations.

846

Woodrow, R. Brian, and Kenneth B. Woodside, eds. **The Introduction of Pay-TV in Canada: Issues and Implications**. Montreal: The Institute for Research on Public Policy/L'Institut de Récherches Politiques. 1982. 240p.

From its inception to the present, Canadian pay-TV has been a subject of controversy. In these essays a variety of authorities bring together their viewpoints on such aspects as its history, regulation, technological possibilities and operational formats, and place in the Canadian broadcasting system. There is also a chapter, "Pay-TV in the United States: Its Growth, Regulation and Prospects." An epilogue contains "A Commentary on the CRTC Licensing Decision of 18 March 1982" which occurred after the publication of the essays. Each chapter has bibliographical notes, and there is a glossary.

Working Press of the Nation. Radio and TV Directory. (See No. 1799.)

World Radio TV Handbook. (See No. 1801.)

847

Woolery, George W. **Children's Television: The First Thirty-Five Years, 1946–1981. Part 1: Animated Cartoon Series; Part 2: Live, Film, and Tape Series**. 2 v. Metuchen, NJ: Scarecrow, 1983, 1985. 386, 788p.

The first part, a filmography of animated cartoon series; traces the origins, growth and development of the genre, giving both network and syndicated history; production credits; principal characters and voices; and a summary delineating theme and component segments and other pertinent facts. Part 2, a compendium of TV series for young people, transmitted live or from film or videotape and syndicated extensively in the U.S. since the start of regular networking, gives for each entry network and syndicated history; production credits; casts; and descriptions of each series. Part 1 contains a four-page chronicle of animated cartoons as televised programming; Part 2 is a 15-page chronicle of children's television in general. In both volumes, descriptions of each show are extensive. Appendixes for Part 1 include numerous other pertinent facts about animated cartoon series, among them being sources on which they are based—comic books, newspaper comics, literary sources, TV programs and others—and a list of animated-film awards. Contained in the appendix of the second volume is a 30-page chronology of children's television, identifying some landmark industry achievements, interesting occurrences, important programming developments, and newsworthy events affecting children's television during the first 35 years. This, combined with the general history, may be one of the most useful features. Also among the other appendixes: awards; longest-running and multi-network series; imported live-action series; animated-cartoon series with live-action components; series with a radio broadcast or cinematic history; and series based on TV programs, literary sources, or comics' characters. Contents of both volumes are covered by a variety of name and subject indexes, with Part 2 cross-referencing Part 1. This compilation is a valuable and thorough reference for anyone needing factual information on children's television programming.

848

Zillmann, Dolf, and Jennings Bryant, eds.
Selective Exposure to Communication.
Hillsdale, NJ: Erlbaum, 1985. 251p.

A great deal of empirical research has been done on the negative effects of television, but little on the reasons why people enjoy whatever they elect to watch or hear, and more fundamentally, why they elect their programs in the first place. This is the contention of the editors in this volume of articles which is concerned with the appeal of entertainment TV. They begin with "Selective-Exposure Phenomena" by the editors, followed by "Cognitive Dissonance in Selective Exposure" by John Cotton; "Measuring Exposure to Television" by James Webster and Jacob Wakshlag; "Informational Utility and Selective Exposure to Entertainment Media" by Charles Takin; "Determinants of Television Viewing Preferences" by Barrie Gunter; "Thought and Action as Determinants of Media Exposure" by Allan Fenigstein and Ronald Heyduk; "Fear of Victimization and the Appeal of Crime Drama" by Dolf Zillmann and Jacob Wakshlag; "Affect, Mood, and Emotion as Determinants of Selective Exposure" by Dolf Zillmann and Jennings Bryant; "Selective Exposure to Educational Television" by Jacob Wakshlag; "Cable and Program Choice" by Carrie Hester and Bradley Greenberg; and "'Play It Again, Sam': Repeated Exposure to Television Programs" by Percy Tannenbaum. Each article has an extensive list of references, and there is an author and a subject index.

Print Media

NEWSPAPERS

849

Abundo, Romeo B. **Print and Broadcast Media in the South Pacific**. Singapore: Asian Mass Communication Research and Information Centre, 1985. 78p.

A UNESCO project designed to study "methods of establishing community newspapers in remote islands of the Pacific in conjunction with other community media, notably radio." An overview of the region gives background, the status and problems of broadcasting and print media, and recommendations, followed by similar overviews of Papua New Guinea, the Solomon Islands, Fiji, Western Somoa, and Tonga. These are accompanied by maps and tables of facts and figures.

850

The Adversary Press. St. Petersburg, FL: Modern Media Institute, Poynter Institute for Media Studies, 1983. 112p.

Have newspapers gone too far as adversaries of government and should they make peace? In this verbatim report of a conference held by the Modern Media Institute 19 prominent journalists and academicians with varying viewpoints discuss the issue.

851

America's Leading Daily Newspapers. A Media Research Institute Survey, Michael Emery, Director. Indianapolis, IN: Berg, 1983. 36p.

The "top ten" newspapers in the U.S., based on results of a poll of more than 3,000 publishers, editors, and journalism professors. A brief discussion of each newspaper gives salient points. Some almost but not quite made the top ten; these are briefly discussed as regional leaders. It was originally published in **Editor & Publisher**, June 11, 1983. A similar review and evaluation of the leading newspapers is also available in **The Press and America** by Michael Emery and his father, Edwin Emery (No. 117).

852

American Newspaper Publishers Association Foundation in cooperation with the Association for Education in Journalism. **Education for Newspaper Journalists in the Seventies and Beyond. Proceedings**. Washington, DC: American Newspaper Publishers Association, 1974. 349p.

Educators and newspaper executives meet and cover the following aspects of journalism education: journalism and a liberal education; non-verbal communication; professionalism of the press; the journalist's body of knowledge; attitude formation; economics of the press; new technology; social science reporting; professional media experience; professional activity beyond the classroom; mastery of a non-journalism discipline; the study of urban life; broad understanding of major issues; objectives of journalism schools; criticism of the press, and an evaluation of journalism schools. Each paper is given in full and verbatim reports of the discussions that followed are also included.

853

American Newspapers, 1821–1936: A Union List of Files Available in the United States and Canada. Ed. by Winifred Gregory. New York: Wilson, 1937. 791p.

A list of newspapers, beginning where Brigham (No. 875) leaves off, giving their location in libraries of the U.S. and Canada, dates when they began and ceased publication (if no longer extant), and changes in names or mergers that have occurred. Information about their history is not, however, as full as in Brigham.

854

American Society of Newspaper Editors. **Newspaper Credibility: Building Reader Trust**. Washington, DC: American Society of Newspaper Editors, 1985. 71p.

Recent years have brought concern about "credibility"—the attitude of the public toward the media. Does the public trust them? and should newspapers be concerned over the problem? The research in this extensive study, consisting of telephone interviews followed by extensive questionnaires and conducted by MORI Research of Minneapolis, focuses on the extent of the problem and possible solutions. After a one-page overview which hits the highlights, specific results are given in detail, with graphs, charts, figures and examples of questions.

855, 856

American Society of Newspaper Editors. **Relating to Readers in the '80s**. Washington, DC: American Society of Newspaper Editors, 1984. 52p.

American Society of Newspaper Editors. **Changing Needs of Changing Readers**. Washington, DC: American Society of Newspaper Editors, 1978. 52p.

Each of these studies centers on learning what kinds of content readers want and expect from their newspapers. Information is based on replies to questionnaires and on discussions with members of the newspaper audience. The many changes in the newspaper industry and the world at large that occurred in the six-year interval between studies are reflected in the answers. Results are both summarized and given in detail. The study was conducted by Clark, Martive and Bartolomeo.

857

Ansah, Paul, et al., **Rural Journalism in Africa**. Paris: UNESCO, 1981. 35p. (Reports and Papers on Mass Communication No. 88.)

An overview; resources for training; origins, development and present situation, country by country; and a brief discussion of African languages in relation to rural newspapers.

858

Arndt, Karl J. R., and May E. Olson. **The German Language Press of the Americas**. New English ed. 2 v. Munich, West Germany: Verlag Dokumentation, 1973, 1976.

The first volume lists by geographic location German-American newspapers published in the U.S.; the second volume lists those published in Argentina, Brazil, Bolivia, Chile, Costa Rica, Cuba, the Dominican Republic, Ecuador, Guatemala, Guyana, Mexico, Paraguay, Peru, Uruguay, and Venezuela, with an addenda to Vol. I on the U.S. Data for each entry vary but usually include frequency, date of founding and expiration date for those no longer extant, top personnel, library holdings, and publisher. Sometimes there is a description of the publication, some of which are direct quotes in German. Vol. II has a lengthy bibliography of works consulted.

859, 860, 861

Ashley, Perry J., ed. **American Newspaper Journalists, 1690–1872**. Detroit, MI: Gale, 1985. 527p. (Dictionary of Literary Biography, Vol. 43.)

Ashley, Perry J., ed. **American Newspaper Journalists, 1873–1900**. Detroit, MI: Gale, 1983. 392p. (Dictionary of Literary Biography, Vol. 23.)

Ashley, Perry J., ed. **American Newspaper Journalists, 1901–1925**. Detroit, MI: Gale, 1984. 385p. (Dictionary of Literary Biography, Vol. 25.)

Patterned after the **Dictionary of National Biography** and the **Dictionary of American Biography**, these three volumes contain biographical sketches of varying length according to the importance of the individual as a writer/journalist or, in some cases like Adolph Ochs or Joseph Pulitzer or William Randolph Hearst, their importance as a publisher or editor. Most of the journalists, however, are primarily or equally well-known as writers, and many of them have become obscure, so that the greatest value of the series perhaps lies in the sketches of lesser-known figures who have escaped the journalism histories and the who's whos. Factual material preceding each sketch, lists some or all of the following data: dates, major positions held, books and articles by and/or about, and for some, personal facts such as education and marriage. In addition to their more scholarly attributes, the articles, all by academics, make interesting reading. Illustrated.

Arterton, F. Christopher. **Media Politics: The News Strategies of Presidential Campaigns**. (See No. 12.)

862

Bailyn, Bernard, and John B. Hench, eds. **The Press & the American Revolution**. Worcester, MA: American Antiquarian Society, 1980. 383p.

Essays on the activities, place, and influence of American printers and journalists during the period of the American Revolution when the two were frequently the same and the man who operated the printing press often determined its content. Chapters include articles on press freedom, the newspaper press' role in the Southern colonies, the Colonial German language press, the Loyalist press, British correspondence in the Colonial press (a study in misunderstanding), statistics on American printing, 1765–1783, and in an Afterword, the legacy of the press in the American Revolution. Footnotes and index.

863

Bainbridge, Cyril, ed. **One Hundred Years of Journalism: Social Aspects of the Press**. London: Macmillan, 1984. 166p.

The greater part of this book is devoted to a history of Britain's IOJ (Institute of Journalists) by Bainbridge in which he has set the role and activities of the professional organization in the context of the development of newspapers and journalism. Preceding this are brief articles on the relationship of the press to freedom of speech, law, public order, industry, the church, and the armed forces (reporting conflicts). Appendixes give the IOJ's Royal Charter, and a list of presidents and of general secretaries. Index.

864

Baistow, Tom. **Fourth-Rate Estate: An Anatomy of Fleet Street**. London: Comedia, 1985. 115p.

A distinguished British journalist takes a hard and not too dispassionate look at the woes that beset British newspapers today. As he himself describes his work: "It is the story Fleet Street doesn't print. I hope that this book will help to throw some light on a problem for our kind of society that transcends Fleet Street's self-interest and, perhaps, encourages wider discussion of potential paths to a healthy pluralist press." He writes both from personal knowledge and extensive documentation. Brief bibliography and index.

865

Balk, Alfred. **A Free and Responsive Press**. New York: Twentieth Century Fund, 1973. 88p.

Consumerism, contends Balk, is too big a force among newspaper readers; they want a better press. He discusses steps that have been taken in this direction, with emphasis on press councils, and laments that too little is accomplished. He describes the British Press Council, tells of American efforts as a whole, and gives the structure of two of the most ambitious in this country—those of Minnesota and Honolulu. Appendixes contain the constitutions of the Minnesota and the British councils and the organization of that of Ontario. Two bibliographies: one of books and one of periodical and newspaper articles.

866

Baran, Paul. **The Future of Newsprint, 1970–2000**. Menlo Park, CA: Institute for the Future, 1971. 49p. (Special Industry Report No. 16.)

Portion of a study which sought to develop a better understanding of the factors that might change the demand for newsprint within the next few decades. As the newsprint business is so much a part of the newspaper business, the report focuses most attention on that area. Among topics surveyed are basic facts about newsprint: its manufacture, distribution, ownership, etc.; substitute media; demographics and economics of the newspaper; and ecological considerations. Information was obtained by polling the opinions of a panel of experts and, except for a five-page introduction, takes the form of graphs and charts.

867

Belford, Barbara. **Brilliant Bylines: A Biographical Anthology of Notable Newspaperwomen in America**. New York: Columbia University Press, 1986. 385p.

An examination of the lives and works of selected newspaperwomen, with samples of their journalism, designed to show "how the careers of women who became journalists (particularly the nineteenth-century pioneers) and what they wrote were shaped by both personal and economic necessity and by the demands of the newspaper editors of their era." In two parts: "Bygone Bylines," featuring 12 women from the last half of the 19th century into the first half of the twentieth, and "Bold Bylines," featuring 12 women from the 20th century. Over and above its insights into journalistic history and the women's movement, and its reference uses, it makes fascinating reading. Bibliography and index.

868

Benjaminson, Peter. **Death in the Afternoon: America's Newspaper Giants Struggle for Survival**. Kansas City, KS: Andrews, McMeel & Parker, 1984. 202p.

Since the 1960s big city afternoon dailies have been a dying breed. Using case studies of some who died and some who are surviving, Benjaminson analyzes possible causes and remedies. Among the papers he studied are the **New York News Tonight** edition which died in 1981, the **Philadelphia Bulletin** (1982), the **Washington Star** (1981) and—surviving—the **New York Post**, the Los Angeles **Herald Examiner** and the Oakland **Tribune**. Contains a list of individuals consulted, periodicals, and books. Index.

869

Berry, Dave, Liz Cooper, and Charles Landry. **Where Is the Other News? The Newstrade and the Radical Press**. London: Minority Press Group, 1980. 79p.

Traces the history of the community and local British radical press during the 1970s, explaining its growth in the context of political and technological developments, and looking at the problems of its survival in the face of inadequate financing, poor distribution, and internal politics. Contains "an idiosyncratic list of (British) 'radical magazines' currently (1980) in print which the authors warn is by no means comprehensive, and brief information about the Publications Distribution Co-operative.

870

Bertrand, Claude Jean, comp. **The British Press, an Historical Survey: An Anthology**. Paris: Office Central de Librairie, 1969. 208p.

Traces through documents and articles from contemporary sources the growth of the British press from the introduction of printing to the present. A chronology, "Landmarks in the History of the British Press," precedes the text. Appendixes in tabular form give circulation figures during the last 30 years; an overview of newspapers broken down into two categories—quality and popular—with circulation, political tendency, and controlling interest; the periodical press divided into journals of opinion and mass magazines, with political tendencies and circulation over the last ten years. Bibliography.

871

Black Press Handbook. Washington, DC: National Newspaper Publishers Association, 1977. 116p.

A commemorative booklet to celebrate the 150th anniversary of the founding of the first black newspaper, **Freedom's Journal**, in 1827. A number of brief features describe various aspects, happenings, and personalities within the black press. The main feature is a list of black newspapers which are NNPA members, with addresses, advertising rates, personnel, date of publication, year of founding, and number of employees. This was preceded by a 1974–75 edition with much of the same information.

872

Bogart, Leo. **Press and Public: Who Reads What, When, Where, and Why in American Newspapers**. Hillsdale, NJ: Erlbaum, 1981. 285p.

The focus of this book is on newspaper readers and the changes in their tastes and habits, based on data Bogart gathered from research done under his direction at the Newspaper Advertising Bureau. He discusses recent demographic and other developments which have affected newspaper circulation; explains the business structure of newspapers; applies his data to audience characteristics tastes in relation to content; and gives his opinion about steps by which marketing and journalism can meet the challenge of change. Other research reference are included to corroborate or amplify some of the findings. He reminds his own readers, however, that the most studies conducted since 1977 were made as part of the Newspaper Readership Project, a special industry-wide effort to boost circulation, and were supported by the newspaper business and its "Establishment." In conclusion is a briefly annotated list, "More Reading." Index.

873

Bohere, G. **Profession: Journalist. A Study on the Working Conditions of Journalists**. Geneva, Switzerland: International Labour Office, Publications Branch, 1984. 177p.

Discusses features of employment, ethical standards, career problems, pay, industrial relations and other pertinent aspects of the profession for journalists, who are defined as those handling current news on a daily basis. Attention is focused throughout on the ways in which they have been affected by recent transformations in communications and information, and the implications of the replacement of traditional by advanced technological methods. The present study is the fifth the ILO has devoted to journalists. The four previous ones were made half a century ago, with two in 1928, another in 1929, and the third in 1931. Contains chapter notes, and tables of facts and figures.

874

Boyce, George, James Curran, and Pauline Wingate, eds. **Newspaper History: From the 17th Century to the Present Day**. Beverly Hills, CA: Sage, 1978. 425p.

Inclusive histories of the British press are few, and for this reason as well as for the quality of the 19 articles which comprise it, this one, which the editors describe as an interim rather than a definitive history, is especially welcome. Part One provides different perspectives on historical development; Part Two traces ownership, control and structure; Part Three examines the changing organization and occupation of journalism; Part Four deals with the role of the press in British society and politics. All in all, it places the British press in a broad cultural perspective. Contains copious notes and references, a seven-page bibliography, a newspaper chronology 1621–1977, and an index.

Among other histories are **English Newspapers: Chapters in the History of Journalism** by H. R. Fox (London: Chatto and Windus, 1887), A. Aspinal's topical **Politics and the Press, c. 1780–1850** (Home & Van Thal, 1949. 511p.), Fredrick Siebert's **Freedom of the Press in England 1476–1776: The Rise and Decline of Government Controls** (No. 401), and Francis Williams' **Dangerous Estate: The Anatomy of Newspapers** (No. 453).

875

Brigham, Clarence S. **History and Bibliography of American Newspapers, 1690–1820**. 2 v. Worcester, MA.: American Antiquarian Society, 1947.

A geographical list of newspapers for the period covered, locating the libraries where they may be found and giving the history of each paper in a concise descriptive annotation. Brought up to date by **American Newspapers, 1821–1936** (No. 853). A 50-page book of additions and corrections appeared in 1961. Each volume contains a list of libraries and of private owners and an index of titles and of printers; Vol. II has a general index.

876

Brown, Lucy. **Victorian News and Newspapers**. Oxford, England: Clarendon Press, 1985. 303p.

A study of news in the latter half of 19th century Britain, and the environment which fostered it. Brown examines Victorian newspaper readership, the new developments in printing and telegraphy, the Victorian journalists and the way they handled the news, and the news sources, including both news agencies and social contacts. Throughout she emphasizes the interplay between politics and journalism, with evidence indicating that influence exerted by politicians or lobbyists met with little effective criticism or resistance. She also finds that newspapers tended to follow current trends rather than introduce them to the public. She concludes with the paradox that as newspapers grew in social acceptance they declined in critical vigor. Footnotes, a bibliography, an index of newspapers and periodicals mentioned in the text, and a name and subject index.

Cannon, Carl L., comp, **Journalism: A Bibliography**. (See No. 1642.)

877

Caspi, Dan. **Media Decentralization: The Case of Israel's Local Newspapers**. New Brunswick, NJ: Transaction, 1986. 154p.

For many years Israel had a nationwide press centered in Tel Aviv, viewing the country as one constituency with a common agenda for economic, political and cultural affairs. Recently, however, local papers—weekly tabloids sold or distributed free throughout their respective cities—are springing up. Caspi's primary concern in this study of the diffusion of a local press is to determine whether these weekly tabloids reflect and in turn contribute to a process of social and political decentralization. Underlying this are two more abstract concerns: relations between social and communication systems, and relations of the various mass media to one another. Elihu Katz has written the Foreword. Chapter notes, bibliography, and index.

Circulation: The Annual Circulation Penetration Analysis of Print Media. (See No. 1737.)

878

Commission of Inquiry into High School Journalism. **Captive Voices: The Report**. Comp. by Jack Nelson. New York: Schocken, 1974. 264p.

The commission investigated four areas of high school journalism: censorship, minority participation, educational and journalistic quality, and interest of editors and other workers in the established media. Appendixes give "A Legal Guide to High School Journalism" and show the methodology, ranging from questionnaires, whose results are shown, to lists of the sources consulted. Indexed.

879

Compaine, Benjamin M. **The Newspaper Industry in the 1980s: An Assessment of Economics and Technology**. White Plains, NY: Knowledge Industry Publications, 1980. 290p.

"This is a study of newspapers, not as an editorial product, but primarily as a business institution." (Introduction) Compaine has gathered together and identified significant trends in major areas affecting newspapers as a business—circulation, advertising, production, labor, and competition, and has analyzed them for present and future trends. In doing so he acknowledges the difficulty in restricting the analysis to the newspaper industry alone, since, as he points out in his conclusions, it is becoming more and more difficult to separate discrete media industries as they rely more and more on similar technology for gathering, processing and storing much of their information.

Among other virtues of this detailed study, it contains a brief section about previous studies, a number of charts and tables, and a bibliography of monographs and articles. Index.

880

Cranfield, G. A. **The Press and Society: From Caxton to Northcliffe**. London/New York: Longman, 1978. 242p.

A survey of the history of the British press in relation to the development of British society, from the time of its introduction into England in 1476 to the twentieth century. Considerable emphasis is placed on the growth of the reading public. Includes not only newspapers proper but also broadsides, ballads, pamphlets, serial fiction, penny dreadfuls, and so on. Notes and bibliography.

881

Curran, James, ed. **The British Press: A Manifesto**. London: Macmillan, 1978. 339p.

Essays by Raymond Williams, Stuart Hall, Anthony Smith, Peter Golding, Philip Elliot, and others of the Acton Society Press Group, which offer a critique of the British press and proposals for reform. They challenge four commonly held assumptions: "the contentional view of press freedom as property right; the belief that 'free market' gives people what they want; the myth of the newspaper 'professional' who can distinguish fact from opinion; and the traditional dictum that, in the words of Macaulay, 'government can only interfere in discussion by making discussion less free than it would otherwise be'." Chapter references and index.

882

Current South African Newspapers/Huidige Suid-Afrikaanse Koerante. Pretoria: The State Library, 1970. 17p.

An alphabetical listing by place. For each entry gives title (with any name changes), date of establishment, address and telephone number, size, frequency, price, and language (whether English or Afrikaans). Preceding this are sections summarizing press law in South Africa, the press union, the South African Press Association, and a history of South African newspapers in broad outline. Indexed.

883

The Daily Press: A Survey of the World Situation in 1952. New York: UNESCO Publications Center, 1953. 45p. (Reports and Papers on Mass Communication No. 7.)

A follow-up, concerned only with newspapers, to the five-volume series, **Press, Film, Radio** (No. 345). Consists of 13 graphs and tables, with detailed explanatory texts, and covers the majority of countries and territories throughout the world. Also lists countries where no daily paper was published at that time.

Danky, James P., ed., and Maureen E. Hady, comp. **Native American Periodicals and Newspapers**. (See No. 1034.)

884

Dann, Martin, ed. **The Black Press (1827–1890): A Quest for National Identity**. New York: Putnam, 1971. 381p.

Although the editor's primary aim in this anthology of the nineteenth-century black press is to provide an insight into black history, it also tells a great deal about the Negro press. A sizable portion—67 pages—is taken up with its role; the five remaining sections—"The Black View of American History," "The Black Man and Politics," "The Black Man and Labor," "The Black Exodus," and "Creating a Black Community"—present in chronological order the articles, editorials, advertisements, and political cartoons of the period. Selections are almost exclusively from newspapers available on microfilm in the Schomburg Collection of the New York Public Library. Indexed.

885, 886, 887, 888, 889

Desmond, Robert W. **The Information Process: World News Reporting to the Twentieth Century**. Iowa City: University of Iowa Press, 1978. 495p.

Desmond, Robert W. **Windows on the World: The Information Process in a Changing Society 1900–1920**. Iowa City: University of Iowa Press, 1980. 608p.

Desmond, Robert W. **Crisis and Conflict: World News Reporting Between the Two Wars 1920–1940**. Iowa City: University of Iowa Press, 1982. 518p.

Desmond, Robert W. **Tides of War: World News Reporting 1940–1945**. Iowa City: University of Iowa Press, 1984. 544p.

Desmond, Robert W. **The Press and World Affairs**. New York: Appleton-Century, 1937. 421p.

A four-volume series which, in Desmond's words, is designed to describe "the evolution of international news reporting from the earliest times. The approach is historical, factual, and perhaps journalistic. It is intended as a descriptive rather than a critical examination of the media. Neither are the volumes designed for use as textbooks, but as accounts of general interest, yet also of value as references in history, political science, and journalism." He describes the various technological developments from the invention of the alphabet, paper and ink

through electronic, periodical and photojournalism, clarifying the process of international news reporting as each invention affected it in relation to the public comprehension of events. Each volume contains a substantial bibliography and an author-subject index.

The Press and World Affairs, a much earlier work by Desmond, "intended to help the average person to read his newspaper with more comprehension," especially where world affairs are concerned, in which the processes and influences involved in reporting are discarded in terms of networks and obstacles as they operated both generally and in various parts of the world. Read today, it provides grounds for analysis of how much has changed and how much remains the same. Footnotes, bibliography and index.

890

Detweiler, Frederick G. **The Negro Press in the United States**. Chicago: University of Chicago Press, 1922. 274p.

In this classic study of the black press in the U.S. from its beginnings to the 1920's Detweiler says, "The purpose has been to describe rather than interpret, to set forth facts in as straightforward a way as possible, and to let the Negro press speak for itself." Arrangement is topical: volume and influence; the press in slavery days and in freedom; favorite themes; content; demand for rights and other possible solutions to the race problem; "Negro Life"; and "Negro Criticism, Negro Life." Although he apologizes that "the author has probably failed of that degree of objectivity he desired to attain," his personal insights lend interest and value. Bibliography and index.

891

Directory of the College Student Press in America. Ed. by Dario Politella. 6th ed. NY: Oxbridge, 1986. 300p.

Lists more than 5,000 student-run newspapers; art, news, literary, and humor magazines; handbooks and year books in thousands of institutions of higher learning in the U.S. Arrangement is by state, with institutions and their publications alphabetical. Gives brief information about each institution, followed by its publications, with data about each varying according to type, but generally including adviser, date founded, frequency, advertising rates, budget or method of financing, size, method of production, and for larger publications, incorporation, copyright and method of distribution.

892

Duscha, Julius, and Thomas Fischer. **The Campus Press: Freedom and Responsibility**. Washington, DC: American Association of State Colleges and Universities, 1973. 115p.

Part I, by Duscha, outlines the history and development of the campus press, with an analysis of similarities and differences between it and the general press. Part II, by Fischer, is a historical and legal perspective on freedom of speech and the press, with a discussion of the particular problems in this area which may affect campus presses. Important cases involving campus publications are abstracted. Contains a section listing footnotes.

893

Fenby, Jonathan. **The International News Services: A Twentieth Century Fund Report**. New York: Schocken, 1986. 275p.

In response to criticism from Third World countries about monopoly over the flow of news by Western news agencies—specifically the Associated Press, United Press International, Reuters and Agence France-Presse which together account for more than 80 percent of the international news diet of non-Communist countries—the Twentieth Century Fund arranged for a British journalist, Jonathan Fenby, to review the history and current role of the wire services, demonstrating how they are structured financially and editorially, how they operate, and the steps they have taken to meet complaints of Third World customers. His work is based on interviews, factual evidence, documentation, analysis of agency services and his conclusions as to prospects for resolving the conflict are sobering. Contains chapter notes, a bibliography and an index.

894

Filler, Louis. **The Muckrakers**. New and enl. ed. University Park: Pennsylvania State University Press, 1976. 456p.

This classic history of the muckraking era, first published in 1939 covering the years 1902–14, was expanded in 1968 under the present title to cover the New Deal, and has now been brought up to date to include Ralph Nader, the women's liberation movement, and the Watergate era, with muckraking now called investigative reporting. Contains a chronology, a bibliographic essay, and an index.

895

Finkle, Lee. **Forum for Protest: The Black Press during World War II**. Rutherford, NJ: Fairleigh Dickinson University Press, 1975. 249p.

An analysis of the response of the black press to the wartime emergency, based upon the opinion and news it disseminated. Emphasis is on news content, editorials, and columnists. Preceding this is a 40-page section giving a brief history of the black press in the U.S. Contains a bibliography and an index.

896

Fisher, Charles. **The Columnists**. New York: Howell, Soskins, 1944. 317p.

The columnists whom Fisher so aptly describes are now history—most of them (with the exception of Dorothy Thompson and Walter Lippmann) forgotten or vaguely remembered like Walter Winchell. They were of all types, from the serious political analyst to the gossip columnist, and they commanded a large readership and exerted an influence on journalism and popular culture. Fisher's portraits, though undocumented, present vivid pictures.

897

Flint, Leon Nelson. **The Conscience of the Newspaper: A Case Book in the Principles and Problems of Journalism**. New York: Appleton-Century, 1925. 470p.

Although this early text dealing with journalistic ethics in the first years of journalism education may now appear simplistic and dated, it is very useful as an example of the ethical problems and public criticism besetting the newspapers of the 1920s—most of which are still with us on a larger scale—and as a glimpse into the newspaper industry in the U.S. by a former journalist and teacher. The first portion, "Newspaper Practice and the Editor's Conscience," consists of discussions of case studies which approach editorial problems from various angles; next is a more general examination of "The Thing We Call Journalism," dealing with its nature and function in relation to the public; and finally, "The Newspaper of Tomorrow"—Flint's glimpse of the influences he sees as shaping its future. An appendix gives codes of ethics set out by associations, organizations, and some of the more prominent newspapers. Index.

898

Ghiglione, Loren, ed. **The Buying and Selling of America's Newspapers**. Indianapolis, IN: Berg, 1984. 200p.

"The daily newspapers of the United States are being put in chains, newspaper chains," says Ghiglione. Ten insightful articles, each about an outstanding small to medium-sized, family newspaper sold to a major chain, describe changes both good and bad (but mostly the latter) that have occurred in terms of quality, editorial freedom, relations to the community, and other important factors. The articles also give incidental insight into the ways newspapers are organized and run. All of them are by practicing journalists.

899

Glessing, Robert J. **The Underground Press in America**. Bloomington: Indiana University Press, 1970. 207p.

Covering 15 years of the underground press from its beginning through the 1960s, Glessing traces its history and shows how it influenced American lifestyle by changing music, clothing, hair styles, sexual mores, politics, advertising, and so on. There are illustrations of writings from the press, a bibliography of sources, a directory of underground newspapers, and an index.

Goldwater, Walter. **Radical Periodicals in America, 1890–1950**. (See No. 1053.)

900

Gormley, William T., Jr. **The Effects of News-paper-Television Cross-Ownership on News Homogeneity**. Chapel Hill: University of North Carolina Publications, Institute for Research in Social Science, 1976. 276p.

This study provides a detailed examination of the results of cross-ownership of newspapers and broadcast stations in the same market, based on a study of 10 markets of different sizes. The author examines effects in three likely situations: when station and newspaper are located in the same building, when both use the same reporters, and when the station uses the stories from the newspaper. There are tables, footnotes, and a bibliography.

901

Gustafsson, Karl Erik, and Stig Hadenius. **Swedish Press Policy**. Stockholm: The Swedish Institute, 1977. 127p.

In Sweden, perhaps more than in any other country, the state has actively intervened to maintain diversity in the press through a program of subsidies. The authors, who both served on the 1972 Parliamentary Commission on the Press, describe the structure of the press policy and its effects since its introduction ten years ago. They also summarize press history, newspaper economy, and newspaper market. An appendix lists Swedish newspapers since 1975. There is a bibliography of references in both English and Swedish.

902

Hale, Oron J. **The Captive Press in the Third Reich**. Princeton, NJ: Princeton University Press, 1964. 353p.

A thoroughgoing examination of the way in which the Nazis gained possession of the German press and the way in which they maintained it and used it for their own purposes. There are charts on the organization of the Eher Verlag in 1944. Contains notes on records, interviews, and books, a bibliography, and an index.

903

Handbook of International News Agencies Around the World. Prague, Czechoslovakia: International Organization of Journalists, 1986. 167p.

Lists approximately 80 news agencies by continent and country. Data, which is supplied by the agency, varies, according to pertinence, including some or all of the following: address; telephone, cable, telex; branches in country of origin; branches abroad; staff; number of transmission hours; extent of daily service; way of transmission; special services; number of foreign agencies received and number of recipients; central editorial office; character of agency. This directory supercedes the **Handbook of News Agencies**, also published by the Inter-national Organization of Journalists as a looseleaf in 1969.

904

Harris, Michael, and Alan Lee, eds., **The Press in English Society from the Seventeenth to the Nineteenth Centuries**. Rutherford, NJ: Fairleigh Dickinson Press, 1986. 261p.

A collection of essays on various subjects which brings together facets of newspaper and periodical history over two centuries. Although economics are not neglected, emphasis is on the identification and analysis of selected content areas in relation to readership, which in turn opens up the larger issue of the complex relationship between the press and society. Contributors are historians of the 18th and 19th centuries who, though not concerned with the press of the period, have special interests which leads to extensive use of contemporary newspapers and periodicals. Individual essays deal with religion, politics, industry (through controversy over the export of wool), children, advertising, sports, and imperialism. The concluding essay is "Content Analysis and Historical Research on Newspapers." Prolific notes, bibliography, and index.

905

Harrison, Stanley. **Poor Men's Guardians: A Record of the Struggles for a Democratic Newspaper Press, 1763–1973**. London: Lawrence and Wishart, 1974. 256p.

Traces the story of the radical and working-class press in Britain from the time of John Wilkes and the "Wilkes and Liberty" agitation in the 18th century to the present. The author surveys the struggle for press freedom between the haves and the have nots, the conflicts of definitions of freedom that marked it from the beginning, and the tremendous stakes in the outcome of these struggles for the labor and progressive movement over the last 200 years. The story is told in terms of the newspapers which led the fight for progress. Contains a bibliography, an index to the newspapers mentioned, and a general index.

906

Here Is the Other News: Challenges to the Local Commercial Press. London: Minority Press Group, 1980. 80p.

An analysis of Britain's local, radical press (a term which the authors use to avoid the more limiting implications of the terms 'community' or 'alternative' press). Parts I and II provide an overview based on a survey of over 50 newspapers, relating the press to community politics. In part III, employees of six such newspapers write about the problems, both political and organizational, involved in producing alternative or radical news coverage. Appendixes discuss legal restraints and local radical papers, with a list of useful addresses and publications.

907

Heren, Louis. **The Power of the Press?** London: Orbis, 1985. 208p.

A history of the British and American newspaper press as revealed through the careers of press barons in both countries, and the way they influenced—even shaped—the role of the press, beginning with Thomas Barnes, appointed editor of the London **Times** in 1817 and John Delane who succeeded him ("Barnes and Delane") and ending with Lord Thomson and Rupert Murdoch ("The British Overseas, Thomson 'Over There', and Murdoch Everywhere"). In between came "Bennett and Greeley," "The Levy/Burnhams and W.T. Steed," "Pulitzer and Hearst," "Northcliffe and Rothermere," "McCormick-Patterson Axis, Scripps-Howard Empire and the UP," "Rothmere and Beaverbrook," "Adolph Ochs and the Sulzbergers," "Katherine Graham and the Washington Post." Documenting with episodes, Heren shows how these publishers determined news and policy, and in some cases made history or changed its course. There is, for example, a long account of the role of the **New York Times** in its coverage—or rather, lack of it—of the Bay of Pigs attack which had far-reaching consequences both to the **Times**, the government and the country. Heren is a good story teller and this is a hard book to put down. "Select Bibliography" and index. Heren does not cite his sources.

908

Hogan, Lawrence D. **The Black National News Service: The Associated Negro Press and Claude Barnett, 1919–1945.** Cranbury, NJ: Associated University Presses, 1984. 260p.

The history of Afro-American journalism in the United States since World War II needs to be updated, but this history, which goes beyond Claude Barnett's news service, does an excellent job of covering the '20s, '30s and into the '40s, an era of strong black press with newspapers, such as the Chicago **Defender** and the Baltimore **Afro-American**, receiving national recognition. In addition it contains an excellent bibliography of manuscript collections, books and periodical articles. Indexed. For an earlier history see Frederick Detweiler's **The Negro Press in the United States** (No. 890).

Hohenberg, John. **The Pulitzer Prizes.** (See No. 194.)

Horowitz, Irving Louis. **Communicating Ideas.** (See No. 1065.)

909

Hughes, Helen MacGill. **News and the Human Interest Story.** New Brunswick, NJ: Transaction, c1940, 1981. 313p.

Today the study of reality in relation to news has become a popular subject, but Hughes, in 1940 at the University of Chicago, was one of the first to examine this now popular dimension of communication study. In this account of the growth of newspapers in modern industrial society, she traces the development of a mass audience through analysis of the origins and development of the human interest story, or more broadly, the human interest aspects of news, pointing out that newspapers not only respond to popular taste but also play their part in a social construction of meaning. Contains notes, a bibliography, and indexes of names and of subjects.

910

The International Directory of News Libraries and Buyers' Guide, 1985–86. Bayside, NY: LDA Publishers, 1985. 118p.

Since the first directory of newspaper libraries was published in cooperation with the Special Libraries Association in 1976, membership in the Newspaper Division of SLA has doubled. This directory includes information for 611 news libraries, primarily from the U.S. and Canada. A special section lists the on-line information retrieval systems with the names of the news libraries using the services classified by the systems. The directory also includes a buyer's guide of library supplies and services. A new edition is to be published in 1987.

911

Jenkins, Simon. **Newspapers: The Power and the Money.** London: Faber & Faber, 1979. 130p.

"This book is about the business of newspapers, about the men who run them and the workers who produce them," says Jenkins in describing his analysis of the upheaval national British newspapers have undergone in the past few years. Emphasis is on the proprietors—past and present—"The Great Proprietors" as he calls them in his introductory chapters—who dominated them and whose managerial style he feels is responsible for their present state, both for better and (at present) for worse. His overall outlook, however, is optimistic. Jenkins, a London journalist, is political editor of **The Economist.** Bibliography and index.

Johnson, Michael L. **The New Journalism.** (See No. 1066.)

912, 913

Journalists and Readers: Bridging the Credibility Gap: An APME Credibility Report. Associated Press Managing Editors Association, 1985. 80p. Obtain from Robert W. Ritter, Executive Editor, **The Sun,** San Bernardino, CA.

The People & the Press: A Times Mirror Investigation of Public Attitudes Toward the News Media, Conducted by the Gallup Organization. Los Angeles, CA: Times Mirror, 1986. 80, 16p.

Two studies, both involved with an investigation of

the credibility of the news media. The Associated Press Managing Editors study concerns attitudes of journalists—1,333 of them, all with responsibility for newspaper content, who were asked "to do a lot of soul searching" about ways to improve newspaper credibility. Their attitudes were compared with those of a sample of the general public as to certain aspects of news coverage.

The Times Mirror study, on the other hand, is concerned only with the public's attitude. The Gallup organization which did the polling used sophisticated techniques on the public at large for opinions on news media. Findings of the two studies are difficult to compare since the APME study is limited to newspapers while the Times Mirror study includes news media generally, and the AMPE focused on journalists' attitudes while the Times Mirror study focused on readers and viewers.

914

Kaplan, Frank L. **Winter into Spring: The Czechoslovak Press and the Reform Movement, 1963–1968**. Boulder, CO: East European Quarterly, 1977. 208p.

During its brief existence as an independent state, Czechoslovakia has been subjected to distinctly different forms of political ideology and government. Focusing on a critical four-year period, Kaplan has analyzed the role played by a traditionally Western-oriented and pluralistic press in a society which becomes Communist-oriented. Appendixes give numerous facts and figures about the press, including a list of daily and weekly newspapers and periodicals (as of 1968). There are copious footnotes, an extensive bibliography, and an index. Kaplan's 54-page monograph, **The Czech and Slovak Press: The First 100 Years**, also appeared in 1977 as **Journalism Monograph** No. 47 (Association for Education in Journalism).

915

King, Frank H. H., and Prescott Clarke, eds. **A Research Guide to China-Coast Newspapers, 1822–1911**. Cambridge, MA: Harvard University Press, 1965. 235p.

"This research guide is designed primarily to facilitate the use of Western-language newspapers published in China, including Hong Kong and Macao, during the late Ch'ing period. It contains information on several related topics, including those newspapers published in London concerned with news of China, and certain Chinese-language sheets published as an integral part of or in close connection with the Western-language newspapers. There is also an appendix listing Japanese-language newspapers published in China during the period through 1911." (Introduction) Contains a bibliography.

916

Kneebone, John T. **Southern Liberal Journalists and the Issue of Race, 1920–1944**. Chapel Hill: University of North Carolina Press, 1985. 312p.

Kneebone bases his work primarily on the writings of five leading southern liberal journalists and the changing patterns of their thinking on race, reform, and history through the decades preceding the Civil Rights protest movement—Gerald W. Johnson, George Fort Milton, Virginius Dabney, Ralph McGill, and Hodding Carter. An epilogue carries the work of McGill and Carter into the latter part of the '40s and the '50s. Notes, bibliography and index.

917

Knudson, Jerry W. **Bolivia: Press and Revolution 1932–1964**. Lanham, MD: University Press of America, 1986. 487p.

A social history of the interaction between the press and Bolivian society, based on a study of Bolivian newspapers over the 12-year period of the Bolivian National Revolution, during which the press played a great part both in fomenting the revolution and carrying it out. This is both an unfolding of the role of journalism and a description of a period of Bolivian history. In Knudson's words: "The historical method has been used in the belief that history is concerned—or should be concerned—not only with what actually happened in any given time and place, but also with what people *thought* was happening, as revealed to them through the means of public information"—in this case, the newspaper. The study is heavily documented. Index.

918, 919

Koss, Stephen. **The Rise and Fall of the Political Press in Britain**. Vol. 1, **The Nineteenth Century**. Chapel Hill: University of North Carolina Press, 1981. 455p.

Koss, Stephen. **The Rise and Fall of the Political Press in Britain**. Vol. 2, **The Twentieth Century**. London: Hamish Hamilton, 1984. 718p.

As Koss evaluates British journalism over two centuries in its party political setting, one factor is constant throughout: the rise and decline of its power and prestige follows that of England. Focus is on the cluster of newspapers—constantly declining in the present century—which have distinct political attributes, objectives and connections, and on the intertwined relationship of prominent politicians and statesmen with prominent newspaper owners and journalists. It is not his aim, he says, to present a full-scale history, nor a survey of events covered by the newspapers, nor a content analysis, nor an account of the internal working of newspapers such as distribution, staffing, labor relations and technology. But even though he has not intended this to be a full-scale history, his scholarly and detailed analysis as he follows the interconnections between press and politics is something of a history both of Britain and of British journalism. Incidentally, throughout the two volumes he discusses differences between the structure of British and American journalism. Footnotes, a list of manuscript sources, and an index.

920

La Brie, Henry G., ed. **Perspectives of the Black Press: 1974**. Kennebunkport, ME: Mercer House, 1974. 231p.

An anthology which gives an eclectic overview of the black press as seen by black—and some white—journalists and journalism educators. Its articles touch on a number of topics: the role of the black press in the past and speculations about its role in the future; experiences of practitioners who have "made it"; pressure groups; testimony before Congress; successful examples of newspapers; the black press as an outlet for poets and fiction writers. Contains a name index and a subject-title index.

921

Lake, Brian. **British Newspapers: A History and Guide for Collectors**. London: Sheppard Press, 1984. 213p.

If you are British (though not necessarily) and have in mind to collect back newspaper accounts of events at the time of their occurrence this guide by an antiquarian bookseller in London should be helpful. First of all Lake initiates the would-be collector with a 93-page profusely illustrated sketch of English newspaper history; next he tells how to approach collection building; and finally he lists British newspaper libraries, dealers in newspapers, and collectors' and dealers' associations. There is a bibliography and an index.

922

Lathem, Edward C. **Chronological Tables of American Newspapers, 1690–1820: Being a Tabular Guide to Holdings of Newspapers Published in America through the Year 1820**. Barre, MA: American Antiquarian Society, 1972. 181p.

The data are presented in a series of tables arranged geographically by state and then chronologically. By consulting columns representing the pertinent year or years, users can determine what papers may exist, either for particular localities or generally. Dates within the tables indicate each newspaper's span of publication and current availability. After consulting the tables the reader can go to Brigham's **History and Bibliography of American Newspapers, 1690–1820** (No. 875) for more detailed information.

923

Lee, Alan J. **The Origins of the Popular Press in England 1855–1914**. London: Croom Helm, 1976. 310p.

Using a broadly Marxist approach focusing on ownership, or control, of the newspaper press at a time when great changes were taking place in England, Lee analyzes it both as an industry and an institution. He deals with English society also, although to a lesser extent—discussing the role of education, prosperity and leisure have played in its development, and, conversely, the role of the press in English society. The study is limited to England, rather than treating Great Britain as a whole. There are tables and maps, a bibliography, and an index.

924

Lee, Alfred McClung. **The Daily Newspaper in America: The Evolution of a Social Instrument**. New York: Octagon Books (Farrar, Straus and Giroux), 1973 (c1937). 797p.

Half a century has not outdated this sociological, or in Lee's words, "natural" history of the daily newspaper in which he has brought together many of the interrelated forces shaping its institutional structure. Organization is topical, including the newspaper in society; the pre-daily paper; the physical basis of the newspaper; labor, ownership, and management; chains and associations; advertising; weekly and Sunday issues; propaganda and public relations tie-ins; the gathering of world news; feature syndicates; the editorial staff; crusades; invasion of privacy. His broad approach, unusual at the time, offers an interesting contrast to Mott's more orthodox chronological one (No. 937).

925

Lent, John A., ed. **Newspapers in Asia: Contemporary Trends and Problems**. Hong Kong: Heinemann Asia, 1982. 597p.

Articles dealing with daily, and in some cases non-daily, newspapers from the late 1960s through the late 1970s in 23 Asian countries, ranging from Afghanistan in the area Lent calls West Asia, to Japan in East Asia. Not included are the Asian portion of the Soviet Union, countries of the Middle East, and the South Pacific territories and countries. Press freedom is described in three additional chapters, broken down by regions. In four parts: Part I is a general description which includes information about production, technology, newsprint, personnel, consumption capabilities, purchasing power, literacy rate, relevant contents, and news agencies. Part Two describes newspapers in East Asia; Part 3, Southeast Asia; and Part 4, South Asia. Contributors, all of whom are affiliated in some way with the Asian press and many of whom are Asians, write from personal backgrounds and were given detailed guidelines concerning content, form and style which they generally followed but often with a different approach or emphasis. Contains many tables throughout. Notes are incorporated in a bibliography. Lent calls attention to some unevenness in documentation.

926

Lewis, Roger. **Outlaws of America; The Underground Press and Its Context: Notes on a Cultural Revolution**. Harmondsworth, England: Penguin, 1972. 204p.

The author, an Englishman who attended an American university, traveled across the U.S. gathering his material. He has identified the main groups and tied in their publications with various counter-culture movements. One chapter discusses the underground press in England. There is a listing, "Underground Press Syndicate—Members and Friends, June, 1971," and a name and subject index.

Linton, David, and Ray Boston. **The Newspaper Press in Britain: An Annotated Bibliography.** (See No. 1669.)

927, 928, 929

Littlefield, Daniel F., Jr., and James W. Parins. **American Indian and Alaska Native Newspapers and Periodicals, 1826–1924.** Vol. 1. Westport, CT: Greenwood, 1984. 482p.

Littlefield, Daniel F., Jr., and James W. Parins. **American Indian and Alaska Native Newspapers and Periodicals, 1925–1970.** Vol. 2. Westport, CT: Greenwood, 1984. 553p.

Littlefield, Daniel F., Jr., and James W. Parins. **American Indian and Alaska Native Newspapers and Periodicals, 1971–1985.** Vol. 3. Westport, CT: Greenwood, 1986. 629p.

An alphabetical listing of each publication, giving a narrative history, a bibliography if existent, index sources to help locate copies, and a publication history with dates, personnel, etc. The editors have also included "those publications by non-Indian or non-Alaska Natives who concern themselves, for better or worse, with the contemporary Indian or Alaska Native and his affairs," but not those that treat "ethnohistorical archaeological, or historical subjects, and those published in Canada or Mexico." Appendix A lists titles by chronology, Appendix B by location, and Appendix C by tribal affiliation or emphasis. Subject index. (See also Danky and Hady, **Native American Periodicals and Newspapers 1828–1982: Bibliography, Publishing Record, and Holdings, 1828–1982,** No. 1034.)

930

Liu, Alan P. L. **The Press and Journals in Communist China.** Cambridge, MA.: Massachusetts Institute of Technology, Center for International Studies, Research Program on Problems of International Security, 1966. 121p. (Distributed by Clearinghouse of Federal Scientific and Technical Information, National Bureau of Standards, Institute for Applied Technology.)

Succinct analysis of the background, structure, function, and content of news and news reporting, newspaper reading patterns, and periodicals, with a concluding chapter on the effectiveness of the press. The author has documented his study (necessarily from secondhand sources) with extensive footnotes and a bibliography.

931

Manoff, Robert Karl, and Michael Schudson, eds. **Reading the News.** New York: Pantheon, 1986. 246p.

"In a world where the news media provide so much of our information about what lies beyond our immediate ken, and at the same time offer unspoken guidelines about how to read that information, how to absorb it, how to take it into our lives, it is important to know how to read not only the news, but journalists and journalism itself. The essays that follow take this as their task." (Introduction) This they do by examining the social, economic, and political constraints under which journalists work, and the literary or narrative structure of news writing itself that constrains them. Leon V. Sigal discusses "WHO? Sources Make the News"; Carlin Romano, "WHAT? The Grisley Truth about Bare Facts"; Michael Schudson, "WHEN? Deadlines, Datelines, and History"; Daniel C. Hallin, "WHERE? Cartography, Community, and the Cold War"; James W. Carey, WHY AND HOW? The Dark Continent of American Journalism"; in summary Robert Karl Manoff, "Writing the News ('By Telling the Story')". The style and penetration of these essays is exceptional. Notes.

932

Martindale, Carolyn. **The White Press and Black America.** Westport, CT: Greenwood, 1986. 204p.

Through an examination of the content of four papers—the **New York Times,** the **Boston Globe,** the **Atlanta Constitution** and the **Chicago Tribune,** Martindale analyzes the role of the media in race relations, the difficulties of covering racial news, and deficiencies in its coverage. Appendixes show in tabular form the percentage of blacks in New York, Boston, Atlanta and Chicago, percentage of news holes given to blacks in the four papers, and topics covered in stories about black problems. Bibliography and index. Notes, bibliography and index.

Marty, Martin E., et al. **The Religious Press in America.** (See No. 1078.)

933

Marzolf, Marion. **Up from the Footnote: A History of Women Journalists.** New York: Hastings House, 1977. 310p.

The story of women journalists from colonial widow-printer to TV anchorwoman. The author discusses pioneers and latter-day figures in their many roles—reporters, printers, editors, publishers, foreign correspondents, researchers, columnists, news directors, and teachers, with sections on the feminist press then and now and on the situation in Europe. There is a bibliography at the end of each chapter and an index.

934

Mayer, Henry. **The Press in Australia**. Melbourne: Lansdowne, 1964. 281p.

"This book attempts three main tasks: *First*, to give the basic facts about the history, structure and content of the Australian press; *second*, to argue that newspapers, given the technical and business conditions under which they work, and granted my view about why they are read, are bound to be much as they are; *third*—and this is my major interest—to analyze common attitudes toward the Press and criticize the assumptions made both by its critics and its defenders." (Preface.)

The author further states that he is not aiming to bring out the special flavor of the Australian press or to compare it with the press of other countries. He deals only with capital-city dailies and gives considerable information about content and readership. Although no bibliography, there are detailed footnotes at the end of each chapter. Indexed.

935, 936

Merrill, John C., ed. **Global Journalism: A Survey of the World's Mass Media**. New York: Longman, 1983. 374p.

Merrill, John C., and Harold A. Fisher. **The World's Great Dailies: Profiles of Fifty Newspapers**. New York: Hastings House, 1980. 399p.

In **Global Journalism** Merrill and contributors take a sweeping look at global journalism and mass communications by regions of the world. In Part 1, "The Global Perspective," Merrill himself does an overall survey of problems, news flow, philosophies, and relations with government for both print media and telecommunications, ending with his analysis of the demand by developing nations for a new information order. In Part 2, "The World's Regions and Journalism," Paul S. Underwood treats Europe and the Middle East; John Luter and Jim Richstad, Asia and the Pacific; L. John Martin, Africa; Marvin Alisky, Latin America, and Ralph D. Barney and Deanna Nelson, the U.S. and Canada. All regions receive the same broad treatment as the general section, with no emphasis on particular newspapers, magazines or broadcast agencies, but rather on philosophy and structure. Education and training for journalism in each area is discussed. Although there is a great deal of pertinent data about journalism throughout the world—of necessity and perhaps (to some) superficial, says Merrill—the book is geared to "the neophyte, the inquisitive beginner" rather than the specialist. It is also intended as a text. There is an excellent bibliography. For those desiring more extensive information about the various countries, see Kurian (No. 239).

The World's Greatest Dailies is an outgrowth of Merrill's **Elite Press** (Pitman, 1968). A completely rewritten and expanded version which makes no attempt to rank the dailies as was done in the earlier book, it presents 50 separate profiles of outstanding dailies—ten more than appeared in **The Elite Press**. Choice is subjective, including those newspapers which the editors believe "represent the very best in the world's journalism, regardless of how differently this journalism may manifest itself in different cultures and ideological contexts." The editors were aided in their selection by national experts and by articles. Bibliography and index.

937

Mott, Frank Luther. **American Journalism: A History of Newspapers in the United States through 260 Years, 1690–1950**. New York: Macmillan, 1941. 835p. Revised, 1950, 1962.

For generations of journalism students, Mott's chronological account was the standard text for the history of American newspapers. The various editions of the Emery history, **The Press and America** (No. 117) have replaced Mott as the standard textbook, but Mott's history remains an excellent source of information on the American press up to the 1960's. An especially useful feature is the "Biographical Notes" following each chapter which describe in some detail the works covering the period, which if taken together form a bibliography of American journalism from its beginning through the 1950s. The first chapter, "The Beginners, 1690–1765," contains a discussion of earlier histories of American journalism. Index.

938

Murthy, Nadig Krishna. **Indian Journalism: Origin, Growth and Development of Indian Journalism from Asoka to Nehru**. Mysore, India: "Presaranga," University of Mysore, 1966. 506p.

Traces the development of India's press against the background of her history, with special emphasis upon the problem of the country's various languages and its struggle for independence from England. Contents include an overall introduction; the history of English daily newspapers; journalism in Indian languages; periodicals; and a general section including government publicity, news agencies and syndicates, newsprint and technical problems, teaching of journalism, professional organizations, press laws, and the Indian Press Commission. A Bibliography and appendixes give tables of facts and figures.

939

Newspaper Libraries in the U.S. and Canada. An SLA Directory. 2d ed. Ed. by Elizabeth L. Anderson. New York: Special Libraries Association, Newspaper Division, 1980. 321p.

An alphabetical listing by state or province and within state or province, by city, giving address, telephone number, circulation and group affiliation (if any) of the newspaper, and the following information about the library: date of establishment, name(s) of librarian(s), public access, limitations of use, services available, hours, resources, microform holdings, indexes, special collections, automation, and products for sale. The U.S. and Canada are listed separately. There is also a list of Washington Bureau libraries, a U.S. and a Canadian city index of libraries, a U.S. and a Canadian newspaper group index, and a joint personnel index. Updated by **The International Directory of News Libraries . . .**, No. 910.

940

O'Dell, De Forest. **The History of Journalism Education in the United States**. New York: Columbia University, Teachers College, Bureau of Publications, 1935. 116p.

For anyone interested in the beginnings of journalism education in the U.S., this is a gem. De Forest goes as far back as 1869 when the concept of professional education for journalism resulted from four decades of conflict between "the American social order and the penny press." Discussing the pioneers in journalism and the emergence of philosophies about it, he shows how it established itself as part of the curriculum in higher education by the 1930s. Findings are based on questionnaires and interviews. Appendixes include an early article, "The Hosmer Pamphlet: The Making of a Journalist: Why a Technical and a Professional School is Needed," "The Pulitzer-Columbia Agreement," and "The Pulitzer Will as It Pertained to the Columbia Endowment." Bibliography.

941

Oey, Hong Lee. **Indonesian Government and Press during Guided Democracy**. Zug, Switzerland: Inter Documentation Company, 1971. 401p. (Hull Monograph on Southeast Asia No. 4.)

Traces the development of the Indonesian press in relation to politics from the beginning of the Dutch period in 1594 through the regime of President Sukarno. Emphasis is on the newspaper press during Sukarno's period of "guided democracy." Contains a bibliography and a brief index.

942

Olson, Kenneth F. **The History Makers: The Press of Europe from Its Beginnings Through 1965**. Baton Rouge: Louisiana State University Press, 1966. 471p.

The growth of the press in 24 nations of Europe, with an evaluation of the European press in the mid-1960s. Contains a list of papers for each country and a comprehensive bibliography.

943

One Hundred Years of the Yiddish Press in America, 1870–1970: Catalogue of the Exhibition. Comp. by Z. Szajkowski. New York: YIVO Institute for Jewish Research, 1970. 20p.

This listing of items, with notes about each, forms an outline history of the Yiddish press in the U.S.—its weeklies and dailies, including the labor press, its writers, compositors, newsdealers, readers, advertisements, and its social role. It is not limited to the past; one section gives dailies appearing in 1970. There is also a section on the Yiddish press of various cities and various groups. All items are available at the YIVO Institute.

944

Paneth, Donald. **Encyclopedia of American Journalism**. New York: Facts on File, 1983. 548p.

In examining this reference book the question arises: is it possible to produce an adequate one-volume encyclopedia of journalism? In the case of this book, the answer is probably no. It is useful for identification of prominent figures, newspapers and periodicals, awards, chains, legal decisions, events and movements. However it does not—probably cannot—go into its articles, even the longer ones, in depth, and many of them, especially in the case of events, issues and movements, are essentially bibliographic essays—i.e., journalism history. In many ways this resembles a dictionary rather than an encyclopedia. Although a true dictionary would not need a name index this one does, but is not provided. There is instead a subject index with a rather unusual arrangement.

945

Patten, David A. **Newspapers and the News Media**. White Plains, NY: Knowledge Industry Publications, 1986. 137p.

Burgeoning new communications technologies are creating a brand new climate for newspapers. This is a precise and thorough examination of necessary adaptions and of possible outcomes. Patten identifies the new media, discusses newspaper-cable marriages, evaluates new media ventures newspapers are making, and speculates on the consequences for advertising, the need for community television, the possibilities for videotex, the changing role of newspapers, and lastly, technology and the journalist. It is a brave new world.

946

Penn, I. Garland. **The Afro-American Press and Its Editors**. New York: Arno Press/New York Times, c1891, 1969. 569p.

Reprint of a book originally published in 1891. To quote from the introduction to the new edition: "The first part takes all of the Afro-American newspapers and magazines, from **Freedom's Journal** (1827) to 1891. The second part, which is very long, consists of many sketches of editors and newspapers, opinions of eminent Negro men on the Afro-American press, its editors' mission, and other chapters on the relation of the Negro press to the white press (including Negroes who write for white newspapers and magazines), the Afro-American League, and the Associated Correspondents of Race Newspapers. There are scores of photographs." Magazines as well as newspapers are included. Indexed.

947

Pineda-Ofreneo, Rosalinda. **The Manipulated Press: A History of Philippine Journalism since 1945**. Manila: Cacho Hermanos, 1984. 256p.

An in-depth analysis from a global perspective of the problems, the trends, and the forces affecting the post-World War II Philippine press, describing its development and showing how the results were the logical offshoots of broad economic, political and cultural trends. A great deal is said about American influences. Appendixes contain "A List of Major Periodicals—1945–1972" and "A List of Provincial Publications." Chapter notes.

948

Potter, Elaine. **The Press as Opposition: The Political Role of South African Newspapers**. London: Chatto and Windus, 1975. 228p.

The author, a South African living in England, explains how the newspaper press, both Afrikaans and English, has to this point preserved a degree of openness and freedom, and how and why she feels that this is threatened. The book, however, is full of other useful information in addition to the issue of politics and the press; there are sections on the history and ownership structure of the press and the results of readership surveys. Contains a lengthy bibliography and an index.

949

Reddick, Dewitt C. **The Mass Media and the School Newspaper**. 2d ed. Belmont, CA: Wadsworth, 1985. 448p.

Dewitt Reddick's name is synonymous with, among other subjects, the teaching of high school journalism. In this text, revised after his death by his son, Bryan Dewitt Reddick, we find his philosophy as well as his techniques. In the first part he discusses the interplay between a changing society and the media; the forces influence the change; and the significance of freedom of the press—all in relation to the school press. The other parts stress techniques. A list of selected readings and an index.

Righter, Rosemary. **Whose News? Politics, the Press and the Third World**. (See No. 354.)

950

Rosengarten, Frank. **The Italian Anti-Fascist Press (1919–1945)**. Cleveland, OH: Press of Case Western Reserve University, 1968. 263p.

Traces the development from the legal opposition press to the underground newspapers of World War II, which were carried on with considerable success by the resistance forces. An appendix gives some key aspects of the laws and principles governing the exercise of freedom of the press in Italy after fascism, and there is a detailed bibliography, most of which is in Italian. Indexed.

951

Rosewater, Victor. **History of Cooperative News-Gathering in the United States**. New York: Appleton, 1930. 430p.

Gathering much of the material from original sources, this covers the first random efforts at newsgathering in Colonial times and continues through the 1920s, with emphasis on organizations and personalities. In addition to the customary print sources, the author says that he drew upon a lifetime of experience on newspapers and as a member of several press associations, and also upon "inside information and original papers, relating to preceding associations, accumulated and preserved by my father during his long career as an old-time telegrapher and as an editor of force and prominence, beginning with the pre-Civil War era." Appendixes give regulations of the General News Association of the City of New York, 1856, and by-laws of the Associated Press of New York. Chapter notes and bibliography.

952

Rosten, Leo. **The Washington Correspondents**. New York: Harcourt Brace, 1937. 436p.

Based on interviews and questionnaires involving 127 Washington reporters, this "a picture, an analysis, and an interpretation of the Washington newspaper correspondents." This is interesting both as the first piece of research on the subject and also to contrast their role more than half a century ago with their present role. His aim is not specifically to show the influence of the Washington press corps on politics, but rather to analyze their function, techniques and composition, but in doing the latter he sheds light on the former. Appendixes give details on the information on which Rosten based his findings. See also Douglass Cater's **Fourth Branch of Government** (No. 59). Reference notes and an extensive bibliography. Index.

953

Royal Commission on Newspapers. **Research Studies on the Newspaper Industry**. Ottawa: Canadian Government Publishing Centre, 1981. Vol. 1–8.

A series of eight volumes, each containing the research material on which the Commission's Report **Royal Commission on Newspapers** (the Kent Report) was based. Authors and titles include: Volume 1, **Newspapers and Their Readers**, by the Communications Research Center; Volume 2, **The Journalists**, by Robert Fulford and others; Volume 3, **Newspapers and the Law**, by Walter Tarnopolsky and others; Volume 4, **The Newspaper as a Business**, by Eugene Hallman and others; Volume 5, **Labor Relations in the Newspaper Industry**, by Gerard Hebert and others; Volume 6, **Canadian News Services** by Carman Cumming and others; Volume 7, **The Newspaper and Public Affairs**, by Frederick J. Fletcher and others; Volume 8, **Newspapers and Computers: An Industry in Transition**, by Peter Desbarats and others.

954

Rutherford, Paul. **A Victorian Authority: The Daily Press in Late Nineteenth-Century Canada**. Toronto: University of Toronto Press, 1982. 292p.

By the end of the 1890s, the number of daily and weekly editions of Canadian newspapers exceeded the number of Canadian families. As Rutherford charts their growth he gives a micro view of the personalities, events and business routines that shaped their content and a macro view of the underlying cultural factors that shaped their growth and Canada's. An appendix lists by place and with pertinent data the leading dailies 1870–1900, and there are chapter notes and an index.

955

Saito, Shiro, and Alice W. Mak. **Philippine Newspapers: An International Union List**. Honolulu: University of Hawaii, Center for Asian and Pacific Studies, Philippine Studies Program, 1984. 273p. (Philippine Studies Occasional Paper No. 7.)

Part I lists 432 newspaper titles by place of publication; Part 2 lists their repositories in Australia, Canada, England, the Philippines and the United States. Title index to Part I.

956

Sarkar, R. C. S. **The Press in India**. New Delhi: S. Chand, 1984. 320p.

An encyclopedic study of the Indian newspaper press, dealing with its existing state, its growth and development, the constitutional and legal framework within which it functions, its role as a business and a public utility, its Press Council, its news flow, and a number of other aspects. An appendix gives some pertinent facts, including statistics. Bibliography and index.

Schudson, Michael. **Discovering the News**. (See No. 392.)

957

Simpson, D. H. **Commercialization of the Regional Press: The Development of Monopoly, Profit and Control**. Aldershot, Hants, England: Gower House, 1981. 224p.

The author contends that the Roy Thomson revolution in British provincial newspapers has led to a downgrading of journalists and editors and to domination by a new breed of commercial managers—in advertising, circulation, accountancy, new production technology and computing, and in personnel.

958

Smith, Anthony, ed. **The British Press Since the War**. Totowa, NJ: Rowman and Littlefield, 1974. 320p.

A collection of articles, documents, selections from books, and other materials, which show the evolution of the continuing newspaper crisis in Britain from World War II into the early 1970s. In four parts: "Fleet Street—Finance, Ownership and Structure;" "The Press and the Law—The Erosion of Newspaper Freedom;" "The Principles and Practice of the Press;" and "Newspapers and Workers' Participation." Smith's aim is to indicate the issues around which general readers and students interested in newspapers may build their reading. He concludes with a bibliographic essay, "Suggestions for further reading." Index.

959

Smith, Anthony. **Goodbye Gutenberg: The Newspaper Revolution of the 1980s**. New York: Oxford, 1980. 367p.

Smith looks at the newspaper in the light of its new technology and changing function, which are interrelated, and casts a broad net. "What one can see in the newspaper is a microcosm of a new social information, in which computers help information to be stored and circulated in ways profoundly different from those which have been employed since the Renaissance, when printing first established itself in Western societies. That is why it has been necessary, in a book primarily about the newspaper, to show the parallels between the present transformation in printing methods to certain earlier transformations in human communications systems, in particular to the advent of printing and writing. The computerization of print is truly a third revolution in communications of similar scale and importance, in that it raises certain fundamental issues—concerning the social control of information, the nature of the individual creative function, the ways in which information interacts with human memory." Within this context he discusses various aspects of the newspaper in the U.S., the new media which affect it, and the broad social implications. An appendix lists the electronic newspaper systems used in Australia, Canada, Finland, France, Germany, Japan, Sweden, the U.K. and the U.S.A., with type, source and operators. Chapter notes, glossary and index.

960

Smith, Anthony, ed. **Newspapers and Democracy: International Essays on a Changing Medium**. Cambridge, MA: MIT Press, 1980. 368p.

A group of essays whose purpose is, in Smith's words "to investigate the ways in which the familiar medium of the newspaper is altering in the closing decades of the century in the countries of the developed world." Essays in the sections "Technology and the Press" and

"Editorial Content" are general; those in "The Press and the State in Established Democracies" and "Press and State in the Newer Democracies" deal with specific countries—Norway, Sweden and France in the former; Spain, Portugal, Japan and Italy in the latter. Together they point how changes in technology and in the economic organization of the newspaper affect its historic purpose in societies which accept the principles of a free press. The various articles contain references, and there is an index.

961

Smith, Anthony. **Subsidies and the Press in Europe**. London: PEP (Political and Economic Planning), 1977. 113p.

In certain European countries the government subsidizes its newspapers in varying ways. For each of 13 countries which do, Smith provides "a synopsis of the particular dilemma of each society toward its press" and "the interim solutions or propositions which are now in use." Countries are: France, West Germany, Italy, Sweden, Norway, Denmark, Finland, the Netherlands, Belgium, Switzerland, Austria, Republic of Ireland, Britain. Supplementing the material are many tables, and appendixes containing a chart summarizing forms of subsidy by country and a copy of the Council of Europe Resolution (74) 43 on Press Concentration.

962

Stamm, Keith R. **Newspaper Use and Community Ties: Toward a Dynamic Theory**. Norwood, NJ: Ablex, 1985. 210p.

An examination of the relationship between newspaper use and the individual's ties with a local community, as shown through research on the subject. Stamm traces the historical development of traditional ideas about community ties and newspaper use; reviews past and current research; and in conclusion "is concerned with developing a broader, historical view of changes in communities, community ties, and newspaper use." Throughout he opts for "a new ('dynamic') paradigm" which he feels could lead to more productive research. Notes, bibliography and index.

963

Steinby, Torsten. **In Quest of Freedom: Finland's Press, 1771–1971**. Tr. by Fred A. Fewster. Helsinki: Government Printing Centre, 1971. 163p.

An historical survey concentrating on the newspaper press—its regulations, the emergence of a party press, its struggles with Russia, its national background, and its present status. An appendix gives a list of Finnish newspapers in 1971.

964

Suggs, Henry Lewis, ed. **The Black Press in the South, 1865–1979**. Westport, CT: Greenwood, 1983. 465p.

A scholarly state-by-state history of the black press from Emancipation to the present, beginning with an "Introduction: Origins of the Black Press in the South" and concluding with a summary chapter. "South" is broadly interpreted to include all the slave-owning states—Alabama, Arkansas, Florida, Georgia, Louisiana, Mississippi, Missouri, North and South Carolina, Tennessee, Texas and Virginia—with detailed essays on each, followed by extensive footnotes. There is, in addition, a 13-page bibliographical essay and a detailed index.

965

Swain, Bruce M. **Reporters' Ethics**. Ames: Iowa State University Press, 1978. 153p.

Sixty-seven reporters of widely varying levels of experience on 16 metropolitan dailies in ten cities talk about questions of ethics they have faced, from freebies to conflict of interest. Appendixes give codes for the American Society of Newspaper Editors, the Associated Press Managing Editors Association, the Society of Professional Journalists (Sigma Delta Chi), and seven newspapers. Notes, bibliography and index.

Switzer, Les, and Donna Switzer. **The Black Press in South Africa and Lesotho: A Descriptive Bibliography**. (See No. 1703.)

966

Taft, William H. **Encyclopedia of Twentieth-Century Journalists**. New York: Garland, 1986. 408p. (Garland Reference Library of the Humanities, Vol. 493.)

". . . a collection of personalities in the media world" is how Taft describes his **Encyclopedia** of editors, publishers, photographers, bureau chiefs, columnists, commentators, cartoonists, artists and a few authors of books—all selected for "significance of achievement as well as reputation." Information focuses entirely upon careers; such personal details as family and education, for instance, are not given unless pertinent to work. Entries are succinct, to the point, and vary in length according to the importance of the journalists, running from two to four on a page. Families famous in American journalism are treated as a whole—i.e., The Hearst Family, The Reed Family, The Pulliam Family. Prefacing the **Encyclopedia** is an identification of all awards mentioned, with brief comments. In his Introduction Taft says that he hopes that later volumes will focus on another large group of media personalities from advertising, public relations, management, and a broad group of "behind-the-scenes" operators, executives, and producers. Index.

967

Tataryn, Lloyd. **The Pundits: Power, Politics & the Press**. Toronto: Deneau, 1985. 198p.

How did syndicated political columnists emerge as professional journalists and become an important part of journalism? And what has been their influence on journalism, their colleagues, and the politicians, they cover? And how responsibly do they exercise the opportunity their columns offer to translate their views into public opinion? Limiting himself to print columnists, Tataryn examines answers by comparing and contrasting their activities in three Western democracies—the U.S., Britain, and Canada, where they do the same work but under different systems and in a different manner. Material is based on personal interviews with key columnists, a reading of their work, and an examination of the literature on the subject of political commentary. Bibliography and index.

968

Taylor, Henry A. **The British Press: A Critical Survey**. London: Arthur Barker Ltd., 1961. 176p.

Survey of English journalism, reviewing its history but dwelling chiefly on the report of the Royal Commission on the Press in 1949.

969

Todorov, Dafin. **Freedom Press: Development of the Progressive Press in Western Europe and the U.S.A.** Prague: International Organization of Journalists, 1978(?). 97p.

A Communist journalist discusses the origins, development, and present state of the working-class press in four major capitalist countries from its beginnings in the 1830s to the present. Todorov categorizes and describes the various newspapers and magazines that played, or play, a part. Bibliography.

970

U.S. Bureau of the Census. Census of Manufacturers. **Industry Statistics 1982: Newspapers, Periodicals, Books, and Miscellaneous Publishing.** Washington: U.S. Government Printing Office, 1985. 35p.

Detailed tables covering many aspects of production and consumption of printed media. Compares figures of current with previous editions—in this case 1977, although some tables go back to 1967. It is published every five years and runs several years late.

971

U.S. Library of Congress. Slavic and Central European Division. Reference Department. **Newspapers of East Central and Southeastern Europe in the Library of Congress.** Robert G. Carlton, ed. Washington: U.S. Government Printing Office, 1965. 204p.

Lists holdings of newspapers issued during the period from 1918 to 1965 within the territorial boundaries of Albania, Bulgaria, and Czechoslovakia, and those issued in Estonia, Latvia, and Lithuania from 1917 to 1940. Contains a language index and an index to titles.

972

Walker, Martin. **Powers of the Press: Twelve of the World's Influential Newspapers**. New York: Pilgrim Press, 1982. 401p.

Walker does not pretend to choose *the* 12 most influential newspapers, but rather 12 *of the* most influential; he says that he could have chosen a number of others, including the **Guardian**, for which he reports. His final selections are **The Times** (London), **Le Monde** (France), **Die Welt** (Germany), **Corriere della Sera** (Italy), **Pravda** (Russia), **Al-Ahram** (Egypt), **Asahi Shimbun** (Japan), **New York Times** (U.S.A.), **Washington Post** (U.S.A.), Toronto **Globe & Mail** (Canada), **The Age**, Melbourne (Australia), and **Rand Daily Mail** (South Africa). He discusses each in terms of policies and personnel, and concludes with an analysis of "Each Newspaper's Coverage of Iran." As a whole, he gives an insight into factors that make for an influential—and quality—press, and equally important, in his introduction he discusses a number of other important papers around the world. Each paper contains the author's "Notes." In conclusion is a general bibliography and bibliographies for the 12.

973

Walker, R. B. **The Newspaper Press in New South Wales, 1803–1920**. Sydney, Australia: Sydney University Press, 1976. 272p.

A history which places the press in a social and political context and relates it to overseas development, particularly in Britain. Footnotes and index.

974

Washburn, Patrick S. **A Question of Sedition: The Federal Government's Investigation of the Black Press During World War II**. New York: Oxford University Press, 1986. 296p.

Washburn explores a little known history of the black press in World War II when powers high in the U.S. government tried unsuccessfully to suppress it for sedition. Here he tells the story of the attempt and its failure. His book is also a study of the black press during the war, and on a larger theme, of libertarianism, defined as the freedom to criticize the government. Fifty-nine pages of notes, an extensive bibliography and an index.

975

Weiner, Richard. **News Bureaus in the U.S.** 7th ed. New York: Public Relations Publishing Co., 1984. 182p.

A listing of news bureaus by geographical location of headquarters, giving address, telephone number and editor. Covers trade and news magazines, newspapers and syndicated wire services. Alphabetical index by bureau, newspaper or magazine. The next edition is scheduled for publication in 1987 by Larimi Communications Association.

976

Whatmore, Geoffrey. **The Modern News Library: Documentation of Current Affairs in Newspaper and Broadcasting Libraries**. London: Library Association; Syracuse, NY: Gaylord Professional Publications, 1978. 202p.

A practicing librarian discusses the organization and management of the news information library—the term **news** covering newspaper, radio, and television. He takes up the various kinds of materials to be collected, the organization, the equipment, the new technology, and other aspects. Indexed.

977

Whitaker, Brian. **News Ltd: Why You Can't Read All About It**. London: Minority Press Group, 1981. 176p.

Whitaker takes a hard and thoughtful look at pressures, financial and otherwise, which influence and restrict news coverage, and describes an alternative way of presenting news which, however, faces these and other difficulties. To highlight differences and emphasize difficulties he tells the story of the Liverpool **Free Press**, for several years the biggest-selling alternative press in Britain. A section of extracts from stories in the **Free Press** is included to give readers some idea of the paper's range of coverage and differing styles and reporting techniques.

978

White, Naomi Rosh, and Peter B. White. **Immigrants and the Media: Case Studies in Newspaper Reporting**. Sydney, Australia: Longman Cheshire, 1983. 177p.

Through case studies the authors seek to answer three generalized questions: How have Australia's immigrants been treated by the media? What does the portrayal of immigrants in the media tell about Australia's attitudes toward its large immigrant population? What have been the forces behind the establishment of multicultural radio and television? Data have been developed from reports in mass newspapers of illustrative cases involving immigrants from 1935 to 1977. Chapter notes, three appendixes explaining methodology, a bibliography and an index.

979

Who Was Who in Journalism. Detroit, MI: Gale, c1925, c1928, 1978. 664p.

"A consolidation of all material appearing in the 1928 edition of **Who's Who in Journalism**, with unduplicated biographical entries from the 1925 edition of **Who's Who in Journalism**," is the subtitle of this reprint, which will be of interest to anyone concerned with the history of American journalism and journalism education in the earlier part of the 20th century. It contains approximate-

ly 4,000 biographical sketches of editors, reporters, managers and publishers of newspapers and magazines, syndicate writers, and journalism teachers. Other features include a listing of news and feature syndicates, teaching staffs and courses and other pertinent features about journalism schools in their formative years, newspaper clubs and associations' foreign news agencies and foreign newspapers in the U.S. and foreign correspondents, the Code of Ethics, a bibliography, and classified directories of journalists both by position and geographical area.

980

Who's Who in the Press, 1985–86. 2d ed. London: Carrick, 1986. 133p.

Who's Who in the Press also contains about 1,000 names, most of whom are representative of the national and provincial daily, evening, and Sunday newspapers. The rest are editors of selected periodicals ranging from leading trade and technical journals to mass circulation magazines. Information in both directories contains the same facts; in the case of journalists, any writing done outside of the job is included. All data is based on response to questionnaires.

Williams, Francis. **Dangerous Estate: Anatomy of Newspapers; The Right to Know: The Rise of the World Press; Transmitting World News: A Study of Telecommunications and the Press**. (See Nos. 453, 454, 455.)

981

Wittke, Carl. **The German-Language Press in America**. Lexington: University of Kentucky Press, 1957. 311p.

A history of America's German-language press, from 1732 to the present, with emphasis primarily upon the role it played in American social, political, and economic history rather than upon individual papers. Footnotes, but no bibliography. Indexed.

982

Wolseley, Roland E. **The Black Press, U.S.A.** Ames: Iowa State University Press, 1971. 362p.

The author first discusses the validity of the concept of a black press (there is such a thing, he concludes), then relates its history, examines today's newspapers and magazines, describes its present and past prominent reporters and editors, considers its problems, and goes into several other areas such as circulation, advertising, syndicates, and public relations. Black radio is also treated briefly. There is a bibliography, notes on sources, and an index.

The Working Press of the Nation. Newspaper Directory. (See No. 1799.)

BOOKS AND MAGAZINES

983

Abrams, Alan E., ed. **Media Personnel Directory: An Alphabetical Guide to Names, Addresses, and Telephone Numbers of Key Editorial and Business Personnel at over 700 United States and International Periodicals**. Detroit, MI: Gale, 1979. 262p.

Lists "thousands of editors, publishers, columnists, art directors, book reviewers, foreign and domestic correspondents and bureau chiefs, sales and production managers, and other management personnel serving on over 700 major United States and international magazines and periodicals." Entries are alphabetical by surname and include job title and last reported place of service, with address and telephone number of periodical. Abrams calls this a first edition, but as yet no later one has appeared.

984

Altbach, Philip G. **Publishing in India: An Analysis**. New York; Dehli: Oxford University Press, 1975. 115p.

In spite of the emphasis on India in the title, the author treats all Third World countries, but specifically deals with India by using it as a case study to examine historical development of the industry, its economics, its distribution, copyright, "public" and "private" publishing, foreign influences, regional language publishing, academic publishing, and publishing and the intellectual community. Footnotes and an extensive bibliography.

985

Altbach, Philip G., Amadio A. Aroleda, and S. Gopinathan, eds. **Publishing in the Third World: Knowledge and Development**. Portsmouth, NH: Heinemann, 1985. 226p.

An in-depth look at the "state of the art" of book publishing in the Third World which examines not only the nuts and bolts but also its status as an important part of the knowledge distribution system. The first 50 pages discuss the status of textbook publishing, copyright, and distribution; the rest of the book takes a country-and-region approach, covering Africa as a whole and more specifically Ghana, Kenya and Egypt; India; China; the Philippines; an overview of Latin America and of Brazil in particular; the role of U.S. publishers and textbooks; and finally, the modernization of publishing in Japan. There are chapter notes, an extensive bibliography of monographs and journal articles, a number of tables, and an index.

Altbach, Philip G., and Eva-Maria Rathgeber. **Publishing in the Third World: Trend Report and Bibliography**. (See No. 1633.)

986

Altick, Richard D. **The English Common Reader: A Social History of the Mass Reading Public 1800–1900**. Chicago: University of Chicago Press, 1957. 430p.

"This volume is an attempt to study, from the historian's viewpoint, the place of reading in an industrial and increasingly democratic society," says the author in this systematically analyzed and documented yet eminently readable work which has become a classic on the subject. In his approach he has not fallen back upon anecdotes nor attempted to analyze the appeal of the period's most popular authors. Rather, he has discussed the social background of the century—its religion, its prevailing philosophy, its education, its labor movements, and its book, periodical, and newspaper trade. Appendixes include a chronology of the mass reading public, 1774–1900; a chronology of best sellers with sales figures and notes; and another chronology of periodical and newspaper circulations. Contains a bibliography and an index.

987

Anatomy of an International Year. Book Year—1972. Paris: UNESCO, 1974(?). 37p. (Reports and Papers on Mass Communication No. 71.)

This is "a digest and appraisal of the initiatives taken and techniques employed during International Book Year with a view to making the most advantageous use of this information for the future." Includes need for, origins, mechanics, the ways in which the program was carried out, a program for the future, an appraisal, and a summing up. An appendix gives resolutions adopted by the UNESCO General Conference.

988

Anderson, Charles B., ed. **Bookselling in America and the World: Some Observations and Recollections in Celebration of the 75th Anniversary of the American Booksellers Association**. New York: Quadrangle, 1975. 214p.

The publishers call this commemorative miscellany "a book of praise to booksellers." Its range is wide and roving, including a brief history by John Tebbel, reminiscences by famous booksellers, a musical tribute by Michael Flanders and Donald Swan, and, of course, a history of the American Booksellers Association—this by Chandler Grannis. Contains a list of officers of the ABA from 1900 through 1975 and the Board of Directors from 1930 to 1975.

989

Anderson, Elliott, and Michael York, eds. **The Little Magazine in America, a Modern Documentary History: Essays, Memoirs, Photo-Documents. An Annotated Bibliog-**

raphy. Yonkers, NY: Pushcart Press, 1979. 770p.

Before 1946, when Frederick J. Hoffman, Charles Allen, and Carolyn Ulrich published **The Little Magazine: A History and a Bibliography** (Princeton University Press), there had been no one single source for the history of little magazines in the U.S. and for bibliographic data on specific titles. **The Little Magazine in America, a Modern Documentary History** is a successor, although with a different approach. Whereas the earlier book is a history of the various movements, themes, causes and types of little magazines, the latter is an anthology of essay-memoirs by prominent and representative little magazine editors, publishers and contributors, with a large selection of photo-documents and an annotated bibliography of 84 important magazines of the period. The editors explain why they chose a different structure: "Although such a documentary project inevitably lacks the integration of more conventional histories, our basic concern has been for the *phenomenon* of little magazines—for the curious and oftentimes eccentric processes of the field—not for one or another interpretation of their collective merit, however congenial. The field today is so large, the kinds of magazines and attitudes of their editors so diverse, that no literary historian could hope to offer more than a gloss." Some of the essays center around specific magazines; others are general. Nor is the scope entirely limited to the little magazine. There is a discussion of its connection with the small press, and stories about Pushcart Press and the Fiction Collective. The annotated bibliography is almost 100 pages long. To date there has been no update of developments.

990

Balkin, Richard. **A Writer's Guide to Book Publishing**. 2d ed. New York: Hawthorn/Dutton, 1981. 239p.

Although this is primarily a guidebook for would-be authors, it is also valuable for the broad insight it offers into the whole book publishing process. Its eight chapters run the gamut: "How to Approach a Publisher," "How a Publisher Evaluates a Proposal or a Manuscript," "How to Understand and Negotiate a Book Contract," "How to Prepare a Final Manuscript," "How a Manuscript is Processed by a Publisher," "How a Manuscript Is Turned Into a Finished Book," "How a Publisher Markets a Book," "Alternatives: Small Presses, Vanity Presses, and Self-Publishing." Focus is primarily on general trade books, both paperback and hardcover, but there is also information on mass market paperbacks, texts, professional and juveniles, and other specialized areas. A preface discusses the state of book publishing in general, with evidence for two commonly held and opposing viewpoints—that conglomerate concentration and commercialization are limiting the marketplace and lowering quality, and conversely, that the market is more open and

in better shape than ever. Selected bibliography and index.

991

Barker, Ronald E. **Books for All: A Study of International Book Trade**. New York: UNESCO Publications Center, 1956. 102p.

On a worldwide basis, the author covers facts and figures on the structure and economics of book publishing, import and export, tariffs, copyright, translations, libraries, and book exchanges. Contains a bibliography and an index. For an update on trends and statistics, see Peter J. Curwen's **The World Book Industry** (No. 1031), which covers some of the same ground in a different manner.

992

Barker, Ronald E., and Robert Escarpit. **The Book Hunger**. Paris: UNESCO, 1973. 155p.

A brief survey of the role of the book in developing countries in terms of needs, demand, production, distribution, and copyright. An appendix gives the "charter of the book."

993

Benjamin, Curtis G. **A Candid Critique of Book Publishing**. New York: Bowker, 1977. 187p.

Lively and provocative essays that have grown out of the author's half-century in book publishing. They deal with the many facets of the trade—the problem of definition; the attractions; the relationship between author and publisher; the art of keeping—and stealing—authors; marketing and promotion; subject publishing; paperbacks; mergers; foreign markets; multinational publishing; helping indigenous publishers in needy countries; trade associations; the role of government; the number of and the future of books. Notes, references, an excellent bibliography, and an index.

994

Benjamin, Curtis G. **U.S. Books Abroad: Neglected Ambassadors**. Washington: Center for the Book, Library of Congress, 1984. 95p.

"The purpose of this study is to provide a document that endeavors to stimulate renewed and further awareness, first, of the dire need for U.S. books in less developed countries, and, second, of possible ways by which this need may be met, at least partially, under present conditions at home and abroad." Preface by John Y. Cole, Executive Director, The Center for the Book. Obviously, all developing countries could not be covered, nor could all organizations; the author has been selective. He discusses the faltering state of U.S. book exports, the influence of multinational publishing, the impact of English-language publishing in continental Europe, various assistance programs in the U.S. and other countries, and deterrents to U.S. book exporting. "Sources of Information" constitutes a bibliography. Appendixes give the U.S.I.A. book promotion and translation programs in 1982 and statistics on the export of U.S. books by types and on the Informational Media Guarantee Program, the Joint Indo-American Textbook Program; the U.S.I.A.-sponsored book publishing program from 1951 through 1980; and the Asia Foundation's distribution of books and journals by countries, 1954–1981.

995

Bennett, H.S. **English Books and Readers (1475 to 1640).** 3 v. 2d ed. Cambridge, England: Cambridge University Press, 1965, 1969, 1970.

History of the book trade in England for the period covered. Vol. I deals with the years from Caxton to the incorporation of the Stationers' Company; Vol. II, the reign of Elizabeth I; Vol. III, the reigns of James I and Charles I.

The author discusses the kinds of books being published, why they were written, and for whom they were intended; the growth of printers and booksellers; and the relationships of printers, authors, patrons, and readers. Each volume contains a bibliography and an index.

Berry, Dave, Liz Cooper, and Charles Landry. **Where Is the Other News?** (See No. 869.)

996, 997

Bonham-Carter, Victor. **Authors by Profession.** Vol. 1. **From the Introduction of Printing until the Copyright Act 1911.** Los Altos, CA: William Kaufmann, 1978. 252p.

Bonham-Carter, Victor. **Authors by Profession.** Vol. 2. **From the Copyright Act 1911 until the End of 1981.** London: The Bodley Head and the Society of Authors, 1984. 336p.

Bonham-Carter has summarized the contents of both volumes in their subtitles: "How authors and dramatists have practiced their profession; their contractual and personal relations with patrons, publishers and promoters; their situation under the law of copyright; their standing with the public; their part in the trade of books and periodicals and presentation of stage plays." And "How authors, dramatists, and radio and screen writers have practiced their profession in their respective media; their contracts and earnings; their situation under the law in respect to copyright, taxation, defamation, obscene publications, etc.; their professional organizations; their experience of literary patronage." If the subtitles sound heavy and dull except perhaps to copyright lawyers and other specialists in authorship, the books themselves are not. Full of hard (and quite a few soft) facts they are written with grace and wit, making fascinating as well as informative reading to anyone interested in the highlights and sidelights of British literature. Substantial chapter notes and references, and a subject index.

998

Bonn, Thomas L. **UnderCover: An Illustrated History of American Mass Market Paperbacks.** New York: Penguin, 1982. 144p.

"My intent is to illustrate with words and pictures the basic features of American mass market publishing, from its beginnings in the nineteenth century through today, with a focus on the cover art and design," says Bonn. He has emphasized the early years in the U.S.—1929–56, when the present-day pattern was established—with a brief chapter on European and early U.S. "Cover Art and Design" are treated separately in Part II, and Part III is devoted to collecting, with a brief bibliographic essay on the subject. Index.

999

Book Development in Africa: Problems and Perspectives. Paris: UNESCO, 1969. 37p. (Reports and Papers on Mass Comm., No. 56.)

Report on a meeting of experts who discussed problems and implications in terms of what was and should be the economic and social role of books and book publishing in Africa.

1000, 1001, 1002, 1003

The Book Industry in Yugoslavia: Report of the Delegation of U.S. Book Publishers Visiting Yugoslavia October 18-November 1, 1963. New York: American Book Publishers Council and the American Textbook Publishing Institute, 1964. 41p.

The Book Trade in the U.S.S.R.: Report of a Delegation of the Publishers Association Which Visited the U.S.S.R. from 28 September to 11 October 1964. Comp. by John Boon. London: The Publishers Association, 1964. 70p.

Book Publishing the Distribution in Rumania: Report of the Delegation of U.S. Publishers Visiting Rumania October 1–10, 1965. New York: American Book Publishers Council and American Textbook Publishers Institute, 1966. 60p.

Book Publishing in the U.S.S.R.: Report of the Delegation of U.S. Book Publishers Visiting the U.S.S.R. August 20-September 17, 1962. New York: American Book Publishers Council and American Textbook Publishers Institute, 1963. 112p.

Four studies of the book trade in the 1960s in countries which have a common, although somewhat differing, Communist orientation—three of the studies made by American publishers, one made by British. Each deals comprehensively with the many aspects of production and distribution of trade books, belles lettres, scientific, technical, and professional books. There are also sections on translations, exports and imports, copyright, and similar important subjects. Statistics accompany texts.

Book Publishing Annual. (See No. 1727.)

Book Publishing Career Directory. (See No. 1728.)

1004

Book Publishing Worldwide. **Special Reports on: Germany, Scandanavia, Portugal, Spain, Australia, Soviet Union, Great Britain, Japan, and Export-Import Statistics.** New York: Bowker, 1979. 2,160p.

A compilation of **Publishers Weekly**'s international country profiles in 1977 and 1978. The articles, each slightly different, all cover structure, major publishing houses, publishers and special features of the book trade.

1005, 1006, 1007, 1008

The Book Trade of the World. Vol. I. **Europe and International Section.** Ed. by Sigfried Taubert. New York: Bowker, 1972. 543p.

The Book Trade of the World. Vol. II. **The Americas, Australia, and New Zealand.** Ed. by Sigfried Taubert. New York: Bowker, 1976. 377p.

The Book Trade of the World. Vol. III. **Asia.** Ed. by Sigfried Taubert and Peter Weidhaas. New York: Bowker, 1981. 284p.

The Book Trade of the World. Vol. IV. **Africa.** Ed. by Siegfried Taubert and Peter Weidhaas. New York: Bowker, 1984. 391p.

A country-by-country systematic description of some of the basic facts about book publishing which are necessary to know in order to conduct business on an international level and useful other purposes as well. Each country gives information about itself under the following categories: general, history, retail prices, organization, the trade press, book trade literature and address services, sources of information, international membership, market research, books and young people, taxes, clearing houses, training, copyright, national bibliographies and national libraries, book production, translation, book clubs, paperbacks, design, publishing houses (not a listing), literary agents, wholesale trade, retail trade, mail order, antiquarian book trade and auctions, imports, exports, book fairs, public relations, bibliophilism, literary prizes, book reviews, and miscellaneous. Obviously, not all of these facts were filled out by every country, and in a few cases, countries failed to reply at all, but nevertheless the total adds up to a great deal of data. In addition, the first volume has an international section in which much of the information in that volume is summarized under these same categories. Vol. II has a long section on book production and number of translations, 1968; the UNESCO Florence Agreement;

the book trade answer code; and a listing of members of the Berne and the Universal Copyright conventions. Maps locating publishing houses accompany the accounts of the various countries. Vol. IV has an inclusive index.

1009

Books for the Developing Countries. Asia. Africa. Paris: UNESCO, 1965. 31p. (Reports and Papers on Mass Communication No. 47.)

Consists of two articles: "The Production and Flow of Books in South East Asia" by Om Prakash and "The Production and Flow of Books in Africa" by Clifford M. Fyle. Both authors emphasize such social aspects as literacy level and language difficulties and such economic aspects as copyright, trade barriers, and raw materials.

1010, 1011

Books in East Africa. Alden H. Clark. New York: Franklin Books Programs, 1964. 16, 9p.

Books in West Africa: Report and Recommendations. Comp. by William E. Spaulding, Simon Michael Bessie, and Datus C. Smith, Jr. New York: Franklin Books Programs, 1964. 44p.

Both reports assess socioeconomic, geographic, and other conditions in East and West Africa as they relate to the possibility of setting up an indigenous book publishing and distribution system.

1012

Books in Our Future. A Report from the Librarian of Congress to the Congress. Washington: Library of Congress, 1984. 49p.

In an introductory chapter Daniel Boorstin, then Librarian of Congress, discusses in general terms "The Culture of the Book: Today and Tomorrow," and in more specific terms describes what is being done by Americans through private organizations, Congress, the Executive branch, and the Library of Congress to promote reading and combat illiteracy. There is a directory of the 31 organizations cited in the text. For further information on other organizations and programs see **The Community of the Book**, edited by John Y. Cole. (No. 1024.)

1013

Bowker Lectures on Book Publishing. New York: Bowker, 1957. 389p.

This book is an eclectic collection of the first 17 annual Bowker Memorial Lectures on Book Publishing, covering 1935–1956, and delivered by distinguished publishers, literary agents, authors and others connected with the profession. Following its publication future lectures were issued as pamphlets by Bowker through 1967 when the series was dropped. These later lectures were never compiled. Some years afterward in 1976, another lecture was given and made into a pamphlet (No.

1119), but no more followed. Even though they are now dated they have attained historical value in addition to their other merits. Taken as a whole they give an overview of American book publishing for 30 years from the mid-1930s through the mid-1960s, as seen by some of its most interested and interesting participants.

1014

Braithwaite, Brian, and Joan Barrell. **The Business of Women's Magazines: The Agonies and the Ecstasies**. London: Associated Business Press, 1979. 176p.

This survey by two co-workers in the National Magazine Company (London) was designed to give insight into the inner workings of contemporary women's magazine publishing in Britain through an examination of the patterns many of the magazines follow or have followed. This is preceded by a historical summary of some length, emphasizing the period from the first World War through the 1970s. Appendixes give data on mergers; ownership; tabular biographies of the main women's magazines in the post-1939–45 war period, including those that have died since the war; and readership information about 12 major titles. The book is an extension of the authors' work on numerous presentations to advertisers, agencies and news-agents, and is not strictly speaking, scholarly. Among other things, there is no documentation. (For a scholarly presentation, see Cynthia White's **Women's Magazines, 1693–1968**. No. 1123.) Nonetheless it provides useful information. Name and title index.

1015

Brownstone, David M., and Irene M. Franck. **The Dictionary of Publishing**. New York: Van Nostrand, 1982. 302p.

A concise dictionary of publishing and allied terms drawn from printing, journalism, art, photography, computer science, sales, marketing and book selling, including a number which relate to old and rare books. Special emphasis is given to terms in the new technologies affecting the publishing process.

1016

Bullock, Penelope L. **The Afro-American Periodical Press 1838–1909**. Baton Rouge: Louisiana State University Press, 1981. 330p.

A narrative history of the beginnings and the early development of periodical publishing among black Americans, discussing the individuals and institutions responsible for the magazines, and suggesting the circumstances in American history and culture that helped shape this press. Appendixes tell where the periodicals may be located today, and two separate listings give their chronology and their geography, alphabetically state by state. Contains notes, a bibliography and an index.

Cain, Michael Scott, ed. **Co-op Publishing Handbook**. (See No. 1740.)

1017

Carter, Robert A., ed. **Trade Book Marketing: A Practical Guide**. New York: Bowker, 1983. 339p.

For various reasons—chief among them, so Carter feels, that book publishing is more art than business and that books are unlike other products—trade book marketing and its practitioners have never had the close and detailed attention they warrant and that virtually every other aspect of publishing has received. In today's climate, however, there is emphasis on marketing, and to meet the needs Carter has assembled this collection of articles by experienced professionals who deal with trade book marketing from a variety of angles, including "even market research, traditionally anathema to trade publishing." Part One takes up "The Marketing Environment;" Part Two, "The Marketing Process;" and Part Three, "Channels of Distribution." The older, more conventional processes and channels are not neglected, but clearly this is intended for the new generation of trade book publishers who know the realities of chain bookstores and mass market paperback racks in supermarkets. An epilogue discusses "Trade Book Marketing in the 1980s," and there is a bibliography, a glossary, and a name-subject index.

1018

Cassell & The Publishers Association. **Directory of Publishing 1985**. 11th ed. London: Cassell, 1984. 2,858p.

A "guide and reference to mainstream publishing and book trade activity throughout the UK, Commonwealth and—with the exception of the USA—other major English-language publishing countries in the world." (For the U.S. the **Literary Market Place**, No. 1767, serves much the same purpose.) Coverage, based on questionnaires, is of necessity selective, not exhaustive. Information includes a listing of publishers in the United Kingdom and the Commonwealth and overseas, with data for each giving address, telephone, chief personnel, specialization, number of new titles, parent company if pertinent, associated and subsidiary companies, overseas representatives, and book trade association membership; authors' agents; packagers in the U.K.; trade and allied services such as translators, representatives, distributors, remainder merchants, book wholesalers and library suppliers, book clubs, literary and trade events, etc. Appendixes include U.K. publishers classified by field of activity; names and addresses of publishers' overseas representatives; overseas publishers represented in the U.K.: overseas authors' agents; index of ISBNs; and an index of personal names. A main index lists publishers, imprints, authors' agents; and trade and allied associations, agencies, societies and services.

1019

Cave, Roderick. **The Private Press**. London: Faber & Faber, 1971. 376p.

Since the invention of printing, private presses have played an important part in literary and political history as well as in the graphic arts. In this handsome and comprehensive book Cave describes some of the most important presses and amateur printers, and the social or aesthetic roles they have played from the beginning of printing to the present. Among these are the quasi-official or patron's press; the scholarly press; the aristocratic plaything; the author as publisher; bibliomania; clandestine presses used for religious and political reasons and such illegal work as counterfeiting; printing as a hobby; William Morris and his Kelmscott Press, and later fine presses in Britain; fine printing in America and on the European continent, etc. Concluding chapters discuss the contemporary scene. There are handsome illustrations of presswork, a lengthy bibliography, and an index of names and titles.

1020

Cawelti, John G. **Adventure, Mystery, and Romance: Formula Stories as Art and Popular Culture**. Chicago: University of Chicago Press, 1976. 335p.

In this study of popular story formulas Cawelti has, in his own words, "tried to define the major analytical problems that confront us when we seek to inquire more fully into the nature and significance of formulaic literature, and to use a variety of different formulas to illustrate with some specificity how these problems might be explored." Although he includes a discussion of the various popular genres and their formulas in an early chapter, he limits himself to three: the detective story, the Western, and best-selling melodrama narrative in books and, lately, in films, to define major technical problems involved in analyzing the nature and significance of formulaic literature. He uses a number of specific masters of these genres as examples—among them, Agatha Christie, Simenon, Dashiell Hammett, Micky Spillane, Zane Grey, James Fenimore Cooper, John Ford, Irving Wallace. However, this is not a critique of their work per se but rather a definition of new approaches to the content analysis of popular narrative.

1021

Cazden, Robert E. **German Exile Literature in America 1935–1950: A History of the Free German Press and Book Trade**. Chicago: American Library Association, 1970. 250p.

Describes the growth of a large and dynamic anti-Nazi press and book trade on an international scale; tells how thousands of German-language books and journals published outside the Third Reich were imported to the U.S.; and discusses the fate of the German emigre author in America. There are three bibliographic appendixes: "Retail Distributors of Free German Publications in the United States 1933–1950"; "Free German and Free Austrian Newspapers and Periodicals in the United States 1933–1950—A Checklist"; "Free German Books and Pamphlets Published in the United States 1933–1954—A Checklist." There is also an extensive bibliography, footnotes following each chapter, and an index.

1022

Cheney, O.H. **Economic Survey of the Book Industry 1930–31**. New York: Bowker, c1931, 1960. 356p.

Since Cheney wrote his economic analysis of book publishing five decades ago, many changes have taken place: the paperback revolution, the decline of the independent publisher, the concept of the book as a product to be tied in with motion pictures and television shows and often written both for and from them, and other trends too numerous to enumerate. But some of the problems remain the same—for example: too many titles? what to do about remainders? who buys books? are popular books bad? the good book without a market. Cheney touches tellingly upon these and many others, ending each chapter with recommendations and making final overall recommendations. Newer books, notably Dessauer's (No. 1036), do not displace this; it remains essential for anyone wanting a knowledge of the past as a frame for the present or for its own sake. The 1960 reprint contains a new bibliography and an introduction by Robert Frase comparing the book industry in 1930 with the industry in 1960.

1023

Clair, Colin. **A Chronology of Printing**. New York: Praeger, 1969. 225p.

". . . being an attempt to set in chronological order those matters judged most important in the history of the printed book, its manufacture, design and dissemination," says the author as he follows printing year by year from its introduction into Europe and its spread throughout the world to the present. His aim is to give a wide spread of information rather than to study any portion in depth. Entries are grouped nationally. A comprehensive index of more than 10,000 items pulls the facts together.

1024

Cole, John Y., ed., and Carren O. Kasten, comp. **The Community of the Book: A Directory of Selected Organizations and Programs**. Washington: Library of Congress, 1986. 123p.

A descriptive directory of organizations that promote books and reading, administer literacy projects, and encourage the study of books. Emphasis is on the United States; international book programs, while included, have been described in greater detail in Cole's **U.S. International Book Programs 1981** (No. 1025) and Curtis Benjamin's **U.S. Books Abroad: Neglected Ambassadors** (No. 994). Taking as a point of departure the 31 organizations listed in the 1984 Library of Congress publication, **Books in Our Future** (No. 1012), it describes an additional 85 major organizations and programs. Among those represented are publishers, booksellers, librarians, book researchers, scholars, teachers, and writers concerned with reading skills, the book industry, the relationship of the book with other media, the history of books, and their international role. Name/subject index.

1025

Cole, John Y., ed. **U.S. International Book Programs 1981**. Washington: Library of Congress, 1981. 61p.

The Library of Congress' Center for the Book surveys 32 book and book-related programs carried out by governmental, inter-governmental and private agencies in the U.S. to promote books and reading. In an introductory essay John B. Putnam discusses "The Book Crisis in the Developing World," and an appendix describes the activities of two important but now defunct organizations, Franklin Book Programs, Inc. (1952–78) and the U.S. Government Advisory Committee on International Book and Library Programs (1962–77). Two earlier government publications are **Books in Human Development**, a 1965 report on a conference sponsored by American University and the U.S. Agency for International Development, and **Who Is Doing What in International Book and Library Programs** (1967), the proceedings of a conference sponsored by the International Relations Office of the American Library Association. For a later report see **U.S. Books Abroad: Neglected Ambassadors** by Curtis G. Benjamin (No. 994).

1026

Compaine, Benjamin M. **The Book Industry in Transition: An Economic Study of Book Distribution and Marketing**. White Plains, NY: Knowledge Industry Publications, 1978. 235p.

Those who fear that the book will soon become antiquated should take heart at an expert's appraisal of the book-publishing industry in which he is guardedly optimistic that there is room for the production of books of all kinds. Drawing from market research that Knowledge Industry Publications has done for its clients, he has updated some of the topics Cheney (No. 1022) tackled four generations previously in the first analysis of the industry. In his words, the study is meant to be "a detailed description of how general books get to various markets, how the economics of this distribution work, what the strengths and weaknesses of the current practices are, what changes are affecting the book industry, and what may be the future of the industry." He includes a number of tables and charts and a brief bibliography. Index.

1027

Compaine, Benjamin M. **The Business of Consumer Magazines**. White Plains, NY: Knowledge Industry Publications, 1982. 197p.

Describing his study as "something of a snapshot of what the industry looked like in 1981," Compaine describes in detail how it works, how it is changing, and how it is staying the same. Specifically, he deals with fact rather than theory—i.e., size and structure, circulation and distribution, advertising, audience research, differences between special and general interest publications, entrepreneurship, group ownership and competition, production, paper and printing. He sums up his data with outlook and conclusions, and following this, with profiles of 15 of the larger publishing groups of magazines. Appendixes give "Circulation for Selected General and Special Interest Consumer Magazines, 1973 and 1978" and "Consumer Magazines Published by Major Groups." Bibliography and index.

1028

Cook, Michael L. **Mystery, Detective, and Espionage Magazines**. Westport, CT: Greenwood, 1983. 795p.

A hefty encyclopedia of mystery, detective and espionage magazines, published in the U.S., Britain and Canada, interpreted broadly to include the frequently overlapping fantasy, horror and supernatural genre as well as fan and semiprofessional magazines which Cook regards as valuable sources of information. The principal portion consists of an alphabetical arrangement of profiles which gives for each a narrative history in detail, with background information, circumstances of founding and (where necessary) of cessation, bibliographical material, location of holdings when known, dates, title changes, editors and publishers, and other relevant information. Other materials include an overview of foreign magazines; book clubs in profile; magazines by category—i.e., dime novels, pulps, digests, etc.; key writers; a chronology; American true-detective magazines; Canadian true-detective magazines; etc. There is a selected bibliography, and an index.

1029

Coser, Lewis A., Charles Kadushin, and Walter W. Powell. **Books: The Culture and Commerce of Publishing**. New York: Basic Books, 1982. 411p.

The authors embarked on this study "at a moment when a variety of voices were beginning to question whether recent developments in the publishing industry—mergers, takeovers, and bureaucratization—might not endanger the key cultural functions of publishing" by upsetting the delicate balance between commerce and culture that has always characterized book publishing. Part I of the text, "History and Structure of the Industry," is an overview. Part II, "The People Who Make Books," discusses personnel, manuscript acquisition, women in book publishing, organization of publishing houses, and marketing and promotion. Part III, "Key Outsiders in the Book Trade," examines the role of literary agents, book reviewers, and bookstores involved with distribution. All this, however, adds up to much more than a description. Rather, it is an analysis of the book publishing industry as an important modal point in the production and dissemination of ideas and a vital part of the distribution of knowledge. Research consisted of interviews and observations of people involved, with methodology described in an appendix. There are chapter notes and an index.

In 1985 one of the authors, Walter W. Powell, published **Getting Into Print: The Decision-Making Process in Scholarly Publishing** (No. 1094), an offshoot of the earlier book. Here he deals at much greater length with the process of manuscript selection. Chapter notes and index.

1030

Curwen, Peter J. **The UK Publishing Industry**. Oxford; New York: Pergamon, 1981. 167p.

A survey—the first, Curwen claims—which takes in the entire spectrum of the UK publishing industry, not only book publishers but also printers, booksellers, libraries, learned societies, and journals as well as books. First comes a statistical overview, then "Publishing," "The Net Book Agreement," "Innovation and Copyright," "Printing," "Marketing and Distribution," "Bookselling," "Price Indices," "Quantitative Aspects of Journal Publishing," "Journal Production," and "Journal Publishers," (these last three by Alan Singleton). This is a detailed and excellent reference, with tables of figures accompanying the facts. There is a 12-page bibliography, and an author and a subject index.

1031

Curwen, Peter J. **The World Book Industry**. London: Euromonitor Publications, 1986. 290p.

Contending that book publishing, whether viewed as a business or as an art, needs to be examined on a supra-national level, Curwen combines research and insight to construct a clearer picture that shows "how the pieces of the worldwide book industry fit together." Rather than breaking it down country by country he takes it by its components. Two introductory chapters, "The Structure of the Book Industry," and "International Trade in Books," are followed by "Market Trends," "Book Distribution," "Libraries," "Reading and Owning Books," "The Price of Books," "Copyright," "Book Printing," and "Electronic Publishing." Conclusions are backed by numerous tables and charts, and statistical appendixes give country-by-country figures. Although there is no bibliography, Curwen shows in his tables the sources of his statistics.

1032

Dahl, Svend. **History of the Book**. 2d English ed. Metuchen, NJ: Scarecrow Press, 1968. 270p.

The author describes his aim in the preface: "Most of the existing works on the history of the book present its various phases—manuscripts, printing, binding, illustration, the book trade and libraries—separately. In this work I have attempted to present them all in a unified account so that their interrelationship will become apparent and the history of the book will appear in perspective as an essential factor in the history of culture." Contains a bibliography and an index.

1033

Daniel, Walter C. **Black Journals of the United States**. Westport, CT: Greenwood Press, 1982. 432p.

"Historical and descriptive profiles of more than 100 Afro-American periodicals—excluding newspapers—published between 1827 and the 1980s." The author says that profiles have been chosen on the basis of available periodicals and a mix of those which seem to him to reflect the broad scope of the Afro-American experience during the years covered. All entries include a historical essay giving information on the periodical's development and editorial policies, and the people involved in its development, followed by "Information Sources" and such relevant data regarding publication history as title changes, publisher, place of publication, editors with their dates, and circulation. Each entry is footnoted. There are two appendixes: "Selected Chronology of Events in Black History as Related to Founding of Black Journals" and "Geographical Distribution of Black Journals." Indexed.

1034

Danky, James P., ed. and Maureen E. Hady, comp. **Native American Periodicals and Newspapers 1828–1982: Bibliography, Publishing Record, and Holdings**. Westport, CT: Greenwood, 1984. 352p. (In association with the State Historical Society of Wisconsin.)

A holding list of American Indian periodicals, newspapers, and magazines, prepared by the State Historical Society of Wisconsin, going back to the earliest newspapers of the Five Civilized Tribes and locating precisely almost every item, current and extant, printed since Indians adopted the white's way of communicating. In all, it presents a guide to the holdings and locations of 1,164 periodical and newspaper titles covering literary, political, and historical journals as well as general newspapers and feature magazines. Information about each item is detailed. Main entry is under title, with the following indexes: subject; editors; publishers; geographic; catchword and subtitle; and chronological. Preceding the title entries are: a list of indexes included in the compilation; sources for purchase of microfilm; libraries included in the compilation; and about 50 reproductions of newsletter and periodical covers.

1035

Davis, Kenneth C. **Two-bit Culture: The Paperbacking of America**. Boston: Houghton Mifflin, 1984. 430p.

"To many people, the paperback book has always been little more than second-rate trash. Literary flotsam. . . . And that view, to a considerable extent, is accurate. But not exclusively so. The point of this history is to paint another portrait of the paperback, one that shows its better side (although not ignoring its warts, crooked teeth, cross-eyes, and cauliflower ears)". Thus Davis focuses on "quality" titles made available for the first time in quantity, describing them in terms of their authors, publishers and readers. These latter he discusses in sweeping strokes through societal trends. And since publications of the "better" mass media paperbacks was made possible through the publication of a vast majority of "lessers," he also gives a picture of the structure of the mass market industry, beginning in 1939 when Robert deGraff successfully launched a varied list of ten titles at 25 cents each.

No broad general history of paperback publishing in 20th century America has yet appeared, and meantime this helps fill the gap. Davis, a journalist who has worked within the publishing industry for many years and contributes regularly to **Publishers Weekly**, writes interestingly and has been able to document many of his facts first-hand. The book has an appendix pretentiously titled "Fifty Paperbacks that Changed America." Contains bibliographic notes, a bibliography and an index.

1036

Dessauer, John P. **Book Publishing: What It Is, What It Does**. 2d ed. New York: Bowker, 1981. 230p.

An ideal introduction to the structure of a complicated subject by a foremost authority on the economics of the industry, first published in 1974, with few changes in the 1981 edition. Dessauer treats book publishing under the following categories: "The Past Is Prologue," a short history; "A Broad Perspective," a discussion of the issues, activities, and associations; and more specifically, "How Books Are Created," "How Books Are Manufactured," "How Books Are Marketed," "How Books Are Stored and Delivered," "How Publishers Finance, Plan and Manage," and in conclusion, "What Does the Future Hold?" Glossary of terms, index, and bibliographic notes.

1037

Dinan, John A. **The Pulp Western: A Popular History of the Western Fiction Magazine in America**. San Bernadino, CA: The Borgo Press, 1983. 128p.

"This book covers a generation—the pulp era of the 1920s, '30s, and '40s of pulp fictioneers who cranked out millions, perhaps even hundreds of millions, of words for the several hundreds of the western pulp magazines then active. I have also tried to produce some sense of continuity of the development of a genre by providing a short history of the origins of Western American fiction, plus a brief commentary on the genre's evolution into the paperback era." Foreword. Bibliography and index.

1038

The Directory of Private Presses and Letterpress Printers and Publishers. Sacramento, CA: Press of Arden Park, 1979. 56p.

Contains 305 listings of U.S., Canadian, British, German, and Latin American private presses. Each entry tells proprietor, address, phone number, type of equipment used, typefaces, kinds of work produced, willingness to exchange with other presses, date of establishment, and goals and philosophy.

Directory of Small Press and Magazine Editors & Publishers. (See No. 1745.)

1039

Duke, Judith S. **The Children's Literature Market, 1977–1982**. White Plains, NY: Knowledge Industry Publications, 1976. 241p.

An analysis of the structure of the juvenile publishing industry as it is today: the demographic, economic, and social trends affecting it and the economics of the industry itself: market trends; book clubs; magazines; the audiovisual market; current trends; predictions for future sales. There are also profiles of 25 of the leading publishers in the field.

Duke, Judith S. **Religious Publishing and Communications**. (See No. 112.)

1040

Educational Publishing in Developing Countries. New Dehli, India: National Book Trust, 1980. 284p.

Report of a four-day Seminar on Educational Publishing in Developing Countries organized in connection with the Third World Book Fair, 1978, in which 83 participants from 24 countries, representing the public and private sectors in developed as well as developing countries, discussed relevant aspects of educational publishing. Subjects covered ranged from textbooks to out-of-school reading material, problems of copyright and translation rights, and such controversial issues as the role of government and multinational firms. One of the aims throughout was to relate educational publishing to complex socio-economic issues like free and compulsory education, adult literacy, development of Indian languages, more money for education, education for science and research, equalization of educational opportunity, and creation of increasing awareness of education as a means of modernization.

Eisenstein, Elizabeth L. **The Printing Revolution in Early Modern Europe**. (See No. 1041.)

1041

Eisenstein, Elizabeth L. **The Printing Press as an Agent of Change: Communications and**

Cultural Transformations in Early-Modern Europe. 2 v. New York: Cambridge University Press, 1979. 794p.

In this scholarly and detailed work Eisenstein focuses on the shift from script to print in Western Europe. In the first volume she deals with the main features of the communications revolution and the relationship between these changes and other developments conventionally associated with the transition from medieval to early modern times. In the second volume she views familiar developments "from a new angle of vision." Concentration is on cultural and intellectual movements rather than on political ones, which she says she will take up in another book. Her primary concern is with the effects of printing on written records and on the transmission of views from one already literate culture to another (rather than from an oral to a literate culture). Contains footnotes, a detailed bibliography, and an index.

A one-volume abridgement, **The Printing Revolution in Early Modern Europe** (New York: Cambridge University Press, 1983. 297p.), has been issued for the general reader with footnotes dropped and illustrations added. The index and bibliography have been retained.

1042

Escarpit, Robert. **The Book Revolution**. London: Harrap; Paris: UNESCO, 1966. 160p.

Although intended as a sequel to Barker's **Books for All** (No. 991), **The Book Revolution**, by a well-known French sociologist, makes no effort to update statistics but rather focuses on broad trends in general and the fate of the literary book in the mass market in particular. The result is a series of provocative essays about the way in which belles lettres fare in various countries. There is no bibliography as such, although notes at the end of each chapter contain references to other works, many of them European. There is no index.

1043

Feather, John. **A Dictionary of Book History**. London: Croom Helm, 1986. 278p.

Emphasis here is on the point of view of the bibliographer and the book trade, encompassing terms relevant to the history of the industry—trade practices, aspects of trade history, trade organizations and prominent printers, publishers and booksellers; specialized terms about the history of book production such as technologies of graphic and textual reproduction, papermaking and book binding; and important books about the trade. Libraries with collections of interest to book historians are also listed. Topics central to the subject merit essays intended to provide both an introduction and an overview. Persons included are members of the trade, illustrators, bookbinders, inventors or developers of techniques or equipment, book collectors and bibliographers, and librarians who have been prominent in the history of bibliography, with entries including a brief biography and an explanation of their significance. Those included have

in common the fact that all but two are dead (Feather found it too difficult to assess the achievements of the living). Entries are in alphabetical order with many cross references and at least one bibliographical reference.

1044

Febvre, Lucien, and Henri-Jean Martin. **The Coming of the Book: The Impact of Printing 1450–1800**. Tr. by David Gerard. London: NLB; Atlantic Highlands, NJ: Humanities Press, 1976. 378p.

This volume, first published in French in 1958, goes far beyond the history of printing; it is a cultural history of the book by a distinguished French historian whose approach is interdisciplinary. In his preface he states that his object is to study the changes the printed book brought into the world, their causes and effects, and to show how the printed book became something the manuscript could never become, for reasons which he analyzes in detail. He takes up the introduction of paper into Europe; technical problems of printing and their solution; the visual appearance of the book; the book as a commodity; journeymen, masters, printers, booksellers, and authors; the geography of the book as it spread from western and middle Europe into the Slavic countries, the New World, and the Far East; the book trade; and the book as a force for change. Febvre died before completing his work; the completion was done by his collaborator and disciple, Martin. There is an introductory chapter on manuscripts by Marcel Thomas. Contains extensive notes and an index.

1045

Feehan, John M. **An Irish Publisher and His World**. Cork, Ireland: Mercier, 1969. 137p.

Books about contemporary Irish publishing are rare. The author emphasizes the problems that differentiate book publishing there from publishing in other countries and concludes with a chapter about his own press, Mercier.

1046

Ferguson, Marjorie. **Forever Feminine: Women's Magazines and the Cult of Femininity**. London: Heinemann, 1983. 243p.

"This study is concerned with those messages which women's magazines have been transmitting to women over the post-war period, principally in Britain, but where relevant in the United States. It looks at how those messages have responded to the impact of social, cultural and economic changes upon the female audiences. It also looks at how those messages came about: the interaction between editors, their teams, their organizations and their audiences." The author, a sociologist, has combined content analysis, interviews, observation, documentation, statistical data and her own prior experience as a journalist. Contains notes, a statistical appendix on women's magazine readership, a bibliography and an index.

1047

First National Directory of "Rightist" Groups, Publications and Some Individuals in the United States (and Some Foreign Countries). 6th ed. Los Angeles: Noontide Press, 1968. 128p. **Supplement**, 1974.

Compiled by an organization called the Alert American Association, **The First National Directory . . .** is an alphabetical listing of several thousand educational, social and religious organizations and their publications where they exist—all of which represented a protest of some sort against prevailing "leftist" political or social trends. Publications are entered under name and again under organization.

1048

Fishman, Joshua A. **Language Resources in the United States. Vol. I. Guide to Non-English-Language Print Media.** Rosalyn, VA: Inter-America Research Associates, Inc., National Clearinghouse for Bilingual Education, Inc., 1981. 51p.

The Guide to Non-English-Language Print Media lists more than 800 ethnic community periodical publications in the U.S. in numerical order by NCBE accession number, with name, address, language, and when available, circulation, frequency, and contact person. This is preceded by an alphabetical list giving NCBE number, and followed by two other alphabetical indexes—one to geographical locations and the other to language.

1049

Fulton, Len. **The Psychologique of Small Press Publishing.** New Brunswick, NJ: Rutgers University, Graduate School of Library Science, 1976. 16p. (Occasional Papers No. 76–3.)

An authority whose life has been devoted to the small press movement and whose small publishing house, Dustbooks, has been called "The R.R. Bowker-H.W. Wilson of the small presses" briefly traces the growth of the movement. In discussing his own house he describes the directories Dustbooks publishes (Nos. 1745 and 1757) and other valuable reference books it alone has made available.

1050

Geiser, Elizabeth A., and Arnold Dolin, with Gladys S. Topkis, eds. **The Business of Book Publishing: Papers by Practitioners.** Boulder, CO: Westview, 1985. 445p.

"Our goal was the definitive work on the business of book publishing, and although this collection may have some gaps and imbalances, it is clear that it also provides a lot of valuable information on most of the phases and functions of the publishing process," says Geiser. Leading figures from the book publishing world provide articles about editorial, production, marketing and distribution aspects. Valuable assorted information comprises Part IV which includes major categories of publishing—i.e., children's books; textbooks; international mass market; professional and scientific publishing; reference books; and university presses. In conclusion are articles telling about careers in publishing; courses to assist newcomers entering the book publishing industry; and a most useful 18-page annotated bibliography by Chandler Grannis, "Books about the Book Industry." Index.

1051

Ghai, O.P., and Narendra Kumar. **International Publishing Today: Problems and Prospects.** Delhi, India: The Bookman's Club, 1984. 237p.

An anthology on international publishing including such aspects as freedom to publish, publishing for human development, international book fairs, piracy, children's publishing, global problems of scholarly publishing, educational publishing, and—specifically for developing countries—training and collection development. Articles also deal with various phases of book publishing in the U.S.S.R., India, Japan, Australia, the Arab countries, Latin, Spain, Mexico and French-speaking Africa. The volume is a festschrift honoring Maueul Salvat, President of the International Publishers Association.

1052

Glaister, Geoffrey Ashall. **Encyclopedia of the Book.** New York: World Publishing Co., 1960. 484p.

"Terms used in paper-making, printing, bookbinding and publishing, with notes on illuminated manuscripts, bibliographies, private presses, and printing societies." Subtitle. In its coverage of book publishing, it not only defines terms but also identifies trade journals, prizes and awards, private (but not commercial) presses, and organizations from the Stationers' Company to the American Book Publishers Council (now the Association of American Publishers). Although the emphasis is British, coverage for the U.S. is thorough. Much of the contemporary information has of course dated as private presses, trade journals, printing societies, and organizations have gone and new ones have come, but terminology has changed little, and enough of the information is historic to make the book still useful.

1053

Goldwater, Walter. **Radical Periodicals in America, 1890–1950: A Bibliography with Brief Notes.** Rev. ed. New Haven, CT: Yale University Press, 1966. 51p.

Lists 321 periodicals with a genealogical chart and a

concise lexicon for daily newspapers, purely trade union publications, local or sectional publications, literary magazines with a dominant political aspect, and periodicals appealing to special groups—all of which have in common an anarchist, Communist or Socialist viewpoint. Each entry has a brief annotation describing content. Contains a bibliography, "A Short List of Useful Books."

1054

Gorokhoff, Boris I. **Publishing in the U.S.S.R.** Bloomington: Indiana University Research Center in Anthropology, Folklore and Linguistics, 1959. 306p.

"This study seeks to present a survey of book, periodical, and newspaper publishing in the Soviet Union, including some related topics such as censorship, copyright, and the book trade" Preface. Emphasis is on science and technology. Contains bibliography and index.

1055

Grannis, Chandler, ed. **What Happens in Book Publishing**. 2d ed. New York: Columbia University Press, 1967. 491p.

"This edition, like the first, is an outline of procedures in book publishing, not a how-to book," says the editor of this anthology. Many changes have taken place since 1967, but enough holds true to make it valuable still, especially for organizational structure. Aspects included are the creation of the trade book: securing and selecting the manuscript, copy-editing, design, production and manufacturing; distribution of the trade book: selling, advertising, publicity, business management and accounting, order fulfillment, subsidiary rights and permissions; and special areas of publishing: children's books, religious books, textbooks, technical, scientific, and medical publishing, university presses, mass-market paperbacks, trade paperbacks, mail order, reference books, "vanity" publishing. There are also articles on the legal aspects and distribution of American books abroad. Indexed.

1056

Greenfeld, Howard. **Books from Writer to Reader**. New York: Crown, 1978. 211p.

Not "how to" but rather "how it is done" by an author and publisher who obviously does not feel that the book is about to be supplanted by the computer. He takes the book through its various stages at a fast gallop—the writer, the literary agent, the publishing house, the decision to publish, the editor, the illustrator, the copyeditor, the designers, including jacket designer, the production supervisor, the compositor, the proofreader and the indexer, the printer, the color printer, the binder, the route from the warehouse to the bookstore and from the bookstore to the reader. There is a glossary, a bibliography, and an index.

1057

Gross, Gerald, ed. **Publishers on Publishing**. New York: Bowker, 1961. 491p.

"The basic editorial concept of **Publishers on Publishing** was to present a series of professional self-portraits of the great publishers, past and present, active and inactive," says Gross. Taking his selections from memoirs, autobiographies, and articles, sometimes by the publisher under discussion, Gross shows attitudes of (in most cases) yesterday's publishers toward such aspects of the business (and art) as agents, writers, editors, and advertisers. Some of the excerpts deal with the history of publishing. Gross has added commentaries and biographical notes about author-publishers.

1058

Gussow, Don. **The New Business Journalism: An Insider's Look at the Workings of America's Business Press**. New York: Harcourt Brace Jovanovich, 1984. 240p.

The history, structure and functioning of the business press and the role of business communications in areas such as marketing, merchandise, public relations and advertising. Appendixes include a glossary of terms, a suggested training program for circulation personnel, a list of colleges and universities offering courses in business journalism, a list of selected business publications, and a bibliography.

1059

Hackett, Alice Payne, and James Henry Burke. **80 Years of Best Sellers 1895–1975**. New York: Bowker, 1977. 265p.

This compilation appeared each decade from the 1950s into the 1970s under the appropriate decade's title. Its purpose is to present facts and figures based on **Publishers Weekly**'s count and to interpret and comment briefly upon the statistics and trends, but not to evaluate from a literary viewpoint. The main portion is a year-by-year listing, followed by brief comments; shorter sections organize best sellers by sales figures into hardbound, paperbound, and combined; and also by subject. Other features include a history of best sellers, a discussion of them before 1895, and books and articles about best sellers. This is not for those wanting a depth study of the phenomenon, but is very useful for breadth. Figures before 1912 come from **The Bookman**; after that, from **Publishers Weekly**. Users should be aware that **PW** includes only books distributed to bookstores and libraries, not those sold through mail order or book clubs. There are no present plans for a 1985 update. For other books on best sellers see Hart's **The Popular Book** (No. 1061) and Mott's **Golden Multitudes** (No. 1081).

1060

The Handbook of Magazine Publishing. Comp. by the editors of **Folio**. 2d ed. New Canaan, CT: Folio Publishing Corp., 1983. 790p.

A compilation of articles from **Folio: The Magazine for Magazine Management** containing articles written by magazine publishing specialists and by **Folio** editors which have appeared from 1972–1982, intended as a guide to an understanding of the industry. In 13 sections: "Advertising Management and Marketing," "Selling Advertising," "Circulation Management," "Circulation Promotion," "Single-copy Sales," "Fulfillment," "Ancillary Activities," "Editorial," "Graphics," "Production," "Printing," "Management," and "Starting the New Magazine."

Harris, Michael, and Alan Lee, eds. **The Press in English Society from the Seventeenth to the Nineteenth Centuries**. (See No. 904.)

1061

Hart, James D. **The Popular Book: A History of America's Literary Taste**. New York: Oxford University Press, 1950. 351p.

Relates America's popular reading to the social background of the times, from the mid-sixteenth century (**Institutes of Christian Religion** by John Calvin) to the late 1940s (**This I Remember** by Eleanor Roosevelt). The author pegs his discussions around specific books. Contains a bibliographical checklist, a chronological index of books discussed (but no sales figures), and an index.

1062

Hartman, Joan E., and Ellen Messer-Davidow, eds. **Women in Print: Opportunities for Women's Studies Research in Language and Literature**. 2 v. New York: Modern Language Association of America, 1982. Vol. 1, 198p.; Vol. 2, 173p.

Articles in the first volume of this study sponsored by the Modern Language Association Commission on the Status of Women in the Professions, point out areas where research and publication by and about women are needed—in the study of language, in the national literatures, and in the literature by women writers whose works of good quality have been neglected because of grounds associated with sex or race. Articles in the second volume examine the ways and means of publication in language and literature studies, including the nature, requirements and resources of both establishment and alternative publishing. Although emphasis is on women, men too could find this work useful, especially the second volume. Chapter notes.

1063

Hasan, Abul. **The Book in Multilingual Countries: A Survey Based on the Proceedings of the Symposium on the Publication of Books in the Various Languages of Multilingual Countries (Moscow-Alma Ata, USSR, 6–10 September 1976)**. Paris: UNESCO, 1978. 40p. (Reports and Papers on Mass Communication No. 82.)

Discussion of the creation, manufacture, distribution and promotion of books in indigenous languages in Europe, Asia, Africa, the Arab countries and Latin America. Appendixes include "Guidelines for the Promotion of Books in the Various Languages of Multilingual Countries" and a bibliography.

Hoffman, Frederick, Carolyn Ulrich, and Charles Allen. **Little Magazine: A History and a Bibliography**. (See No. 989.)

Hoggart, Richard. **The Uses of Literacy: Aspects of Working-Class Life with Special Reference to Publications and Entertainment**. (See No. 193.)

1064

Honey, Maureen. **Creating Rosie the Riveter: Class, Gender and Propaganda during World War II**. Amherst: University of Massachusetts Press, 1984. 251p.

"How did the strong figure of Rosie the Riveter become transformed into the naive, dependent, childlike, self-abnegating model of femininity in the late forties and 1950s." Maureen Honey seeks the answers to these and related questions about the differing roles of women during and after World War II through a case study of wartime fiction, advertising, and propaganda as it appeared in **Saturday Evening Post** and **True Story**. Although this is the main focus, a by-product is an exploration of some of the dimensions of popular culture—its functions, its characteristics, its relationship to social realities. Chapter notes and bibliography.

1065

Horowitz, Irving Louis. **Communicating Ideas: The Crisis of Publishing in a Post-Industrial Society**. New York: Oxford University Press, 1986. 240p.

This study, says Horowitz in this analysis of academic publishing, is an attempt to bring together what he refers to as the dualism, or "two worlds," of the literature on book publishing which tends either toward "an excessive pragmatism, a how-to-mentality which defines the publishing world in strict 'nuts and bolts' terms and defies any analysis of long-term trends," and on the other hand a "bland idealism," an intellectualization which downgrades all aspects of book publishing except the editorial. He deals at length with the new technologies—and other aspects of present-day academic scholarly publishing—among them, scientific information and democratic choice; technological impact on scholarly publishing; the political economy of database publishing; copyright legislation and its consequences; the reproduction of knowledge and maintenance of property; from computer revolution to intellectual counter-revolution; scholarly communication and academic publishing; the politics of global knowledge; scientific access; advertising ideas and marketing products; gatekeeping functions;

the social structure of scholarly communication; social science as scholarly communication; and experts, audiences, and publics. Notes and index.

Industry Statistics 1982: Newspapers, Periodicals, Books and Miscellaneous Publishing. (See No. 970.)

International Directory of Little Magazines and Small Presses. (See No. 1757.)

International Literary Market Place. (See No. 1759.)

1066

Johnson, Michael L. **The New Journalism: The Underground Press, the Artists of Nonfiction, and Changes in the Established Media.** Lawrence: University Press of Kansas, 1971. 171p.

The author believes that the new journalism is a new genre. The first two chapters are devoted to the underground press from its beginnings to the mid-1960s. Next is a critical survey of the new journalism as an evolving literary form. Following this the author discusses its effect on the established press. Notes and an index.

Kaplan, Frank L. **Winter into Spring: The Czechoslovak Press and the Reform Movement, 1963–1968.** (See No. 914.)

1067

Kingsford, R. J. L. **The Publishers' Association 1896–1946, with an Epilogue.** London: Cambridge University Press, 1970. 228p.

This story of England's book trade association from its founding to the mid-1940s, with an epilogue of six pages bringing it up to 1962, is also the story of the major events of the British book trade during the period. Appendixes give the first rules of the Association, the founding members and first Council, and the officers and secretaries from 1896 to 1962. There is a bibliography and an index.

1068

Kurien, George Thomas. **The Directory of American Book Publishing from Founding Fathers to Today's Conglomerates.** New York: Simon and Schuster, 1975. 386p.

A reference book modeled on J. Kirchner's **Lexikon des Buchwesena.** "Publishing," says the author, "is basically a mosaic and does not lend itself easily to an integrated narrative," but rather to a dictionary-type reference book. He has grouped his entries under the following headings: "Founding Fathers and Their Enterprises"; "Today's Publishing Houses"; "Conglomerates"; "Multiple Publishing Houses"; "Book Trade Associations"; "Major Prizes, Awards, Events." Each entry contains a succinct account of salient facts. Although an attempt has been made to include publishing houses founded before 1968 and all university presses irrespective of size, the list is by no means all-inclusive nor intended to be. Appendixes give commonly used publishing abbreviations; a glossary of publishing terms; and two bibliographies—one of general references, biographies, and memoirs; the other of company histories and company addresses. Indexed.

1069

Kurian, George, ed. **Worldwide Markets for English-Language Books.** 2 v. White Plains, NY: Knowledge Industry Publications, 1978. 327p.

A description of the book trade in the seven major English-speaking countries of the world, which, grouped by size of market, are the United States, the United Kingdom, Canada, Republic of South Africa, Australia, India, and New Zealand. A special section gives eleven minor markets in alphabetical order; they are Bangladesh, Ghana, Ireland, Jamaica, Kenya, Malaysia, Nigeria, Pakistan, Philippines, Singapore, and Sri Lanka. The aim is "to develop indicators of the strengths and weaknesses of the constituent markets, to analyze the general state and direction of growth of the book industry, and to interrelate these factors so as to provide a firm basis for decision-making in public." Information for each country is accompanied by numerous tables, and for the seven major countries, by profiles of a few representative publishing houses. An Executive Summary condenses the total findings, and a 13-page Introduction summarizes the findings in terms of certain important trends. At the end of the second volume are conclusions. Index.

1070

Lane, Michael, with Jeremy Booth. **Books and Publishers: Commerce Against Culture in Postwar Britain.** Lexington, MA: Lexington, 1980. 148p.

"In this book, I have tried to record and understand how publishers are being affected by and respond to a time of fundamental crisis in the culture in which they are either entrepreneurs or gatekeepers, and what their response means for that culture," says Lane. He begins with the examination of the book itself—as a cultural object; its varieties; its course through publication. He then examines book publishing—its economics; its models; traditional versus modern publishing; the power structure; selection; organization; and the place of book publishers in today's culture. In addition to the bibliographical sources Lane has listed he has drawn upon an intensive case study and fieldwork over a ten-year period, placing book publishing throughout in a larger context. In addition to the extensive bibliography there are chapter notes and an index.

1071

Lehmann-Haupt, Hellmut, in collaboration with Lawrence C. Wroth and Rollo G. Silver. **The Book in America: A History of the**

Making and Selling of Books in the United States. 2d ed. New York: Bowker, 1951. 431p.

A history in which the author chronicles book production and distribution from the colonial period, beginning in 1638, to about 1950. Excellent for its identification and discussion of printers, publishers, and publishing houses in the U.S. during the time covered. For a much fuller account of the years between 1630 and 1980, see Tebbel's multi-volume history (Nos. 1114–1117).

Lewis, Roger. **Outlaws of America: The Underground Press and Its Context**. (See No. 926.)

1072

Lippy, Charles H., ed. **Religious Periodicals of the United States: Academic and Scholarly Journals**. Westport, CT: Greenwood, 1986. 599p.

A survey of 100 out of the more than 2,500 periodicals in the field of religion in print in the United States, intended to provide students and scholars with an introduction to the kinds of periodical literature available on the subject and the kinds of concerns revealed. Taken together, they provide a history of religious periodical publishing in the U.S. and the way they mirror changes in religious scholarship over the years. The range of content includes Protestant, Catholic, Jewish, humanist, and sectarian denomination or groups. Each profile gives a capsule history of the periodical, including the factors that instigated it, its focus, important articles that have appeared, and its contribution. Following this description is a bibliography, index sources, availability of reprint or microfilm editions, and libraries which carry it. In conclusion is a summary publication history—title changes, volume and issue data, publishers and places of publication, editors, estimated circulation. Arrangement is by title of publication; appendixes provide a chronological listing by date of founding and by religious orientation. Name/subject index.

Littlefield, Daniel F., Jr., and James W. Parins. **American Indian and Alaska Native Newspapers and Periodicals**. (See No. 927.)

Liu, Alan P.L. **The Press and Journals in Communist China**. (See No. 930.)

1073

Machlup, Fritz, and Kenneth Leeson. **Information Through the Printed Word: The Dissemination of Scholarly, Scientific, and Intellectual Knowledge. Vol. 1, Book Publishing. Vol. 2, Journals**. New York: Praeger, 1978. 301, 338p.

First intending to update **The Production and Distribution of Knowledge in the United States** (No. 261), Machlup became deeply involved instead in an overlapping three-volume project, **Information Through the**

Printed Word, in which he analyzed the dissemination of scholarly, scientific and intellectual knowledge through books, journals and libraries. Two kinds of data were used: Primary, consisting of unpublished information obtained from firms and organizations, and secondary, chiefly statistical from published sources. To obtain the primary data, the authors had the cooperation of learned and professional societies, 28 commercial publishing houses and university presses, and an unnamed number of periodicals, not identified. Volume 1, **Book Publishing**, Part 1, is a 63-page General section which gives information pertinent to all three volumes, much of it dealing with terminology and methodology. The rest of Volume 1 concerns aspects of book publishing: scope, structure, and markets; data; sales; incomes and expenses; inventory policies; total sales and sales broken down by subject; incomes and expenses; inventory policies; and profiles of individual but unnamed books in various disciplines, with manufacturing costs, price, sales, and free copies. Biography and books of fiction are not included.

Volume 2, Part 3, "Journal Publishing," is limited to academic and scholarly publishing—no "magazines." It includes scope and structure of the industry and its market; type data used; nominal and real sales; costs; and subscription rates, circulation and revenue. Part 4, "Use of Journals," gives published research on use of scientific and scholarly journals in the physical sciences, psychology and economics; methodology of the study; general evaluation of the economics journals as to the study and use of individual articles; and policy issues.

The third volume in the series deals with libraries.

1074

Madison, Charles A. **Irving to Irving: Author-Publisher Relations 1800–1974**. New York: Bowker, 1974. 279p.

As Madison examines author-publisher relations of 30 or so famous authors from the U.S. and Britain he gives from an unusual and interesting angle an insight into the intricacies and changes within book publishing itself. Among his authors are Hawthorne, Longfellow, William James, Robert Frost, Kipling, Conrad, Santayana, Edith Wharton, James Joyce, Thomas Wolfe, John Steinbeck, F. Scott Fitzgerald and Margaret Mitchell. His sympathies, he states, are frankly with publishers who strove to maintain high literary standards. He highlights what he considers the deterioration of the relations with a hoax perpetuated on McGraw-Hill by a minor writer named Clifford Irving who represents to Madison an example of the worst as Washington Irving had represented the best. A list of source material and an index.

1075

Madison, Charles A. **Jewish Publishing in America: The Impact of Jewish Writing on American Culture**. New York: Sanhedrin Press, 1976. 294p.

A straightforward account, beginning with early

publishing by and about Jews in Colonial days, and continuing with the Jewish Publication Society and other organizational and commercial publishers; early Yiddish periodicals, magazines and literature; the flowering of Yiddish literature in the early 20th century; major Yiddish writers; Yiddish book publishing; English-language contemporary Anglo-Jewish periodicals; and finally the influential New York publishing houses of the 1920s–1970s whose founders were Jewish although their output was only incidentally so. Emphasis is on Jewish writers as well as their publishers. Bibliography and index.

1076

Magazine People '84. William E. Barlow, Publisher; Terence Poltrack, ed.; Victoria Wood, associate editor. New York: Min Publishing Co., 1984. 122p.

Brief biographies of key personnel in the magazine/advertising community. Advertising personnel is limited to managerial and marketing directors. Information for each item varies, but all include past and present employment, address, and telephone number; most of them also include one or more of the following: education; membership in organizations; awards; and authorship where pertinent. There are approximately 600 entries. Contains an "Index to Biographies by Employer." Intended to be an ongoing publication.

Magazine Publishing Career Directory. (See No. 1769.)

1077

Malhotra, D. N., and Narendra Kumar, eds. **Indian Publishing Since Independence**. Delhi, India: The Bookman's Club, 1980. 182p.

An anthology whose articles, written by members of the Bookman's Club of Delhi, when taken together review the status of book publishing in today's India. Among topics: regional language publishing; Hindi publishing; educational publishing; paperback publishing; children's books publishing; professionalism, authors, publishers and booksellers; writing as a profession; libraries and book development; book production; state publishing; promotion; cooperation; international publishing.

1078

Marty, Martin E., and others. **The Religious Press in America**. New York: Holt, Rinehart & Winston, 1963. 184p.

The aim of the authors is to familiarize readers of denominational publications, both newspapers and magazines, with the ways in which these publications interpret the world in terms of religious commitments. In chapters both descriptive and broadly analytical, they discuss the Protestant, Catholic, and Jewish presses and the secular uses of the religious press. Footnotes. Marty is among the best of the writers on religion in contemporary America, and his findings hold over the decades since their publication here.

1079

McMurtrie, Douglas. **The Book: The Story of Printing and Bookmaking**. 3d ed. New York: Oxford University Press, 1943. 676p.

Because of the close relationship between printing and publishing, this account of book design from the time of primitive human records to the present is a good source for information about the historical development of the book, early printers, publishers, and presses, and so on. Contains extensive bibliographies and an index.

1080

Meeting of Experts on Book Development Planning in Asia, Singapore, 1968. Final Report. Paris: UNESCO, 1968. 15p.

Skeletal resume which pinpoints what had been done to develop a book-publishing industry in those Asian countries where little existed, with recommendations for the future.

1081

Mott, Frank Luther. **Golden Multitudes: The Story of Best Sellers in the United States**. New York: Bowker, c1947, 1960. 357p.

The author establishes a simple arithmetical formula for determining best sellers and discusses them chronologically in their social and literary context, from Michael Wigglesworth's **Day of Doom** in 1662 to Kathleen Winsor's **Forever Amber** in 1945.

1082

Mott, Frank Luther. **A History of American Magazines**. 5 v. Cambridge, MA: Harvard University Press, 1930–68. (Vol. I, 1741–1850; Vol. II, 1850–65; Vol. III, 1865–85; Vol. IV, 1885–1905; Vol. V, 1885–1905.)

A thorough and comprehensive history of the American magazine from pre-Revolutionary times to 1900. Arrangement is chronological. Vol. V, published posthumously and edited by the author's daughter, Mildred Mott Wedel, assisted by Theodore Peterson and John T. Frederick, is somewhat different, consisting of a series of sketches of 25 of the most prominent magazines of the period.

The appendixes of the first four volumes contain a chronological list of magazines covered, with dates of establishment and demise (except in the rare cases where they are extant). Vol. V indexes the entire series. For the period from 1900 on see Peterson's **Magazines in the Twentieth Century** (No. 1092).

1083

Mumby, Frank A., and Ian Norrie. **Publishing and Bookselling**. 5th ed. London: Jonathan Cape; NY: Bowker, 1974. 685p.

Frank Mumby's first edition, which is a classic on the subject, appeared in 1930 with three more editions updating it to 1956. This latest is a hefty volume in which Norrie uses Mumby's first 13 chapters—up to 1870—and carries it into contemporary times. Mumby has dealt (chronologically) with publishing and bookselling in the ancient world and the Middle Ages, and from that point on orients himself strictly around England. Norrie goes into more modern times, discussing among other topics, the acceleration of takeovers and mergers, the obscenity laws, international copyright, and restrictive practices. Both authors have written in detail about individual British firms. Appendixes contain sales figures and membership lists to trade organizations. There is a 60-page bibliography and an author-title index with occasional subject entries.

Murthy, Nadig Krishna. **Indian Journalism**. (See No. 938.)

1084

Myers, Robin. **The British Book Trade from Caxton to the Present Day**. London: Deutsch in Association with the National Book League, 1973. 405p.

"This book consists of a classified and annotated selection of works indicating the way in which the book trade evolved, with a historical bias which reflects that of the libraries (the National Book League and St. Bride's Institute) on which it has been based. I took the invention of printing from movable type in Europe as a starting point, although trading in books goes back at least to the fifth century B.C. The contents are limited to organized commerce in books, excluding the non-commercial book world such as libraries and librarianship . . . , and other forms of printed communication . . . ." Introduction. Emphasis is British, but the book trade being what it is, other countries are inevitably drawn in. Contents include authorship, bookselling, binding, design and production, illustration, history of the book trade, children's books, laws relating to the book trade, the Net Book Agreement, printing paper and ink, private presses, publishing. Each section and some subsections have introductions which summarize and explain where necessary. Annotations are detailed and often evaluative. Author-title-subject index.

1085

Nunn, Godfrey Raymond. **Publishing in Mainland China**. Cambridge, MA: M.I.T. Press, 1966. 83p. (M.I.T. Report No. 4.)

"This study attempts to analyze the organization of book and periodical publishing in China from 1949 to the end of 1964, with particular reference to publications in the natural, applied, and social sciences." Introduction. It gives as much information as could be obtained from sources at Hong Kong about the structure of the industry, the size of publishing houses, the relative amounts of literature published in minority and foreign languages, and the relative amounts published by subjects. It also deals with distribution systems—retail, direct, and through libraries. Contains four appendixes, a bibliography, and an index.

1086

The Oxbridge Directory of Ethnic Periodicals: The Most Comprehensive Guide to U.S. & Canadian Ethnic Periodicals Available. Ed. by Patricia Hagood. New York: Oxbridge, 1979. 247p.

Some 3,500 ethnic newspapers, magazines, journals, newsletters, bulletins, directories, yearbooks, bibliographies and association publications published in the U.S. and Canada by some 70 ethnic groups. Arrangement is by ethnic group, with a general section and a title index. Information includes address, telephone, top personnel, description of editorial content, year established, frequency, rates, circulation, distribution of readership, method of printing, number of pages per issue, and use of color.

1087

The Oxbridge Directory of Religious Periodicals. Ed. by Howard Greenberg. New York: Oxbridge, 1979. 148p.

A guide to over 1,900 religious periodicals in the U.S. and Canada, giving for each all or some of the following information: affiliation, address, telephone, key personnel, frequency, cost, circulation, type of material it publishes, and whether or not it accepts advertising. Arrangement is alphabetical by title, with an alphabetical index by title which seems superfluous.

1088

Page, Roger. **Australian Bookselling**. London: Deutsch, 1970. 175p.

A survey, including a historical retrospect, of the Australian book trade as it affects booksellers. Contains chapters on educational and library business and the trade in English, American, and locally published books. The author is manager of the Royal Melbourne Institute of Technology bookshop and a former president of the Australian Booksellers Association. Contains appendixes, a bibliography, and an index.

1089

Parnell, Frank H., with Mike Ashley, comps. **Monthly Terrors: An Index to the Weird Fantasy Magazines Published in the United States and Great Britain**. Westport, CT: Greenwood, 1985. 602p.

The compilers' aim is to provide an index to all weird fantasy magazines published in the English language, with "weird fantasy" defined as "fiction that deals with non-everyday happenings—the bizarre, the outre, the macabre—all tinged with an infusion of the supernatural." Borderline cases have been included, as have small press 'semi-professional' magazines. The index is divided into two main and several small (though not lesser, say the compilers) parts. The first main part lists the magazines by issue, giving contents of each—168 different magazines running to 1,733 issues—with some basic publishing data on each title; the second main part lists and very briefly identifies the authors and their contributions, telling in which magazine each story can be found. There are in addition artists and editor indexes. Four appendixes index series; describe certain magazines selected for Honorable Mention because, although not devoted exclusively to weird fantasy, they carry stories in the genre; and list magazines chronologically and geographically. Preceding the main portion is a historical survey of the genre from 1919 through 1983 in the U.S., Canada and the United Kingdom.

1090

Pellowski, Anne. **Made to Measure: Children's Books in Developing Countries**. Paris: UNESCO, 1980. 129p.

A part of UNESCO's efforts within the framework of the International Year of the Child, this small book is both an explanation of standard book publishing procedures intended for the uninitiated in the Third World and, more instructively and interestingly to the initiated, discussions by Third World citizens who work with children's books as to the state of the children's book publishing industry in their countries. Trade and educational books are considered. In conclusion is a bibliography of the works mentioned.

Penn, I. Garland. **The Afro-American Press and Its Editors**. (See No. 946.)

1091

Peters, Jean, ed. **The Bookman's Glossary**. 6th ed. New York: Bowker, 1983. 223p.

The Bookman's Glossary first appeared in serial form in the July 12, 1924 **Publishers Weekly**. Since then it has been revised and enlarged to reflect the expanding and changing terminology of the book trade, but its object has not changed. Like its predecessors this edition is designed to provide a practical guide to the terminology used in the production and distribution of books in words in common usage in the bookstore, in the publisher's office, in a library, or among book collectors. The 5th and 6th editions are broadened to include relevant computer terms. Names of organizations, associations, and prominent people in the book trade are included. There is a selected reading list and a list of proofreaders' marks.

1092

Peterson, Theodore. **Magazines in the Twentieth Century**. 2d ed. Urbana: University of Illinois Press, 1964. 484p.

The best single source for detailed information on trends in consumer magazines for the first 60 years of the

century and for the history of specific ones. The author deals with special-interest as well as big-name magazines, tracing their development and placing them in broad historical and economic context. Arrangement is broadly by aspects of magazine publishing and types of magazines—for example, "Advertising: Its Growth and Effects," "The Economic Structure of the Industry," "The Old Leaders That Died," "The New Leaders That Survived," "New Leaders: The Missionaries," "New Leaders: The Merchants," "Success by Compression," "Magazines for Cultural Minorities." As the headings suggest, Peterson's style is witty and incisive. The first edition (1956) contained a lengthy bibliography which has been omitted from the second. However, footnotes somewhat replace it. There is an index, Mott (No. 1082) and Peterson are giants among magazine historians; no one has replaced nor updated their work.

Pineda-Ofreneo, Rosalinda. **The Manipulated Press: A History of Philippine Journalism since 1945**. (See No. 947.)

1093

Plant, Marjorie. **The English Book Trade: An Economic History of the Making and Sale of Books**. 3d ed. London: Allen & Unwin, 1974. 520p.

The author's comprehensive historical analysis is mainly economic and British, as the title states. It is divided into two parts—the age of hand printing and the age of the mechanical printer. This latter section extends to 1970. Among topics discussed in a depth often lacking in publishing histories are labor, labor organizations, paper and binding materials, and an extensive treatment of copyright. Statistical and other data have been revised, and new sections have been included on public lending rights, paperbacks, photocopying, and the rise of international publishing. Extensive footnotes and a subject index.

1094

Powell, Walter W. **Getting Into Print: The Decision-Making Process in Scholarly Publishing**. Chicago: University of Chicago Press, 1985. 260p.

Using case studies of two small scholarly houses, Powell shows how as a whole editors in such houses decide what books to select, and, in the process, the ways in which publishing departs from many of the assumptions commonly found in the literature of other types of organizations. Copious notes, a bibliography, and an index.

1095

Publishing in Africa in the Seventies. Ed. by Edwina Oluwasanmi, Eva McLean, and Hans Zell. Ife-Ife, Nigeria: University of Ife Press, 1975. 377p. (Proceedings of an International Conference on Publishing and Book Development held at the University of Ife, Ife-Ife, Nigeria, 16–20 December, 1973)

The recommendations, summaries of the various sessions, and a selection of the papers read at this conference attended by more than 100 African writers, publishers, booksellers, librarians, printers, and teachers give a succinct account of the history and hopes of African publishing. Among topics discussed are the cultural and social factors of book reading and publishing in Africa; a frank explanation as to why indigenous publishing has trouble getting started; the mechanics of acquiring library materials—African and otherwise; the role of government; the role of Christian publishing houses; and the problems faced by writers, distributors, and booksellers.

Publishers' International Directory. (See No. 1781.)

1096

Radway, Janice A. **Reading the Romance: Women, Patriarchy, and Popular Literature**. Chapel Hill: University of North Carolina Press, 1984. 274p.

The research reported here is intended to explain why women find reading romance novels enjoyable and "emotionally necessary." To this end Janice Radway has constructed a fascinating study of a complex social process beginning with the publication of romantic fiction within an institutional structure and culminating in its meaning and importance to a sample of dedicated readers in a particular social world. As a result of her belief that "the semiotic view of reading as a process must ground new research into the cultural meaning of texts" she has developed a research method heavily dependent on questionnaire responses and on intensive interviews. This is an important contribution to the theory of contemporary mass culture. Notes, bibliography and index.

1097

Reilly, Mary Lonan. **A History of the Catholic Press Association, 1911–1968**. Metuchen, NJ: Scarecrow, 1971. 350p.

Tells how the Catholic Press Association came into being, its changing interests over the years, the evolution of the organizational structure, and cooperative efforts with other groups. Appendixes include membership statistics, convention dates and sites, and prominent officials. There is a lengthy bibliography which also includes archival material. Indexed.

1098, 1099

Riley, Sam G. **Magazines of the American South**. Westport, CT: Greenwood, 1986. 346p.

Riley, Sam G., comp. Index to **Southern Periodicals**. Westport, CT: Greenwood Press, 1986. 459p.

"In writing this book [**Magazines of the American South**] and in compiling a companion volume entitled **Index to Southern Periodicals**, which is a reasonably complete list of the region's magazines and other non-newspaper periodicals from 1764 to 1984, I hope to make a start in supplying a missing chapter in the cultural history of the South," Riley says of these two guides.

The major purpose of the **Index** is to identify and locate. It consists of a chronological list of periodicals with place of publication, dates and present location. This is followed by an alphabetical listing of titles, and by a listing by state. There are roughly 7,000 titles, including not only consumer magazines but also legal, medical, religious, business and other specialized types as well.

Magazines of the American South profiles in considerable detail about 90 magazines, including the development of each and its editorial policies and content. This is followed by a bibliography of sources, and a publication history showing title changes, volume and issue data, publisher and place of publication, editors, and circulation. Riley's criterion for selection is general rather than literary appeal. In his words: "The focus of this book is not on the magazine as literature, but simply on magazines as magazines, admitting that peoples' literary needs are only one area of a magazine's usefulness, and that practical information or amusement are also important components of the total picture." Religious periodicals and those published by and for blacks are excluded because they are covered by Charles H. Lippy's **Religious Periodicals** in the United States (No. 1072) and Walter C. Daniel's **Black Journals of the United States** (No. 1033). Profiles are arranged alphabetically; appendixes give chronological and geographical listings by state.

In both volumes "The South" is operationally defined as the states of the Confederacy plus Maryland. Each volume is indexed.

1100

Sankaranarayanan, N., comp. and ed. **Book Distribution and Promotion Problems in South Asia**. Paris: UNESCO, 1964. 278p.

Survey of distribution and promotion in Ceylon, Burma, Iran, East and West Pakistan, North and South India, as well as in three highly developed countries by way of contrast—Holland, the United Kingdom, and the U.S.

1101

Scholarly Communication: The Report of the National Enquiry. Baltimore, MD: Johns Hopkins University Press, 1979. 176p.

Popularly known as the National Enquiry into Scholarly Communication, this study evaluates the means by which scholarly knowledge in the U.S. is published, disseminated, stored, and used. Two of its four parts concern scholarly journals and presses. Index.

1102

Scholarly Publishing in Asia: Proceedings of the Conference of University Presses in Asia and the Pacific Area. Ed. by Shigeo Minowa and Amadio Antonio Arboleda. Tokyo: University of Tokyo Press, 1973. 172p.

". . . the (two) types of (existing) university presses, the medieval (i.e., Cambridge and Oxford models) and the modern (i.e., the American university press model) are being supplemented in certain countries by a third type, a new concept of university press," says Minowa. These proceedings—in two parts, "The Asian Experience" and "The International Experience"—discuss problems particular to 16 countries in the Asia-Pacific region and the possibilities of international cooperation. Not all countries are "developing"—for example, India, Australia, and Japan—although the rest qualify. Of particular interest is an appendix, "Report on the Formation of the Asian University Presses and Scholarly Publishers Group."

1103

Schreuders, Piet. **Paperbacks, U.S.A.: A Graphic History, 1939–1959**. San Diego, CA: Blue Dolphin, 1981. 259p.

Schreuders emphasizes that this is not intended as a history of American paperback publishing, but rather a sketch of its graphic development over the years. In his words: "It may seem to you as though you're on the wrong side of Alice's looking-glass, but in this volume the designers and artists of book **covers** will receive more attention than will authors, editors, printers, binders, distributors and salesmen." He does, however, give a 96-page history of paperbacks as background and a section of distribution of paperbacks in America. Appendixes contain a year-by-year chronology from 1929 through 1959; an overview of publishing houses, with commentary; a list of the first 100 titles; a "who's who" in cover art; and notes on collecting paperbacks. Numerous illustrations in color, a bibliography, and an index.

A Select Bibliography of Books About Books. (See No. 1692.)

1104

Simon, Rita J. **Public Opinion and the Immigrant: Print Media Coverage, 1880–1980**. Lexington, MA: D.C. Heath, 1985. 239p.

Public attitudes and beliefs about the impact of immigrants on American society, as shown in the coverage of the subject by leading magazines from 1880 to 1980, when about 30 million immigrants from diverse lands settled in the U.S. Part I is an overview: about who came when and from where; major legislation; and public opinion as shown by national polls from 1937 when they were first taken to 1980. Part II gives brief general profiles of the magazines surveyed then, in the major portion, discusses contents of articles. **New York Times** editorials

are also included. There is a chronology of major immigration legislation. Chapter notes and index.

Slide, Anthony, ed. **International Film, Radio & TV Journals**. (See No. 1480.)

1105, 1106

Smith, Datus C., Jr. **A Guide to Book Publishing**. New York: Bowker, 1966. 244p.

Smith, Datus C., Jr. **The Economics of Book Publishing in Developing Countries**. Paris: UNESCO, 1977. (Reports and Papers on Mass Communication No. 79.)

Two books which treat from different angles book publishing in developing countries. The 1966 volume deals explicitly with techniques which will help developing countries to establish book-publishing programs. It traces the various steps from beginning to end, including economics and specialized publishing, encouragement of literacy and reading development, the role of libraries, rights and contracts, and distribution, this latter encompassing retail bookstores and training. It contains a bibliography and an index.

The 1977 publication is based on the findings of a detailed survey of publishers in Africa, Asia, Latin America, and the Middle East, which pinpoints problems and gives a general picture of publishing in each of these areas. Contents include, first, an overview containing facts from the survey—manufacturing, editorial and overhead cost, list price, discount, sales income, profit, loss, and break-even point; and second, an analysis and commentary, consisting of such subjects as pricing policy and long-term planning, book development, the issues of national languages and self-sufficiency, possibilities of co-publishing, cooperation with government, and determination of greatest needs. In his preface Smith lists six books he considers basic to the subject.

1107

Smith, Roger H. **Paperback Parnassus**. Boulder, Co: Westview, 1976. 111p.

Although a number of paperback publishers have gone and others have come since the publication of **Paperback Parnassus** it remains one of the best sources for a brief summation of the structure of the industry. Appendixes give statistical tables (now out-of-date but easily updated in **Publishers Weekly**). Index.

1108

Stern, Madeleine B., ed. **Publishers for Mass Entertainment in Nineteenth Century America**. Boston: G.K. Hall, 1980. 358p.

". . . this volume—with its encyclopedic histories of publishing houses, their founders, their development, their purposes, and their achievements—is also a survey of the cheap book and its effect upon American literary taste," says Madeleine Stern in her Introduction, which in itself constitutes a brief factual history of popular reading taste in a pre-radio-TV century. Forty-five selected firms are described by contributors from academic and book publishing, and some by Stern herself, with references following each entry. It is not the aim of this book to place the popularity of this type of reading in a broader social context, but it will provide a good starting place for such an analysis.

1109

Stiehl, Ulrich. **Dictionary of Book Publishing with 12,000 Sample Sentences and Phrases, German-English**. Munich: Verlag Dokumentation, 1977. 538p.

A German-English dictionary covering books and other media (periodicals, newspapers, and audiovisual materials), authors and readers, the book industry in general, book publishing in specialized fields, book art, editing and copyright, production, marketing, and library science. Includes as examples 8,000 complete sample sentences in English and several thousand illustrative phrases drawn from various sources.

1110

Studies on Books and Reading. Paris: UNESCO, Book Promotion and International Exchanges Division. No. 1, [1981]–.

A series of research reports which vary geographically from single countries to entire continents, with statistical data and ideas about reading, book publishing and distribution:

No. 1. **The Role of Children's Books in Integrating Handicapped Children into Everyday Life**, by Tordis Orjasaeter. [1981]. 46p.

No. 2. **The Latin American Book Market: Problems and Prospects**, by Alberto E. Augsburger. 1981. 122p.

No. 3. **International Circulation of Books**, by Edward Wegman. [1981]. 29p. (See No. 1121.)

No. 4. **Promoting National Book Strategies in Asia and the Pacific: Problems and Prospectives**, Abdul Hasan. [1981]. 33p. and appendixes.

No. 5. **Book Production and Reading in the Arab World**, by Abdelkader Ben Cheikh. 1982. 50p.

No. 6. **Trends in Worldwide Book Development, 1970–1978**, by Robert Escarpit. [1982] 40p.

No. 7. **Textbook Production in Developing Countries: Some Problems of Preparation, Production and Distribution**, by Douglas Pearce. 1982. 51p.

No. 8. **The Future of the Book. Part I.: The Impact of New Technologies**, Ed. by Priscilla Oakeshott and Clive Bradley. 1982. 115p.

No. 9. **The Future of the Book. Part II: The Changing Role of Reading**. A report prepared by Michel Gauolt for the French National Commission for UNESCO, 1982. 34p.

No. 10. **Books and the Mass Media: Modes of Interaction in the USSR**, by V. D. Stelmakh. 1982. 33p.

No. 11. **Bibliography of Books for Handicapped Children**, Comp. by the International Youth Library of Munich. Part I. [1982]. 103p. Part I. [1982]. 95p.

No. 12. **Books and Reading in Bulgaria**, by Vladimir Simeonov, et al. [1983]. 53p.

No. 13. **Books and Reading in Kenya**, by Henry Chakava. [1983] 55p.

No. 14. **Le Livre et la Lecture en Yugoslavia**, by Milos Nemangic and Jovan Janicejevic. [1983] 73p.

No. 15. **Publishing and Book Development in Africa: A Bibliography**, Comp. by Hans M. Zell. 1984. 143p.

No. 16. **Books and Reading in China**, by the Publishers Association of China. [1983]. 43p.

No. 17. **Le Livre et la Lecture en Irak**. (In French and Arabic), by Nawaf Adwan. [1980–81]. 36p.

No. 18. **The Future of the Book. Part III: New Technologies in Book Distribution: The United States Experience**. Prepared for the Center for the Book, Library of Congress. 1984. 34p.

No. 19. **Books and Reading in Jamaica**, by Marlene A. Hamilton. 1984. 50p.

No. 20. **Books for Language-Retarded Children: An Annotated Bibliography**, Comp. by the International Board of Books for Young People. [1985] 114p.

No. 21. **Books and Reading in Ghana**, by S. A. Amu Djaleto. 1985. 43p.

No. 22. **Le Livre et la Lecture en Algerie**, by Mahmoud Bouayed. 1985. 43p.

No. 23. **Directory of Institutions and Organizations Specializing in Children's Literature**, Comp. by the International Board on Books for Young People. Pts. 1 and 2, 1985. 213p.

No. 24. **Le Livre et la Lecture en Roumanie**, by Joan Dragon and Angela Popescu-Brendicini. [1982–1986]. 60p.

No. 25. **Books and Reading in Tanzania**, by Walter Bgoya. [1986]. 76p.

1111

Sutherland, J.A. **Fiction and Fiction Industry**. Atlantic Highlands, NJ: Humanities Press, 1978. 231p.

In his social study of fiction, Sutherland examines the material conditions under which the contemporary English novel is produced and consumed. The first section, "Crisis and Change," considers the economic and institutional conditions under which novels are produced in both England and the U.S. The second, "State Remedies," dealing with public lending right, the Arts Council, and writers in universities, discusses England in the first two chapters and both countries in the third. The final section, "Trends, Mainly American," selects several major trends affecting both—paperbacks, packaged literature, book clubs, genre fiction, independent publishing, the telenovel. Throughout, Sutherland is always concerned with the economics of authorship, with libraries as a market, and with whether or not, in Kingsley Amis's phrase, "more makes worse." A literate and provocative book by an author who knows contemporary literature and its economic background.

1112

Sutherland, J.A. **Bestsellers: Popular Fiction of the 1970's**. London: Routledge & Kegan, 1981. 268p.

In his study of best sellers Sutherland asks: what qualities make a best seller? How do we define it? Is it antithetical to literature? Does it harm literature in the marketplace? A number of authors have set out to answer the first two and sometimes the last two—Hacket (No. 1059) among them. Now Sutherland takes on all four questions, using best sellers of the 1970s, especially those which have benefited from tie-ins with film and television, as a tool to answer some broad questions about literary culture. His approach is by "an examination of the apparatus which produces them (bestseller lists, the publishing industry, publicity)." Both British and American bestsellers are included, and are discussed in terms of authors and genres. Bibliography and index.

1113

Taubert, Sigfred. **Bibliopola: Pictures and Texts about the Book Trade**. 2 v. New York: Bowker, 1966.

Vol. I includes 306 illustrations with texts arranged by themes such as symbols of the book trade, the antiquarian bookman, the author, bookshop interiors, and even headings like "Drink" (the bibulous bookseller, with woodcut, captioned "An early specimen, this woodcut suggests that drinking is another tradition among booksellers, though less violent than the 16th century artist would have us believe"). Vol. II contains 258 plates arranged chronologically, along with an anthology of writings covering the book trade over the past 2,000 years. Text is in French and German as well as English; illustrations are charming.

1114, 1115, 1116, 1117

Tebbel, John. **History of Book Publishing in the United States**. Vol. 1. **The Creation of an Industry 1630–1865**. New York: Bowker, 1972. 646p.

Tebbel, John. **A History of Book Publishing in the United States**. Vol. 2. **The Expansion of an Industry, 1865–1919**. New York: Bowker, 1975. 813p.

Tebbel, John. **A History of Book Publishing in the United States**. Vol. 3. **The Golden Age Between the Wars, 1920–1940**. New York: Bowker, 1978. 744p.

Tebbel, John. **A History of Book Publishing in the United States**. Vol. 4. **The Great Change, 1940–1980**. New York: Bowker, 1981. 830p.

Tebbel's encyclopedic history of American book publishing traces its development from small and eclectic beginnings to its growth as a major American industry (though still small in comparison with such other American industries as automotive or food, for instance). His method is chronological and narrative; his approach, which varies somewhat from volume to volume, centers around firms, figures, and categories of subject specialization, with sections devoted to such trends and aspects as censorship, copyright, technology, advertising, graphics, etc. Vols. 1 and 2 each have appendixes: "American Book Title Output, 1880–1918," "A Graphic Survey of Book Publication," and "Directories of Publishers, 1888, 1900, 1919," "An Economic Review of Book Publishing, 1915–1945," "**PW** Profiles of Children's Editors," by Muriel Fuller and "Best Sellers, 1920–1940." All volumes are fully indexed. In his Preface to the fourth volume Tebbel describes in broad terms major sources of research into the book industry. All chapters contain notes, and all volumes are fully indexed. This is a formidable addition to the literature of book publishing in the U.S. and a valuable reference tool. In addition it contains vignettes about various colorful personalities which make good reading. **Between Covers: The Rise and Transformation of Book Publishing in America**, is a one-volume edition of this larger work.

1118

Tymn, Marshall B., and Mike Ashley, eds. **Science Fiction, Fantasy, and Weird Fiction Magazines**. Westport, CT: Greenwood, 1985. 970p.

An extensive analytical and historically focused bibliography which extends from 1882 to the early 1980s. Its purpose is "to provide scholars, researchers and the general reader with a useful tool for evaluating the science fiction, fantasy and weird fiction magazines as a historical and literary phenomenon, and to furnish a bibliographic apparatus for documenting the appearance of these magazines in all their various phases." It is divided into four sections: Section I contains all of the important and most of the less significant English-language magazines (279 titles); Section II, anthology series (15 titles); Section III, Academic periodicals and major fanzines (72 titles); and Section IV, non-English language magazines, by country (184 titles). Two appendixes include an index to major cover artists and a chronology by founding date. Comprehensive data is given for each periodical, including a narrative on the magazine's history and development, basic details of its publication history, location sources, and sources for further information. In each section, periodicals are listed alphabetically. A name/subject index provides general access to titles in Sections I, II, and III, but not to the non-English magazines in Section IV. In conclusion is a bibliography of indexes, surveys and histories.

1119

Vaughan, Samuel S. **Medium Rare: A Look at the Book and Its People**. New York: Bowker, 1977. 39p. (Fourth of the R.R. Bowker Memorial Lectures, New Series, November 4, 1976.)

Are too many books published? What are the book's unique characteristics? Will it survive in competition with other media? What is its role in journalism, history, politics? The author brings his long experience in book publishing and his knowledge of communication history and theory to bear as he speculates on these questions. Bibliography.

1120

Walker, Gregory. **Soviet Book Publishing Policy**. Cambridge, England: Cambridge University Press, 1978. 164p.

An examination of the operations and management of the vast Soviet publishing industry in the light of governmental policy and its effects on creation, content, production, manufacture, and distribution. Appendixes give authors' fee scales and all-union book retail prices. There are notes, a bibliography, and an index.

1121

Wegman, Edward. **International Circulation of Books**. Paris: UNESCO, 1982. 29p. (Studies in Books and Reading No. 3.)

An examination of ". . . the position of books in the service of international understanding and international trade in books, including distribution networks and problems. It then turns to the standards that have been set and other measures to liberalize the flow of books." Introduction. A long list of various kinds of information is given: facts and figures on production, exports and imports, and trade by category of book; distribution networks and problems, such as rights, language, transport charges, and quotas and frontier formalities; brief descriptions of agreements that set standards, such as the Berne and Universal Copyright Convention; and measures to ease the flow of books, such as GATT, UNCTAD, the UNESCO Coupon Scheme, the Universal Postal Union, the International Air Transport Association, government initiatives, and activities by book professionals. Contains a select bibliography.

1122

West, Celeste, ed. **Words in Our Pockets: The Feminist Writers' Guild Handbook on How to Gain Power, Get Published, & Get Paid**. Paradise, CA: Dustbooks, 1985. 361p.

Works in Our Pockets, says Celeste West, "is about becoming a writer in a world women never scripted. (It is not about how to write; there are countless books on technique.)" Rather, she continues, "it is a women writer's survival chest; a collection of spiritual and economic tools. More than forty women discuss their craft from 'submission' to revolution; the passion, the philosophy, the adventure, the magnificent absurdity of it all." The 40 essays—all, of course, by women—are grouped under "Finding Your Way Around Establishment Publishing," "Women's Publishing," "A Spectrum of Genres," and "The Community of the Book & Our Support System." This is both informational and inspirational. Some of the articles contain bibliographies, and there is an index.

1123

White, Cynthia Leslie. **Women's Magazines, 1963–1968**. London: Michael Joseph, 1971. 348p.

A sociological study of women's magazines in Britain, tracing their growth as an industry and relating their character and function to economic change. A final chapter of 25 pages is devoted to the women's press in the U.S. The major part of the text is taken from the author's doctoral thesis at the University of London. Contains a number of appendixes giving circulation charts and graphs. There is a bibliography and an index.

1124

Whiteside, Thomas. **The Blockbuster Complex: Conglomerates, Show Business, and Book Publishing**. Middletown, CT: Wesleyan University Press, 1980. 207p.

In the 1960s trade book publishing, which had always been considered "a gentleman's profession," half literature, half trade, underwent drastic changes to de-emphasize literature and emphasize trade. Here Whiteside describes these changes, the reasons behind them, and the results as book publishing was metamorphosed from small, often family-held and distinguished firms characterized by a concern for the arts into a part of the conglomerate structure. Whiteside's style is smooth and elegant as he creates from the nitty-gritty of the transformation an absorbing but sad story, which first appeared in the **New Yorker**. Although an accurate, well-researched and valuable profile of an industry it is not the sort of academic publication that carries references. The book, however, is indexed.

Who's Who in the Press, 1985–86. (See No. 980.)

Wolseley, Roland E., and Isabel Wolseley. **The Journalist's Bookshelf**. (See No. 1708.)

1125

World Congress on Books. 2pts. Paris: UNESCO, 1982. 22pp.

In two parts: **International Book Year Plus Ten** and **Toward a Reading Society: Targets for the 80s**. The first of these is an analysis of present trends and forecasts for the future such as problems facing governments and all who are concerned with the production and distribution of books in an increasingly complex and interdependent world. The second takes into consideration the results of national and international action over the past two years, puts forward measures to overcome the obstacles to book development identified in the first part, and proposes a new program.

1126

Worpole, Ken. **Reading by Numbers: Contemporary Publishing and Popular Fiction**. London: Comedie, 1984. 119p. (Comedia series, No. 22.)

Worpole is obviously a confirmed reader who knows the publishing industry, literature, and the history of the book—all of which he brings together in an eclectic collection of essays about the book trade. But unlike most scholars who tend toward a dim view of the future for works of literary merit in today's highly commercial market, he seems quite comfortable, regarding the trend away from literary value as merely another in a long series of developments. Topics he discusses are "Books, Money and Meanings," "The Best Seller Industry," "Why Romance?," "Watching the Detectives," "Rediscovering Rhyme," "Childhood Dreams and Stories," "The Price on the Cover," "The Rules of the Distribution Game," and "Literature: Garden or Workshop?" Although his orientation is British, his remarks are pertinent to book publishing and reading in general. Chapter notes.

1127

Zell, Hans M., and Carol Bundy, eds. **The African Book World & Press: A Directory**. 3d ed. Munich, Germany: Hans Zell Publishers (an import of K.G. Saur), 1983. 285p.

The editors attempt to provide "comprehensive, accurate and up-to-date information, in both English and French, on libraries, publishers and the retail book trade, research institutions with publishing programs, book industry and literary associations, major periodicals and newspapers, government as well as commercial printers, throughout Africa, South Africa excepted for the last name group." In all, 4,621 institutions and organizations are represented. Data varies according to the type of organization or institution and completeness and accuracy also vary because, the editors tell us, 45 percent of addresses failed to update their entries or return the questionnaire. These cases are indicated with a dagger or asterisk. Even so, it provides a formidable amount of information. Librarians proved the best respondents; consequently data about libraries is more likely to be the most complete. Arrangement is alphabetical by county.

Appendixes include a subject index to special libraries and to periodicals and magazines, and listings of book clubs, awards and principal dealers in African books in Europe and the U.S. Text is in English and French.

Film

4

1128

Adair, Gilbert. **Vietnam on Film: From the Green Berets to Apocalypse Now**. New York: Proteus, 1981. 192p.

An analysis of war films produced in the U.S., made during the 1960s and 1970s and centering upon Vietnam. An introductory chapter, "Apocalypse Then," discusses earlier war films. Many illustrations, a filmography, and a title index.

1129

Aldgate, Anthony, and Jeffrey Richards. **Britain Can Take It: The British Cinema in the Second World War**. London: Blackwell, 1986. 312p.

Through detailed examination of 11 key films made in England during World War II the authors show the relationship between the official propagandists and the filmmakers and demonstrate the role of the movies in maintaining British morale. An opening chapter discusses the overall effect of the war on the British film industry. Chapter notes and a filmography for the 11 films analyzed. Index.

1130

Allan, Elkan. **A Guide to World Cinema**. London: Whittet Books in association with the British Film Institute, 1985. 682p.

Includes the programs of the National Film Theatre, London, covering the 7,200 films shown there between 1950 through 1984. For each film there is a still, a brief synopsis, the country of origin, the date, the director, and for some, the outstanding members of the cast. Arrangement is by title, with an index of directors.

1131

Allen, Nancy. **Film Study Collections: A Guide to Their Development and Use**. New York: Ungar, 1979. 194p.

A comprehensive guide to film study resources, intended for librarians and scholars, which covers such aspects as the relationship between university film study programs and supporting libraries; a descriptive list of major U.S. collections of film study documentation; information on publishers who specialize in film books and other materials; and film reference services, including recommendations on building a basic collection, the impact of computer technologies on film services, and a list of accessible data bases. Special features are a survey of some 100 university libraries, detailing size and description of their film study collection, especially unpublished filmscripts, and a cataloging/classification scheme for film-related materials by Michael Gorman. There is also a bibliography of 100 titles and an index.

1132

Allen, Robert C., and Douglas Gomery. **Film History: Theory and Practice**. New York: Knopf, 1985. 276p.

This discussion of methodological approaches to the historical study of film is intended as a text to enable the student to place film history within the context of historical research in general; acquaint the reader with problems confronting film historians; survey the approaches that have been taken; and provide examples of various types of historical research. Focus is on American film. Chapter notes, comprehensive bibliographical essay by chapters, and an index.

Alvarez, Max Joseph. **Index to Motion Pictures Reviewed by** *Variety*, **1907–1980**, see *Variety* Film Reviews (No. 1797).

1133

The American Film Institute Guide to College Courses in Film and Television. Ed. by Charles Granada, Jr., and Margaret G. Butt. 7th ed. Princeton, NJ: Peterson's Guides, 1980. 334p.

An alphabetical list of U.S. colleges offering television and/or film curricula, with pertinent details followed by names and addresses of foreign schools; grants and scholarships; student film/video festivals and awards; a selected list of film and video centers; national and international organizations; a directory of useful information on careers, and indexes of graduate degrees by state and of degrees offered by state and indexes of types of degrees offered by state, and a general index. Even though this is now almost a decade out of date, curricula do not change rapidly, so that much is still pertinent. The publishers have no plans to update.

1134, 1135

American Screenwriters. Ed. by Robert Morsberger, Stephen O. Lesser, and Randall Clark. Detroit, MI: Gale, 1984. 382p. (Dictionary of Literary Biography, Vol. 26.)

American Screenwriters. Ed. by Randall Clark. 2d series. Detroit, MI: Gale, 1986. 464p. (Dictionary of Literary Biography, Vol. 44.)

Companion volumes containing career studies and biographies of a total of 129 writers who wrote primarily for the screen, selected as representative samples "of the hundreds of screenwriters who have worked in Hollywood, ranging from the artistically important to the commercially successful to the relatively obscure." Each entry begins with a list of credits, including television plays; continues with an analytical discussion of the screenwriter's body of works; and ends with a bibliography which in some cases includes letters, interviews and papers as well as books and articles. Entries are written by specialists and accompanied by excellent illustrations.

1136

Anderson, Joseph I., and Donald Richie. **The Japanese Film: Art and Industry**. Rutland, VT: Charles Tuttle, 1959. 456p.

This book, written at the end of a decade during which Westerners had first become aware of Japanese films, is the first full study to appear about films in a foreign language. The first portion deals in chronological fashion with its structure and development, technologically and socially; the second with the content, technique, directors, actors and actresses and theaters and audiences. There are many plates, and two charts: the first, "Directors as Pupils and Teachers," is designed to show the recruiting and training of directorial talent in Japan; the second, "Development at Major Companies," traces the origin and development of all important production companies since the introduction of motion pictures into Japan. Index.

1137, 1138

Andrew, J. Dudley. **Concepts in Film Theory**. New York: Oxford, 1984. 239p.

Andrew, J. Dudley. **The Major Film Theories**. New York: Oxford, 1976. 278p.

In his introduction to **Concepts in Film Theory**, Andrew says of this and his earlier book, **The Major Film Theories**: "In **The Major Film Theories** I gave attention to several powerful individual thinkers who constructed complete views of the cinema. In writing now about contemporary theory, I find it far more useful and honest to treat key concepts rather than key personalities and to build an overall view of film based on positions taken in relation to those concepts, specifically to perception, representation, signification, narrative structure, adaptation, evaluation, identification, figuration, and interpretation. Why have these issues come to dominate our era in film theory? More important, why has a method based on such reflective concepts dominated other, more direct approaches to film?" This is the matter Andrew treats and the questions he sets out to answer. Chapter notes, a classified bibliography and an index.

Annual Index to Motion Picture Arts and Credits. (See No. 1715.)

1139

Armes, Roy. **A Critical History of the British Film**. New York: Oxford, 1978. 374p.

"The primary aim of this present history—in addition to providing a synthesis of the available knowledge—is . . . to provide a genuinely critical perspective on eighty years of British filmmaking," says Armes, who uses a chronological framework to illustrate the economic and cultural factors which have shaped the British film, both entertainment and documentary, over this period. He relates its social functions, defined largely in terms of economic structure, and the artistic achievements of its individual filmmakers (colored by their personal beliefs and values) to the enormous technological changes that have taken place and the particular formal pattern of communication which has become dominant—the narrative structure of the 90 minute feature film. Notes, bibliography, and index.

1140, 1141

Armes, Roy. **French Cinema**. London: Secker & Warburg, 1985. 310p.

Armes, Roy. **French Cinema Since 1946**. Vol. I, **The Great Tradition**; Vol. II, **The Personal Style**. New York: Barnes, 1966.

Armes says of **French Cinema**: "This present book attempts an analogous history of French cinema, setting out to offer a study of the successive styles of film production adopted by groups of filmmakers in response to changing theoretical conceptions of cinema and differing economic, social and cultural circumstances." Arrangement is chronological, with period divisions determined by the internal economic developments of production, distribution and control within the industry, or on occasion, coinciding with national and world events. In selecting the films to exemplify styles or trends he has chosen works which have attracted critical attention for their artistic merit.

His earlier **French Cinema Since 1946** is a critical survey centered around the creative role of the director and of the film as a narrative medium like novels and plays, rather than strictly visual. Contains filmographies, with credits for directors and a bibliography for each. Both volumes are indexed.

1142

Arnheim, Rudolf. **Film as Art**. Berkeley: University of California Press, 1957. 230p.

A collection of Arnheim's writings from the 1930s. In the first part, or major portion, of the essays Arnheim explores the relationship between reality and art as demonstrated by the motion picture—"to show how the very properties that make photography and film fall short of perfect reproduction can act at the necessary molds of an artistic medium." In the final portion he discusses the properties of television and talking pictures.

1143, 1144

Aros, Andrew A. **A Title Guide to the Talkies, 1975 through 1984**. (As conceived by Richard B. Dimmitt.) Metuchen, NJ: Scarecrow, 1986. 347p.

Aros, Andrew A. **A Title Guide to the Talkies, 1964 through 1974**. (As conceived by Richard B. Dimmitt.) Metuchen, NJ: Scarecrow, 1977. 336p.

The two recent volumes build on the earlier work, **A Title Guide to the Talkies: A Comprehensive Listing of 16,000 Feature-Length Films from October, 1927 until December, 1963**, compiled by Richard B. Dimmitt and published in two volumes (2,133p.) by Scarecrow in 1965. The primary purpose of this series is to give the origins of the screenplay from which the talkie was derived. In the two latter editions, novels written from screenplays are also identified, foreign films exhibited in this country have been included, and in addition to the distribution company, year of general release, pagination, and director's name have been given when available. Arrangement is alphabetical by titles, with an index of proper names.

Austin, Bruce A. **The Film Audience: An International Bibliography of Research with Annotations and an Essay**. (See No. 1636.)

Austin, Bruce A., ed. **Current Research in Film: Audiences, Economics, and Law**. (See No. 1742.)

1145

Auty, Martyn, and Nick Roddick, eds. **British Cinema Now**. London: BFI Publishing, 1985. 168p.

An attempt, say the editors, "to avoid the twin poles of much (British) film writing, which has veered from the gushingly aesthetic to the snottily dismissive, and to fill the gap in writing on British cinema between history (of which there is plenty) and sociological analysis (of which there is too much.)" Against the background of "an industry simultaneously renascent and in crisis," contributors look at the varying contexts of film production—government policy or lack of it, finance, production, distribution, independent filmmaking, ideology. Chapter notes and index.

1146

Babitsky, Paul, and John Rimberg. **The Soviet Film Industry**. New York: Praeger, 1955. 377p.

Shows the principal steps by which the Communist party consolidated its power over the Soviet motion picture industry; gives the economic base and central administration; discusses scenarios and writers, imports and exports, and production under the five-year plan; and makes a quantitative content analysis of heroes and villains in Soviet films, 1923–50.

1147

Baechlin, Peter, and Maurice Muller-Strausse. **Newsreels across the World**. New York: UNESCO Publications Center, 1952. 100p.

"This book seeks to present an objective, worldwide survey of news films as they are today, and the problems they raise—from the production of the actual newsreels to the projection on the cinema. It deals both with international organization for production and exhibition of newsreels and with the machinery for exchange of newsreels between countries. It was also considered useful to include an analysis of the impact of television and certain types of documentary films upon the newsreel industry."—Preface. Its thoroughness, its international scope, and the scarcity of other materials on the subject make it extremely valuable for this aspect of communication. Contains a bibliography and an index.

1148

Bálázs, Bela. **Theory of the Film: Character and Growth of a New Art**. Tr. from the Hungarian by Edith Bone. New York: Dover, 1970. 291p.

Bálázs was one of the first major film theorists, beginning his writings in the 1920s. Much of his work has not been translated; this one, his last, sums and brings into focus his other works, in all of which he searches for an aesthetic of film art. Index.

1149

Balio, Tino, ed. **The American Film Industry**. Rev. ed. Madison: University of Wisconsin Press, 1985. 664p.

A systematic survey of the history of the film industry, this extensively revised book of readings discusses the range of factors—economics, legal restraints, technological advances, studio organization and procedures, financing, distribution trade practices, and exhibitor preferences—which have influenced the form and content of the movies. Organization is chronological. Part I describes the period from 1894 to 1908 when motion pictures changed from a novelty into a business. Parts II and III, from 1908 through 1948, discuss the growth of the industry into an oligarchy, and its behavior and organization. Part IV (1948 to the present) describes certain monumental developments and the effects on the industry—i.e., the Supreme Court's Paramount decision, the witch hunt of the House Un-American Committee, and the competition of foreign exports and television. It is intended as a collateral text for undergraduate courses dealing with the development of American film. Contains a bibliography of books and articles, an index of motion picture titles and a general index.

1150

Ballantyne, James. **Researcher's Guide to British Newsreels**. London: British Universities Film and Video Council, 1983. 119p.

Abstracts of articles, books and pamphlets about the British newsreel in particular and cinemagazines incidentally, arranged chronologically to chart their genesis, development and eventual demise. Along with serious articles, the author has listed popular comments and brief trade notices to help build an overall picture of how the newsreel companies operated and how the reels were and are regarded. A listing of pertinent information follows, including such information as organizations; newsreel companies and their staffs; libraries and archives; and a list of films and videos about the British newsreels. There is a subject index to the abstracts.

This is a companion volume to **Researcher's Guide to British Film and Television Collections**, edited by Elizabeth Oliver. (See No. 1446.)

1151

Bardeche, Maurice, and Robert Brasillach. **The History of Motion Pictures**. Ed. and tr. by Iris Barry. New York: Norton and Museum of Modern Art, 1938. 412p.

This classic "attempts to survey the entire history of filmmaking in Europe and in America and to describe the exchange of influences to which the film as a whole has been subject. That it surveys the field from a European angle, even from a distinctly French angle, rather than from our own native viewpoint, makes it a useful check on other accounts of this art-industry."—John E. Abbott, director of the Museum of Modern Art Film Library. Beginning in 1895, it encompasses prewar and World War I films; the emergence of film as an art (1919–23); the silent film (1923–29); the talking film (1929–35); the film as a world industry; and, in conclusion, a summary of 40 years of film, "The Music of Images." There is also an editorial postscript for the years 1935–38, an index to film titles, and a general index.

1152

Barnes, John. **The Beginnings of Cinema in England**. New York: Barnes & Noble, 1976. 240p.

Combining information gathered from the literature of the time with that obtained by direct examination of surviving apparatus and films, Barnes has pieced together the two years from October 1894 to the end of 1896, when film grew from a single Kinetoscope parlor in London into a main attraction in major music halls of Great Britain. There are detailed discussions with illustrations of the early technology and its inventors. Appendixes include a catalog of news, nonfiction, and fiction films made during the two-year period, again with illustrations; a chronology; notes; an index of films; and a general index.

1153

Barnouw, Erik. **Documentary: A History of the Non-Fiction Film**. Rev. ed. New York: Oxford University Press, 1983. 360p.

Traces the documentary over almost a century from its beginnings in the 1890s into the 1980s. Barnouw follows it in the leading centers where it is made, showing its various forms such as direct cinema, *cinema verite*, and the TV documentary; its well-known creators; its subject matter—exploration, animals, aspects of war, human behavior, social problems, propaganda—and its recent technological breakthroughs, including video cassettes and cable TV. He lays special stress on the attempts of governments and large corporations to influence and control content. Contains chapter notes, a bibliography and an index.

1154

Barnouw, Erik, and Subrahmanyam Krishnaswamy. **Indian Film**. New York: Columbia University Press, 1963. 301p.

Development of the motion picture industry in India—its economics structure, its censorship problems, its content.

1155

Barr, Charles, ed. **All Our Yesterdays: 90 Years of British Cinema**. London: BFI Publishing in association with the Museum of Modern Art, 1986. 446p.

A series of essays which trace British film history by bringing together "a number of *diachronic* studies of particular traditions and other aspects and strands of British national cinema, tracing them through the decades," and exploring the connections between cinema and other media: theater, literature, music hall, broadcasting. In doing so it deals with the relation of the film industry and the state; the realist and non-realist conceptions of cinema; and divergent strands such as independent cinema, animation, regional, "underworld films." There is also a set of shorter, illustrative case studies. An appendix lists and gives brief information about all films mentioned in the text. Chapter notes, a short bibliography and a general index.

1156

Barsam, Richard Meran. **Nonfiction Film: A Critical History**. New York: Dutton, 1973. 332p.

Barsam chronicles the documentary in terms of personalities, trends and the films themselves, starting with "The American, Russian, and Continental Beginnings" and concluding with "The New Nonfiction Film: 1960–1970." Major emphasis is on films produced in the U.S. and Great Britain, and on "idea" films which attempt to pose solutions to major social problems, with discussion and analysis on content rather than technique. Within these limitations he has set about to establish certain basic traditions and to locate major films in their own tradition where applicable and in their own time frame. Omitted are discussions of films of the USIA and UNESCO, and films made for television, although there is reference to them in the extensive bibliography. Two appendixes: "Production Facts on Major Films," and "Major Nonfiction and Documentary Awards." Index.

1157

Basinger, Jeanine. **The World War II Combat Film: Anatomy of a Genre**. New York: Columbia University Press, 1986. 373p.

A history of World War II combat films, based on a study of the films themselves, which traces their origin and evolution and indicates important information about the system that produced them, the individuals who created them, and the technological developments that changed them. In a larger context it presents an analytical approach to one genre, particularly one with a specific beginning point in film history, and by tracing it forward in time, sheds light on the larger topic of genre itself. Basinger includes an "Annotated Chronological Filmography of World War II and Korean Combat Films" from December 7, 1941 through 1980." An appendix lists "Selected Titles Relevant to Prior History of World War II Combat Films." Notes, a bibliography, a film index and an extensive subject index.

1158

Batille, Gretchen M., and Charles L. P. Silet, eds. **The Pretend Indians: Images of Native Americans in the Movies**. Ames: Iowa State University Press, 1980. 202p.

An anthology containing 25 reprints of articles and film reviews, all by authorities, grouped under four headings: "The Native American: Myth and Media Stereotyping," "The Indian in the Film: Early Views," "The Indian in the Film: Later Views," and "Contemporary Reviews," with an additional non-print section, "Photographic Essays on the American Indian as Portrayed by Hollywood," and followed by a 17-page annotated checklist of articles and books. Vine Deloria has written the introduction, and each section has a short to-the-point introduction by the editors. All in all this is a wonderfully comprehensive, authoritative and interesting coverage of

the subject on which a number of articles but few books exist.

1159

Batty, Linda, comp. **Retrospective Index to Film Periodicals 1930–1971**. New York: Bowker, l975. 425p.

"Indexed herein are the entire contents of fourteen English-language film journals from their beginnings through December 1971, plus the film reviews and articles from **Village Voice**. Selection . . . was based on the author's judgment of their excellence, coverage, and lasting interest."—Preface. Articles are divided into three sections: "Index to Reviews of Individual Films," "Index of Film Subjects," containing names of directors and actors and actresses among other topics, and "Index to Book Review Citations." All entries list date, volume number and pagination of articles; the subject index gives a brief annotation. The 14 periodicals covered are among those in the yearly **International Index to Film Periodicals** (No. 1928) which begins in 1972 where Batty leaves off.

1160, 1161

Baxter, John. **The Gangster Film**. New York: Barnes, 1970. 160p.

Baxter, John. **Science Fiction in the Cinema**. New York: Barnes, 1970. 240p.

Two books on film genres, each with a different approach. **The Gangster Film**, defined by Baxter as "films that deal, even in a general way, with **organized** as opposed to conventional crime," is a reference-type work, listing actors, directors, and others engaged in the production of gangster films, with a "who's who" type of information and filmographies where pertinent, along with some subject information—e.g., Private Detectives, and Saint Valentine's Day Massacre. **Science Fiction in the Cinema**, on the other hand, surveys the genre on an international scope, dealing with its history, its themes, and some of its best-known examples along with their actors, directors and producers. Beginning with the very early **A Trip to the Moon (Le Voyage dans la Lune)**, a 16-minute production, and H.G. Wells' **First Men in the Moon**, Baxter concludes with **2001: A Space Odyssey**, and a note on science fiction for television. He points out the different attitudes toward science in cinema science fiction and in written science fiction. **The Gangster Film** has an index; **Science Fiction in the Cinema** has a short bibliography and a selected filmography.

1162

Bazin, André. **What Is Cinema?** Essays Selected and tr. by Hugh Grey. 2 v. Berkeley: University of California Press, 1967. 176p.; 200p.

Bazin, a film critic and early realist theorist, laid the groundwork for much of the theory that followed. This two-volume edition of his essays is a selection from his influential four-volume **Qu'est-ce que le cinéma?**, published shortly before his death. Index.

1163

Beattie, Eleanor. **A Handbook of Canadian Films.** Toronto: Peter Martin, 1973. 280p.

The author describes this as "an attempt to bring together and to make accessible all information about film and filmmaking in Canada." It is in essence a directory, but with a lengthy introduction which gives a history and analysis. About half of the contents is taken up with information about Canadian filmmakers—a brief biography, a filmography, and a bibliography. Following are sections on writing and writers; actors; music in films; film people; emerging filmmakers; professional associations; film societies; film study centers; media and film courses; children's films; video and community film; film festivals and competitions; cooperative distribution and production; technical equipment and services; technical information and assistance; film and photography archives; educational material; film collectives; trade journals and periodicals; directories and film catalogs; addresses; a bibliography; and an index of films.

1164, 1165

Beaver, Frank E. **Dictionary of Film Terms.** New York: McGraw-Hill, 1983. 383p.

Beaver, Frank E. **On Film: A History of the Motion Picture.** New York: McGraw-Hill, 1983. 530p.

Through definition, explanation, and when applicable illustration, Beaver's **Dictionary of Film Terms** defines terms relevant to both the contemporary and historical cinema. Emphasis is on the aesthetic, although technological terminology has been incorporated. A bonus is an extensive chronological outline of film history. Entries are cross-referenced to other relevant entries, and there are a "Term and Film Title Index" and a "Topical Index."

In **On Film . . .** his intention is "to trace the development and progress of an art form that was born of technological innovation, nurtured by commercial enterprise, and brought to full stature by a host of international visionaries: directors, producers, studio chieftains, cinematographers, editors, performers, and writers." Primary focus is on their aesthetic and stylistic contributions, with particular emphasis given to the ones who helped to discover the language and syntax of cinema and those who stood apart as important individualists. Coverage is extensive. There are suggested readings following each chapter, a glossary, and an index.

1166

Behind the Scenes: Equal Employment Opportunity in the Motion Picture Industry. Washington, DC: U.S. Commission on Civil Rights, 1978. 48p.

A report, prepared by the California Advisory Committee, which explains the background of the film industry in terms of the work force, unions, and the hiring process; discusses the Equal Employment Opportunity Commission Hearings in 1969; analyzes the major studies in terms of affirmative action and the effort being made by the federal government to enforce it; and concludes with findings and recommendations. Appendixes list producers of TV prime time shows in 1977 and give a table, "Contract Services Administration Trust Fund, Industry Experience Rosters."

Bennett, Tony, et al., eds. **Popular Television and Film.** (See No. 503.)

1167

Bergan, Roger. **Sports in the Movies.** London: Proteus, 1982. 160p.

On the theory that sports are an integral element of social life which illuminate much of the character of a people and that "their depiction in the movies, aside from purely entertainment value, provides insights into the psychology of a nation," Bergen has analyzed them as a genre from as far back as the 1920s to the present. Classifying them by specific sport—boxing, football, baseball, riding, driving, the Olympics, tennis, golf, soccer, rugby, cricket, hunting, shooting, fishing, basketball, wrestling, water sports, and so on—he discusses the films within each category, and he also discusses themes and treatment as they relate to society. In the introduction, he treats the subject as a whole. After each chapter is a list of films with relevant data and a brief annotation for each. Many illustrations and an index of films mentioned.

1168

Bergman, Andrew. **We're in the Money: Depression America and Its Films.** New York: New York University Press, 1971. 200p.

What was there about movies in the 1930s which drew audiences in droves when money was scarce? Obviously they represented cheap entertainment in bad times, but Bergman assumes that the need went deeper and sees Depression films as a serious reflection of a specific time and culture. In this context he examines the intent of the producer and the relationship between audience, society and filmmaker. Part One covers trends in 1930–1933 films—gangster and shyster films, comedies, sex, musicals; Part Two covers 1933–1939 with variations of the same types and several of the most prominent producers—Warner Brothers, King Vidor, Frank Capra. Chapter notes; a list of the many films Bergman viewed, and a bibliography of books and articles. Index.

1169

Berton, Pierre. **Hollywood's Canada: The Americanization of Our National Image.** Toronto: McClelland and Steward, 1975. 303p.

A well-known Canadian writer has documented and

analyzed the 575 films Hollywood has set, although not necessarily made, in Canada and has found them to be stereotyped, distorted, and narrow in their focus upon the North Woods and Mounted Police almost exclusively. His conclusion is that Canada has been exploited financially and culturally. An appendix lists "Hollywood Movies about Canada." Includes notes and a name-title index.

1170

Bertrand, Ina, and Diane Collins. **Government and Film in Australia**. Sydney: Currency Press and the Australian Film Institute, 1981. 200p.

Two Australian film historians collaborate on this retrieval of the shifting and often stormy relationship between filmmakers and government—a period of half a century, beginning with the 1920s, which set the conditions, by default and otherwise, in which films could or could not be made or, if made, seen or not seen. Chapter notes, a bibliography and an index.

1171

Besas, Peter. **Behind the Spanish Lens: Spanish Cinema under Fascism and Democracy**. Denver, CO: Arden Press, 1985. 291p.

Using a chronological approach, Besas writes about the Spanish cinema in terms of its directors. Although his orientation is focused primarily on the film as art, he does not neglect the important role played by its socio-economic and political background which, he says, has always influenced films made in Spain. He explains that he has gone into this in more depth than he might otherwise have done because this is the first book on the Spanish cinema written in English and intended for an English-speaking audience. For the same reason he has included material intended to give readers a better insight into and "feel" for the country. There is a filmography of directors interviewed, a selected bibliography which in all but a few cases includes Spanish works, and an index.

1172

Birkos, Alexander S., comp. **Soviet Cinema: Directors and Films**. Hamden, CT: Archon, 1976. 344p.

On one level this book may be regarded as a reference guide to films and careers of Russian filmmakers from 1918 to the mid-seventies; on another level the abstracts of the films give insight into the Russian political thought and value system. In two alphabetical sections: the first lists films released during the period covered and describes content, critical reception, and often political manifestations; the second lists all directors by name and gives brief career histories and titles of their films. Many cross references bring both sections together. A 14-page introduction surveys the history of Soviet film after 1918. Contains a list of Soviet film studios and a selected annotated bibliography.

1173

Björkman, Stig. **Film in Sweden: The New Directors**. London: Tantivy, 1977. 127p.

In the 1960s Sweden enacted a subsidy which resulted in a number of films of high artistic quality, until the 1970s when financial assistance was modified and weakened. Björkman writes a history of outstanding filmmakers and their films during that decade when he feels a high artistic quality was reached which could not be achieved again because of the strained resources of the 70s. He prefaces his discussion with a Foreword explaining briefly but in detail the economic structure of Swedish film. Contains filmographies.

1174

Bluestone, George. **Novels Into Film**. Berkeley: University of California Press, 1957. 237p.

In this broad and theoretical study Bluestone "begins by finding resemblances between novel and film and ends by loudly proclaiming their differences." The 64-page initial chapter, "The Limits of the Novel and the Limits of the Film," is a comprehensive survey of relevant aesthetic principles; the next six chapters each analyze a well-known film of the times made from a novel: "The Informer," "Wuthering Heights," "Pride and Prejudice," "The Grapes of Wrath," "The Ox-Bow Incident," and "Madame Bovary." Although time has brought cultural changes since Bluestone made his study—for example, the Production Code which in the 1950s was a powerful factor in transition from book to novel is negligible today—his conclusions that the movie takes on an entity of its own still holds. "Selected Bibliography" and index.

1175

Bogle, Donald. **Toms, Coons, Mulattoes, Mammies and Bucks: An Interpretative History of Blacks in American Films**. New York: Viking, 1973. 260p.

The author, himself black, has screened and researched every film he could find in which black actors appeared from 1905 to the early 1970s. His purpose is not only to ferret out facts but also to appraise the performances they gave, and he concludes that "the essence of black film history is not found in the stereotyped role but in what certain talented actors have done for the stereotype, showing how they progressed from jester to servants to militants." There are many illustrations and a name-title index.

1176

Bondanella, Peter. **Italian Cinema: From Neorealism to the Present**. New York: Ungar, 1983. 440p.

An analysis of major trends in the Italian cinema which assesses what the author feels to be "its many, many achievements and sometimes spectacular failures." While Bondanella has provided general economic trends within the industry, he has primarily written about Italian cinema as an art form, with the director playing the key role, and has linked the films to Italian literature and social problems. Contains chapter notes, a selected bibliography, rental information on sources for Italian film, and an index.

1177, 1178

Bordwell, David, Janet Staiger, and Kristin Thompson. **The Classical Hollywood Cinema: Film Style & Mode of Production to 1960.** New York: Columbia University Press, 1985. 506p.

Bordwell, David, and Kristin Thompson. **Film Art: An Introduction.** 2d ed. New York: Knopf, 1986. 400p.

The Classical Hollywood Cinema expounds the theory that filmmaking is a blend of aesthetic norms and modes of production, each interacting with the other. The authors have examined in detail Hollywood filmmaking from 1917 to 1960 to isolate the elements of film style and the economic, technological and social factors which mutually shaped them over four decades. A final section, "Since 1960: The Persistence of a Mode of Film Practice," suggests the historical influence and the current state of this mode of film practices, and considers alternative modes. Appendixes include the sample of films examined; "A Brief Synopsis of the Structure of the American Film Industry;" "Principle Structure of the U.S. Film Industry," this time in chart form; and "Lighting Plots and Descriptions," showing how lighting can be used to achieve special effects. There are 64 pages of chapter notes, a lengthy bibliography, and an index.

Film Art is an introduction to the aesthetics of film intended for students, both beginning and advanced (a text for the former and an outline of principles, issues, and concepts and suggestions for the latter). The approach emphasizes film as an artifact—made in particular ways, having a certain wholeness and unity, existing in history—and is divided into sections stressing production, form, style, history, and methods of critical analysis. A history section includes Japan, Germany, France, the U.S.S.R. and Italy as well as the U.S. Contains many stills throughout, a glossary, a bibliography, several reference books with rental sources, and a name/subject index.

1179

Brady, Anna, comp. and ed. **Union List of Film Periodicals: Holdings of Selected American Collections.** Westport, CT: Greenwood, 1984. 316p.

The aim of this union list is to give subject and title access to film periodicals by identifying relevant ones, locating them historically and geographically, and supplying information as to where these can be accessed either through on-site visits or interlibrary loan. Al-
though the list is extensive, the compiler says that it is not definitive; some libraries were unable to participate, and of the 39 who did, not all gave complete holdings, and sometimes information is incomplete. Nonetheless, the list is formidable. Bibliographic information for each title is as full as possible, indicating any changes in title; country of publication; ISSN number if available; publication dates; appropriate notes; and as complete as possible data for holdings. There is an index of title changes and a geographic index.

1180

The British Film Catalogue 1895–1985: A Reference Guide. Ed. by Denis Gifford. New York: Facts on File, 1986. Unpaged.

A vast though unpaged compilation which includes "the first complete catalogue of every British film produced for public entertainment since the invention of cinematography," with the exception of those untraceable before the Cinematographic Act of 1927, and with "British" defined as the ones made in the British Isles. Arrangement is chronological, so that the catalog as a whole is a skeletal history of British cinema. Information for each entry is terse but prolific, becoming more prolific as the years advance, and including some or, when available, all of the following information: date, title, length, censor's certificate, silent or sound, color systems, screen ration, stereoscopy, production company, distribution company, reissue, producer, director, story source, screenplay, narrator, cast and characters, subject (i.e., action, adventure, children, comedy, crime, fantasy, etc.), a single-sentence summary, awards, series or serials for films made in groups, and any pertinent additional information. Each film is given a catalog number in the title index for ease in retrieving. In all, films number 15,289. Not included are those made especially for television. The catalog is in two parts: from 1895 through 1970, representing an earlier work, and an update from 1971 through 1985, continuing in chronological order.

1181

The British Film Industry. London: PEP (Political & Economic Planning), 1952. 307p.

A report containing the results of a study carried out at the suggestion of the British Film Institute, intended to give the interested layman and members of the industry a comprehensive account of the development, organization and problems of the British film industry up to the 1950s, with special reference to the economics. It follows the industry closely and comprehensively, and contains its first official statistics, published by the Board of Trade. This is one of the most detailed and comprehensive sources on the various aspects of British cinema in its first half century. Footnotes, chronological table and index.

British National Film Catalogue. (See No. 1730.)

1182

Britton, Andrew, Richard Lippe, Tony Williams, and Robin Wood. **American Nightmare: Essays on the Horror Film**. Toronto: Festival of Festivals, 1979. 99p.

An in-depth discussion of the horror film, in which the four authors each contribute analytical essays on various examples, indicating trends, types, themes, and underlying psychology and significance. Title index.

1183, 1184

Brosnan, John. **Future Tense: The Cinema of Science Fiction**. New York: St. Martin's Press, 1978. 320p.

Brosnan, John. **The Horror People**. New York: St. Martin's Press, 1976. 304p.

Future Tense is a history of the science fiction film, beginning with 1900. Brosnan, like John Baxter (No. 1161) [**Science Fiction . . .**], emphasizes the difference between written and filmed science fiction, claiming the former draws from science and the intellect and appeals to a specialized audience while the latter draws from entertainment and emotions and appeals to a more generalized audience. He feels, however, that the two forms can be, and indeed have often been, successfully merged. An appendix lists chronologically science fiction shows on TV and summarizes each show. There is also a bibliography and an index.

The Horror People is more than a popular book about a genre; it is a serious discussion, written in terms of its actors, directors, writers and producers. Brosnan defines "horror" broadly as any film basically concerned with the bizarre, so that it includes non-supernatural films like **Psycho** as well as traditional ones like **Dracula**. Chronological in arrangement, it also serves as a history. Reference notes and index.

1185

Brosnan, John. **Movie Magic: The Story of Special Effects in the Cinema**. New York: St. Martin's Press, 1974; reissued by New American Library, New York, 1976. 300p.

"Basically, special effects, whether optical or physical, are concerned with creating illusions on the screen—such as the illusion that two actors are travelling in a car when in reality they have been filmed inside a studio, or the illusion that a giant ape is climbing up the Empire State Building," writes Brosnan. He discusses the pioneers, early sound, the British special effects men, developments in the 1950s and 1960s, Disney's live cartoons, war films and special effects, model animators, science fiction and disaster films, and special effects in the early 1970s (at the time of writing). Appendixes identify some of the movie magicians, as he calls them, and their works, and Academy Awards for special effects are listed. Reference notes, bibliography and index.

1186

Brownlow, Kevin. **The Parade's Gone By**. New York: Knopf, 1968. 577p.

"The silent era is regarded as prehistoric, even by those who work in motion pictures. Crude, fumbling, naive, the films exist only to be chuckled at—quaint reminders of a simple-minded past, like Victorian samplers. This book is an attempt to correct these distortions, for the silent era was the richest in the cinema's history," says Brownlow, whose aim is to recapture the spirit of the era through interviews with those who created it. He has supplemented the interviews by reviewing many of the silents and by documenting from publications of the period. There are many illustrations. This is one of the most important books on the early history of American cinema, and in addition, very readable. Footnotes and index.

1187

Brunsdon, Charlotte, ed. **Films for Women**. London: BFI Publishing, 1986. 236p.

While the movie industry has increasingly emphasized the role of women as consumer of movies and products, an alternative movement with a different emphasis has resulted from the feminist movement of the late 1960s. This collection of retrospective articles traces the shifts in the discussions about women and film since that time, looking at the representation of women in cinema; at films by women; and at films for women and for the different types of audience that has emerged. An appendix lists three statements made by British feminist exhibition and distribution organizations. Filmography and index.

1188

Bucher, Felix. **Germany**. New York: Barnes, 1970. 298p.

Directory of actors, actresses, and others important in German films, with preference given to those made before 1945 because Bucher believes most of the important films were before that time. Gives brief biographical data and a filmography. Some of the leading movements in film—e.g., "avant-garde"—are discussed. There is a detailed index to names and films.

Burton, Julianne. **The New Latin American Cinema: An Annotated Bibliography 1960–1980**. (See No. 1641.)

1189

Butler, Ivan. **Religion in the Cinema**. New York: Barnes, 1969. 208p.

Surveys the treatment of Biblical history and Christian practice in the commercial film, from the layman's point of view. As the author says in his Introduction, it is "a study of religion in films rather than films in religion." Only the Christian religions are represented, although there are chapters on witchcraft and Satanic rites. A few foreign films are included. An appendix lists organizations and church groups which make or sponsor films or religious content. Select bibliography and index of films.

1190

Butler, Ivan. **The War Film**. New York: Barnes, 1974. 191p.

"This book is a study of the main trends in the treatment of war by the fictional cinema," says Butler. "It is not intended as a sociological or fictional treatise—though such aspects are of course inseparable from such a theme; neither does it touch on film aesthetics, a subject with which most war films are notably—and perhaps not unmercifully—concerned." Films included are those shown, and mostly made, in Britain and the U.S., and they are grouped according to the period they were produced rather than by specific war. Balancing this is a chronological list, beginning with the Napoleonic Wars and ending with Vietnam and a section called "The Atomic Threat." (These latter two sections, however, are scanty because in the early 1970s not too many films on the subjects existed.) Though not complete, the list is reasonably comprehensive, including significant films in English or subtitled versions, "good or bad." A title index lists all movies mentioned.

1191

Campbell, Craig W. **Reel American and World War I: A Comprehensive Filmography and History of Motion Pictures in the United States, 1914–1920**. Jefferson, NC: McFarland, 1985. 303p.

The book begins with a historical discussion of the themes and genres of popular films, with descriptions of plots and players, to show how movie-going helped to build new attitudes and reinforce existing ones during the World War I and post-war period. Part 2 is an extensive filmography for the period 1914–1919, grouped under various categories: feature films and serials; short war-related films; films in which the war is peripheral to the plot; documentaries; selected newsreel and screen magazine items; cartoons; Liberty Loan specials; films on military Americana, the Civil War and Westerns related to the military; and "Bolshevik" films. Sandwiched between the two parts are about 40 illustrations. Indexed.

1192

Campbell, Edward D. C., Jr. **The Celluloid South: Hollywood and the Southern Myth**. Knoxville: University of Tennessee Press, 1981. 212p.

"This is not a study of film as film per se, but of film as a reflection of popular perceptions of the South in plots, visual images, advertising, reviews—and how these perceptions may reveal the uses to which the region has been put and the needs the South has met in the

popular culture of cinema." Preface. The opening chapter, "The Growth of a Mythology," sets the scene with a broad discussion of popular culture in the South, beginning with early Southern authors and ending with "Roots." The other chapters are chronological: "A Black Defense of a White World: The South in Silent Film, 1903–1927"; "The South and Hollywood's Golden Era: Enterprise and Entertainment, 1929–1939"; "The South as National Epic, 1939–1941: Gone With the Wind"; and "Hollywood and the Reinterpretation of the South: Reform as Good Business, 1941–1980." We see throughout how the mythology adapts to the times. Footnotes, bibliography and index.

1193

Casty, Alan. **Development of the Film. An Interpretive History**. New York: Harcourt Brace Jovanovich, 1973. 425p.

An interpretation of the progress of film as an art form. Arrangement is chronological; scope is international. Casty treats both people and movements—i.e., the emergence of a film style, D.W. Griffith, the Russians and epic montage, realism, comedy, genres and stars, sound, Orson Wells, Renoir, Antonioni, France's New Wave, Britain's "angry young men," and so on. Indexed by person and film.

Cawelti, John G. **Adventure, Mystery, and Romance**. (See No. 1020.)

Cawelti, John G. **The Six-Gun Mystique**. (See No. 60.)

1194

Ceram, C. W. **Archaeology of the Cinema**. New York: Harcourt, Brace & World, 1965. 264p.

An "ancient history of the theater which begins circa 1830 with the technology of motion when the first drawn pictures "moved," and ends where most cinema histories begin, circa 1879 with the development of cinema as an industry. In between, Ceram describes the assemblage of technical apparatus that was invented and discovered and the inventors and discoverers—all of it profusely illustrated by 293 pictures. Apart from the research value of the many chapter notes, mainly in French, German and English, the book makes fascinating reading for film fanciers. Bibliography and index.

1195

Ceplair, Larry, and Steven Englund. **The Inquisition in Hollywood: Politics in the Film Community 1930–1960**. New York: Anchor Press/Doubleday, 1980, 536p.

Although this is primarily a history of the stormy years when Washington combed the film industry for Communists, it is also an analysis of the relationship between Hollywood and government. "The times change, the names change, the films change, above all, the tactics and strategy of repression change, as they are continually refined. Only the goal of government remains the same: control." Thus the authors sum up their conclusions, as they focus on the search for subversives, the spy trials, the loyalty oaths, the Attorney General's lists, and the general hysteria that swept Hollywood. Much of their material is based on interviews with the people concerned. There are copious "Notes" of these and other sources, and a long bibliography, including the names of those they interviewed; archives consulted; and books and articles. Appendixes list other pertinent material covering the period. Index.

1196

Chaikin, Judy, and Lucinda Travis, comps. **Film/Television: Grants, Scholarships, Special Programs**. Rev. ed. Los Angeles, CA: American Film Institute, Education Services, 1984. 33p. (Factfile No. 12.)

Lists and gives pertinent information about foundations, organizations and other places where film/videomakers can apply for grants; programs of study for scholars, researchers, writers, and American and foreign students; and helpful periodicals, newsletters, guidebooks and yearbooks.

1197, 1198

Chanan, Michael. **The Dream That Kicks: The Prehistory and Early Years of the Cinema in Britain**. London: Routledge & Kegan Paul, 1980. 353p.

Chanan, Michael. **Cuban Image: Cinema and the Cultural Politics in Cuba**. Bloomington: Indiana University Press, 1985. 314p.

The Dream That Kicks is a different sort of history of the early years of the motion picture, not primarily because it is written from a Marxist perspective, but also because it goes minutely into those first decades, tying the cultural with the technological in considerable detail. In various chapters Chanan explores "The Dialectic of Inventions" involving conditions of invention, theories of perception, the development of photography, patents, celluloid, and the production of consumption; "Music Hall and Popular Culture" which examines cinema in light of its origins, milieu and its reflection of the collective experience of the working class; "Middle Class Culture and Its Influences" with "middle class" translated in the American idiom to "highbrow" or at least upper-middle-brow; "The Early Years," detailing the expansion of the motion picture market, the accumulation of capital, and the development of aesthetic theories; and the final chapter, "The Dream That Kicks," describing a mix of technological and aesthetic properties linking fantasy and reality which gives the cinema power to be exploited for better or worse. Bibliography and index.

Cuban Image is also written from a Marxist perspec-

tive. "If anyone wants to call this book a partisan history, I will make no apology for it," Chanan says of this study of Cuban film and its place in the social and political structure, which resulted from his visit there at the invitation of the Cuban Film Institute, the ICAIC. "Trekking through the historical undergrowth in order to answer the question how it was that the Cuban revolutionaries learnt to place such a high value on cinema," he traces it from the pre-Castro period to the present against the background of Cuban history in general, with emphasis on the cultural and political history of the revolutionaries who promoted cinema through governmental decree and channels. Throughout, he analyzes the films themselves, stressing both political and social qualities. Chapter notes, title index, and general index.

1199

Cinema 1900–1906. 2 v. Brussels: Federation Internationale des Archives du Film, 1982. 658p.

An analytical study of the National Film Archive and the International Federation of Film Archives (FIAF) containing results from a symposium conducted by historians from Great Britain, France, Italy, Czechoslvakia and the United States which sheds new light on a little known period. Volume One, compiled by Roger Holman, concerns their discussions and papers; Volume Two, compiled by a team of historians under the supervision of Andre Gaudreault, is a detailed analytic filmography of the films viewed, with known production facts, shot descriptions, contents, and sources.

1200

Cline, William C. **In the Nick of Time: Motion Picture Sound Serials**. Jefferson, NC: McFarland, 1984. 281p.

The motion picture serial from 1930 through 1956 when television took over—"what it was, who the people were who made it what it was, and—much as we can [determine] with a layman's knowledge—how they did it." Cline has broken serials down into their various components, with chapters on the formula, the sources, the types, the writers, the heroes and heroines, the assistants, the villains, the henchmen, the citizens, the pawns, the stuntmen, the technicians, the music, the directors, and the alumni stars. For his data he apparently depended upon an examination—in his case a loving one—of the serials themselves. In an appendix he has included a filmography of all serials released from 1930 through 1956 with pertinent information about each, including chapter titles. There is also a name index.

1201

Cinematographic Institutions: A Report by the International Film and Television Council (IFTC). Paris: UNESCO, 1973. 98p. (Reports and Papers on Mass Communication No. 68.)

Primarily "a study of institutions of the public or public utility character whose purpose is to promote the art and technique of the cinema and their applications in education, science and culture." Thus, film and trade associations and trade union types of associations are not dealt with. It uses as examples detailed descriptions and charts of organizations in Britain, India, Sweden, and Poland, with an annex giving names and addresses of national branches of the International Council for Educational Media (ICEM) and the International Scientific Film Association (ISFA) throughout the world. There is also a list of the membership of the International Newsreel Association (INA).

1202

Clarens, Carlos. **Crime Movies: From Griffith to** *The Godfather* **and Beyond**. New York: Norton, 1980. 351p.

Although this history of the crime movie and its players can serve as a detailed account of this particular genre in the United States, Clarens makes the point that the genre film as a whole is presently in crisis as society changes because "the values and certainties that were intrinsic in the form are no longer there for the filmmaker to use." Although he is basically concerned with the crime film he devotes considerable attention to the Western as an example of a declining genre for reasons he makes evident.

1203

Conant, Michael. **Antitrust in the Motion Picture Industry: Economic and Legal Analysis**. Berkeley and Los Angeles: University of California Press, 1960. 240p. (Publications of the Bureau of Business and Economic Research.)

A detailed assessment of the break-up of the studios, which analyzes and evaluates the impact of antitrust actions on the structure, behavior, and performance of the industry. Updates Huettig (No. 1295). Contains a bibliography, an index of cases, and an index.

1204

Contemporary Theatre, Film & Television: A Continuation of *Who's Who in the Theatre*. Vol. 1. Ed. by Monica M. O'Donnell. Detroit, MI: Gale, 1984. 545p.

Subtitled "A Biographical Guide Featuring Performers, Directors, Writers, Producers, Designers, Managers, Choreographers, Technicians, Composers, Executives, Dancers, and Critics in the United States and Great Britain," this new series contains over 1,100 biographies, with information under the following headings: Personal, Career, Writings, Awards, and Sidelights. Primary emphasis is given to people currently active, although some who have made significant contributions in the past but are not longer active are also included. A cumulative index interfiles references to this volume with references to **Who's Who in the Theatre** 17th ed. Subsequent editions will cover primarily new, entirely different personalities, with those in previous volumes made accessible by a cumulative index.

1205

Contemporary Polish Cinematography, a collective work by Wladyslaw Banaszkiewicz and others. Warsaw: Polonia Publishing House, 1962. 173p.

Excellent source for information about the film in Poland from the 1890s to the 1960s, dealing briefly with history, organization, clubs, press and publications, and feature, short and amateur films. An appendix lists chronologically feature films produced after World War II through 1961 with credits; and short and medium-length films awarded at International festivals and competitions.

1206

Cook, David A. **A History of Narrative Film**. New York: Norton, 1981. 721p.

"The language of film has become so persuasive in our daily lives that we scarcely notice its presence. And yet it **does** surround us, sending us messages, taking positions, making statements, and constantly refining our relationship to material reality. We can chose to live in ignorance of its operations, and be manipulated by those who presently control it. Or we can teach ourselves to read it . . .," says Cook in his Preface to his encyclopedic history of film, worldwide in scope, whose aim is to teach us to learn its new and different language. He starts with its technological origins in Europe and America and continues with its international expansion 1907–1918; Griffith and the narrative form; the contributions of Germany, Russia and Hollywood in the 1920s; the coming of sound; the American studio system; Europe in the 1930s; post World-War cinema in Italy, the U.S. and Hollywood in the 1950s; the French New Wave; the European renaissance; Japan; and the film in the 1970s. There is much mention of specific actors, directors, films, and changes technology constantly makes. Chapter references, a glossary, a chapter-by-chapter bibliography, and an author-title-subject index.

1207

Corrigan, Timothy. **New German Film: The Displaced Image**. Austin: University of Texas Press, 1983. 213p.

An examination of the aesthetics of West German film over a 15-year period beginning with the manifesto issued at Oberhausen in February 1962, and concluding in 1977 with **Germany in Autumn**, a film made by multiple teams of directors and technicians. Together, says Corrigan "these two documents describe symbolic poles in the development of what is commonly called the New German Cinema." He has illustrated his points by an analysis of six important films. Contains notes, a filmography, a bibliography, and an index.

1208

Coursodon, Jean-Pierre, with Pierre Sauvage. **American Directors**. 2 v. New York: McGraw-Hill, 1982. 456, 424p.

American Directors consists of two volumes of original, comprehensive essays on 118 American film directors "of recognized (in quite a few instances, under-recognized) stature," preceded by a chronological filmography of his pictures. A number of the directors selected go back to the "silent" days. Excluded are directors who died or were otherwise inactive after 1940, which eliminates some major names such as Buster Keaton, D. W. Griffith, Eric von Stroheim and some lesser but not negligible ones. Also excluded are some well-known Hollywood names who directed only three or fewer pictures. And only directors of feature films are considered. Within these limitations, however, coverage is thorough and the essays are lengthy, critical and comprehensive. Although the majority of them were written by Coursodon and Sauvage, 20 other contributors did from between one to three each. Each volume has a general index and an index of movie titles.

Andrew Sarris' earlier volume of essays, **The American Cinema** (No. 1462), contains much shorter examinations of a larger number of directors (200), with capsuled facts and evaluations about each.

1209

Crafton, Donald. **Before Mickey: The Animated Film 1898–1928**. Cambridge, MA: MIT Press, 1982. 413p.

A carefully researched and interestingly written history of the origins and early development of the animated film up to the time of Walt Disney, set against the background of the industrial and cultural environment of the period. Sources are listed in a lengthy bibliography, and there are copious notes. Index.

1210, 1211

Cripps, Thomas. **Slow Fade to Black: The Negro in American Film, 1900–1942**. New York: Oxford University Press, 1977. 447p.

Cripps, Thomas. **Black Film as Genre**. Bloomington: Indiana University Press, 1978. 184p.

Slow Fade to Black is a social history which chronicles, against the background of the times, the slow impact of Afro-American films on American ones in terms of who act in them or take part in other ways. Footnotes and subject and title indexes.

In **Black Film as Genre** Cripps defines "black film" and gives its history from the 1890s to the present, with an analysis of six well-known examples. In conclusion he discusses the state of criticism and scholarship. Contains a bibliography, a filmography, and an index.

1212

Cross, Robin. **The Big Book of B Movies: Or, How Low Was My Budget**. New York: St. Martin's Press, 1981. 208p.

Genre by genre—thrillers, series and serials, westerns, horrors, science fiction, musicals and comedies, epics and costume dramas, and the teenage market—Cross describes examples, accompanied by many, many pictures. An opening chapter, "Spirit of the B Hive," discusses the industry generally. Better for breadth than depth, it could be a useful reference to the almost forgotten stars of the "B" period—Ronald Reagan being the outstanding exception. Brief bibliography and index.

1213

Curran, James, and Vincent Porter, eds. **British Cinema History**. Totowa, NJ: Barnes & Noble, 1983. 445p.

"This book is not intended to be a definitive history of the British cinema, even if such a history were possible to produce. Rather it attempts to illuminate certain key developments and movements in the history of the British cinema through nineteen essays, some of which are surveys and others of which are case studies." Introduction. Part One provides two linked overall perspectives of film history; Part Two traces the evolution of the British film industry and parallel government policy toward it; Part Three examines different aspects of the organization and practice of filmmaking through a series of case studies; Part Four considers the ideological and cultural significance of some of the important movements and genres since the 1920s. Among the authors: Raymond Williams, Philip Corrigan, Michael Chanan, Margaret Dickinson, Stuart Hood, Vincent Porter, Janet Woollacott, Sue Aspinall. An appendix gives a statistical survey of the British cinema industry, and a 60-page "Select Bibliography" lists articles and books (mostly the latter) by subject.

1214

Curtis, David. **Experimental Cinema**. New York: Universe Books, 1971. 168p.

Traces the development of cinema experimentation from pioneer efforts in the early years of the century to the underground filmmakers of the 1960s. Bibliography and index of names.

1215, 1216

Cyr, Helen W. **A Filmography of the Third World: An Annotated List of 16mm Films**. Metuchen, NJ: Scarecrow, 1976. 319p.

Cyr, Helen W. **A Filmography of the Third World, 1976–1983: An Annotated List of 16mm Films**. Metuchen, NJ: Scarecrow, 1985. 275p.

These volumes provide titles with annotations, producer, length, date, distributor and whether color or black/white for films about the undeveloped areas of the world and also—although the title does not indicate this—major ethnic minorities in the northern nations of North America and Europe. Among the topics it covers are customs, geography, history, science, economics, politics, fine arts, religion, sports, technology and travel, with a few appropriate fictional films included. Geographic coverage is wide: the Third World (general), Africa, Asia, the Pacific, North America, Latin America, and England because of its Third World population. List of distributors and title index.

1217

Davies, Brenda, ed. **International Directory of Film and TV Documentation Sources**. 2d ed. Brussels, Belgium: Federation Internationale des Archives du Film (FIAF), 1980. 86p.

Holdings in 37 countries, most of which belong to FIAF. Information for each entry includes address, telephone, staff, hours of service, reproduction service, and description of collection. There is an index to special collections.

1218

Derry, Charles. **Dark Dreams: A Psychological History of the Modern Horror Film**. South Brunswick, NJ: Barnes, 1977. 143p.

A detailed study of the horror film in the 1950s, 1960s and 1970s, examined mainly in terms of the prime sources of horror. Derry categorizes these sources into three broad types: horror of personality, horror of Armageddon, and horror of the demonic. The first category includes psychological thrillers and dark drama, including some black comedy; the second, mainly frightening science fiction, in which the horror derives from an outside threat to humanity and the familiar world; the third involving the supernatural as represented by a malign non-human force for evil. With few exceptions (the most notable being several Japanese made in the Toho studios) practically all of the approximately 200 films covered are made in the U.S. There is a filmography for each and an index.

1219

Dick, Bernard. **The Star-Spangled Screen: The American World War II Film**. Lexington: University of Kentucky, 1985. 294p.

"**The Star-Spangled Screen** is an attempt to examine the American World War II film from the standpoint of the studio system that created it and the culture that embraced it." Preface. Looking at about 180 films which Dick checked for historical accuracy and, wherever archives were available, studied their production history, he evaluates them as a whole in terms of the myth of a united America. He focuses mainly on the 1940s when the most memorable World War II films appeared. An appendix gives a list of the films discussed and their availability, and there are extensive chapter notes, a bibliographical essay, and a film and a subject index.

1220

Dickinson, Margaret, and Sarah Street. **Cinema and State: The Film Industry and Government 1927–84**. London: BFI Publishing, 1985. 280p.

Why does the British film industry follow a commercial course rather than one modeled after the BBC's public service/public control concept? Dickinson and Street examine the question in this policy study of Britain's film trade, showing the various forces that have been responsible over the years for its present structure. They have not, however, attempted to explore the way in which the economics and power structure of the industry has affected the character of the films produced. This, they say, would be too difficult to assess and would require a different approach. Chapter notes; a bibliography of unpublished archival sources, special collections, official papers and secondary sources; and an index.

1221

Dickinson, Thorold. **A Discovery of Cinema**. London: Oxford, 1971. 164p.

A discussion of film in terms of four factors: the political and social climate; the creative capacity of the artist and the number of these artists; the flexibility of film equipment; and the audience. Although the first three factors are treated chronologically in terms of "The Silent Film," "The Early Sound Film," and "The Modern Sound Film," the author disclaims it as a history of the cinema, saying that it is "a personal view of a medium of expression which already in the short span of seventy-five years has often revealed itself as an art." Scope is international. Bibliography and index.

1222

Dickinson, Thorold, and Catherine De La Roche. **Soviet Cinema**. London: Falcon Press, 1948. 136p.

An analysis of the Soviet film, beginning shortly before the revolution and ending in the mid-1940s. Discusses techniques, specific pictures and producers, and the interplay between government and filmmakers.

Directors Guild of America, Inc. Directory of Members. (See No. 1743.)

1223

Dixon, Wheeler W. **The "B" Directors: A Biographical Directory**. Metuchen, NJ: Scarecrow, 1985. 594p.

"The world of the 'B' film is imperfect, riddled with shortcomings and compromises. It could not be otherwise. To create something of lasting beauty and worth when all economic circumstance conspire against you takes talent, desperation, and faith that one's ideas will transcend the physical realities of cheap and hurried production. But the best "B" films do exactly that. . . ."

Dixon has selected some 350 of their directors whom he considers outstanding, from 1929 to the mid-1980s, for inclusion in his directory. Each entry contains a listing of works, with distributor and date of release and/or copyright, followed by a discussion varying in length according to his estimate of importance. In conclusion is a list of the major films cited and another of the major serials, with distributor and director. There is a brief bibliography giving sources for general information about films.

1224

Drabinsky, Garth H. **Motion Pictures and the Arts in Canada: The Business and the Law**. Toronto: McGraw-Hill Ryerson, 1976. 201p.

A comprehensive treatment of Canadian law as it applies to film production. It explains each stage of the production process, outlines the differences between Canadian and American copyright law, and deals in detail with the various kinds of contractual agreements required. The author, a lawyer, has also been a film producer and publisher. Bibliography and index.

1225

Druxman, Michael, **Make It Again, Sam: A Survey of Movie Remakes**. South Brunswick, NJ: Barnes, 1975. 285p.

For reference purposes the most valuable part of this book is a lengthy compendium which lists more than 500 remakes (by no means all, says Druxman), with year of release, producer, distributor, stars (if known, as they often were not in early films), and country of origin if other than the U.S. The main portion, however, consists of a fascinating analysis of 33 of the most famous remakes—**An American Tragedy**, **Les Miserables**, **Wuthering Heights**, **Stagecoach**, for example—with commentary on the various versions, a synopsis, and quotes from reviews.

1226, 1227

Durgnat, Raymond. **Films and Feelings**. Cambridge, MA: M.I.T. Press, 1967. 288p.

Durgnat, Raymond. **The Crazy Mirror: Hollywood Comedy and the American Image**. New York: Dell, 1972. 280p.

"Beyond what interest it may possess as a collection of different cinematic topics, this text is offered also as a basis for re-exploring an art-form which seems to pose certain aesthetic problems more consistently than other media have done," says Durgnat of **Films and Feelings**. Exploring the question of aesthetics in the opening chapter, "Putting on the Style," he then examines what he terms "a second source of confusion—the function of the motion picture as entertainment versus its function as an art form." He does not attempt to solve the problems involved, but rather to present them with pertinent comments. "Citations and References" and index.

In a second book, **The Crazy Mirror**, Durgnat again examines the tensions between art and entertainment as exemplified by the Hollywood comedy tradition, exploring it in terms of certain specific types and examples from them. Contains references, suggestions for further reading, and an index.

1228

Dwoskin, Stephen. **Film Is . . . : The International Free Cinema**. London: Owen, 1975. 268p.

Something of a history of the underground film, something of a contemporary survey, and something of the author's reminiscences of his own experiences as an independent filmmaker. The range of his recollections includes a number of countries and goes back in time to the beginning of the movement. Over 700 films are discussed, many for the first time. Includes a bibliography, "Books and Magazines Consulted"; an index of films; a list of illustrations, and a general index.

1229

Dyer, Richard. **Stars**. London: BFI Publishing, 1979. 204p.

A critical examination of stardom as a phenomenon. Dyer, seeking a theory for empirical investigation, has approached it through what he feels to be two mutually interdependent concerns—sociology and semiotics. Part One, "Stars as a Social Phenomenon," deals with the former; Part Three, "Stars as Signs," deals with semiotics; and Part Two, "Stars as Images," brings the two together as human beings, types, and images. He makes his analysis through examples of specific stars in specific films. Chapter notes, a long bibliography, and an index.

1230, 1231, 1232

Eisenstein, Sergei M. **The Film Sense**. Tr. and ed. by Jay Leyda. New York: Harcourt, Brace, 1942. 288p.

Eisenstein, Sergei M. **Film Form: Essays in Film Theory**. Tr. and ed. by Jay Leyda. New York: Harcourt, Brace and World, 1949. 279p.

Eisenstein, Sergei M. **Film Essays and a Lecture**. Ed. by Jay Leyda. New York: Praeger, 1970. 220p.

Eisenstein is both a filmmaker and a writer. **The Film Sense**, his first book of theory, is primarily for the use of other filmmakers but is equally valuable to the scholar or to the layman who wants to go deeper than general appreciation of the medium. Throughout he investigates the ways in which the spectator's reactions can be fused with the creative process both to produce a richer emotional expression of the film's theme and also, as is typical of other art forms in the Soviet Union, to emphasize social responsibility. Appendixes have been selected which show the stages of various of his film concepts on their way to completed form, including sketched structures, notes for picture and sound images, blue prints, and so on. There are also a list of his sources and a bibliography of his writings available in English. Index.

Film Form was Eisenstein's second and last book (he died shortly before it was published), an anthology from his hundreds of essays selected to show certain key-points in the development of his film theory, and, in particular, of his analysis of the sound-film medium. Notes and index.

Several decades after Eisenstein's death Leyda brought together more of his work in **Film Essays and a Lecture**. In his Introduction Ledya says: "Students of Eisenstein's growth as the cinema's foremost theoretician will find in these essays the first suggestions of his two richest theories: his view of the film as a synthesis of all arts and all sciences, and his vision of an 'intellectual cinema'—a conveyance in film of ideas and principles to change and charge the audience." Contains "Sources and Notes" and a bibliography, "The Published Writings of Sergei Eisenstein," with notes on their English translations. Index.

1233

Ellis, Jack C. **A History of Film**. 2d ed. Englewood Cliffs, NJ: Prentice-Hall, 1985. 447p.

Ellis' history is international, essentially aesthetic, and interpretive more than descriptive or critical. Following introductory chapters about the characteristics and methodologies of film history in general and its early beginnings internationally, he concentrates on its development by country or regions and in terms of various aesthetics, treating Scandinavia, Germany, the U.S.S.R., Italy, Eastern Europe, Britain, Asia, the Third World, and the U.S. At the end of each chapter is a bibliography and a list of outstanding films. Index.

Ellis, Jack C., Charles Derry, and Sharon Kern. **The Film Book Bibliography 1940–1975**. (See No. 1648.)

1234

Ellis, John. **Visible Fictions: Cinema, Television, Video**. London: Routledge & Kegan Paul, 1982. 295p.

"Cinema and broadcast TV are often taken to be interchangeable media, in direct competition with each other. This book argues their differences from each other: differences in their social roles, their forms of institutional organization, their general aesthetic procedures," says Ellis, who sees them not as competitive media, but as distinct and interdependent forms, with different functions. He also speculates about the possible effects of video on both media. Lists films and programs cited, and contains a select bibliography for each chapter.

1235

Emmens, Carol A. **Short Stories on Film and Video**. 2d ed. Littleton, CO: Libraries Unlimited, 1985. 337p.

A sourcebook listing all films, theatrical and non-theatrical, adapted from short stories between 1920 and 1984—1,375 entries in total, including those available on video. Arrangement is alphabetical by author, subdivided by an alphabetical list of the story and film titles, with technical information (i.e., length, black and white or color, and date), production credits, cast credits, and a brief annotation. A directory of current distributors and indexes for story and film title follow.

1236

Enser, A.G.S. **Filmed Books and Plays: A List of Books and Plays from Which Films Have Been Made, 1928–1974**. London: Deutsch, 1975. 549p.

Consists of three indexes: the film title index, which lists under title the name of the maker or distributing company, the year the film was registered, the author, the publisher, and any change of title; the author index; and a change-of-original-title index.

Ensign, Lynne Naylor, and Robyn Eileen Knapton. **The Complete Dictionary of Television and Film**. (See No. 599.)

1237

Erens, Patricia. **The Jew in American Cinema**. Bloomington: Indiana University Press, 1984. 455p.

A decade-by-decade description of the presentation of Jews in American studio films between 1903 and 1983, with a discussion of the number and types of characters identified as Jewish and a chronicle of the narrative context in which the characters appeared. Within this framework Erens analyzes the ways in which the films relate to American society in general and to the American-Jewish community in particular, and shows the rise and fall of specific types, genres and themes, along with the persistence of certain conventions while others disappear, and the modifications that occur in accordance with socio-historic and artistic pressures. There are notes, a bibliography, and a filmography giving title, year, director, and distributor/producer. More than 300 films are examined. Index.

1238

Erens, Patricia, ed. **Sexual Stratagems: The World of Women in Film**. New York: Horizon, 1979. 336p.

Erens has come up with a neat stratagem; she has arranged the contents in two sections: "Part One: The Male Directed Cinema" and "Part Two: The Women's Cinema," dealing respectively with films directed by men and films directed by women. These articles, which represent and separate the thinking of men and women in the United States and Europe, are concerned not only with the images of women on film and the complicated factors underlying their creation, but also with the nature of feminist art and the criteria of a feminist aesthetic. Most of the articles were written during the seventies, but the relevance of their ideas dates back to the beginnings of film. In conclusion is a selective listing of major international women directors. Bibliography.

1239

Everson, William K. **American Silent Films**. New York: Oxford University Press, 1978. 387p.

A scholarly reassessment of the film industry from the era of the nickelodeon to sound. Everson analyzes the history in terms of its actors and actresses, its producers and directors, its genres, its technological changes, its influences from Europe. From the perspective of the mid-1970s he views the place and influence of women before sound came, and other topical areas. Contains an appendix, "The State of Film Scholarship in America: The Silent Film—Books, Films, Archives and Other Reference Tools," and a chronology, "The Movies in America: Art and Industry—A Chronological Survey of Highlights in the Silent Period." Indexed.

1240, 1241

Everson, William K. **The Bad Guys: A Pictorial History of the Movie Villain**. New York: Citadel, 1964. 241p.

Everson, William K. **The Detective in Film**. Secaucus, NJ: Citadel, 1972. 247p.

Everson says of **The Bad Guys**: "... its principal object is not a sociological one, but is rather to offer a nostalgic and light-hearted, but withal a respected survey of one aspect of the movies—the wonderful heavies, brutes, monsters, mad doctors, train robbers, gangsters, and pirates—good badmen and *bad* badmen—who have made those movies so exciting, and such fun." General index and picture index.

Much the same thing can be said of **The Detective in Film**. It is a survey whose principal object is to describe rather than analyze films about well-known fictional detectives, with emphasis on the actors and supporting casts. It too is well-illustrated.

1242

Factfile. Los Angeles: American Film Institute, Education Services, 1977–. (Nos. 1–16.)

An ongoing series of reference documents listing organizations, significant books, periodicals, holdings and services and activities specific to film, video, or television subject areas:

No. 1. **Film and Television Periodicals in English**. Rev. ed. 1979. 60p.

No. 2. **Careers in Film and Television**. Rev. ed. 1983. 57p.

No. 3. **Film/Video Festivals and Awards**. 2d ed. 1981. 88p.

No. 4. **Guide to Classroom Use of Film/Video**. 2d ed. 1981. 56p.

No. 5. **Women and Film/Television**. Rev. ed. 1979. 83p.

No. 6. **Independent Film and Video**. 1979. 70p.

No. 7. **Movie and TV Nostalgia**. 1977. 26p.

No. 8. **Film Music**. 1977. 24p.

No. 9. **Animation**. 1977. 26p.

No. 10. **Third World Cinema**. 1978. 27p.

No. 11. **Film/Television: A Research Guide**. 1977. 28p.

No. 12. **Film/Television: Grants, Scholarships, Special Programs**. Rev. ed. 1984. 22p. (See No. 1196.)

No. 13. **Films about Motion Pictures and Television**. 1981. 54p.

No. 14. **Screen Education Resources**. 1982. 81p.

No. 15. **Broadcast Television: A Research Guide**. 1983. 62p. (See No. 775.)

No. 16. **Asian-American Cinema**. 1987. 20p.

No. 17. **Blacks and American Film/Video**, in process.

1243

Feinstein, Peter, ed. **The Independent Film Community: A Report on the Status of Independent Film in the United States**. New York: Anthology of Film Archives, Committee on Film and Television Resources and Services, 1977. 97p.

The result of four years of study based on conferences and contributions by a number of authorities across the country and sponsored by the John and Mary Markle Foundation, the Rockefeller Foundation, and the National Endowment for the Arts, this small book is packed with information on a subject about which too little exists. It discusses the nontheatrical film in terms of filmmaker, distribution, funding, exhibition, preservation, and places where it may be studied. There are conclusions and recommendations.

1244

Fell, John L., ed. **Film Before Griffith**. Berkeley: University of California Press, 1983. 395p.

As cinema has grown in scope and importance as a field of study, so have the research materials and methodologies. In the belief that the formative pre-Griffith years lend themselves particularly well to both, Fell has gathered articles which are especially important in this respect. In fact, he says, they comprise a small compendium of methodologies for future work. In most of the articles represented, "we glean new understandings from the past through new sources, less exclusively dependent than earlier histories on aging memories and crumbling movie reviews." The book falls into three sections: "Places and Productions," which emphasizes a few early companies, filmmakers, and screenings; "Exhibitions and Distribution," which describes how and where the early movies were systematically viewed and how such situations were inflected by matters like copyright law and distribution practices; and "The Films," which concentrates on the product itself—early movies viewed 70 or 80 years after their first, often very transient appearance, and some not viewed at all. Introductions precede each section. Authors of the 28 articles range from graduate students to big names in the field. Notes, bibliography, film index and general index.

1245

Fenin, George N., and William K. Everson. **The Western: From Silents to the Seventies**. Rev. ed. New York: Penguin, 1977. 396p.

The authors say that in this, as in their first edition (Grossman, 1973), they have attempted a detailed history of the Western which will show the aesthetic and industrial growth of the genre, along with a critical analysis. Fenin has added two final chapters to the second edition. Several chapter headings from the contents give an idea of its range and scope: "Western History and the Hollywood Vision," "Contents and Moral Influence of the Western," "The Primitives: Edward S. Porter and Broncho Billy Anderson," "William Surrey Hart and Surrealism," "Tom Mix and Showmanship," "Stuntman and Second Unit Director," "The Western's International Audience and the International Western," "Spaghetti Western and the Western 'Made in Japan.'" Index.

1246

Fielding, Raymond. **The American Newsreel, 1911–1967**. Norman: University of Oklahoma Press, 1972. 392p.

History of a vanished genre. The author appraises the newsreel critically and indicts it for having failed to live up to its potential. Contains illustrations, notes, a bibliography, and an index.

1247

Fielding, Raymond, ed. **A Technological History of Motion Pictures and Television**. Berkeley: University of California Press, 1967. 255pp.

"This anthology," says Fielding, "is designed to fill a need for a historical survey whose perspective is distinctly technological," ignoring the purposes to which film and television are put, but emphasizing the means by which ends are achieved. In three sections consisting of a compilation of historical papers whose individual publication covered an extended period of time, it includes "Autobiographical Reminiscences;" Historical Papers" on motion picture cinematography and film stocks, laboratory practice, and sound; and "Historical Papers—Television." All articles are concerned with the technology of the media and were originally published in the **Journal of the Society of Motion Picture and Television Engineers**. A few carry extensive bibliographies; some are footnoted; and many have detailed illustrations.

Film Canadiana. (See No. 1749.)

Film Literature Index. (See No. 1920.)

Film Review Annual. (See No. 1750.)

1248

Film Vocabulary. London: Western European Union, 1958. 224p.

Multilingual vocabulary of some 900 cinema terms in common use among those who work in the fields of cultural and educational film and audiovisual education. In cases where a word in one language has no equivalent in the other languages, a short description in the other language is given.

1249, 1250

Filmography: Catalogue of Jewish Films in Israel. Vol 3. Jerusalem: Abraham F. Rad Jewish Film Archives, Institute of Contemporary Jewry, Hebrew University, 1972. 427, 5p.

Fox, Stuart, comp. **Jewish Films in the United States: A Comprehensive Survey and Descriptive Filmography**. Boston: C.K. Hall, 1976. 359p.

These two major surveys were carried on cooperatively between the Institute of Contemporary Jewry at Hebrew University and the Division of Cinema at the University of Southern California. The Hebrew University catalog lists feature and various types of shorter films which are located in Israel archives or other institutions, with pertinent information about each. This listing is followed by an index of film titles, an index of subjects, an index of Hebrew titles, and a list of institutions with code numbers. Specific subjects warranting special attention are: afforestation, aliya, Arab countries, Jewish customs, Germany, the way of life in Israel, famous personalities, philanthropy, pioneers, public opinion, recreation, romance, scenery, Israeli settlements, and Israeli towns.

The American filmography is somewhat broader in its inclusions, containing not only films made in the U.S., but also those released or distributed there, including television showings. Although Fox found most of his entries in film and television archives he includes fugitive material located through references in sources like movie magazines which may not now be in existence. He has accumulated 4,000 titles in all, consisting of feature films, documentaries, newsreels, Yiddish features, and various types of television shows. The listing of these films constitutes the main portion of the filmography. This is followed by an index to titles and an index to subjects. The main entry gives location.

1251

The First Ten Years. Washington, DC: American Film Institute, John F. Kennedy Center for the Performing Arts, 1978. 96p.

A report of the American Film Institute's organization, services, and program from its inception in 1967 through 1977.

Fisher, Kim N. **On the Screen: A Film, Television and Video Research Guide**. (See No. 1649.)

Fox, Stuart, comp. **Jewish Films in the United States**. (See No. 1250.)

1252, 1253

Frank, Alan. **The Horror Film Handbook**. Totowa, NJ: Barnes & Noble, 1982. 194p.

Frank, Alan. **The Science Fiction and Fantasy Film Handbook**. Totowa, NJ: Barnes & Noble, 1982. 187p.

Although Frank says he has had to be "ruthlessly selective" in his choices, his aim is to provide a comprehensive guide to major actors and filmmakers in the three genres and to cover in detail several hundred films in each book. A filmography is given for each entry, followed by a critical annotation and excerpts from reviews. At the end of both volumes is a discussion of critical themes with a list of illustrative films. Alternative titles are given and an index provided.

1254

French, Philip. **Westerns: Aspects of a Movie Genre**. Rev. ed. New York: Oxford University Press, 1977. 208p.

In this book, which deals with the Western since 1950, the author says that his approach is largely "social, aesthetic and moral." Setting the genre against this background, he discusses, among other topics, politics, heroes and villains, women and children, Indians and blacks, landscape, violence, and poker. There is a final chapter on the post-Western. Contains a brief filmography of the directors mentioned and a bibliography.

1255

French, Warren, ed. **The South and Film**. Jackson: University of Mississippi Press, 1981. 258p.

An anthology bringing together essays on films which depict the southern United States in its varied historical and regional aspects and demonstrate the ways in which well-known filmmakers have envisioned it. There are discussions of the classics, exemplified by **The Birth of a Nation**, **Jezebel**, and (of course) **Gone with the Wind**; genres such as Civil War, hillbillies, plantations and post-Reconstruction; auteurs—John Ford's South, Robert Altman's, Martin Ritt's; the treatment of Southern white and black women; William Faulkner and film; and the presentation of regionalism. All of which, the editor feels, constitute attempts to create a genre—the "Southern"—which may replace the Western.

1256

Friedman, Lester D. **Hollywood's Image of the Jew**. New York: Ungar, 1982. 390p.

Friedman suggests that ". . . in a very real sense the images of Jews in American films were created by Jews themselves; at the very least, Jews had a hand in the process by virtue of the vast number of Jewish studio heads and producers, as well as the writers, directors, and performers. By examining how Jews were presented in movies, one might learn what some Jews thought about themselves, how the image of Jews in the national consciousness changed over the years, and what Jews were willing to show of themselves to a largely Gentile audience." From the "silents" through the "eighties," Friedman traces the portrayal of Jews in American film. Contains "Notes," "A Chronological Listing of Jewish-American Films," "16mm Rental Information," a bibliography, and an index.

1257

Gabriel, Teshome H. **Third Cinema in the Third World: The Aesthetics of Liberation**. Ann Arbor, MI: UMI Press, 1982. 147p.

"Third Cinema filmmakers equate film with a weapon and view the act of filming as more than a political act," says Gabriel in this explanation of a new cinematic movement based on the rejection of traditional Hollywood films in favor of those of social and political relevance, especially where the Third World is concerned. Treating the movement in terms of both style and ideology, he suggests a direction for Third World film criticism and offers a view that unless repressed, it can establish an instructive cinema leavened with folk humor. Notes, bibliography and index.

1258, 1259

Garbicz, Adam, and Jacek Klinowski. **Cinema, The Magic Vehicle: A Guide to Its Achievement. Journey One: The Cinema Through 1949**. Metuchen, NJ: Scarecrow, 1975. 551p.

Garbicz, Adam, and Jacek Klinowski. **Cinema, the Magic Vehicle: A Guide to Its Achievement. Journey Two: The Cinema of the Fifties**. Metuchen, NJ: Scarecrow, 1979. 551p.

Film-by-film discussions of movies from various parts of the world which, in the opinion of the editors, are of interest to the serious student of the cinema. Again the approach is aesthetic and stylistic, with the main portion a year-by-year listing of the 317 films selected, with a mini-essay, preceded by title, running time and credits. For this edition the editors have provided an introductory "Comparison of Length and Running Times for Projection in Cinema and Television" and an "Outline of the Main Events in Cinema History of the Fifties." In both books, there is an index to directors and an index to films.

1260

Geduld, Harry M. **The Birth of the Talkies: From Edison to Jolson**. Bloomington: Indiana University, 1975. 337p.

How and why the transition from silent to sound cinema came about, beginning with the invention of the phonograph in 1877 and ending with the first sound film in 1927. Although emphasis is on American contributions, Geduld also includes foreign ones. Appendixes give some notable opinions on the subject in 1928–1929; a list of Hollywood feature films produced in 1929; and information about patents. Chapter notes and index.

Gerlach, John C., and Lana Gerlach, comps. **The Critical Index: A Bibliography of Articles of Film in English, 1946–1973.** (See No. 1651.)

1261

Giannetti, Louis. **Understanding Movies**. 3d ed. Englewood Cliffs, NJ: Prentice-Hall, 1982. 500p.

"Because films can express so many ideas and emotions simultaneously, viewers are sometimes overwhelmed by the sheer density of information they are bombarded with," says Giannetti. This book is an attempt to simplify some of these complex elements for the viewer by separating them and approaching them individually. Beginning with what he considers a relatively simple element, "Photography," he continues with chapters on "Mise-en-scene," "Movement," "Editing," "Sound," "Player," "Drama," "Literature," "Documentary," and "Avant-Garde," and ends with what is probably the most complicated of the elements, "Theory." Many of Giannetti's points are made through analysis of specific films. Each chapter has suggestions for further readings, and a glossary further facilitates understanding. There is a name/title index. (A new fourth edition was published in 1987.)

1262

Giannetti, Louis, and Scott Eyman. **Flashback: A Brief History of Film.** Englewood Cliffs, NJ: Prentice-Hall, 1986. 528p.

Although 500 pages can scarcely be considered brief, this book really is brief in that it covers an impressive amount of ground in terms of time and territory, hitting on the basics of American, European and international fiction film history by decades, beginning with "Griffith and His Contemporaries" in 1908 and ending with "American Cinema Since 1970." The methodology is purposefully eclectic; Giannetti and Eyeman say that "we have adhered to a broad consensus tradition of film history and criticism; except for a humanist bias, we have no theoretical axes to grind." The main focus is on film as art, although in keeping with their eclectic approach they also discuss it when appropriate as industry and as a reflection of popular audience values, social ideologies, and historical epochs. The text is clean, neat and free of jargon, with technical terms in boldface to indicate that they are in the glossary. Each chapter ends with "Further Reading," and there is a name and title index.

1263

Gifford, Denis. **British Cinema: An Illustrated Guide.** Cranbury, NJ: Barnes, 1968. 176p.

"This book is the first attempt to put between handy covers at a handy price the complete story of British films

in factual form. It is a kind of All Time Who's Who of stars and directors, 546 of them, selected for their contribution to the overall seventy-year scene." So says the author in his Introduction. His description is accurate except for the use of the word *complete*. As he later states, he has dealt with stars and directors who have a substantial body of work in film rather than with bit players or minor directors. For each entry he gives a filmography. Writers and producers are generally omitted. Contains a title index.

1264

Gifford, Denis. **Movie Monsters**. London: Studio Vista, 1969. 158p.

Paperback history of the monster from 1896 to the present. The author has gathered film monsters into 12 classifications and discusses some of the leading examples, illustrating with numerous stills. Pictures predominate over text. At the end is a chronological filmography of every known monster in each of the 12 categories.

1265

Goldberg, Judith N. **Laughter Through Tears: The Yiddish Cinema.** Rutherford, NJ: Fairleigh Dickinson University Press, 1983. 171p.

Although the Yiddish culture has vanished and the language no longer used, a rediscovery is taking place which has brought with it, among other facets, a growing interest in the relatively small volume of Yiddish film produced between 1910 and 1961 when the last was made. This review of them, placed in a historical context and with background information on the film industry, is in response to the revival. In addition to the text is a filmography listing films made in the Soviet Union, Poland and the United States, the chief producers. There is also a bibliography and an index.

1266

Goldstein, Ruth M., and Edith Zornow. **Movies for Kids: A Guide for Parents and Teachers on the Entertainment Film for Children.** Rev. ed. New York: Ungar, 1980. 268p.

"Not a textbook, not a work on the art of film, not an introduction to film study, it is a guide for parents, teachers, and librarians—for anyone looking for good movies to entertain children," say the authors of this useful compilation of 430 feature films, featurettes, and documentaries in 16mm, for rental or sale, which they think suitable for non-theatrical showings in homes, schools, libraries, churches, synagogues, camps and clubs. The films are in three listings: the first consists of about 300 titles considered best; the second is a shorter "not prime but choice" selection; and the third contains 36 features which are a representative selection from the Children's Film Foundation of Great Britain available in the U.S. Each film in the first section is lengthily annotated, with shorter annotations for those in the other two sections. Long or short, all annotations are well-written and to the point. Supplementary materials include a brief prefatory essay, "How to Look at a Movie," a directory of film companies and distributors, a list of organizations, and the two bibliographies, "One Hundred Good Books about Film," and "A Selected List of Film and Television Periodicals." Title index to films.

1267

Gomery, Douglas. **The Hollywood Studio System**. London: Macmillan/British Film Institute, 1986. 213p.

"**The Hollywood Studio System** strives to be a one-volume guide to the economics of the studio era, incorporating significant reinterpretations of the history of the U.S. film industry at present found only in specialized journals or books," says Gomery, as he examines the workings of the major studios between 1930 and 1949, the so-called Golden Age when the U.S. motion picture dominated the mass entertainment business worldwide, to show how the profit motive dictated the nature of production, exhibition and distribution. He concludes with an impressive bibliographic essay. Index.

1268

Gottesman, Ronald, and Harry Geduld. **Guidebook to Film: An Eleven-in-One Reference**. New York: Holt, Rinehart & Winston, 1972. 230p.

This excellent reference book begins with a comprehensive annotated bibliography broken down by subject: reference works, history, theory, criticism and reviews, genre studies (including documentary), adaptation, film and society, film techniques, screenplays, film personalities, Hollywood novels, film magazines, special series, and teaching materials. There are also the following miscellaneous listings: theses and dissertations about film; museums and archives in the U.S., Canada, Central and South America, Europe (including Great Britain and the U.S.S.R.), the Middle East, Asia, and Australia; film schools in the U.S. and other countries; equipment and supplies; distributors; bookstores, publishers, and sources for stills (the latter two in the U.S. only); film organizations and services; festivals and contests in the U.S. and other countries; awards; and terminology. In the past it has been necessary to dig out this kind of material from a variety of books; this one accumulates it succinctly.

1269

Goulding, Daniel J. **Liberated Cinema: The Yugoslav Experience**. Bloomington: Indiana University Press, 1985. 190p.

"This study focuses upon a thematic and critical analysis of the most significant feature films produced in Yugoslavia from the end of the Second World War to the present, with primary emphasis given to the period from 1961 to 1972—a period widely regarded by Yugoslav and foreign critics as Yugoslavia's most innovative and fecund period of film development and achievement—and to the period from 1977 to the present, which some critics are now referring to as a 'new Yugoslav cinema,' as a 'second new wave,' or more simply as a period of 'resurgence' or 'rebirth' of a nationally and internationally significant Yugoslav cinema," Golding says in his Introduction. Primary emphasis is upon feature films which represent "liberated" or "liberating" tendencies in the evolution of film content and in varying modes of stylistic expression. Notes, bibliography and index.

1270

Graham, Peter. **A Dictionary of the Cinema**. Rev. ed. New York: Barnes, 1968. 175p.

Hundreds of short biographical listings of international film actors and actresses, directors, script writers, and others prominent in films, with a list of their films and dates. Also discusses certain of the terms which describe cinema trends—neo-realism, new cinema, nouvelle vague, expressionism, for example—in fact-packed prose reminiscent of "who's who" entries. There is a two-page "Guide to Technical Terms." Scope is international.

1271

Grierson, John. **Grierson on Documentary**. Ed. by Forsyth Hardy. Berkeley: University of California Press, 1966. 411p.

"In this book I have made a selection from Grierson's vast volume of writing on mass communication," says Hardy in his Introduction to the essays of the man who, perhaps more than any other, established the documentary as an art form. "The earlier chapters include some of the film reviews contributed by Grierson to various journals in the early thirties. . . . The most important statements on documentary principles follow: they have been widely quoted and reproduced in many languages. Grierson's wartime writings on the interrelations of education, propaganda and democracy are included. Chapters added to the volume since its first appearance in 1947 include his annual surveys of world documentary and his analysis of television." Hardy's 20-page introduction discusses Grierson's life and contributions. An appendix lists the dates and original sources of the articles, reviews, writings and addresses. Index.

1272

Griffith, Mrs. D.W. (Linda). **When the Movies Were Young**. New York: Dutton, c1925, 1965. 266p.

". . . one of the earliest volumes containing eyewitness testimony to the conditions under which early motion pictures were made."—Introduction to the Dover reprint edition, 1969. Indexed.

1273

Griffith, Richard. **The Movie Stars**. New York: Doubleday, 1970. 498p.

A mammoth, coffee-table-type book which attempts to analyze the factors which constitute "star appeal," using past and present examples and many photographs. Beginning with "Early Fanfare" and going into "The Heydey of the Stars," it concludes with "Death and Transfiguration," the diminution of the system. The author does more than tell a story; he delves into the reasons for the rise and fall of the institution of stardom. Indexed.

1274

Guback, Thomas H. **The International Film Industry: Western Europe and America Since 1945**. Bloomington: Indiana University Press, 1969. 244p.

"The object of this study is to uncover and analyze relationships between the American and European film industries, keeping in mind the financial stake American companies have in Europe." Introduction. To accomplish his aim, the author penetrates economic, sociological, and cultural factors which have a bearing. Contains a bibliography of books, monographs, pamphlets, documents, reports, and articles. Also has a particularly useful index with a minute subject breakdown.

1275, 1276

Halliwell, Leslie. **Halliwell's Film Guide**. 4th ed. New York: Scribner, 1983. 936p.

Halliwell, Leslie. **Halliwell's Filmgoer's Companion**. 8th ed. New York: Scribner, 1985. 1,150p.

The **Guide** is a delightful and scholarly reference book in which Halliwell gives a great deal of information about the 15,000 English language and foreign films 90 minutes or over in length, including title; a star rating system within its genre; whether black, white or color; country of origin; the writer or other original source; director; photographer; composer of musical scores; other credits as available and applicable; for some of the titles, quotes from critics; a thumbnail synopsis; and brief, often pithy comment which adds flavor to the facts, as in **A Fistful of Dollars**: "An avenging stranger, violent and mysterious, cleans up a Mexican border town. A film with much to answer for: it began the craze for 'spaghetti westerns,' took its director to Hollywood, and made a TV cowboy into a world star. In itself, it is simple, brutish and actionful." In conclusion are two brief essays: "A Word on Shape," and "The Decline and Fall of the Movie."

"I have continued to seek, digest and present information about producers, small part actors, silent stars, cinematographers, art directors, composers, original authors, screenwriters, and indeed anyone who has had a creative role to play in the history of the cinema. Trade matters are virtually ignored." Thus Halliwell describes the scope of this eighth edition of his **Filmgoer's Companion**. A chatty, eclectic sort of encyclopedia, it provides mini-essays on general topics, as for example:

"Abortion, unmentionable on the screen for many years save in continental dramas like **Carnet Del Bal**, 37 and officially ostracized exploitation pictures like **Amok**, it was first permitted as a Hollywood plot in **Detective Story**, 51." Under "amnesia" he lists all actors who have suffered from this affliction on film with names of films in which they did so. He has continued the practice of including descriptions of a selected number of films from the **Guide** in cases where they underline trends or are especially significant in cinema history. The main text contains a special list of these. Another list gives fictional screen characters and series, like **Fu Manchu** and **The Thin Man**. Themes explored—i.e., abortion, concentration camps, religion, private eye—are listed, and so are title changes. Finally come Halliwell's "Recommended Books" and his 100 favorite films. (New editions were published in 1988.)

1277

Hames, Peter. **The Czechoslovak New Wave**. Berkeley: University of California Press, 1985. 322p.

A study of the brief flowering of Czechoslovakian films in the 1960s which, in spite of its brevity, occupies a place of primary importance in the history of cinema. Through a detailed analysis of the work of individual directors, Hames places the movement in an aesthetic context linked to the social and cultural conditions of the period as he answers his own question: "How had it all started, and what were the traditions from which the films had been born?" Notes, bibliography, index of films, and general index.

1278

Hampton, Benjamin B. **History of the American Film Industry from Its Beginnings to 1931**. New York: Dover, c1931, 1970. 456p. (Formerly titled **A History of the Movies**. New York: Covici, Friede, Inc. 1931.)

Benjamin Hampton was a vice-president of American Tobacco who became actively involved also in the film industry in 1916. His history is founded on his experience in it (unsuccessful; he believed in the separation of production, distribution and exhibition which was defeated in the 1920s) and his wide knowledge of the business practices of the time as he looks back on his involvement retrospectively. The result is both personal and scholarly. Richard Griffith, in his introduction to the 1970 Dover edition, calls it the best history of the movie business up to that date. Indexed.

1279

Hanhardt, John G., ed. **Video Culture: A Critical Investigation**. Layton, UT: Gibbs M. Smith, Peregrine Smith Books in association with Visual Studies Workshop Press, 1986. 296p.

An anthology which brings together a wide range of critical, theoretical and historical writings on film, video, and television as art. The editor's aim is "to provide the reader with a collection that will address issues pertaining to art and technology and, more specifically, the definition of a 'video culture' as it is determined by the distinctive features of the medium and the forces acting as history." In three sections: "Theory and Practice," "Video and Television," and "Film and Video: Differences and Futures." Contributors are artists, writers and academics, including Walter Benjamin, Bertolt Brecht, Louis Althusser, Hans Magnus Enzensberger, Jean Baudrillard, David Antin, David Ross, Rosalind Krauss, Stanley Cavell, Nam June Psik, Gene Youngblood, Jack Burnham, John Ellis and Douglas Davis. Most of the essays have notes. Bibliography.

1280

Hardy, Forsythe. **Scandinavian Film**. London: Falcon Press, 1962. 62p.

As the author points out, Sweden and Denmark have contributed to world cinema far out of proportion to their size. He traces the development of their film industry, stressing the influences that have made its products different from those of other countries.

1281, 1282, 1283

Hardy, Phil. **The Western**. New York: Morrow, 1983. 395p.

Hardy, Phil, ed. **Science Fiction**. New York: Morrow, 1984. 400p.

Hardy, Phil. **The Encyclopedia of Horror Movies**, by Tom Milne and Paul Willemen. New York: Harper & Row, 1986. 406p.

These three volumes are among the most definitive—if not the most definitive—works in their various genres and are part of what Hardy planned—or plans?—as a nine-volume encyclopedia set. Each volume begins with an essay putting the genre in perspective, followed by the main section—"the heart"—which is a title-by-title arrangement by decades. Information for each film is extensive, ranging from 50 to 1,000 words, and including detailed credits, a brief synopsis, critical comments, and (for many) a photograph. **Science Fiction** and **Horror Movies** each contain 1,300 entries and **The Western** 1,800. For this latter genre silents are not included—"space being at a premium because the Western is the most prolific genre Hollywood has produced" and because few silents are available for viewing. A valuable feature of each are the appendixes. Those for **Science Fiction**: all-time best rentals; most successful films financially; critics' top ten; Oscars; and Trieste Festival selection. Those for **The Western**: all-time best rentals; most successful films financially, most successful stars financially; critics' top ten; Oscars; selected sound Westerns and their novel sources; and a chronological listing of sound westerns which could not be covered in detail. Those for **Horror Movies**: all-time best rentals, critics' top ten; Oscars; and a select bibliography. All are indexed.

1284

Harmon, Jim, and Donald F. Glut. **The Great Movie Serials: Their Sound and Fury**. New York: Doubleday, 1972. 384p.

Informal social history of the serial, 1930–60. Serials are analyzed by categories—science fiction, jungle stories, aviation, detective thrillers, Westerns, etc.—with casts, story synopses, and evaluations. Jim Harmon is a special consultant on old-time radio to the Hollywood Museum and the Canadian Broadcasting Co.; Donald Glut is a professional free-lance writer. Both live in Hollywood, where they researched the book, drawing from scripts, anecdotes, interviews, and photographs. Indexed.

1285

Haskell, Molly. **From Reverence to Rape: The Treatment of Women in the Movies**. New York: Holt, Rinehart and Winston, 1974. 388p.

Decade by decade from the 20s through the 60s Haskell makes an impressionistic analysis of sexism in movies, analyzing women's roles in hundreds of films. Her prose is dense, her findings pessimistic. Index.

1286

Hayes, R. M. **Trick Cinematography: The Oscar Special-Effects Movies**. Jefferson, NC: McFarland, 1986. 370p.

Chronicles the special-effects awards from their first annual presentation in 1929 through 1984. Hayes' intention is "to acknowledge the many craftspersons who have received Academy recognition over the years as well as bring to notice the various other individuals who have done so much with seldom a mention in the screen billing." He has covered all special effects nominations as well as scientific, technical and special awards, with each film represented by as complete a credit listing as he could research. Preliminary sections cover alphabetical listings of all pictures mentioned, and all technicians. Hayes has commented, often at some length, on the awards. An extensive index gives individuals, companies, film titles, working titles, etc., which appear.

1287, 1288, 1289

Hendricks, Gordon. **The Edison Motion Picture Myth**. Berkeley: University of California Press, 1961. 216p.

Hendricks, Gordon. **Beginnings of the Biograph: The Story of the Invention of the Mutoscope and the Biograph and Their Supplying Camera**. New York: The Beginnings of the American Film, 1964. 11, 78p.

Hendricks, Gordon. **The Kinetoscope: America's First Commercially Successful Motion Picture Exhibitor**. New York: The Beginning of the American Film, 1966. 182p.

This series of three monographs is intended to throw light on the early technological history of the motion picture and to clear up some misconceptions. The author in his preface hopes that they will be a "beginning of the task of cleaning up the morass of well-embroidered legend with which the beginning of the American film is permeated." Much of it centers around W.K.L. Dickson, an employee of Thomas Edison, whom Hendricks feels has not been given sufficient credit, and other employees of the early days. His beliefs are well documented; some of the evidence is included in the appendixes. All three volumes are indexed.

1290

Hibben, Nina. **Eastern Europe: An Illustrated Guide**. Cranbury, NJ: Barnes, 1969. 239p.

Brief factual information about the postwar work of film directors, players, and technicians in Albania, Bulgaria, Czechoslovakia, East Germany, Hungary, Poland, Romania, the Soviet Union, and Yugoslavia. Since the territory is large, considerable selection was required. A criterion was the knowledge of the personalities and films in the West. There is also emphasis on the specialities of each country—for example, the high proportion of animators in the Yugoslav section and of documentation in the German section. In dealing with the U.S.S.R., the compiler omitted information available in Peter Graham's **A Dictionary of the Cinema** (No. 1070). Data on each country precedes the discussions of its films and personalities. There is an index to film titles.

1291, 1292

Higham, Charles. **Hollywood at Sunset**. New York: Saturday Review Press, 1972. 181p.

Higham, Charles. **The Art of the American Film, 1900–1971**. New York: Doubleday, 1973. 322p.

Higham's theme in both books is Hollywood's struggle to maintain artistic integrity. In **Hollywood at Sunset** he presents his answer to those who wonder what has caused its decline. He analyzes the events that have taken place and forces that were at work from the peak years of 1946 to the 1970s—the government antitrust actions which resulted in the consent decree, the House Un-American Activities investigation of alleged Communists in the film industry, the advent of TV, and other lesser-known factors he deems disastrous. Higham meant this for an interesting bit of reading rather than a depth study, but it nevertheless gives good background on social aspects of the film industry.

In **The Art of the American Film** his approach is different but his interest is the same. "Since this book is concerned with the art of American film, an art which has survived the businessmen who run it, I have been chiefly concerned with their enemies, the men who have fought them to achieve a measure of personal expression," he says. He has written about Hollywood films in terms of certain traditions—the pastoral tradition as ex-emplified by Griffith, King Vidor, and others; the epic Belasco-like tradition of DeMille and Ince; the Viennese-Berliner sophisticated boudoir-comedy tradition introduced by Lubitsch; the emergence of entirely new traditions. There are many stills and an index.

1293

Hillier, Jim, ed. **Cinema in Finland**. London: BFI Publishing, 1975. 67p.

Designed to serve as an introduction—the first in English—to the traditions, history, and achievements of the Finnish cinema in general, emphasizing social, political, and economic factors. The final section provides a guide to most of the films in the Finnish Film Archive.

1294

Huaco, George A. **The Sociology of Film Art**. New York: Basic, 1965. 229p.

To be analyzed sociologically, says Huaco, who is a philosophically oriented social scientist, a film style must be describable and analyzable in a context comprised of professional personnel; of common social characteristics; of a commonly shared technology; of a specific industrial and commercial organization; and of a public climate responsible to a given film style. Here he applies this framework to the history of German, Russian and Italian movies. Selected bibliography and index.

1295

Huettig, Mae D. **Economic Control of the Motion Picture Industry: A Study in Industrial Organization**. Philadelphia: University of Pennsylvania Press, 1944. 163p.

Approaching the American film from the economic angle, Huettig analyzes its financial structure, including exhibition and distribution, up to the early 1940s. Contains a bibliography. Conant (No. 1203) is useful for information up to 1960. Jobes (No. 1312) takes the subject to 1966. Less and Berkowitz (No. 1339) describe the economics of filmmaking in the 1970s. For an analysis of British film finances published in 1937, See Klingender (No. 1322), which has an appendix "A Summary of American Film Finances."

1296

Hull, David Steward. **Film in the Third Reich: A Study of the German Cinema, 1933–1945**. Berkeley: University of California Press, 1969. 291p.

Carefully documented study based on years of research during which the author tracked down and screened virtually all important films of the period. Arranged chronologically beginning with 1933, it shows the takeover of the film industry by Goebbels as he abolished critics and absorbed it, and the trends in German films, such as war, escapism, and anti-semitism. Several useful sections are the prologue, which reviews the literature on the subject, the notes, the bibliography, and the index.

Hyatt, Marshall, comp. **The Afro-American Experience: An Annotated Bibliography & Filmography**. (See No. 1658.)

1297

Index to Critical Film Reviews in British and American Periodicals. Ed. by Stephen E. Bowles. 3 v. in 2. New York: Franklin, 1974, 1975, 781p.

Retrospective index, mainly of feature length theatrical films, but also including documentary, experimental, short, and educational films which were criticized in the periodicals selected for inclusion—"the leading English language journals of film scholarship, both American and British, active or defunct," as well as a few other sources not strictly journals (**Filmfacts** and **International Film Guide**). Coverage begins with first issue and continues either through its termination or December 1971 for the first three volumes. A fourth volume, in preparation for many years, is forthcoming from publisher Burt Franklin. Entry is by name of film, with source of review, author and approximate length. Volume 2 goes from A through M; volume 3 from N through Z, and also contains an index to critical reviews of books about film, and indexes to directors, film reviewers, authors, and book reviewers; a subject index to books about film, and a union list of film periodical locations.

1298

Inglis, Ruth A. **Freedom of the Movies: A Report on Self-Regulation from the Commission on Freedom of the Press**. Chicago: University of Chicago Press, 1947. 241p.

"... the movies can realize their full promise only by unremitting effort from all concerned: the government, the industry and the public—each in his own sphere." Thus Inglis summarizes her rosy view stressing self-regulation, which has not worked out. As background, she discusses the social role of film, the history and economics, the attempts to control, the evolution of self-regulation, and self-regulation in action—largely through the Production Code Administration. An appendix gives the production code. Source notes and index. This is a part of the Commission on Freedom of the Press report (No. 81).

1299

Insdorf, Annette. **Indelible Shadows: Film and the Holocaust**. New York: Random House, 1983. 234p.

An exploration of the growing body of films about the Holocaust—primarily fiction—that "illuminates, distorts, confronts, or reduces the Holocaust," showing the degree to which they manifest artistic and moral integrity. Focus is on cinema of the U.S., France, Poland, Italy and Germany—countries which have produced significant, accessible and available films on the subject. (Eastern Europe has also produced films treating the effects of World War II, but they are difficult to see in the U.S.) The approach is thematic: "Finding an Appropriate Language," "Narrative Strategies," "Responses to Nazi Atrocity," "Shaping Reality." Notes, a filmography which includes Eastern European films, and a bibliography. Index.

1300, 1301, 1302

The International Dictionary of Films and Filmmakers, Ed. by Christopher Lyon. **Films**. Vol. 1. Chicago: St. James Press, 1983. 526p.

The International Directory of Films and Filmmakers, Ed. by Christopher Lyon. **Directors/Filmmakers**. Vol. 2. Chicago: St. James Press, 1984. 611p.

The International Directory of Films and Filmmakers, Ed. by Christopher Lyon. **Actors and Actresses**. Vol. 3. Chicago: St. James Press, 1986. 670p.

First three of a projected four-volume series, the fourth to be **Writers and Production Artists**. The aim of volumes 2, 3 and 4 (when published) is to provide factual and critical information about principal creative figures in the history of film. The first volume, **Films**, gives a background of a comprehensive reference source, with bibliographies, on the "most widely studied films," selected by experts, oriented toward the film as art, and including current concerns of North American, British, and European film scholarship and criticism. Similar criteria are used in the other volumes. All entries include a succinct but in-depth appraisal. Other information—for **Film** (Vol. 1), filmography and bibliography; for **Directors** (Vol. 2), biographical information, publications and works by and about; for **Actors and Actresses** (Vol. 3), biographical information, roles, and works by and about.

1303

The International Encyclopedia of Film. Ed. by Roger Manvell. New York: Crown, 1972. 574p.

The major portion of this work consists of over 1,000 alphabetical entries giving biographies, national film histories, general topics, and technical terms. Preceding this is a chronological outline of film history, indicating selected events year by year. Films are not entered separately but can be easily found through an index. There are two other indexes—one to names and one to principal title changes. The bibliography is broken down by subject. Contributors include such well-known film writers as Lewis Jacobs, David Robinson, Jay Leyda, and a number of others, who treat the subject both as an art and as an industry. Although there are numerous illustrations, this is primarily a reference rather than a picture book.

International Film Guide. (See No. 1297.)

International Index to Film Periodicals: An Annotated Guide. (See No. 1928.)

International Motion Picture Almanac. (See No. 1760.)

1304

Jackson, Kathy Merlock. **Images of Children in American Film: A Sociological Analysis**. Metuchen, NJ: Scarecrow, 1986. 223p.

A look at the portrayal of children to determine latent cultural attitudes being expressed in American society. Jackson approaches the analysis in two chronological sections: "Images of Children in Pre-World War II Films: Unqualified Innocence," covering America before World War I through World War II, and "Images of Children in Post-World War II Films—New Variations," covering post-World War II and the baby boom into the age of Spielberg. Jackson is particularly concerned with the transition in portrayal from the good child in earlier films to the bad child in later ones, as society lost much of its innocence and with it the vision of childhood innocence. Notes, bibliography, filmography and index.

1305

Jacob-Arzooni, Ora Gloria. **The Israeli Film: Social and Cultural Influences 1912–1973**. New York: Garland, 1983. 387p.

Reprint of a dissertation from the University of Michigan which traces social, cultural and historical influences on the development of the Israeli feature film from its beginnings up to and including the Yom Kippur War in 1973. It also deals with the Israeli stage and the documentary film when these have influenced the feature film. Appendixes include a list of full-length Israeli films produced through 1972, giving the number of persons attending, and the tax returns awarded producers; milestones in the Hebrew theater and lists of productions in major theaters; best Israeli films in the opinion of certain of the people connected with the industry; and some pertinent points from the Law for the Encouragement of the Israeli Film, enacted in 1954. There is a bibliography but no index.

1306

Jacobs, Lewis. **The Documentary Tradition, from Nanook to Woodstock**. New York: Hopkins & Blake, 1971. 530p.

Examines 50 years of documentaries through discussions by 90 filmmakers and critics and 80 illustrations. Arrangement is chronological and coverage is international. Selected bibliography and index.

1307, 1308, 1309

Jacobs, Lewis. **The Rise of the American Film: A Critical History with an Essay, "Experimental Cinema in America, 1921–1947."** New York: Teachers College Press, 1948, 1967 (c1939). 585p.

Jacobs, Lewis, ed. **The Emergence of Film Art: The Evolution and Development of the Motion Picture as an Art, from 1900 to the Present**. 2d ed. New York: Norton, 1979 (c1969). 544p.

Jacobs, Lewis, ed. **The Movies as Medium**. New York: Farrar, Straus & Giroux, 1970. 335p.

The Rise of the American Film tells the story of the motion picture in the U.S. from its beginning at the turn of the century to 1947. Although as in all Jacobs' works the main stress is on film as art and entertainment, he has placed considerable emphasis on economic development, with discussions of individual directors and pictures that have helped shape its history. "Experimental Cinema in America, 1921–1947" has been added to the 1967 edition. There is an extensive bibliography and a film, name and general indexes.

"The purpose of this book is two-fold," Jacobs says of **The Emergence of Film Art**. "First to provide insight into creative film expression, and second, to present an historical overview of the medium's artistic development." It is divided into three sections—the silent film, the sound and color film, and the creative process—with each part consisting of essays by eminent filmmakers, critics, and historians, and an introduction by Jacobs. Scope is international. Index to names and titles.

The Movies as Medium is a compilation of articles, presented in interlocking order: "Directors Speak," "Image," "Movement," "Time and Space," "Color," and "Sound," whose purpose as a whole is to enable the lay film enthusiast to recognize and appreciate the nature of cinematic art and craft.

1310, 1311

Jarvie, Ian C. **Movies as Social Criticism: Aspects of Their Social Psychology**. New York: Basic Books, 1970. 394p.

Jarvie, Ian C. **Toward a Sociology of the Cinema: A Comparative Essay on the Structure of a Major Entertainment Industry**. London: Routledge & Kegan Paul, 1970. 394p.

What is the role of the movies in society, Jarvie asks in **Movies as Social Criticism**. Do they serve as pacifier or catalyst? Social pap or an engine of criticism and reflection? After posing and examining some historical and theoretical questions he discusses their changing relation to society and to reality, their diverse audiences and functions, and in conclusion, their role as social criticism. He himself views their role as moderate, somewhere between the extremes. There is a short bibliography of articles and books, a name and a subject index, and an index of films.

In an earlier book, **Toward a Sociology of the Cinema** (published in the United States by Basic as **Movies and Society**) he first evaluates sociology as a tool to examine the cinema, then discusses at length its structure, its audience, and its content (genre films), ending with a sociological evaluation about the ways we learn about and appraise film. An important feature is an annotated bibliography of articles and books over 100 pages long. There are also indexes to subject, personal names and films.

1312

Jobes, Gertrude. **Motion Picture Empire**. Hamden, CT: Archon, Shoe String Press, 1966. 398p.

Economics-based history, coupling careful research with firsthand knowledge. Contains an index of names and a bibliography. For other earlier studies of the economics of film see Huettig (No. 1295) and Conant (No. 1203).

1313

Johnson, William, ed. **Focus on the Science Fiction Film**. Englwood Cliffs, NJ: Prentice-Hall, 1972. 182p.

The editor's aim is to define the film genre and to examine its relationship to science fiction writing. Arrangement is roughly chronological: "Beginnings: 1895–1940," "Popular Years: The 1950s," "Taking Stock: Some Issues and Answers," and "Moving On: The 1960s and After." In a separate section, "Further Comments," prominent writers and filmmakers who are not among the contributors give their views on science fiction films. Contains a chronology, a filmography and an index.

Contributors vary in their approaches. Some emphasize aesthetics and effects, others emphasize production, a few probe deeper into science fiction as a genre, and a few are anecdotal.

1314

Jowett, Garth S. **Film: The Democratic Art**. Boston: Little, Brown, 1976. 518p.

A social history packed with both facts and ideas, which the author describes as "an attempt to chronicle and analyze some of the ways in which the motion picture affected the lives of the American people, and those forces, both positive and negative, which shaped the final product seen on the screen." Jowett has grouped film around broad topics—recreation, censorship and control, for example—beginning with the very late 19th century. His concern is with the accommodation between films and the American people—the obstacles that have slowed the process, and the social, political, and cultural adjustments that have been required. The book ends with a chapter, "The Uncertain Future," dealing with the present. A lengthy section of appendixes contain valuable reference material: the industry codes in 1921, 1924, 1927, and 1930–34; box office receipts from 1929 to 1973 in relation to personal consumption expenditures; the growth of attendance from 1922 to 1965; profits from 1932 to 1972 by individual companies; a great deal of information about audiences; and various other facts and statistics. There are chapter notes, a bibliography of books, articles, and other materials of major significance, and a comprehensive index.

1315

Jowett, Garth, and James M. Linton. **Movies as Mass Communication**. Beverly Hills, CA: Sage, 1980. 147p. (Sage CommText Series.)

The authors feel that in spite of the wealth of material on the movies as art, too little of it is concerned with their place as a mass medium, and they offer this text as an attempt to examine movies in this light. They deal with its economics, its audience and symbols, its techniques in terms of psychology, its social and cultural aspects. Finally they discuss its role in relation to television and newer technologies. Though slight, this is packed with information, presented in an easily understandable way suitable for undergraduates or other interested layman, yet in no wise written-down. References and index.

1316

Kael, Pauline. **5001 Nights at the Movies: A Guide from A to Z**. New York: Holt, Rinehart and Winston, 1982. 676p.

An assemblage of thousands of movie synopses, going back to the days of silent film, written over the years for the "Going on About Town" department of **The New Yorker**, which are masterly pieces of condensation, giving the full flavor of plot, cast and direction, and a critical appraisal of quality. Handy to keep by the TV set for ready reference. The entries are alphabetical by title; there is no index.

1317

Kaminsky, Stuart M. **American Film Genres**. 2d ed. Chicago: Nelson-Hall, 1985. 238p.

Kaminsky's argument is that popular work has significant meaning and can be analyzed. The method he has adopted to prove his point is to examine various ways in which genre analysis can be approached. In one case, for example, he takes an individual film and indicates some of its contributions; in another, he deals with comparisons of source and film versions; in others, he studies literary adaptation, historical perspective, psychological perspective, social perspective, the genre director. In each he applies the method to actual works. Examples are exclusively American films and non-American generic films that have been popular in the United States. Each chapter contains a bibliography where pertinent. Index.

1318

Kauffman, Stanley, with Bruce Henstell, eds. **American Film Criticism from the Beginnings to "Citizen Kane": Reviews of Significant Films at the Time They First Appeared**. New York: Liveright, 1972. 443p.

This chronological anthology of skillfully selected reviews gives insight into the development of an art and an industry. Kauffman has preceded each review with editorial notes, usually brief. There is a bibliography in the form of the books and articles cited and an index.

1319

Kelly, Terence. **A Competitive Cinema**. London: Institute of Economic Affairs, 1966. 204p.

Study of the economics, structure, and institutions of the British cinema industry, ranging from the financing of production to the exhibition of the film in theaters throughout the country. Contains a bibliography.

1320

Kerr, Walter. **The Silent Clowns**. New York: Knopf, 1975. 372p.

Kerr explores the aesthetics of silence in film as exemplified in the movies of the great comedians of the pre-sound era. He emphasizes the particular qualities that were lost with the coming of the talkies and makes the point that the effect of sound upon serious drama was quite different. Beautifully written and illustrated. Index.

1321

Kindem, Gorham, ed. **The American Movie Industry: The Business of Motion Pictures**. Carbondale: Southern Illinois University Press, 1982. 448p.

A collection of case studies which surveys the history of the American movie industry. Organization is both chronological and topical. The first three parts follow the history of the film industry's marketing strategies, structural changes, and product innovations. The last two parts examine major topics such as regulation and censorship, interaction with television, Canada as a feature film producer, and the role of the U.S. in the international film industry. The essays deliberately represent diverse methods and perspectives to suggest that the history of the American film industry is really a collection of histories rather than a monolithic, single-strand chronology of events. There are extensive footnotes; a list of trade papers, journals and yearbooks; and a long bibliography which includes both books and articles.

1322

Klingender, F.D., and Stuart Legg. **Money Behind the Screen: A Report Prepared on Behalf of the Film Council**. New York: Arno, c1937, 1978. 79p.

A detailed analysis of British film finances filled with facts and figures, useful to show the economic state of the industry in pre-World War II days. Because of the important role of American film companies in British cinema, an appendix gives "A Summary of American Film Finances." Originally published in England by Lawrence & Wishart.

1323

Klotman, Phyllis Rauch. **Frame by Frame—A Black Filmography**. Bloomington: Indiana University Press, 1979. 700p.

A compendium of over 3,000 film items from around the world with black themes or subject matter or substantial participation by blacks as writers, actors, producers, directors, musicians, animators, or consultants or who even appeared in ancillary or walk-on roles. Klotman sought—but did not always get—the following information for each: film title/series title; narrator/cast; writer, whether screenplay or adaptation; producer, director, studio/company; technical information encompassing film size/color/sound or silent; number of reels/time; date/country or origin; type; distributor/archive; annotation. The approximately 3,000 films are listed alphabetically with the above information, with separate indexes of black performers, author, screenplay writers, producers and directors. It includes not only feature films but also anthropological, avant-garde, experimental and documentary films worldwide.

1324

Knight, Derrick, and Vincent Porter. **A Long Long Look at Short Films: An A.C.T.T. Report on the Short Entertainment and Factual Film**. New York: Pergamon Press and the Association of Cinematograph, Television and Allied Technicians, 1967. 185p.

Factual report, written for a British trade union, the Association of Cinematography, Television and Allied Technicians, which documents both the social and aesthetic need for short films and their present plight. Contains many facts and figures, both in the main body and in the appendixes. Bibliography and index.

1325

Kobal, John, comp. and ed. **Fifty Years of Movie Posters**. New York: Bounty Books, 1973. 175p. (Distributed by Crown.)

A big book reproducing in all their glory posters from Hollywood's early days to its heyday in the 1950s. David Robinson has written an introduction in which he details the economic importance of the posters. There is an index to movie titles represented.

Kowalski, Rosemary Ribich. **Women and Film: A Bibliography**. (See No. 1662.)

1326

Kracauer, Siegfried. **Theory of Film: The Redemption of Physical Reality**. New York: Oxford University Press, 1965. 364p.

"In sum, my book is intended to afford insight into the intrinsic nature of photographic film," says Kracauer. He sees film as an extension of photography, sharing with it an ability to capture the visible world and coming into its own as a medium when it records the ephemeral movement of the life about us. With this as his thesis he discusses general characteristics such as basic concepts and establishment of physical existence; areas and elements including fantasy, actors, dialogue and sound, music, audience reaction; the various kinds of film—experimental, factual, theoretical; and relationship between the novel and film. Throughout the book a number of movies are analyzed to bring out the various points, and in a final chapter, "Epilogue," "the cinema itself is set in the perspective of something more general—an approach to the world, a mode of human existence." Contains notes, a bibliography of material cited, and an index.

1327

Kracauer, Siegfried. **From Caligari to Hitler: A Psychological History of the German Film**. Princeton, NJ: Princeton University Press, c1947, 1966. 361p.

Although Kracauer says that he is not concerned with German films merely for their own sake but rather as a means to increase knowledge of pre-Hitler Germany in a specific way, he nevertheless gives a great deal of information about structure and content of the motion picture in Germany and about individual films.

"Propaganda and the Nazi War Film," which with a few changes is a reprint of the author's pamphlet of the same title issued in 1942 by the Museum of Modern Art Film Library, is included as a supplement. There is also a structural analysis giving specific examples of the ways in which propaganda is used, an excellent bibliography, and a name-subject index.

1328

LaBeau, Dennis. **Theatre, Film and Television Biographies**. Detroit, MI: Gale, 1979. 477p.

Subtitled "A consolidated guide to over 100,000 bibliographical sketches of persons living and dead, as they appear in over 40 of the principal biographical dictionaries devoted to the theatre, film and television," this index to biographical material on performing artists scrupulously covers a variety of biographical dictionaries, directories and filmographies. For each entry the date of birth (and death) and location of biographical materials is given. When information on name or date differs, all entries are included. Arrangement is alphabetical.

1329, 1330

Lahue, Kalton C. **Continued Next Week: A History of the Moving Picture Serial**. Norman: University of Oklahoma Press, 1964. 203p.

Lahue, Kalton C. **A World of Laughter: The Motion Picture Comedy Short, 1910–1930**. Norman: University of Oklahoma Press, 1966. 240p.

Histories of two bygone genres. **Continued Next Week** is a chronological story of the old-time serial. Following the text, a 123-page appendix traces various serials from 1912 to 1930, with director, cast, release date, company and chapter titles for each. There is an index. Lahue followed this in 1968 with a picture book, **Bound and Gagged: The Story of the Silent Serials** (Barnes), designed primarily to entertain and to promote nostalgia in those old enough to remember its heyday.

The World of Laughter is an account of the major films, firms, actors, and directors of short comedy up to the advent of sound. An appendix lists by date the films of selected major comedians. In conclusion is a very brief bibliography and a name-title index.

1331

Lansell, Ross, and Peter Beilby, eds. **The Documentary Film in Australia**. North Melbourne: Cinema Papers, 1982. 205p.

The output of the documentary sector of Australia's film industry has always outstripped feature film production and, according to the editors, is the backbone of the industry. The irony is that while Australia feature film is well-known in and outside of the country, the documentary has received too little attention. The editors are doing their bit to remedy the situation with this survey which includes a brief history, production, case histories, market-place, some themes, preservation and repositories of documentaries, a glimpse of the future, and assorted other useful information, such as producers and directors, government film and TV organizations, distributors, government film libraries, sales agents, documentary film festivals and award winners. Index of personal names and film and program titles.

1332

Leab, Daniel J. **From Sambo to Superspade: The Black Experience in Motion Pictures**. Boston: Houghton-Mifflin, 1975. 301p.

A history and interpretation of the black in American motion pictures which presents a bleak and well-documented picture. Illustrations, footnotes, bibliography, and index.

1333

Le Grice, Malcolm. **Abstract Film and Beyond**. Cambridge, MA: MIT Press, 1977. 160p.

A theoretical and historical account of the trends in abstract filmmaking which covers not only nonrepresentational forms but also experiments into film's manipulation into time. Beginning with Cezanne, whom Le Grice considers influential because of his preoccupation with pictorial space, he discusses the Futurists' cinema; the early abstract film experiments in Germany, France and the U.S. in the 1920s; post-World War II experimental film, and finally the present. There are many illustrations, footnotes, a list of catalogs, and an index.

1334

Leiser, Erwin. **Nazi Cinema**. Tr. from the German by Gertrud Mander and David Wilson. New York: Macmillan, 1975. 179p.

The author examines notorious and forgotten German films to show how Hitler's Minister of Popular Enlightenment converted German cinema to a highly efficient cog in the Nazi propaganda machine to help sell the German people on his government and its policies. Contains a bibliography, a selected filmography, and an index of names.

1335

Lejeune, Caroline A. **Cinema**. London: Alexander Maclehose, 1931. 255p.

Even the contemporary portions of these perceptive essays have now become history, and as history as well as for themselves alone, they are excellent. Most of the essays are about film personalities—actors, actresses, directors, producers—and about types of film, such as war, travel, the soil, experimental, and so on, grouped into three sections—American, European, and miscellany—in which latter category Lejeune has placed the various genres. Contains a bibliography and an index.

1336

Lenihan, John H. **Showdown: Confronting Modern America in the Western Film**. Urbana: University of Illinois Press, 1985. 214p.

Lenihan has analyzed the content of the Western as an important cultural formula, using it to demonstrate its relation to major political, intellectual and social issues and trends since World War II, and likewise to explore some of the assumptions, concerns and attitudes of American society that have made the genre so popular. After an analysis of the formula he applies it in terms of events and trends following the war, with chapters on "Cold War-Wrath," "Racial Attitudes," "Postwar Alienation from the Good Society," "Society in the 1950s: Complacent or Plaintive?" "Against the Establishment." There is a bibliography of the films, books, articles and unpublished materials examined and of the interviews conducted; a film title index; and a subject index.

1337

Lentz, Harris M., III. **Science Fiction, Horror & Fantasy Film and Television Credits: Over 10,000 Actors, Actresses, Directors, Producers, Screenwriters, Cinematographers, Art Directors, and Make-Up, Special Effects, Costume and Other People; Plus Full Cross-References from All Film and TV Shows**. 2 v. Jefferson, NC: McFarland, 1983. 730p., 1,374p.

The first volume (730 pages) gives in outline form for each character a listing of the play or plays involved, with dates, and in cases of actors and actresses, the role. Volume II (1,374 pages) is an index to all plays and television shows in Volume I, with a filmography for each. If the television production is a serial, each sequence is included, with date and cast.

1338

Leprohon, Pierre. **The Italian Cinema**. Tr. from the French by Roger Greaves and Oliver Stallybrass. New York: Praeger, 1972. 256p.

Traces Italian film from its beginnings in 1895, relating its directions to the social, cultural, and political crises in Italy, and ending with the year 1969. Arrangement is chronological. There is a three-page section, "Notes and References," a lengthy biographical dictionary, and an index to people and film.

1339

Lees, David, and Stan Berkowitz. **The Movie Business**. New York: Vintage, 1981. 196p.

"The primary goal of each of these chapters," the authors say of their behind-the-scenes explanation of the economics of filmmaking, "is to outline the more important chores usually involved in deciding how films are made and marketed. Beyond that we also explore the central role played by uncertainty in determining the character of most of the decision making that goes on before and after the cameras have rolled." As they tell it, economics, not art, is the determining factor. Aspects they discuss in economic terms include credits; components of filmmaking; ground crews; major, minor and independent studios; tax shelters; domestic and foreign distribution; blind bidding; marketing; merchandising; Oscars and the future. The authors, long-time film reporters, gathered their evidence from interviews with toilers in the movie vineyard, ranging from high executives to theater owners. For a historical perspective on the subject of movie economics, see Huettig (No. 1295).

1340

Leyda, Jay. **Dianying: An Account of Films and the Film Audience in China**. Cambridge, MA: MIT Press, 1972. 515p.

The author traces Chinese films and filmmaking chronologically, tying it in with history. Within this framework he discusses important films and their casts. He includes both the films made with the endorsement of the political party and those made by the underground forces, and attempts to show the influence of politics and the reactions of the Chinese audiences. There are a number of appendixes: "Contributors to the Art and History of Chinese Film," "Important Chinese Films Made by Chinese and Foreign Groups from 1897 to 1966," "A Counter-Revolutionary Record Aimed at the Restoration of Capitalism." Contains a list of sources and a detailed index.

1341

Leyda, Jay. **Kino: A History of the Russian and Soviet Film**. New York: Macmillan, 1960. 493p.

An intensive treatment of the background, personalities, political interests, industrial growth and artistic development, concluding with the death of Eisenstein in 1948. There are five appendixes, one of the most useful of which is "Fifty Years of Russian and Soviet Films 1908–1958, a Select List." The list of sources for each chapter forms a bibliography, and there is an index.

1342

Lieberman, Susan, and Frances Cable, comps. **Memorable Film Characters: An Index to Roles and Performers, 1915–1983**. Westport, CT: Greenwood, 1984. 291p.

Identifies alphabetically and describes briefly over 1,500 screen characters from both silents and talkies, predominantly from American but also from foreign films, giving title of the film, release date, and a brief description of the role. This is followed by an index to characters by title of film and an index by name of performer. Thus, each character may be identified in three different ways: by character, by title of movie, or by name of actor or actress portraying the role. Selection—a difficult task—was on the basis of nominations for prominent awards and a questionnaire sent to 75 film buffs. Obviously, as the authors admit, it is not definitive. In spite of omissions, it should prove helpful to film students, movie enthusiasts, nostalgia buffs and Trivial Pursuiters. A selective bibliography of sources and a list of helpful periodical indexes are included.

1343

Liehm, Antonin. **Closely Watched Films: The Czechoslovak Experience**. White Plains, NY: International Arts and Science Press, 1974. 485p.

"No other film industry—or only those of the largest countries—received so many prizes and awards, so much recognition, in the sixties as did that of Czechoslovakia," says Liehm. "Today it is forgotten," halted by the Soviet invasion, he continues. These 33 interviews with leading filmmakers represent his effort to perpetuate the memory of this renaissance. Contains a filmography of their productions, along with a small list of other Czechoslovak films with U.S. distribution. Index of names and films.

1344

Liehm, Mira, and Antonin Liehm. **The Most Important Art: East European Film after 1945**. Berkeley: University of California Press, 1977. 467p.

What effect does the nationalization of an art have upon it? Surveying films and filmmakers of Bulgaria, Czechoslovakia, the German Democratic Republic, Poland, Romania, the U.S.S.R., and Yugoslavia, this comparative study shows how the history of their film industries has been one of conflict between the potentialities of a publicly supported art (not dependent on box office) and the limitations and interests of the political forces controlling state support. Films discussed include lesser known ones which did not achieve foreign notice as well as the better known which circulated through much of the world. Contains many illustrations, a bibliography, and an index.

1345

Limbacher, James L. **Feature Films: A Directory of Feature Films on 16mm and Video Available for Rental, Sale, and Lease**. 8th ed. New York: Bowker, 1985. 734p.

Lists 22,205 feature films available in various formats, with the following information for each: title, alternate title, translated title, number of parts, part number, version, series title and subtitle, original title, current and original languages (if other than English), cast, director, release date, producer or country of origin, special information (i.e.—documentary, etc.), number of items, running time, sound statement, size/format, color/B&W, dubbing/narration statement, and distributor. Arrangement is by title, with an index of 4,570 directors, a foreign language films index, and index of 1,436 films under 43 foreign languages. There is also a "Film Reference Bibliography" and a directory of names and addresses.

Two earlier books by Limbacher with self-explanatory titles which make available some rather uncommon information are **Haven't I Seen You Somewhere Before? Remakes, Sequels and Series in Motion Pictures and Television, 1896–1978** (Ann Arbor, MI: Pierian Press, 1979. 295p.), and **Film Music: From Violin to Video** (Metuchen, NJ: Scarecrow, 1974. 835p.).

1346

Lindsay, Vachel. **The Art of the Motion Picture**. New York: Macmillan, 1915. 324p.

A delightful contemporary account by a famous American poet of the early 20th century about the early days of movies. Lindsey's aim is to supply viewers with a social and aesthetic way of regarding them. One chapter, "California and America," deserves special mention, for in it he makes the prophecy that California, "as the natural moving picture playground, has the possibility of developing a unique cultural leverage upon America."

1347

Liu, Alan, P.L. **The Film Industry in Communist China**. Cambridge, MA: Massachusetts Institute of Technology, 1965. 92p. (Distributed by the Clearinghouse for Federal Scientific and Technical Information, U.S. Department of Commerce, National Bureau of Standards, Institute for Applied Technology.)

Report, based almost exclusively on Chinese publications, which analyzes the dynamics of the film industry. Deals briefly with Chinese films in the pre-Communist era and discusses at length the development, production, and audience under the later government, as well as the role of foreign film in the country. An appendix charts the distribution of the Film Copy System, and a bibliography lists Communist Chinese books, Chinese books from Hong Kong and Taiwan, articles in Western journals, and Western books on China.

1348

Low, Rachael. **The History of the British Film**. 7 v. London: Allen & Unwin, 1948–.

Thus far this multi-volume series spans the period from 1896 through 1939. Volume 1, co-authored with Roger Manvell, covers 1896–1906; Volume 2, 1906–1914; Volume 3, 1914–1918, and Volume 4, 1918–1929. The 1930s is treated in three volumes: Volume 5, **Documentary and Educational Films of the 1930s**; Volume 6, **Films of Comment and Persuasion of the 1930s**; and Volume 7, **Film Making in 1930s Britain**, dealing with feature films. Publication is under the auspices of the British Film Institute. Each volume discusses production and distribution in general and specific films in particular, and each contains a bibliography, a list of films, and an index.

1349

Lyon, S. Daniel, and Michael J. Trebilcock. **Public Strategy and Motion Pictures: The Choice of Instruments to Promote the Development of the Canadian Film Industry**. Toronto: Ontario Economic Council, 1982. 132p.

The authors state that their primary purpose is "to discover what policy or policies the government seeks in developing the film industry, why particular instruments were chosen, and whether these instruments accomplish their stated goals," one of which is to foster a sense of Canadian identity. Gives an excellent overall picture of the state of the industry from its inceptions to the 1980s, including a chapter on the National Film Board, the Canadian Film Development Corporation, provincial and municipal programs, tax advantages (the capital cost allowance) and regulation. Footnotes and bibliography.

MacCabe, Colin, ed. **High Theory/Low Culture: Analyzing Popular Television and Film**. (See No. 700.)

1350

MacCann, Richard Dyer, ed. **Film: A Montage of Theories**. New York: Dutton, 1966. 384p.

There can be no final theory of the film, says Mac-Cann, but "the medium and its limits can be described, differentiated from other media, found to possess unique characteristics." Here he has put together in an anthology a variety of theories from Europeans and Americans designed to put the art of the film in better perspective as part of the knowledge of contemporary civilization. Among the approximately 40 contributors are Eisenstein, Rene Clair, Alfred Hitchcock, Vachel Lindsay, Parker Tyler, Hollis Alpert, Rudolf Arnheim, Ingmar Bergman, Mack Sennett, Herbert Read, Arnold Hauser, Susanne Langer, John Grierson, Siegfried Kracauer, Pauline Kael, Francois Truffaut, Federico Fellini.

1351

MacCann, Richard Dyer. **The People's Films: A Political History of U.S. Government Motion Pictures**. New York: Hastings House, 1973. 238p.

In his preface the author says: "I am concerned . . . with the questions: What factual motion pictures have been produced by the United States Government? When? How? But I am also concerned with the question: Why? What pressures and personalities produced the decisions which produced these films? And beyond this, it is important to make some attempt at criticism of the 'why.'" The author stresses the public relations and propaganda aspect of government films, and devotes a chapter to the documentary in Canada and England. The U.S.I.A., too, comes up for discussion in connection with films and foreign policy. Person, film, and subject-index.

1352

MacPherson, Don, with Paul Willemen, eds. **British Cinema: Traditions of Independence**. London: British Film Institute, 1980. 226p.

Essays which analyze the independent film movement in Britain as represented by political organizations, trade unions, and the Left Book Club which produced and showed films with an alternative voice. Also includes documents of the period showing the debate about film and politics, reprinted with contextual comment. Contains a filmography and a selective bibliography.

1353, 1354, 1355, 1356, 1357

Magill's Survey of Cinema: English Language Films. First series, 4 v. Ed. by Frank N. Magill. Englewood Cliffs, NJ: Salem Press, 1980. 1,906p.

Magill's Survey of Cinema: English Language Films. Second series, 6 v. Ed. by Frank N. Magill. Englewood Cliffs, NJ: Salem Press, 1981. 2,752 p.

Magill's Survey of Cinema: Silent Films. 3 v. Ed. by Frank N. Magill. Englewood Cliffs, NJ: Salem Press, 1982. 1,338p.

Magill's Survey of Cinema: Foreign Language Films. 8 v. Ed. by Frank N. Magill. Englewood Cliffs, NJ: Salem Press, 1985. 3,504p.

Magill's Cinema Annual. Ed. by Frank N.

Magill. Englewood Cliffs, NJ: Salem Press, annual. (1982– .)

This set provides a comprehensive examination of thousands of films which the editor considered outstanding. Each motion picture is analyzed in depth in a signed essay of from 1,000 to 2,500 words written by a specialist who treats cinema as a serious art form, stressing the various elements that have gone into its making. The first and second series, the 10-volume set of **English Language Films**, deals with films released in the U.S., Britain, Canada, Australia and Jamaica after 1927. **Silent Films** contains those released between 1902 and the advent of the talkies, and is preceded by essays on important people, developments and events, including some "lost" films. **Foreign Language Films** includes similar signed essays on over 2,250 major motion pictures from around the world which originated in languages other than English. **Cinema Annual** keeps **English Language Films** and **Foreign Language Films** updated. Each series is arranged alphabetically and is thoroughly indexed, often by separate volumes.

1358

Maltin, Leonard. **TV Movies 1985–86**. 6th ed. New York: New American Library, 1984. 1,021p.

In 1969 Maltin began his **TV Movies**, a handy series to keep by the TV set and equally handy for reference. Originally intended as a guide to both made-for-TV and made-for-Hollywood movies presented on TV, this selection of 16,000 films in the current edition also indicates availability on video. Each film is briefly and critically annotated, with Maltin's own star ratings, year of release, country of origin, running time, and title change when indicated. (Running time can be complicated because videodiscs are often time-compressed.) Annotations are terse and informative. Films go back to the 1930s. Whether for trivial or higher pursuits this can be useful. Frequently updated. (A seventh edition was issued in 1988.)

1359

Maltin, Leonard, ed. **The Whole Film Sourcebook**. New York: Universe, 1983. 454p.

"When I was asked to produce this film directory, I agreed only on condition that I could flesh out our facts with descriptive prose. I wanted to provide something more than the reader could find in a computer printout," says Maltin in his Introduction. He has succeeded admirably in carrying out his aim. Coverage is wide-ranging: "Education and Careers," including the study of film in American colleges and universities, the underpinnings of support such as grants (and grantsmanship), loans, and resources, and film unions and guilds; "Access," broadly covering 16mm rental sources, distributors and production companies, archives, specialized exhibition, and festivals; and "Research and Reference," with a selected

bibliography of film books, and an extensive listing of film periodicals, research libraries and special collections, bookstores and photo sources. Contributors represent experts from each area. All entries are annotated or discussed at some length. The fabled traveler, stranded on a desert island with only one book on film, might do well to pick this.

1360

Maltin, Leonard. **Movie Comedy Teams**. New York: New American Library, 1970. 352p.

In **Movie Comedy Teams** Maltin pictures a bygone Hollywood through biographies, peppered with anecdotes, of such famous tandem comedians as the Marx brothers, Burns and Allen, Abbott and Costello, and the Three Stooges. There are also synopses of major films by comedy teams, along with painstaking filmographies and over 200 still photographs.

1361

Manvell, Roger, ed. **Experiment in the Film**. New York: Arno, 1970. 273p.

An anthology, originally published in 1948, in which contributors take stock of the achievements of the experimental and in some cases the genre film during the first five decades of the century in France, the U.S., the U.S.S.R., Germany and Austria, and Britain. A final short essay deals with the contributions of film to science. Indexes to titles and to novels.

1362

Manvell, Roger. **Film**. London: Penguin, c1944, 1950. 288p.

A survey, interesting not only in itself but also as a study of the state of the art shortly after World War II. Manvell discusses the motion picture as art and entertainment and shows some of the problems its international popularity created. He ends with an annotated booklist and "Fifty Years of Film," a selected list of directors and their work from the U.S., Britain, France, Germany, Italy and Russia. Indexes of film titles, subjects, and personal names.

1363

Manvell, Roger. **Films and the Second World War**. Cranbury, NJ: Barnes, 1974. 388p.

"The purpose of this book is to discuss and illustrate a cross-section of films about the Second World War, both fiction films and factual films—the picture of war and its motivation from the popular viewpoint as it was (and sometimes still is) presented to the public of the principal nations involved, both during and after the actual years of fighting. The few films that anticipated the coming struggle for power are also discussed in a preliminary chapter."—Preface. Notes, a bibliography, and indexes of films and of titles.

1364

Manvell, Roger, and Heinrich Fraenkel. **The German Cinema**. New York: Praeger, 1971. 159p.

This first survey of German movies to be published in English analyzes films from their origins in 1895 through the 1960s, discussing the trends and developments, detailing the Nazis' use of the film as propaganda and subsequent "deNazification" of the industry, and examining the post-World War II cinema. There is also a survey of younger German directors. Bibliography and index.

Manvell, Roger, ed. **The International Encyclopedia of Film**. (See No. 1303.)

1365, 1366

Manvell, Roger. **New Cinema in Europe**. New York: Dutton, 1966. 60p. (Vista Paperback.)

Manvell, Roger. **New Cinema in the USA: The Feature Film Since 1946**. New York: Dutton, 1968. 160p. (Vista Paperback.)

The first of these two books deals with film in Europe after World War II, with emphasis on the realistic and naturalistic approach of major filmmakers. Among nations included are Italy, Britain, France, Russia, and Poland. Indexed.

The second contrasts American film with that in other parts of the world and fills in the 1950s background of U.S. films. It then discusses films and directors in terms of traditionalism and experimentation, and has a chapter on the musical. Indexed.

1367

Manvell, Roger, and Peter Day. **The Technique of Film Music**. 2d ed. New York: Hastings House, 1975. 310p.

Addressed to filmmakers and musicians, this traces the development and function of all kinds of music in the silent and sound film up to about 1955. After that date an analytical approach stressing contemporary achievement is substituted for the historical one. Further chapters discuss the music director and sound recordist, and give the composer's view. Appendixes include "An Outline History of Film Music," "Film Music Criticism," and a bibliography. Indexed.

1368

Mapp, Edward. **Blacks in American Films: Today and Yesterday**. Metuchen, NJ: Scarecrow Press, 1972. 278p.

After a brief history of the Negro in motion pictures from the earliest appearances through 1961, the author examines the content of Negro portrayals in films of each year from 1962 through 1970, comparing old and new stereotypes and changing screen images. Bibliography and index.

1369

Marill, Alvin H. **Movies Made for Television: The Telefeature and the Mini-Series**. New York: New York Zoetrope, 1984. 452p.

Covers nearly 1,700 films and mini-series made expressly for television that premiered between the 1964–65 season and the 1983–84 one on the three commercial networks, Home Box Office, Showtime, or on independent stations (in the case of Operation Prime Time attractions and a handful of other features). PBS is not included. The majority of the films filled a two-hour time slot, including commercials, although some fit into 90-minutes. A few are three hours or longer. Films are arranged chronologically by premier date in New York, with cast and credits, story line, notes of interest when necessary, and award notations where applicable. Indexed by title, by cast, by director, by producer, and by writer. There is a list of alternative titles.

1370

Mast, Gerald. **The Comic Mind: Comedy and the Movies**. 2d ed. Chicago: University of Chicago Press, 1979. 369p.

Speculating that the serio-comic tradition in the arts is a necessary counter-influence to the chaos of modern life, Mast shows how certain films reveal serious thought through comic form as he discusses and evaluates comedies both silent and sound, American and foreign, which fit into a broad framework of comic structures and traditions. Like any discussion dealing with old movies, this can evoke nostalgia, but its range is much broader and deeper. Chapter notes, a short bibliography, and a list of distributors of comic films. Index.

1371

Mast, Gerald, and Marshall Cohen, eds. **Film Theory and Criticism: Introductory Readings**. 3d ed. New York: Oxford University Press, 1985. 852p.

"This collection of readings gathers together under one cover the most significant theories and theorists of films," the editors say in their first (1974) edition of their text. Although the intervening 11 years between this and the third edition have seen new theoretical and critical developments their statement of purpose still holds. In this latest edition they take note of the growing distinction between "classical film theory" as opposed to "contemporary film theory," and the division of the former into two historical waves. Emphasis is on the former, which has been around longer and had a better chance to demonstrate its usefulness. Discussions fall under the following categories: "Film and Reality," "Film Image and Film Language," "The Film Medium," "Film, Theater, and Literature," "Film Genres," "The Film Artist," "Film: Psychology, Society, and Ideology." There are 53 selections in all.

1372

Mast, Gerald, ed. **The Movies in Our Midst: Documents in the Cultural History of Film in America**. Chicago: University of Chicago Press, 1982. 764p.

A backward look at the social and cultural history of American film through primary and secondary documents past and present which reveal six important issues central to the development of American film—technology, economics, politics, social implications of film content, censorship, and influence of film on American life. Arrangement is chronological: "Beginnings (1882–1900)"; "Nickelodeon (1900–1913)"; "Feature Films and Hollywood (1914–1927)"; "The Talkies (1924–1930)"; "The Thirties (1931–1940)"; "The War Abroad, A War at Home (1941–1952)" and "Hollywood in the Television Age (1953–1977)." Documents are limited to the U.S., although a few in the later periods involve the impact of foreign film. Many of them are long out of print and difficult to obtain. In conclusion is a detailed bibliography of books, government hearings and articles.

1373

Mast, Gerald. **A Short History of the Movies**. 4th ed. New York: Macmillan, 1986. 562p.

Mast places the achievements of film art within the context of social practice and cultural convention, using various outstanding examples of pictures, directors, actors and actresses to show the way our culture defines social, sexual, and personal relationships. Coverage is broad, as illustrated by chapter headings: "Birth"; "Film Narrative, Commercial Expansion"; "Griffith"; "The Comics: Mack Sennett and the Chaplin Shorts"; "Movie Czars and Movie Stars"; "The Golden Age"; "Soviet Montage"; "Sound"; "France Between the Wars"; "The American Studio Years: 1930–1945"; "Hollywood in Transition: 1946–65"; "Neorealism and New Waves"; "Emerging National Traditions 1: The 1950s and 60s"; "Hollywood Renaissance, 1964–1976"; "Emerging National Traditions 2: The 1970s and 80s"; and "The Return of the Myths: 1977– ." The final chapters reflect four decades of international films—beginning with Italy, France, Japan, India, and Central Europe, and continuing with Germany, the Third World, Australia and other Commonwealth nations. In conclusion Mast discusses the emergence of video and its possible future implications for movies. Two appendixes: a 30-page bibliography, "For Further Reading and Viewing," correlating references with each chapter and containing a representative sampling of the major films of each director mentioned; and a very short history of 16mm film distribution since 1980 (earlier editions contain earlier periods) followed by a list of distributors with addresses and phone numbers. There is a title/name/subject index.

1374

May, Lary. **Screening Out the Past: The Birth of Mass Culture and the Motion Picture Industry**. New York: Oxford University Press, 1980. 304p.

An investigation of the part the motion picture industry played in forging a new and different mass culture pattern that came in with the twentieth century when rebellion against Victorian styles and moral standards spurred a new sort of creativity. Against this backdrop May looks at the relationship among artists, their audiences, and the commercial energy of urban life as together they created a unique new form of entertainment and (sometimes) art, the American movie as exemplified by Hollywood. Appendixes contain "Historiography and New Sources," and tables of statistics and other factual information. There are copious source notes which can also serve as a bibliography, and an index.

1375

Mayer, Michael F. **The Film Industries: Practical Business/Legal Problems in Production, Distribution and Exhibition**. 2d ed. New York: Hastings House, 1978. 230p.

While teaching a course in film industry management, Mayer, a theatrical lawyer, wrote the first edition of this book as a text to chart the way for students and any other interested laymen through the complicated processes of production, distribution, and exhibition. Among the numerous aspects he discusses are contracts, financing agreements, markets abroad and at home, non-theatrical as well as theatrical film, conglomerates, antitrust, copyright, and problems of context. An excellent guide for the novice.

1376

McArthur, Colin, ed. **Scotch Reels: Scotland in Cinema and Television**. London: BFI Publishing, 1982. 122p.

Although Scotland and the Scots have been depicted in cinema since the turn of the century, and although Scotland has had its own distinctive cinematic institutions since the 1930s, it has always been portrayed in stereotype and cliche, McArthur contends. These essays discuss Scotch film culture, examining its lacks and misinterpretations, and suggesting the reasons. They also deal with television because of the kinship and interpenetration of the film and television and more particularly, because of its increasingly important role in presenting Scotland.

1377

McCaffrey, Donald W. **The Golden Age of Sound Comedy: Comic Films and Comedians of the Thirties**. New York: Barnes, 1973. 208p.

Basically a picture book, coffee table variety, but useful because it describes in some detail the films and their stars. There is an annotated bibliography consisting mostly of works on specific stars. Indexes of names and films.

1378

McCarthy, Todd, and Charles Flynn, eds. **Kings of the Bs: Working Within the Hollywood System: An Anthology of Film History and Criticism**. New York: Dutton, 1975. 561p.

The editors of this anthology believe that American B (and C and Z) movies are as necessary to the economics of the Hollywood system as the works of master directors. With this in mind they tour the slums of U.S. filmmaking, digging out figures and facts as well as making observations. Contains filmographies for 325 directors hard to find elsewhere, 75 illustrations, and an index.

1379

McClure, Arthur F., comp. and ed. **The Movies, an American Idiom: Readings in the Social History of the American Motion Picture**. Rutherford, NJ: Fairleigh Dickinson University Press, 1971. 435p.

Collection of articles, drawn from the writings of journalists, critics, historians, sociologists, and humorists, which describe the historical relationship between the American motion picture and the environment of the twentieth century. Articles are arranged chronologically in three parts: "Admission and Ascendancy, 1900–1949"; "Retrenchment and Renewal, 1950–1969"; and "Whither Hollywood?" Among the contributors are Foster Rhea Dulles, Terry Ramsaye, Richard Schickel, Lewis Jacobs, Siegfried Kracauer, Richard Dyer MacCann, Hollis Alpert, Arthur Mayer, Paul Reynolds, Ben Hecht, John Cassavetes, Bosley Crowther, Arthur Knight, and Olivia de Havilland.

1380

McGee, Mark Thomas, and J.R. Robertson. **The J.D. Films: Juvenile Delinquency and the Movies**. Jefferson, NC: McFarland, 1982. 197p.

A critical examination of films about juvenile delinquency which flourished from the 1950s into the 1970s, discussed within the context of the cultural events that inspired them. Beginning with the background, the youthful rebellion of the jazz generation and moving to the inner city delinquents of the 1930s and 1940s, it focuses on the 1950s which brought **The Wild One**, **Blackboard Jungle**, **Rebel Without a Cause** and many lesser examples, and moves on to the turbulent 60s with their throwbacks to the earlier years and the motorcycle and youth rebellion films. The films of the 1970s are summed up in an epilogue. Although no attempt is made to judge the films aesthetically, quality or its absence influences emphasis placed on individual ones. It does,

however, explore the formulas and the genres juvenile delinquent films are derived from. Filmography, bibliography and index.

1381

Mehr, Linda Harris. **Motion Pictures, Television and Radio: A Union Catalogue of Manuscripts and Special Collections in the Western United States**. Boston: G.K. Hall, 1977. 201p. (Sponsored by Film and Television Study Center.)

This is the first effort to collect a checklist of sources of archival materials in these relatively new media. It locates, identifies, and describes research collections currently available for use in established institutions, libraries, museums, and historical societies in Arizona, California, Colorado, Idaho, Montana, Nevada, New Mexico, Oregon, Utah, Washington, and Wyoming. There is a general index and an index by the occupations of the individuals represented in the collections.

1382, 1383

Mellen, Joan. **The Waves at Genji's Door: Japan Through Its Cinema**. New York: Pantheon, 1976. 436p.

Mellen, Joan. **Voices from the Japanese Cinema**. New York: Liveright, 1975. 295p.

In both books Mellen's desire is to introduce Westerners to the Japanese film. Believing that they have been intimidated by the degree to which it is concerned with a national history which seems unfamiliar and even unappealing to the West, she has written **The Waves at Genji's Door** "in the hope of dispelling the myth of inaccessibility which has denied the Japanese film its due." Within this framework she centers upon various aspects of national history from medieval times to the present, as well as more specific aspects like the role of women and the family today and yesterday. There are footnotes and an index.

In **Voices from the Japanese Cinema** she presents an inside view of films, directors, and actors, with emphasis upon the cultural factors which shape Japanese filmmaking.

1384, 1385, 1386

Metz, Christian. **Film Language: A Semiotics of the Cinema**. Tr. by Michael Taylor. New York: Oxford, 1974. 268p.

Metz, Christian. **Language and Cinema**. Tr. by Donna Jean Umiker-Sebeok. The Hague: Mouton, 1974. 304p.

Metz, Christian. **Psychoanalysis and the Cinema: The Imaginary Signifier**. Tr. by Celia Britton, et al. Bloomington: Indiana University Press, 1982. 327p.

Metz is famous for his application of the science of

semiotics to the theory of film, which he elaborates in the first two of the above volumes. In **Film Language**, a collection of his essays, he is concerned with differences and similarities between film and language, using specific films as examples. In **Language and Cinema** he investigates the system of codes that govern cinematic meaning. **The Imaginary Signifier** moves into psychology, applying psychoanalysis to the cinema. All three require previous knowledge of linguistics and semiotics. Each book has notes and indexes.

1387

Miller, Randall M., ed. **Ethnic Images in American Film and Television**. Philadelphia: The Balch Institute, 1978. 173p.

Contains 27 short articles on representation of eight ethnic groups in the U.S.—blacks, Jews, German-Americans, Irish, Italian-Americans, Poles, Puerto Ricans and Asian-Americans. Obviously no author goes into the subject in any depth or even breadth, and for some groups, especially blacks and Jews, other and better material exists. On the other hand, the remaining six groups are not well-represented in the literature, and these essays can serve as a beginning. In a few of the articles notes serve as brief bibliographies.

Milne, Tom, and Paul Willemen. **The Encyclopedia of Horror Movies**. (See No. 1283.)

1388

Monaco, James. **American Film Now: The People, the Power, the Money, the Movies**. 2d ed. New York: Oxford University Press, 1984. 544p.

In his first edition which appeared in 1979 Monaco said: "Anthropologists unearthing **Jaws**, **Heaven Can Wait**, **Grease**, **Close Encounters of the Third Kind**, and other popular films of the seventies a thousand years from now will be hard-pressed to divine from this evidence just what the 1970s were all about," and he finds nothing in the subsequent five years to alter his opinion in this new edition. One of the most revealing portions of both editions is his analysis of Hollywood's economic structure, which he feels dominates its aesthetics. Two chapters have been added to cover the 1980s. One of the most useful features is a 100-page section, "The Data," containing a discussion of film critics and their choices, ten major filmographies of important directors, a long and detailed subject bibliography, chapter references, and a lengthy "Who's Who in American Film Now." Index.

1389

Monaco, James. **How to Read a Film: The Art, Technology, Language, History and Theory of Film and Media**. New York: Oxford University Press, 1977. 502p.

Why do we need to *read* a film? Because, says Monaco, film along with television so closely mimic reality that we apprehend them much more closely than we comprehend them, and it is important to know how they tell us what they tell. To assist he has written a virtual encyclopedia—"an essay on understanding . . . on several levels" which covers the film as art; the technology of the film: image and sound; its language: signs and syntax; its history; its theory in relation to form and function; and a concluding section on related media such as radio, records, TV and video. Each section is clearly written and fully developed, and can be understood independently. Monaco has managed to combine depth with breadth— no mean feat—which makes it one of the best available all-round sources on the subject. Appendixes contain a glossary, a 25-page bibliography and a chronology. Index.

1390

Monaco, James. **Who's Who in American Film Now**. New York: New York Zoetrope, 1981. 221p.

This is different from the average biographical directory whose main concern is with vital statistics and other assorted facts. Rather than a "who's who," this is a "who does what," in which Monaco gives a skeleton structure of the industry by classifying the 13 major crafts, or components of each film, in the sequence usually followed in production, beginning with "Writer" and ending with "Editor," and listing alphabetically under each sequence the names of people "who should and usually do have significant input to a movie," followed by the titles with dates of his or her films. All in all, there are about 4,000 names. A revised edition was published in 1987.

1391

Montgomery, John. **Comedy Films, 1894–1954**. 2d ed. London: Allen & Unwin, 1968. 286p.

Factual history of comedy film in the U.S. and England.

1392

Mora, Carl J. **Mexican Cinema: Reflections of a Society 1896–1980**. Berkeley: University of California Press, 1982. 297p.

"My main reason for writing this book is simply to provide an introduction to the Mexican commercial cinema for American and other English-speaking readers," says Mora of his chronological history of "the largest and most important" cinema in the Latin-speaking world. Emphasizing its role as entertainment and as an influential factor in popular culture, he discusses various films within the context of Mexican society and social movements. Although very much concerned with players and plots, he does not go into economics. There is a 115-page chronological filmology, 1896–1980 (with the exception of 1967–69 when film production lists were not available) giving title, producer and director. Note on sources, bibliography and index.

1393

Moran, Albert, and Tom O'Regan, eds. **An Australian Film Reader**. Sydney: Currency Press, 1985. 391p.

This collection of 50 articles is at the same time a survey and a rather unorthodox history of Australian film. It is divided into four sections in accordance with four distinct types of cinema: the feature films of the silent and early sound period up to World War II; the documentary work of Film Australia and its numerous precursors; the commercial features produced by the re-established industry from 1971; and the range of independent/oppositional/avant-garde film practices, with their diverse political affiliations, from the early 1960s to the present. Comment from the present is often juxtaposed with material from earlier sources, emphasizing that issues around the film work of each period spill over into the present one, and authors sometimes present opposing viewpoints, so that the anthology as a whole departs from the usual documentary history. Throughout, however, it is unified in its central aim to show what is generically Australian about Australian film. Bibliography and index.

1394

Morin, Edgar. **The Stars**. Tr. by Richard Howard. New York: Grove Press, 1960. 189p.

Study of stardom as an institution in which the author, using famous film personalities as examples, discusses the sociology of stardom. There is a table of chronological landmarks.

Morella, Joe, et. al., **Those Great Movie Ads**. (See No. 1596.)

1395

The Motion Picture Guide, by Jay Robert Nash and Stanley Ralph Ross. 12 v. Chicago: Cinebooks, 1985–87.

The statement made by Nash and Ross in the Introduction that theirs is "the only definitive and all-encompassing film encyclopedia in the world" is no idle boast. Its 12 volumes contain more than 50,000 entries for English-speaking and notable foreign films released theatrically and on video cassette. The first eight volumes, A through Z by title, contain entries for releases from 1927 through 1983, with the ninth volume (the end of the alphabet) carrying into 1984. The tenth volume by Robert Connelly consists entirely of silent films, and is in two parts, with those he considers the best receiving full treatment and remaining titles briefly noted. The final two volumes list alternate titles, series, awards and proper names. Entries carry detailed information, including credits, ratings by the author as well as by PR and MPAA, date of release, running time, producing and/or distributing companies, color or black and white, remakes and sequels, genre, and a critical analysis which is often long.

The authors say that the encyclopedia represents 50 years—25 apiece—of joint research into tens of thousands of sources and a viewing of each film, and there is in addition Connelly's work on the silent films. The result is a monumental source of information and enjoyment.

Moulds, Michael, ed. **International Index to Film Periodicals: An Annotated Guide**. (See No. 1928.)

1396

Murray, James P. **To Find an Image: Black Films from Uncle Tom to Superfly**. Indianapolis: Bobbs-Merrill, 1973. 205p.

The film editor of **Black Creation** magazine surveys the treatment of blacks in film from the earliest days of Oscar Michaux and other black filmmakers of the 1920s through Stepin Fetchit, Sidney Poitier, and Shaft. He includes films made by both white and black production companies. An appendix lists the "establishment," labor unions, black films from 1904 to the present (produced by both black and white companies), and representative black producers, directors, screenwriters, scorers, and production companies. Indexed.

1397

Nachbar, John G., ed. **Focus on the Western**. Englewood Cliffs, NJ: Prentice-Hall, 1974. 150p.

Essays, which present an alternative to the assumption that Westerns should recreate history, assembled under four headings—"Origins and Development," "What Is a Western?," "The Western as Cultural Artifact," and "The Contemporary Western." Each develops in a different way the idea that Westerns are not artifacts of actual history but of American idealization of its history. Contributors are John Cawelti, Michael Marsden, Peter Homans, James K. Folson, T.J. Ross, Frederick Elkin, Ralph Brauer, Kathryn Esselman, Richard Etulain, Jon Tuska, Robert Warshow, Jim Kitses and the editor. Includes a selected chronology, "Seventy Years on the Trail," an annotated bibliography of books, articles and periodicals, and an index.

Nachbar, John G. **Western Films: An Annotated Critical Bibliography**. (See No. 1677.)

1398

National Film Archive Catalogue. Volume One: Non-Fiction Films. London: British Film Institute, National Film Archive, 1980. 808p.

A guide to 10,000 nonfiction films from 61 countries held in the National Film Archive. Entries are arranged by country of origin and date and are also accessible through title and subject indexes. Most of the films listed are complete but some, particularly those from early years, are fragments whose origins and titles are unknown. Each entry gives details, where known, of the director, sponsor, production company, footage and a brief synopsis. The Cataloging Section of the National Film Archive can give further information.

1399

National Film Archive Catalogue of Viewing Copies. London: British Film Institute, 1985. 129p.

A complete guide to the films and television material held in the National Film Archive of which copies are available for viewing by students and researchers on Archive premises. Eight thousand fiction and nonfiction films and television programs are listed, with each entry giving length in feet and running time, and date of release or transmission date. All entries are cross-indexed by director and production company.

1400

Naylor, David. **American Picture Palaces: The Architecture of Fantasy**. New York: Van Nostrand, 1981. 220p.

The story of the movie "palaces" that flourished in the '20s, '30s, and '40s, declined with the coming of television, and are being partially rescued, although put to different uses. The text is accompanied by stunning photographs. An appendix is a listing, alphabetical within a chronological framework, of each theater by year, location, architect, seating capacity, and status as of 1981. There is also a bibliography and an index.

1401

Neale, Steve. **Cinema and Technology: Image, Sound, Colour**. Bloomington: Indiana University Press, 1985. 171p.

Neale discusses a number of the technologies that feature prominently in the history of the cinema—photography and early visual entertainments that preceded cinema proper, the camera, the projector, sound recording and reproduction, and finally, color—giving for each an outline of the scientific and technical principles involved and appraising some of the economic, aesthetic and psychological factors. Overall he emphasizes the impact of these various technologies upon the cinema as both an industry geared toward the production of profits and an institution geared toward the production of meaning and pleasure. Bibliography and index.

1402

New York Times Encyclopedia of Film, Ed. by Gene Brown. 13 v. New York: Times Books, 1984.

Facsimiles of all articles in their entirety reproduced from the **New York Times** between 1896 and 1979. Arranged chronologically, they give a view of film history as it happened. The 13th volume is an index.

1403, 1404

New York Times Film Reviews 1913–1968. 6 v. New York: New York Times Library and Information Division, 1970.

New York Times Film Reviews 1969–1982. 6 v. New York: Arno, 1971–1984.

The first five volumes contain approximately 18,000 film reviews as they appeared in the **New York Times** in chronological order. Volume Six indexes the films by title, by persons, and by corporation, with an appendix preceding which includes a substantial section of reviews inadvertently omitted from early volumes; the **Times'** choice of the Ten Best from 1924 through 1968; the New York Film Critics Circles Awards, 1935–1968; the Academy Awards from 1927 to 1968; and a Picture Gallery of portraits of 2,000 movie stars.

The second set of six volumes were issued biennially, ending with 1982. For one man's choice from the earlier set, see George Amberg's **The New York Times Film Reviews: A One-Volume Selection 1913–1970**. (Quadrangle, 1971, 495p.)

1405

Nichols, Bill. **Ideology and the Image: Social Representation in the Cinema and Other Media**. Bloomington: Indiana University Press, 1981. 334p.

Focusing on narrative and documentary film, Nichols attempts to define the relations between art, broadly interpreted, and ideology to probe what the patterns found in films and other images had to do with life. To explore these and similar pertinent questions he draws from a number of traditions: Marxist cultural criticism, structuralism, semiology, psychoanalysis, communication theory, the psychology of perception, and the philosophy of science.

1406, 1407

Nichols, Bill, ed. **Movies and Methods: An Anthology**. Vol. I. Berkeley: University of California Press, 1976. 640p.

Nichols, Bill, ed. **Movies and Methods: An Anthology**. Vol. II. Berkeley: University of California Press, 1985. 753p.

Each volume examines a range of critical methods applicable to film study, with examples of how these methods can be applied to the study and appreciation of actual films by "setting older traditions alongside newer ones, throwing light on the limits of methods that were once pervasive and establishing a historical context for methods that are still being formulated." Nichols intends the essays in the first volume, made in the early 1970s, to mark the emergence of film as a new area of scholarship with its own distinctive methodologies, and the essays in the second, mostly from the early 1980s, to confirm film as an established field of study. Essays in Volume I are arranged under "Contextual Criticism" with subheads "Political Criticism," "Genre Criticism," and "Feminist Criticism"; "Formal Criticism" with subheads "Auteur Criticism" and *Mise-en-scène* Criticism"; and "Theory" with subheads "Film Theory" and "Structuralism-Semiology."

Essays in the second volume are grouped without subheads under "Historical Criticism," "Genre Criticism," "Feminist Criticism," "Structuralist Semiotic," "Psychoanalytic Semiotic" and "Countercurrents." There are about 100 essays in all. In the first volume Nichols has written a short introduction to each group, accompanied by a bibliography; in the second volume he has omitted the group introductions in favor of a 24-page general introduction covering the content of both volumes, and he has brought the references together in a general bibliography. Each volume is indexed.

1408

Nicholls, Peter. **The World of Fantastic Films: An Illustrated Survey**. New York: Dodd Mead, 1984. 224p.

"This is a book about seven hundred of the most interesting fantasy films ever made," says Nicholls. Fantasy, Nicholls tells us, is difficult to define, including among other types, tales of monsters, cavemen, star ships, and even—stretching not too fine a point—James Bond who employs science fiction paraphernalia not of this world. However, he settles upon five categories for his discussion—science fiction, monster, supernatural horror, settings in an imaginary past, and sword-and-sorcery—with a long chapter on each. Preliminary to these are four chapters dealing with the history of the fantasy—the final one discussing 13 key directors and producers since 1968. A chronology from 1902 through 1983, constitutes a third of the book; a detailed filmography and an index conclude it.

1409

Noble, Peter. **The Negro in Films**. London: Skelton Robinson, 1948. 288p.

Some years before the treatment of blacks in the entertainment world became the issue it is today, their status was undergoing examination in Britain. This book looks at portrayals of and by Negroes on the stage beginning with the Federal period, and moves on to the silent and then the sound film. It takes up the Negro in song and dance roles, in independent and government films, and in European films; discusses some of the leading Negro players; and assays what the future may hold. Appendixes give a brief historical background of the American Negro, a bibliography, a list of films featuring Negroes or containing important racial themes—American, British, and continental—and a defense of D.W. Griffith's **The Birth of a Nation**. Indexed.

1410

Oakley, Charles Allen. **Where We Came In: Seventy Years of the British Film Industry**. London: Allen & Unwin, 1964. 245p.

A chronological history told largely in terms of films and the people connected with them, set against the background of the times. Oakley never loses sight of the economics of the industry. Documentary as well as theatrical films are included. Contains a 12-page chronology, "The Sequence of Events,"; many illustrations, and an index.

1411

Ohrn, Steven, and Rebecca Riley, comps. **Africa from Real to Reel: An African Filmography**. Waltham, MA: African Studies Association, Brandeis University, 1976. 144p.

A listing, with descriptive annotations, of approximately 1,300 16mm films on Africa distributed in the U.S. and Canada. The compilers describe the selection of films as follows: "a curious mixture of some of the best and some of the worst films ever made about Africa and Africans. Most of the films are of historic value only, being biased presentations shedding more light on ethnocentrism than Africa; more telling of the attraction to the strange and exotic than to the search for truth in other people's cultures and lives. Yet for those interested in the study of Africa, especially the history of Africa on film, this filmography should provide clues to a rich and exciting resource." For each entry is given title, date, producer and filmmaker, characteristics, location, distributors, and any further pertinent information. Additional material includes a geographical and area index, a list of films, and an annotated bibliography of African filmography.

Oliver, Elizabeth, ed. **Researcher's Guide to British Film and Television Collections**. (See No. 1446.)

1412

Oshana, Maryann. **Women of Color: A Filmography of Minority and Third World Women**. New York: Garland, 1985. 338p.

"This book aims to acquaint the reader with English-language films whose characters include a woman of color, specifically an American woman character who belongs to a minority group or a woman of the Third World," explains Oshana. Even, as in many cases, when the role is played by a white woman, it is included; emphasis is on character of women's roles rather than on the actresses. Coverage is from 1930 to 1983, and consists mainly of films from the U.S., with a few from Britain. No attempt is made to be comprehensive; this, says the author, would be almost impossible because of the number of black and Hispanic women playing servants. Nor are silent films listed. Even so, there are more than 1,700 entries, each of which contains a filmography and brief synopsis. An actress index giving only actresses playing minority roles is followed by a director's index, and a minority/Third World classification index beginning with the **Arabian Nights** and ending with the South Sea Islands.

1413, 1414, 1415, 1416, 1417

Parish, James, and Michael R. Pitts. **The Great Gangster Pictures**. Metuchen, NJ: Scarecrow, 1976. 431p.

Parish, James, and Michael R. Pitts. **The Great Science Fiction Pictures**. Metuchen, NJ: Scarecrow, 1977. 382p.

Parish, James, and Michael R. Pitts. **The Great Spy Pictures**. Metuchen, NJ: Scarecrow, 1974. 585p.

Parish, James, and Michale R. Pitts. **The Great Spy Pictures**. Vol. 2. Metuchen, NJ: Scarecrow, 1986. 430p.

Parish, James, and Michael R. Pitts. **The Great Western Pictures**. Metuchen, NJ: Scarecrow, 1976. 455p.

The main portion of each of these volumes consists of an alphabetical list of motion pictures which the authors consider typical of the genre. Each title is discussed, with date, running time, credits, synopsis, and comments, often from reviews. This is preceded by an introduction and followed by lists of radio and TV series, and a selected bibliography. There are no indexes. A second volume of **The Great Gangster Pictures** was scheduled to appear in 1987.

1418, 1419, 1420, 1421

Parish, James R. **Actors' Television Credits, 1950–1972**. Metuchen, NJ: Scarecrow, 1973. 869p.

Parish, James R., with Mark Trost. **Actors' Television Credits. Supplement 1**. Metuchen, NJ: Scarecrow Press, 1978. 423p.

Parish, James R., with Vincent Terrace, **Actors' Television Credits. Supplement 2, 1977–1981**. Metuchen, NJ: Scarecrow Press, 1982. 327p.

Parish, James R., with Vincent Terrace, **Actors' Television Credits. Supplement 3, 1982–1985**. Metuchen, NJ: Scarecrow Press, 1986. 449p.

Detailed credits on a selected list of TV performers ("those who have contributed most uniquely to the industry. Due to space limitations the author has had selectively to eliminate some of the more hardworking but less essential actors . . . ," says Parish in the first volume). The main source used to gather the information is **TV Guide**, which has been virtually indexed by player. Names are arranged alphabetically, with information as to type of program series, single episode, pilot, and so on, and the nature of the role (host, hostess, narrator, etc.). Certain areas are not covered—documentaries, game shows, live special events, news shows, quiz shows, sports shorts, talk shows, theatrical motion pictures, variety shows. Even so there are thousands of entries. Supplements add new ones and amplify, correct, and delete information where necessary.

1422, 1423

Parish, James R., and Michael R. Pitts. **Film Directors: A Guide to Their American Films**. Metuchen, NJ: Scarecrow, 1974. 436p.

Parish, James R., et al. **Film Directors Guide: Western Europe**. Metuchen, NJ: Scarecrow, 1976. 292p.

These volumes are intended as a checklist of directors who have contributed feature-length films to the U.S. cinema; and in the case of the second, a checklist of directors from Western Europe countries. (Sweden is omitted from the latter, because the authors at that time planned to produce a similar volume on Eastern Europe which was to include Sweden.) Information for each entry includes the director's name, dates, birthplace, and films, with production company, distributor, and release date when this information was available.

Patterns of Discrimination Against Women in the Film and Television Industries. (See No. 741.)

1424

Patterson, Lindsay, comp. **Black Films and Film-Makers: A Comprehensive Anthology from Stereotype to Superhero**. New York: Dodd, Mead, 1975. 298p.

Approximately 30 articles divided into six sections moving from early criticism of the black as a caricature and the controversy over **Birth of a Nation** to an examination of black movies of the 1970s. Emphasis is on the place of black films in the black culture and on the blacks who have acted in or produced the films. Contains a filmography and a bibliography.

1425

The Payne Fund Studies. **Motion Pictures and Youth**. W.W. Charters, Chairman. New York: Macmillan, c1933, 1935. (Reprinted by Arno.)

This series of empirical studies is the first major undertaking on the effects of film on youth—in this case the youth of the 1930s. It has historical value both for its findings and because it is seminal. Charters, Dale, Blumer, and others of the authors were among the best-known early researchers in this field. A list of individual volumes—in some cases, two titles are combined in one book—are:

Blumer, Herbert. **Movies and Conduct**, 1933.

Blumer, Herbert, and Philip M. Hauser. **Movies, Delinquency, and Crime**, 1934.

Charters, W. W. **Motion Pictures and Youth: A Summary**, 1933, together with P. W. Holday and George D. Stoddard, **Getting Ideas from the Movies**, 1933.

Cressey, Paul G., and Frederick M. Thrasher. **Boys, Movies, and City Streets**, 1934.

Dale, Edgar. **Content of Motion Pictures**, published

together with Edgar Dale's **Children's Attendance at Motion Pictures**, 1935.

Dale, Edgar. **How to Appreciate Motion Pictures**, 1934.

Dysinger, W. S., and Christian A. Ruckmick. **The Emotional Responses of Children to the Motion Picture Situation**, 1933.

Dysinger, W.S., Christian A. Ruckmick, and Charles C. Peters. **Motion Pictures and Standards of Morality**, 1933.

Forman, Henry James. **Our Movie-Made Children**, 1933.

Peterson, Ruth C., and L. L. Thurstone. **Motion Pictures and Social Attitudes of Children**, published 1933; together with Frank K. Shuttleworth and Mark A. May, **The Social Conduct and Attitude of Movie Fans**, 1933.

Renshaw, Samuel, Vernon L. Miller, and Dorothy Marquis. **Children's Sleep**, 1933.

1426, 1427

Peary, Gerald, and Roger Shatzkin, eds. **The Classic American Novel and the Movies**. New York: Ungar, 1977. 356p.

Peary, Gerald, and Roger Shatzkin, eds. **The Modern American Novel and the Movies**. New York: Ungar, 1978. 461p.

Companion volumes which together and from an aesthetic viewpoint use 59 motion pictures (27 in the first volume, 22 in the second) as case studies to follow the transformation from book to film and the numerous factors that create a difference. To pick their examples the editors select "classics" in terms of chronology rather than literary merit as books published before 1930, and "modern"as between that date and 1930–70. Essays are by film and literary critics and all treat the film as art, although they point out economic and cultural determinants. For an earlier work see George Bluestone's **Novels into Film** (No. 1174). Each volume contains "Sources for Films Listed in Film Credits and Filmography," "Film Credits," "Selected Filmography" and "Selected Bibliography." Indexes.

1428

Perlmutter, Tom. **War Movies**. New York: Hamlyn, 1974. 156p.

From World War I propagandistic war films to bitterly realistic ones, some of which were made quite early, this book examines and illustrates trends. Newsreels, documentaries, and anti-war films are also included. The format is very large—18-by-11-inches—and illustrations outweigh texts, but both work well together and the text is analytical. Title/name index.

1429

Perry, George. **The Great British Picture Show**. Boston: Little Brown, 1985. 386p.

A history of the British film in which the author searches to find characteristics and contributions which differentiate it from the film of other nationalities, discussing specific films, directors, and players. In his Introduction he tells the reasons that he feels lie behind "the failure of the British cinema to achieve an independent status." A detailed "Biographical Guide to the British Cinema" gives the author's commentary on some of the leading performers and producers of British film, with a list of productions and dates. Revised and updated from a 1974 edition. Bibliography and index.

1430

Phillips, Klaus, ed. **New German Film-makers: From Oberhausen Through the 1970s**. New York: Ungar, 1984. 462p.

". . . explores the directions of the New German Cinema by concentrating on twenty-one filmmakers whose films, individually and collectively, convey a sense of the forces and concerns that gave form to the new cinema and helped propel it to worldwide prominence" Introduction. Those included are Herbert Achternbusch, Hark Bohm, Alf Brustellin and Bernhard Sinkel, Hullmuth Cistard, Rainer Werner Fassbinder, Hans S. Geissdorfer, Reinhard Hauff, Werner Herzog, Alexander Kluge, Peter Lilienthal, Edgar Reitz, Volker Schlondorff and Margarethe von Trotta, May Spils and Werner Enke, Ula Stockl, Jean-Marie Straub and Daniele Huillet, Hans-Jurgen Syberberg, and Wim Wenders. In an introductory chapter the editor gives a background. There are filmographies and bibliographies for each of the filmmakers, and a general bibliography.

1431

Pilkington, William T., and Don Graham, eds. **Western Movies**. Albuquerque: University of New Mexico Press, 1979. 157p.

Twelve essays featuring 14 films which the editors consider landmarks within the genre—"a classic or a near classic or, in some cases, an interesting failure." The essayists and their films are: **The Virginian**—Joseph Trimmer; **Stagecoach**—David Clandfield; **Fort Apache**—William Pilkington; **High Noon**—Don Graham; **Shane** and **Hud**—James Folsom; **Rio Bravo**—Robin Wood; **The Wild Bunch**—Arthur Pettit; **Little Big Man**—John W. Turner; **A Man Called Horse**—Dab Georgakas; **The Great Northfield Minnesota Raid**—Don Graham; **Ulzana's Raid**—John Nachbar; and **The Missouri Breaks**—Floyd Lawrence. The editors have contributed an analytical introduction and a brief annotated bibliography.

1432

Pitts, Michael R., comp. **Hollywood and American History: A Filmography of Over 250 Motion Pictures Depicting U.S. History**. Jefferson, NC: McFarland, 1984. 332p.

"In **Hollywood and American History** I attempted to study not only the individual films based on our nation's past but how these events have been interpreted to the public, either right, wrong, or in-between, on celluloid," says Pitts. In addition to Hollywood products he has included films from the East Coast and other parts of the country as well as a few foreign movies about events in U.S. history. Entries are in alphabetical order by title, followed by a listing of cast and chief production staff, the plot, and Pitts' comments. In cases of important films these comments are often of some length, including facts about the film and Pitts' evaluation. Bibliography and subject/name/title index.

1433

Pitts, Michael R. **Western Movies: A TV and Video Guide to 4200 Genre Films**. Jefferson, NC: McFarland, 1986. 623p.

The author's intent is to provide the Western film viewer with a comprehensive handbook of films available, including television films, 16mm, 8mm and Super 8mm films; and video cassettes and video discs, along with brief information about each. Entries include film title, release company and year, running time and whether black, white or color, a cast listing, plot synopsis, and brief critical review. Only feature films are included, and x-rated films are not. Those available on video—several hundred in all—are indicated. Following the text is a list of horses and the cowboys who made them famous; a list of pseudonyms; and a list of video sources. Bibliography and name index.

Powers, Anne, ed. **Blacks in American Movies: A Selected Bibliography**. (See No. 1687.)

1434

Pratt, George C. **Spellbound in Darkness: A History of the Silent Film**. Rev. ed. New York Graphic Society, 1973. 548p.

A compilation of original readings about the silent film from 1896 to 1929, collected from contemporary sources and bound together by the compiler's commentary. Scope is both American and foreign. Though most are reviews, there are also articles, particularly in the early portion.

1435

Prawer, S.S. **Caligari's Children: The Film as Tale of Terror**. New York: Oxford University Press. 1980. 307p.

"The ghost story is alive and well and living in the cinema," says Prawer, who believes that today's horror story has found its home in the motion picture. In this serious study of the genre in print and in film, he examines its genesis and progress, discussing early examples like **Frankenstein** and **Murders in the Rue Morgue**, which have become classic, and more modern ones like **The Cabinet of Dr. Caligari** and **The Exorcist**, created for film. He has included hundreds of titles—the less well known along with the familiar—demonstrating the changes that occur in the metamorphosis into film and explaining the tricks of the trade commonly used in

the making of all horror (or terror, as he prefers to call them) movies. Bibliography, name index, and film title index.

1436

Quart, Leonard, and Albert Auster. **American Film and Society Since 1945**. New York: Praeger, 1984. 156p.

"In writing this book we set out, influenced by genre, auteur, psychoanalytic, Marxist and other critical perspectives (but not wedded to any one of them) to observe and evaluate, both politically and aesthetically, how American film conveys its social and cultural values and commitments, and even what solutions it sometimes offers for society's problems," say the authors. The approach is decade by decade, beginning with 1945, examining specific films they feel to be "public classics," among which are **The Best Years of Our Lives**, **Rebel Without a Cause**, **Bonnie and Clyde**, **M*A*S*H**, **The Deerhunter**, and **Coming Home**. Chapter notes, bibliography, and index.

1437

Quigley, Martin, Jr. **Magic Shadows: The Story of the Origin of Motion Pictures**. New York: Biblo & Tannen, c1960, 1969. 191p.

A pre-history of the motion picture, from ancient times through the kinetoscope. Contains a chronology from 6000 B.C. through 1986, a bibliography, and an index.

1438

Quinlan, David. **British Sound Films: The Studio Years 1928–1959**. London: Batsford, 1984. 406p.

"This book is both an attempt to look at an era of filmmaking through its product, and a record of the product itself," said Quinlan of his filmography of the entertainment feature films of three decades. In addition to cast lists and credits each entry has a synopsis and rating. An introduction precedes the decades and a list of short fictional films follows. Arrangement is alphabetical by title within each decade, but unfortunately there is no name index. Brief bibliography.

1439, 1440, 1441

Quinlan, David. **Quinlan's Illustrated Directory of Film Stars**. 2d ed. London: Batsford, 1986. 475p.

Quinlan, David. **The Illustrated Directory of Film Character Actors**. London: Batsford, 1985. 325p.

Quinlan, David. **The Illustrated Guide to Film Directors**. London: Batsford, 1983. 334p.

Quinlan's **Illustrated Directory of Film Stars** and . . . **Film Character Actors** are a pair. In both he has tried, not always too successfully, to capture the appearance and personality of the actor/actress in a few pithy and evaluative adjectives, followed by a short career description including dates and marital status. After this brief identification is a long, inclusive filmography. The **Guide to Film Directors** is different, with a much longer but again evaluative description of their work, followed by a filmography. All three are concerned with professional careers rather than personal biographical details. Each volume contains hundreds of entries and each ends with a short bibliography.

1442

Quinn, James. **The Film and Television as an Aspect of European Culture**. Leyden: Sijthoff, 1968. 168p.

Survey of the educational and cultural significance of film and television, commissioned by the Council for Cultural Co-operation of the Council of Europe. Gives different forms of governmental support, steps taken by educational bodies in various countries to develop film and television studies, use of film and television in education, attitudes of the church and the public, and attitude of film industries of different countries toward the film as art.

1443

Rachty, Gehan, and Khalil Sabat. **Importation of Films for Cinema and Television in Egypt**. Paris: UNESCO, 1980. 78p. (Communication and Society 7.)

In four parts: "The Social Effects of Imported Films and Telefilms" which surveys relevant literature to make a case for Western cultural imperialism in developing countries; "Foreign Films in Egyptian Cinemas and on Television Screens," giving facts and figures on distribution and regulations; "Analysis of Foreign films Projected in Cinemas or Transmitted by Television in Egypt (April, May and June 1979)" a content analysis; and "Flow of Foreign Programmes to the Egyptian Television Organization (Importation Bases—Censorship Rules—Sources)".

1444

Ramsaye, Terry. **A Million and One Nights: A History of the Motion Picture**. New York: Simon & Schuster, c1926, 1964. 868p.

First published in 1926, at a time when many of the founders of the film industry were alive, this book goes into detail about the history of the motion picture in the U.S. from its inception to 1926. The author, first connected with the industry in 1913 as a journalist, used original sources whenever possible and interviewed every person then living whom he mentioned. Contains an index but no bibliography or footnotes. Over the years certain historical inaccuracies have been found in Ramsaye, but it is still a useful and interesting source.

Rehrauer, George. **The Macmillan Film Bibliography**. (See No. 1690.)

1445

Renan, Sheldon. **An Introduction to the American Underground Film**. New York: Dutton Paperback, 1968. 318p.

Renan's work is substantial. Beginning with a lengthy definition of the underground film in its many aspects, he then gives its history in the U.S. and its earlier European background and a gallery of its chief filmmakers, its stars, and its "establishment"; and finally he discusses "expanded cinema," which he defines as a spirit of inquiry leading in many directions.

An appendix lists the 400 to 500 films mentioned, telling their length, whether in color or black and white, silent or sound, and availability for sales or rental, with sources from which they may be obtained. Contains a bibliography and an index.

1446

Researcher's Guide to British Film & Television Collections. Ed. by Elizabeth Oliver. 2d ed. London: British Universities Film & Video Council, 1985. 176p.

A directory of locations of film holdings in Britain, arranged according to national archives; regional collections; television companies; newsreel, production and stock shot libraries; specialized collections; and associated information and documentation sources. Information for each holding varies in length and detail, but includes as much of the following information as is pertinent: person to contact, history, holdings, components, storage, cataloging; documentation; junking; access. Following the Introduction, several essays proceed the Directory proper: "Reflections on Film Research" by James Barker; "Copyright in Films" by Geoffrey Crabb; "Postgraduate Academic Film Research" by Timothy Hollins" and "Researching for a Television Series" by Christine Whittaker. Appendixes include a bibliography of books, periodicals and Acts of Parliament and Government and other reports and surveys relevant to the British film and television industries; and a listing of organizations, conferences and festivals. There are two indexes: by collection, and by subject.

1447

Rhode, Eric. **A History of the Cinema: From Its Origins to 1970**. New York: Hill & Wang, 1976. 674p.

A history of the film in major countries of the world where the industry has developed, with stress on Europe and the U.S. Rhode has systematically attempted to relate movies to the societies from which they emerge, and he treats them in a social, economic, and artistic context, with much attention to individual directors and films and an analysis of the techniques used. Contains footnotes and a bibliography for each chapter, and a name-title index, but unfortunately none for subject.

1448

Richie, Donald. **The Japanese Movie**. Rev. ed. Tokyo: Kodansha International, 1982. 212p.

Pictures and text cover a span of over 80 years to re-create the story of the Japanese film in its social and aesthetic setting, paralleling its development in Japan with its development in the West. This is an excellent book to help Europeans and Americans understand and appreciate Japanese motion pictures. Many of the illustrations are from stills. An index of names and film titles, with the latter given both in Japanese and English.

1449

Robinson, David. **The Great Funnies: A History of Film Comedy**. New York: Dutton, 1969. 156p.

"This essay pretends to be no more than a bird's-eye view, only lingering from time to time over a figure of particular importance or special attention," says the author with too much modesty. For, building his history around various well-known comedians, he packs in a great deal of material in a succinct and interesting fashion. The scope is international. Indexed.

1450

Rose, Ernest D. **World Film & Television Study Research: A Reference Guide to Major Training Centres and Archives**. 2d ed. Bonn-Bad, Germany: Fredrich-Ebert-Stiftung, 1978. 420p. (Mass Media Manual.)

Describes in some detail approximately 375 schools and 85 archives in 76 countries around the world. Information under each entry varies, including for schools all or some of the following items: address, telephone, date of founding, sources of support, language of instruction, program emphasis, length of program, award upon completion, number admitted annually, school year calendar, application procedures and deadline, special requirements for foreign students, and estimated living expenses. For research centers, information includes size and type of holdings, address, director or curator, sources of support, description of library, publications screenings, and other pertinent items. Contains a bibliography: "Selected Readings in the International Area."

1451

Rosow, Eugene. **Born to Lose: The Gangster Film in America**. New York: Oxford, 1978. 422p.

"I have rooted the study of gangster movies in American social history in order to reach a better understanding of how and why gangster films became a significant force in our culture. I have also concentrated on the formal and technical evolution of gangster movies in order to give as complete a picture as possible of the

origin and development of the film genre," says Rosow in his Preface which neatly summarizes his study of the genre. Beginning with its mythic origin he takes it through the 1920s, the Depression, and the succeeding years to 1976. There are notes, a bibliography of books and articles, an annotated filmography, a list of gangster films by year, beginning with 1912, and an index.

1452

Rosten, Leo C. **Hollywood: The Movie Colony; the Movie Makers**. New York: Harcourt, Brace & World, 1941. 436p.

"This book is primarily concerned with putting Hollywood under the microscopes of social science. For Hollywood is an index to our society and our culture." Preface. The result is one of the earliest systematic analyses of the modern motion picture industry, in which the author and a staff of social scientists combine statistical documentation with perception. Appendixes contain data on such items as: the movies and Los Angeles; production costs, analysis of movie companies, comparison with other industries; annual earnings, weekly salaries, and spending patterns; social data; marriage and divorce data; comments and preferences of movie makers; dogs, yachts, resorts; fan mail. Useful both historically and for certain eternal verities. Reference notes form a bibliography, and there is an index of subjects.

1453

Rotha, Paul. **Documentary Film**. 3d ed. London: Faber & Faber, 1952. 412p.

Subtitled "The use of the film medium to interpret creatively and in social terms the life of the people as it exists in reality," this is an intensive study. Limiting himself to no one country, the author first gives a general introduction to the cinema, then treats the following aspects of documentary film: its evolution; certain basic principles; techniques; developments, policies, purposes; and a history from 1939 to the early 1950s. Three appendixes include the use of films by the U.S. Armed Forces, 100 important documentary films, and a select bibliography. Fully indexed. Sinclair Road and Richard Griffith collaborated with Mr. Rotha.

1454

Rotha, Paul. **The Film till Now: A Survey of World Cinema**. 3d ed. London: Spring Books, 1967. 831p.

Published in its first edition in 1930, this has become a classic. A history and analysis of the motion picture, worldwide in scope, it treats the factual and theoretical backgrounds. Part I, "The Actual," discusses its development, its various forms, and its growth and characteristics in the U.S., the U.S.S.R., Germany, France, Britain, and a number of other countries. Part II, "The Theoretical," discusses it aims and influence of form upon dramatic content. Part III, by Richard Griffith, brings the first edition up to 1948. An epilogue in the third edition goes to 1958 and covers about 35 Western and Eastern countries, and a "Postscript" takes it into the 1960s. Index.

1455

Roud, Richard, ed. **Cinema: A Critical Dictionary: The Major Film-Makers**. 2 v. New York: Viking, 1980. Vol. 1, Aldrich to King; Vol. 2, Kinugasa to Zanussi.

This two-volume work consists of critical essays, most of them lengthy, on the work of major filmmakers, interspersed with a few shorter accounts of the contributions of major actors and actresses and longer accounts of national and topical film trends—i.e., "Czechoslovak Cinema of the 60s," "Italian Silent Cinema," and "Dance in Film." Essays are by prominent film critics and represent various schools. The editor says, "My own critical position has been expressed in the choice of entries and writers. But the opinions expressed by these writers are as varied as their personalities and backgrounds. Most of the critical schools are represented; there has been no attempt to impose a monolithic point of view." Among these schools are the Marxist/materialist, the structuralist, the semiological and the psychoanalytical. There are roughly 150 entries. Arrangement is alphabetical. Name/title index.

1456

Sadoul, Georges. **The Cinema in the Arab Countries**. Beirut, Lebanon: InterArab Centre of Cinema & Television, 1966. 290p.

Anthology, prepared for UNESCO, which provides the first general view of the cinema in the Arab world. It is divided into six sections: the cinema and Arab culture, history of the Arab cinema, geography of the Arab cinema, problems and future development, recommendations, film lists and statistics.

1457, 1458

Sadoul, Georges. **Dictionary of Film Makers**. Tr., ed., and updated by Peter Morris. Berkeley: University of California Press, 1972. 288p.

Sadoul, Georges. **Dictionary of Films**. Tr., ed., and updated by Peter Morris. Berkeley: University of California Press, 1972. 432 p.

Film Makers provides compact biographical information on some 1,000 directors, writers, editors, animators, composers, art directors, and cameramen, giving country of citizenship, birth and, where appropriate, death dates, biography, filmography, and assessment of role. Even though several decades old this is a valuable reference book because data on behind-the-scenes film workers can be hard to find.

Films covers more than 1,000 films produced in 50 countries over a 70-year period. Information includes title, country of origin, year, major credits, a brief synopsis, and a brief discussion of the film's role in cinema history. The two volumes are designed to be used together.

1459

Salmane, Hala, Simon Hartog, and David Wilson, eds. **Algerian Cinema**. London: BFI Publishing, 1976. 58p.

Declaring that this is not intended as a comprehensive study of Algerian cinema, the editors state their aims: to provide basic information on a national cinema little known outside of French-speaking countries and to assess it in the context of Algerian history. In a still broader context this small book throws light on the effects of colonialism on national film.

1460

Sampson, Henry T. **Blacks in Black and White: A Source Book on Black Films**. Metuchen, NJ: Scarecrow, 1977. 333p.

Presents relatively little-known facts concerning films with all-black casts independently produced between 1910 and 1950. Contains a historical overview, a discussion of two important black companies and of white and black independents, a synopsis of some of the black films produced between 1910 and 1950, and biographies of leading black actors and filmmakers. Appendixes list all-black films by independent film producers between 1904 and 1950, a partial list of individuals and corporations organized to produce black-cast films in the years 1910–50, and film credits for featured players in black-cast films, 1910–50. Indexed.

1461

Samuels, Stuart. **Midnight Movies**. New York: Collier, 1983. 224p.

A history, analysis, and exploration of the midnight movie phenomenon in the context of American culture and society of the 1970s, exemplified by seven classics and two supercult films—**El Topo**, **Night of the Living Dead**, **The Harder They Come**, **Reefer Madness**, **Pink Flamingos**, **The Rocky Horror Picture Show**, **Eraserhead**, **Harold and Maude**, and **King of Hearts**—each of which he describes in detail, probing their appeal. Notes and scripts for the films and their recordings.

1462

Sarris, Andrew. **The American Cinema: Directors and Directions, 1929–1968**. New York: Dutton, 1968. 383p.

A brief but pointed examination of 200 American film directors. The author, a film critic, rates his directors in categories ranging from "pantheon" to "strained seriousness," "less than meets the eye," and "oddities, one-shots, and newcomers," and gives sound judgments as well as facts. Taken as a whole, the book constitutes an excellent survey of the American sound film. Special features are a directional chronology of the most important films of each year from 1929 through 1967 and an alphabetical list of over 600 films with year of release and director.

1463

Schatz, Thomas. **Hollywood Genres: Formulas, Filmmaking, and the Studio System**. Philadelphia: Temple University Press, 1981. 297p.

Divided into two parts. Part One is primarily theoretical, concerned generally with the essential characteristics and cultural role of genre filmmaking, stressing the formal and narrative features common to all genres and their relationship to the culture at large. Part Two treats the six specific genres which Schatz feels are the most significant: the Western, gangster, hard-boiled detective, screwball comedy, musical, and family melodrama. He concludes with an Epilogue: "Hollywood Film Making and American Myth Making." Chapter notes, bibliography and index.

1464

Scheuer, Steven H., ed. **Movies on TV, 1986–87**. 11th ed. New York: Bantam, 1985. 829p.

Brief, literate appraisals of thousands of feature films, old and new, intended to guide the discriminating TV viewer. Over 1,000 new reviews of theatrical, made-for-TV and films have been added to the many reinserted from previous editions. Each is listed alphabetically by title, with date, cast, a rating by asterisks, succinct annotations which capture plot, mood, and quality, and—new to this edition—a dagger to indicate those available on videocassette. Some of the entries go as far back as 1935. Listing is alphabetical by title. Appendixes give brief essays on various film genres and a list of Academy Awards through 1984. (**Movies on TV, 1988–89** was published in 1987.)

1465

Schmidt, Georg, and others. **The Film: Its Economic, Social, and Artistic Problems**. London: Falcon Press, 1948. [124p.]

A study of the contemporary film of the '40s, limited to what the authors term the fiction film rather than the documentary, the newsreel, or the advertising film, and showing its present function, its technical and artistic means, and the nature of its economic and social structure. Some history is also given as background.

1466

Schnitman, Jorge A. **Film Industries in Latin America: Dependency and Development**. Norwood, NJ: Ablex, 1984. 134p.

Within the larger framework of economic, politics and culture of the film industry in Argentina, Mexico, Brazil, Chile and Bolivia, Schnitman discusses problems of production, distribution and exhibition 1930–1980, showing emergent patterns which are both contradictory and complementary. Background chapters describe "The

Silent Years, 1896–1930" and "The International Context," featuring the film industry in the U.S., 1930–1948. An appendix gives statistics on Latin American film. Contains a list of references and a name and a subject index.

1467

Schnitzer, Luda, Jean Schnitzer, and Marcel Martin, eds. **Cinema in Revolution: The Heroic Era of the Soviet Film**. Tr. and with additional material by David Robinson. New York: Hill & Wang, 1973. 208p.

In the 1920s—the early days of the Russian Revolution—a new and exciting generation of filmmakers interacted to found a Soviet cinema which reached its height during those years. Here some of them recall their work and their youth. Although the essays do not constitute an exact history of the times they present a vivid picture of a unique and influential epoch of filmmaking. The section introductions have been augmented and revised by Robinson, who has added a glossary of persons and an index.

Screen International Film and TV Year Book. (See No. 1787.)

Screen World. (See No. 1788.)

1468

Shale, Richard, comp. **Academy Awards: An Unger Reference Index**. 2d ed. New York: Unger, 1982. 691p.

A listing of the Oscar Awards given annually by the Academy of Motion Picture Arts and Sciences from 1927/28 through 1981 compiled, in Shale's words, "to make more accessible the names of those performers, craftsmen, and scientists—all artists in their respective fields—and the films they created." After a beginning chapter on the history of the Academy, the body of the book is taken up by a list of the awards by categories—best pictures, best actors and actresses, best writing, best musical scores and songs, best costuming, etc. year by year, followed by a straight chronological list of winners within categories. 1978–81 awards are added as supplements to the proper sections. Appendixes include names of the Academy founders, presidents, and best-picture directors. Bibliography and name/film index.

1469

Sharff, Stefan. **The Elements of Cinema: Toward a Theory of Cinesthetic Impact**. New York: Columbia University Press, 1982. 187p.

Sharff sets out to demonstrate the existence of uniquely cinematic elements of structure which cast light on cinema's creative processes and on its aesthetic potential, and to distinguish between film as a medium of mass communication and cinema as a potential art form. Through his analysis of cinematic structures he hopes to teach the audience to "read" cinema as a form of communication which exists on a syntactic continuum. Glossary and index.

1470

Short, K.R.M., ed. **Film & Radio Propaganda in World War II**. London: Croom Helm, 1983. 337p.

Experts on film and radio propaganda examine the content of the propaganda put out by the various nations involved in World War II. Part I deals with propaganda in international politics, 1919–1939; Part 2 the Allies, including the Soviet Union; Part 3, Fascist Europe; Part 4, Japan. Notes and an index.

1471

Sigoloff, Marc. **The Films of the Seventies: A Filmography of American, British and Canadian Films 1970–1979**. Jefferson, NC: McFarland, 1984. 424p.

An overview of the decade, concentrating on mainstream filmmaking. Excluded are animated films and documentaries and some but not all films which are primarily sex-oriented. Those included have either "broken through their origins or were early works by filmmakers who have themselves achieved major status." Listings are alphabetical by title, and under each is the following information: date; cast and production credits; ratings by the Motion Picture Association of America; domestic (U.S. and Canada) box-office rentals of four million dollars or more (source—**Variety**). Entries conclude with a brief summary of major plot details and characters and an evaluation of its virtues or flaws. Index of names.

1472, 1473

Sitney, P. Adams, ed. **The Avant-Garde Film: A Reader in Theory and Criticism**. New York: New York University Press, 1978. 295p.

Sitney, P. Adams. **Visionary Film: The American Avant-Garde, 1943–1978**. 2d ed. New York: Oxford University Press, 1979. 463p.

In the first of these two books Sitney uses a diversity of materials—manifestoes, letters, a scenario, program notes, lectures, interviews—to present an extensive survey of the theoretical contributions and the achievements of avant-garde filmmakers. Several texts appear in print, or in English, for the first time in this collection. Among contributors in addition to the editor are Sergei Eisenstein, Hans Richter, Jean Epstein, Germaine Dulac, Antonin Artaud, Joseph Cornell, Maya Deren, Signey Peterson, James Broughton, John and James Whitney, Harry Smith, Carel Rowe, Stan Brakhage, Peter Kubelka, Stephen Koch, Annette Michelson, Michael Snow, Jonas Mekas, Ernie Gehr, Anthony McCall, Paul Sharits, Tony Conrad and Hollis Frampton. Index.

As a taking-off point to survey the avant-garde film in the U.S. the author has interviewed 24 filmmakers and analyzed their works, from which he has devised a theory. He relates the avant-garde tradition to the larger film context, which he connects to the subjective European films of the 1920s. There are 66 still photographs, footnotes for each chapter, and a name-subject index.

1474

Sklar, Robert. **Movie-Made America: A Social History of American Movies**. New York: Random House, 1975. 340p.

"The advent of the movies on the American cultural scene . . . clearly posed a challenge to existing cultural policies and institutions," says the author, who examines, among other topics, the invention of motion picture technology; the nature and evolution of the audience, the organization and business tactics of the movie trade; the design and economics of theaters; the social and professional lives of movie workers; government policies toward movies, the attitudes and strategies of censorship groups; and the cultural influence of movies at home and overseas. Contains chapter notes and an index.

1475

Skvorecky, Josef. **All the Bright Young Men and Women: A Personal History of the Czech Cinema**. Tr. by Michael Schonberg. Toronto: Peter R. Martin Associates, 1971. 280p. (Take One Film Book Series.)

"It is not a scholarly work, just a personal remembrance," says the author. Nonetheless, it is a fascinating account of the flowering of an art under considerable odds for all too brief a period, and of the young men and women who made it possible. In spite of the author's statement that the history is not scholarly, he has referred to the writings of the Czech film critics and historians for background facts, although he has not documented the sources. There are almost 200 photographs—many of them never before seen in the West and available nowhere outside a book. A chronological list, of "The Most Interesting Czech Feature Films, 1898–1970," follows the text. Indexed.

1476, 1477, 1478, 1479

Slide, Anthony. **The American Film Industry: A Historical Dictionary**. Westport, CT: Greenwood, 1986. 432p.

Slide, Anthony. **Early American Cinema**. Cranbury, NJ: Barnes, 1970. 192p.

Slide, Anthony. **Aspects of American Film History Prior to 1920**. Metuchen, NJ: Scarecrow, 1978. 161p.

Slide, Anthony. **Early Women Directors**. Cranbury, NJ: Barnes, 1977. 119p.

Slide is one of the most interesting of the film historians as he investigates unusual angles. Among the best illustrations is his **American Film Industry** which he calls a "What's What." A dictionary of American producing companies, technological innovations, film series, industry terms, studios, genres, and organizations, it contains more than 600 entries "on everything from the Academy of Motion Picture Arts and Sciences to the Zoom Lens, from Astoria Studios to Zoetrope." They vary in length according to the importance of the subject matter, with an address for companies and organizations still active, a short bibliography, and, where appropriate, information as to institutional holdings of the subject's films, papers, or still photographs. In conclusion is a list of resources for libraries and institutions, a bibliography, and an index. Each entry has its own bibliography, in addition to the general one. This not only fills a gap in the literature but also makes good browsing.

Early American Cinema is a brief history from 1900 to about 1915, constructed around the people and companies who helped create it. There is a useful bibliography and an index.

Aspects of American Film History Prior to 1920 covers much the same ground but from a different vantage point. An eclectic series of essays, it includes among its subjects the evolution of the star, child stars, forgotten directors, film magazines, the first motion picture bibliography, certain companies (including Kalem, the first to shoot films on location abroad), and a fascinating three-page vignette of Katherine Anne Porter's brief employment with the motion picture industry. Appendixes include bibliographies on nine of the companies and a list of source material on American film production during the period. Contains an index.

In **Early Women Directors** Slide contends that in this early period the film industry was controlled by women. The importance of women stars, some of whom had their own production organizations, is well known, but not so the importance of women directors, of whom there were more than 30. Slide tells about their lives and works, some in much greater detail than others. Bibliography.

1480

Slide, Anthony, ed. **International Film, Radio, and Television Journals**. Westport, CT: Greenwood, 1985. 428p. (Historical Guide to the World's Periodicals & Newspapers.)

Contains profiles of major journals and a considerable number of minor ones which, in the opinion of Slide and his contributors, have research value, whether scholarly or popular. Categories include: fan magazines, in-house journals, national film periodicals, technical journals, trade papers, and popular/academic journals. Entries are alphabetical, with descriptions of varying length giving history and content, followed by a listing of information sources, reprint edition editions, location sources and all of some of the following publication facts (title changes, volume and issue data, publisher and location, editor). There is a brief historical introduction and six appendixes which include short essays on fan club journals, fan magazines and in-house journals, and a listing by country and another by type and subject matter. In his introduction Slide says that although radio and television are well-covered, film periodicals dominate the book because they dominate the publishing field in this area. Numerous bibliographies. Index.

1481

Slusser, George, and Eric S. Rabkin, eds. **Shadows of the Magic Lamp: Fantasy and Science Fiction in Film**. Carbondale: Southern Illinois University Press, 1985. 259p.

"Fourteen critics, using very different methods and with widely varying ideas of what fantasy is and where its center in the corpus of world cinema might lie, have written essays addressing the general question of fantasy in film" Introduction. Fantasy is interpreted broadly to include sub-genres such as horror, the Arthurian romance, Gothic expressionism, the animated film, even the musical—in all of which they find a common link to science fiction. Historically, the articles cover a broad span, from Melies and Lang to very recent films like **E.T. the Extra-Terrestrial** and **Raiders of the Lost Ark**. Notes and index.

1482

Smith, John M., and Tim Cawkwell. **The World Encyclopedia of the Film**. New York: World Publishing Co., 1972. 444p.

"From Hollywood and the great national cinemas to documentary and the 'Underground' every aspect of the film is covered through its creators—the directors, actors, writers, cameramen, set designers and many others are well represented," say the co-authors. The book takes the form of a biographical dictionary with pertinent facts about careers and listings of credits with dates. An index section, which constitutes a reference work in itself, includes all films mentioned in the biographical section, with dates, main credits, technical specifications, releasing organizations (in most cases), and alternative titles.

1483

Smith, Paul, ed. **The Historian and Film**. New York: Cambridge University Press, 1976. 208p.

Eleven contributors from Britain, France, Holland, and the U.S. discuss the uses to which historians may put films of various types, from newsreel to feature. Among subjects examined are preservation and archives, evaluation as to historical evidence, and value in the interpretation and teaching of history. Contains a select bibliography, a list of addresses of organizations involved with film and history, and an index.

1484

Smith, Sharon. **Women Who Make Movies**. New York: Hopkinson & Blake, 1975. 307p.

A survey which shows that women have contributed substantially to filmmaking in its early years, both in this country and abroad, and again in the 1960s with the increased use of 16mm films. The author identifies individuals and describes their role. Contains a directory of filmmakers throughout the U.S., a listing of organizations to which most of them belong, and a bibliography and index of names.

1485

Sobchack, Vivian Carol. **The Limits of Infinity: The American Science Fiction Film 1950–1975**. New York: Barnes, 1980. 246p.

Unlike Baxter (No. 1161) and Johnson (No. 1313), who surveyed the field broadly, Sobchack sets geographical and time limitations in order to make a depth analysis in terms of the visual and aural qualities which she feels set it apart and define it formally as a genre. Using as examples those films produced in the U.S. beginning with the 1950s, she comes up with a theory and aesthetic. Chapter notes; a selected bibliography of books, articles and unpublished materials, and an index. A second and enlarged edition was due in 1987, to be called **Screening Space: The American Science Fiction Film**.

1486

Solomon, Stanley J. **Beyond Formula: American Film Genres**. New York: Harcourt Brace Jovanovich, 1976. 310p.

In his preface Solomon succinctly describes his study of the Western, musical comedy, horror, crime, detective, and war film genre. "A good genre film works because it is art as well as genre. . . . Equally important, such a film is *of its genre*, and therefore to understand its meaning we must also understand its relationship to a hundred similar minor films, and even to some dreadful films. For this reason, the first half of each chapter describes the relevant categories of a genre, and the second half treats individual works of art within these categories. My ultimate aim is to explore the key associations between the unique elements of a particular work of genre art and the conventions and traditions within which the work exists." His introduction defines genre and relates it to popular culture. There is a bibliography, an index of films which he has examined, a list of film distributors and a general index.

1487

Spehr, Paul C. **The Movies Begin: Making Movies in New Jersey, 1887–1920**. Newark, NJ: The Newark Museum and Morgan & Morgan, 1977. 190p.

The roots of the Hollywood movie industry were in New Jersey. This book, which grew out of an exhibit at the Newark Museum, examines the movies from their beginnings in Edison's day until 1920, when the extensive studio facilities built in the state began to shut down. Much space is devoted to Edison's contribution. Chapters include the pre-cinema, invention of the motion picture and its early development, early filmmaking in New Jersey, the studios, the personalities. Many illustrations, a bibliography, and an index.

1488

Spraos, John. **The Decline of the Cinema: An Economist's Report**. London: Allen & Unwin, 1962. 168p.

One of the best economic studies of the film industry in Britain, which the author contends is declining—a contention he bolsters with facts and figures. He then proceeds to give the reasons, some of which directly pertain to the American film industry. Indexed.

1489

Squire, Jason E., ed. **The Movie Business Book**. Englewood Cliffs, NJ: Prentice-Hall, 1983. 414p.

"The movie industry works on money. It's important to know how the money is arranged, spent, protected, and returned. This work is an effort to organize, simplify, and examine all that," says Squire. In case this statement seems crass, Squire explains that "The responsible filmmaker learns early to mix the creative and business sense out of self-defense." To cover the economic nut-and-bolts of the broad spectrum of feature filmmaking he has turned to industry specialists with specific expertise for the detail and scope of their particular areas under the following headings: "The Creators," "The Property," "The Money," "The Management," "The Deal," "The Shooting," "The Selling," "The Distributors," "The Exhibitors," "The Audience," and "The Future." Squire's introduction briefly makes some interesting points. Although there is an ever-increasing multitude of books on the history, aesthetics and other aspects of film, few have tackled it from this angle. This, along with the high quality of its contributions, makes it a valuable addition to the literature. Index.

Stedman, Raymond William. **The Serial: Suspense and Drama by Installment**. (See No. 795.)

1490

Steinberg, Cobbett S. **Film Facts**. New York: Facts on File, 1980. 476p.

Is film primarily an art, an industry, or, more practically, a mix? Treating it as a mix, Steinberg has compiled a reference book of statistics, lists and surveys and legislation which take into account the diverse aspects, covering from beginnings to 1979. Sections include "The Marketplace," "The Stars," "The Studios," "The Festivals," "The 'Ten Best' Lists," "The Awards," "The Codes and Regulations." Information includes data and statistics (the marketplace), lists (awards, "bests," etc.) with preliminary introductions, descriptions and histories (the studios), and texts (codes and regulations). There is a name/title index.

1491

Stewart, John. **An Encyclopaedia of Australian Film**. Frenchs Forest, NSW: Reed, 1984. 304p.

"This is a book mainly about the people of the Australian Film Industry, with the emphasis on feature filmmakers and modern film," says Stewart. The main portion consists of alphabetical entries on actors and actresses, producers, directors of photography, editors, composers, writers and soundmen, with short annotations summarizing their careers. Other features include a filmography, "Australian Films Year by Year" giving date, director and cast; a listing by author of novels which have been filmed, with year of filming and change of title, if any; photographic credits; and an index.

1492

Stewart, John. **Filmarama**. 2 v. Metuchen, NJ: Scarecrow, 1975, 1977. 398, 733p. Vol. 1 **The Formidable Years, 1893–1919**; Vol. 2 **The Flaming Years, 1920–1929**

Lists screen and stage credits for motion picture actors and actresses, along with such other information as is available about these early players—for example, birth and death dates, dates of production of films, roles played. A title index follows the name index in each volume.

1493

Stoddard, Karen M. **Saints and Shrews: Women and Aging in American Popular Film**. Westport, CT: Greenwood, 1983. 174p.

On the theory that motion pictures reflect the fears, values, myths and assumptions of their society, Stoddard analyzes the depiction of women in terms of aging as shown through the portrayal of both leading and character roles from the 1930s into the 1980s. Her reason for choosing women over men or aging in general is her assumption (which she substantiated) that in film as well as society there is a double standard. Bibliography, an annotated list of films cited, and an index.

1494, 1495

Stoil, Michael Jon. **Balkan Cinema: Evolution after the Revolution**. Ann Arbor, MI: University Microfilm International Research Press, 1982. 160p.

Stoil, Michael Jon. **Cinema Beyond the Danube: The Camera and Politics**. Metuchen, NJ: Scarecrow, 1974. 198p.

In **Balkan Cinema** Stoil examines film in Bulgaria, Rumania, Yugoslavia, and to a lesser extent Albania (where cinema is scarce and the authorities only minimally cooperative), conducting interviews, viewing films and searching through archives and other materials in order to explain long-term changes in content because of its use by the regimes as a policy-making tool. The first half of the book discusses the impact of the national cinematic traditions, ideology and industry structure on political content of film in general; the latter half examines changing trends in content over the years through

a genre-by-genre look at Balkan feature films. Notes, bibliography, filmography and index.

Cinema Beyond the Danube is an account of filmmaking in Eastern Europe in which Stoil has combined film criticism with political and social analysis. The film history of the Soviet Union is considered apart from that of other Communist states in the region: Poland, Czechoslovakia, Hungary, Yugoslavia, Bulgaria, Rumania and Albania, with East Germany omitted because it is basically in the Western tradition. Intended as an introduction for students and laymen unfamiliar with the subject. There is a bibliography of works available in English, an index of films, and a general index.

1496

Stratton, David. **The Last New Wave: The Australian Film Revival**. Sydney: Angus and Robertson, 1980. 337p.

Between 1970 and 1980 Australian film underwent a feature film renaissance. Basing his study on the comments of the directors and producers themselves, Stratton pieces together the "how" and "why" 120 feature films were made. After a synopsis of the plot of each film comes a discussion of the nuts-and-bolts of production and its fate in the marketplace. Aesthetics are not included. This latter approach, says Stratton, "will become the responsibilities of others in other books." There is a "Chronology: Ten Years of the New Australian Cinema" and a detailed filmography. Lack of an index can cause difficulties in finding specific films in the main section.

1497

Sullivan, Kaye. **Films For, By and About Women**. Series I and II. Metuchen, NJ: Scarecrow, 1980, 1985. 552p., 780p.

Sullivan's aim is to provide "a historical view of sex roles—a view that allows a better perspective on the relationship between being human and being a woman or a man," and "to present women filmmakers and identify the genre of films made by each one." After each entry is a brief description of content, followed by credits, running time, date and availability. European films and many documentaries are included. The first volume has early as well as more recent films; the second has mostly current productions which Sullivan feels to be exceptional in content and in technical and artistic quality. Appendixes contain a "Directory of Film Sources and Filmmakers" and "Bibliography." Concluding is an "Index to Women Filmmakers" and a subject index.

1498

Svenska Filminstitutet; the Swedish Film Institute. Stockholm: Svensk Film Industri, 1964. 20p.

Pamphlet packed with facts about the Swedish film reform of 1963, giving economic and legal status of the industry and the effect upon quality. In both French and English languages.

1499

Svensson, Arne. **Japan**. Cranbury, NJ: Barnes, 1971. 189p.

Guide to the work of the major directors, players, technicians, and other key figures in the Japanese cinema. Filmographies are given as completely as possible. Complete careers of directors have been covered, but it was more difficult, the author states, to do so in cases of actors and actresses, where information about the early stages of their careers was not always known. He also would have liked to have included more technicians and scriptwriters, but again had difficulty acquiring relevant information. Filmographies list those connected with the film and give plot, comments, and an illustration. There is an index of 2,000 titles, and in the introduction a list of materials on the Japanese film used in the compilation.

1500

Thompson, Kristin. **Exporting Entertainment: America in the World Film Market 1907–1934**. London: BFI Publishing, 1985. 238p.

Thompson goes back to the early days of film to examine the reasons the American industry gained worldwide hegemony during World War I. Concentrating on exhibition and distribution, she probes the degree to which audiences were seeing American films as opposed to those of other countries and showing how the American takeover occurred. Data is based on government publications, contemporary trade papers, customs statistics, and archival material. Appendixes give a detailed chronology, "Foreign Companies' American Agents or Branches and Major American Import/Export Films, 1902–1927"; tables showing American exports and shares of the foreign market; and illustrative charts. Chapter notes and index.

1501

Thorp, Margaret Farrand. **America at the Movies**. New Haven, CT: Yale University Press, 1930. 313p.

A perceptive series of articles on the social influence of the motion picture in America which the author wrote during the years before TV, when movies were at a peak. Indexed.

1502

Trojan, Judith. **American Family Life Films**. Metuchen, NJ: Scarecrow, 1981. 425p.

The author states as her goal "to provide a single, comprehensive resource of easily accessible 16mm films that cover the broad spectrum of family dynamics in America, past and present." Target audiences include social workers, family and guidance counselors and therapists, medical personnel, community programmers, librarians, and teachers on the primary through college and adult school levels. Selection is limited to films produced in the U.S. with an American viewpoint and setting, although a few specially selected Canadian and internationally produced films are included which touch on universal themes. Of the 2,103 films, the majority—1,573—are shorts and documentaries; the other 530 are dramatic features. Information for each includes length, color or black and white, date, producer or director, and/or distributor, and a brief annotation. Additional material, "Useful Resources," lists articles, books and periodicals, and media distributors and publishers. Arrangement of the films is alphabetical, with a subject and a title index.

1503

Truitt, Evelyn Mack. **Who Was Who on Screen**. 3d ed. New York: Bowker, 1983. 788p.

Contains more than 13,000 entries covering the years 1905 to 1982, and representing primarily American, British, French and German screen players—great and near great as well as bit players in important features and headliners in lesser-known films. Also lists persons who, while they appeared at least briefly on screen, are better known for other achievements—for example, fighter Joe Lewis, artist Pablo Picasso, and authors Somerset Maugham and George Bernard Shaw. Animal performers like Rin Tin Tin, Tony the Wonder Horse, Lassie and the less famous Trigger, Flipper and Petey make it, too. Roles with dates are listed chronologically under each name, preceded by very brief biographical data about birth and death dates and marriages. In conclusion is a selected bibliography.

1504

Tucker, Richard. **Japan: Film Image**. London: Studio Vista, 1973. 144p.

An examination of the Japanese film industry from a social and aesthetic viewpoint. After a historical survey noting important change and key films, there follows the major portion in which Tucker groups Japanese films by types and examines the social attitudes underlying the groupings and the prominent filmmakers involved. The last section deals with recent major changes. Contains a bibliography.

1505

Tudor, Andrew. **Image and Influence: Studies in the Sociology of Film**. New York: St. Martins Press, 1975. 260p.

Attempting to avoid "the scientism and objectivism which has so long characterized media research," Tudor has produced a general text which explores the relationship between the cinema and society through abstract discussion and empirical detail drawn from examples like the workings of the Hollywood community, the German silent film, the star system, and similar characteristics and manifestations. Bibliography and index. For other studies see I.C. Jarvie's **Toward a Sociology of the**

Cinema (No. 1310), and his **Movies as Social Criticism** (No. 1311).

1506

Tulloch, John. **Australian Cinema: Industry, Narrative and Meaning**. Sydney: Allen & Unwin, 1982. 272p.

A study of Australian cinema in the 1920s and 1930s in which the author's aims are to extend the analysis of film beyond the work of individual directors, and to widen the social context beyond the 'media imperialism' thesis. In the first two sections Tulloch discusses the film industry in cultural and economic terms, combining fact and theory; in the last section he analyzes narrative and textual meaning. His interpretations draw heavily upon the Frankfort School and Britain's Open University media studies, among other sources. Chapter notes and index.

1507

Tuska, Jon. **The American West in Film: Critical Approaches to the Western**. Westport, CT: Greenwood, 1985. 303p.

An evaluation of Western films in terms of their ideological content in which Tuska contrasts the fantasies generated by them to the historical realities. Addressing the Western in terms of structure, or *auteurisme*, of frontier legends, and of stereotypical contents, he has made historical reality the standard against which he measures degrees of deviation as a means to understand the motivations behind the distortions which he feels to be calculated. Part I, "Varieties of Montage," is a discussion of critical theories about Western films and their structure; Part II, "Six Studies in Authorship (*auteurisme*) is devoted to the works and themes of well-known directors John Ford, Howard Hawks, Henry Hathaway, Anthony Mann, Budd Boetticher and Sam Peckinpah; Part III analyzes prevalent frontier legends— Jesse James, Billy the Kid, "Wild Bill" Hickok, Wyatt Earp, heroes in defeat, and legendary and historical reality. Part IV, "Types and Stereotypes," takes up treatment of women and images of Indians. Chapter notes, bibliography and index. In an earlier work, **The Filming of the West** (Doubleday, 1976), Tuska reviewed the history of Western film production. He has withdrawn this book and has planned to issue a revised and updated edition.

1508, 1509

Tyler, Parker. **Underground Film: A Critical History**. New York: Grove Press, 1969. 249p.

Tyler, Parker. **Screening the Sexes: Homosexuality in the Movies**. New York: Holt, Rinehart and Winston, 1972. 367p.

Underground Film is intended as a definitive history of the experimental film movement. The author, a prominent film critic, assesses the work of the leading directors, discusses specific films, and shows the variety of current aims and techniques, tracing the origins. Contains a filmography.

Although in **Screening the Sexes** Parker focuses on the treatment of homosexuality in films he extends his range to take in various forms of sexual behavior, especially deviant ones. As he examines appropriate American and European movies he analyzes them within a framework of literature and myth. Index.

1510

Vallance, Tom. **The American Musical**. Cranbury, NJ: Barnes, 1970. 192p.

". . . a guide to the artists who gave Hollywood supremacy in the forms of the musical. It lists their musical credits with a small amount of biographical material and comment. Though complete objectivity is probably impossible, I have generally tried to keep any controversial views in check and have given what are mainly widely held judgments and opinions on the artists involved." Introduction. Not all the entries are under performers. Some deal briefly with subjects—e.g., "Animation in the Musical," "Band Leaders," "Ghosting," "Composers on the Screen." Choreographers, directors, composers, and various others connected with the musical are listed along with the actors. Indexed.

1511

Variety's **Complete Science Fiction Reviews**. Ed. by Donald Willis. New York: Garland, 1985. 479p.

All science fiction film reviews that have appeared in **Variety** from 1907 through 1984, reproduced in their entirety. Where the genres of science fiction and horror overlap, the editor's criterion for inclusion was whether emphasis was on scientific means or horrific ends. A filmography precedes each review.

Variety **Film Reviews**. (See No. 1797.)

Index to Motion Pictures Reviewed by *Variety*, **1907–1980**. (See No. 1797.)

1512

Vronskaya, Jeanne. **Young Soviet Film Makers**. London: Allen & Unwin, 1972. 127p.

Much has been written about the giant Russian filmmakers of a generation or more ago, but less about the strictly contemporary ones. Jeanne Vronskaya, a Soviet film critic living since 1969 in London, deals with the filmmakers who began their work in the 1950s. She gives a short history of the Russian film and tells of its departure from social realism in the 1960s, illustrating her point by a discussion of some of the leading directors. The latter part of the book takes up the cinema of national minorities. Appendixes list Soviet film studies and main films, and give filmographies of directors. Bibliography and index.

Wade, Graham. **Film, Video and Television, Market Forces, Fragmentation and Technological Advance**. (See No. 442.)

1513

Waldron, Gloria. **The Information Film**. New York: Columbia University Press, 1949. 281p. (A Report of the Public Library Inquiry.)

"This survey is concerned primarily with film as an instrument for adult education and culture. It is necessarily concerned, too, with the institutions—particularly the public library—that are making films an educational force," says the author. She investigates production, distribution, and possibilities and finds that possibilities far exceed production and distribution, which had many problems to overcome. A comprehensive and critical overview which has now become historical. Contains appendixes, a glossary, a bibliography, and an index.

1514

Walker, Alexander. **Stardom: The Hollywood Phenomenon**. New York: Stein & Day, 1970. 392p.

The author, film critic for the **London Evening Standard**, examines stardom and its implications, illustrating, with case studies of past and present Hollywood stars, how they are made and broken, often at the expense of their talent. Contains a bibliography and an index.

1515

Walsh, Andrea S. **Women's Film and Female Experience 1940–1950**. New York: Praeger, 1984. 257p.

Underlying the author's research is the assumption that popular culture, through the mediation of myth and symbol, reflects significant themes within popular consciousness. In this case she has used top-grossing women's films of the 1940s—a period when World War II was changing women's roles—to trace and interpret main currents and undercurrents within American female consciousness. First she shows the evolution and development of Hollywood's women's films; then she describes the social history of American women in the 1940s; and finally she analyzes dominant narrative patterns within popular women's films of the 1940s: the maternal drama, the career woman comedy, and the films of suspicion and distrust toward men, especially husbands. Appendixes compare charts of marquee values of women's film stars for audiences by sex, age, and socio-economic status; give the 1930 Production Code; and list by year selected popular women's films of the 1940s. Filmography, bibliography, and index.

1516

Wasko, Janet. **Movies and Money: Financing the American Film Industry**. Norwood, NJ: Ablex, 1982. 247p.

"Film is a commodity, and exchange value sets the broad parameters that determine not only how the medium will be used, but also the shape of the industrial structure that makes, distributes, and exhibits it," says Thomas Guback in his Foreword to Janet Wasko's penetrating analysis of the relationship between the motion picture and banking industries. General focus is on the production and distribution branches of the film industry, with little emphasis on exhibition. After an initial chapter showing early ties between the film industry and banking, Wasko approaches the subject chronologically through case studies of banks and production companies. Sample chapters are "A New Era in Film Financing (1919–1926) . . . Case Study: D. W. Griffith," and "The Transitional Period and the Growth of Independent Production (1940–1960) . . . Case Study: The Bank of America." Much of the documentation is primary. Included are charts and voluminous chapter notes; an extensive bibliography of monographs, government documents, legal documents and court cases, unpublished materials, manuscripts and various miscellaneous sources; a list of interviews; and an index.

Wasserman, Steven R., ed. **The Lively Arts Information Directory**. (See No. 443.)

1517

Weatherford, Elizabeth, ed. **Native Americans on Film and Video**. New York: Museum of the American Indian, 1981. 152p.

A listing of approximately 400 films and videotapes, chosen by the Museum of the American Indian's Film and Video Project staff. Considerations for inclusion were clarity of viewpoint, the input of American Indians, technical quality, and the documentation of critical issues and of information formerly unavailable on film or videotape. Listings are alphabetical by title; information for each film includes date of production, running time, credits, language spoken (other than English), format, and distributor/s. Each entry has a descriptive annotation. Following this are lists which include special film collections, resources where media organizations can be found, film festivals, tribal and regional centers, production companies, media training courses, and distributors. There is also a brief bibliography of readings and of film catalogs, and a subject index.

1518, 1519

Weaver, John T., comp. **Twenty Years of Silents, 1908–1928**. Metuchen, NJ: Scarecrow Press, 1971. 514p.

Weaver, John T., comp. **Forty Years of Screen Credits, 1929–1969**. 2 v. Metuchen, NJ: Scarecrow Press, 1970. 1,458p.

Twenty Years of Silents lists actors, actresses, directors, and producers with birth and death dates and the films in which they appeared or which they made, with dates. Other features include listings of names of individuals in some of the popular series shows, such as the **Keystone Kops**, the **Sennett Bathing Beauties**, the original **Our Gang** kids, the **Wampus Babies**. There is also a list of silent film studio corporations and distributors.

Forty Years of Silent Screen Credits lists approximately 4,800 players with birth or birth and death dates and screen credits. Other features are Oscar and special awards winners, and the names of the children in series or a group context such as the Dead End Kids.

1520

Weiss, Ken, and Ed Goodgold. **To Be Continued . . .** New York: Crown, 1972. 341p.

A chronological guide to 231 motion picture serials from 1920 through 1956, giving for each serial a brief synopsis, the number of episodes, the director, the cast, and some stills. Indexed.

1521

White, David. **Australian Movies to the World: The International Success of Australian Films Since 1970**. Sydney: Fontana and Melbourne: Cinema Papers, 1984. 143p.

White, a publicist for Australia films, traces the transformation of the Australian film industry from the 1960s when there was virtually none to its worldwide success of the 1970s and 80s, describing how its came about and the break-through into the international market. Emphasis is on the films themselves and on the Australian and overseas directors, producers, actors, distribution executives and critics who were instrumental. Profiles of actors and directors are by Debi Enker. Designed as a success story rather than a critique, it nevertheless makes a useful reference about Australian films and those involved.

1522

Who Wrote the Movie and What Else Did He Write? An Index to Screen Writers and Their Film Works, 1936–1969. Los Angeles: Academy of Motion Picture Arts and Sciences and Writers Guild of America, 1970. 401p.

Two organizations concerned with screen writing have collaborated on this reference book which identifies authors of film scripts. It is composed of three indexes— the "Writers Index," listing approximately 2,000 authors with titles of motion pictures they wrote or were in some way involved in, followed by other data about their careers; "Film Title Index," with approximately 13,000 listings, each giving their producing or distributing company, year of release, and any other titles by which the film may have been known; and the "Awards Index," including films which either were nominated for writing awards or won other honors, with date. Few reference books are devoted entirely to screen writers and their works, which makes this one uniquely valuable.

1523

Whyte, Alistair. **New Cinema in Eastern Europe**. New York: Dutton, 1971. 159p.

In spite of the severe political pressures to which the nationalized cinema in this part of the world has been subjected, some very interesting films have emerged. Whyte concentrates on certain of these films and their directors in Poland, Hungary, Czechoslovakia, Yugoslavia, and with briefer treatment, Albania, Rumania, Bulgaria and East Germany. His concern is only with the films as art—not with the history or economics or other social aspects of the industry. For this see Nina Hibbin's **Eastern Europe: An Illustrated Guide** (No. 1290), which it supplements. Brief bibliography and index.

1524

Williams, Christopher, ed. **Realism and the Cinema: A Reader**. London: Routledge & Kegan Paul in association with the British Film Institute, 1980. 285p.

Acknowledging that there is as yet no single theory of film, Williams has chosen to explore realism as a theory by placing a number of representative statements by filmmakers, critics and theoreticians together to bring out their similarities and contradictions. His approach is primarily conceptual rather than contextual, concerned with juxtaposing ideas rather than giving thorough accounts of the specific historical context in which the ideas are produced. Among the contributors are André Bazin, Bertolt Brecht, Eisenstein, John Grierson, Siegfried Kracauer, Jean Renoir, Roberto Rossellini. There are notes, suggestions for further reading, a list of 16mm film available in Britain, and an index.

1525

Wolfenstein, Martha, and Nathan Leites. **Movies: A Psychological Study**. Glencoe, IL: Free Press, 1950. 316p.

A study of the movies as shared day dreams common to a culture in which the authors look systematically at regularities and variations in the treatment of certain major relationships—lovers and loved ones, parents and children, killers and victims, performers and onlookers. Throughout they point up what is characteristic in American films by comparisons with British and French films. Although almost half a century old it is still valuable not only for its findings, many of which still hold, but as a classic in the literature and as history of film content at a given period. In 1970, a reprint was published by Hafner Publishing Co., New York. "Note on Data and Interpretations" and Index.

1526

Wood, Robin. **Hollywood from Vietnam to Reagan**. New York: Columbia University Press, 1986. 328p.

Labeling himself a gay, a feminist and a political radical influenced by Marx and Freud, Wood brings together a series of his essays on specific films and trends over two decades in which he seeks to show how the industry has been affected by the social transition from the radical and questioning late 1960s and early 1970s of Vietnam and Watergate to the late '70s and early '80s of Carter and Reagan when reaction set in. Bibliography and Index.

1527

Wright, Will. **Six Guns and Society: A Structural Study of the Western**. Berkeley: University of California Press, 1975. 217p.

Using a framework of structural theory and economic and political history, Wright studies the Western film as a cultural genre, a popular set of stories, and a myth of contemporary American society. There is a "Methodological Epilogue" and an appendix which deals in particular with Levi-Strauss' theory of myth. Selective bibliography and index.

1528

Wright, Gene. **The Science Fiction Image: The Illustrated Encyclopedia of Science Fiction in Film, Television, Radio and the Theater**. New York: Facts on File Publications, 1983. 336p.

Intended as a reference source, this surveys hundreds of science fiction films and radio and television programs, with several plays and one opera thrown in for good measure. Listings include plot summaries, cast, filmmakers credits, and critiques that focus on the contributions of the productions to the genre. Interspersed with the productions are biographies of prominent directors, actors and writers (Lewis Carroll among them; this goes back a long way), and techniques of the trade. There are over 200 illustrations, some in color. Arrangement is alphabetical. A name and subject index would have made this more useful as a reference tool.

1529

Adler, Richard P., et al. **The Effects of Television Advertising on Children: Review and Recommendations**. Lexington, MA: Lexington Books, 1980. 367p.

Based on a project supported by the National Sciences Foundation, this reviews existing research and recommends a plan for the future, and in doing so provides a comprehensive review of the state of knowledge up to the 1980s about television advertising and children. Contributors include Ronald Faber, Laurence Kransy Meringoff, Gerald Lesser, John Rossiter, Scott Ward, Thomas Robertson and Adler. The concluding chapter summarizes findings. Two appendixes: "Evaluation of Individual Studies" and "Industry Codes and Guidelines for Children's Television Advertising, Set Forth by the National Association of Broadcasters and the National Advertising Division, Inc." Bibliography and index.

1530

The Advertising Agency Business Around the World: Reports from Advertising Agency Associations and Agency Leaders in Fifty-One Countries. 7th ed. New York: American Association of Advertising Agencies, 1975. 244p.

Information about each country varies, with most of them including expenditure by media and product classification. Australia, for example, gives brief economic background; expenditure as a whole and by media and industrial classification; amount of agency-placed advertising; agency statistics; recognition (accreditation) and compensation; cash discount; acceptance of foreign commercials; taxes on advertising; and restrictions; government relations; self-regulation; liability for payment; major problems; total expenditure broken down by media and product. Developing countries obviously give less information and sometimes dwell on demography and plans. All reflect to a greater or lesser degree their economic and governmental concerns. Useful not only for the facts about individual countries but also to show the development of advertising on a world scale.

Advertising Career Directory. (See No. 1712.)

1531, 1532

Albion, Mark S., and Paul W. Farris. **The Advertising Controversy: Evidence on the Economic Effects of Advertising**. Boston: Auburn House, 1981. 226p.

Albion, Mark S. **Advertising's Hidden Effects: Manufacturers' Advertising and Retail Pricing**. Boston: Auburn House, 1983. 311p.

The Advertising Controversy, say the authors, is an attempt at "an objective, albeit at times critical, evaluation of the research on the economic effects of advertising," considered from the perspectives of economists, business people and consumers. They examine the research of both marketers and economists, whose viewpoints often differ, to bring out the important problems and underlying debates. In the final chapter they present their own opinions. There are notes, a bibliography, and an index.

In a second book intended primarily for both advertisers and retailers, Albion deals in detail with one economic aspect of advertising—its effect upon pricing. Contains a glossary, a bibliography and an index.

1533

Andy Awards Annual. New York: Advertising Club of New York, annual. (1964– .)

A glossy cumulation of illustrations of the yearly winners according to media—"Magazine"; "Other Print Media: Specialty, Packaging, Book Covers, Direct Mail, Billboards, Transit, Posters"; "Television: Single Entry, 30 seconds, 60 seconds, over 60 seconds"; "Campaign: 30 seconds, 60 seconds, over 60 seconds"; "Cable TV"; "Animation"; "List of Radio Awards: Single Entry, Campaign"; "Winning Entries Not Illustrated." Information accompanying each entry tells category where applicable (national, regional, local, institutional, corporate, specific product, etc.), advertiser, agency, art director, copywriter, photographer. Indexed by advertisers, agencies, and individuals.

1534

Atwan, Robert, Donald McQuade, and John W. Wright. **Edsels, Luckies, and Frigidaires: Adver-**

tising the American Way. New York: Delta, 1979. 363p.

A stunning collection of over 250 magazine ads spanning 100 years, assembled to show on one level "the essential as well as the superfluous goods of industrialized society" and on another level "the cultural assumptions and behavioral values reflected in the language, settings, plots and characters of most advertising." Together they reflect the changing nature of American society. Part One, "Advertising and Social Roles," features ads about women, men and blacks; Part Two, "Advertising and Material Civilization," features ads about inventions, transportation, the American diet, and fashion; and Part Three, "Advertising and the Strategies of Persuasion," afflictions and anxieties, heroes, heroines, celebrities, and sex. Commentary preceding each section is incisive and eloquently written.

1535

Ayer Glossary of Advertising and Related Terms. 2d ed. Philadelphia: Ayer Press, 1977. 219p.

Half of the book is given over to general terms used in advertising. The other half includes terms used in television and radio, printing, photography and graphic arts, computer and data-processing research in advertising media and in marketing, associations, unions, government bureaus, and similar allied areas.

Bacon's International Publicity Checker. (See No. 1721.)

Bacon's Publicity Checker: Vol. 1 Magazines; Vol. 2 Newspapers. (See No. 1723.)

1536

Baker, Michael J., ed. Macmillan Dictionary of Marketing & Advertising. New York: Nichols, 1984. 217p.

Terms, phrases and proper names are defined tersely, clearly and where necessary at length for agencies, organizations, methodological research techniques, and persons actively connected with advertising and marketing through their theories and/or practices. Includes Britain and the U.S.

1537

Barnes, Michael, ed. The Three Faces of Advertising. London: The Advertising Association, 1975. 277p.

A series of articles, extracts, and lectures, embracing both "pro" and "anti" views of advertising and spanning the years 1950–73. Part I discusses ethics; Part II, economics; and Part III, effects. Among contributors are

Raymond Williams, Richard Crossman, Nicholas Kaldor, and Julian L. Simon.

1538   HF 6146. T4. B26

Barnouw, Erik. The Sponsor: Notes on a Modern Potentate. New York: Oxford University Press, 1978. 220p.

In this penetrating study of an important and neglected aspect of advertising history, one of broadcasting's finest historians analyzes the pervasive influence of the advertiser on commercial network programming. He sketches the rise of the sponsor on radio and television; examines the sponsor's impact on TV programming; and assesses the dominant role broadcast advertising has played in terms of its influence on society, mores, and institutions. Public TV is not exempt; he discusses the sponsor as an instrument of power in this area as well. Comments are as pertinent today as they were in the '70s. Contains notes and an index.

1539

Bauer, Raymond A., and Stephen A. Greyser. Advertising in America: The Consumer View. Boston: Harvard University, Graduate School of Business Administration, Division of Research, 1968. 473p.

In the 1960s the American Association of Advertising Agencies (AAAA) and faculty members of the Harvard Business School undertook cooperative research "to present an objective examination, comprehensive and systematic, of public attitudes toward advertising and advertisements, and the reasons for these attitudes." The examination is intensive, consisting of many surveys of various kinds (in the appendixes), summaries in the introductions to each of the four parts, and summary sections at the end of each chapter give overviews. The final section, "Summary and Evaluation," explains the meaning of the study as a whole. Apart from its historical value, certain of the findings still hold. Tables, charts and footnotes.

1540

Berman, Ronald. Advertising and Social Change. Beverly Hills, CA: Sage, 1981. 157p.

In this text which critiques contemporary advertising, the author, from the Department of Literature at the University of California at San Diego, takes a hard look at advertising as a major social institution. He discusses its message to a mass society; he examines the society itself; and he tells of ways in which advertising may be evaluated by the public. Emphasis is on television, and his conclusions are not optimistic. Bibliography and index.

Bishop, Robert L., comp. Public Relations, A Comprehensive Bibliography. (See No. 1638.)

1541

Bogart, Leo. **Strategy in Advertising: Matching Media and Messages to Markets and Motivation**. Chicago: Crain, 1984. 406p.

In this challenge to many popular concepts held by the advertising industry, Bogart says advertising is too concerned with numbers—"big, demonstrable, measurable numbers"—rather than with meaning. Numbers, he contends, are only superficial indicators of its success, which lies in "the realm of myth, to which measurements cannot apply." Taking this as his theme and rooting his discussions in psychology he examines such facets as "Advertising on the American Scene," "Is All This Advertising Necessary?," "Deciding How Much to Spend and Where," "Persuasion and the Marketing Plan," "Understanding the Media," "Getting the Message Through," "Reach Versus Frequency, and the Third Dimension," "The Uses of Repetition," "The Concept of Audience," "Advertising Models and Advertising Realities," "On Measuring Effects," and several other pertinent topics. In arriving at his thought-provoking conclusions he draws upon scores of research as well as other more general literature which he notes after each chapter. Index.

1542

Borden, Neil H. **The Economic Effects of Advertising**. Homewood, IL: Irwin, 1942. 988p.

A classic factual analysis of the economics of advertising, which, though decades old, has not lost its value. It contains background information about the development and use of advertising by businessmen, gives its relation to price and pricing practices, and discusses its effect on the range and quality of products and on investment and volume of income. It also takes up ethical aspects. Appendixes and index.

1543

The British Code of Advertising Practice. 7th ed. London: Code of Advertising Practice Committee, 1985. 82p.

Gives as body of general rules and of rules applying to particular categories of advertising—i.e., health claims, children, vitamins and minerals, mail order, etc. Two appendixes contain stipulations for cigarettes and tobacco. Not covered are television and radio, which are subject to a similar Code operated by the Independent Broadcasting Authority. Index.

1544

Brozen, Yale, ed. **Advertising and Society**. New York: New York University Press, 1974. 189p.

This series of lectures on the impact of advertising, delivered in 1973 at the Graduate School of Business at the University of Chicago, comes out with a vigorous defense of advertising as a social force for good. Among aspects dealt with are: its place in American civilization (here Daniel Boorstin tells us how "outrageous overstatements" by enterprising advertisers helped entice settlers to America), advertising and the consumer, economic values, advertising in an affluent society, institutional advertising by nonprofit organizations (Philip Kotler believes that they pose a threat), brand loyalties, advertising and the law. Some of the articles are footnoted.

1545

Bryden-Brown, John. **Ads That Made Australia: How Advertising Has Shaped Our History and Lifestyle**. New York: Doubleday, 1981. 239p.

Selecting ads from newspapers and magazines, posters, radio and television over the years, Bryden-Brown makes his point: "Kellog changed our breakfast eating habits, the retailers determined how we would furnish and decorate our homes, the airline companies moved us sixteen thousand kilometers closer to the world—all through the power of our advertising." Topics include family life, drinking and smoking, various types of relaxation "Australian style," transportation, banking and insurance, and war propaganda. Commentary accompanies the ads, although there is no effort to link cause and effect. This is an uncomplicated surface look at Australian advertising history. Product index.

1546

Bullmore, J.J.D., and M. J. Waterson, eds. **The Advertising Association Handbook**. London: Holt, Rinehart and Winston with the Advertising Association, 1983. 378p.

Descriptive first edition of a handbook intended as an introduction to the British advertising industry, containing articles by authorities on, first of all, advertising statistics, then the various media, including daily, Sunday and regional newspapers; consumer and business magazines; the ITV companies; independent radio; posters; cinema advertising; and direct mail. This is a new publishing venture for Britain's Advertising Association, and is intended as an introduction to British advertising in its various and varied aspects. Experts, who are all high-ranking advertising practitioners in one form or another (with the exception of two academicians) discuss the different kinds of advertisers; the role of the advertising agency and the huge spread of available media; some problems facing advertising in the 1980s; and criticisms sometimes made about it. Articles are all in essay form, with appropriate graphs, charts, statistics, etc. In addition to its abundant information it makes interesting reading.

1547

Buzzi, Giancarlo. **Advertising: Its Cultural and Political Effects**. Tr. by B. David Garmize. Minneapolis: University of Minnesota Press, 1968. 142p.

Drawing upon a variety of fields—psychology, sociology, politics, history, economics, anthropology, and even works of art and poetry, Buzzi considers advertising as a social phenomenon, underscoring its cultural, political and moral effects. He concludes "Advertising is neither licit or illicit, good or evil in itself, but only relative to a context, to values, to a choice (or group of choices), to an ideology, a vision of life. The only yardstick it can be measured by is *social morality*." This is a stimulating, provocative, challenging, and not altogether comfortable book, not only to those who practice the trade but also to the consumer society which demands it. He does not include a bibliography, which, he apologizes, would be too long and invade too many other areas. He also apologizes to his fellow practitioners: "To those in the field of advertising who are upset by the polemics contained herein, or by the book as a whole, I should like to say only that I have been, and still am, an advertiser who obediently follows the rules of the game in this not always pleasant occupation; the faults I often refer to are also my own." This is a far cry from the usual critique denouncing advertising, and his treatises are even more pertinent in the 1980s than they were in the 1960s.

1548

Cantor, Bill, ed. **Experts in Action: Inside Public Relations**. New York: Longman, 1984. 460p.

An anthology in which Cantor, a public relations practitioner, has collected "the best that the public relations field has to offer in the way of its thoughts about the profession: how it works, how it must face the future, how it should be managed, and what skills it has and needs," presented here by professionals. Cantor warns that it is intended for the initiated rather than the uninitiated. He has contributed an appendix, "Public Relations/Public Affairs Job Guidelines," and a glossary. Name and subject index.

1549

Chapman, Simon. **Great Expectorations: Advertising and the Tobacco Industry**. London: Comedia, 1986. 158p.

Flippant title to the contrary, this is a deadly serious challenge to the tobacco industry's claims that cigarette advertising has no harmful effects. Using examples drawn from around the world, Chapman looks at the industry's justifications for advertising; how its effects can be understood; what the cigarette advertisements are really saying; the legal controls on advertising in different countries; and in conclusion, case studies from the West and the Third World. The author is a member of the World Health Organization's Expert Committee on Smoking Control and a consultant for the International Union against Cancer. Chapter notes and references.

1550

Chiplin, Brian, and Brian Sturgess. **Economics of Advertising**. 2d ed. London: Holt, Rinehart, and Winston with the Advertising Association of Britain. 1981. 145p.

An economic analysis of advertising that raises broad questions, this presents a 20-year review of the state of the art of advertising, both theoretically and empirically. Advertising is treated in the broader context of information to the consumer. The social and economic effects of information and persuasion are explained from both viewpoints of the consumer and seller. "We believe there are no simple solutions to complex issues," say the authors. In the course of this complex examination, advertising's relation to the marketing structure and its social value as information and persuasion come up for appraisal. Intended as a text for upper-level economics students. Chapter references and index.

Circulation: The Annual Circulation and Penetration Analysis of Print Media. (See No. 1737.)

1551

Commercial Radio in Africa. Federal Republic of Germany: German Africa Society/Deutsche Afrika-Gesellschafte, 1970. 307p.

Although the title mentions only radio, TV services are also included in this handbook of broadcasting stations throughout Africa, intended primarily for advertisers and marketers. Arrangement is alphabetical by country. Data for each station includes official address; name; language or languages in which commercials are broadcast; coverage; transmitting power and wave length; times of transmission for commercial programs; time classification; advertising rates; special regulations and services. Alphabetical index of stations.

1552

Craig, C. Samuel, and Brian Sternthal, eds. **Repetition Effects Over the Years: An Anthology of Classic Articles**. New York: Garland, 1986. 186p.

The effect of repetition on the individual's response to advertising has long served as a basis for the design of media strategy and a general understanding of how individuals respond to advertising. The articles selected for this anthology portray the historical development of inquiry pertaining to repetition effects during this century and part of the last, and discuss the appropriateness of various repetition strategies to increase impact. All articles are quantitative; some have references.

1553, 1554

Critchley, R. A. **Television and Media Effect: A Review of the Relevant Research**. London:

British Bureau of Television Advertising, 1974. 134p. (BBTA Occasional Papers No. 9.)

Critchley, R. A. **U.K. Advertising Statistics: A Review of the Principal Sources and Figures**. London: The Advertising Association, 1973. 50p.

In his preface to **Television and Media Effects**, Critchley calls this " . . . essentially a pulling together of the main information—already published in UK and elsewhere—which seems to be relevant" to the knowledge about the effectiveness of TV communication with special reference to advertising. Various theories are discussed, as are the findings from empirical data. In conclusion there is a three-page summary of facts that have been ascertained and a lengthy bibliography.

U.K. Advertising Statistics brings together readership and circulation figures for the press, audience data for television, as much information as is available for other media, and data about advertising billings and employment. Part I gives U.K. advertising expenditure; Part II, advertising rates and audiences; and Part III, advertising agency data. Sources for all figures are included, along with a great deal of explanatory data. Appendix I is "Bibliography and Sources"; Appendix II, "Control Systems in Advertising Practice," or codes.

1555

Current Issues and Research in Advertising. Ed. by James H. Leigh and Claude R. Martin, Jr. Vol. 1 **Original Research and Theoretical Contributions**. Vol. 2 **Review of Selected Areas**. Ann Arbor, MI: University of Michigan, Graduate School of Business Administration, Division of Research, annual. (1985–.)

The first volume consists of five conceptual articles bearing on theory, practice, and current developments and seven illustrating new research. Volume 2 reviews the literature in selected areas. Numerous tables and charts, and chapter references.

Cutlip, Scott M., comp. **A Public Relations Bibliography**. (See No. 1646.)

1556

Cutlip, Scott M., Allen H. Center, and Glen M. Broom. **Effective Public Relations**. 6th ed. Englewood Cliffs, NJ: Prentice-Hall, 1985. 670p. *1964 ed. HM 263. C98*

A tried-and-true text, first published in 1952, which combines public relations practice with factual information, so that in addition to use in class it serves as a dependable guide to a layman wanting a definition and description. Besides "how-to" information it places advertising in its historical, organizational and legal context, its status as a profession, and the variety of trade associations, professional societies, labor unions, volun-

tary organizations, etc. which use it. Obviously, it does not examine critically its place in society, but it does put in one place a great many facts about the profession.

1557

Darmon, Rene Y., and Michel Laroche. **Advertising Management in Canada**. New York: Wiley, 1984. 577p.

Contains a mixture of theoretical knowledge and practical skills required to make advertising decisions from management's point of view within the Canadian environment. In five parts: 1) the role and functions of advertising in the marketing plan; 2) the structure and role of advertising organizations in Canada, 3) an analysis of opportunity, which draws on the behavioral sciences and communication theory; 4) management of advertising programs; and 5) the economic and social effects of advertising in Canada. Intended for business majors, advertising students, users of mass communications, public relations managers in nonprofit organizations, and "anyone in this country or abroad who needs to have a good grasp of what makes advertising different in Canada." Contains charts, tables, statistics. Appendixes give broadcasting regulations and radio advertising and a technical "overview of the most common tools and techniques to produce print and broadcast advertisements." There is also a glossary and a subject and an author index.

1558

A Design for Public Relations Education: The Report of the Commission on Public Relations Education. New York: Foundation for Public Relations Research and Education, 1975. 19p.

Co-sponsored by the Public Relations Division of the Association for Education in Journalism and the Public Relations Society of America, this pamphlet recommends curriculum on the undergraduate, masters, and doctoral level; discusses the role of the educator and his relation with practitioners; and goes briefly into research, and the transition from campus to practice. In 1985, new recommendations for graduate education were published in a pamphlet, **Advancing Public Relations Education**. An update on undergraduate education was to be issued in 1987 as a report of the 1987 Commission on Undergraduate Public Relations Education, co-sponsored by the Public Relations Division of the Association for Education in Journalism and Mass Communication, the Public Relations Society of America, and the Educators Section of PRSA.

1559

Diamond, Edwin, and Stephen Bates. **The Spot: The Rise of Political Advertising on Television**. Cambridge, MA: MIT Press, 1984. 416p. *JF 2112 . A4 . D53*

An analysis of the recent rise and present role of political advertising and marketing (the "pollspot") in American politics. In four parts: Part I shows by example the opening rounds of the 1984 presidential campaign, revealing how media strategy fit into the broader campaign; Part II narrates the role of television and pollspots in the presidential elections from Eisenhower-Stephenson in 1952 to Reagan-Carter in 1980, with emphasis on description and presentation of representative spots; Part III examines major persuasive techniques and visual styles of the pollspot form; Part IV brings together the media techniques to explain how pollspots work and to assess the actual (as opposed to the fanciful) effects of television campaigns. Findings are based on interviews on the pollspots and other political television materials in the archives of the News Study Group in the Department of Political Science at M.I.T. Source notes and index. (A new edition was published in 1988.)

1560

Driver, John C., and Gordon R. Foxell. **Advertising Policy and Practice**. London: Holt, Rinehart and Winston, with the Advertising Association, 1984. 165p.

"Advertising often generates intense feeling, relatively little analysis and immoderate conclusions. This book attempts the reverse," say the authors, who are British lecturers in the subject. They survey the problems and practices from several points of view, with emphasis on economics and behavioral psychology, as they challenge certain accepted ideas and offer a different approach to advertising theory, policy and practice, in the course of which they comment upon considerable analytical and some descriptive literature. They are especially interested in the interrelationship of the economics of the Austrian School with the marketing approach to advertising, which they explain in some detail. This is a thorough examination, densely written and not for laymen. A list of references follow each chapter, with appendixes containing relevant British statutes and statutory instruments and various regulatory and administrative provisions. Indexed.

1561

Dyer, Gillian. **Advertising as Communication**. London: Methuen, 1982. 230p. HF 5821.D99

A text in which Dyer critiques modern advertising in terms of function, origin and development, and effects as shown in research—all from a socialist point of view—and tells how to analyze ads for both overt and covert meaning, using, among other tools, semiotics and ideology. Although intended for the novice it is by no means so strictly limited. Appendixes give statistics, a sample of rates, the titles of the laws affecting it, the code of the Advertising Standards Authority, and useful addresses. References and index.

1562

East Coast Publicity Directory. Ed. by Craig T. Norback. Fort Washington, PA: IMS Press, 1984. 374p.

This is an apparently one-shot directory of daily and weekly newspapers, magazines, and radio and television stations in the Boston, Connecticut, New York state, New Jersey, Philadelphia, Baltimore, Washington, D.C., Atlanta and the Miami/Fort Lauderdale areas. For each entry it gives information pertinent for publicity purposes which varies according to type of media but includes such items as address and telephone number (always), chief personnel, circulation, special editions and price for print and for broadcasting, information about personnel, and acceptable types of material. Following this section is a brief geographic listing, "National Publications," which contains certain special subject interest magazines and broadcasting stations, not limited to the East and with no explanation of the basis for selection; and a list of feature syndicates, and of news and wire services. A complete name index follows.

1563

Elliott, Blanche B. **A History of English Advertising**. London: Business Publications Ltd., 1962. 231p.

The author traces English advertising from its beginning in the late sixteenth century through the 1950s, with most of the emphasis on pre-twentieth century. Her concern is basically with facts rather than with ethical pros and cons. Much of her information comes from original sources, notably the Burney Collection and the Thomason Tracts in the British Museum. Brief bibliography of monographs and an index.

1564, 1565

Ewen, Stuart. **Captains of Consciousness: Advertising and the Social Roots of the Consumer Culture**. New York: McGraw-Hill, 1976. 261p. HF58.3.US.E94

Ewen, Stuart, and Elizabeth Ewen. **Channels of Desire: Mass Images and the Shaping of American Consciousness**. New York: McGraw-Hill, 1982. 312p. HF5813.US.E94

Both of these titles take a hard and critical look at modern advertising within the social structure. In **Captains of Consciousness** Ewen theorizes that it is a conditioning process intended by industry to design a value system suitable to its purposes—to create buyers and consumers. He traces the ways in which this has been done back to its historical roots in the early twentieth century, particularly in the 1920s. Notes, a bibliography, and an author-title-subject index.

Channels of Desire is a companion critique of advertising in Western society today that, the Ewens contend, has become an industrial, consumers' society which has given rise to and depends upon mass imagery to influence public consciousness, often through the subconscious. Tracing the development of this society, they point out its contradictory promises and its blighting effect on the human spirit. Chapter notes and index.

1566

Firestone, O.J. **The Public Persuader: Government Advertising**. Toronto: Methuen, 1970. 258p.

A Canadian study, made independently and later used as a significant portion of the Report of the Canadian Task Force on Government Information, which was tabled in 1969. The author examines in detail the particular methods used by the Canadian government and evaluates their effectiveness, gives details on amounts spent, discusses political patronage in relation to government advertising, and discusses the role of advertising agencies. The book ends with recommendations. There are several appendixes, two of which discuss government advertising in Britain and the U.S. Indexed.

1567

Fox, Stephen. **The Mirror Makers: A History of American Advertising and Its Creators**. New York: Morrow, 1984. 383p. HF5813.U5.F79

Advertising, the author feels, is largely a personal business, reflecting to a greater extent than most businesses its talented and dominant personalities. With this in mind he has written what is largely a chronological biographical history arranged by prevailing trends over the decades. As the title indicates, he feels that advertising reflects rather than creates cultural tendencies within society. There are chapter notes but no bibliography, probably because much of his material is based on interviews and on manuscript collections, which he has listed separately. Indexed.

1568

Gable, Jo. **The Tuppenny Punch and Judy Shows: 25 Years of TV Commercials**. London: Michael Joseph, 1980. 192p.

A solid and witty illustrated history of TV advertising in Britain. Emphasis is on trends rather than economics.

1569

Geis, Michael L. **The Language of Television Advertising**. New York: Academic Press, 1982. 257p. HF6146.T4.G31

A linguist analyzes and documents the various linguistic devices employed by advertisers in their use of language, and the ways consumers can be expected to interpret them. The focus is on the use and abuse of words, phrases and sentences most frequently employed, although not on their effectiveness, because solid information on the latter is hard to come by. The first six chapters are devoted primarily to television advertising directed to adults; the last six to children-oriented television advertising. Bibliography and index.

1570

Goffman, Erving. **Gender Advertisements**. Cambridge, MA: Harvard University Press, 1979. 84p. HF5827.G61

Goffman presents 507 photographs taken from commercials which he analyzes to show the unnatural symbols and rituals which, all too often in the eyes of society and invariably in the eyes of the advertisers, surround the male/female relationship. Chapter references. This first appeared as a monograph in the Fall 1976 issue of **Studies in the Anthropology of Visual Communication**.

1571

Graham, Irvin. **Encyclopedia of Advertising**. 2d ed. New York: Fairchild, 1969. 324p. *HF5803.G73

Defines more than 1,100 entries relating to advertising, marketing, publishing, law, research, public relations, publicity, and the graphic arts. Section I, which is the main body of the book, is devoted to terminology; Section II groups the terms according to subject matter to form a sort of index; Section III is a directory of associations.

1572

Hall, Jim. **Mighty Minutes: An Illustrated History of Television's Best Commercials**. New York: Harmony, 1984. 172p.

On the theory that "commercials present to us, in microcosmic but vivid form, a social and economic record of America during the television age," Hall has arranged about 165 black-and-white stills of successful commercials under various categories: "The Identifiable Characters," "Women in Commercials," "Men in Commercials," "Sex in Commercials," "Kid Vid Commercials," "Humor and Innovation," and "Jingles and Sentimentality." The text which accompany each section tells something about the creation and reception of the TV commercials. Although primarily entertainment, this has a potential reference use. Indexed.

1573

Hanson, Philip. **Advertising and Socialism: The Nature and Extent of Consumer Advertising in the Soviet Union, Poland, Hungary and Yugoslavia**. White Plains, NY: International Arts and Sciences Press, 1974. 171p.

Theoretically, advertising and communism are not compatible, but Hanson explains why this is not necessarily the case. In Part I he treats the Soviet Union, in Part II, Eastern Europe, showing in both parts organization and function and highlighting similarities and differences. Much of the information in Part II comes from a survey in which nationals responded to a questionnaire. A bibliography in the appendix accompanies Part I. The study was originally published in 1971 and 1972 as two separate monographs in the (British) Advertising Association's Research Studies in Advertising series.

1574

Henry, Brian, ed. **British Television Advertising: The First Thirty Years**. London: Century Benham, 1986. 527p.

A glossy tribute to the advertising side of Independent Television from its beginnings in the mid 1950s. It begins with a history of more than 200 pages, which is strong on facts but weak on analysis, by the editor, Brian Henry, who for 20 years was Marketing and Sales Director for Southern Television. This is followed by a number of shorter articles on various aspects by top practitioners connected through advertising, marketing or management—"The Television Commercial," "An Authority View" (two articles), "Medium Built on Research," "Copy Controls from Within," "Commercial Production," "The Effect of Television on Marketing," and "The Agency Viewpoint" (three articles). The one contributor outside the profession is Sir Asa Briggs with "TV Advertising and the Social Revolution." Maps and diagrams accompany the text. Twelve appendixes give codes and documents pertinent to the creation and existence of ITV and its advertising regulations as well as statistics on resources and expenditures. Index.

1575

Hill and Knowlton Executives. **Critical Issues in Public Relations**. Englewood Cliffs, NJ: Prentice-Hall, 1975. 234p.

This anthology, in which contributors are practitioners in the large public relations firm of Hill and Knowlton, Inc., is something of a "how to" book, but it is also an excellent source of information on the structure and operation of public relations. Although obviously very much in favor, contributors also discuss arguments against it. Among topics are financial and government relations, public interest issues, advertising, and international aspects. Max Ways, a **Fortune** editor and the one non-member of the firm, presents an overview, and the conclusion is an article about the role of public relations in society. Indexed.

1576

Hill and Knowlton International. **Handbook on International Public Relations**. 2 v. New York: Praeger, 1967, 1968. HD59.H64

Although concerned with the "how to" aspect of public relations, this handbook also contains a country-by-country discussion of such facts as media, audience, and government regulations. Specialists in each country contribute articles, each covering slightly different aspects. Vol. I treats Belgium, France, Italy, the Netherlands, Scandinavia, Spain, Switzerland, the United Kingdom, and West Germany. Vol. II treats Australia, Hong Kong, India, Japan, Latin America, Malaysia, New Zealand, and Singapore.

1577

Honomichl, Jack J. **Marketing Research People: Their Behind-the-Scenes Stories**. Chicago: Crain, 1984. 190p.

Although this is obviously intended as a text, its valuable insights about the way marketing is conducted makes it valuable to interested laymen, consumer groups and anyone who wants to know how campaigns—political and business—are conducted. The best description is through the table of contents. Part I describes marketing case histories—"The Marketing of Arm & Hammer," "How Detroit Reacted to the Imported Car Threat," "Launching Renault's Alliance," "The Marketing of Cycle Dog Food," "President Reagan's Marketing Plan," and "The Big Four of Political Research." Part Two describes the U.S. marketing research industry—its early history, its trends; its top 30 research companies, with thumbnail sketches of each; its top advertising agencies and their research functions; the amount spent on advertising and marketing research; the world's top ten marketing/advertising research organizations, etc. There is special material about A.C. Nielsen and Arbitron.

1578

Howard, John A., and James Hulbert. **Advertising and the Public Interest: A Staff Report to the Federal Trade Commission**. Chicago: Crain Books, 1973. 96p.

Based mainly upon the transcript of the Federal Trade Commission's hearings in the 1960s on modern advertising practices. The hearings are chiefly concerned with helping to insure that regulation is conducted for the benefit of consumers and competitors; to determine more precisely what constitutes "unfair" and "deceptive" advertising; and to understand more clearly the mechanisms by which advertising works. To these ends the hearings examine the structure and process of advertising; its role in marketing strategy; models of advertising communication; an evaluation of techniques; and regulation and control. At the end are recommendations.

INFA Press and Advertisers Year Book. (India) (See No. 1756.)

1579

Institute of Practitioners in Advertising. **Advertising Conditions**. London: The Institute. (1971–1976.)

This series gives brief and basic facts about such aspects of the countries involved as geography, demography, expenditures, chief media used, research organizations, number of advertising agencies, taxes, laws, regulations, and organizations. After 1978 it was discontinued.
Advertising Conditions in Austria. 1975. 16p.
Advertising Conditions in Belgium. 1971. 20p.
Advertising Conditions in Canada. 1975. 16p.
Advertising Conditions in Denmark. 1975. 16p.
Advertising Conditions in Finland. 1975. 20p.
Advertising Conditions in France. 1974. 20p.
Advertising Conditions in Germany (Federal Republic). 1976. 24p.
Advertising Conditions in Greece. 1975. 24p.
Advertising Conditions in Italy. 1975. 75p.
Advertising Conditions in Norway. 1975. 20p.

Advertising Conditions in the Netherlands. 1972. 24p.
Advertising Conditions in Poland. 1978. 24p.
Advertising Conditions in the Republic of Ireland. 1974. 16p.
Advertising Conditions in Spain. 1978. 24p.
Advertising Conditions in Sweden. 1976. 20p.
Advertising Conditions in Switzerland. 1975. 16p.
Advertising Conditions in the UK. 1976. 24p.

1580

JK524.J32 Jamieson, Kathleen Hall. **Packaging the Presidency: A History and Criticism of Presidential Campaign Advertising**. New York: Oxford University Press, 1984. 505p.

"...how presidential advertising came to be and what it has become, how candidates have shaped it and been shaped by it, what it has contributed, and the ways in which it has contaminated the political process." Focus is on each presidential campaign from 1952 through 1980, with an introductory chapter, "Broadsides to Broadcasts," on methods used by earlier candidates. Notes, an extensive bibliography and a name index.

1581

Jefkins, Frank. **Dictionary of Marketing, Advertising and Public Relations**. 2d ed. London: International Textbook Co., 1983. 311p.

Includes approximately 6,000 acronyms, proper names, and terminologies, with succinct, to-the-point identifications and definitions.

1582

Key, Wilson Bryan. **Subliminal Seduction: Ad Media's Manipulation of a Not So Innocent America**. New York: Prentice-Hall, 1973. 206p.

The idea of manipulation through perception in advertising—"the language within a language"—enjoyed a great vogue in the 1970s by the detractors of advertising and to some extent still does, especially among the young, with whom it is something of a cult book. Much of it consists of the psychoanalysis of specific print and television content, especially ads, which contain subliminal and not-so-subliminal sex symbols. Most of the titles are cute: "Sex Is Alive and Embedded in Practically Everything," "The Castrating Cosmovogue," "Video's Victimized Voyeur," "The Man Who Almost Thought for Himself," "The Avarice-Entrapped Media of Mass Communication." Marshall McLuhan has written an introduction, and Key has included "References." For all its superficiality, this book, by popularizing subliminal perception, is a part of the history of advertising.

1583

Kurtz, Bruce. **Spots: The Popular Art of American Television Commercials**. New York: Arts Communications, 1977. 111p.

In this analysis of television advertising Kurtz has as his aim to provide a conceptual framework for studying and understanding "the most pervasive visual imagery of our culture: television commercials," and to do so within the context of art history. Along with his text and illustrations are interviews with four TV commercial directors—Elbert Budin, Mike Cuesta, Rick Levine, Dan Nichols. He has included a wide-ranging bibliography of books on art, popular culture, and film and other media.

1584

Langholz Leymore, Varda. **Hidden Myth: Structure & Symbolism in Advertising**. New York: Basic, 1975. 208p.

Langholz has adapted the basic principles of structural analysis, as advocated by Levi-Strauss, as the focal point to examine "two of the most important processes in any society—the exchange of signs and the exchange of money, goods and services. Advertising uses the discourse of words and images to bring about the dialogue of values." For her study she examines two types of advertising for given products over given periods of time—magazine, or "static," advertising, and television, or "dynamic", advertising—and comes up with the functions of advertising in modern society. Throughout the text and in appendixes she explains her methodology. Bibliography and index.

1585

Leiss, William, Stephen Kline, and Sut Jhally. **Social Communication in Advertising: Persons, Products, & Images of Well-Being**. New York: Methuen, 1986. 327p.   2nd ed (1990) HF5827.L53

In industrial societies in the 20th century, national consumer product advertising has become one of the great vehicles of social communication, the authors contend. Although when looked at superficially its role seems to be the promotion of goods and services, a more penetrating examination shows that it reaches deeply into more serious concerns, among them being interpersonal and family relations, the sense of happiness and contentment, sex roles and stereotyping, the culture of affluence, the life style of younger generations, and the role of business in our society. In three parts: Part One, "Debates on Advertising and Society," gives criticisms and defenses; Part Two, "Advertising and the Media," discusses the development and structure in relation to the media; and Part Three, "The Theater of Consumption," deals with various methodological approaches to the study of advertising, with emphasis on content analysis and semiology. Bibliography and index.

Lipstein, Benjamin, and William J. McGuire, comps. **Evaluating Advertising: A Bibliography of the Communication Process**. (See No. 1670.)

1586

Liu, Peter Yi-Chih. **The Development of the Advertising Industry in Japan and Taiwan: A**

Comparison, 1945–1975. Taipei, Taiwan: International Advertising Agency, 1975. 141p.

A comparison of the development and status of advertising in the two countries, taking into account the similarities and differences of each. The author's conclusions are liberally bolstered by statistics and regulatory documents. Footnotes, a bibliography, and appendixes containing pertinent laws and codes.

1587

Lodish, Leonard. **The Advertising & Promotion Challenge: Vaguely Right or Precisely Wrong?** New York: Oxford University Press, 1986. 188p.

"The challenge of this book is to create a new mode of thinking about advertising and promotion," says Lodish. He contends that advertising and promotion are full of rationales that lead to very precise methods and decisions that are very easy to implement but are "precisely wrong," while other much better and less precise methods are "vaguely right" and produce better results. His book is an exploration of the "vaguely right" to greater productivity—its roles and objectives, its alternative ways of obtaining advertising and promotional services, its decision support through research, testing and experiments. Lodish is Professor and Chairman of the Marketing Department at the Wharton School, University of Pennsylvania. Glossary and index.

1588

Marchand, Roland. **Advertising the American Dream: Making Way for Modernity, 1920–1940**. Berkeley: University of California Press, 1985. 448p. HF 5813 . U5 . M315

Marchand scrupulously examines in depth the content of a wide selection of advertisements of the 1920s and 1930s to determine their relation to social reality, revealing the ways in which advertising as a whole influenced American society through reflection, distortion, and perhaps most of all, promise. Elegantly written and illustrated, this is an outstanding example both of advertising as social history and of qualitative content analysis. There are 53 pages of notes and a bibliographical essay which examines many books about and pertinent to advertising. Sources for the ads are cited. Name-subject index.

1589

Martineau, Pierre. **Motivation in Advertising: Motives that Make People Buy**. New York: McGraw-Hill, 1957. 210p.

Although advertising has always had its share of the nonrational and nonutilitarian, Martineau was one of the first to call attention to the effectiveness of this approach. Drawing upon psychology and the social sciences in general he examines techniques that go beyond the purely informative and verbal and advocates greater use of symbolic, emotional and aesthetic appeals to create "a rich positive product image or institutional image with many desirabilities." Today Martineau's suggestions have become truisms, but this book remains important in the literature of advertising history. Bibliography and index.

1590

Masson (Peter), and Partners. **Television Advertising Conditions in Europe**. 4 v. London: British Bureau of Television Advertising Ltd., 1973.

Four booklets which discuss briefly, with accompanying tables, the following aspects for each of the countries covered: background, availability of advertising time, allocation system, flexibility of system, rate card, advertising restrictions, cancellations, TV research. A summary for each follows. Vol. I includes Germany and France; Vol. II, Austria, the Netherlands, Switzerland; Vol. III, Finland, the Republic of Ireland, Spain; Vol. IV, Cyprus, Greece, Italy.

1591

Mayer, Martin. **Madison Avenue, U.S.A.**. New York: Harper, 1958. 332p.

Since 1958 Madison Avenue, Mayer's metaphor for advertising, has changed, but Mayer's book remains a classic, an important "first" in the history of its literature. A reporter rather than an advertising man, he visited Madison Avenue's leading agencies where he interviewed about 400 practitioners and read about 30,000 pages to gather material for his critique of the profession. His observations are informative, challenging, and stylishly written; where there is controversy he has given both sides but lets his sympathies show, and except in the last two chapters, which are avowedly editorial, he has generally avoided expression of his own opinion. Much of what he says are eternal verities.

1592

McLuhan, Marshall. **The Mechanical Bride: Folklore of Industrial Man**. Boston: Vanguard, 1951. 157p. 1967 ed. HM 291 . M16

This—McLuhan's first and unheralded book—is a pioneering content analysis of advertisements. Although he makes no mention of the term "semiotics" he employs the disciplines of literature, anthropology, psychology and aesthetics, among others, to dissect 154 ads of the 1940s to uncover their appeals in terms of carefully embedded social values. With a keen sense of good and evil, or, if you will, value judgment, he ends each of the 154 essays accompanying the ads with a message of warning against manipulation.

Measuring Payout: An Annotated Bibliography on the Dollar Effectiveness of Advertising. (See No. 1674.)

Melody, William H. **Children's Television: The Economics of Exploitation.** (See No. 719.)

1593

Meyers, William. **The Image Makers: Power and Persuasion on Madison Avenue.** New York: Times Books, 1984. 242p.

This examination of the advertising business which follows in the footsteps of Vance Packard's **Hidden Persuaders** (1957) and Martin Mayer's **Madison Avenue** (1958) contends that it has become more of a science than an art and that imagination and creativity have been replaced by commercial psychoanalysis and statistical research. Meyers, who has worked both in advertising and publishing, demonstrates his thesis with descriptions of the campaigns of various types of products, as for example, "Giant-Killers: Philip Morris Takes On the Advertising Establishment," "Sour Grapes: Wine Tries to Become Our National Drink," "Gold Mine: Computers Get Personal," in which he delivers his punches in an easy, free-wheeling style. Bibliography and author-subject-title index.

1594

Millum, Trevor. **Images of Women: Advertising in Women's Magazines.** Totowa, NJ: Rowman and Littlefield, 1975. 206p.

A study of visual advertising in women's magazines in the late 1960s which probes the nature of the advertisement as a cultural artifact, with meanings above and beyond the sales message. Through a detailed and systematic examination, Millum considers and connects the role of advertising itself as it portrays the role of women. In addition to its content the study is interesting for its methodology which he details throughout. Bibliography, subject index, and index of authors cited.

1595

Morais, Benedict, and Hamdan Adnan, eds. **Public Relations: The Malaysian Experience.** Kuala Lumpur, Maylasia: Institut Perhubungan Raya Malaysia (Institute of Public Relations), 1986. 259p.

A compilation of articles by Malaysian academicians and public relations professionals from the public and private sectors, intended both as a text and as a survey for the interested layman. In two parts: the first deals with public relations in several types of business, in government and in some of its more general aspects; the second contains a history of the Institute, its goals, code, membership, and other specific features.

1596

Morella, Joe, Edward Z. Epstein, and Eleanor Clark. **Those Great Movie Ads.** New Rochelle, NY: Arlington House, 1972. 320p.

Reproductions of film posters from the 1930s through the 1960s, divided into subdivisions to illustrate various trends: "Stars," "Comic Strip Features," "Misleading Ad Lines," "Movies from Other Media," "Logos," "Tie-ins and Endorsements," "Films from Other Lands," "Classics," "Censorship and Advertising," and so on. Brief text precedes each section, and Judith Christ has written the introduction.

1597

Myers, Kathy. **Understains: The Sense and Seduction of Advertising.** London: Comedia, 1986. 152p.

Myers plays devil's advocate as she examines the uses and abuses of current British advertising, with emphasis on the latter, analyzing its growth and methods "from 'branding' to 'target markets', its calculated appeal to women ('the black magic system')," and its use by England's political parties. She ends with a theory of consumption. Bibliography.

1598

The New World of Advertising. Ed. by Vernon Fryburger. Chicago: Crain Books, 1973. 230p.

On January 15, 1963, **Advertising Age** published **The World of Advertising**, an extra-thick issue devoted entirely to facts, figures, and articles designed to broaden the knowledge of practitioners and the general public about advertising. This proved a valuable reference tool, but by the end of the 1960s was out of date except for historical purposes.

Ten years later, in its November 21, 1973, issue, **Advertising Age** brought out **The New World of Advertising**, designed "to put the changes of the past decade into perspective" and to attempt to show that advertising and marketing are necessary to the U.S. economy. In five parts, the first contains an introductory statement by the Council of Economic Advisers, a report on the state of the advertising business, and an essay defining advertising. The second part discusses the role of the advertiser, the agency, marketing research, advertising and regulatory associations, and the functions of the various media. The third tells the uses made of advertising by government, agricultural associations, labor unions, states and cities, and so on. It also defines the work of the Advertising Council. A fourth surveys aspects of international advertising, and the fifth debates pros and cons of advertising with Tom Dillon, president of BBD&O, pro, and Arnold Toynbee, con.

In 1975, a 129-page supplement appeared, also edited by Fryburger, with 20 selections from the 1973 edition, some of which are up-dated, and ten articles from more recent issues of **Advertising Age**.

1599

Nolte, Lawrence W. **Fundamentals of Public Relations: Professional Guidelines, Concepts and Integrations.** 2d ed. New York: Pergamon, 1979. 511p.

Although designed as a basic text for college students, with emphasis on techniques, this book nevertheless provides a synthesis of theory and practice which shows how public relations serves, whom it serves, and what it views as its function in society. Bibliography and index.

1600

O & M Pocket Guide to Media. 8th ed. New York: Ogilvy & Mather, 1982. 101p.

A handbook designed as a reference tool for quick estimates of the dimensions, audiences, and costs of the various media. The information, in tabular form, is compiled from many sources and is organized under the headings of Television, New Technologies, Radio, Magazines, Newspapers and Supplements, Out-of-Home Media, Direct Response, Yellow Pages, Minority Markets, Reach and Frequency, and a glossary of terms in an appendix. Data are compiled from syndicated services and special studies and subject to rapid change.

O'Dwyer's Directory of Corporate Communications. (See No. 1774.)

O'Dwyer's Directory of Public Relations Firms. (See No. 1775.)

1601

O'Toole, John. **The Trouble with Advertising: A View from the Inside**. New York: Chelsea, 1981. 245p.

For someone wanting to learn more about advertising, this is an excellent source, not least among the reasons because it is so well written. Much too sophisticated for a "how-to" book, it nevertheless is full of professional pointers. O'Toole, chairman of Foote, Cone & Belding, explains what 34 years in the business have taught and defends advertising against what he sees as popular misconceptions. Part I, "Advertising—A Four-Syllable Occupation or a Four-Letter Word," describes its basic nature; Part II, "What Goes Down the Elevator Determines What Goes Up the Flagpole," discusses personnel; Part III, "Making Better Advertising While Making Advertising Better," deals with process; and Part IV, "Aspects and Varieties of the Species," concerns structure. Since he has drawn largely on experience there is no bibliography. There are, however, three indexes: Subjects and Proper Names; Advertising Agencies; and Advertisers and Brands. (A second edition was issued in 1985.)

1602

Packard, Vance. **The Hidden Persuaders**. Rev. ed. New York: Washington Square Books, 1980. 228p.

When the first edition of **The Hidden Persuaders** appeared in 1957 (McKay) Packard said of it: "This book is an attempt to explore a strange and rather exotic new area of American life. It is about the large scale efforts being made, often with impressive success, to channel our unthinking habits, our purchasing decisions, and our thought processes by the use of insights gleaned from psychiatry and the social sciences. Typically these efforts take place beneath our level of awareness; so that the appeals which move us are often, in a sense, 'hidden.' The result is that many of us are being influenced and manipulated, far more than we realize, in the patterns of our everyday lives." Step by step he pointed out various techniques which, in his opinion, bewitched the public by instilling desires for "wants" over and above "needs." Today his findings no longer seem unnatural and strange, but his book, one of the first of its kind, has become something of a classic. In the revised edition Packard has appended an epilogue, "A Revisit to the Hidden Persuaders in the 1980s" in which he finds that "virtually all the strategies described are still being used, some more than others." Although he has apparently based his findings on reading, research and interviews, he has not used chapter notes nor given a bibliography. There is an index.

1603

Paletz, David L., Robert E. Pearson, and Donald L. Willis. **Politics in Public Service Advertising on Television**. New York: Praeger, 1977. 123p.

The authors analyze public service advertising on television through interviews, questionnaires, telephone polls, and content analysis to show how akin it can be to advocacy and propaganda. They approach the analysis on two levels: the operation of production, distribution, and airing; and a more speculative discussion of the values espoused in the spots and their political relevance. To demonstrate values and political relevance they analyzed the content of public service announcements aired during a given period. Particular attention is given to the question of selection. Since there is not nearly enough air space for all the institutions, organizations, agencies, and groups who request time, how are choices made? The structure of the Advertising Council in particular is examined. Footnotes and index.

1604

Pease, Otis. **The Responsibilities of American Advertising: Private Control and Public Influence, 1920–1940**. New Haven: Yale University Press, 1958. 232p.

This is one of the first broad, in-depth studies of advertising in its cultural and political context. Emphasizing the period between 1920 and 1940, Pease analyzes the attitude of the industry toward the public, its concept of responsibility, and the intellectual assumption underlying its operation. Included also is the public's attitude toward advertising, as manifested in the consumer movement. Though confined to the newspaper and magazine, the study is to a considerable extent applicable to the radio of the period. The concluding 17-page bibliographical essay is a valuable feature. There are chapter notes and an index.

1605

Perlongo, Bob, Comp. **Early American Advertising**. New York: Art Directions, 1985. 184p.

A light-hearted and random collection of mid-to-late 19th through early 20th century ads, good for a laugh or for advertising history or as examples of popular culture. In three sections: "A Gallery of Advertising and Commentaries" (the commentaries by the compiler); "Samples from Two Random Years: 1896 and 1906," and "Potpourri." Dates are given when available; sources are not identified. No index, although an index of product type would have been interesting and perhaps useful. But this anthology was not meant for reference.

Pollay, Richard W., ed. and comp. **Information Sources in Advertising History**. (See No. 1685.)

1606

Pope, Daniel. **The Making of Modern Advertising**. New York: Basic Books, 1983. 340p.

Pope approaches advertising as an aspect of business history. As he puts it: "We may or may not get the advertising we deserve; we most certainly get the kind of advertising corporations require." Although he does not neglect other forces—legal regulations, ethical and aesthetic beliefs, external pressures for reform, the social background of its professional men and women—he explains the evolution of modern advertising in terms of the business needs it fulfills. Unlike some other recent books on the history of American advertising—Marchand (No. 1588) and Fox (No. 1567) for example, which deal primarily with the 1920s and beyond, Pope concentrates on the period before the 1920s on the theory that its institutional context was formed earlier in the century. Using economic determinism as a theory, he explores industry's demand for advertising; advertising's effect on industry; and the agencies, ethics and messages of persuasion. He closes with "Advertising Today: The Era of Market Segregation." Copious chapter notes and an index, but no bibliography.

1607

Presbrey, Frank. **The History and Development of Advertising**. New York: Doubleday, Doran, 1929. 642p.

"This book expresses the culmination of many years of work in the gathering of material and many hours spent in weaving the story of one of the world's most potent instruments for the development of manufacture, trade and industry," says Presbrey in his Foreword. "This volume is not one of theories and does not seek to give instruction," he continues. Its text adheres closely to what is expressed in its title. The first hundred pages concern "Ancient Advertising and Development of Advertising in England"; the rest of the book chronologically details "Development of Advertising in the United States" through the 1920s, concluding with an appendix giving an address by Calvin Coolidge on the economic aspects of advertising, delivered in 1926 to the American Association of Advertising Agencies. Granted that Presbrey's uncritical enthusiasm is dated, this remains a valuable and monumental repository of factual information. Not the least of its useful features are more than 350 illustrations. Index.

1608

Preston, Ivan. **The Great American Blow-Up: Puffery in Advertising and Selling**. Madison: University of Wisconsin Press, 1975. 368p. HF5813.US.P

A head-on attack on puffery, defined as "advertising statements which are not illegal though they cannot be proven to be true." Attacking the conventional wisdom among advertising practitioners that puffing cannot be deceptive, he traces its history and suggests ways to treat it. This is an excellent case-by-case record of the relationship between advertising and the law. Chapter notes, a table of cases and an index.

1609

Price, Jonathan. **The Best Thing on TV: Commercials**. New York: Viking/Penguin, 1978. 184p. HF6146.T4.P94

"More fun than a gorilla with a suitcase, more explosive than a camera that blows up, more entertaining than the programs they interrupt, more informative than most network news, commercials are often the best thing on TV. And the best commercials out-pace the programs they interrupt in at least a dozen ways." After analyzing the commercial and its environment, Price elaborates on the ways which, in his opinion, commercials accomplish these feats. Whether you agree with him or not, this is an unorthodox, entertaining, and illuminating book.

Public Relations Career Directory 1986. (See No. 1778.) *HF5382.M84.P9

1610

Ramond, Charles. **Advertising Research: The State of the Art**. New York: Association of National Advertisers, 1976. 148p.

Designing his book for practitioners and students rather than for hard-core researchers, Ramond summarizes and appraises in layman's language studies in the field of advertising which give practical knowledge. Arrangement is topical under aim and scope: how advertising communicates; how it sells; how brand attributes and corporate images are arrived at and how they work; the selection of target audiences; copy, media, and budget research; studies of advertising frequency; and the future of advertising research. Appendixes contain an annotated bibliography of reviews of advertising research and a 20-page bibliography of the references cited. Indexed.

1611

Rijkens, Rein, and Gordon E. Miracle. **European Regulation of Advertising: Suprana-**

tional Regulation of Advertising in the European Economic Community. New York: Elsevier Science, 1986. 375p.

"To recall the past and help the reader prepare for the future," a European advertising executive and ex-president of the European Association of Advertising Agencies and an American advertising professor review and analyze supranational regulatory activities affecting advertising, focusing on advertising regulation as proposed by the Commission of the European Community, the response to it by the business world, and the influence of other inter-governmental bodies covering a wider area than the Common Market. Beginning with conditions leading to the post World War II development of the consumer movement in Europe with its criticisms of advertising, the study continues into the 1960s when the movement gained momentum, the 1970s when the height of regulatory activity was reached, and the 1980s when it subsided, leading to the adoption of certain principles which guided united action by the business community. In addition to numerous articles, books, official documents and other published materials, the authors drew upon Rijkens' professional experience and files, private correspondence and personal interviews with officials of consumer organizations, current and former officials and staff of governments and of the European Economic Community, business leaders, representatives of industry associations, international advertising executives, and many others. An "Executive Summary and Recommendations" distills main points and recommendations; appendixes reproduce some of the principle documents, and 20 pages of "References" lists sources. There is a subject index.

1612

Rotzoll, Kim B., James E. Haefner, and Charles H. Sandage. **Advertising in Contemporary Society: Perspectives Toward Understanding**. Cincinnati, OH: South-Western, 1986. 155p.

HF 5821 . R85

This text probes beneath the surface to background the why's and wherefore's rather than explain the how-to's. Part I, "Basic Perspectives," examines various theories of society that may influence the climate of advertising: the classical liberal world view, the neo-liberal world view, and five views of advertising's social role as an institution. Part II deals with "Issues of Consequence," economic theories and effects; the audience; the relationship with the various media; regulation; and ethics. An "Afterword" is a tentative exploration of advertising's future and the factors which may determine it. Chapter notes.

1613, 1614

Sandage, Charles H., Vernon Fryburger and Kim Rotzoll. **Advertising Theory and Practice**. 11th ed. Homewood, IL: Irwin, 1983. 509p.

Sandage, Charles H., and Vernon Fryburger, eds. **The Role of Advertising: A Book of Readings**. Homewood, IL: Irwin, 1960. 499p.

Although much of **Advertising Theory and Practice**, first published in 1948, is concerned with techniques and market analysis, an almost equal part is given to an analysis of the place of advertising in our society as the authors see it—its evolution, its regulation, its possible effects, its possible future. Over the years the subject matter has been reorganized and where necessary updated, with account taken of new trends, strategies, and research. Footnotes, an index, and well-chosen illustrations. A 12th edition is forthcoming.

The Role of Advertising, a reader, discusses pertinent facts and theories, such as advertising's place in society, its responsibility, its appeals, its function, and its impact. Its evaluation of advertising's role has dated surprisingly little. Includes a bibliography at the end of each section and gives "Standards of Practice of the American Association of Advertising Agencies" and the Television Code.

1615

Schudson, Michael. **Advertising, the Uneasy Persuasion: Its Dubious Impact Upon American Society**. New York: Basic Books, 1984. 288p.

HF 5813.U5.S38

"What is the work that advertising does? Where does it fit into the culture? . . . What kind of a culture has been historically required to nurture it?" In this analysis that has been by and large praised by advertising's supporters and panned by its detractors, Schudson explores these questions, orienting his investigation around the place consumption holds in our culture, the kind of consumption it is, and the role of advertising in it. Throughout he rejects the claims of practitioners and the fears of critics, believing, as the subtitle implies, that we lack proof of effect. Notes and index.

1616

Schwartz, Tony. **Media: The Second God**. New York: Random House, 1981. 206p.

Schwartz, who has written television and radio commercials for more than 300 major corporations, four presidential campaigns and dozens of senatorial and gubernatorial campaigns, analyzes in a very readable way his creative process against the background of the communication process. An easy writer with a clever turn of phrase, he combines wide experience with the broadcast media and a knowledge of Marshall McLuhan's theories. Index.

In an earlier book, **The Responsive Chord** (Anchor/Doubleday, 1973), Shwartz discusses the use of sensory perception in constructing commercials.

1617

Selling Dreams: How Advertising Misleads Us. Penang, Malaysia: Consumers Association of Penang, 1986. 149p.

This book, the result of monitoring Malaysian advertisements in both print and broadcast media, looks into three main issues: misleading advertisements that make dangerous products seem harmless, or make extravagant claims, or exploit women and children, or use false psychological tactics; effects of advertising, economically, environmentally, culturally, and even morally; and the ineffectiveness of the various codes, guidelines, and laws related to advertising in Malaysia. Ads that illustrate the points are included. In conclusion are recommendations to the government on ways to improve advertising standards.

1618

Sharp, Harold S. **Advertising Slogans of America**. Metuchen, NJ: Scarecrow Press, 1984. 543p.

If for whatever reason you need information about advertising slogans, this is your source. About 15,000 of them used by some 6,000 businesses and other organizations are shown in a single alphabetical listing under organization, product, service or business, and under the slogan itself.

1619

Simon, Morton, J. **Public Relations Law**. New York: Appleton-Century-Crofts, 1969. 882p.

"We have sought to produce for the PR practitioner a basic book which will also guide the layman when he ventures into the legal sectors of public relations," says the author, a lawyer. Gives legal basics of such areas as copyright, privacy, libel, trademarks, photography, deception, contests, industrial espionage, government relations, lobbying, employee-employer relations, and similar aspects, some of which have changed over the decade. Enough, however, remains the same to make the references useful.

1620

Singer, Benjamin D. **Advertising & Society**. Don Mills, Ontario, Canada: Addison-Wesley, 1986. 240p.

A Canadian academic probes the social role of advertising in general, and on a smaller scale in Canada in particular, examining it in terms of the values and norms that guide human behavior, the roles and statuses occupied by people, the collective behavior in which people engage, and the processes of social control. Part 1 deals with the most relevant structural, historical, and economic issues such as financing and key social organizations like agencies, advertisers, media, and control institutions. Part 2 focuses on explicit and implicit mechanisms of social control with children, women, the elderly, and visible minorities used as examples. Part 3 gives the other side of the coin: control exerted over advertising by the advertisers themselves and by society. An epilogue speculates on the future. Appendixes contain "Rules and Regulations for Alcoholic Beverage Advertising in Canada, by Province (December 1984)," and "A New Code of Advertising for Lawyers." Chapter references and name/subject index.

Standard Directory of Advertisers. (See No. 1789.)   *HF5805.S78.1990 v.1-2.

Standard Directory of Advertising Agencies. (See No. 1790.)

1621

Standard Rate and Data Services, Inc. Wilmette, IL. (ca. 1919– .)

At present SRDS, as it is known, publishes 13 guides which bring together comprehensive information on advertising rates and specification for the media listed below. Data for each varies slightly according to the medium, but generally includes, in addition to rates and specifications, information about circulation or listenership, and demography. The report of advertising rates has recently become spotty for the broadcast media. In the SRDS publications for radio and television, many stations—in several instances stations clustered in the same markets—are not giving ad rates for publication. The publishing frequency also varies from annual to monthly, or annual with frequent updates. Geographics likewise vary; at one time European media were included, whereas now volumes are limited to the U.S. and Canada. New titles are published following media trends. The 13 current volumes are:

1. **Business Publication Rates and Data**
2. **Newspaper Rates and Data**
3. **Newspaper Circulation Analysis**
4. **Consumer Magazine & Agri-Media Rates and Data**
5. **Spot Television Rates and Data**
6. **Spot Radio Rates and Data**
7. **Spot Radio Small Markets Edition**
8. **Direct Mail List Rates and Data**
9. **Co-op Source Directory**
10. **Print Media Production Data**
11. **Community Publication Rates and Data**
12. **Canadian Advertising Rates and Data**
13. **Print Media Editorial Calendars**

1622

Stewart, David W., and David H. Furse. **Effective Television Advertising: A Study of 1000 Commercials**. Lexington, MA: Lexington Books, 1986. 175p.

"Much of contemporary advertising research has severe limitations," say the authors. "No convincing theory has emerged to guide research in the field. Theories have been borrowed from other fields, but little in those borrowed theories suggests precise testable hypotheses. It appeared to us that a large, well-executed descriptive study would be a useful contribution to the literature and the progress of theory development. . . ." With this in mind they have produced a set of measures of advertising effectiveness for TV commercials, based on consumer choice and designed around three outcome measures: related recall, key message comprehension, and persuasion (measured as a shift in brand choice). The concluding chapter suggests the need for a new paradigm for research emphasizing choice behavior and the use of reliable measures. This is a broad but detailed statistical analysis with many tables and charts, geared toward the initiated rather than the layman. Appendixes show the codes used by the designers, the results of the study in tabular form, and sampling procedures. There is a valuable literature review and an index.

1623

Stridsberg, Albert B. **Effective Advertising Self-Regulation: A Survey of Current World Practice and Analysis of International Patterns**. New York: International Advertising Association, Inc., 1974. 181p.

Study of the possibilities and problems of voluntary self-regulation. The first part is general: basic issues, how to organize, and future of self-regulation. The second part gives profiles of what 29 countries have done. There are four appendixes: "International Code of Advertising Practice, 5th ed., 1973"; "International Code of Marketing Research Practice, 1971"; "International Code of Sales Promotion Practice, 1973"; "World Chart of Advertising Self-Regulation."

1624

Taplin, Walter. **The Origin of Television Advertising in the United Kingdom**. London: Pitman, 1961. 106p.

When the Independent Television Authority was authorized in Britain in 1954, bringing commercial television to the public, advertisers were by no means certain whether they should invest in the new medium. Their final decision to do so was crucial to the survival of the ITA. In this study Taplin has traced the history of this decision, which he feels was an important one not only for the historical record but also because it throws light on how such decisions are made, and in a broader way, how advertising works. Appendixes give the questionnaire on which some of the material is based and statistical tables to supplement those in the text. Index.

Thompson (J. Walter) Co. **Advertising: An Annotated Bibliography, 1972.** (See No. 1704.)

1625

Turner, E. S. **The Shocking History of Advertising**. New York: Dutton, 1953. 351p.

A light-hearted history of advertising in Britain and America, full of interesting examples and anecdotes but no economics. This is an excellent place to learn what products were advertised and how from the 17th century to 1953, when Turner concludes with a seven-page chapter on "TV—the 'Salesman's Dream'." Although seemingly well-researched, Turner does not give sources nor a bibliography. There is, however, an index.

1626

Urdang, Laurence, ed. **The Dictionary of Advertising**. Lincolnwood, IL: NTC Business Books, 1986. 209p.

Contains over 4,000 definitions used in marketing, planning, copywriting, art direction, graphic supply, print production, commercial production, program production, media planning, media research, media analysis, media buying, marketing research, consumer research, field interviewing, statistical analysis, merchandising and promotion planning, public relations counseling, data processing and advertising finance. Included are special meanings of ordinary words, names of services and organizations, and cross-references for abbreviations, acronyms and synonyms. The author is the managing editor of the **Random House Dictionary of the English Language**.

1627

Vestergaard, Torben, and Kim Schroder. **The Language of Advertising**. Oxford, England: Blackwell, 1985. 182p.

An examination of the socio-linguistic characteristics of advertising, backed by discussions of its role in society—its economic structure, its techniques and strategies, its ideology. Examples are taken from a wide range of British magazines—**News of the World, The Sunday Times, Titbits, Reader's Digest, Woman, She, Cosmopolitan,** and **Mayfair**. Meant for the layman; the professional already knows the tricks of the trade.

1628

Ward, Scott, Daniel B. Wackman, and Ellen Wartella. **How Children Learn to Buy: The Development of Consumer Information-Processing Skills**. Beverly Hills, CA: Sage, 1977. 268p. HC79.C6.W26

The authors take a long-range unemotional view of the effect of television advertising on children's behavior as consumers by stressing their information-processing capabilities within the framework of a large class of information-processing behaviors and by seeking to learn the conditions that foster or interfere with the development of these skills and attitudes. Data for their theory is based on interviews with 615 kindergarten, third-grade and sixth-grade children and their mothers from blue-collar and middle-class in Boston and Minneapolis-St. Paul. Their conclusions neither apologize for nor attack television advertising directed at children, but rather show both its abuses and its benefits. Appendixes reproduce the experiment and its results. Bibliography and index.

1629

Watkins, Julian Lewis. **The 100 Greatest Advertisements: Who Wrote Them and What They Did**. 2d rev. ed. New York: Dover, 1959. 232p.

"I think, as you go through these pages, you will feel a new pride in the business of advertising, for you will realize again what it has meant to the building and preservation of American free enterprise . . . *and how little of its surface in that direction has been scratched.*" With these words Watkins sums up the philosophy that led him to compile the advertisements he considered "greatest" in terms of aesthetic appeal and effectiveness. Although today there are those who may take issue with his philosophy, few will do so with his selection, and this is where the value of the book lies. Most of the ads—the "100" in the title—are representative of print advertising in the 1940s; in the 2d edition, 13 have been added as a supplement to cover the 1950s. The advertisements, with his brief comments on each, show the climate of advertising in the pre-TV days.

1630

Williamson, Judith. **Decoding Advertisements: Ideology and Meaning in Advertising.** London: Marion Boyers, 1978. 179p.

In this content analysis of advertising Williamson combines the insights of Freudian and post-Freudian psychology with the techniques of semiology to demonstrate how advertisements achieve their effects. She dissects over 100 print illustrations, examining them critically from a Marxian standpoint for grounds of dishonesty and exploitation. Contains a bibliography of 13 titles dealing with theory and methodology.

1631

Wood, James Playsted. **The Story of Advertising.** New York: Ronald Press, 1958. 512p.

A chronological history, with several early chapters about its beginnings in England but centering thereafter on the U.S. Largely descriptive, it discusses advertising within the framework of the period. Bibliography and index.

Working Press of the Nation. (See No. 1799.)

World Advertising Expenditures. (See No. 1800.)

Bibliographies

6

1632

Abrams, Alan E., ed. **Journalist Biographies Master Index**. Detroit, MI: Gale, 1979. 380p.

This biographical index contains reference to sources of information in over 200 standard biographical dictionaries and directories of European and American journalists, past and present, going as far back as Daniel DeFoe, but with heavy concentration on the present. A journalist is defined as "a person who has devoted a significant part of his or her career to work related to newspapers, magazines, or the broadcast media." In addition to the sources for further information, data for each includes birth, and if deceased, death dates. Some journalists are included for whom no information exists in cumulated biographies; in these cases a NF follows. By rough estimate about 35,000 names are included.

1633

Altbach, Philip G., and Eva-Maria Rathgeber. **Publishing in the Third World: Trend Report and Bibliography**. New York: Praeger, 1980. 186p.

The book is primarily a 969-item bibliography about publishing in the Third World, which includes a reference to both scholarly and trade literature, divided into geographic and topical sections with sub-headings. A lengthy, analytical essay on the state of publishing in the Third World defines the geographic area and surveys the literature about publishing. A cross-reference index links the essay and the bibliography.

1634

An Annotated Bibliography of UNESCO Publications and Documents Dealing with Space Communication 1953–1977. Paris: UNESCO, 1977. 102p.

Provides a consolidated list of papers, reports, articles, and publications produced by UNESCO in the field of space communication, incorporating two previous bibliographies compiled in 1970 and 1973. Most of the documents are no longer available for free distribution or for sale. They can be consulted in UNESCO's Mass Communication Documentation Centre and are also in most UNESCO depository libraries.

1635

Asian Mass Communication Bibliography Series. Singapore: Asian Mass Communication Research and Information Centre, irregular. (1975–1983.)

In these annotated bibliographies communication is defined broadly to include relevant material from such areas as agriculture, anthropology, community development, economics, education, law, political science, population, public administration, sociology, social psychology, and urban studies. Types of material covered are books, pamphlets, conference reports, seminar papers, theses and dissertations, research studies, surveys, government annual reports, commission reports, and periodical materials. Some of these are unpublished. The series is complete with No. 11, 1983.

Mass Communication in Malaysia. Comp. by Lim Huck Tee, assisted by V. V. Sarashandran. 1975. 91p. (No. 1.)

Mass Communication in India. Comp. and coordinated by R. K. Mehotra, The Indian Institute of Mass Communication. 1976. 216p. (No. 2.)

Mass Communication in Hong Kong and Macao. Comp. by Timothy L. M. Yu. 1976. 30p. (No. 3.)

Mass Communication in the Philippines. Comp. by Emilinda V. de Jesus, assisted by Amerla J. Gloria and Aida B. Pecana. 1976. 335p. (No. 4.)

Mass Communication in Taiwan. Comp. by Shou-Jung Yang. 1977. 65p. (No. 5.)

Mass Communication in Singapore. Ed. by Christina Y. Espejo and Guy De Fontgalland. 1977. 60p. (No. 6.)

Mass Communicaton in Nepal. Comp. by Narendra R. Panday. 1977. 34p. (No. 7.)

Mass Communication in Korea. Comp. by Taeyoul Hahn. 1977. 67p. (No. 8.)

Mass Communication in Sri Lanka. Comp. by H.A.I. Goonetileke. 1978. 77p. (No. 9.)

Mass Communication in Indonesia. Comp. by Mastini Hardjo Prakoso. 1978. 61p. (No. 10.)

Mass Communication in Thailand. Comp. by Sanan Padmadin. 1983. 80p. (No. 11.)

1636

Austin, Bruce A. **The Film Audience: An International Bibliography of Research, with Annotations and an Essay.** Metuchen, NJ: Scarecrow, 1983. 177p.

In this bibliography on the relationship of commercial cinema to its audience Austin has concentrated on empirical studies using social science methodology and available in non-book form, although he has included certain speculative or advocacy pieces based on his value judgment. With the exception of certain material it was impossible to obtain, all entries are annotated. Each entry includes the following information: entry number, author's name, title of article, and the necessary publication information. Arrangement is alphabetical by author, and there is a subject and a title index. Sources searched are listed. Preceding the bibliography is an essay by the compiler, "The Motion Picture Audience: A Neglected Aspect of Film Research."

1637

Bibliography of Media Management and Economics. Comp. by Rita Du Charme. Minneapolis: Media Management and Economics Resource Center, School of Journalism and Mass Communication, University of Minnesota, 1986. 113p.

A comprehensive bibliography of over 400 titles, primarily for books although including some annuals and journals, related to the field of mass media management and economics. This is the first bibliography of what is expected to be an annual publication, and it marks a new area of bibliography in the study of media. The 35 subject categories are broad, including these examples: book publishing, desktop publishing, ethics/social responsibility, journalists, media law, news, organization, personnel, unions and minorities. An author index is included. The entries are not annotated.

1638

Bishop, Robert L., comp. **Public Relations, a Comprehensive Bibliography: Articles and Books on Public Relations, Communication Theory, Public Opinion, and Propaganda, 1964–1972.** Ann Arbor, MI: A.G. Leigh-James Publishers, 1974. 212p. (Obtain from Publications Distribution Service, University of Michigan Press.)

A wide-ranging list, comprised of over 4,000 entries from dissertations, surveys, and an assortment of other sources in addition to books and periodicals. Entries are grouped under about 1,800 headings, with numerous cross entries and an author index. There are annotations when needed. Updated by Bishop in two supplements in **Public Relations Review**—Vol. 1 (1975–76) and Vol. 3 (1977)—and continued by Albert Walker, beginning in Vol. 4 (1978), as an annual supplement in the journal.

1639

Bol, Jean-Marie van, and Abdelfattah Fakhfakh. **The Use of Mass Media in the Developing Countries.** Brussels: International Center for African Social and Economic Documentation, 1971. 750p.

Contains 2,500 annotated citations in many languages. The late-lamented **Aspen Handbook of the Media** (1978–79) calls it "the best bibliography on the subject to date."

Brigham, Clarence S. **History and Bibliography of American Newspapers.** (See No. 875.)

1640

Broadcasting Bibliography: A Guide to the Literature of Radio & Television. 2d ed. Washington: National Association of Broadcasting, 1984. 66p.

An unannotated listing of 360 books, most of them published after 1975, intended as an introduction to the broadcasting field. Entries are grouped under seven categories, representing major areas of interest within the industry: reference sources, business, regulation, technology and production techniques, societal concerns, comparisons with other systems, and the newer related technologies. With the exception of the unit on regulation, each is divided into more specialized units, with some overlapping of necessity. A list of trade periodicals, newsletters, and journals follows. Author-title index.

1641

Burton, Julianne. **The New Latin American Cinema: An Annotated Bibliography 1960–1980.** New York: Smyrna Press, 1983. 80p.

Includes bibliographies; filmographies; books in Spanish, Portuguese and English; general articles and articles on Argentina, Bolivia, Brazil, Chile, Cuba, Jamaica, Mexico, Nicaragua and Venezuela; Hispanic cinema in the U.S.; and a listing of film periodicals in Spanish, Portuguese and English. About 150 entries in all.

1642

Cannon, Carl L., comp. **Journalism: A Bibliography.** New York: New York Public Library, 1924. 360p.

Annotated list of books and magazine articles "intended to be useful to the American newspaper man actively engaged in his profession, or to the student of journalism." The author has emphasized the present rather than the historical in his selections, which means that his bibliography is now an excellent source for references to the state of journalism in the early 1920s.

1643

Cassata, Mary, and Thomas Skill. **Television: A Guide to the Literature**. Phoenix, AZ: Oryx Press, 1985. 148p.

This bibliographic essay carefully selects, describes and evaluates approximately 450 titles under three headings: "Test Patterns," "The Environment," and "Directions," each of which is preceded by an introductory essay. "Test Patterns" is general, giving the literature of the mass communication process and the historical development of television, along with bibliographies, source books and program guides for radio as well as TV. "The Environment" deals with the literature of processes and effects in general and in terms of children, television news, and television politics. "Directions" includes the literature of the television industry, television criticism, and collected works. Each chapter lists the books that have been discussed. There is an author index, a title index, and a subject index. Bibliographical essays such as this are rare and difficult; in addition to requiring a knowledge of the literature it also takes an ability to synthesize. This is an outstanding example and a valuable addition to the field.

1644

Ceulemans, Mieka, and Guido Fauconnier. **Mass Media: The Image, Role, and Social Conditions of Women: A Collection and Analysis of Research Materials**. Paris: UNESCO, 1979. 78p. (Reports and Papers on Mass Communication No. 84.)

Covers a wide range of books and articles, broken down by media—advertising, broadcasting (radio, television, film), and print (Newspapers and magazines); and within the various media by geographic location—North America, Europe, Asia and Africa. Contains a list of the research studies analyzed.

1645

Chin, Felix. **Cable Television: A Comprehensive Bibliography**. New York: IFI/Plenum, 1978. 285p.

The major portion is an annotated bibliography of books, documents and periodical articles divided into seven areas: "General and History," "Cable Television Regulation and Policy," "Cable Technology and Channel Capacity," "Cable Television Regulation and Policy," "Cable Technology and Channel Capacity," "Cable Television Finance and Economics," "Uses of Cable Television," "Cable Television and Education," "Community Control and Franchises of CATV." A smaller but equally useful portion contains appendixes giving the 50 largest U.S. systems; the 50 largest companies; a chronology of major decisions and actions affecting cable; federal agencies and Congressional committees dealing with it; national, regional and state associations and other organizations; state regulatory agencies; section headings

of FCC rules; and a glossary of terms. Although no longer up-to-date, it is still an excellent source for information about the important formative years of cable. There is an author and subject index.

1646

Cutlip, Scott M., comp. **A Public Relations Bibliography**. 2d ed. Madison: University of Wisconsin Press, 1965. 305p.

"Books, articles and other related material written about public relations since it first emerged as an identifiable vocation in the early 1900s are classified under seventy-four subject categories," says **Marketing Information Guide**. Public relations is interpreted broadly to include theory as well as practice and includes such allied fields as communications and opinion change. The second edition reflects changes in attitude toward the profession, with more attention paid to substantive issues and to self-justification, tools, and research. Indexed. Cutlip's bibliography was updated by Robert L. Bishop in **Public Relations: A Comprehensive Bibliography** (No. 1638) and later bibliographic work in a journal, **Public Relations Review** (No. 1884).

1647

Danielson, Wayne A., and G. C. Wilhoit, Jr., comps. **A Computerized Bibliography of Mass Communication Research, 1944–1964**. New York: Magazine Publishers Association, 1967. 399p.

Notable as the first computerized bibliography in the field and also for its historical value, this leads the user to thousands of articles from 48 periodicals relating to the mass media when it was emerging as a discipline.

1648

Ellis, Jack C., Charles Derry, and Sharon Kern. **The Film Book Bibliography 1940–1975**. Metuchen, NJ: Scarecrow, 1979. 752p.

A subject-organized listing of 5,442 English-language books, monographs and published doctoral dissertations between 1940 and 1975 dealing with various aspects of the motion picture. It is divided into ten major classifications: Reference; Film Techniques and Technology; Film Industry; Film History; Film Classifications (genres); Biography, Analysis and Interview; Individual Films; Film Theory and Criticism; Film and Society; Film and Education. Each of these classifications has been further subdivided into more specific categories. Entries are arranged alphabetically to show the evolution of film literature within the area, with the exception of the sections on biography and individual films, which are arranged alphabetically according to person or film title. Each citation contains author, title, publication information and pagination. Annotations are included only if the title gives no indication of contents or is misleading. There is a name and a title index.

The authors consider their bibliography as complementary to two earlier ones: **The Film Index**, a series begun in 1941 and edited by Harold Leonard (New York: Museum of Modern Art Film Library and H.W. Wilson Co.), which gives information on both books and periodicals, and **The New Film Index** (1975), by Richard Dyer MacCann and Edward S. Perry which is annotated in this chapter (No. 1672).

Factfile. [A series of reference guides about film and television.] (See No. 1242.)

1649

Fisher, Kim N. **On the Screen: A Film, Television and Video Research Guide**. Littleton, CO: Libraries Unlimited, 1986. 209p.

". . . designed to acquaint the student, researcher, librarian and anyone interested in motion pictures and television with the important English-language reference works in these fields." Introduction. Fisher has indeed accomplished this. The 731 carefully selected and comprehensively annotated entries of resources include bibliographic guides; dictionaries and encyclopedias; indexes, abstracts and databases; biographies and credits; film reviews and television programming; catalogs; directories and yearbooks; filmographies and videographies; bibliographies; handbooks and miscellaneous sources; core periodicals; research centers and archives; and societies and associations. Emphasis is on the U.S., but some publications from England, Canada and Australia are included. As a general rule each entry contains author/s, title, place of publication, pagination, date and, where available, Library of Congress and ISSN or ISBN information. An appendix gives database service suppliers, with addresses and telephone numbers. Author/title and subject indexes. This is an essential sourcebook.

1650

Friedman, Leslie J. **Sex Roles Stereotyping in the Mass Media: An Annotated Bibliography**. New York: Garland, 1977. 324p.

Brings together some 1,000 studies, content analyses and published opinions concerning sex stereotypes in articles and books, under "Media Socialization and Sex Roles," "Advertising," "Print Media," "Popular Culture," "The Media Image of Minority Group Women," "Children's Media," "Educational Material," and "The Impact of Media Stereotypes on Occupational Choices." Writers come from many different backgrounds and points of reference, from academic to "feminism's early, but justifiable, tones of outrage." Entries include "entertaining speeches, statistical evidence gathered by women's and church groups, consciousness raising slide programs and films, and works tracing the imagery of womanhood throughout the history of film, rock music and women's magazines." Annotations are clear and concise. Author index and subject index.

1651

Gerlach, John C., and Lana Gerlach, comps. **The Critical Index: A Bibliography of Articles of Film in English, 1946–1973, Arranged by Names and Topics**. New York: Teachers College Press, 1974. 726p.

". . . a guide to articles about directors, producers, actors, critics, screenwriters, cinematographers, specific films and 175 topics dealing with the history, aesthetics and economics of film, the relation of film to society, and the various genres of film." There are in all 5,000 items from 22 British, U.S., and Canadian periodicals and more than 60 general ones. Contains an author and a film index.

Gottesman, Ronald and Harry Geduld. **Guidebook to Film**. (See No. 1268.)

1652

Gray, Peggy, comp. **Register of Current and Recently Completed British Research on Mass Media and Mass Communication**. Leicester, England: University of Leicester, Lester Documentation Centre for Mass Communication Research, Centre for Mass Communication Research, 1983. unpaged.

Contains 197 entries arranged by medium: television, radio, broadcasting in general, the press, books, film, music, cartoons, and multi-media, and in four special cases—advertising, new technology, communication and social policy, and research and development—by subjects. There is a residual category, "Other Research," to include studies that do not fit elsewhere. Projects are numbered sequentially in alphabetical order of main researcher. Information includes researcher/s, an annotation summarizing project, sponsor, duration of research, research institution, degree, and any other pertinent information. This latter topic sometimes tells form and source of publication. The list is followed by three indexes—a subject index; a list indicating inclusion of audience, content, or international studies; and an alphabetical list of contributors.

Hachten, William A. **Mass Communication in Africa: An Annotated Bibliography**. (See No. 164.)

1653

Head, Sydney W., and Lois Beck. **The Bibliography of African Broadcasting: An Annotated Guide**. Philadelphia: Temple University, School of Communications and Theater, 1974. 60p.

Lists major books and articles from newspapers and magazines—458 items in all, with a list of periodicals in the field and a topical index.

1654

Higgins, Gavin, ed. **British Broadcasting 1922–1982: A Selected and Annotated Bibliography**. London: BBC Data Publications, 1983. 279p.

Contains some 1,200 items, arranged alphabetically by author under broad subject headings, with brief descriptive annotations for most. Each entry is numbered. Subjects include: Broadcasting and society; cable and satellite broadcasting; engineering; external broadcasting; the Fourth Television Channel; general; government publications; organization policy and control; personalities; pirate broadcasting; production and programming techniques; books about programs (mostly analytical, but with a few scripts included); and government publications. Appendixes list periodicals, BBC's Engineering Division monographs; and the BBC's Lunchtime Lectures. An alphabetical index refers back to all entries, except those in the appendixes.

1655, 1656, 1657

Hill, George H. **Black Media in America: A Resource Guide**. Boston: G.K. Hall, 1984. 333p.

Hill, George H. **Blacks on Television: A Selectively Annotated Bibliography**. Metuchen, NJ: Scarecrow, 1985. 223p.

Hill, George H., and Lenwood Davis. **Religious Broadcasting 1920–1983: A Selectively Annotated Bibliography**. New York: Garland, 1984. 243p.

Three bibliographies concerned with blacks in the media. The first, **Black Media in America**, a compilation of more than 4,000 entries for books and other monographs, including dissertations and theses, as well as periodicals and newspaper articles, covers major aspects of media—book publishing, newspapers, magazines, radio, television, public relations and broadcasting. Practically all monographs are annotated, as are a few of the articles.

Blacks on Television spans the years from 1939 through 1984, with more than 2,800 entries taken largely from periodicals in the black consumer market where, the authors say, most of the material lies. Shorter sections list books, dissertations and theses, and journals and newspaper articles. A brief introductory article gives a thumbnail history of blacks in television. Three appendixes: "Black-Owned Television Stations," "Black-Owned Cable Companies," and "Emmy Winners." Program index and subject-author index.

Religious Broadcasting is more specialized in subject matter and broader in scope in that it is not limited to blacks. Subject matter, which is divided into books, dissertations and theses, and articles, covers a variety of subjects, ranging from personality profiles and studies of leaders to technical examinations of how the stations and programs function. Again, annotations are mostly for monographs. Subject/author and programs indexes.

1658

Hyatt, Marshall, comp. **The Afro-American Experience: An Annotated Bibliography & Filmography**. Wilmington, DE: Scholarly Resources, 1983. 260p.

The major portion of this publication consists of a bibliography of 977 articles and books "ranging from scholarly treatises analyzing film content to editorials castigating the industry for its insensitivity to black images and a black aesthetic," selected to recount "the history of the Afro-American cinematic experience." This is followed by a 577-item filmography of full-length films which blacks either act in or direct, or in which a black image is presented. Some shorter films of exceptional quality or importance are included. As a whole, it is intended to represent a carefully screened study that comments upon the most worthy, the most controversial, and the most useful works. Bibliographical entries are listed alphabetically, with a name/subject index. The filmography section lists films by category, giving name and date only.

1659, 1660

Kaid, Lynda Lee, Keith R. Sanders, and Robert O. Hirsch. **Political Campaign Communication: A Bibliography and Guide to the Literature**. Metuchen, NJ: Scarecrow Press, 1974. 206p.

Kaid, Lynda Lee, and Anne Johnston Wadsworth. **Political Campaign Communication: A Bibliography and Guide to the Literature 1973–1982**. Metuchen, NJ: Scarecrow, 1985. 216p.

Companion volumes, each consisting of journal and periodical articles, pamphlets, public documents (primarily hearings and reports of the U.S. Congress and specific federal agencies), and unpublished materials (primarily dissertations, theses, and papers presented at meetings and conventions. Coverage is limited to the United States except for a supplement of French and German materials in the first volume. The first volume also contains an annotated list of 50 books the authors consider seminal to the subject; the second has included books within the unannotated main body of materials. While annotations are always desirable, their lack throughout is compensated by the wealth of periodicals, articles, etc.—about 4,000 in all—which are included. Each volume contains a section, "Guide to the Literature," and a subject index.

1661

Kittross, John M., comp. **A Bibliography of Theses and Dissertations in Broadcasting, 1920–1973**. Washington: Broadcast Education Association, 1978. 238p.

Has more than 4,300 main entries, each containing

author and title, degree awarded, institution, and date. A serial number precedes each entry. There is a key word index, a title-by-year index, and a topical index. Preceding the main entries Kittross has analyzed the theses and dissertations according to schools and years and has drawn some observations.

1662

Kowalski, Rosemary Ribich. **Women and Film: A Bibliography**. Metuchen, NJ: Scarecrow Press, 1976. 278p.

Divided into four major sections: women as performers, women as filmmakers, images of women presented on the screen, and women as columnists and critics. Many entries are annotated, especially when necessary to convey contents. Subject and name index.

1663

Landrum, Larry N. **American Popular Culture: A Guide to Information Sources**. Detroit, MI: Gale, 1982. 435p.

Annotated bibliography of approximately 2,200 monographs covering a variety of aspects of the popular arts and of life style in general under 22 wide-ranging headings. One section is devoted to the media; various other sections are pertinent. Name and subject indexes.

For an abstracted bibliography on periodical articles on popular culture see **American Popular Culture: A Historical Bibliography** by Arthur Frank Wertheim (No. 1707).

1664, 1665, 1666

Lasswell, Harold D., Ralph D. Casey, and Bruce Lannes Smith, comp. **Propaganda and Promotional Activities: An Annotated Bibliography**. Chicago: University of Chicago Press, c1935, 1969. 460p.

Smith, Bruce Lannes, Harold D. Lasswell, and Ralph D. Casey, comp. **Propaganda, Communication, and Public Opinion: A Comprehensive Reference Guide**. Princeton, NJ: Princeton University Press, 1946. 435p.

Smith, Bruce Lannes, and Chita M. Smith, comp. **International Communications and Political Opinion: A Guide to Literature**. Princeton, NJ: Princeton University Press, 1956. 225p.

These three bibliographies covering the early days of communications bring together thousands of references from books and periodicals in both English and foreign languages, especially French and German. Although they concentrate largely on propaganda and public opinion, in doing so they deal with symbols, channels, contents, and effects of communication in general. While not up-to-date they are certainly not out-of-date.

In the first volume Lasswell, one of the most distinguished scholars to pioneer the field, has written a long essay, "The Study and Practice of Propaganda." In the second volume, Smith, Lasswell, and Casey have contributed four essays on the nature, contents, and effects of communications, with special emphasis on propaganda.

1667

Lent, John A. **Asian Mass Communications: A Comprehensive Bibliography**. Philadelphia, PA: Temple University, School of Communications and Theater, 1975. Supplement, 1978. 619p.

Lent calls **Asian Mass Communications** "the first attempt to make available in one place as much as possible of what has been written on all aspects of mass communications, both in Asian institutions and abroad." It is divided by region into four sections—Asia (general), East Asia, Southeast Asia, and South Asia—and subdivided by country, with research institutions, type of research conducted, and bibliographies and periodicals published about or in the respective nations. Entries, of which there are thousands, are unannotated. Contains a number of references which would be difficult to find elsewhere.

1668

Lichty, Lawrence W., comp. **World and International Broadcasting: A Bibliography**. Washington, D.C.: Association for Professional Broadcasting Education (now Broadcast Education Association), 1971. 800p. (approx.)

A massive work encompassing close to 100,000 entries from 1920 through the 1960s, geographically and chronologically organized, and covering about 150 countries and territories, excluding Great Britain, Canada and the U.S., but including 13 pages on China. Preceding and following this geographical listing are sections on bibliographies and general references; on general works; and on international ones. In addition to books and periodicals, there are articles from the **New York Times**. Lichty says he has not been selective nor has he verified items, but has depended upon other bibliographies, indexes, and listings.

1669

Linton, David, and Ray Boston. **The Newspaper Press in Britain: An Annotated Bibliography**. London: Mansell, 1986. 361p.

A fine-tuned scholarly work which gathers together monographs and articles (mostly the former) on the history of the British newspaper beginning with Caxton in 1476, with "British" defined as the present-day United Kingdom and Northern Ireland, and "press" defined to include photojournalism and cartoon illustration but not magazine or periodical publishing. Entries are annotated, often critically, except in cases where the title is self-explanatory. Many of the entries, in addition to the critical comments, give information on the author. Arrangement is alphabetical by author or title, with a detailed name/subject index. An appendix provides a chronology of British newspaper history from 1479 to 1986, showing the major events and principal personalities and publications over a period of more than 500 years. Another appendix indicates where papers and other archives relating to individual authors, newspapers, etc., can be located. The introduction deserves special comment for its succinct analysis of the state of the art of British newspaper press history.

1670

Lipstein, Benjamin, and William J. McGuire, comp. **Evaluating Advertising: A Bibliography of the Communications Process**. New York: Advertising Research Foundation, 1978. 362p.

The title is a misnomer. Actually, this 7,000-entry bibliography is limited to an evaluation of periodicals and various forms of monographs with findings applicable to TV commercials, and does not include research on print media. Nonetheless, it is a massive compilation. Entries, which abstract the material, cover a range of literature that has evolved from TV researchers as well as from professionals in related disciplines who are studying effects—evaluation, comprehension, persuasion, learning behavior, and similar pertinent topics. The largest portion consists of annotated author entries. There is a topical index and an alphabetical list of access words. Each compiler has written an essay—Lipstein on "Some Observations about the Literature," and McGuire on "Retrieving the Information from the Literature."

1671

Marxism and the Mass Media: Towards a Basic Bibliography. Bagnolet, France: International Mass Media Research Center, dist. by International General, irregular. (1978–.)

An ongoing series whose aim is to compile a global, multilingual, annotated bibliography of Marxist studies on all aspects of communications. Entries date from the 19th century and cover capitalist and socialist countries and the Third World, in English, French, German and Italian. Nos. 1, 2 and 3, published in 1972, 1973 and 1974 went out of print and were replaced by a 3-volume-in-one revised edition in 1978. Numbers 4–5 and 6–7 appeared in 1976 and 1980. The publishers at present (1986) have planned 17 numbers, some of which are special subject issues: Nos. 8–10, **Toward An International Left Bibliography on the Film**; Nos. 11–12; Nos. 13–15: **A World Bibliography of Left Writings on Photography, Typography, Design, and Posters**, Ed. by Bert Hogenkamp; and Nos. 16–17, **Portugal: Political Struggle and the Mass Media**. Most of the entries are annotated, and are arranged numerically by date of receipt in the organization's library in Bagnolet, France, with subject, author and country index to specifically locate items. An appendix lists organizations, groups and reviews mentioned, with addresses.

1672

MacCann, Richard Dyer, and Edward S. Perry. **The New Film Index: A Bibliography of Magazine Articles in English, 1930–1970**. New York: Dutton, 1975. 522p.

An annotated subject index to periodical articles about film, listed under nine major headings: Introduction and Reference, Motion-Picture Arts and Crafts, Film Theory and Criticism, Film History, Biography, Motion Picture Industry, Film and Society, Nonfiction Films, and Case Histories of Film Making. Each section is subdivided into various subheadings. Reviews of specific films or books about film are not included. The fourth section, Film History, includes foreign coverage. Although there is a proper name index there is none for film titles, so that the user cannot get back to individual films except through the rather broad subject arrangement.

1673

McKerns, Joseph P. **News Media and Public Policy: An Annotated Bibliography**. New York: Garland, 1985. 171p.

Seven hundred thirty-one annotated references covering a range of material, including philosophical and theoretical speculation, historical and quantitative research, and selected popular writings. Books, articles and doctoral dissertations are included. Author and subject index.

1674

Measuring Payout: An Annotated Bibliography on the Dollar Effectiveness of Advertising. New York: Advertising Research Foundation, 1973. 39p.

One hundred forty-three books, articles, and speeches, arranged chronologically from 1965 to 1972, with a separate section of the classics in the field. There is an author and a subject index.

Mowlana, Hamid, ed. **International Flow of News: An Annotated Bibliography**. (See No. 309.)

1675

Müller, Werner, and Manfred Meyer, comp. **Children and Families Watching Television: A Bibliography of Research on Viewing Processes**. Munich and New York: K.G. Saur, 1985. 159p.

Four hundred fifty-four titles, most in the English language and some in German, including articles, papers and books, which use empirical methodology to determine the active involvement (or lack of it) the viewer brings to the communication process—reception research as it is called in Germany. Each entry is described by subject catchwords. In four parts: "Bibliographies, Introductory Literature"; "Reception Processes"; "Viewing Situation"; and "Media Education." Author and subject indexes.

1676

Murray, John P. **Television & Youth: 25 Years of Research & Controversy**. Boys Town, NB: Boys Town Center for the Study of Youth Development, 1980. 278p.

A comprehensive bibliography citing about 3,000 items appearing from 1955 to 1980, covering the subject of television and youth. Among them are original reports, research reviews and commentaries on research, discussions of the policy implications of research for various segments of industry, government and the public, "and for all who are concerned with the well-being of children." Emphasis is on English-language publications from Australia, Great Britain, Europe and Scandinavia as well as North America. Part I, "Television & Youth: A Review of Research, Commentary and Controversy," is a bibliographic essay; Part II, "The Master Bibliography: 1955 to the Present," contains all entries mentioned; Part III, "Thirteen Specialized Bibliographies," breaks the titles down by subject; Part IV, "Hither, Thither, and Yon," contains suggestions for policy, guide lines for action, and bibliographies.

Murray plans a companion volume, "Television and Youth: International Perspectives on Television and Research," which will survey the non-English language research and commentary.

1677

Nachbar, John G. **Western Films: An Annotated Critical Bibliography**. New York: Garland, 1975. 98p.

The author's aim is, through his bibliography, "to sum up what has been discovered about Western films and their relationship to their culture," and more important, to provide a tool for research. In his introduction he surveys the evolution of the genre through various popular culture forms, narrative dramas, and spectacles that came together in the early 1900s in the Western film. In the bibliography that follows, articles and books are listed under nine categories: reference sources, pre-1950 criticism, specific films, specific performers, specific producers, Western film history, the audience, comparative studies, and Westerns in the classroom. Author and subject indexes.

1678

Nafziger, Ralph O., comp. **International News and the Press: Communication, Organization of News Gathering, International Affairs, and the Foreign Press—An Annotated Bibliography**. New York: Arno, c1940, 1972. 193p.

Nafziger has examined thousands of books, articles, proceedings, documents, memoirs, occasional papers, and various fragmentary and episodic bits and made them into a topical bibliography which covers the U.S. and

foreign news gathering from the turn of the century to World War II. Name index.

1679, 1680

A New World Information and Communication Order: Toward a Wider and Better Balanced Flow of Information: A Bibliography of UNESCO Holdings. Paris: UNESCO, 1979. 73p.

A New World Information and Communication Order: Toward a Wider and Better Balanced Flow of Information: A Bibliography of UNESCO Holdings. Supplement 1980–81. Paris: UNESCO, 1982. 46p.

The titles in these bibliographies are available for on-site use at the Communication Documentation Centre, UNESCO, Paris. The bibliography lists UNESCO-published material and material published elsewhere. The UNESCO material may be purchased as the stock permits. Full bibliographic information and a subject index is provided.

The material dates form the late 1960s, although some earlier documents are included to indicate "that UNESCO's concern about the problem of information imbalance can be traced back as far as the fifties." Forward, 1979. The supplement updates the list of UNESCO holdings for 1980–81.

1681

Newspaper Libraries: Bibliography, 1933–1985. Comp. by Celia Jo Wall. Washington, DC: Special Library Association, 1986. 126p.

A bibliography of books, journal articles, reports, and pamphlets about library services to news organizations. The main contribution of the bibliography is that it brings together citations about the application of computers in newspaper libraries.

1682

Parker, Elliott S., and Emelia M. Parker, comps. **Asian Journalism: A Selected Bibliography of Sources on Journalism in China and Southeast Asia**. Metuchen, NJ: Scarecrow, 1979, 471p.

This bibliography listing general descriptive and historical works in Asian journalism is intended to fill a gap by complementing and sometimes backgrounding other subject matter on China and Southeast Asia which are written about more frequently, such as development communications, use of media in population planning, and the place of the media in contemporary Asian society. The Parkers do not claim consistency. They say that their selection is eclectic and their scope ambiguous, and it is impossible not to agree, although they have stuck close to certain important features. The period covered is 1910–1960 throughout; the nature of the material is historical and descriptive, as claimed; and geographic coverage is limited to China and Southeast Asia—primarily Malaysia, Singapore and Indonesia. Primary stress is on newspaper articles, but some pertinent books and magazine articles are included—Western as well as Eastern. Most entries are print, with a few from radio, television and film. Language is English unless otherwise specified. Main entries are by author when stated (otherwise by the periodical or newspaper when these appear), with a chronological subject index by country. An appendix contains material from **The China Weekly**. This is not an easy book to use from the standpoint of either arrangement or graphic design, but it contains references to a great deal of material, much of which is otherwise obscure. All sources are extant.

1683

Picard, Robert G., and James P. Winter. **Press Concentration and Monopoly: A Bibliography**. Baton Rouge, LA: Association for Education in Journalism and Mass Communication, Mass Communication and Society Division. 1985. 23p.

Contains entries for more than 300 books, articles, government reports and documents, and unpublished material categories compiled as a coordinated effort by nine faculty members from journalism programs to gather important literature which assesses the extent and impact of chain ownership, joint operating agreements, and local monopolies. Topic areas include the effects of concentration and monopoly on news coverage, diversity of opinion, labor relations and management activities, and economic behavior and performance. Items are not annotated.

1684

Picard, Robert G., and Rhonda S. Sheets. **Terrorism and the News Media: Research Bibliography**. Columbia, SC: Association for Education in Journalism and Mass Communication, Mass Communication and Society Division, 1986. 33p.

Contains more than 450 unannotated entries divided into books, articles, government reports and documents, and unpublished material categories. Arrangement is alphabetical by author within each category. Although not all-inclusive, the bibliography contains the most important literature and major differing views of and approaches to terrorism and terrorism and the news media. A subject index would make it even more valuable.

1685

Pollay, Richard W., ed. and comp. **Information Sources in Advertising History**. Westport, CT: Greenwood, 1979. 330p.

This is a welcome addition to the literature of advertising. It presents an exhaustive list of about 1,600 titles, arranged by subject and including reference books,

general histories, texts, and books on advertising psychology, criticism, and ethics. There is even some fiction. It is particularly strong in representing primary sources, many of them rare, from the pre-1940 era. All entries are annotated.

Preceding the bibliography are four essays, the first outlining the state of the available literature and the other three giving sources of economic data, commercial sources of advertising data, and contributions of the trade press to the literature. A special feature gives directories to collections of advertising materials housed in archives, museums, trade associations, and agencies themselves. Indexed.

1686

Poteet, G. Howard. **Published Radio, Television, and Film Scripts: A Bibliography**. Troy, NY: Whitston, 1975. 245p.

The author tells us that although a few incomplete listings of film scripts exist, there is no index to the scripts used in radio and TV. This is the first attempt to index all three media. Both excerpts and complete scripts have been included. Texts come from monographs and collections. Arrangement is alphabetical by media. For radio and TV, transcripts as well as scripts are listed, as are dates on which each program was broadcast and the name of the author when available. For films, both complete works and fragments have been included, but no novelized scripts, music sheets, or picture books. Contains an author index.

1687

Powers, Anne, ed. **Blacks in American Movies: A Selected Bibliography**. Metuchen, NJ: Scarecrow, 1974. 157p.

A listing of books, articles, and other materials on blacks in American films, intended as a guide to periodical information on the subject. The first part, however, is a brief list of general non-periodical listings, followed by a lengthy listing of articles by subject; by periodical; and chronologically. In conclusion is a filmography, "Features by and about Blacks 1909–1930," included either because they were landmarks or as specimen of the films black filmmakers of the era were producing. Entries are annotated when needed or to make a point. The author's purpose centers on the social significance of black involvement in film in the U.S., although she has included a few articles dealing with blacks in foreign-made films. An introductory article summarizes her findings. Author/subject index.

1688, 1689

Price, Warren C. **The Literature of Journalism: An Annotated Bibliography**. Minneapolis: University of Minnesota Press, 1959. 489p.

Price, Warren C., and Calder Pickett. **An Annotated Journalism Bibliography, 1958–1968**.

Minneapolis: University of Minnesota Press, 1970. 285p.

Price's work, along with its update by Pickett, remains one of the most valuable bibliographic sources for British and American journalism prior to the 1970s. Price's table-of-contents indicates the emphasis of his coverage: "General Histories of Journalism in the United States and Canada," "Special-Period Histories of Journalism in the United States," "General Histories of British Journalism," "Histories of Individual Newspapers and Associations in the United States and Canada," "Histories of Individual Newspapers in Great Britain," "History," "Biography," "Narratives of Journalists at Work and Anthologies of Journalistic Writing," "Appraisals of the Press, Ethics of the Press, and Law of the Press," "Techniques of Journalism, Including Textbooks," "Magazines," "Management of the Press," "Public Opinion, Propaganda, and Public Relations," "Radio and Television," "Foreign Press and International Communication Facilities," "Bibliographies and Directories." Each entry is annotated in detail and many contain a literary quality. Arrangement is in the broad categories indicated, with a name/subject index.

In 1970, after Price's death, his bibliography was updated by Pickett, who broadened the scope to include new developments in the field. Entries total 2,172. Unlike Price, Pickett has used an alphabetical arrangement with an extensive subject index. Together the two volumes give comprehensive coverage of the time-span.

1690

Rehrauer, George. **The Macmillan Film Bibliography: A Critical Guide to the Literature of the Motion Picture**. 2 v. New York: Macmillan, 1982. 969, 532p.

In the first volume of this critical two-volume work Rehrauer has identified and evaluated a total of 969 books in what he describes as "An attempt . . . to include the entire spectrum of film books, ranging from original paperbacks to commercialized doctoral dissertations." It consists by and large of critical works, guides and directories, biographies and autobiographies, scripts in book form, and bibliographies and filmographies. Sometimes portions only concern film, but they are nevertheless included. Novels with Hollywood or motion picture themes are omitted, as are fictionalized film scripts. Rehrauer's selection is as inclusive as he could make it, and his annotations are well-written, critical, and often lengthy. In cases where he was unable to examine the book, he noted as many bibliographical details as possible.

The second volume is a single-alphabet author-title-subject index.

1691

Rubin, Rebecca B., Alan M. Rubin, and Linda J. Piele. **Communication Research: Strategies**

and Sources. Belmont, CA: Wadsworth, 1986. 233p.

As the title indicates, this guide is intended to introduce the beginning student and others among the uninitiated to the art and science of searching and researching the areas of speech and mass communication. Included are valuable listings and discussions of general sources, finding aids, communication periodicals, and information compilations, with explanations of some length for each group and annotations for individual entries. There is a glossary, a source index and a subject index.

1692, 1693

A Select Bibliography of Books about Books. Karachi, Pakistan: UNESCO Regional Office for Book Development in Asia and the Pacific, 1978. 89p.

A Select Bibliography: Book Publishing and Related Subjects—1982. Karachi, Pakistan: UNESCO Regional Office for Book Development in Asia and the Pacific, 1982. 85p.

The 1978 booklet contains about 600 entries on various aspects of books, from authorship to readership. The 1982 booklet contains more than 900 entries on book publishing, including development and promotion; production processes like composition, copy preparation, editing; distribution; marketing; bookselling, copyright; graphic arts, lithography; paper, printing; seminars and training courses; typography; general aspects; and reference books.

1694

Shearer, Benjamin F., and Marilyn Huxford, comps. **Communications and Society: A Bibliography on Communications Technologies and Their Social Impact**. Westport, CT: Greenwood, 1983. 242p.

"The purpose of this selected bibliography is to explore the diversity of communications technologies and their impact on society from a humanistic perspective." Preface. There are 2,732 entries, including books, articles, theses and dissertations, listed under (1) Theory and Process of Media: Technologies as Media and Messages; (2) History of Technological Development and Innovation in Communications; (3) The Shaping of Mass Media Content: Media Sociology; (4) The Social Effects of Mass Media; (5) The Mass Media as Creators and Reflectors of Public Opinion; (6) Politics and Mass Media; (7) Buyer Beware: Advertising and the Mass Media; (8) Glimpses Beyond: The Future of Mass Communications; (9) Fine Art and Literature in the Technologized Society. Entries are not annotated. Mass media covered include books, magazines, newspapers, radio, television, film and in the early chapter on history—telegraph and cable, telephone, photography and wireless telegraphy. There is an author index and a subject index.

1695

Signitzer, Benno. **Bibliography of Austrian Mass Communication Literature, 1945–1975**. Salzburg, Austria: Wolfgang Neugebauer, 1978. 349p.

Contains approximately 4,600 annotated entries from monographs, journal articles, and newspapers, covering the newspaper, broadcasting, film, book, and recording industry as well as the more general areas of communication research, news agencies, public relations, journalism education, advertising, communication policy, and law. Contains subject, author, and name indexes. In both German and English.

1696

Signorielli, Nancy, comp. and ed., with assistance of Elizabeth Milke and Carol Katzman. **Role Portrayal and Stereotyping on Television: An Annotated Bibliography of Studies Relating to Women, Minorities, Aging, Sexual Behavior, Health, and Handicaps**. Westport, CT: Greenwood, 1985. 214p.

Consists primarily of articles published in scholarly and popular journals, books, and government reports. Each annotation consists of a bibliographic citation, a description of the sample used in the research (if described and/or appropriate), and an abstract of the results. Among the authors whose works have been analyzed are George Gerbner, Larry Gross, Michael Morgan, Bradley Greenberg, F. Earle Barcus, Mary Cassata, Thomas D. Skill, and the editor, Signorielli. Author and subject index.

Slide, Anthony. **International Film, Radio and Television Journals**. (No. 1480.)

Smith, Bruce Lannes, Harold D. Lasswell, and Ralph D. Casey, comps. **Propaganda, Communication, and Public Opinion**. (See No. 1665.)

Smith, Bruce Lannes, and Chita M. Smith, comps. **International Communications and Political Opinion**. (See No. 1666.)

1697

Smith, Myron J., Jr., comp. **U.S. Television Network News: A Guide to Sources in English**. Jefferson, NC: McFarland, 1984. 233p.

A bibliography of books and monographs, scholarly papers, periodical and journal articles, government documents, doctoral dissertations and masters theses, covering the period from the late 1940s through most of 1983. Smith says that the guide is not definitive, but "attempts comprehensiveness in that virtually all factors concerning network television news are covered." Sources are English-language, and 99% are from the U.S. There are brief annotations for book titles and certain periodical articles. Each entry is serially numbered, with detailed author and subject entries. Book titles and certain periodicals are briefly annotated. There are nine categories, with over 3,000 entries numbered serially, and detailed author and subject indexed.

1698

Snorgrass, J. William, and Gloria T. Woody. **Blacks and Media: A Selected, Annotated Bibliography 1962–1982**. Tallahassee: Florida A&M University Press, 1985. 150p.

"Lists over 700 books, journal and magazine articles, and other printed materials concerning blacks in America and their relationship to mass media," covering print and broadcast journalism, advertising and public relations, film and theater. Some of the materials were published prior to 1962 but were reprinted during the interval covered. Chapters and sections of books as well as whole books are included. Annotations are not evaluative. Index to authors and titles. For an earlier bibliography the compilers suggest that done by Armistead S. Pride (December 1968), including material from 1890 to that date, published in the Winter 1977–78 issue of **Journalism History**.

1699

A Sourcebook on Radio's Role in Development. Washington, DC: The Clearinghouse on Development Communication, 1976. 85p. (Information Bulletin No. 7.)

A bibliography, international in scope, which abstracts about 600 items in an attempt to bring together in a single source the various project reports, country surveys, research and evaluation studies, bibliographies, and discussions concerning the application of radio to problems of education and development.

1700, 1701, 1702

Sterling, Christopher H. **Telecommunications Policy: A Survey Bibliography**. 5th ed. Washington, DC: Communication Booknotes, George Washington University, Department of Communication, 1986. 17p. (Basic Bibliography No. 1)

Sterling, Christopher H. **Mass Communication and Electronic Media: A Survey Bibliography**. 11th ed. Washington, DC: Communication Booknotes, George Washington University, Department of Communication, 1986. 17p. (Basic Bibliography No. 2.)

Sterling, Christopher H. **Foreign and International Communications Systems: A Survey Bibliography**. 3d ed. Washington, DC: Communication Booknotes, George Washington University, Department of Communication, 1986. 19p. (Basic Bibliography No. 3.)

An ongoing list of current books and documents, by an expert with outstanding knowledge of the literature of the various aspects of telecommunications which provides a selective introduction of an ever-growing field. Stresses the most recent material but includes a section on historical background. Items are briefly annotated. Periodical citations are not included. (New editions of this series were published in 1989.)

1703

Switzer, Les, and Donna Switzer. **The Black Press in South Africa and Lesotho: A Descriptive Bibliographic Guide to African, Coloured and Indian Newspapers, Newsletters and Magazines 1836–1976**. Boston: G.K. Hall, 1979. 307p.

In assembling this bibliographic guide of 712 items the authors' primary aim was to find material which had received little or no attention from researchers writing about the black experience in South Africa and Lesotho. Selection was made in terms of black rather than white readership, and includes newspapers, newsletters and magazines issued serially with a frequency anywhere from daily to annual. Publications are arranged according to subject matter, with each entry containing full title, place of publication, dates, frequency, language, contents, and holdings. In addition to English and Afrikaans nine major African languages are represented, as well as four major Indian languages, and French, Dutch, Portuguese and Arabic. Added features are a section of bibliographies and a history. Index.

Television and Social Behavior: An Annotated Bibliography of Research Focusing on Television's Impact on Children. Ed. by Charles K. Atkin, John P, Murray, and Oguz B. Nayman. (See No. 808.)

1704

Thompson (J. Walter) Co. **Advertising: An Annotated Bibliography, 1972**. London, England: National Book League, 1972. 35p.

A 35-page pamphlet containing over 300 entries (all books), annotated and arranged by subject. Emphasis is British.

1705

Twomey, John E. **Canadian Broadcasting History Resources in English**. Toronto: Ryerson Polytechnical Institute, Canadian Broadcasting History Research Project, 1978. 72p. and appendixes.

Results of a broadcast educator's investigation into the size and scope of available material reflecting Canadian broadcasting. Includes monographs, journals, bibliographies, scripts, archival materials in official sources, and private collections.

1706

Wedell, George, Georg-Michael Luyken, and Rosemary Leonard, eds. **Mass Communications in Western Europe: An Annotated Bibliography**. Manchester, England: The European Institute for Media, The University, 1985. 327p. (Media Monograph No. 6.)

An international multi-lingual bibliography in 20 European countries, encompassing 757 entries, dating from 1980 to 1985, including legislation and official documents as well as scholarly and policy-oriented texts. Countries covered include Austria, Belgium, Switzerland, Cyprus, Federal Republic of Germany, Denmark, Spain, France, United Kingdom, Greece, Italy, Republic of Ireland, Iceland, Luxembourg, Norway, Netherlands, Portugal, Sweden, Finland and Turkey. There are separate sections for intergovernmental organizations (UNESCO, Council of Europe, Commission of the European Communities, European Parliament) and for non-governmental organizations. Scholarly publications and publications by independent institutions and individuals are briefly annotated; texts of documents, statutes, official reports and policy statements are not. The main portion is arranged geographically, followed by a subject index according to media, and an author index. In most cases annotations are in the language of the country with the exception of some that have English translations.

1707

Wertheim, Arthur Frank. **American Popular Culture: A Historical Bibliography**. Santa Barbara, CA: ABC-Clio Information Services, Inc., 1984. 246p.

Contains 2,719 abstracted entries under the following headings: The Popular Arts; Mass Media and Communications; Folk Culture; Customs, Behavior and Attitudes; Science and Religion; Theory, Research & the Classroom. All entries are from periodicals selected from a large data base. Arrangement is alphabetical under the various headings, with a 67-page subject index, an author index, and a list of the periodicals which formed the data base.

For an annotated bibliography of books on popular culture see **American Popular Culture** by Larry N. Landrum (No. 1663).

1708

Wolseley, Roland E., and Isabel Wolseley. **The Journalist's Bookshelf: An Annotated and Selected Bibliography of United States Print Journalism**. 8th ed. Indianapolis, IN: Berg, 1986. 400p.

This bibliography consists of 2,368 carefully chosen and well-annotated entries arranged alphabetically under 34 headings with an "Index to Authors, Editors and

Compilers" and an "Index to Titles." Many of the books concern techniques and specific kinds of journalism, and are practical rather than theoretical. For example, "Religious Journalism" contains 57 titles instructing about ways to use the media for religious purposes, without inclusion of any of the growing number of critical and analytical works. However, emphasis here and under other headings is deliberately on the practical, not the theoretical type. But by no means all of the titles are primarily techniques; there is a 99-page section, "Biography: Autobiography, Biography, Memoirs, and Reminiscences," followed by 19 pages on "By or About More Than One Journalist"; 38 pages on "History," and shorter sections on such non-technique-oriented subjects as "Evaluation and Problems" and "Ethics." The first edition of **Journalist's Bookshelf** was published in 1939; each subsequent edition has been extensively revised and updated. Other bibliographies by Roland Wolseley include **The Changing Magazine: Trends in Readership and Management** (New York: Hastings House, 1973) and **The Black Press, U.S.A.** (Ames: Iowa State University Press, 1971).

1709

Yamanaka, Hayato, et al., comps. **Japanese Communication Studies of the 1970s: Bibliographic Abstracts of Studies Published Only in Japanese**. Honolulu: University of Hawaii Press for the East-West Center, Institute of Culture and Communication, 1986. 251p.

An anthology of 100 abstracts grouped by principal theme or subject. Priority has been given to research involving the collection and analysis of primary data, including surveys of mass media effects and uses, analyses of media structures and development, and case studies of community and group media behavior. Sources include research articles and bibliographical lists in key journals of Japanese communication research and annual subject and title bibliographies issued by the Japanese Diet Library. Author and subject indexes.

This is the third of a series of translations. **Japanese Research on Mass Communication** appeared in 1974 and **Research on Mass Communication in Taiwan and Hong Kong** in 1977.

1710

Advertisers' Annual: An Annual Director for All Engaged in Advertising and Selling. East Grinstead, West Sussex, England: Thomas Skinner Directories, annual. (1925–.)

Includes lists of daily, weekly, and local (provincial) newspapers; consumer publications classified by subject, with data about each; information about outdoor advertising, commercial radio, and television; advertising agencies and public relations companies; services and suppliers; and British advertisers in England, Wales, Scotland, the Channel Islands, and the Isle of Man, with information about each. There is a lengthy "who's who" section and a geographic overseas section.

1711

Advertising Age Yearbook. Chicago: Crain, annual. (1981–1984.)

A review of the past year, culled from the pages of **Advertising Age**, covering the events in more than 60 subject areas, accompanied by charts, tables and graphs showing statistics for current trends in growth and investment worldwide, with related disciplines included as well. In addition to hard facts, some of the most pertinent articles are reproduced. Name/subject index. The last yearbook was published in 1984.

Advertising and Press Annual of Southern Africa. (See No. 1587.)

1712

Advertising Career Directory. New York: Career Publishing Corp., annual. (1986–.)

Well-known practitioners from various segments of the advertising profession contribute articles to present practical facts about entering the field to young aspirants. Included is an overview section, "Advertising—Yesterday, Today & Tomorrow," followed by chapters on account management, creative (art & copy), media, research, and alternatives and options. Special sections include "How to Get the Agency Job You Want," entry-level job listings, and internships and training programs. Appendixes list colleges offering advertising majors/sequences, and industry trade organizations and publications. This is the first of a yearly series. Index.

1713

The Alternative Press Annual. Philadelphia, PA: Temple University Press, annual. (1983–.)

Three volumes (1983, 1984, 1985) have been published of this anthology of the year's most provocative articles from the magazines and newspapers dedicated to social change and which are generally outside the commercial mass media channels. The 1985 volume reprints articles on medical problems, alternative awards, environment, peace, and feminist and gay issues. The editor, Patricia J. Case, of the SourceNet in Santa Barbara, invites alternative press editors and publishers to send their publications for consideration. Each volume is indexed in detail.

Annual Review of BBC Broadcasting Research Findings. (See No. 1729.)

1714

American Book Trade Directory. New York: Bowker, biennial. (1915–.)

Deals primarily with the various agencies involved in all phases of the retailing and wholesaling of books in the U.S. and Canada—some 25,000 according to the 1987–88 edition. An annual introductory statistical section provides totals by categories on booksellers, gross sales, average transactions per customer, paperback sales and other breakdowns which are useful not only in themselves but for annual comparisons. Five sections follow: Section 1 is a breakdown of booksellers by type—i.e., antiquarian, religious, etc.—with specifics for each as to address, key personnel, date of establishment, specializations, sidelines, and service; Section II lists wholesalers, jobbers and distributors, with similar specifics; Section III is an alphabetical list of foreign book dealers, exporters and importers, export representatives, rental library chains, appraisers of library collections, auctioneers, and national and regional organizations; Section IV indexes stores by type; and a fifth section is a general index.

1715

Annual Index to Motion Picture Arts and Credits. Beverly Hills, CA: Academy of Motion Picture Arts and Sciences, annual. (1937–.)

Includes any film for a given year which is feature length and has run in a commercial motion picture theater in the Los Angeles area for not less than one week. In four sections: Section One, "Film Titles," with information including date of release, length, production credits in detail, and cast; Section Two, "Credits," including the information given under "Film Titles" but in separate alphabetical categories—"Actors," "Art Direction," "Cinematographers," "Costume Designers," "Directors," "Film Editors," "Music," "Producers," "Sound," and "Writers"; Section Three, "Releasing Companies"; and Section Four, "Alphabetical Index of Individual Credits," by personnel, with name of film and role in production.

1716

APME Red Book. New York: Associated Press for the Associated Press Managing Editors Association, annual. (1948–.)

An account of the annual convention of the Associated Press Managing Editors Association. The 1984 volume initiates an editorial change from printing the entire convention proceedings to a condensation of events, organized by subject. Certain programs which were not directly journalistic, such as a discussion of foreign affairs, are not included. Much information about the association is included: past presidents and convention sites, beginning in 1933; committee reports, AP staff awards, special panel discussions, AP membership list (personal).

1717

The Associated Church Press Directory. Geneva, IL: Associated Church Press, annual. (1951–.)

Lists current member publications' personnel, statistics, style and advertising. Also contains "Statement of Ethics and Standards of Professional Practice of the Associated Church Press, and its officers, board of directors and committees.

1718

ASNE. Washington, DC: American Society of Newspaper Editors, annual. (1923–.)

In the beginning, this annual report was called **Problems of Journalism: Proceedings of American Society of Newspaper Editors**. The recent issues are simply entitled **ASNE-1986**, etc. It is a verbatim report of the major speeches at the annual meeting and the year's end reports of the standing committees. The report is historically useful for the committee reports and rosters, annual awards, and it is interesting because of the speeches by prominent politicians, leaders and journalists.

Ayers Directory of Publications, see **Gale Directory of Publications**. (No. 1782.)

1719

B & T Yearbook. Sydney, Australia: Greater Publications Pty Ltd., annual. (1957–.)

Even though B & T presumably stands for broadcasting and telecasting, this can serve as a directory for Australian media generally. There are four sections: "Radio," "Television," "Press," and "General"—the latter concerned with advertising and public relations. Information is prolific; some specific areas are lists of commercial and public broadcasting stations, networks, production units, services and equipment; business and consumer magazines, ethnic newspapers, national newspapers for the various states; advertising agencies, consultants, media representatives, media ownership and a great deal of other information relevant to advertising and public relations. Index.

1720

BBC Annual Report and Handbook. London: British Broadcasting Corporation, annual. (1928–1987.)

As can be expected, contents of this annual report and handbook have varied somewhat over the years, but all of them hit the essentials of the BBC's activities in England, Scotland, Wales, and Northern Ireland, as well as its external broadcasting. Jeremy Tunstall, in **The Media in Britain** (No. 436), has described this as "the most fact-packed annual report." Among the many hard facts in the 1986 report are programming, financing, structure, audience, sales and services, personnel, publications, awards, and engineering information. An annual feature is the bibliography of works about the BBC. There is also a subject index. The glossy stills are fun but nonessential. Extensive appendixes list summaries of regular series broadcasted by the BBC. Title variations over the years: **BBC Yearbook**, 1928–34; **BBC Annual**, 1935–37; **BBC Handbook**, 1938–42; **BBC Yearbook**, 1942–1952; 1953/54 was never published; **BBC Handbook**, 1955–1980; **BBC Annual Report and Handbook**, 1981–87.

1721

Bacon's International Publicity Checker. Chicago, IL: Bacon's Publishing Co., annual. (1975–.)

A guide to Western European publicity markets which lists by country more than 10,000 technical and trade publications and over 1,000 national and regional daily newspapers. Within every country magazines are classified by subject; newspapers are listed separately following the magazines. For each, the **Checker** gives address, telephone and Telex numbers, translation requirements and publicity coding. Each country has an alphabetical index. The guide is published with the Media Information Group of London.

1722

Bacon's Media Alerts. Chicago, IL: Bacon's Publishing Co., annual. (1983–.)

One of four Bacon directories published for the business of public relations described here, **Media Alerts** is a directory of the editorial calendars of magazines and newspapers in the U.S. and Canada. This information tells the public relations professional about special editions and seasonal features to be published by a specific magazine or newspaper.

1723

Bacon's Publicity Checker: Vol. 1, Magazines; Vol. 2, Newspapers. Chicago, IL: Bacon's Publishing Co., annual. (1933–.)

Intended for public relations professionals, these two volumes list over 7,500 business, trade, consumer and farm magazines in the U.S. and Canada, organized into 195 market classifications, with alphabetical index; and over 1,600 daily and 7,600 weekly newspapers, organized geographically. Information for both magazines and newspapers includes address, editor/s, circulation and telephone and Telex, followed by pertinent editorial coding for magazines and news department coding for newspapers. This title continues **Bacon's Publicity Manual**, which began in 1933, and replaces **Bacon's Newspaper Directory**, which was published for a few years in the mid 70s.

1724

Bacon's Radio/TV Directory. Chicago, IL: Bacon's Publishing Co., annual. (1983–.)

Used primarily by public relations practitioners, this directory lists geographically more than 9,000 radio and 1,300 television stations, including PBS and college radio, giving the following information for each entry: station call letters, phone number; format; programming information on all locally produced shows, network news, and talk shows; network affiliation; key contacts with profiles; and point of view. Other features are maps of the top 30 markets, and cable networks and outlets.

1725

Benn's Media Directory. 2 v. Tonbridge, Kent, England: Benn's Publications, annual. (1852–.)

One of the world's oldest press directories and one of the most comprehensive. Intended primarily to serve advertisers and, in the case of the second volume, anyone interested in international trade, it is otherwise useful for names of specific media in the United Kingdom and abroad. Volume I lists newspapers (including free distribution ones); trade periodicals; directories and other reference series; and organizations, agencies and services for the media industry. Brief comments are made on each entry, always including address and Telex, and where appropriate, more specific information about subject matter and intended readership. Arrangement of the sections is for the most part alphabetical, except for local newspapers which is geographic, and each section has its own index, which in the case of periodicals, is classified by subject. There is also a master index.

When information about international advertising and trade first appeared in the 1877 **Benn's Press Direc-** **tory** (as it was known until the 1987 issue) it occupied two pages. Today it includes a second volume, geographically divided into Europe, Africa/Middle East, the Americas, and Australasia/Asia/Far East with appropriate newspapers and trade publications for each country within the area, preceded by an international area section. Information for each publication is brief and varies, including often only name and address, and in cases of larger publications, Telex and circulation. For the smaller countries arrangement is straight alphabetical; for the larger countries, newspapers are listed geographically and periodicals by subject matter. Preceding the main body is a general international section: "A Survey of Central Sources with Information about Each"; a list of the national representative bodies of the Commonwealth Union; overseas press and media associations; other U.K. advertisement representatives for overseas publications; and international organizations, with selected official periodicals. There is no index.

1726

Best of Photojournalism. Philadelphia, PA: Running Press, annual. (1976–.)

An annual publication of journalistic photographs which emanate from the "Pictures of the Year" competition sponsored by the National Press Photographers Association and the University of Missouri.

1727

Book Publishing Annual. New York: Bowker in collaboration with the staff of Publishers Weekly, annual. (1983–85.)

The Preface identifies the 1984 publication as the second volume of its predecessor, **Publishers Weekly Yearbook**, with the coverage of book publishing extended to include "scholarly, high education, school, and small press publishing." The purpose of the annual series is to provide a full profile of the book publishing industry. The content is a mixture of summaries of trends written by various experts, for example, John P. Dessauer writes a section on book industry economics, lists (awards, best sellers, book fairs, mergers, salaries) and statistics (production, exports, financial summaries of 14 major companies). The chapter headings are: "The Year in Review," "The Year in Books," "The Business of Books," "Books and the Law," "Design and Technology," "Retailing," "Computer Software," "Milestones," "The International Year," "Educational and Professional Reading." Index to the annual and a separate index to **Publishers Weekly** (magazine). The series ceased with the third volume.

1728

Book Publishing Career Directory. New York: Career Publishing Corp., annual. (1986–.)

A compilation of articles by experts in book publishing intended to present practical facts about their own particular vineyard to young aspirants seeking a career in the industry. Section I offers an overview and a look at three specialized areas—university presses, book clubs and scientific/technical publishers. Sections II through IV offer detailed discussions of the three major areas of job specialization—editorial, marketing sales, and production; and sections V-VI talk about the job search and job possibilities. Appendixes contain a listing of industry trade organizations, industry trade publications, and book publishing courses. Among the 15 contributors: Samuel Vaughan, formerly editor-in-chief of Doubleday; Chandler Grannis, former editor-in-chief of **Publishers Weekly**; Herbert Addison of Oxford University Press; Jessica Weber, executive art director of Book-of-the-Month Club; Michael Pratt, vice-president in charge of marketing and sales at Random House; Diane Kuppler, director of college advertising at Prentice-Hall and Zlate Paces, vice-president and design director of Macmillan. This is the first of a yearly series. Index.

1729

British Broadcasting Corporation. **Annual Review of BBC Broadcasting Research Findings**. London: Broadcasting Research Department, British Broadcasting Corporation House, annual. (1975–.)

Annual reports of BBC radio and television audience studies for radio and television. Ad hoc research studies, such as television sct ownership, campaign coverage on referenda, are also reported. Recent volumes report on the research to monitor the public's knowledge and understanding of teletext (Ceefax and Oracle) and viewdata (Prestel) services.

1730

The British National Film Catalogue. Ed. by Maureen Brown. London: British Film Institute, quarterly, with annual cumulations. (1963–.)

Includes all nonfiction and short films generally available in Britain for hire, loan, or sale; films available to specialized or limited audiences only; fiction and nonfiction TV programs available in film for nontheatrical release for loan or hire; film magazines and certain nonfiction shorts which, though made for theatrical release, frequently become available on 16mm at a later date; British films distributed abroad through British Information Services and the British Council. Straight advertising, home movies and features covered by the **Monthly Film Bulletin**, and newsreels are excluded.

The catalogue lists entries by subject, with a subject-title and a production index. For each title information is given on distribution, date, production company and sponsor, technical data, language version, credits, length, and a synopsis.

1731

Broadcasting Cablecasting Yearbook.
Washington, DC: Broadcasting Publications, Inc., annual. (1935–.)

One of the indispensable directories for the mass media, **Broadcasting Cablecasting Yearbook** offers current and historical information about "The Fifth Estate." (**Editor & Publisher Yearbook** is its counterpart for "The Fourth Estate.") This yearbook is organized into nine sections. The major sections are the detailed, station-by-station directories for radio, television, and cable companies. The radio directory information includes the call letters, date of beginning operations, address and telephone, programming information, corporate and station personnel. The television directory information includes similar information plus the ADI's and the Arbitron circulation figures. An important feature in the television section is the presentation of the ADI Market Atlas, showing each of the 212 area maps. The cable section summarizes the industry and provides information about the cable systems similar to that given for television and radio stations. The satellite section lists satellites currently used by North American owners and operators and a directory of cable programming services. Other sections in the yearbook feature programming with a directory of producers, distributors and production services; an advertising and marketing section with a directory of advertising agencies; a technology section with a directory of international equipment and software manufacturers and suppliers; and a large three-part section on professional services, associations, and education including directories of consultants, research services and attorneys, an annotated, lengthy bibliography of books about broadcasting and electronic media, and a list of educational programs; a short course on broadcast history; a listing of FCC rules; and radio and television stations with pending applications for license.

1732

Cable and Satellite Yearbook: Europe. London: 21st Century Publishing Ltd., annual. (1985–.)

The yearbook provides directory information for the companies in the European cable and satellite industry. The directory is organized in three sections: a summary of the year's satellite developments, including a descriptive list of international organizations; a country-by-country (Europe only) summary and directory of agencies and companies; and a calendar of conferences and exhibitions. Statistical information is limited.

1733

Cable & Station Coverage Atlas. Washington, DC: Warren Publishing, Inc., annual. (1966/67–.)

Shows state-by-state grade-B contour maps; state-by-state 35-mile and 55-mile radius for television markets maps; and location of all cable systems. Among the variety of other features are state regulatory agencies; regional and state cable associations; FCC cable rules; copyright law and regulations; cable brokerage and financing companies; management and technical consulting services; pay-TV and satellite services; manufacturing and suppliers; construction and installation services; multichannel multipoint distribution service; instructional TV stations by state; low power TV stations by state and their ownership; and a list of cable communities not on the maps. There are also lists of the top 100 cable system operators and Arbitron cable penetration estimates. The former title of this yearbook was **CATV and Station Coverage Atlas and Zone Maps**.

1734

Cassell and Publishers Association Directory of Publishing in Great Britain, the Commonwealth, Ireland, South Africa and Pakistan. London: Cassell, irregular. (1960–.)

The British counterpart of **Literary Marketplace** (No. 1767). In two parts: "The Publishing and Promotion of Books" and "Representatives and Services." The first part lists publishers with thumbnail information about address, personnel, subsidiaries, overseas representatives, etc.; classifies them by field of activity; and gives government, trade and other associations connected with the industry, as well as societies, foundations, book clubs, events, and even literary luncheons. Under "Representatives and Services" comes agents of various kinds; TV and radio organizations; remainder merchants; translators; packagers; indexers; and a variety of similar services. There are indexes of subjects and of names of publishers and literary agents.

1735

Catholic Press Directory. Rockville Center, NY: Catholic Press Association, annual. (1923–.)

Official media guide to Catholic newspapers, magazines, general publishers, diocesan directories, membership of the Catholic Press Association, and names of other religious associations. Gives for each media entry the address, key personnel, rates and circulation. Index to publications.

1736

CEBA Exhibit Journal: The Black Media and Marketing Source. New York: World Institute of Black Communications, Inc., annual. (1978–.)

"CEBA" abbreviates Communications Excellence to Black Audiences, and CEBA Awards have been presented annually since 1978 for outstanding advertising design and execution to U.S. corporations, and agencies and individuals. The annual publication thoroughly illustrates, in black and white, the winning advertisements in each category: print, radio, television, film and video, and merchandising and sales promotion. A final 20-page section of the annual is given to reference information statistics of black consumer spending and a directory of black-owned media, advertising agencies and production companies.

1737

Circulation. Malibu, CA: American Newspaper Markets, annual. (1962–.)

"A comprehensive print analysis showing circulation and penetration in every U.S. county, in every U.S. metro section, and television viewing area for every U.S. daily newspapers, every U.S. Sunday newspapers, all regional sales groups, five national supplements, and 22 leading magazines." (Title page) In addition to circulation figures, it also gives demographic information for all areas. This wealth of tightly packed statistics is designed to aid the practitioner in placing advertisements and would be difficult for the layman to interpret. For market research purposes, the data present a picture of the circulation of print media in small geographic units, such as the county level.

1738

Commonwealth Broadcasting Association Handbook. London: Broadcasting House, biennal. (1945–.)

The Association, which consists of 56 national broadcasting organizations in 51 Commonwealth countries in Europe, Asia, Africa, and Caribbean, Pacific and North and South America, cooperates in the professional improvement of broadcasting among its members. Their **Handbook** records the origins of the Association, gives examples of the kind of practical cooperation that goes on, and summarizes the proceedings of the General Conferences held from 1945 onward. It also provides background information on each of the member states, with a thumbnail description of its broadcasting system: history, funding, programming, audience, and technical facilities.

1739

Communication Yearbook. Newbury Park, CA: Sage Publications with the International Communication Association, annual. (1977–.)

A series, sponsored by the International Communication Association, whose purpose is to give an annual overview and synthesis of the field. The content reflects the broadly representative membership of the association, where the behavioral science perspective on communication research has been encouraged. The review publishes two types of articles: (1) general commentary; these critiques are usually solicited articles; and (2) reports of research and scholarly review competitively selected for presentation at the annual meeting of the association. Divisions of ICA represented in the yearbook are information systems, interpersonal communication, mass communication, organizational communication, intercultural and development communication, political communication, instructional communication, health communication, philosophy of communication, and human communication technology (interest group). In the first volume, an appendix gives a history of ICA. The editorial policy changed beginning with Volume 11 to publish solicited summaries of current research. The ICA research papers are expected to be published in a separate volume. Author and subject index.

1740

Co-op Publishing Handbook. Ed. by Michael Scott Cain. Paradise, CA: Dustbooks, annual. (1978–.)

As major-league book publishing becomes more and more a conglomerate industry with emphasis on mass-market best sellers and the book as a packaged product, a substantial number of writers have found an alternative in cooperative publishing. Here a number of such groups tell why and how they got started. The book is both philosophical and practical, exploring the impetus and needs behind the growth of co-ops and describing the nuts and bolts. Various kinds of cooperative publishing are represented—large well-established ones like Fiction Collective, the regional groups, the social-political groups, the oddities, the independents, the unclassifiable. The editor has written a substantial introduction about the movement and a summing-up.

1741

CPB Public Broadcasting Directory. Washington, DC: Corporation for Public Broadcasting, annual. (1982–.)

Separate geographical listings by state of public radio stations and public television stations, giving for each address, telephone, licensee type (radio only), date on air, power coverage, and personnel. Following this is a personnel index for both radio and television, with an index by licensee type for radio and by call letters for television. Preceding this are lists of "National and Regional Organizations and Networks," "Organizations by State," and "Related Organizations/Agencies." This directory was preceded by **CPB Qualified Public Radio Station Directory**.

1742

Current Research in Film: Audiences, Economics, and Law. Ed. by Bruce A. Austin. Norwood, NJ: Ablex, annual. (1985–.)

An annual series on film which focuses, as the title of the series indicates, on research about the film audience, motion picture economics, and legal concerns relevant to film as a mass medium. The first volume contains 12 original articles concerning marketing and advertising, early audience research, the history of drive-ins, factors influencing selection and attendance, financing, and censorship. The second volume has 13 original articles, six of which are about audiences and cultural aspects of film. The topics of the remaining seven articles vary from economics to ethics to antitrust legislation. The 13 articles published in the third volume take on an international outlook and include studies about the South

African cinema, television and film industries in Latin America, and film exports to Britain and France. Several of the remaining articles in the third volume are historical analyses of film economics and law. The series is particularly important because, while a great deal of research is done on film, little of it centers on the audience and the economic and legal aspects.

1743

Directors Guild of America. **Directory of Members**. Hollywood, CA: Directors Guild of America, Inc. (1967/68–.)

A directory of guild members with varying information about each. In most cases this includes home and/or business address, telephone number, title, and film or TV credits. Types of directors and their locations range widely, although many are centered around Hollywood and New York and most but not all are in commercial film and TV. Other information: National Board of Directors, bylaw provisions; a brief chronological history of the organization; a geographic breakdown by name of members in each area, which includes 15 foreign countries as well; DGA award winners for television and theatrical direction; recipients of the D.W. Griffith Award and the Critics Award; honorary life members; and an index of agents, attorneys, and business managers.

1744

Directory of Asian Mass Communication Institutions. 4th ed. Singapore: Asian Mass Communication Research and Information Centre, irregular. (1986–.)

An ongoing series which provides information about 90 mass communication institutions active in research, teaching and training in Asia, including address, telephone number, date founded, aims, activities, names of staff members, and a list of selected research and publications. The countries included are Bangladesh, Hong Kong, India, Indonesia, Japan, Korea, Malaysia, Pakistan, Philippines, Singapore, Sri Lanka, and Thailand. First published in 1973 as the **Asian Mass Communication Institutions, Teaching, Training and Research: A Directory**, the 1986 directory is the fourth edition and the "most drastically revised." (Introduction) The second and third editions were published in 1975 and 1981.

1745

Directory of Small Press and Magazine Editors & Publishers. Ed. by Len Fulton and Ellen Ferber. Paradise, CA: Dustbooks, annual. (1970–.)

An alphabetical index listing by name of all the editors and publishers of small presses and magazines appearing in the companion volume, the **International Directory of Little Magazines and Small Presses** (No. 1757). Information for each entry includes the press or publication with which the individual is associated, with address and phone number.

1746

Editor & Publisher International Yearbook. New York: Editor & Publisher Co., Inc., annual. (1924–.)

Properly subtitled "The Encyclopedia of the Newspaper Industry" and annually issued by the publisher of the weekly trade magazine **Editor & Publisher**, the yearbook is divided into seven sections. Perhaps the most used is "Daily Newspapers Published in the United States," a directory of all U.S. dailies, with data on address, circulation, personnel, advertising rates, date of founding, special editions, mechanical facilities, broadcast affiliates, news agency features, Sunday magazine if any, political leanings, and groups and mergers. Section II, "Weekly and Special Newspapers Published in the United States," includes detailed information—location, publication days, circulation, personnel, advertising rates—for weeklies, black newspapers, foreign language newspapers, religious newspapers, and college and university newspapers published in the U.S. The third section gives detailed information for daily, weekly and foreign language newspapers published in Canada. Section IV gives pertinent information about foreign newspapers. The fifth section, "News and Syndicate Services," includes news services, feature syndicates, comic section groups, magazine sections, art and mat services. The "Mechanical Equipment, Supplies and Services" section gives directory information for companies and American Newspaper Publishers Association statistics for mechanical forces pay scales and top minimum pay scales for reporters. The final section gives information about other organizations and industry services, such as a membership roster for the American Newspaper Publishers Association, foreign correspondents, journalism schools, brokers and appraisers, newsprint statistics, clipping bureaus, and thumbnail descriptions of films about newspapers.

1747

Editor & Publisher Market Guide. New York: Editor & Publisher, annual. (1924–.)

A compilation of marketing information for every city or community in the U.S. and Canada where a daily newspaper is published—more than 1,500 in all. All newspapers are listed, with descriptions of the population and commerce of the locations. Arrangement is alphabetical by state province with information about towns and cities including transportation; population; number of households; banks; number of cars, electric meters and gas meters; principal industries; climate; retailing; and newspapers. Other data include national newspaper representatives of daily and selected newspapers; demographic information by state or province and town, for income, households, and farm products; and a similar section for retail sales.

1748

Editor & Publisher Syndicate Directory. New York: Editor & Publisher Co., annual. (1925–.)

Every year **Editor & Publisher** magazine carries a special issue on syndicated services, listing them in the following ways: by syndicate, giving name, address, telephone, and chief executives and/or editors; by title of byline features, giving author or artist; by author or artist; and by subject.

1749

Film Canadiana. Montreal, Quebec: National Film Board of Canada, biennial. (1969–.)

This national periodic filmography includes films produced by Canadian companies or independent producers, as well as co-productions with foreign companies, TV productions released for general distribution, and video productions if available on film. Also, an attempt is made to trace earlier productions not included in previous editions. Data vary, including always title, year, running time, producer, as many credits as possible, and a summary. This is followed by an index of films in English; films in French, films by subject category; a series index; a director index; a producer index; a production agency index; a listing of feature films 1970–1984; a title listing; and a directory of producers and distributors. In both English and French. The publishing history has varied: 1969–1972, quarterly; 1972–73 to 1979–80, annual; 1980–82, triennial; 1983–84, biennial.

Film Literature Index. (See No. 1920.)

1750

Film Review Annual. Ed. by Jerome S. Ozer. New York: Ozer, annual. (1981–.)

". . . provides, in a convenient format, a single reference volume covering important reviews—*in their entirety*—of full-length films released in major markets in the United States in the course of the year." (Preface) Films are reviewed in alphabetical order by title, followed by information which includes production, cast, crew listings, running time, and MPAA ratings, and the reviews themselves in alphabetical order by name of publication, with date, pagination, and reviewer. Because of restrictions on obtaining reviews from some publications an "Also Reviewed" section is included for each film. In conclusion is a full listing of major film awards, giving nominees as well as winners. Ten indexes lead back to specific information in the reviews: Film Critics; Publications; Cast; Producers; Directors; Screenwriters; Cinematographers; Editors; Music; and Production Credits.

1751

Folio: 400. Stamford, CT: Folio Publishing, annual. (1978–1986.)

Now defunct, **Folio: 400** was designed for the advertising and marketing community and presented a quantitative analysis of the year's 400 top revenue-producing publications in the U.S. There are pages of composite materials illustrated by graphs and charts, followed by detailed profiles under subject categories—i.e., Business and Financial, Health and Fitness, Black, Science and Nature, etc. Under each publication is statistical data, followed by detailed profiles.

1752

Gale Directory of Publications. Detroit, MI: Gale Research, annual. (1869–.)

This is the authoritative directory of print media published in the United States, Canada and Puerto Rico. It lists detailed information about newspapers and magazines organized by the geographical place of publication. Information about the publisher, editor, address, circulation, subscription price and advertising rates are given. Statistical tables also offer comparative data about newspapers and periodicals. The older editions of this directory, first published in 1869 as Rowell's **American Newspaper Directory** are extremely useful. Most recently called **IMS Directory of Publications**. Formerly called **Ayers Directory of Publications**.

1753

The Gallup Poll: Public Opinion. Wilmington, DE: Scholarly Resources, annual. (1978–.)

A chronological arrangement, day by day, of the various polls released by the Gallup Poll Organization to newspapers from January through December, including questions, tabular data, and interpretative notes such as "Selected National Trends" or "Presidential Performance Ratings." Yearly volumes have been continuous since 1978. They were preceded by two multi-volumed sets, **The Gallup Poll: Public Opinion 1935–1971** in three volumes, published by Random House in 1972, and **The Gallup Poll: Public Opinion, 1972–1977**, published in two volumes by Scholarly Publishers in 1978. Prefatory material in each set or volume has a record of Gallup's accuracy, a chronology of events, and a summary of the year according to Gallup findings. Each is indexed. Although the primary purpose of this comprehensive work is to give the views of the American public on social and political issues, it has a secondary use equally important—it shows what the issues were for a given year.

1754

Hudson's News Media Contacts Directory. Ed. by Howard Penn Hudson and Helene F. Wingard. Rhinebeck, NY: Hudson's Directory, annual. (1968–.)

An organized listing of the Washington news media, giving in the present edition 3,735 news outlets (bureaus, newspapers, news services, radio-TV, magazines, newsletters, syndicates and names of 3,937 correspondents and editors. All material is well arranged, so that media, features and personal names may be easily found through indexes. There is also an Assignment Locator to enable the user to find quickly the correspondents who

have special beats and assignments. Revisions are provided three times a year.

1755

IENS Press Handbook. New Delhi: Indian & Eastern Newspaper Society, annual. (1940/41–.)

Intended primarily as an aid for media space buyers, this lists Indian and Eastern Newspaper Society members, with full particulars about participating newspapers and periodicals; assorted rules and information concerning advertising agencies and a list of accredited agencies with selected personnel and accounts; press organizations in India and abroad; accredited correspondents; departments of journalism; and an assortment of documents and production information. (See also **INFA Press and Advertisers Yearbook**, No. 1756.)

1756

INFA Press and Advertisers Yearbook. New Delhi, India: INFA Publications, annual. (1961–.)

Published by the India News and Feature Alliance, the yearbook emphasizes newspapers, magazines and advertising. Among the contents are a review of the year; accredited correspondents; news and feature agencies; journalism courses; trade and professional associations; newsprint agents and laws; information services by state; a who's who in Indian journalism, advertising and public relations; circulation and demographic figures; and rates and data for newspapers, consumer magazines, trade, technical and professional publications, theaters, radio, video, outdoor railway and airport advertising. Index to press media and index to advertisers. (See also **IENS Press Handbook**, No. 1755.)

1757

International Directory of Little Magazines and Small Presses. Ed. by Len Fulton and Ellen Ferber. Paradise, CA: Dustbooks, annual. (1965–.)

This directory is indispensable to anyone interested in the status of alternative publishing. Although its primary use is for writers searching out a market and for libraries verifying subscriptions or answering reference questions, it can serve also as a source of knowledge about the little magazine/small press world. Earlier editions had an introduction by Fulton on this subject which has been dropped, perhaps in favor of international coverage. The body of the directory lists publications alphabetically, with varying information about each, according to whether the entry is a magazine or a book publisher. Also, entrants send in their own data, which makes for an unevenness but gives greater individuality. Some entries are quite long and descriptive, others short and factual. Following the publications is a subject index and a geographical index. The **Directory of Small Press and Magazines Editors & Publishers** (No. 1745) serves as a proper name index.

1758

International Film Guide. Ed. by Peter Cowie. London: Tantivy Press, annual. (1964–.)

Each year this estimable and hardy annual varies somewhat in the topics it treats, but its basic structure remains much the same. The main feature is always "World Survey" which in the 1986 edition reports on the cinema of 65 countries. Other contents in 1986 include a special article on Australian film and a tribute to the Sydney Film Festival; a guide to leading festivals; film archives; animation; film schools; film bookshops, posters and records; book reviews; and magazines.

1759

International Literary Market Place. New York and London: Bowker, annual. (1965–.)

Contains information about book publishing in 160 countries from Afghanistan to Zimbabwe, with pertinent facts for each, including publishers, book trade organizations, book trade reference books and journals, remainder dealers, literary agents, book clubs, major libraries and library associations, library reference books and journals, literary associations and societies, literary periodicals and prizes, translations agencies and associations, and brief information about the country (language, population, currency, export-import regulations, copyright, etc.) An international section records copyright conventions, international organizations, international bibliographies about the book trade, international literary prizes, a book trade calendar, and information about the ISBN system. Index.

1760

International Motion Picture Almanac. New York: Quigley Publishing Co., annual. (1929–.)

This is a companion volume to the **Television & Video Almanac**, (No. 1794). There is duplication of material in both, notably in the lengthy "Who's Who in Motion Pictures and Television," "Credit for Feature Films" of the year, "Film Distributors in Key Cities," "Services for Producers," "Feature Films from 1955" to the current year. Also the term *International* used in both titles is misleading; except for a relatively few pages at the end of the book—"The World Market," "The Industry in Great Britain and Ireland," and "International Film Festivals," emphasis is on the U.S. and Canada. This is not to put down the usefulness of these yearbooks, for both of them contain much that is not readily available elsewhere, but to forewarn the user.

The "Who's Who" section is broad, including, in addition to actors and actresses, directors, writers, executives, set designers, and other categories of workers in film and broadcasting. Among other features are various kinds of statistics; awards and award winners; distributors; talent and literary agents (duplicated); motion picture corporations, giving structure, organization, executive personnel; government film bureaus; theater circuits in the U.S. and Canada; a list of drive-in theaters with locations, owners, and capacity; the film press, including trade publications, newspapers with film departments, and fan magazines; and the motion picture code.

1761

The Japanese Press. Tokyo: Japan Newspaper Publishers and Editors Association (Nihon Shinbun Kyokai), annual. (1949–.)

The first part of this annual consists of miscellaneous material about the Japanese press—for example, in the 1986 edition, advertising and newspaper sales codes, general trends, awards, newspapers in the year 2000, the rising credibility of newspapers, and organization and activities of the Nihon Shinbun Kyokai. The second part, "Facts about Japanese Newspapers," gives statistics which also include advertising. The third part is a directory of newspapers, news agencies, broadcasting stations, and a geographic listing of newspaper correspondents overseas.

1762

Journalism Abstracts. Columbia, SC: Association for Education in Journalism and Mass Communication, University of South Carolina, annual. (1963–.)

The unique feature of this annual compilation of abstracts of graduate student dissertations and theses in mass communication programs in the U.S. and Canada is the publication of the abstracts of the masters-level theses. The dissertation abstracts also appear in **Dissertation Abstracts**. The publication provides a hunting ground for research topics for graduate students. An extensive subject index is used.

1763

Journalism and Mass Communication Directory. Columbia, SC: Association for Education in Journalism and Mass Communication, University of South Carolina, annual. (1983–.)

The directory is in several parts: (1) Schools and Departments of Journalism and Mass Communication, (U.S., Australia, Canada, England and Puerto Rico) giving address, faculty, and information about the educational offerings; (2) Journalism Educational Organizations, which includes detailed information about the Association for Education in Journalism and Mass Communication (AEJMC), affiliated organizations, and the accrediting organization; (3) National Funds Fellowships and Foundations in Journalism; and (4) the AEJMC Membership Roster, including, position title, education, academic and professional interests, address and telephone numbers.

1764

Journalism Career and Scholarship Guide. Princeton, NJ: Dow Jones Newspaper Fund, annual. (1962–.)

This useful directory gives a rundown of colleges and universities in the United States with programs in journalism. In three Sections: the first, "A Newspaper Career for You," discusses (in rather glowing terms) some of the facts about journalism as a career; the second, "Universities that offer Journalism Majors," is a state-by-state chart of the universities and their programs; and the third, "Directory of Journalism Scholarships," is a school-by-school listing of scholarships, with a special section on minority and general scholarships, fellowships and programs. There is also information about how to apply. No attempt is made to evaluate the various programs, but some general facts about journalism as a profession are included.

Journalism Directory. (See No. 1763.)

1765

Knowledge Industry 200. White Plains, NY: Knowledge Industry Publications, Inc., 1983. (Distributed by Gale Research Company)

Although **Knowledge Industry 200** is not published annually, the book's contents is timely and should be regularly issued. It is an economic analysis of America's 200 largest media and information companies, ranking each according to revenue and profiling it as to number of employees, total assets (media and otherwise), media revenue breakdown, corporate officers, directors, company description, divisions, recent acquisitions and divestitures, financial ratios and other pertinent information which varies somewhat from company to company. An introduction summarizes the state of the industry by newspapers, periodicals, television broadcasting, motion pictures, book publishing, radio broadcasting, records, cable television, data base publishing, newsletters and loose-leaf services, and sheet music. The two final sections list officers' and directors' names and telephone numbers, and gives an alphabetical list of secondary companies followed by parent company to provide the user easy access. Information is detailed and specific—for example, under each corporation is listed by name newspapers, broadcasting stations, periodicals, etc., held. An invaluable aid in tracking down facts and figures, many of which are otherwise obscure. (A more recent edition was published in 1987.)

1766

The Korean Press. Seoul: The Korean Press Institute, annual. (1984–.)

For the first time, in 1984, an English edition of the **Korean Press Yearbook** was published. Contents include "A Brief History of the Korean Press," largely devoted to ethics, guidelines and codes; "Pressdom Today," giving the present structure of newspapers, broadcasting, the news agency, and sales and circulation; "Press Workers," describes training, the Korean Institute, working conditions; "Press-Related Organizations," with various associations, committees, commissions, etc., and "Directory," listing news agencies, broadcasting companies, press societies, awards,

1767

Literary Market Place: The Directory of American Book Publishing. New York: Bowker, annual. (1940–.)

An appropriate subtitle for this compendium might also read **The Bible of American Book Publishing**. Perhaps its most used feature is an alphabetical list of the most active book publishers in the U.S. (vanity publishers excluded), with addresses, telephone numbers, and personnel; a concise summary of the kinds of publications each firm produces; the number of yearly titles; foreign representatives; and trade associations to which each firm belongs. (This information varies somewhat according to the size of the firm and other factors.) Further lists classify the publishers both by location and by type. Another important feature is "Names and Numbers," an alphabetical list of firms and leading figures in book publishing, with addresses and telephone numbers.

A partial list of other information includes: book clubs, rights and representatives (including literary agents), associations and other organizations; book trade events, conferences, and courses; literary awards, contests and grants; services and suppliers; direct mail promotion; book reviews, book selection, and reference books; radio and television networks and programs featuring books; wholesale, export and import formation; book manufacturing; paper merchants and mills; and newspapers, newspaper magazine sections, newspaper representatives, and news services and feature syndicates which offer opportunity for publicity.

1768

Magazine Industry Market Place: The Directory of American Periodical Publishing. New York, NY: Bowker Co., annual. (1980–.)

This does for the magazine industry what the **Literary Market Place** does for book publishing. Information includes the following sections: publications and publishers which lists and classifies them by subject and records cessations, mergers and acquisitions, publishers of multiple periodicals and micropublishers; reference literature; associations and organizations; events and exhibits; agents and agencies; services and suppliers; direct mail promotion services; publication manufacturing; and fulfillment and distribution services. In conclusion is "Names & Numbers," a telephone and address directory that lists the names of the firms and most of the personnel found in the text, with the exception of newsletters for the trade, and associations and organizations.

1769

Magazine Publishing Career Directory 1986. New York: Career Publishing Corp., annual. (1986– .)

Articles and advice on entering the profession by

executives with some of the biggest and best known magazines and magazine chains in the U.S. Following an overview of the industry are chapters on various aspects of it—sales, art and design, circulation, production (manufacturing and distribution), promotion, public relations, and starting your own magazine. Special sections include job hunting, entry-level job listing, internships and training programs, and publishers to contact in the consumer, trade and professional/scientific/technical fields. Appendixes include industry trade organizations and publications. This is the first issue of a yearly series. Index.

Magill's Cinema Annual. (See No. 1357.)

1770

Mass Communication Review Yearbook. Newbury Park, CA: Sage Publications, Inc., biennial. (1980–1987.)

This yearbook represents a synthesis of current "scholarly enterprise" published by mass communication scholars primarily from two continents, Europe and North America. Nominations of recent articles are solicited from the members of the large international editorial advisory board. In addition, a few original manuscripts are invited. The yearbook, which switched from annual to biennial publication with Volume 5, 1985, is perhaps the only one that represents a sifting of the current research literature and that imposes a theoretical framework on the chosen representations of that collective work. For another approach to yearbooks of communication research, see **Communication Yearbook**, (No. 1739) and **Progress in Communication Science** (No. 1776). This series ceased with Vol. 6, 1987.

1771

National Directory of Community Newspapers. Brooklyn, NY: American Newspaper Representatives, Inc., annual. (1927/28–.)

The information in the main section of this directory, "Directory of Weekly Newspapers, Alabama through Wyoming," is similar to information given in the **Editor & Publisher International Yearbook** in its special section on weekly newspapers. The **National Directory of Community Newspapers** presents the same data in a more spacious tabular format than does **E&P** and adds more detail, such as symbols to reflect the newspaper's policy on alcoholic beverage advertising. This directory also publishes a state-by-state table of weekly newspaper statistics: number of weekly newspapers by state, total circulation, and total readership. Formerly, **National Directory of Weekly Newspapers**.

National Press Photographers Association. **Directory.** (See special Spring issue of **News Photographer**, a monthly journal. No. 1871.)

1772

Newspaper Guild: Proceedings of Annual Convention. Washington, DC: The Newspaper Guild, (AFL-CIO, CLC), annual. (1940–.)

A verbatim report of the annual convention of the Newspaper Guild, including financial and budget reports, committee reports, all resolutions, debates, remarks and formal addresses made at the convention. The Newspaper Guild is a labor union, founded in 1933, of over 30,000 newspapers employees, including reporters. The annual convention is traditionally held in June, and the proceedings are published early in the next calendar year.

1773

Newsprint Data: Statistics of World Demand and Supply. Montreal, Quebec, Canada: Canadian Pulp and Paper Association, annual. (1930–.)

Tables and charts, many of them comparative, showing newsprint capacity, production, exports, imports and demands.

1774

O'Dwyer's Directory of Corporate Communications. New York: J.R. O'Dwyer, annual. (1975–.)

An extensive survey showing how America's largest companies and trade associations (3,000 of the former and 500 of the latter) have defined, organized and staffed their public relations/communications operations. The main body lists alphabetically the corporations, with address, sales totals, product produced, chief public relations personnel, and a very brief description of public relations channels. Preceding this is a list of the corporations grouped by type of industry, and a state-by-state geographical index to corporate headquarters. Following it is a list of national associations.

1775

O'Dwyer's Directory of Public Relations. New York, NY: J. R. O'Dwyer Co., annual. (1969–.)

The standard of public relations companies. The main directory lists all 1,800 companies alphabetically and provides, in addition to the usual information given in business directories, a round figure of net fee income (when available and when judged to be reasonably accurate) and a listing of the firm's accounts. Geographical and subject indexes are prominent among several special indexes. Financial rankings of the top 50 companies appear for the first time in the 1986 edition. Jack O'Dwyer, publisher and editor, writes an interesting section, "How To Hire and Get the Most Outside PR Counsel."

1776

Progress in Communication Sciences. Ed. by Brenda Dervin and Melvin J. Voight. Norwood, NJ: Ablex Publishing, annual. (1979–.)

The focus of this annual review ranges widely from interpersonal to mass media. From the first volume through the current issue, the review has kept its pledge "to present a high quality state of the art review of the literature in the fields of communication and information science." (Preface, Volume 7, 1986) A short list of the reviews in the latest volume gives evidence of the diversity of the research: Emile G. McAnany, international cultural industries; Hak Soo Kim, co-orientation and communication; Gavan Duffy, broadcast policy debates; Christine L. Borgman, human-computer interaction; Payson Hall, cross-cultural research; Beth J. Haslett, theory of discourse; Myles Breen and Farrel Corcoran, mythic themes in mass media studies; Donald P. Cushman and Sarah Sanderson King, communication in life crises; and Charles T. Salmon, consumer communication. Each review has a full bibliography. Each annual review lists the table of contents of all the previous volumes. The early volumes were published somewhat irregularly. The first volume was edited by Voight and Gerhard J. Hanneman.

1777

Promodata: Promotions Marketing & Advertising Data. London and Capetown, South Africa: Clarion Communications Media, annual. (1981–.)

Incorporating **Advertising and Press Annual of Southern Africa: The Blue Book of Advertising in Southern Africa** (1968?-1980), this serves as a press as well as an advertising directory in that it lists, with pertinent information, South Africa media which accept advertising—daily, weekly, fortnightly, etc. newspapers; consumer and trade periodicals, general and specialized; and radio and TV stations and networks and cinemas. Additional listings include advertising agencies, marketing services; direct mail firms; and supplies and other services. All listings are alphabetical under appropriate headings, but there also is a classified and a straight alphabetical index.

1778

Public Relations Career Directory 1986. New York: Career Publishing Corp., annual. (1986–.)

Practitioners in the field contribute articles to present young aspirants with the job possibilities, techniques of job hunting, scope of the field and its specializations, and other pertinent facts to consider when planning and hoping to enter public relations. Contributors represent practically all types of work in public relations—agencies, corporations and businesses, associations and public service organizations, and government. A special section discusses entry-level jobs, internships and training programs, and special places to contact. A chart shows the 50 largest U.S. public relations operations in the U.S. both independent and ad agency affiliated. Appendixes give industry trade organizations and publications. This is the first of a yearly series. Index.

1779

Public Television Programming by Category. Washington: Corporation for Public Broadcasting, biennial. (1975–.)

Reports the numbers and characteristics of public television content, based on data provided by public television licenses to CPB. Statistical data is given in terms of hours for various kinds of programming—instructional, general, news/public affairs, special or target audiences, etc. It does not deal with individual programs. For many years the data were compiled by Nathan Katzman. Appendixes give "secondary" schedules, methodology, and instructional grade level by subject matter. Previous to the first of the series, **Public Television Content 1974**, also by Katzman, was a series of volumes starting in 1961, **One Week in Educational Television**, produced by a variety of different people and organizations.

1780

Publishers Directory: A Guide to Approximately 12,000 New and Established Commercial and Nonprofit, Private and Alternative, Corporate and Association, Government and Institution Publishing Programs and Their Distributors. Includes Producers of Books, Classroom Materials, Reports, and Databases. Detroit, MI: Gale, annual. 2 v. (1979–.)

The first thing that should be said about this relatively new directory of publishing is that it does not overlap with **Literary Market Place** (No. 1767). In fact, publishers listed there are excluded; those included here tend to be smaller, regional, more specialized and often dealing with non-book materials. To provide convenient access to firms listed in **Literary Market Place**, **Publishers Directory** has included citations of publishers and imprints in **LMP** in their Publishers, Imprint, and Distributors Index.

In its first four editions **Publishers Directory** appeared as **Book Publishers Directory**, but its Fifth Edition (1985) was expanded to include publishers of non-book materials of the types described in the subtitle. Information varies slightly with each entry; among the items are address, telephone number, date founded, principal officials and managers, affiliations, number of new titles, subject, discounts, return policy, and selected titles. The current edition lists 11,600 publishers in the U.S. and Canada, and contains a separate section which identifies over 250 distributors, wholesalers, and jobbers. As in the case of book publishers, information varies, but among items are principal officials and managers, description, subjects, special services, discounts, percentage of sales broken down by bookstores, libraries, etc., returns policy, type customers served, and territory. There is a publishers/imprints/distributors index; a subject index; and a geographic index.

1781

Publishers' International Directory with ISNB Index. Internationales Verlag Addressbuch mit ISNB Register. 2 v. Munich, Germany: Saur, annual (irregular until 1984). (1964–.)

The 12th edition (1985) lists about 160,500 firms, including publishers of periodical literature, alternative publishers, and various institutes, institutions, organizations and individuals engaged in publishing, both print and software. In all, 194 countries are included. Volume One is alphabetical by country, with firms in alphabetical order; Volume Two is numerical by prefix. The main entry, in the first volume, gives details for each firm as to address, telephone and Telex numbers, branches, distributors, and wherever available, areas of specialization. In both English and German.

1782, 1783

Radio Financial Report. Washington, DC: National Association of Broadcasters, annual. (1953–.)

Television Financial Report. Washington, DC: National Association of Broadcasters, annual. (1950–.)

The radio and television reports give revenue, expense, and income by types of markets and types of stations, and by income and expense item. Data is based on replies received from financial questionnaires sent to all U.S. commercial television and radio stations requesting revenue sources, department expenses and specific line items. These are valuable as the only consistent source of financial information since it is no longer collected by the FCC. There are some problems with incompatible responses from the stations.

1784

Radio Programming Profile. 2 v. Glenn Head, NY: BF Communication Services, three issues per year. (1967–.)

A geographic listing of AM and FM stations, intended to provide advertisers and public relation specialists with detailed programming in capsule form—for example, contemporary music, country music, ethnic shows, talk shows, news, etc. The stations themselves have supplied comments along with data. Covers approximately 200 markets.

1785

Roper Organization. **America's Watching: Public Attitudes Toward Television**. New

York: Television Information Office, biennial. (1959–.)

A series of pamphlets, each numbering around 20 pages, about surveys conducted for the Television Information Office by the Roper Organization which are designed to show how commercial television stands with the public by tracking changes over time in perceptions of the mass media and also measuring responses to specific issues which have come up periodically. They are useful not only for the statistics they provide but also for interpretations and editorial comments which indicate commercial TV's attitudes toward its product and its public.

1786

Sage Annual Reviews of Communication Research. Newbury Park, CA: Sage Publications, annual. (1972–.)

The first of the annual reviews of communication research, this series has published consistently outstanding monographs. Each volume is devoted to a single research area, which distinguishes the series from other annual reviews: **Communication Yearbook** (No. 1739.), **Mass Communication Review Yearbook** (No. 1770.) and **Progress in Communication Sciences** (No. 1776.). The monographs in the **Sage Annual Reviews of Communication Research** are:

Kline, F. Gerald, and Phillip J. Tichenor, eds., **Current Perspectives in Mass Communication Research**. Vol. 1, 1972. 320p. (See No. 234.)

Clarke, Peter, ed. **New Models for Mass Communication Research**. Vol. 2, 1973. 307p.

Blumler, Jay G., and Elihu Katz, eds. **The Uses of Mass Communications: Current Perspectives on Gratifications Research**. Vol. 3, 1974. 318p. (See No. 39.)

Chaffee, Steven H., ed. **Political Communication: Issues and Strategies for Research**. Vol. 4, 1975. 319p. (See No. 61.)

Miller, Gerald R., ed. **Explorations in Interpersonal Communication**. Vol. 5, 1976. 278p.

Hirsch, Paul M., Peter V. Miller, and F. Gerald Kline, eds. **Strategies for Communication Research**. Vol. 6, 1977. 288p.

Wartella, Ellen, ed. **Children Communicating: Media and Development of Thought, Speech, Understanding**. Vol. 7, 1979. 286p. (See No. 827.)

Roloff, Michael E., and Gerald R. Miller, eds. **Persuasion: New Directions in Theory and Research**. Vol. 8, 1980. 311p.

Rosengren, Karl Erik, ed. **Advances in Content Analysis**. Vol. 9, 1981. 283p. (See No. 370.)

Ettema, James S., and D. Charles Whitney, eds. **Individuals in Mass Media Organizations: Creativity and Constraint**. Vol. 10, 1982. 259p. (See No. 120.)

Wiemann, John M., and Randall P. Harrison, eds. **Nonverbal Interaction**. Vol. 11, 1983. 288p.

Rowland, Willard D., Jr., and Bruce Watkins, eds. **Interpreting Television: Current Research Perspectives**. Vol. 12, 1984. 293p. (See No. 766.)

McPhee, Robert D., and Phillip K. Thompkins, eds. **Organizational Communication**. Vol. 13, 1985. 296p.

1787

Screen International Film and TV Yearbook. London: King Publications, annual. (1945–.)

The emphasis of this yearbook is not international but British. The major section, the 500-paged "International Who's Who," lists mostly British actors, directors and other film and television personnel. A few U.S. residents, usually from Los Angeles, are included. A second section of the yearbook, the "British Directory" gives names and addresses of British film and television companies—studios, distributors, laboratories, and other services. A third and much smaller section, the "International Directory" gives limited information for 10 countries: Australia, Austria, Canada, France, Germany, Israel, Italy, Japan, Saudi Arabia, and U.S.A.

1788

Screen World. New York: Crown, annual. (1949–.)

Lists domestic and foreign films released during the year, with credits and shots. Among other features: Academy Award winners of current and previous years, and obituaries.

1789, 1790

Standard Directory of Advertisers. Wilmette, IL: National Register Publishing Co., annual. (1899–.)

Standard Directory of Advertising Agencies. Wilmette, IL: National Register Publishing Co., three issues per year. (1917–.)

Companion volumes. **Advertisers** tell which agency advertises a specific product; **Advertising Agencies** tells which accounts a specific agency carries.

The **Standard Directory of Advertisers** is issued in two editions—the classified edition (April) and the geographical edition (May)—and lists more than 17,000 corporations doing national and regional advertising, classified by type of product. Information about each corporation includes name, address, telephone number, heads of divisions, products and services, and not only the advertising agency employed by also the media used and in some cases the appropriation. There are several indexes—one by name of corporation, one by trade name and two by classification—one by SIC (Standard Industrial Classification) code, one by geographical area, and one by alphabetical order.

The **Standard Directory of Advertising Agencies** lists approximately 4,000 agencies, with address, telephone number, and some or all of the following: year founded, number of employees, specialization, approximate annual billing and a breakdown of gross annual billing by media, account executives, and accounts carried. Other features include the 40 largest advertising agencies, ranked according to annual billing; mergers and acquisitions, name changes, and a geographical index. Also: a market index to agencies specializing in various markets—blacks, Hispanic, financial, medical, resort, travel, etc.; and a geographical index, both U.S. and foreign.

1791

Standard Periodical Directory. New York: Oxbridge, irregular. (1964–.)

A subtitle, **The Most Complete Guide to U.S. and Canadian Periodicals**, is not boastful. "Periodicals" is defined as any publication with a frequency of at least one every two years. Types include consumer magazines; trade journals; newsletters; government publications; house organs; directories; transactions and proceedings of scientific societies; yearbooks; museum, religious, ethnic, literary and social group publications; and several other categories. Information for each varies, giving all or in the majority of cases some of the following: title, publisher, address, telephone number, editor and several other key personnel, capsule description of content, indexing/abstracting information, year established, frequency, subscription rate, circulation, advertising/audit information, distribution of readership (national and international), advertising rates, format, catalog numbers of government publications. Arrangement is by subject, with an alphabetical index.

1792

Television & Cable Factbook. 2 v. Washington, DC: Television Digest, Inc., annual. (1945–.)

Together the two volumes of this industry directory measure over six inches of bound pages. Part 1 is a compendium of data about the television stations, including Arbitron data about station penetration. A full description of the information in the station directory prefaces that section. The data are presented in a format that is easy to read. An abundance of detail is given for U.S. (including Puerto Rico and the Virgin Islands) and Canadian stations. A substantial amount of information about foreign televisions stations is provided. Part 2 is devoted to detailed information about cable companies and descriptive data that represent cable agreements listed community-by-community. In both volumes directories about related services supplement the main section on television stations and cable companies.

1793

Television & Radio. London, England: Independent Broadcasting Authority (London), annual. (1979–.)

In addition to being informative, this may well be the most beautiful annual on record and with its glossy paper and handsome colored illustrations would decorate any coffee table. Emphasis is on programming, which does not mean reference material is slighted. Preliminary pages describe the structure of IBA; in the back are 50 pages of data which include: finance; reception; transmitters; program production and output; awards; sales overseas, detailed rundowns on the various companies which comprise IBA; Independent Local Radio areas with maps; and listing of IBA's personnel and advisory bodies. Sandwiched between and constituting the major portion is information about types of programming with descriptions and vivid illustrations of specific programs, most of them in color. There is a detailed index.

1794

Television & Video Almanac. New York: Quigley, annual. (1929–.)

Formerly **International Television Almanac**, this almanac has been reconstituted to include 110 pages of data about home video, with statistics, production and distribution, trade associations, trade and consumer periodicals and various other pertinent information. A broad "who's who" section includes biographical information about producers, directors, writers, set designers, and other kinds of workers in film and broadcasting in addition to actors and actresses. Among other features are a variety of statistics, and listings of companies (networks, set manufacturers, major producer, and major group station owners), cable data, producers-distributors, stations, advertising agencies and station representatives, programs, organizations, publications, and a few concise pages on "The Industry of Great Britain & Ireland" and "The World Market," which constituted its chief claim to the misleading **International** in its former title.

This is a companion volume to the **International Motion Picture Almanac** (No. 1760), which, like **Television & Video Almanac**, contains very little about the international scene. In each volume the "who's who" section is the same. But both volumes contain a great deal of highly packed, useful information about the American market.

Television Financial Report. (See No. 1783.)

1795

Ulrich's International Periodicals Directory: A Classified Guide to Current Periodicals, Foreign and Domestic. New York: Bowker, Biennial. (1932–.)

The 22d edition (1983) includes 64,800 periodicals published throughout the world and currently in print, arranged by subject classification, with alphabetical index. Each entry contains basic information about title, frequency, publisher's name and address, classification code, and Dewey Decimal number, and when available, further information about editor, format, circulation, advertising policy, inclusion of book reviews and various other kinds of reviews, availability on microform, and whether indexed. It also tells which, if any, of the periodical indexes analyze its contents. Recent editions contain "Index to Publications of International Organizations." **Ulrich's Quarterly**, which began in 1977, brings up-to-date information on new serial titles, title changes, and cessations.

1796

The Underground and Alternative Press in Britain. Ed. by John Spiers. Brighton, England: Harvester Press, annual. (1972–.)

An index to the Harvester Press' collection of microfiche and microfilm underground and alternative publications which in itself constitutes a bibliography. For each entry is given date of founding and often—too often, for small publications have a high death rate—of ending; address; and a full descriptive annotation about contents and slant. The 1972 volume contains an essay on the underground and alternative press in Great Britain by John Spiers. Entries continue in microfilm.

1797

Variety **Film Reviews**. New York: Garland, biennial. (1907–1980.)

Multi-volume set, beginning in 1907 when **Variety** "first took note of the film branch of show business." Reviews are reproduced in their entirety. Coverage was spasmodic in the early years and was discontinued between March 1911 and January 1913, at which time reviews became a regular, permanent feature. Volume 16 (1907–1920) is an index for those years; later volumes, issued at approximately two-year intervals, contain their own indexes. A separate publication, **Index to Motion Pictures Reviewed by** *Variety*, **1907–1980**, by Max Joseph Alvarez (Metuchen, NJ: Scarecrow, 1982. 510p.) lists all the titles in one volume, with the date the review appeared.

1798

Willing's Press Guide: A Guide to the Press of the United Kingdom and to Principal Publications of Europe, Australasia, the Far East, Middle East, and U.S.A. East Grinstead, West Sussex, England: Thomas Skinner Directories, annual. (1874–.)

One of the oldest continuous directories on record, this is an alphabetical listing of newspapers, general and specialized periodicals, and even some annual publications published in the United Kingdom and 28 other countries, giving for each the year established, frequency, price, and publisher's name and address. Publishers of the United Nations are also included. Among other features is a list of some reading periodical publishers with their periodicals and a list of reporting, news, and press clipping agencies. Publishers in the U.K. section are in alphabetical order and in the Overseas Section, geographical. Classified index and directory of services and suppliers.

1799

The Working Press of the Nation. 5 v. Chicago: National Research Bureau, Division of Information Products Group, Automated Marketing Systems, annual. (1947–.)

This series, which has grown from one volume, is intended primarily for publicists but includes detailed information pertinent to media personnel, especially advertisers, and to librarians answering reference questions. Vol. 1, **Newspaper Directory**, contains listings of daily and weekly newspapers by state and community, giving circulation, frequency, wire services, material requirements, deadlines, and much other useful data, including over 7,000 management and editorial personnel who are also indexed by subject; an index of newspapers by metro areas; and indexes of newspapers with Sunday supplements and TV supplements. Vol. 2, **Magazine Directory**, lists more than 4,700 consumer, farm and agriculture, service, trade, professional and industrial publications grouped by subject area, with an alphabetical index. Prolific data is given for each including a thumbnail description of its contents and its readers. Vol. 3, **Radio and TV Directory** is divided into "Radio" and "Television," giving for each the stations by metro and non-metro areas, commercial stations, personnel by subject, local programming, and public/educational stations; and for television, a listing of networks. Vol. 4, **Feature Writer and Photographer Directory**, contains over 1,900 feature writers and photographers, their home addresses, subject areas, and publications accepting their work. They are also indexed by subject areas, and publications accepting their work. They are also indexed by subject specialties. Vol. 5, **Internal Publications Directory**, provides detailed information about internal and external publications of more than 3,100 U.S. companies, government agencies, clubs and other groups.

1800

World Advertising Expenditures: A Survey of World Advertising Expenditures in 1985. Mamoroneck, NY: Starch INRA Hooper in cooperation with the International Advertising Association, annual. (1965–.)

Consists of tables designed to enable country-by-country comparisons of media advertising in 46 countries. Expenditures figures are in U.S. currency, with one table showing equivalency for local currencies. Market information for the various media is also included in two of the tables. Unlike previous editions where data were often extrapolated from past estimates, in the 20th edition (1985) the data have all been provided by local practitioners. Categories may vary somewhat from year to year.

1801

World Radio TV Handbook. New York: Billboard Publications, annual. (1946–.)

This compact compendium of technical and nontechnical data on international broadcasting gives a detailed country-by-country description of both radio and television stations, listing personnel, program information, frequencies, transmitter powers, operating times, languages, and addresses along with other information pertinent to a particular station; maps of principal transmitter sites; names and addresses of international radio listeners' clubs; data on reception conditions; and Time Signal Stations. Other specialized aspects are tucked away in fine print. Each volume has a section of featured articles. There is no index (to index this type of reference book would be an impossible task), but the detailed table-of-contents somewhat compensates.

1802

Writer's Market. Cincinnati, OH: Writer's Digest Books, annual. (1930–.)

Aptly subtitled "When and How to Sell What You Write: 4,000 Places to Sell Your Articles, Books, Fillers, Gags, Greeting Cards, Novels, Scripts and Short Stories," this is a comprehensive guide to editorial requirements for aspiring writers or for those who for whatever reasons need an introduction to the marketplace. First of all comes a 174-page alphabetical listing, "Book Publishers," a summary of editorial policies and requirements, followed by a concise subject index to speciality types of writing. The bulk of the volume is a subject breakdown of periodical possibilities, again summarizing needs and requirements. Other features include the market for syndicated material; author's agents; and contests and awards. The Appendix contains an essay, "The Business of Free Lancing," filled with practical facts about such things as taxes, copyright, manuscript requirements, and suggested charges for editorial services. There is a glossary and index. **Writer's Market** provides all the assists; the only thing the user need provide is talent.

Journals

(The journals about film are *not* covered in this chapter. Anthony Slide's bibliography of film journals, **International Film, Radio, and Television Journals**, c.1985 (No. 1480), is outstanding in scope and detail.)

8

1803

AEJMC News. Columbia, SC: Association for Education in Journalism and Mass Communication, bimonthly. (1967–.)

The membership of the Association for Education in Journalism and Mass Communication is predominately faculty from mass communication programs in North American colleges and universities. This newsletter is the source of unique information, such as the place and dates of the annual convention, the association's membership application, and convention registration forms. The July issue publishes titles and some abstracts of the research papers to be presented at the August convention.

1804

AIM Report. Washington, DC: Accuracy in Media, Inc., biweekly. (1969–.)

Published as a brief, four-paged newsletter, **AIM** is a highly critical review of the national news media, including the network television news programs, public television, and the major newspapers and magazines. The opinions are those of the editor, Reed Irvine.

1805

Access Reports/Public policy and mass media. Washington, DC: Monitor Publishing Co., bimonthly. (1975–.)

This 8–12 page newsletter reports in detail all federal government activity involved in the Public policy and mass media Act. Legislative bills and hearings, federal court decisions, and agency responses to requests for information make up the bulk of the news. Because the press receives fee waivers for information, the newsletter carefully reports all matters about FOI of interest to the news media. FOI issues in Canada are also reported. Annual subject index and table of cases are included.

1806

Advertising Age. Chicago, IL: Crain Communications, Inc., weekly. (1930–.)

This "international newspaper of marketing" carries much information about the mass media. Especially helpful are annual special features published in the regular weekly issues which provide statistical, directory, and background information: 100 Leading National Advertisers, Second Leading National Advertisers, and the newer annual, 100 Leading Media Companies.

1807

American Journalism. University, AL: American Journalism Historians Association, School of Communication, University of Alabama, quarterly. (1982–.)

The journal is limited to articles about journalism in the U.S. Histories of the broadcast media as well as the older print media of newspapers and magazines are included. Articles on the history of ideas and movements, in the development of journalism, with recent emphasis on the contributions of women, are regularly published.

1808

American Printer. Chicago, IL: MacLean Hunter Publishing Corp., monthly. (1883–.)

International in outlook, this journal has been publishing trade information about the business of printing for over 100 years. Today's issues emphasize computer technology, paper quality, color graphics, and management problems.

1809

APF Reporter. Washington, DC: Alicia Patterson Foundation, quarterly. (1977–.)

This publication is a showcase for lengthy journalistic articles, often investigative pieces, written by current fellows of the Alicia Patterson Foundation. The fellows, who are print journalists, are supported for a year to write about public affairs issues.

1810

APME News. Los Angeles, CA: The Associated Press Managing Editors, irregular. (1964–.)

Similar in content to the American Society of Newspaper Editors' publication, **The Bulletin**, the Associated Press Managing Editors' magazine is lively with issues of interest to newspaper editors—ethical and legal issues about news, how to win the Pulitzer, sabbaticals for editors, and the annual convention program.

1811

AP World. New York: The Associated Press, three issues per year. (1945–.)

A heavily illustrated magazine, **AP World** tells who and how the Associated Press staff reported the news. The personnel news items are presented with candid photographs.

1812

Australian Journalism Review. St. Lucia, Australia: Journalism Education Association, University of Queensland, biannually. (1979–.)

The physical appearance of the **Australian Journalism Review** suggests that it is a traditional academic report of scholarly thought and research, and this is true but not all true. It is a fascinating mixture of the traditional reports of scholarly investigation and news and essays about Australian mass media events, trends and controversies. The news items about Rupert Murdoch's media companies are of special interest to U.S. readers. The articles are short and are contributed by university teachers, journalists, and government officials (or former officials). In recent volumes both of the two issues were published as a single volume.

1813

Broadcasting. Washington, DC: Broadcasting Publications, Inc., weekly. (1931–.)

For recent information about the U.S. broadcasting industry—its upcoming meetings, legislation, radio and TV stations sold, audience ratings of programs, programming trends, news of the networks, and so forth—this is the publication to use. The "help wanted" classified ads are used by university students seeking their first jobs in broadcasting. For directory information and annual summaries of trends and information published in the weekly **Broadcasting**, see **Broadcasting Cablecasting Yearbook**, (No. 1731) issued by the same publisher. See also **Broadcasting Index** (1972–1981) (No. 1914).

1814

The Bulletin. Reston, VA: American Society of Newspaper Editors, nine issues per year. (1970–.)

The Bulletin is a journal for newspaper editors and publishes short essays and articles on current press controversies. The issues are usually devoted to a central topic, for example, the crisis orientation of journalism, analysis of newspaper readership, ethics of investigative reporting, journalism educational programs, and practical problems of newspaper editing.

1815

Cable & Satellite Europe. London: Cable & Satellite Magazine Ltd., monthly. (1984–.)

The focus of this trade journal is Europe, particularly the United Kingdom, and the value of the journal in U.S. library collections lies in its report of the European industry. Also important for the same reasons is its sister publication, **Cable and Satellite Yearbook**, (No. 1732) an annual industry directory.

1816

Cable Marketing. New York: Associated Cable Enterprises, monthly. (1980–.)

The subtitle—**The Marketing/Management Magazine for Cable Television Executives**—describes this oversized (11 x 14 inches) magazine. The content is devoted to cable television programming news and marketing strategies.

1817

Cable Television Business. Englewood, CO: Cardiff Publishing Co., biweekly. (1976–.)

A trade journal that reports a broad spectrum of cable television industry issues, **Cable Television Business** has covered cable topics for 25 years. The three large areas of current news coverage are customer service, programming, and technology. The information—practical, specific, and timely—is directed to cable television management. Former titles are **TVC**, **TV Communications**, and **Television Communications**.

1818

Cable Vision. Denver, CO: International Thomson Communications, Inc., biweekly. (1975–.)

A trade publication, this magazine reports industry trends, technological developments, the cable industry on Wall Street, and personnel news. A regular feature, "Cable Stats," gives a variety of information, including the number of households subscribing to cable systems and the percentage of the market saturation.

1819

Canadian Journal of Communication. Calgary: University of Calgary Press, quarterly. (1974–.)

The journal publishes scholarly articles about communications research and policy in Canada. As Canadian mass communication issues are closely linked with broadcast media in the United States, communication practice and policy for both countries is often a subject of interest. A recent editorial decision is to focus each issue on a single, broad topic. Edited by Gertrude Robinson at McGill University, the journal is independently published, but it carries news about the Canadian Communication Association and publishes the Gordon Sinclair (Foundation) essay series. Book reviews appear regularly. The journal is published in English with summaries in French and English.

1820

Channels: The Business of Communications. New York: C.C. Publishing Inc., bimonthly. (1981–.)

A lively industry journal, **Channels** reports the news about television and cable programming—trends, syndicates, distributors, market saturation and growth, work styles of important people in the industry, and statistics. The journal regularly publishes information usually found in handbooks, such as a glossary of industry buzzwords and an annual field guide that is data-rich with details about sales, forecasts, and the companies involved. Formerly entitled **Channels of Communication**.

1821

Columbia Journalism Review. New York: Graduate School of Journalism, Columbia University, bimonthly. (1962–.)

The standard among media review journals, **CJR** criticizes the performance of the U.S. news media. **CJR** is probably the most widely read of all the journalism review journals and can be depended upon to comment on or initiate discussion of important journalistic issues. The "Lower Case," a regular backpage feature, displays bloopers, usually in the form of headlines, made by the U.S. daily press.

1822

Comm/ent. San Francisco, CA: Hastings College of Law, quarterly. (1977–.)

Subtitled: **A journal of communications and entertainment law**. This unique law journal was begun by students at the University of California Hastings College of Law, which has a joint degree program with the University of California at Berkeley School of Journalism. Among the topics covered in the first seven volumes are the Fairness Doctrine, Copyright Law of 1976, international legal implications of satellite broadcasting, and the "right" of publicity.

1823

Communication. London: Gordon and Breach Science Publishers S.A., quarterly. (1975–.)

With the 1986 volume, this journal changed editors—James Carey of the University of Illinois, the editor, associate editors (all from Illinois), and the editorial advisory board. The editorial policy changed to broaden the journal's forum to include a wider sweep of academic disciplines contributing to the study of communication. The journal has traditionally published articles by authors from multiple continents. The number of issues per volume increased from two to four with Volume 9, 1986.

Communication Abstracts. (See No. 1917.)

1824

Communication Booknotes. Comp. by Christopher H. Sterling. Washington, DC: George Washington University, Department of Communication, bi-monthly. (1969–.)

This bibliography, formerly called **Mass Media Booknotes**, is an indispensable guide to the current literature in mass communications, which Sterling defines to include various aspects of telecommunications and technology, advertising, film, journalism, pop culture and research, interpreted broadly. Geographically, he is also broad, covering works from Canada, Australia, Britain, the Third World, France and Germany, and sometimes Italy and Spain. With the help of contributors he covers between 25–30 books an issue, each with descriptive and often evaluative annotations. Each year there are two single topic issues—on government documents in August and on cinema books in December. The annual issue on government documents deserves special mention because documents are not well-publicized, nor is the literature about them easy to follow. Anyone buying in the mass communication field or keeping up with it will find Sterling's monthly bibliographies invaluable.

In addition **Communication Booknotes** publishes a series of three annotated and regularly revised bibliographies on telecommunications policy, media, and international/foreign communications.

1825

Communication Research. Newbury Park, CA: Sage Publications, Inc., bimonthly. (1974–.)

An academic journal, **Communication Research** publishes articles about research in the broad definition of communication studies and is not limited to mass media research. The book review section is written in essay form and reviews current and older books.

1826

Communications and the Law. Westport, CT: Meckler Publishing Corp., bimonthly. (1979–.)

Freedom of the press, copyright law, and public access to the broadcast media are among the topics discussed in this journal, a lawyer's journal.

1827

Communications Lawyer. Chicago, IL: American Bar Association, Committee on Communications Law, quarterly. (1983–.)

This newsletter publishes brief essays or review articles about communications law developments. For example, the first issue has a one-page essay summarizing the AT&T consent decree. The essay is written by a telecommunications lawyer based in Washington, DC. Longer essays, on points about free speech, for example, are also published.

1828

Critical Studies in Mass Communication. Annandale, VA: Speech Communication Association, quarterly. (1984–.)

A quarterly journal contributing to the body of literature characterized as critical studies." The journal publishes cross-disciplinary research about mass communication systems and the relationship of culture and mass media and provides a forum for the dialogue between critical studies and empirical approaches to understanding mass communication. (See also, **Journal of Communication Inquiry** and **Journal of Communication**.) Illustrative themes drawn from the first five volumes are as follows: (1) television content—rhetorical analysis of political news, reality, and aesthetics of entertainment programs; (2) concepts of mass communication audiences—children watching television, relationships between community and local media; (3) international communication—ideology and analyses of news flow, Marxist interpretation of media studies; and (4) technological and economic aspects of mass media—general implications of technology, economic interpretation of the Penny Press.

1829

Current. Washington, DC: Current Publishing Committee: Education Broadcasting Corporation, bimonthly. (1982–.)

The newsletter, published 23 times per year, was formerly published from 1978–1980 under two different titles: **NAEB Letter** and **National Association of Educational Broadcasters Newsletter**. The news is about public television and radio stations, programming, personnel, national trends, legislation, fund raising, and open positions and a calendar of meetings and events. It is indexed in **Reader's Guide to Periodical Literature** (No. 1937).

1830

Deadline. New York: Center for War, Peace, and the News Media, New York University, bimonthly. (1986–.)

In a newsletter format, **Deadline** publishes essays critical of media coverage of issues relating to arms and disarmament, or more broadly, war and peace. The essays, clearly written and edited, are detailed with facts and examples of media misdeeds as well as citations of exemplary reporting.

1831

Editor & Publisher. New York: Editor & Publisher Co., Inc., weekly. (1884–.)

The purpose of this journal, the key one of its kind, is to provide a weekly report on the business of newspaper publishing. In short articles it publishes information about the economics of publishing and issues confronted by editors and reporters. The format of this journal is unchanging which helps to overcome the problem created by an inadequate table of contents. Annual sections include preconvention news about the American Newspaper Publishers Association and the **Syndicate Directory** (No. 1748) which gives all the information about national syndicated columnists, except what you really want to know: her or his address and telephone number and which newspapers publish the syndicated column.

1832

Electronic Media. Chicago, IL: Crain Communications, weekly. (1982–.)

A tabloid-sized publication that easily lends itself to large color advertising, **Electronic Media** covers the national news of television, cable, and radio. It provides some help in answering requests for the Nielsen audience ratings by publishing Nielsen data in varying formats, usually by individual program titles and by networks within seasonal boundaries.

1833

Electronic and Optical Publishing Review. Medford, NJ: Learned Information Ltd., quarterly. (1981–.)

The journal publishes articles that touch many international institutions—telecommunications, computing, libraries, and publishing. When this journal was founded, videotext was of keen interest and in a healthy stage of international development. Since 1981, several major exploratory videotext systems have been abandoned. The editorial focus of the journal has shifted with the technological development of electronic publishing. Current interests in 1986 are desk top publishing and optical disc publishing. The former title was **Electronic Publishing Review: The International Journal for the Transfer of Published Information Via Videotex and Online Media**.

1834

European Journal of Communication. London: Sage Publications Ltd., quarterly. (1986–.)

This new quarterly brings together both East and West European scholars. The three editors represent universities in England, The Netherlands and Sweden. In the essay which introduces the new journal, the editors describe their view of communication, ". . . the central phenomena are processes of public communication within and between societies and thus primarily to do with mass media and mass communication." The journal is published in English.

1835

Federal Communications Law Journal, Los Angeles, CA: UCLA School of Law, three times per year. (1977–.)

Formerly published as the **Federal Communications Bar Journal** (1937–1976), the **Federal Communications Law Journal** is jointly published by the UCLA School of Law and the Federal Communications Bar Association.

A variety of topics receive scholarly review. Among them are First Amendment issues involved in cable franchises, pornography and newsgathering; telephone divestiture and public policy; regulation of the telecommunications industry; and new communication forums, such as computer bulletin boards. The journal also carries reviews of books and articles. Most of the authors have legal credentials.

1836

Feed/back: The California Journalism Review. San Francisco: Journalism Department, San Francisco State University, quarterly. (1974–1986.)

Feed/back was one of the few "watchdog" reviews of journalism and the only one in the West. Other reviews listed among the journals in this chapter are the **Columbia Journalism Review**, the **St. Louis Journalism Review**, and the **Washington Journalism Review**. Feed/back focused attention on the best and the bad of journalism in California. Lou Cannon and Ben Bagdikian were among its nationally known contributors. The editors, unpaid volunteers, announced in the Spring 1986 issue that they were resigning.

1837

F.O.I. Center Report. Columbia, MO: Public Policy and Mass Media Center, University of Missouri, monthly. (1959–.)

Taken as a whole, the individual reports discuss topics about information and the public's right to know. Individually, the reports, which run about eight pages, summarize timely topics—state laws on access to information, access to broadcast air time, news organizations' uses of computer databases and the regulation of the advertising industry. The reports are often overlooked in an ordinary literature search because they are not indexed by the standard services. Occasionally an issue will include a listing of the most recent titles. For special assistance with locating these reports by subject, contact the library of the University of Missouri School of Journalism, 117 Walter Williams Hall, Columbia, MO 65201–5149. (314) 882–7502.

1838

Folio: The Magazine for Magazine Management. Stamford, CT: Folio Publishing Corp., monthly. (1972–.)

Although much of the content of **Folio** is used to discuss the sales, promotion and distribution of magazines, some attention is given to editorial issues involved in magazine management. The ethical question of retouching photographs is one example; libel law, another. **Folio: Source Book**, an annual directory of magazine-related business is issued in June. The directory is divided into a classified listing of businesses under three subsections, "Production," "Circulation," and "Management/Marketing/Editorial," and a telephone directory of all the businesses listed in the classified section. Brokers of illustrations and photographs do not appear to be included in this source book.

1839

Gannetteer. Arlington, VA: Gannett Co., Inc., monthly. (1955–.)

The **Gannetteer** is the most interesting of the house organs published by the large media corporations. The color and graphic flair, similar to the brightness of the Gannett newspaper **USA Today**, is used in this employee magazine on every page, not just the cover. The upbeat attitude is also maintained by the strong promotion of the achievements of Gannett employees and executives. It provides an informal history of the organization and a sense of who works there. Al Neuharth, CEO, is frequently interviewed and reported on by the magazine.

1840

Gazette. The Netherlands: Martinus Nijhoff Publishers, three issues per year. (1955–.)

Traditionally, the **Gazette** has paid special attention to communication in developing countries. The articles are scholarly and scientific; the subjects range widely and are also about communication issues in developed countries. Founded in 1955, the journal has one of the longer publishing histories in the field of mass communication. Bibliographies, often annotated ones, are another area of special interest.

1841

Grassroots Editor: A Journal for Newspeople. DeKalb, IL: International Society of Weekly Newspaper Editors. Available: Donald F. Brod, Editor, Department of Journalism, Northern Illinois University, quarterly. (1960–.)

Essays and reports about community weekly newspapers, mostly in the United States, but also from Canada and England, are published in this small quarterly journal. The authors are the newspaper publishers and editors themselves and faculty members whose academic interests fall in with weekly newspapers. Annually a report of two awards, the Quill and the Cervi, is included. See also **Publisher's Auxiliary** (No. 1885) for a report of the business side of weekly newspapers.

1842

Guild Reporter. Washington, DC: The Newspaper Guild (AFL-CIO,CLC), 22 issues per year. (1933–.)

Published on newsprint in newspaper format, the **Guild Reporter** covers the news about labor in the newspaper publishing industry—strikes, contracts, new members, safety on the job (i.e., radiation of VDT's), newspaper ownership changes. Salary data is published for job groups, for example, library positions at "guild" newspapers.

1843

Historical Journal of Film, Radio and Television. International Association for Audio-Visual Media in Historical Research and Education. Available: Carfax Publishing Co., Abingdon, Oxfordshire, England, three issues per year. (1980–.)

The journal has had a recent increase in the submission of high quality papers and a gain in subscriptions. The focus of the content is the historical study and teaching of film and to a lesser extent television and radio.

1844

Human Communication Research. Austin, TX: International Communication Association, quarterly. (1975–.)

Human Communication Research was founded by the International Communication Association. The papers in the first issue of the journal help to define the editorial boundaries. The articles are about the personal act of communicating, the development of language, and the social nuances of human communication. In more recent issues, human communication with the mass media is explored.

1845

Information Economics and Policy. The Netherlands: Elsevier Science Publishers, quarterly. (1983–.)

Most contributors to this journal are based in academic departments of economics and are interested in the international economic patterns of information. Information is frequently delivered via mass media systems and that is where the two areas of study converge. An example of a mass communications topic is an article by three Australian economists, "The Impact of Economic Cycles on the Demand for International Telecommunications in Australia," (Vol. 2, No. 2, June 1986).

1846

Intermedia. London: International Institute of Communications, bimonthly. (1973–.)

Issue after issue of **Intermedia** explores the impact of communications technology on mass media in particular and broadly on national and continental societies. The tone of the journal is humanistic, and the articles are presented from a broad viewpoint, although the subject of the article may be specific, for example, a measure of international communication by comparing AT&T long distance usage units. Bibliography receives regular attention, and the major papers of the annual meeting of the International Institute of Communications are usually summarized.

1847

IPI Report. London: International Press Institute, monthly. (1952–.)

News of government restrictions on press freedom (print and broadcast media) is reported in this monthly magazine. The reports are most often about specific problems, such as censorship in Sri Lanka, journalists' arrests in South Africa, and Nicaraguan editors in exile in Costa Rica. Formal protests to heads of government filed by the IPI's director are reprinted regularly. The general financial health of the world news media is also reported. Short items about trade union negotiations, folding newspapers, and newspaper property sales are presented.

1848

IRE Journal. Columbia, MO: Investigative Reporters & Editors, Inc., quarterly. (1978–.)

This journal is about the affairs of the Investigative Reporters & Editors, Inc. It contains news about members and articles by members about doing the job of investigative journalism—how to get the story, hot topics, dynamics of team reporting projects. It is published on newsprint, tabloid style, and as newsprint is self-destructive it is doomed to a limited shelf life in research libraries.

1849

Journal of Advertising Research. New York: Advertising Research Foundation, bimonthly. (1960–.)

Intended for practitioners and users of advertising research, this journal solicits reports of research findings and research measurement tools. Among the currently published topics of advertising research are the reliability of the people meters used for broadcast audience research, advertising strategies of multinational corporations, behavior of VCR owners, and a gender analysis of readership of newspaper advertisements. In the 28 years of the life of the journal, it has greatly influenced the direction and the standards of advertising research.

1850

Journal of Broadcasting and Electronic Media. Washington, DC: Broadcast Education Association, quarterly. (1956/57–.)

A primary journal for full research articles, brief research reports and reviews of scholarly books about the traditional broadcasting media and the newer electronic ones. The study of television dominates the journal's content. Formerly called **Journal of Broadcasting.** A special index, **Journal of Broadcasting Author & Topic Index to Volume 1 through 25 (Winter 1956/57 through Fall 1981**, was issued by the Broadcast Education Association in 1982. This index updated an earlier index published in 1972, covering Volumes 1–15.

1851

Journal of Communication. Fair Lawn, NJ: Oxford University Press, quarterly. (1951–.)

An essential journal in the study of communication,

Journal of Communication publishes research and review articles on the full range of topics under the communication umbrella; a few examples are linguistics, UNESCO communication policies, effects of television on children, oral traditions, public relations for developing countries, international and technology-based communication systems. It is widely indexed by the standard services, including **Psychological Abstracts, Social Sciences Index**, and **Historical Abstracts**. The "Intercom" section is useful for bibliographers as it describes conference and research reports otherwise easily missed. Nicely edited, designed and printed, the journal is part of a membership package in the International Communication Association.

1852

Journal of Communication Inquiry. Iowa City: Iowa Center for Communication Study, School of Journalism and Mass Communication, University of Iowa, biannual. (1974–.)

The journal has maintained its editorial policy to publish articles taking the broad cultural and historical view of communication, not limited to mass communication or mass media. The articles are intellectual and interdisciplinary. Recent issues have been devoted to single themes, for example, music television as a popular culture form of communication.

1853

Journal of Mass Media Ethics. Provo, UT: Department of Communications, Brigham Young University, two issues per year. (1985/86–.)

The journal's editorial purpose represents an area of strong current interest among journalism educators, the study of the ethical standards and practices of the mass media institutions and the standard-bearers.

1854

Journal of Popular Culture. Bowling Green, OH: Popular Culture Association, quarterly. (1967–.)

The institutional support for this journal is complicated. It is the official publication of the Popular Culture Association, the Popular Literature Section of the Modern Language Association of America, and the Popular Culture Section of the Midwest Modern Language Association. A scholarly and eclectic journal, recent issues are devoted to communication, culture and development in Latin America. This issue was "double"—all the articles in English and all also in Spanish. Several of the dozen articles are mass media studies, for example, a gatekeeper study about news from South America and a report about radio programming in Columbia. In addition to media studies, the journal publishes scholarly comment on advertising, humor, popular fiction, comics, art, and music. It is widely indexed, including the **Humanities Index** and the **Arts and Humanities Citation Index**.

1855

Journal of Popular Film & Television. Washington, DC: Heldref Publications, a division of Helen Dwight Reed Educational Foundation, quarterly. (1971–.)

Former title: **Journal of Popular Film**. The journal is edited at the Popular Culture Center at Bowling Green State University in Ohio. Its editorial emphasis is on commercial film and television. The scholarly articles range from historical studies of television series and film genre to broader thematic analyses, such as creativity in TV production companies. The journal is well illustrated with black and white stills from film and television.

1856

Journalism Educator. Columbia, SC: Association for Education in Journalism and Mass Communication, University of South Carolina, quarterly. (1945–.)

The main purpose of the journal is to provide a forum for ideas about teaching journalism. A regular feature of interest is the listing of new faculty appointments, promotions, leaves, retirements and deaths. One of the annual features is the presentation of unique enrollment data from a national survey of journalism and mass communication programs in U.S. colleges and universities. The data have been collected annually for more than 15 years. Other annual features include the publication of official business of the Association for Education in Journalism and Mass Communication (AEJMC) the financial statement and a report of the annual convention. AEJMC does not publish convention proceedings, however, the refereed papers given at the annual meeting are accepted by the ERIC system and can be located through the ERIC indexes (No. 1938).

1857

Journalism History. Northridge, CA: Journalism Department, California State University, quarterly. (1974–.)

Journalism History publishes articles, both research and essays, about the "full range of the historical development of American media. . . ." (Vol. 1, No. 1). Among the early volumes is a two-part, lengthy bibliography about women and outstanding individual women in the history of the American press. The James Carey essay, "The Problem of Journalism History," which was published in the inaugural issue, was revisited in Vol. 12, (Summer 1985).

1858

Journalism Monographs. Columbia, SC: Association for Education in Journalism and Mass Communication, University of South Carolina, four issues per year, varies. (1966–.)

For more than 20 years, **Journalism Monographs** has issued these lengthy reports of scholarship that are "longer than those normally accepted by quarterly journals..." Bruce Westley, founding editor, 1966. The series provides an important publishing forum for work that falls between the journal article and the book. Many of the titles are historical analyses of journalistic and scholarly trends.

1859

Journalism Quarterly. Columbia, SC: Association for Education in Journalism and Mass Communication, University of South Carolina, quarterly. (1924–.)

The oldest of the scholarly journals devoted to the study of journalism, **Journalism Quarterly** publishes refereed research articles and brief reports of research projects. Several cumulative indexes to the journal have been issued: **Volumes 1–40, 1924–63; Volumes 41–50, 1964–73;** and **Volumes 51–60, 1974–83.** In recent years, the annual index is published in the first issue of the next-published volume.

1860

Mass Comm Review. Philadelphia: Mass Communications and Society Division, Association for Education in Journalism and Mass Communication. Available: Department of Journalism, School of Communication and Theater, Temple University, three issues per year. (1973–.)

Mass Comm Review publishes a wide spectrum of essays and research articles about the mass media. The journal reflects a high quality of academic research and thought. Under new editor Diana Tillinghast, the journal has published a cluster of articles under a broad research theme, for example, political campaigns. Although the journal continues to be a refereed publication, it is also publishing invited essays.

1861

Masthead. Rockville, MD: National Conference of Editorial Writers, quarterly. (1948–.)

A lively trade journal, **The Masthead** reports the affairs and opinions of the members of the National Conference of Editorial Writers. It mixes practical articles on how to do the job of producing an editorial page in the newspaper, surveys of newspaper editorial stances on national issues, and features on particular editorial writers and cartoonists. Informal reports of annual conventions are included.

1862

Media Asia. Singapore: Asian Mass Communication Research and Information Centre, quarterly. (1974–.)

The journal has remained steadfast to its editorial purpose, as well as its graphics and format, since the first issue in 1974, which published an open letter from Wilbur Schramm, then Director of the East-West Communication Institute in Hawaii, calling for application of social research to communication problems in developing countries. The journal publishes a variety of articles about communication problems in Asian developing countries. The book review section and the AMIC Documentation List section provide continuous bibliographic and descriptive information about unique publications.

1863

Media and Values: A Quarterly Resource for Media Awareness. Los Angeles, CA: Media Action Research Center, quarterly. (1977–.)

This small publication is sponsored by a confederation of religious denominations and national organizations and offers resource material to stimulate criticism of the overarching values represented by the mass media. Each issue is centered on a theme, for example, advertising, rock music, access to media, sports. High school and college level students will find it useful for essays about the mass media.

1864

Media, Culture and Society. London: Sage Publications, quarterly. (1979–.)

A cosmopolitan, scholarly journal, publishing research and essays about cultural aspects of national mass media and media content. Examples of recently published articles include those about political communication in Northern Ireland, the composition of crime news, the operation of the Australian Press Council, and Mexican television news. The journal is edited in England by Richard Collins, James Curran, Nicholas Garnham, Paddy Scannell, Philip Schlesinger, and Colin Sparks. Although most of the corresponding editors are based in Europe, India, Mexico, Canada and the U.S. are also represented. The U.S. corresponding editors are Herbert Schiller and Dan Schiller.

1865

Media Development. London: World Association for Christian Communication, quarterly. (1970–.)

Media Development presents a definite viewpoint about one of the broadest subfields in mass communications, that is the area of international communications which embraces the study of the international flow of news and entertainment as well as national communication policies and practices. The editorial policy of the journal is to publish information and commentary about the human values which are reflected in mass media content and how the media affect values held by their audiences. The journal is open to an international roster of contributors, including church professionals and secular university professors and journalists. Recent issues have been devoted to communication about political change in the Philippines, grassroots communication development, and the mass media in China.

1866

Media Institute Forum. Washington, DC: The Media Institute, quarterly. (1984–.)

A newsletter in form but not in content, **Media Institute Forum** publishes lengthy commentary and opinion about current problems in the mass media industry rather than short news items printed in most publications using an eight-page format. Each of the six issues per year focuses on a single topic—changes in the monolith of network television news—is a recent example. The contributors are usually executives from media organizations. Formerly called the **Business-Economic News Report**.

1867

Media Law Reporter. Washington, DC: Bureau of National Affairs, weekly. (1977–.)

Media Law Reporter is the most useful guide to legal decisions relevant to mass communications law in the United States. The weekly issues provide full-text of all U.S. Supreme Court decisions and selected federal and state court decisions and administrative agency decisions. Annual volumes compile the weekly issues. The material is extensively indexed. The Topic Index is a subject analysis which leads to the Classification Guide. The Classification Guide provides a detailed outline of the Index Digest, where the decisions are annotated on their legal and factual points. The Index Digest is also an index to the full-text presentation of the decisions.

1868

Media Report to Women. Washington, DC: Women's Institute for Freedom of the Press, bimonthly. (1972–.)

This newsletter plays a special watchdog role on the problems encountered by women working in the mass media and in academic journalism and mass communication programs in the United States and, with less frequency, in foreign countries. Employment for women is a strong theme of the newsletter, and to this end, it regularly publishes notices of open positions in academe and statistics on the employment of women in the media.

1869

Multichannel News. Denver, CO: Fairchild Publications, weekly. (1980–.)

Subtitle: **The Newspaper for the New Electronic Media**. A tabloid news report of the cable industry plus a scattering of brief items about network television and large multi-media companies, Time, Inc. for example.

1870

News Media and the Law. Washington, DC: The Reporters Committee for Freedom of the Press, quarterly. (1977–.)

The magazine reports the practical effects of legal controversies involving the U.S. media. Accounts of journalists jailed to protect the identities of news sources, incidents of prior restraint, and guidelines for journalists challenged on their right to report are examples of the articles published in this journal. Written for working journalists—reporters and editors—it is a fruitful source of information about state laws on confidentiality of sources and Public policy and mass media laws.

1871

News Photographer. Durham, NC: National Press Photographers Association, monthly. (1946–.)

The photographs in this professional journal enliven each issue, and the older issues are immediately interesting because of the photographs. For information about contests on news photography, reproductions of the winning photographs, and background on the winning photographers, this is the source. Over the long span of years the journal has been publishing, the changes in the profession are well documented in **News Photographer**. The influx of women in the profession and the modern use of color in photographs are two important changes. The special directory, published in the spring, includes an alphabetical list of the membership of the National Press Photographers Association with the members' mailing addresses. The section on competitions gives a list of all the recipients of the awards for picture of the year, military photographers of the year, picture editing quarterly contest, college photographers of the year, Pulitzer prizes, etc. News photographers' codes of ethics are part of this annual directory.

1872

Newspaper Research Journal. Newspaper Division of the Association for Education in Journalism and Mass Communication. Available: Journalism Department, Memphis State University, Memphis, TN, quarterly. (1979–.)

Each quarterly issue of this relatively new journal publishes eight or so research articles about newspaper problems and a few short book reviews. A sample of the research reported in recent volumes yields articles about newspaper management styles, newsroom computerization, reporting state government, reader perception of changes in newspaper design, and newspaper carrier turnover. The content of **Newspaper Research Journal** is similar to an earlier series of the **News Research Report**, published from April 8, 1977 to December 30, 1983, by the American Newspaper Publishers Association.

1873

Nieman Reports. Cambridge, MA: Nieman Foundation, Harvard University, quarterly. (1947–.)

A journal of essays, addresses, news, and book reviews about public affairs journalism. The writers are members of an elite group of journalists, the Nieman Fellows of Harvard University, a program dating back to 1937. In this journal the fellows speak provocatively about prevalent journalism issues. Occasionally space in the journal is given to alumni news and reunions.

1874

Political Communication and Persuasion. New York: Crane, Russak & Co., Inc., quarterly. (1980–.)

This small academic journal is widely abstracted and indexed in the standard social sciences services, **Communication Abstracts**, being among them. The subtitle, **An International Journal**, is descriptive of the range of subjects considered by this journal. Rhetorical analyses of the content of the mass media—often the television news programs—describe communication of military and political events, environmental issues, and cultural values.

1875

Political Communication Review. Norman, OK: Department of Communication, University of Oklahoma, quarterly. (1975–.)

A quarterly publication of the Political Communication Division of the International Communication Association co-edited by Keith R. Sanders and Lynda Lee Kaid. Recent volumes have published research articles and essays about political campaigns, television networks and access issues, and political debates. Book reviews and a strong bibliographic section are regular features. The journal has an irregular publishing history; beginning with Volume 4, 1979, it has been published as a single-issue annual. In the early volumes several issues of the "quarterly" were not published (Vol. 1, No. 4; Vol. 2, Nos. 3–4; Vol. 3, Nos. 3–4).

1876

Press Woman. Blue Springs, MO: National Federation of Press Women, Inc., monthly. (1937–.)

Written for professional women working in mass media positions, this magazine cogently surveys the workplace to present practical information. Discrimination in the newsroom, how to negotiate, jobs in the next century, salary surveys are examples of the articles in this well-edited journal. Convention information for the National Federation of Press Women is published regularly. Formerly called **PW: Press Woman**.

1877

Presstime. Reston, VA: American Newspaper Publishers Association, monthly. (1979–.)

Presstime was established to consolidate nine separate ANPA publications published in staid, newsletter style. **Presstime** is slick and sparkles with color graphics, photographs, clean layout, and a variety of articles, all aimed to get the attention of busy newspaper executives. The articles in **Presstime** are broader than those in **Editor & Publisher** (No. 1831), which is a weekly trade journal; both journals cover the newspaper business. **Publisher's Auxiliary** (No. 1885), a biweekly publication, covers the industry from the point of view of the community, weekly press.

1878

PRO/COMM: The Professional Communicator. Austin, TX: Women in Communications, Inc., bimonthly. (1915–.)

In a profession which now employs more females than males, professional magazines for women in the communications industry provide a bulletin board about current issues and happenings and about the persons involved. Historically, these professional journals present a sociological pattern of female employment in the journalism and promotional communications fields. See also **Press Woman** (No. 1876).

1879

Public Opinion. Washington, DC: American Enterprise Institute for Public Policy Research, bimonthly. (1978–.)

A journal of essays and reports of research for the lay reader, **Public Opinion** organizes its publication around large themes for each bimonthly issue. Recent themes have been ethnicity, the efficacy of the media, Presidential elections, and ethics among common professional groups (clergy, doctors, journalists). Each issue features graphic summaries of the results of opinion polling about the issue's particular theme.

1880

Public Opinion Quarterly. American Association for Public Opinion Research. Available: Elsevier Science Publishing Co., Inc., New York, quarterly. (1937–.)

A widely read academic journal, **Public Opinion Quarterly** is central for scholars interested in opinion polling, how public attitudes are formed, and refinements of the research methods. The proceedings of the annual conferences of the American Association for Public Opinion Research and the World Association for Public Opinion Research are published here, including the presidential address, a brief description of the conference program and a report of the business meeting.

1881

Public Relations. Harlow, Essex, England: Longman Group Ltd. with the Institute of Public Relations, quarterly. (1982–.)

A professional public relations journal from the British viewpoint, **Public Relations** publishes case studies, essays and research about the problems, procedures and results of public relations efforts. Public communication about AIDS and nuclear power are examples of recently published research and critical review articles.

1882

Public Relations Journal. New York: Public Relations Society of America, monthly. (1945–.)

A slick trade journal, **Public Relations Journal** publishes articles about industry trends and bulletin board information about workshops and personnel news. For the last 15 years, an annual survey of corporate advertising expenditures is published in the November or December issue. The expenditure information specifies the dollar figures for expenditures by mass medium and by the names of the top ten corporate advertisers. The information is given in greater detail and depth in **Advertising Age** (No. 1806) special sections.

1883

Public Relations Quarterly. New York: Public Relations Quarterly, quarterly. (1955–.)

Historical research, critical essays, reports and reviews of public relations campaigns, summaries of the professional literature, and discussions of the latest trade tools, such as office computerization and video communication, create an interesting mix of information published in this attractive quarterly. The authors are either practitioners or educators or both. Edward L. Bernays, an early proponent of public relations education and research, is listed among the contributing editors.

1884

Public Relations Review: A Journal of Research and Comment. Silver Springs, MD: Foundation for Public Relations Research and Education, quarterly. (1975–.)

The fourth issue of the first volume of **Public Relations Review** (1975–76) is a 200-paged comprehensive bibliography of "Articles and Books on Public Relations, Communication Theory, Public Opinion, and Propaganda, 1973–74" by Robert L. Bishop. The bibliography is organized by subject and updates earlier bibliographies by Scott Cutlip (No. 1646), which were revised in a "third edition," **Public Relations Comprehensive Bibliography, 1964–72** by Bishop (No. 1638). Brief descriptions of the article or book are often provided in the **Public Relations Review** bibliography. Albert Walker has continued to compile this annual bibliography since 1976, and it is now in the 14th edition (Vol. 12, No. 4, Winter 1986). In addition to this useful bibliographic series, the journal publishes the research and comments of both academics and practitioners.

1885

Publisher's Auxiliary. Washington, DC: National Newspaper Association, biweekly. (1865–.)

Although the content of **Publishers' Auxiliary** is similar to that of the weekly **Editor & Publisher** (No. 1831)—both report on the newspaper business—**PA** publishes more news about the weekly, community press.

1886

Publishers Weekly. Riverton, NJ: Bowker Magazine Group, weekly. (1872–.)

Publishers Weekly reports the book publishing industry. It is useful for statistics, information about legal issues, technological changes in publishing, and marketing plans. The forecasts of non-fiction are used for selecting "trade" books of interest to mass communication scholars.

1887

Quill. Chicago, IL: The Society of Professional Journalists, Sigma Delta Chi, monthly. (1912–.)

The **Quill** stirs the ever present mix of controversies about news reporting in a democratic society with a free press. Articles about banning tobacco advertising in newspapers, the biases that constrict female sports reporters and broadcasters, the ethics of and practical tips for using anonymous sources are recent examples of its editorial coverage.

1888

Righting Words. New York: Righting Words Corp., bimonthly. (1987–.)

The subtitle is **The Journal of Language and Editing**. The founding editor, Jonathan S. Kaufman, and the founding publisher, Don R. Hecker, write in a preface to the inaugural issue that the journal is for persons interested in modern usage of the English (American) language and, in particular, for copy editors, who do not otherwise have a professional journal. Rudolf Flesch, known for Flesch Readability Formula, wrote the lead article, "If you can't be careful, be good." He died in October 1986 before the first issue of the journal was published. Also included in this issue is a report of a national survey of newspaper copy editors concerning salaries and job satisfaction.

1889

RTNDA Communicator. Washington, DC: Radio Television News Directors Association, monthly. (1946–.)

The official organ of an association of radio and television news directors, the **RTNDA Communicator** regularly publishes information of interest beyond the association's membership. One example is Vernon Stone's annual survey on salaries and employment in the news departments of U.S. radio and television stations which provide unique data and are usually published in the February or March issue. Another example is the membership directory in the January issue. Discussions of ethical questions arising on the job and larger criticisms of the broadcast media, such as these given in a recent reprinting of Ed Murrow's 1958 speech to the association, are other articles of interest to readers outside the membership.

1890

Scripps-Howard News. Cincinnati, OH: Scripps Howard Corp., 10 issues per year. (1948–.)

As the corporate publication for Scripps Howard, the **Scripps Howard News** chronicles the business, personnel, and philanthropic news of the organization. It is an excellent source of directory information about the corporation. For example, the "Answerbook 1987," inserted in the January-February issue, gives information about newspapers, broadcasting cable, foundations and service companies owned by Scripps Howard.

1891

Southwestern Mass Communication Journal. San Antonio, TX: Southwest Education Council for Journalism and Mass Communications, Department of Communication, Trinity University, semiannual. (1985–.)

The journal is published by a regional journalism educational organization, but the contents of the two issues of the first volume address topics of wide interest in the study of mass communication. The contents of the first volume and the three prototypes (1982, 1983, and 1984) are based on scholarly papers given at the annual symposia of the Southwest Education Council of Journalism and Mass Communication.

1892

Spectra. Annandale, VA: Speech Communication Association, monthly except July. (1964–.)

Subtitle: **To Promote Study, Criticism, Research, Teaching, and Applications of the Principles of Communication**. A newsletter of the Speech Communication Association, **Spectra** reports on convention business, personnel changes in the leadership of the organization, academic appointments, awards, leaves, changes in title, and positions open.

1893

St. Louis Journalism Review. St. Louis, MO: St. Louis Journalism Review, monthly. (1970–.)

Subtitle: **A Critique of Metropolitan News Media**. Until 1986 the **St. Louis Journalism Review** had competing daily newspapers to criticize. When the **St. Louis Globe-Democrat** folded in 1986, the city was left with the **St. Louis Post-Dispatch**, a newspaper legacy begun by Joseph Pulitzer in 1878. The **St. Louis Journalism Review** also surveys the city's broadcast media. The review has performed its media surveillance with enthusiasm and savvy. In 1974 the **Review** published excerpts from documents submitted to the FCC when the FCC denied licenses to local radio and television stations. The tabloid **Review** is published on newsprint.

1894

Target: The Political Cartoon Quarterly. Wayne, PA: R. S. West and K. B. Mattern, Jr., quarterly. (1981–1987.)

During its short publishing life, the journal promoted, reviewed, reprinted, criticized and reveled in political cartoons. The U.S. and Great Britain were the main geographical areas of interest.

Bull's Eye: The Magazine of Editorial Cartooning, a new publication endorsed by the editors of the defunct **Target**, began publishing on an erratic basis in 1988. Its aim is to present the best of political cartooning in the U.S.

1895

Telecommunications Policy. Sussex, England: Butterworth Scientific Ltd., quarterly. (1977–.)

The journal discusses the policy implications of the technological and international changes in telecommunications. The articles in a recent issue illustrate the tension between technological changes and national communications policy. Topics discussed are: conducting foreign policy via telecommunications; telecommunication systems in France and Great Britain; the growth factor of the information sector in developing countries; and an argument against the industry position that long distance telephone service subsidizes local service.

1896

Telematics and Informatics: An Information Journal. Elmsford, NY: Pergamon Journals, Inc., quarterly. (1984–.)

Telematics represents the merger of telecommunications and computers; informatics means data processing. The two concepts are converging, and hence, a new journal, designed to reach allies in academia, government and business. The articles report about the issues involved in the broad topic of technology and communication and the transfer of information. Specifically, the articles discuss national and international communication policies, costs and market segmentation of national and private communication systems, equipment and software.

1897

Television and Families. Princeton, NJ: National Council for Families and Television, quarterly. (1978–.)

Formerly called **Television & Children**, the journal title was altered in 1985 to recognize the context of the family in the relationships between television and the audience of children and adolescents. The journal is a forum for discussions of television programming and its effects on the pre-adult audience by television writers, educators, and researchers.

1898

Television Broadcast. Overland Park, KS: Globecom Publishing Ltd., monthly. (1978–.)

This trade journal appears to be dedicated to the promotion of new equipment in telecommunications. Describing the unfolding of technology in the broadcast industry is a breathless and serious experience—breathless because of the quick pace of the development of new equipment and serious because of the financial investment involved. The journal provides limited guidance about quality and industry standards.

1899

Television Digest with Consumer Electronics. Washington, DC: Television Digest Inc., weekly. (1945–.)

A newsletter covering the broadcasting industry and consumer electronics. The weekly publication provides statistical data and other details gathered from its base in Washington, by reporting on national legislation and regulation and the interaction between government and industry. In-depth reports on the FCC and special reports about the television, radio and cable industries are issued regularly. It is the publication to check for full-text reports of FCC decisions and significant speeches by officials in government and business. Indexed in **INFOTRAC**. (See No. 1927.)

1900

Television Quarterly. New York: National Academy of Television Arts and Sciences, quarterly. (1962–.)

Television Quarterly, the journal of the National Academy of Television Arts and Sciences, is an interesting collection of essays and reviews, and its contents are difficult to categorize or to predict. The general subject of the journal is television program content, and it reviews television programming trends in Chicago as well as Moscow; broadcasting museums; academic journal articles; television programs and series; contributions of outstanding individuals; and books.

1901

Television/Radio Age. New York: Television Editorial Corp., biweekly. (1953–.)

A magazine for broadcasting executives, **Television/Radio Age** has been reporting the industry for more than 30 years. **Television/Radio Age** concentrates on the broadcast advertising business and summarizes recent developments in the larger broadcast industry, as reports, for example, the FCC report, Wall Street report, cable report, spot advertising reports, and so forth. In recent years, the magazine has closely recorded the growth of the cable industry to the extent of producing an occasional special section called "Cable Age." The convention of the National Association of Television Program Executives is reported in detail. Indexed in **Business Periodicals Index**.

1902

Third Channel: IBS Journal of International Communication. Seoul, Korea: International Broadcasting Society, biannual. (1985–.)

A journal of research and commentary, **Third Channel** publishes studies of issues and problems relating to broadcasting in the Third World and, therefore, internationally. The articles are solicited by a general notice about the theme of the forthcoming issue. The Third World broadcast audience and the social status and influence of Third World broadcasters are two examples of themes. The contributors represent the international world of communication scholars.

1903

TV World. London: Alain-Charles Publishing Ltd., monthly. (1977–.)

Subtitle: **International Business Magazine for Television and Video**. The intended readers are persons in management in television broadcasting and video production and distribution. The distinctions between film and video and between theater box office and television sales are blurring, and this trade journal illustrates the convergence of the two media and the two distribution vehicles. **TV World** features news about changes in national television broadcast policy, about entrepreneurs in production and distribution, and about sales of the entertainment programs, which includes sports. While names and production specifics are published by the journal, statistics about international sales of programs are not found here. International audience ratings are provided.

1904

Typographical Journal. Colorado Springs, CO: International Typographical Union, monthly. (1889–.)

The **Typographical Journal** is the official paper of the International Typographical Union, and for many years carried that description as the subtitle. It has faithfully reported in detail the business of the union since 1889. For example, the names of the delegates and the alternates to the annual convention, representing each of the 600 local unions are printed by order of the number and place of the local, i.e., No. 1, Indianapolis. The financial reports, national and local unions, are recorded. Officers' reports and opinions are given regularly.

1905

Variety. New York: Variety, Inc., weekly. (1905–.)

A weekly newspaper, **Variety** covers the national and international news of the entertainment industry, emphasizing the big three, film, television, and music. The entertainment elements of the industry, content, writers, producers, artists, are the central story. The economic barometers of the industry are also recorded in detail because they sustain the writers, actors, musicians, promoters, agents, lawyers and the many others. The January "Show Business" annual illustrates **Variety's** rich storehouse of information, including lists of ranking rental films of the previous year (a measure of box office sales), Academy Award nominees and winners, the many film awards in festivals at Berlin, Cannes, Venice, etc., and indexes to **Variety's** reviews of films, television programs, music releases, circuses, ice shows, and on-and-off Broadway theater. Convention news of related associations such as the National Association of Television Program Executives is published here. Related journals include **View** (No. 1907), **Electronic Media** (No. 1832), **Television/Radio Age** (No. 1901), and **Channels** (No. 1820).

A publication easily confused with the weekly **Variety** is the **Daily Variety** published in Hollywood, California. The **Daily Variety** is a tabloid newspaper, issued daily Monday through Friday, covering the entertainment business worldwide.

1906

Videography. New York: Media Horizons, Inc., monthly. (1976–.)

A trade magazine covering the news of the video production industry, **Videography** focuses on the creative aspects, including the process, the equipment, and the people. Computer graphics and animation and quality sound equipment are topics of current emphasis. Annual features include an equipment directory in the fall, a production facilities directory in December, and a who's who of the people involved in production in January. In the special section on the creative persons in videography, the blending of the film and television production industries is underscored as the producers create for both media.

1907

View: The Magazine of Television Programming. New York: View, 21 times a year. (1980–.)

This trade journal publishes an annual profile of the "top" 25 persons in television programming and related areas. (In 1986, the profiles were published in an October issue.) These articles provide background information about persons rarely included in the standard reference directories.

1908

Washington Journalism Review. Washington, DC: College of Journalism, University of Maryland, monthly. (1977–.)

A review of American journalism with emphasis on national and international political reporting, **WJR** also includes articles about the news media industry and short items about individual editors and journalists. The national coverage of this journal is similar to that of the **Columbia Journalism Review** (No. 1821).

1909

Witty World: International Cartoon Magazine. North Wales, PA: Witty World Publications, quarterly. (1987–.)

A new professional magazine for the international business of comic and cartoon art. Industry information about syndicates, techniques, equipment, materials, meetings, publications, and exhibitions as well as features about the art and the artists is given.

1910

World Press Review. New York: The Stanley Foundation, monthly. (1961–.)

An anthology of material published by the press outside the U.S., **World Press Review** is intended "to foster international information exchange." All articles are published in English translations. The journal is *not* a critical review of the world press. It is an excellent source of cartoons from the press abroad.

Indexes to Mass Communication Literature

9

This list of indexes to the literature of mass communication reflects the variety of sources about the field, extending over publications about general analyses of the mass media, the business and technology of media, and the academic and theoretical approaches. There are also indexes to the content of the mass media. Those commonly known are for newspapers and magazines, such as the **New York Times Index** and **Readers' Guide**. Printed indexes to content of the broadcast media and of the alternative press are also available.

A new approach to the massive content of the mass media is provided through computer-held files of the "full-*text*" of newspapers, broadcast programs, news service copy, legal and government reports, journals, newsletters, dictionaries and encyclopedia. These files can be approached without using the prescribed subject headings of the traditional printed indexes. This means that the content of the **New York Times** can be accessed by a computer search on words or phrases, specified by the researcher, which may be found any place in the text of the publication. The full-text computer-based services as well as the CD-ROM computer products, which can be a repackaging of the traditional printed indexes, are described in this section.

1911

ABC News Index. Woodbridge, CT: Research Publications, quarterly with annual cumulations. (1969–1986—.)

Complete transcripts of ABC daily news and public affairs programs are issued on microfiche and are indexed by a quarterly, printed publication. The news programs included are: **Business World, Closeup, This Week with David Brinkley, The Health Show, Nightline, ABC News Specials, 20/20, Viewpoint, The Weekend Report, World News Saturday and Sunday**, and **World News Tonight**. The subject index uses indexing terms adapted from the Library of Congress Subject Headings and provides a brief abstract of the news report as well as the location of the program transcript in the microfiche files. The backfiles of the index and the transcripts are available for the years 1969–1986. The regular publication of the index and transcripts began with the year 1987. At this time, the **ABC News Index** is decidedly more current than its sister publication, the **CBS News Index**. **ABC News Index**

publishes about four to six months after the broadcast date, i.e. index for April-June is issued in October.

1912

Abstracts of Popular Culture. Bowling Green, OH: Bowling Green University Popular Press, quarterly. (1976–1982.)

This interesting index has ceased publication. For the period it covers, it is useful for periodical literature and unpublished conference papers about American culture and mass media. The topics are indexed under broad terms such as film, TV, sports, music, and comics. The abstracts are not topically organized in the publication, and because the subject headings are broad and cite only accession numbers of the abstracts, the index can be discouraging to use if the selected subject has many abstract numbers assigned to it.

1913

Alternative Press Index. Baltimore, MD: Alternative Press Center, Inc., quarterly. (1969–.)

Publishing about four months behind the indexing date, this service provides a unique access to periodical literature on subcultures and mass media (blacks, gays/ lesbians, feminists, ethnic groups, religious alternatives, environmental groups, and political activists). Indexes about 240 alternative and radical publications, including international and foreign language publications, by subject and proper names. Covers articles, columns, editorials, reviews of books, films, television programs, plays, poetry and music, and bibliographies and other lists.

1914

Broadcasting Index. Washington, DC: Broadcasting Publications, Inc., annual. (1972–1981.)

Now historical, this highly specific index to **Broadcasting** (No. 1813) magazine, the weekly chronicle of the industry, is no longer published in hardcover book format. The publisher is offering the annual index as a computer printout, unbound (not seen). The entire content of the magazine is included, among them personnel items and license renewals. The articles are briefly abstracted, with entries for personal and organization names included. For example, an article about a FCC decision is indexed in four (or more) ways—the legal issues, the call letters of the station involved, the station owner's name, and the FCC. The **Business Periodicals Index** (No. 1915), **Infotrac** (No. 1927) and **Topicator** (No. 1944) also index **Broadcasting** magazine.

1915

Business Periodicals Index. New York: Wilson, monthly with annual cumulations. (1958–.)

The standard index to the business periodical literature in the English language, formerly published as the **Industrial Arts Index** (1913–1957). General areas of emphasis important to mass communication are advertising, communications, printing and publishing, and public relations. As many as 18 periodicals indexed by **Business Periodicals Index** are primary journals in these areas. Especially useful for accessing the voluminous information in three key trade journals, all published on a weekly schedule, **Advertising Age**, **Broadcasting**, and **Editor and Publisher**. The subject index includes entries for specific companies and persons (i.e., Orion Pictures, Gannett, Cable News Network, Rupert Murdoch, Allen Neuharth) and such topics as "Motion picture industry," "Newspapers," "Public relations," "Public television," "Telecommunication," and "Television broadcasting." **Business Periodicals Index** is also available as an online computer database in **Wilsearch**, beginning June 1982 and continuing to present. See **Wilsearch** (No. 1947).

1916

CBS News Index. Ann Arbor, MI: University Microfilms International, quarterly with annual cumulations. (1975–.)

A printed index to the four daily news broadcasts and other public affairs programs on the Columbia Broadcasting Service network. Public affairs programs include presidential press conferences and speeches, **Face the Nation**, and **60 Minutes**. A descriptive phrase is assigned to each news item to provide the main thrust of the story. The transcripts of the news are published on microfiche. If the visual portion of the news is also needed, video cassettes of the CBS news are available from the National Archive or may be borrowed from the Vanderbilt Television News Archive (evening news only). At this time, there is a time delay in the index of 18 months which is expected to be temporary.

1917

Communication Abstracts. Newbury Park, CA: Sage Publications, Inc., quarterly. (1978–.)

The best abstracting service in the communications field, **Communication Abstracts** covers the scholarly literature in over 250 journals. The abstracting of journal articles is selective and therefore does not necessarily abstract all articles from any one journal. About 25 abstracts per quarterly issue are devoted to books and book chapters, when the book has discrete chapters by different authors. The subject emphasis is communication, broadly interpreted to include also small group, organizational, and inter/intrapersonal communication, as well as mass media studies. The coverage has been expanded in the areas of new communication technologies and international research.

1918

Current Index to Journals in Education. Phoenix, AZ: Oryx Press, monthly with semi-annual and annual cumulated indexes. (1969–.)

The articles in 780 journals are summarized and indexed by the staff at the 16 ERIC clearinghouses in the U.S. with the Reading and Communication Skills and the Social Studies/Social Science Education clearinghouses generating most of the summaries of mass communication and communication articles. This abstracting and indexing service is useful for coverage of the journal literature about the scholastic press/journalism. **Journalism Educator** and **Journalism Quarterly** are frequently cited, and **Journal of Communication**, **Communication Research**, **Journal of Broadcasting & Electronic Media**, and **Public Relations Review** are more selectively indexed. For a description of the same service available as a computer database, see **Resources in Education** (No. 1938).

1919

Facts on File. New York, NY: Facts on File, Inc., weekly with quarterly and annual cumulations of the index. (1940–.)

A summary of the news reported in more than 50 foreign and U.S. newspapers and magazines is published weekly by **Facts on File: the World News Digest with Index**. Government publications, press releases and other documents are used to verify and expand the information gleaned from the news media.

A table of contents identifies the events covered in the weekly digest. A news summary gives the sequence of events, the facts and statistics, the names, companies, organizations, and associations involved, and the historical and geographical context. Much of the information, including the personal and corporate names, is used as entries in the subject index.

The weekly digest includes international news, U.S. news, news of Europe, and "Other World News." The "Miscellaneous" section is of special note as it covers major sporting events, lives and deaths of well-known persons, New York film releases, best selling books and music records and tapes, top-profiting films, and most-watched television programs, a short list which includes the rating points assigned by the A.C. Nielsen Company.

1920

Film Literature Index. Albany, NY: State University of New York at Albany, Film and

Television Documentation Center, quarterly with annual cumulations. (1973–.)

A subject/author index to the international film and television literature appearing in over 300 well-known established film journals and specialized, exotic or fugitive film publications. (Periodicals of purely fan interest, totally technical data and extremely short pieces of release information are excluded.) Articles are indexed under 1,000 subject headings, as well as by names of individual screenwriters, performers, directors, cinematographers, professional societies and corporations. The entries include information about filmography, credits, biographical data or interviews; the entries for film titles and television programs include original language title, original release date, American release titles, director's name, and country of publication. Book reviews appear under both subject and author entries.

The depth of indexing, the fullness of the information in the entries, and the large number of journals indexed make this an important index.

1921

Graphic Arts Abstracts. Pittsburgh, PA: Graphic Arts Technical Foundation, monthly with annual index. (1947–.)

Subtitled: **A Digest of Scientific, Technical and Educational Information for the Graphic Communications Industries**. Each month about 100 articles are abstracted and published under 32 subject categories. Examples of the subject categories are: Advertising and Marketing, Book and Magazine Production, Education and Training, Newspaper Production, Photography, and Typesetting and Typography. The abstracted articles are selected from 96 technical and trade journals, such as **Graphic Arts Monthly**, **Folio**, **Functional Photography**, **Printing Impressions**, **Presstime**, and **Editor & Publisher**. The annual index lists each article by title organized by the 32 subject categories and includes an author index.

1922

Graphic Arts Literature Abstracts. Rochester, NY: Technical and Education Center of the Graphic Arts, Rochester Institute of Technology, monthly with an annual index. (1954–.)

This abstracting service selects articles from "250 domestic and foreign trade publications, scientific and technical journals, annuals, and conference proceedings." The abstracts are organized by ten main sections: Printing and Publishing, Management, Composition, Preparatory Operations, Reproduction Processes, Postpress Operations, Inks and Coatings, Paper and Other Substrates, Science and Technology, and Education. Each monthly issue has a keyword index and an author index. While similar to the **Graphic Arts Abstracts** (No. 1921), the **Graphic Arts Literature Abstracts** survey a larger number of journals and other publications.

1923

Humanities Index. New York: Wilson, quarterly with annual cumulations. (1974–.)

Preceded by the **International Index** (1907–1965) and the **Social Sciences and Humanities Index** (1965–1974), this indexing service focuses on the periodical literature of several areas related to the mass media—history, performing arts, language, and literature—and is a useful tool for almost any literature search about print and broadcast journalism and film studies. Topical subject entries include "Mass Media," "Women and Mass Media," "Media Use," "Journalistic Ethics," and "Television and Politics." Five basic journals—**Columbia Journalism Review**, **Journal of Broadcasting & Electronic Media**, **Journalism History**, **Journalism Quarterly**, **The Quill**—are among the 295 English-language periodicals indexed. As the performing arts is an area covered by the **Humanities Index**, film literature, particularly articles about film genres and film reviews, is also indexed, with the **Quarterly Review of Film Studies** among the journals.

The **Humanities Index** is also available on compact digital disk (CD-ROM), a database beginning with February 1984 and continuing to the present with quarterly updates, and "online" in the **Wilsearch** computer database service, beginning with February 1984 and continuing with regular updates. See **Wilsearch** (No. 1947).

1924

Index to Journalism Periodicals. London, Canada: Graduate School of Journalism, University of Western Ontario, biennially on microfiche. (1986–.)

An index to a broad coverage of mass media trade journals, journalism reviews, and mass communication scholarly journals. The citations are organized under a subject framework, which is direct, uses current language, and is easy to use. The subject entries do not include "see" and "see also" references. The citations include the title of the article, the name of the publication, the volume, the issue number, and the year, but not author's name or authors' names and the pagination of the article.

The strength of the indexing service is the breadth of the coverage of the periodicals. The index does not index all articles published in the periodicals.

1925

Index to Legal Periodicals. New York: Wilson, monthly with three-year cumulations. (1908–.)

This index to 500 legal journals, yearbooks, and annual reviews published in the English language is useful for locating articles on issues of communications law and public policy for broadcasting. Pertinent subjects include copyright, censorship, First Amendment rights of the press, and governmental and legal decisions involving telecommunications.

To locate specific legal decisions and developments in communications, the **Media Law Reporter** (No. 1867) is useful because it indexes and prints the texts of decisions by federal and state courts and selected administrative agencies.

The **Index to Legal Periodicals** is also available as an online service through several companies, Mead Data Central, H.W. Wilson, and West Publishing Co. The online product corresponds to the printed index and covers from 1981 to date, with monthly updates.

1926

The Information Bank Abstracts. Produced by the New York Times Company and vended by the Mead Data Central Inc. as the ABS file of the **NEXIS** online service, daily. (1969–.)

This computer online database contains abstracts of all news and editorial material from the final Late Edition of the **New York Times**, selected news and editorial material from nine other newspapers, including the **Washington Post**, **Christian Science Monitor**, **Los Angeles Times**, **Miami Herald**, and **Chicago Tribune**, and selected news articles from 43 business, scientific, news and trade periodicals published in the U.S. and internationally. The periodicals cover a wide range of interests; among the publications are **Editor & Publisher**, **New Yorker**, **World Press Review**, **Latin American Weekly Report**, and **Economist of London**. The "bank" of current news items is useful as a resource for the most recent information about issues, individuals and organizations. The **New York Times** abstracts are available 24–48 hours after publication in the newspaper. See also, **NEXIS** (No. 1934).

1927

InfoTrac. Belmont, CA: Information Access Company. A four-year database with monthly updates. (1981/84–.)

InfoTrac is a videodisc index, providing access to three databases of citations to periodicals, newsletters, newspapers, 720 legal publications and U.S. government publications. The three are **InfoTrac Database**, **Government Publications Index**, and **LegalTrac Database**, and each yields citations about the mass media. They are accessed through a dedicated microcomputer workstation. First-time users are generally so successful they become repeaters, and **InfoTrac** is for many users the beginning place for any literature search.

The **InfoTrac Database** indexes many periodicals—the list is still growing—about business, management, social sciences, humanities, and the general sciences, also articles in two newspapers, **Wall Street Journal** for the last six months and **New York Times** for the last 60 days. Book and movie reviews are included in the citations. The original database covers the years 1981–1984, with annual and monthly updates. The search strategy defaults to the most recent years and provides the option of repeating the search on the 1981-1984 database. The

database covers the trade and professional journals in broadcasting and advertising; the list is similar to the journals indexed by the **Business Periodicals Index**, only larger. For example, **Folio** is here but not in **BPI**. The publisher has recently announced a list of 235 journal titles to be added to the database. Three on the list, **Columbia Journalism Review**, **Journal of Communication**, and **Journalism Quarterly**, and quite a few film journals, are of much interest.

Government Publications Index is the **Monthly Catalog of U.S. Government Publications**, from 1980 and continuing to the present with monthly updates. Citations to the Federal Communications Commission reports and papers and to Congressional reports and hearings about the mass media are provided with the speed of a "computer search."

LegalTrac Database contains citations to 750 legal publications, including law reviews, bar journals and seven legal newspapers. The database begins in 1980 and continues to the present with monthly updates.

1928

International Index to Film Periodicals: An Annotated Guide. Ed. by Michael Moulds. New York: Bowker, with International Federation of Film Archives, annual. (1972–.)

The 1984 volume indexes articles from approximately 170 periodicals selected worldwide under the headings "General Subjects," "Individual Films," and "Biography." Each entry contains the following information when applicable: author(s); title; name of periodical; volume and issue number; date; page(s); indication of special features such as filmography or statistics; whether article, interview, review, etc.; and a descriptive annotation. The "General Subjects" section is subdivided by topic and where appropriate by country. There are many cross references and indexes both to film directors and authors of articles. For an index to periodicals which predates 1972 see **Retrospective Index to Film Periodicals 1930–1971** (No. 1159).

Journal of Broadcasting Author and Topic Index. (See No. 1850.)

1929

Journalism Abstracts. Columbia, SC: Association for Education in Journalism and Mass Communication, annual. (1963–.)

Abstracts of masters' research theses and doctoral dissertations about mass communication written in graduate programs of cooperating universities in the U.S. and Canada. The abstracts are presented in two sections, dissertations followed by the more numerous theses, in alphabetic order by author. The unique offering here is the publication of the abstracts of master-level research theses. **Journalism Abstracts** is one of the first sources to consult for graduate students in search of ideas for thesis or dissertation proposals. The detailed subject index carries along the terminology used in the last five annuals to alert the users to previously published abstracts. **Dissertation Abstracts** should also be consulted for relevant Ph.D. work from academic departments other than communications.

Journalism Quarterly Cumulative Index. (See No. 1859.)

1930

Linguistics and Language Behavior Abstracts. LaJolla, CA: Sociological Abstracts, Inc., quarterly. (1967–.)

The abstracts provide access to the world's scholarly literature of language behavior and linguistics. Articles from foreign journals not indexed elsewhere, especially German journals, appear in the Communication Sciences section under the subdivision "Mass Media." Formerly called **LLBA: Language and Language Behavior** (1967–1984). Also available as a computer database on the DIALOG system. The computer database begins in 1973.

1931

The (London) Times Index. Reading, England: London Times, monthly with annual cumulations. (1907–.)

An excellent index to the **Times** and related publications: the **Sunday Times and Magazine**, the **Times Literary Supplement**, the **Times Educational Supplement**, and the **Times Higher Education Supplement**. The subject categories are not as broadly defined as in the **New York Times Index**, and like the New York index, this one is a reliable source for personal and organizational names.

1932

The New York Times Index. New York: New York Times Company, biweekly with quarterly and annual cumulations. (1913–.)

Because the **New York Times** is the national newspaper of record and because the index abstracts each article in detail, the index is frequently consulted to verify names, numbers, dates, and events, and used as a guide to the contents of other newspapers. The newspaper's coverage of the arts is excellent and is, therefore, a source for original information about film and television. An index for the years 1851–1912 has been issued, thus completing the retrospective indexing. See also the description of the newspaper as a full text file on the **NEXIS** service (No. 1934).

1933

Newspaper Index. Wooster, OH: Bell & Howell, monthly with annual cumulations. (1972–.)

Issued in four separate volumes: **Chicago Tribune Index**, **Los Angeles Times Index**, (New Orleans) **Times**

Picayune Index, and **Washington Post Index**. The news content of the microfilmed editions of the newspapers is described and indexed. The coverage includes syndicated columns, reviews, and obituaries which appear as news stories. Advertisements, classified obituaries, society personals, routine sports events, food, and hobby stories are omitted. These indexes are also available as computer databases in the **National Newspaper Index**, one of the DIALOG files. This database is updated monthly by a transfer from a second database on DIALOG called **Newsearch**, a daily index of the four newspapers.

1934

NEXIS. Dayton, OH: Mead Data Central, Inc. An online computer information service, updated daily. (1980–.)

The **NEXIS** service was organized in 1980, but the information in the databank is far older than 1980. In 1983, Mead Data Central became the exclusive distributor of the databases developed by the New York Times Company (see **Information Bank Abstracts**, No. 1926).

NEXIS is a full-text retrieval service of a computerized warehouse information best described as general, business, economic, technical and financial news. The information is organized by 145 files: newspapers, magazines, news wire services copy, newsletters, financial reports, and government publications. The file names correspond to a known publication or information service, for example, BBCSWB is the **BBC Summary of World Broadcasts and Monitoring Reports**, MACLEH is **The MacNeil/Lehrer NewsHour**, and UPST is the **United Press International State and Regional Wires**.

The information is retrievable in computer-measured speed by searching the entire contents of the file for words specified by the searcher. Retrieving the full document is costly, but the availability of the quantity and variety is unmatched by other full-text news services (see **VU/TEXT**, No. 1945) as well as the holdings of traditional research libraries. Although some research and public libraries subscribe to the **NEXIS** service, it is usually available at law libraries because Mead Data is also a major vendor of legal information.

1935

Psychological Abstracts. Arlington, VA: American Psychological Association, monthly with a cumulated annual index. (1927–.)

A major index for international social science serial literature, **Psychological Abstracts** surveys about 1,450 journals from more than 50 countries. "Communication Systems" with its two subdivisions, "Language & Speech" and "Literature & Art," is one of 16 divisions used to present the abstracts. The subject index is excellent for finding citations on specific research subjects, such as "Television advertising," "Newspapers," "Motion pictures," "Mass media," "Books," and "Television viewing." An excellent guide to the subject entries is the **Thesaurus of Psychological Index Terms** (4th ed., 1985).

Psychological Abstracts selectively indexes and abstracts the following journals: **Communication, Communication Research, Human Communication Research, Journal of Broadcasting and Electronic Media, Journal of Communication,** and **Public Opinion Quarterly.** The abstracts are also available on a compact digital disk (CD-ROM) as **PsycLit,** beginning 1974 and continuing with quarterly updates to the present. The dates of the coverage of the disk product may vary. The database is also available as an online computer service called **PsychINFO** through several major vendors. The online database corresponds to the printed **Psychological Abstracts** from 1967 to 1979, and beginning in 1980, contains more citations than the printed abstracts. It is updated monthly.

1936

Public Affairs Information Service Bulletin

(PAIS). New York: Public Affairs Information Service, Inc., weekly with annual cumulations. (1915–.)

The strength of this weekly indexing bulletin is its selectivity from a variety of published international sources (in English)—books, periodicals, pamphlets, government documents, and reports from public and private agencies. The sources cited by PAIS generally represent significant statements on the topic. Coverage is broadly defined as issues relating to economic and public affairs. Specific topics of interest to media scholars include press criticism and analysis, broadcasting, advertising, film industry, and communications law and regulation. The database is also available as a compact digital disk product and as an online database through DIALOG.

1937

Readers' Guide to Periodical Literature. New York: Wilson, biweekly with annual cumulations. (1900–.)

An index to general literature in 180 popular periodicals ranging in purpose from hobby magazines and weekly news magazines to scholarly publications. Journals indexed here which frequently publish articles on media topics are **The Atlantic, Commentary, Esquire, Harper's, The Nation, The New Yorker,** and **Publisher's Weekly.** Personal and corporate names, used as authors or as subjects of journal articles, are given as entries in the subject index. **Readers' Guide** is also very useful for citations to movie and television program reviews. See also **InfoTrac** (No. 1927) and **Wilsearch** (No. 1947).

1938

Resources in Education. Washington, DC: Educational Resources Information Center (ERIC), U.S. Department of Education, Office of Educational Research and Improvement, published by U.S. Government Printing Office, monthly with semiannual indexes. (1975–.)

Previous title: **Research in Education, 1966–1974.** An abstract and guide to the research reports in the ERIC system, a national program to disseminate research related to education. Copies of the actual research reports are available on microfiche, a large collection usually held by academic libraries. The refereed research papers presented at the annual meeting of the Association for Education in Journalism and Mass Communication are included in this service. A previous problem of a two-year time lag in the appearance of the AEJMC convention papers has much improved; an abstract of a research paper at the 1986 AEJMC convention is cited and described in the November 1986 issue of **Resources in Education.**

The abstracts of periodical articles published in the printed index, **Current index to Journals in Education** (CIJE) and the research report literature published in the print version of **Resources in Education** (RIE) are also available online in the **ERIC** database, vended by several standard online services. The **CIJE** online files cover from 1969 to date, with monthly updates. The **RIE** online files cover from 1966 to date, with monthly updates. The **ERIC** database is also available as a compact disk product with coverage approximately the same as the online service.

1939

Social Sciences Citation Index: An International Multidisciplinary Index to the Literature of the Social, Behavioral and Related Sciences. Philadelphia: Institute for Scientific Information, three issues a year. (1973–.)

This index is probably the broadest in the social sciences in terms of inclusion and also one of the most difficult to use in the printed edition, but it is well worth mastering. The index cites and analyzes thousands of journals, monographs, and other types of print materials, among which are letters to journal editors, corrections, editorials in journals, abstracts of scholarly and professional meetings, footnotes, book reviews, bibliographies, and information about individuals, such as obituaries, biographies, awards and tributes.

The citation of footnotes is particularly useful for advanced scholars who may, among other things, use it to track the history of a concept; a second use is to measure how often an individual scholar is cited in footnotes. The field of mass communication and communications is often cited. The index is also available as a computer database in the DIALOG service.

1940

Social Sciences Index. New York: Wilson, quarterly with annual cumulations. (1974/75–.)

For a note on predecessors to this index, see the entry for **Humanities Index.** One of five Wilson Company indexes to periodical literature cited in this bibliography, the **Social Sciences Index** uses many of the same subject headings as the other Wilson indexes, "Reporters and Reporting" and "Violence in Television," for example. Entries under the personal names of journalists, particularly television correspondents and print columnists, are also included. Because this index covers such journals as **Journal of Communication**, **Public Opinion**, **Public Opinion Quarterly**, and the **Economist**, it is also a useful guide to articles about public opinion, newspaper publishing, government and the press, news agencies, and media performance in foreign countries.

Social Sciences Index is also available on compact digital disk (CD-ROM) and on **Wilsearch** (No. 1947), a computer online database, both databases beginning with February 1984 and continuing to present with frequent updates.

1941

Sociological Abstracts. San Diego, CA: Sociological Abstracts, Inc., co-sponsored by the International Sociological Association, five times a year with annual index. (1952–.)

Abstracts articles selected from more than 1,000 international journals. The abstracts are presented under broad topics, "Mass Phenomena" being the one of interest to mass communications scholars. Three of the categories in this section are "Public Opinion," "Communication," and "Mass Culture." The subject index uses more specific headings such as "mass media," "mass media effects," "mass media violence," "television," and "advertising." Journals which do not have the word "sociology" appearing in the titles are indexed and abstracted selectively. Examples of mass communication journals selectively indexed are **European Journal of Communication**, **Communications** (France), **Journal of Communication**, **Communication Research Report**, **Journal of Communication Inquiry**, **Human Communication Research**, and **Public Opinion Quarterly**.

1942

Television Index. Long Island City, NY: Television Index Inc., weekly. (1949–.)

This is probably the most continuous and comprehensive coverage of commercial network television programming in existence, and certainly the most complicated to use, in spite of excellent indexing. It is in various parts. **The Network Program Report** covers all commercial network series debuting or returning during the current week, with production credits, sponsors, and series history, as well as all network specials including variety shows and documentaries, with credits and sponsors. **News, Public Affairs & Sports Program Record** reports guests and highlights of series in these categories as well as religious events and specials in all of the above. **The Program Performance Record** provides performer, director, writer and other pertinent production credits for the week's network programs. All series are indexed, with cumulative indexes issued quarterly. **Television Network Movies** (quarterly since 1973–74, cumulative with annual index) is a spinoff from **Program Performance Record**. It pulls together movies of 90 minutes or more, whether made for theaters or especially for television, giving for each the network, running time, date of first showing, producer/distributor, stars, writer,

and director. **Television Pro-Log** (weekly since 1972) is four digest-sized pages of news and comment, with periodic special reports in expanded issues based on interviews and surveys of various aspects of the program production. **Network Futures** (weekly since 1966) gives calendar-guide listings for upcoming series, debuts, returns, program specials, and schedule changes.

From 1949 to 1963 the title of this publication was **Ross Reports**; in 1963 it took its present title.

1943

Television News Index and Abstracts. Nashville, TN: Vanderbilt Television News Archive, Jean & Alexander Heard Library, Vanderbilt University, monthly with annual cumulations of the index only. (1972–.)

An index to and abstracts of a video archive of TV network national evening news as broadcast by ABC, CBS, and NBC. Video tapes and audio tapes of the news programs may be borrowed from the archive. The archive staff will compile a video recording using short takes from the news programs as specified by the researcher. These compiled tapes allow the user to study the news about an event or topic with greater efficiency. The abstract of each news story includes the date, time, length of the broadcast, the network and the reporter's name as well as a brief summary of the news. A retrospective index and abstract to the archives collection, which began in August 1968, has been issued on microfilm. The archive also includes tapes of major news events such as presidential speeches, political party conventions and the Watergate and Nixon impeachment hearings.

1944

Topicator. Clackamas, OR: Topicator, monthly with annual cumulated index. (1965–.)

Subtitled **Classified Article Guide to the Advertising/Communications/Marketing Periodical Press**. This indexing service selectively indexes 18 journals, nine of which are indexed extensively by **Business Periodicals Index**; one is indexed by **Readers' Guide to Periodical Literature**; two are indexed by **Humanities Index**, and so forth. The value of **Topicator** is found in its selectivity. Small libraries and reading rooms organized to house the three big trade publications, **Advertising Age**, **Broadcasting**, and **Editor & Publisher** and other standard media industry and journalism publications, such as **TV Guide** and **Columbia Journalism Review**, could use **Topicator** to index the significant articles in these journals.

1945

VU/TEXT. Philadelphia, PA: VU/TEXT Information Services, Inc., a subsidiary of Knight-Ridder Co., daily cumulated by year. (1983–.)

A full-text news computer database of articles from 38 newspapers plus business journals and newswires. The unique aspect of this newspaper database is the inclusion of many state and local newspapers not available elsewhere as computer files. A sample of the newspapers from Alaska to Florida shows the variety available: **Anchorage Daily News** (AK), **Sacramento Bee** (CA), **Wichita Eagle-Beacon** (KS), **Philadelphia Inquirer** (PA), **Charlotte Observer** (NC), and **Miami Herald** (FL). The beginning dates of each of the newspaper files varies—the **Philadelphia Daily News** and **Inquirer** begin in 1983—with most files beginning about 1985.

The articles are retrieved using keywords and free text searching or using a controlled vocabulary and field searching. For example, the search can be limited to editorials within a specified range of dates.

1946

The Wall Street Journal: Index. New York: Dow Jones, monthly with annual cumulations. (1958–.)

The index is divided into two sections: "Corporation News" and "General News." A brief abstract of the newspaper articles is included. Like the **New York Times Index**, this is as much a source of data, particularly for corporate information, as it is an index to the newspaper articles which are frequently about the media institutions and media companies. The index has a two-month lag time.

The full-text of **The Wall Street Journal**, from 1984 to the present day, is available for searching by computer on the Dow Jones News Retrieval service. The text of selected stories from the newspaper are available on the service from June, 1979 to the present.

1947

Wilsearch. New York: H. W. Wilson, an online computer access to multiple indexes to periodical and book literature.

One of the 17 different print-based Wilson indexes to literature is often the best bibliographic tool to begin a search of the literature on any chosen subject. (See also, **InfoTrac**, No. 1927.) The **Wilsearch** service provides the fast and wondrous access to these traditional, print-based indexes that characterizes computer searching of bibliographic databases. Some of the advantages of using the **Wilsearch** system are: several years of an index can be searched at one time; the indexes are updated every two weeks; more than one index can be search at one time; the search approach can be by author, article title, subject, journal title, or a combination of these; the subject terms can be linked together; the search can be limited within a time frame.

The following 17 Wilson indexes available on **Wilsearch** are:

Applied Science & Technology Index, November 1983–.
Art Index, October 1985–.
Bibliographic Index, November 1985–.
Biography Index, July 1984–.
Biological and Agricultural Index, July 1983–.
Book Review Digest, July 1983–.
Business Periodicals Index, June 1982–.
Education Index, September 1983–.
Essay and General Literature Index, 1983–.
General Science Index, May 1984–.
Humanities Index, February 1984–.
Index to Legal Periodicals, August 1981–.
Library Literature, January 1983–.
Modern Languages Association International Biography, January 1983–.
Readers' Guide Abstracts, September 1984–.
Readers' Guide to Periodical Literature, 1983–.
Social Science Index, February 1984–.

Author Index

Numbers refer to annotated entries.

Title Index

Numbers refer to annotated entries.

Subject Index

Numbers refer to annotated entries.

A Note on the Authors

ELEANOR BLUM, professor emeritus of library science and former librarian at the College of Communication, University of Illinois at Urbana-Champaign, was the first recipient of the Eleanor Blum Distinguished Service to Research Award given by the Association for Education in Journalism and Mass Communication. She was contributing editor of the book review of the *Journalism Quarterly* and is the author of *Basic Books in the Mass Media*. She has also served as a library consultant in mass communications at various universities.

FRANCES GOINS WILHOIT is librarian and head of the Journalism Library at Indiana University and assistant professor in the School of Journalism at Indiana. She is the former editor of *Journalism Abstracts*, the author of many articles on mass communications literature, and the co-author of a bibliography on mass media periodicals.